# TROTSKY

# TROTSKY

## A BIOGRAPHY

## ROBERT SERVICE

The Belknap Press
of Harvard University Press
Cambridge, Massachusetts
2009

Printed and bound in the United States of America

First published in the United Kingdom by Macmillan
an imprint of Macmillan Publishers Ltd


Library of Congress Cataloging-in-Publication Data

Service, Robert, 1947–
Trotsky : a biography / Robert Service.
p. cm.
Includes bibliographical references and index.
ISBN 978-0-674-03615-4    4237  4917  1/10
1. Trotsky, Leon, 1879–1940.   2. Revolutionaries—Soviet Union—Biography.
3. Statesmen—Soviet Union—Biography.   4. Exiles—Russia—Biography.
5. Communism—Soviet Union—History.   6. Russia—Politics and government—1894–1917.
7. Soviet Union—Politics and government—1917–1936.   I. Title.
DK254.T6S427 2009
947.084092
[B]
2009025417

# CONTENTS

CONTENTS

# PART TWO: 1914–1919

# PART THREE: 1920–1928

CONTENTS

# List of Illustrations

THE SOUTHERN RIM OF 'NEW RUSSIA'

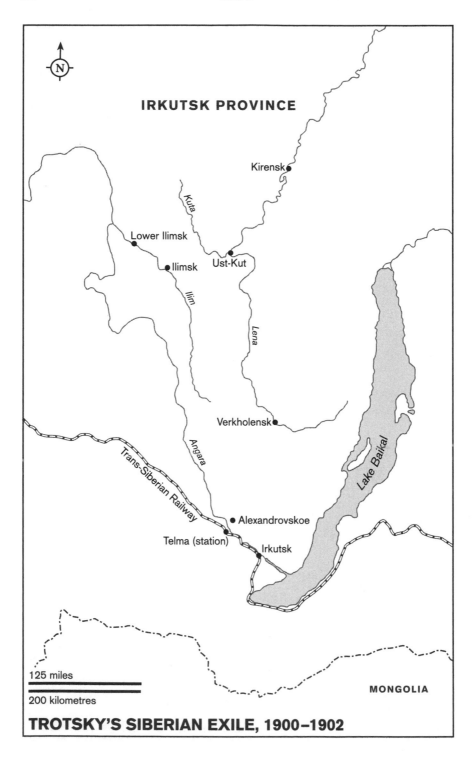

IRKUTSK PROVINCE

Kirensk

Kuta

Lower Ilimsk

Ilimsk

Ust-Kut

Ilim

Lena

Verkholensk

Angara

Trans-Siberian Railway

Lake Baikal

Alexandrovskoe

Telma (station)

Irkutsk

125 miles

200 kilometres

MONGOLIA

**TROTSKY'S SIBERIAN EXILE, 1900–1902**

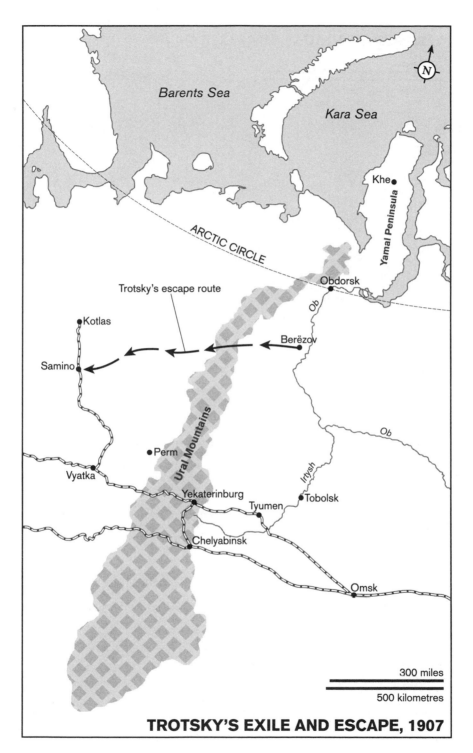

TROTSKY'S EXILE AND ESCAPE, 1907

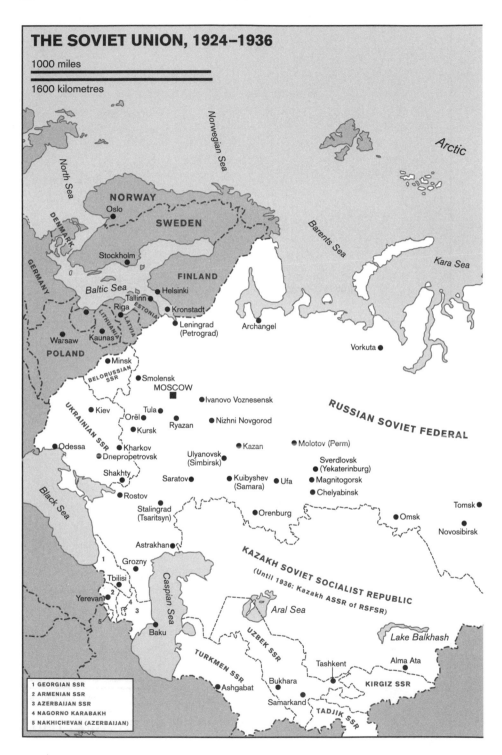

# THE SOVIET UNION, 1924–1936

1000 miles

1600 kilometres

1 GEORGIAN SSR
2 ARMENIAN SSR
3 AZERBAIJAN SSR
4 NAGORNO KARABAKH
5 NAKHICHEVAN (AZERBAIJAN)

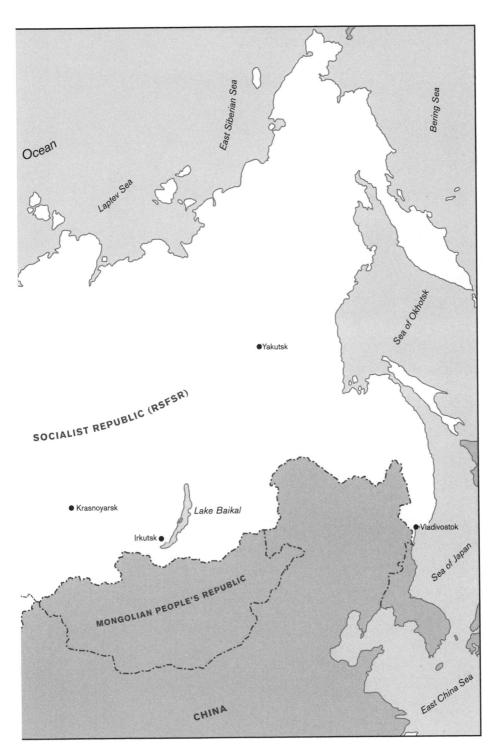

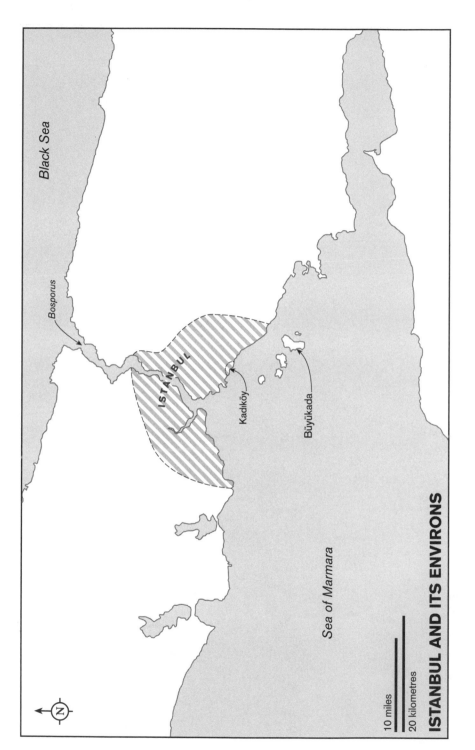

Black Sea

Bosporus

ISTANBUL

Kadıköy

Büyükada

Sea of Marmara

10 miles

20 kilometres

N

ISTANBUL AND ITS ENVIRONS

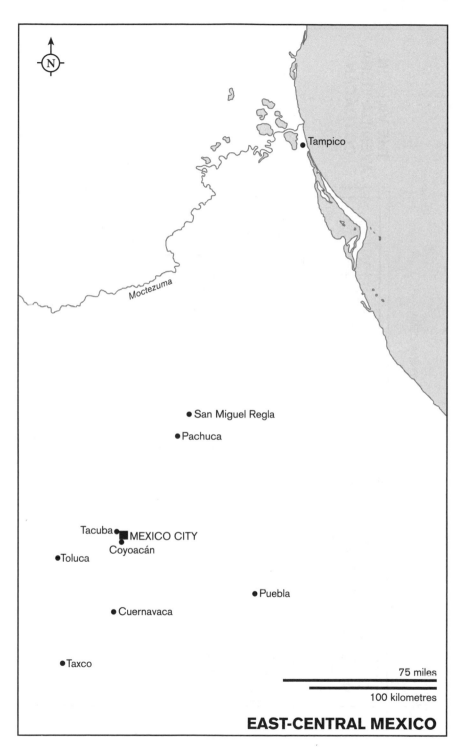

**EAST-CENTRAL MEXICO**

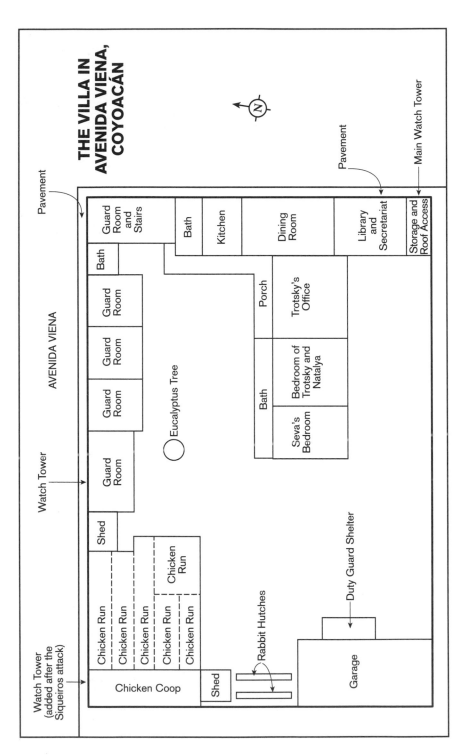

THE VILLA IN AVENIDA VIENA, COYOACÁN

# Preface

This is the third book in a trilogy about the leaders of the early Soviet state. The Hoover Institution has been my base for the archival research, and I am grateful to Director John Raisian, Senior Associate Director Richard Sousa and Board of Overseers member Tad Taube, as well as to the Sarah Scaife Foundation, for the friendly, efficient way they set up the opportunity to carry out the work at Stanford. Deborah Ventura and Celeste Szeto too could not have been more helpful. In the archives I received indispensable assistance from Elena Danielson, Linda Bernard, Carol Leadenham, Lora Soroka, David Jacobs, Ron Bulatoff, Zbigniew Stanczyk, Lyalya Kharitonova, Dale Reed and Anatol Shmelev. They went far beyond the demands of their responsibilities, frequently alerting me to material whose existence was unknown to me. Our conversations about the hundreds of boxes in diverse collections were of inestimable assistance.

The fresh material used in the book includes folders from the Trotsky Collection, the Boris Nicolaevsky Collection, the Bertram Wolfe Collection, the sundry records of Politburo and Central Committee for the 1920s, the papers deposited by Trotsky's assistants and followers and the internal records of the nascent Fourth International. The gem in the Hoover Archives is the first draft of Trotsky's autobiography which has much information he excluded from the printed version. Also of importance are the letters from and to Trotsky as well as the unpublished variants of his works and the correspondence and memoirs by his wife Natalya and other members of his family across several generations. The Hoover Institution Archives, moreover, have invaluable sources on Trotsky from the Paris office of the Russian Imperial Okhrana, from Nestor Lakoba's papers and from Dmitri Volkogonov's papers. Most of such material is used for the first time in this biography. I am grateful too to the staff in the Hoover Institution Library for their diligence in delivering rare contemporary books, articles and newspapers.

Other Trotsky archival holdings consulted for the book include those in Amsterdam, Harvard and Moscow. Whereas Amsterdam and Harvard were mined long ago, the seams in Moscow have been open to prospectors only since 1991. Not only Trotsky's personal file and central party records in the Russian State Archive of Social and Political History (once known as the Central Party Archive) but also the papers from the Russian State Archive of Military History and the Central Archive of the Federal Security Service offer important information. The Houghton Library at Harvard University too contains letters in its holdings which have merited reconsideration, and I thank Jennie Rathbun for obtaining the ones I requested. SSEES-UCL in London has a number of early editions of Trotsky's books which I was able to consult. My wife Adele Biagi visited the National Archives at Kew in search of documents on Trotsky and discovered several interesting police records.

While writing up the research I benefited from exchanges of opinions with Robert Conquest whose capacious knowledge of episodes in Trotsky's life and times gave me plenty of clues to work with. It was also a pleasure to try out ideas on Paul Gregory, Arnold Beichman, Michael Bernshtam, Norman Naimark and Amir Weiner at Hoover and Stanford and on Yuri Slezkine at Berkeley. Paul's annual Soviet archives working group has become a remarkable annual forum for the discussion of questions about the USSR's past. At Oxford I have benefited over many years from working with Katya Andreyev on the courses we have taught together. The Russian and Eurasian Studies Centre and its Library have provided excellent facilities and I am indebted to Richard Ramage, our Administrator, for securing books even during the disruption when our Library was being reconstructed. The Centre's Monday seminar, which has run for over half a century, has been a fecund source of ideas for this book even when the topics had nothing to do with Trotsky.

My thanks go to Elena Danielson who recounted her conversations with Ella Wolfe, Frida Kahlo's great friend; to Anita Burdman Feferman who knew and wrote about Jean van Heijenoort; to Robin Jacoby whose psychiatric and psychological expertise helped towards an understanding of Trotsky's personality; to Tanya Okunskaya, who provided letters from the Turkmenistan party archives; and to the late Brian Pearce who over many years shared his lifetime of reflections on Trotsky and Trotskyism. Olga Kerziouk and Elena Katz gave their informed verdicts on Trotsky's accent and diction after we listened online to his speeches in Russian. Gabriel Gorodetsky shared with me the pages of Ivan Maiski's diary which mention Trotsky. Bob Davies, the late John Klier, Keith Sidwell, Faith Wigzeil, Mikhail Zilikov and Andrei Zorin offered advice on particular matters. I am grateful to Robert Harris for lending me his pre-revolutionary map of Odessa and to Harun Yılmaz for obtaining and translating Turkish historical literature.

Harry Shukman and Ian Thatcher took appreciable time away from their own work to read the entire manuscript. Harry's historical interests touch on crucial themes in this biography and I am grateful for his deft, tactful steerage away from many crudities in the draft chapters. Ian has spent his career writing about Trotsky; I appreciate his generosity of spirit in scrutinizing my draft and making suggestions. Both Harry and Ian also kindly allowed me to come back to them with further queries. Simon Sebag Montefiore and Paul Gregory read large parts of the draft and sharpened the argument. Both Simon and Paul wear their learning lightly: my thanks go to them for their insights. Hugo Service cast his eye over the Introduction. Above all, Adele has gone through the book twice, assisted in cutting out mistakes and advised on the course of the argument and narrative. I cannot thank her enough for all her insight and patience: we have talked endlessly about the problems of Trotsky's life and, as ever, it is to her that I owe the greatest debt.

My literary agent David Godwin and Macmillan editor Georgina Morley have been as active and encouraging as always; and Peter James has done an excellent job of copy-editing the text with his usual mixture of consultative empathy and incisiveness. It has been a pleasure to work with all three of them.

This book is the first full-length biography of Trotsky written by someone outside Russia who is not a Trotskyist. Trotsky himself wrote a vivid set of memoirs in 1930, ten years before he died. His Polish-emigrant follower Isaac Deutscher wrote a trilogy of literary dash in 1954–63 and the French Trotskyist Pierre Broué produced a single-volume study in 1989. Trotsky and Deutscher wrote with brio, and I make no pretence of having matched them in style. But I do contend that Trotsky was selective, evasive and self-aggrandizing in his account and that Deutscher and Broué omitted to ask many of the necessary awkward questions about him. Broué was an idolater; Deutscher, even while believing that the Soviet regime after Stalin could rectify itself and build a humane communist order, worshipped at Trotsky's shrine. Trotsky and Deutscher wrote books which gained a lasting influence far outside the perimeter of the political far left, and their highly disputable judgements have all too often been treated as the last word on the subject. That was how they wanted it. The history of the Russian Revolution deserves a more searching approach and this biography is intended to help in all this.

It would be tedious for everyone if my disagreements with the basic Trotskyist 'line' about Trotsky were to pepper the book's chapters. Over three decades ago, when doing doctoral research on the communist party in the early revolutionary period, I became convinced that Trotsky's diagnosis of the causes of his defeat by Stalin was self-serving and misleading. Several other works on Trotsky have subjected him to sceptical scrutiny. On his tactics in the October seizure of power, Alexander Rabinowitch and James White have made important contributions. On his leadership of the Red Army, Francesco Benvenuti, Evan Mawdsley and Geoff Swain have offered fresh insights. On his economic ideas during the NEP, Richard Day, Bob Davies and John Channon have challenged the old picture. On his China policy in the 1920s, Alexander Pantsov has offered a new analysis. On his activity as revolutionary politician and writer before the October Revolution, Ian Thatcher's studies are fundamental. Two large biographies, by Nikolai Vasetski and Dmitri Volkogonov, have appeared in Russia. Without offering an original interpretation, they have increased the documentary information available.

Time was when Trotsky was a frequent topic of public discussion at least outside the USSR. Those days are gone. But his ideas and activity deserve to be looked at again because they have an importance for the way we understand the past hundred years of Russian and world history. This book is dedicated to the memory of the late Janet Service. Hailing from the Scottish borders, she met our father in wartime Edinburgh before they made the rest of their lives in the English Midlands. For most of her employed life she was a selfless nurse for phyically disabled children; she was a superlative cook and knitter and could turn her hands to almost any practical job around the home. She was an exceptional mother for my brother Rod and me and a wonderful grandmother for her six grandchildren.

Robert Service
*March 2009*

## A Note on Usages

Dates are usually given according to the calendar in official use in the country where Trotsky was living at the time. The Russian authorities employed the Julian calendar until January 1918, when they switched to the Gregorian one. In transliterating from Russian, I have used a simplified version of the US Library of Congress system with the qualification that endnotes are given in line with the full system. The translations of most quotations are mine – Trotsky's own translators did not always serve him well, and anyway it was not the easiest job since he often interfered with their work even when, as was true of English, his grasp of the language was inadequate.

# INTRODUCTION

Trotsky moved like a bright comet across the political sky. He first came to global attention in 1917. By all accounts he was the finest orator of the Russian Revolution. He led the Military-Revolutionary Committee which carried out the overthrow of the Provisional Government in October. He did more than anyone to found the Red Army. He belonged to the Party Politburo and had a deep impact on its political, economic and military strategy. He was a principal figure in the early years of the Communist International. The whole world attributed the impact of the October Revolution to his partnership with Lenin. He and Lenin had their difficulties with each other. Before 1917 Trotsky had been an enemy of Bolshevism, and many Bolsheviks did not let him forget it. When Lenin fell mortally ill in 1922, the rest of the Politburo feared that Trotsky would bid to become his sole successor. The subsequent factional struggles brought disaster upon him and he was deported from the USSR in 1929 and given political asylum in Turkey, France, Norway and Mexico. His analysis of what had gone wrong with the Soviet state continued to have an influence abroad. Trotskyist organizations sprang up wherever political conditions allowed. Stalin depicted Trotsky as a traitor to the October Revolution, laid charges against him in the show-trials of 1936–8 and ordered Soviet intelligence agencies to assassinate him. In 1940 they succeeded.

He lived a life full of drama played out with the world as his stage. The October Revolution changed the course of history, and Trotsky had a prominent role in the transformation. Politics on the left were transfigured in every country; socialists had to decide whether to support or oppose what was being undertaken by the Bolsheviks in Russia. The foes of socialism were no less affected. Governments had to devise ways of counteracting the Communist International; and fascist parties on the political far right sprang up to prevent the further spread of revolutionary Marxism.

Trotsky felt pride about his accomplishment in the years of power and strove to justify the revolutionary measures of the Soviet government as well as the violence it deployed. As soon as he was appointed a People's Commissar he wrote commentaries and memoirs which described Bolshevik activity in the warmest colours. His works were distributed widely in the USSR; they were instantly translated and sold abroad in popular editions. For several years he was a best-selling author. About his literary and analytical brilliance there was never a doubt. After he was expelled from the Soviet Union it was only by his prolific writings that he could support himself and his family in reasonable comfort. He was taken seriously not just by anti-communist socialists but by a large number of influential commentators who detested Stalin's regime. Trotsky's explanation of what had happened since the fall of the Romanov monarchy in February 1917 took root in Western historical works. Trotsky's books stayed in print. His autobiography was a favourite among readers who wanted a general account of the October Revolution and its consequences. His political pamphlets were cherished by communist critics of the Kremlin.

In his lifetime Trotskyist groups made a minuscule impression on political affairs. After his death the movement went into a steady decline. A brief re-ascent occurred in 1968 during the students' disturbances in Europe and North America, but it barely outlasted the year. In the USSR he continued to be reviled until Gorbachëv ordered his posthumous political rehabilitation in 1988. Meanwhile Trotskyists in the West continued to form their querulous groups, often campaigning for ideas that would have alarmed him.

Trotsky's account of his life and times, however, has maintained its deep imprint on Western scholarship. According to him, Stalin was a man of no talent, an ignoramus, a bureaucratic mediocrity. Supposedly Trotsky lost the struggle to succeed Lenin because the balance of social forces in the country was tilted in favour of bureaucracy. The Soviet administrative stratum embraced Stalin and rejected Trotsky. Thus the October Revolution had been doomed from the start unless it could break out of its isolation and link up with communist states in Germany and elsewhere. Stalin's caution allegedly betrayed the international revolutionary cause after Lenin's departure. Trotsky postulated that conditions in the USSR would have been radically different if only he and his faction had gained supremacy. He claimed that they would at least have struggled for the democratization of Soviet politics and held back the tides of counter-revolution, arbitrary rule and terror. He declared that the workers would have come to his side if they had not been prevented by oppressive police action.

The elegance of his prose was not the only reason for Trotsky's influence on subsequent historical thinking. His murder turned him into a political martyr who was often given the benefit of the doubt by authors who might otherwise have exercised their scepticism. A certain mental freewheeling was also at work. Trotsky had provided arguments that discredited the reputation of Stalin and his henchmen, and it was all too easy for writers unthinkingly to adopt them as their own.

Trotsky was wrong in many cardinal aspects of his case. Stalin was no mediocrity but rather had an impressive range of skills as well as a talent for decisive leadership. Trotsky's strategy for communist advance anyway had little to offer for the avoidance of an oppressive regime. His ideas and practices laid several foundation stones for the erection of the Stalinist political, economic, social and even cultural edifice. Stalin, Trotsky and Lenin shared more than they disagreed about. As for the charge that Stalin was an arch-bureaucrat, this was rich coming from an accuser who had delighted in unchecked administrative authority in the years of his pomp. Even Trotsky's claim that Stalin was uninterested in aiding foreign communist seizures of power fails to withstand scrutiny. Moreover, if communism had been victorious in Germany, France or Spain in the inter-war years its banner-holders would have been unlikely to have retained their power. And if ever Trotsky had been the paramount leader instead of Stalin, the risks of a bloodbath in Europe would have been drastically increased. Trotsky prided himself on his ability to see Soviet and international affairs with realism. He deceived himself. He had sealed himself inside preconceptions that stopped him from understanding the dynamics of contemporary geopolitics. (Not that Stalin was without his gross failures of prediction.) The point is that whoever governed the USSR effectively stood in need of deeply authoritarian methods to conserve communist power.

There is no denying Trotsky's exceptional qualities. He was an outstanding speaker, organizer and leader. He could easily have achieved a great career as a journalist or essayist if politics had not become his preoccupation. He had a sensitivity, albeit an intermittent one, for literature. He wrote about everyday life and cultural progress as well as on the more customary Marxist themes of his day. He had unbounded enthusiasm and commitment to revolutionary objectives. He inspired his entourage to feats of sacrifice. More than any other leading Bolshevik he conserved in his head a vision of a future world where each man and woman would have the opportunity for self-fulfilment in service of the collective good. He proclaimed this with passion to the day he died.

Yet his portrait of his life and times involved many distortions – and these have clouded our understanding of Soviet communist history. He exaggerated his personal importance. His ideas before 1917 were nowhere near to being as original and wide-ranging as he liked to believe. His contribution to the Bolshevik advance on power was important but not to the degree that he asserted. Although he brought a unifying authority to the Red Army in 1918–19, he also provoked unnecessary trouble and made avoidable mistakes. In the ensuing years he remained volatile and untrustworthy. He lacked tactical finesse. He was an arrogant individual, and even in times of personal adversity in the 1920s and 1930s he dazzled his followers with his pre-eminence but failed to coax and encourage them to the full. He egocentrically assumed that his opinions, if expressed in vivid language, would win him victory. He was a better administrator than politician. Stalin outplayed him. Trotsky did not go down to defeat at the hands of 'the bureaucracy': he lost to a man and a clique with a superior understanding of Soviet public life. Fine oratory and well-turned pamphlets were no longer enough. Trotsky was addicted to the self-image he had acquired in the year of the Revolution. This did him no favours in later years.

Trotsky is usually regarded as a person with qualities that put him in a different category to Stalin. It is true that Stalin did things of a monstrosity which only a few dictators in the twentieth century matched. But Trotsky was no angel. His lust for dictatorship and terror was barely disguised in the Civil War. He trampled on the civil rights of millions of people including the industrial workers. His self-absorption was extreme. As a husband he treated his first wife shabbily. He ignored the needs of his children especially when his political interests intervened. This had catastrophic consequences even for those of them who were inactive in Soviet public life – and his son Lev, who followed him into exile, possibly paid with his life for collaborating with his father.

Yet Trotsky also had beguiling qualities. It serves no purpose to pretend that he can be cut down to a regular size and shown to be just like the rest of us. So how exactly should we go about assessing him? Although he could be disarmingly frank he kept a lot to himself when publishing his autobiography and releasing selections of documents. This book's purpose is to dig up the buried life. Trotsky had a complex character and career. As with all the leaders of the October Revolution, the evidence starts with the works – his books, articles and speeches – which he published in his lifetime. Trotsky found some of them an embarrassment as his own political interests changed. But even if we examine all such works, we cannot leave the enquiry at that. They tell us about his big objectives without always elucidating his personal or factional purpose at any given moment. As an active politician he could not always afford to spell out what he was up to. His letters, telegrams and other messages offer a way into that inner circle of his thinking. Even so, the dispatched message was often an over-polished object. In order to understand what he was planning it is also necessary to look at the drafts of what he wrote. The excisions and amendments tell us about what he did not want others to know. This is particularly true of his autobiography.

His written legacy should not be allowed to become the entire story. It is sometimes in the supposedly trivial residues rather than in the grand public statements that the perspective of his career is most effectively reconstructed: his lifestyle, income, housing, family relationships, mannerisms and everyday assumptions about the rest of humanity. There is little about this in his autobiography, but the information can be pieced together from his letters and jottings and from what his associates – from his wives and children through to his translators and slight acquaintances – remembered about him. As with Lenin and Stalin, moreover, it is as important to pinpoint what Trotsky was silent about as what he chose to speak or write about. His unuttered basic assumptions were integral to the amalgam of his life.

Trotsky hated to throw things away. He stuffed his filing cabinets with old ferry tickets, expired passports, unpublished memoir fragments and photographs of his rented accommodation; he once chided his long-suffering translator Max Eastman for crumpling up a letter from a woman in Ohio, USA, despite having no intention of answering it.[1] The result is that an abundance of material remains. It was a pleasure for me to unroll the original draft of Trotsky's history of the Russian Revolution which he laboriously glued, page by page, into chapter-length scrolls. Archaeologists who unearthed papyri in Egyptian deserts must have had the same tingling sensation. Yet Trotsky was not an ancient official, priest or trader but a twentieth-century revolutionary with his own typist and industrially produced paper. Acquaintance with his scroll-making eccentricity has helped towards acquiring a feeling for his ways of life and work. The extant films of his speeches prove that, contemporaries as attested, he really was a superb orator. His love letters to his first and second wives provide vivid examples of his passionate nature. Likewise the drafts of his writings, especially his scintillating autobiography, demonstrate just how fluent and exact a writer he was. When he amended a piece of writing it was often only in order to prevent some kind of political or social embarrassment. Stylistically he could shape his thoughts at the first attempt.

He also had mercifully neat handwriting. The beautiful little address book he maintained in internal Soviet exile in Alma-Ata in 1928 confirms that he was fastidious and well organized. Truly he was not much of a conspirator but occasionally he worked on this shortcoming, as is proved by the copy of Alexander Blok's published diary in which he used invisible ink to jot down instructions for his followers. Then there is the book on Marxism and philosophy by his ex-follower Sidney Hook: the exclamation marks he made in the margins testify to angry self-righteousness and intellectual self-regard. Equally remarkable are the hundreds of letters he sent to Trotskyists in dozens of countries, employing a bewildering alternation of pseudonyms (Old Man, Crux, Onken, Uncle Leon, Vidal and Lund) – he needed a very capacious memory to keep abreast of his multiple identities. Trotsky left behind plenty of evidence that he was somebody out of the ordinary in matters great and small.

Like all human beings, he was an unrepeatable phenomenon. A Trotsky could anyway not burst upon us again for the obvious reason that too much has changed in the world, and a political comet of his brilliance would have a different composition and trajectory. Account has always to be taken of his times and his environment. He was born in a generation known for its revolutionary radicalism in the Russian Empire. He rose to prominence inside a party which seized power in October 1917 and proclaimed its determination to turn the world upside down. Trotsky did as much as anyone, except Lenin, to build the Soviet state in the first half-decade of its existence. But he did not have superhuman faculties. He and his comrades benefited from operating in circumstances of profound disruption throughout society. Otherwise they would never have been able to take and consolidate their hegemony in Russia. Once they had won the Civil War they still faced huge difficulties. The administration and the economy was chaotic; hostility to communism was widespread. The communist party itself was not a toy in the hands of the central leadership: it had to be managed and coaxed with care and compromise. For a while, through to the early 1920s, Trotsky behaved as if no constraints existed on communists so long as they showed sufficient will power, unity and readiness to use mass violence. He gradually began to see that this was utopian. But he never completely abandoned the unrealistic agenda he had held out to himself and to the party. He lived for the dream which many people found a nightmare.

That dream acquired its form incrementally over the course of his life. No one – or almost no one – who knew Trotsky as an adolescent or young man guessed what an extraordinary career he would have. Yet in retrospect some of the glimmerings were already visible in those early years, and we must now begin at the beginning.

# PART ONE

# 1879–1913

# 1. THE FAMILY BRONSTEIN

Lev Davidovich Trotsky was born on 26 October 1879 into a farming family at Yanovka in Kherson province in the region then called New Russia and now lying in southern Ukraine. He finished his days in Coyoacán on the outskirts of Mexico City nearly sixty-one years later. His was an extraordinary life. Not until almost the end of its fourth decade did he acquire sustained public prominence. From the October Revolution of 1917 he was a figure with a worldwide impact. For a decade he occupied a place at the apex of Soviet politics. Then his fortunes changed irretrievably and Siberian exile and deportation from the USSR followed. But he remained in the global spotlight until his assassination by an agent of Stalin's security police in 1940.

Trotsky was Leiba Bronstein until the age of twenty-three when he adopted his renowned pseudonym. He remains a more elusive figure than has generally been recognized. Chastising what he called 'the Stalinist school of falsification', he exposed Stalin's campaign of calumniation against him;[1] but although he seldom told outright lies in autobiographical accounts, his own writings were full of serious inaccuracies. He was an active revolutionary, and nothing he stated in public was unmarked by his practical purposes at the time of delivery. He laughed at the very suggestion that things could ever be otherwise.[2] In narrating his life's story, he cut and selected episodes to suit his current political interest. He was persistently unfair about his adversaries. His selectivity was not an entirely conscious process. Trotsky adopted a definite ideology at an early age; his analysis and prognosis underwent development but did not radically change. Seeing the world through the prism of certain basic ideas, he blinkered himself to the merits of alternative options. He was cut from a single stone, rejecting any demarcation of the private man from the public leader. This inevitably influenced how he went about writing autobiography. His account of himself has been accepted uncritically by generations of readers. The reality was different, for whenever inconvenient facts obscured his desired image he removed or distorted them.

As a Marxist he was embarrassed about the wealth of his parents, and he never properly acknowledged their extraordinary qualities and achievements. What is more, the published account of his boyhood in his autobiography tended to drop those passages where he appeared timid or pampered; and without denying his Jewish origin he trimmed back the references to it. By examining the drafts and proofs, we can catch glimpses of aspects of his upbringing that have long lain hidden. Thus he stated publicly only that his father was a prosperous, competent farmer. This hugely understated the reality. David Bronstein, married to Aneta, was among the most dynamic farmers for miles around in Kherson province. By hard work and determination he had dragged himself up the ladder of economic success and had every right to be proud of his achievement.

Yanovka lay on the edge of a Jewish agricultural colony known as Gromokleya in Kherson province's Yelizavetgrad district. The farm was a couple of miles from the nearest village.[3] The soil of New Russia was very fertile. Kherson province lay on the Black Sea coast and near to the great, booming port of Odessa whence cargo ships took Russian and Ukrainian exports out into the Mediterranean. Having defeated and driven out the Turkish forces in 1792, Empress Catherine the Great had set about securing her frontiers. Odessa was a focus of her attention, and it prospered under the governor-generalship of Armand Emmanuel du Plessis, Duc de Richelieu, at the beginning of the nineteenth century. (Frenchmen at that time were welcomed to the empire if they had outstanding expertise.) This city dwarfed Nikolaev and all the other inhabited places of New Russia; and the rural areas in their hinterland were thinly populated for years after the Russian military conquest. The authorities in St Petersburg understood that the threat of an Ottoman return could never be excluded. Catherine's grandson, Emperor Alexander I, therefore resolved to populate the lands of New Russia by opening them to settler–farmers. Appeals went out to army veterans, to Germans and to Jews in the Russian Empire to occupy the virgin territory in the Ukrainian steppes. Thousands of families migrated southwards. There was a boom in cereal production as New Russia acted as a magnet for those who sought to take advantage of the opportunities on offer.

The Imperial government had no liking for its Jews. Millions of them had been scooped into the empire through the three partitions of Poland imposed by Vienna, Berlin and St Petersburg in 1772–95. Jews from the start met with official suspicion. Successive emperors were fearful of letting them 'contaminate' Russia's heartland with their alien religion, commercial acumen and educational prowess. Russians were the empire's demographic and spiritual backbone and their sensibilities had to be taken into account. But the Jews had to live somewhere if they were not going to be deported and the government never dreamed of expelling them as the Spanish had done in 1492. The Jews themselves wanted to stay: there was no mass exodus to the United States until the end of the nineteenth-century and the Zionist movement for a Jewish homeland in Palestine had yet to begin. The Pale of Settlement was the chosen solution of Empress Catherine in 1791. Stretching from the Baltic Sea down to the Black Sea, it covered a vast region. Its purpose was to bar Jews from inhabiting Russian cities, towns and villages unless they happened to be very rich – and even in that instance there were sometimes difficulties in obtaining the required papers of permission. Most Jewish subjects of the tsars went on living in the northern half of the Pale where they had had their homes for centuries.

Their shtetls were townlets or villages where poverty was the norm. The inhabitants held to the faith of their forefathers. Traditions of charity, mutual support and schooling were maintained. Jews, being the people of the book, studied the Torah and their children acquired a level of literacy and numeracy unmatched by Poles, Russians and Ukrainians. Since time immemorial even the poorest Jews put aside money so that their offspring could study the holy books. Kosher dietary rules were followed. The traditional religious calendar was observed. Rabbis and cantors were revered and scholarship was esteemed. Religious effervescence was common in most shtetls, and it was Judaism of the Hasidic variety that was widely popular. Its sects argued with each other as much as with other Jewish believers. Nearly all the adherents kept to a strict dress code. The men with their long black caftans and curly side-locks were easily distinguishable from their Slavic neighbours. Men and women worshipped separately; and Hasidism expected adult males to go several times every day to the house of prayer. Such Jews, unless they belong to the few who were successful entrepreneurs, kept their distance from Gentiles. Crimes and civil disputes were handled by the Jewish religious courts. Once the annual taxes were paid to the government there was little contact with the Imperial administration.

It was not only Hasidism which disconcerted the authorities. Jews in the northern shtetls were concentrated in occupations such as shoe-making, tailoring and other artisanal trades. Economic competition among them was ferocious. Like most Russians and Ukrainians, moreover, they had large families. Couples went on producing children through to the end of the wife's capacity to become pregnant. Poverty seared the lives of most Jewish families in the northern shtetls. The government concluded that, if ever they were to be integrated into general society, something had to be done to reform their spiritual and material conditions.[4]

It was in this situation that Emperor Alexander I introduced a scheme for Jewish agricultural colonies. Empty lands in the provinces of Kherson and Yekaterinoslav near the Black Sea were marked out for them. Proclamations were issued, and Trotsky's Bronstein grandfather was among the first to move from Poltava province to one of the colonies. Many Jews travelled south in search of relief from poverty by starting their lives afresh as farmers.[5] It was this idea that the government decided to encourage. Ministers of the crown hoped to transform the Jews from an indigent, restive, alien community into productive people better integrated into the empire. Free virgin grassland in specially demarcated areas was offered to those who agreed to cultivate it. Over 65,000 Jewish settlers lived in southern, central and western Ukraine by the middle of the nineteenth century, and there were twenty-two Jewish colonies in Kherson province alone.[6] Gromokleya was the last Jewish agricultural colony to be founded there. The Bronsteins were among the plucky Jews who decided to escape the economic trap of the shtetls and take up agriculture.[7]

Legal restrictions were built into the scheme for such colonies and government inspectors made regular trips to ensure compliance. (The man who reported on Gromokleya stayed in the house of Trotsky's uncle Abram.)[8] Officials from the beginning expressed doubts that the Jewish urban artisan was amenable to manual work on the farm.[9] Many settlers seemed to prove the point by trying to sell their land as soon as they arrived. A ban was placed on such attempts (which did not stop people simply absconding from their colonies).[10] The more intelligent administrators recognized the physical conditions to be often of exceptional difficulty. Not every settlement was near a river, which was the fault of the Imperial authorities rather than the arriving Jews. Another annoying factor was the prohibition on setting up shops or stalls.[11] The idea of ministers was that colonists should dedicate themselves wholly to farming. Initially they were banned from taking on Christian labour even at harvest time in case Ukrainian peasants should fall under their economic dominance. Whatever happened, furthermore, the colonies were to be kept separate. Jewish colonists were banned from selling their houses and fields to Gentiles; they were also not permitted to buy the landed property of non-Jews. The whole framework of laws and decrees was pervaded by distrust.[12]

There was to be no attempt to convert them to Christianity; the authorities intended them to remain true to their faith. So the Jews were encouraged to build synagogues.[13] The hope was that the kind of Judaism they practised would acquire a more 'enlightened' and modern character and that Hasidism would be abandoned as their living conditions improved. Official help with setting up Russian-language schools was provided from 1840. But they were not usually a success. Nearly all Jewish settlers went on bringing up their children up speaking Yiddish.[14] The government in St Petersburg was perplexed about this, and ministers considered how best to intervene in the schools established by the colonists. They tried to get Yiddish schools to teach Russian rather than German as a second language. But the Jews for a while resisted this intrusion. Yiddish originated to a large extent in the German language, and it was conventional for the schools in the northern shtetls – if they taught any foreign language at all – to opt for German.[15] Only after much coaxing did the colonies begin to accept Russian teachers and the Russian language.[16]

Respect for Jewish custom was vibrant in the colonies. The settlers felt no desire to change how they lived and worshipped, and soon the Imperial administration in New Russia reported that they were inviting Hasidic rabbis and ritual slaughtermen to join them from the north.[17] Many features of Jewish behaviour were baffling to Christians. It was rare for any colonist to get drunk in taverns. The incidence of criminality was low – administrators noted with awe that 'the shame of punishment has a stronger effect than the punishment.'[18] (Whether such sobriety was maintained in their homes at Succoth and other feasts of the religious calendar may be doubted, but the civil authorities saw little of that.) 'Not even a trace' of Hasidism had previously existed in New Russia. The newcomers changed all that.[19] When a rabbinic scholar spoke on social matters his words had the force of a command: faith and everyday life were intimately connected. The Imperial authorities regarded this as sheer 'fanaticism'. Why, they exclaimed, the Jews gave priority to the calendar of their faith over work and profit! They 'wasted' their money on kosher meat. Every week they 'lost' the entire period from Friday twilight to the moment when the first star was sighted on Saturday evening without doing any work in the fields – indeed usually they resumed their labours only on Sunday morning.[20] Jewish families scrimped and hoarded only to spend their savings on marrying off their daughters. When a relative died they all sat on the floor for a week and mourned the departed. What sort of routine was this if they wanted to become successful at farming?

Soon the annual audits were telling the story that the output of settler communities fell far below official expectations. The reckoning was that only a fifth of settlers around the middle of the century had made a success of farming. A further fifth did reasonably well for themselves, but the rest of them were pretty abject failures. A specialist reported: 'The government's beneficent proposal – to make farmers out of Jews – has not been realized.'[21] Poverty had been transferred from the Polish or Lithuanian shtetl to the farming colonies of Kherson and the neighbouring provinces.

Things changed a little for the better as official policy was adjusted.[22] Ministers in St Petersburg had come to accept that the Jewish agricultural colonies needed to operate with fewer restrictions. In 1857 Jews were at last permitted to hire Christian labourers for seasonal work.[23] Gromokleya, moreover, came into being in the period when Emperor Alexander II was making general reforms to the Imperial order. In 1861 he issued an Emancipation Edict giving personal freedom to peasants who were beholden to the landed gentry. Where the soil was fertile they were accorded a small plot of land to cultivate. Where it was less productive they gained a much larger one. In both instances they had to pay back state loans for their newly acquired property. The special conditions of the Jewish agricultural colonies were not ignored while such a transformation of rural conditions occurred. In 1863 the prohibition on colonists engaging in non-agricultural trade outside the colony was lifted.[24] At the end of the decade, the ban on the permanent employment of Christians was revoked, and Jews were allowed to rent additional land from Gentiles. The colonies ceased to be kept in quarantine from the rest of the agricultural sector. The more successful Jewish farmers were reported as achieving 'a prosperous economic existence', and the inspectors believed they would constitute 'a healthy core of real agriculturalists' as restrictions on activities in the Jewish colonies were eased.[25]

Improvement, slow in starting, seemed at last to be on the horizon – and the Bronsteins were among the families which strengthened official optimism. The average size of a holding when the colonies were set up in Kherson province was 110 acres.[26] The normal procedure was for the head of household to claim title to a continuous area, and there was no pressure to intermingle small strips of land as was usual among peasants in central and south-east Russia.[27] As the regulations on land renting were eased, men like David Bronstein seized their chances to increase the area they owned or rented. By the middle of the century, eight families in Kherson province's Jewish agricultural colonies had accrued enough money and expertise to construct windmills – and the Bronsteins were later to join them.[28] Technical modernity was coming to the local countryside.

The general economic environment was on the side of the Bronsteins and their like. World markets were eager for Russian and Ukrainian cereals. Railways were constructed from the north to Odessa and Kherson. Ports on the great river system on the northern shore of the Black Sea were expanded. Trains and steamships carried wheat and rye to Odessa. Cereal cultivation in New Russia began to thrive. Agricultural techniques had to be developed almost from nothing since both soil and climate in the southern steppes were different from elsewhere in the Russian Empire. Certainly the land was fertile. But otherwise there were problems which had not been anticipated. Rainfall was unpredictable. The conventional strains of wheat did not do well. The Jews who came to Kherson and Yekaterinoslav provinces, unlike the German colonists, had scant experience of ploughing, sowing and harvesting. No scientific advice was made available to them by the authorities. They had to learn on the job. In good years they could do well simply because it was virgin territory for cultivation. Lacking any ecological training, they took few steps to replenish the soil's fertility – and in the twentieth century this led to the steppes in many places being turned into dust bowls. The work was backbreaking. But the immediate rewards were high for the determined few.

New Russia was renowned for its ethnic and religious diversity, and the economy of Kherson province reflected this mélange. Gromokleya, as it happened, lay adjacent to a prosperous German agricultural colony. As the early restrictions on the colonies of Jews were relaxed Poles, Germans and Jews as well as Russians increasingly interacted, and by and large there was peaceful coexistence. Anti-Jewish pogroms and riots were not infrequent in the Russian Empire in 1881–3. Naturally this agitated Jews all over New Russia, especially in trouble spots like Odessa, but those who lived in the countryside saw less of the trouble and held to the hope that the situation would improve.

David and Aneta Bronstein fitted into this broader milieu better than most Jewish colonists. They were oddities among members of the Gromokleya colony in having a somewhat casual attitude to religious observance. Yanovka lay too far from the village synagogue for them to join in worship on a daily basis. Trotsky remembered them as practising their Judaism with a light touch and quietly holding reservations about all religious faith – and Leiba in adolescence supposedly overheard them talking as confirmed atheists. And although they were rural inhabitants, Aneta came from Odessa and had relatives who were making a success of their lives there. Ties of family meant that the couple had a window on to a wider world than the farm and the village. Among their relatives was a factory owner; and Aneta had nephews and nieces who would prosper in the economic expansion of the late nineteenth century. The Bronsteins of Yanovka belonged to an extended family which did well for itself in the surging economy of New Russia. David's parents had once lived in a Poltava province shtetl whereas he and his wife were pioneers of the kind of existence which did not have Jewishness at its forefront.

The remote agricultural life, of course, limited the couple's intercourse with modernity. Aneta had been brought up without much attention to her education. She could read fitfully but not very well. David, a son of the village, could not read or write; he was an unusual Jew in not having had rudimentary schooling. This restricted the Bronsteins' access to the changing urban culture of the Russian Empire, and they were content with the farming life for themselves. Their rising prosperity was a marvel for the entire colony. Geographical distance did not prevent David from making his own trips to Nikolaev and doing his own deals. Nor did Aneta's relatives in Odessa fail to make trips out to Yanovka in the summertime.

Imperceptibly the Bronsteins were becoming less 'Jewish' than their Gromokleya neighbours. At home, if we are to believe Trotsky's account, David Bronstein 'spoke an ungrammatical mixture of the Russian and Ukrainian languages with a preponderance of the Ukrainian'.[29] This was the local vernacular – usually it was referred to as 'jargon'. There was a practical reason why the Bronsteins dispensed with Yiddish. Their labourers and servants were Ukrainians who spoke nothing but Ukrainian 'jargon'. It made sense for them, being stuck out on a farm in Kherson province, to use the local tongue. The similarity of the Yiddish and German languages would have made it easy for David to communicate with the German landowners as well as with friends and relatives in the colony. People across the Pale of Settlement – Poles, Russians, Ukrainians, Germans, Jews and Greeks – got used to muddling through linguistically. David and Aneta were unusual only in giving so heavy a preference to a Ukrainian dialect over all the others. It was a sign of their openness to a world outside their immediate family and community.

Whereas most families in Gromokleya lived and worked on the land over more than one generation, not a single son or daughter of David and Aneta Bronstein stayed on the farm on reaching adulthood. Their parents bought them the best education available. David and Aneta themselves were a couple who could have contributed to the creation of a very different Russia from the one which emerged from the carnage of world war, revolutions and civil war. If we judge by their behaviour, they belonged to the widening stratum of the emperor's subjects who stood for enlightenment, material progress and promotion through merit. New Russia as a name had a social as well as a territorial significance. The old Russia was steadily giving way to a society, economy and culture which did away with traditional attitudes and practices, and the Bronstein household in Yanovka was enthusiastic about the process of change.

# 2. UPBRINGING

The Bronsteins had eight children. Only half of them survived to adulthood. The others died young of scarlet fever or diphtheria, and Trotsky recorded: 'I was born the fifth. My birth was scarcely a joyful event in the family. Life was too full of intensive labour. Children were an inevitability but, for well-off families, not a requirement.'[1] As usual he exaggerated the grimness of conditions at Yanovka; but he was justified in stressing that the family as yet did not enjoy access to all the facilities of contemporary civilization. Leiba Bronstein was the third of the surviving children – a brother and two sisters grew up with him. He scarcely mentioned them in his autobiography except when describing incidents which directly involved them. Their names were Alexander, Elisheba, who was known as Yelizaveta in later life, and Golda who became known as Olga.[2] Alexander was born in 1870, Elisheba in 1875. Then came Leiba, followed by Golda in 1883. The two older children, Alexander and Yelizaveta, paired off for many activities and Leiba and Golda played together, but with a gap of four years between them it was always he who took the lead.

The Yanovka farm took its name from its former owners, a Colonel Yanovski, whose meritorious service had earned the grant of a thousand acres in Kherson province in the reign of Emperor Alexander II. Yanovski had risen from the ranks and was hopelessly inexperienced at farming, and he put the farm up for sale. David Bronstein discerned a good commercial opportunity as well as, perhaps, the chance to break away from the social and religious restrictions of the Gromokleya agricultural colony. He made a tempting offer to buy a parcel of over 250 acres. The Yanovski family was only too happy to accept; they leased a further 400 acres to Bronstein before moving north to Poltava province. The Russian Yanovskis were going back to precisely the same part of the empire from which the Bronsteins had once migrated. Once or twice a year the colonel's widow would return in person to collect her rent and inspect the property. She never needed to complain about Bronstein's tenancy. He cultivated wheat for the thriving export markets in the region. He kept horses for ploughing and for travelling to Yelizavetgrad and other nearby towns. He had many cattle and sheep; he also raised pigs – despite his Jewishness he had no aversion to keeping them and he let them wander near the house, snuffling in the foliage and often making their way into the garden unmolested.

Leiba was a handsome, well-built boy with bright blue eyes like his father's. (Acquaintances in the years to come, including the American communist journalist John Reed, wrongly described them as dark brown. Probably they assumed, from prejudice, that no Jew could have blue ones; this was a source of some irritation to Trotsky.)[3] His parents quickly appreciated his high intelligence. They did not spoil him or their other children. David was gruff, Aneta was demanding. They expected a lot of their sons and daughters and were angry when expectations were not fulfilled – and Leiba usually earned their praise.

His memories of times when he was scolded remained with him. One such occasion was also important because it was when he experienced one of those blackouts that would plague him throughout his life. When he was two or three years old he accompanied his mother to nearby Bobrinets to visit one of her friends who had a daughter of the same age as Leiba. Aneta Bronstein and her friend, deep in conversation, left the children on their own. It was a standing joke for the adults to refer to the little pair as the bride and the groom. The little girl briefly left the room. Leiba, standing next to a chest of drawers, had some kind of blackout. He awoke to find he had left a puddle on the varnished floor. In came his mother: 'Aren't you ashamed of yourself?' Her friend was more forgiving: 'It doesn't matter, doesn't matter. The children were just playing.'[4] Aneta herself was afflicted by blackouts and it was from her that Leiba had inherited the tendency. Generally he sought the protection of his nanny Masha. Later he told how she climbed plum trees for fruit to make into jam. The little boy got worried in case she fell. Masha laughed it off. His mother smiled at the scene but ordered: 'Climb down, Masha!'[5] Everyone on the farm knew that his parents did not want him to do anything physically dangerous. But he loved to go riding. Tumbles were not unknown, and young Leiba kept them secret for a long time from the family 'so that they didn't ban him from getting up on a horse'.[6]

He often got into scrapes:

Grisha [Trotsky's temporary name for himself in the early draft of his autobiography] was very afraid of adders and tarantulas like everyone around him in the family. Despite the fact that Grisha was

a completely rural boy and played with peasant lads, he nevertheless
failed to learn to distinguish adders from grass-snakes and was fearful
about both of them.[7]

He had come upon an adder while walking in the garden with his nanny
at the age of three or four. She had thought it was a snuff box and poked
it with a stick. She shrieked on recognizing her mistake and scooped up
Leiba before running off. He never shook off his trepidation in the face
of snakes.[8] With tarantulas he managed better – and a few years later he
went round the farm with young Viktor Gertopanov catching them with
a thickly waxed string which the pair of them lowered into their holes.[9]

As he grew older Leiba met most of the landowners in the area around
Yanovka, and he remembered them as having been as eccentric as any
described in the stories and novels of Nikolai Gogol (who also came
from Ukraine). The Bronsteins rented land near Yelizavetgrad from a
noblewoman by name of Trilitskaya. She once came on a trip to Yanovka
to renegotiate the deal, arriving with her male companion; and Leiba
observed how he could blow smoke rings from his cigarettes. Leiba learned
to be careful about what was said about this noblewoman in case it was
reported back to her and she reacted badly.[10] Then there was Fedosya
Dembovska, a Polish widow who did not remain a widow for long. She
married her bailiff Casimir. Fat and jolly, Casimir knew only one funny
story which he told Leiba again and again; he brought generous gifts in
the shape of the honeycombs from his own bees when he visited Yanovka.[11]
Another landowner he remembered was Ivan Dorn, who was a fat German
with a brightly painted cart.[12] Richest of all were the brothers Feldzer.
Possessing thousands of acres, they lived in a house that was as sumptuous
as a palace: in Kherson province they were as famous for their wealth as
the Rockefellers were in the rest of the world. (They did not keep it all
since their fraudulent bailiff regularly reported a loss in the annual
accounts.) Ivan Feldzer one day rode out fox-hunting with two companions and a pair of dogs across the fields of Yanovka. The dogs slurped
the water from the Bronsteins' well as the farm labourers expostulated
that no fox was in the vicinity. David Bronstein was angry at seeing his
crops trampled. The hunters were helped into a rowing boat and left to
their own devices on the far bank of the river.[13]

Then there were the Gertopanovs who had once owned an entire
district but then had to mortgage all their property. Although they were
left with over a thousand acres they were hopeless farmers and needed a
tenant to pay their monthly debt to the bank. David Bronstein obliged.

Timofei Gertopanov and his wife would turn up at Yanovka with gifts of tobacco and sugar. Mrs Gertopanov would talk endlessly about her lost youth and her pianos. In a total reversal of family status the Bronsteins took on one of their sons, Viktor, as an apprentice.[14] It is easy to imagine how the Bronsteins shook their heads at the oddities and fecklessness of their neighbours. Trotsky wrote of this like a socialist Anton Chekhov: 'The seal of doom lay on these landowning families from Kherson province.'[15]

David Bronstein was not the only Jew who did well for himself in the neighbourhood. Three miles from Yanovka lay the estate of Moisei Morgunovski (as he called himself in the Russian fashion). The Morgunovskis had learned French and old man Morgunovski played the piano, albeit better with his right hand than with his left. Unfortunately his grandson, David, as a conscript in the Imperial Army, had tried to commit suicide by shooting himself in the head – Jews were given a hard time in the armed forces. Young David had to have his head bandaged for the rest of his life; but his troubles did not end there. The authorities put him on a charge of military insubordination which was removed only when his father paid a large bribe.[16] Leiba and his elder brother Alexander spent days with them. The Morgunovskis, unlike the Bronsteins, did not let livestock into the garden, where they kept peacocks. They lived luxuriously. The family subsequently fell on hard times so that the farm subsided into disrepair. The last peacock died, the fences tumbled and cattle trampled the flowers and even some of the trees. Moisei Morgunovski had to give up his fine phaeton for a peasant horse-drawn cart, which he drove on visits to Yanovka. The sons lived less like lords than like peasants. The Bronsteins became the richest Jews in the neighbourhood.[17]

In the German colony a different social ambience existed. The boys were sent to the towns; the girls worked in the fields. The farmhouses of the Germans were typically of brick construction with red and green iron roofing. They went in for horses of good pedigree.[18] One family, the Falts-Feins, were renowned for developing local breeds of merino sheep, and Trotsky never forgot the bleating of their vast flocks.[19] Generally it was the German colonists who were the wealthiest in Kherson province.

Trotsky liked others to think that the Bronstein family were peasants. Some aspects of the household pointed in this direction. For many years David and Aneta lived in the mud hut constructed by Colonel Yanovski. Being illiterate, David had no capacity for keeping written accounts. He turned for help to his children, as when he called to young Leiba:

'Come on, then, write this down! I received thirteen hundred rubles from the commission merchant. I sent 660 to the colonel's widow and handed over 400 to Dembovski. Put it down too that I gave 100 rubles to Feodosya Antonovna when I was in Yelizavetgrad in the spring.' That is the sort of way the accounts were kept. Even so, my father slowly but doggedly kept climbing upwards.[20]

As David grew in wealth he replaced the original Yanovski hut with a house of brick, and he had the garden, including a croquet lawn, set out in a grand fashion. He built his own mill so that he could grind his own wheat and cut out payments to middle men. He travelled to Yelizavetgrad and Nikolaev to sell his harvest and buy equipment and materials. He stopped using a cart except for tasks around the farm and purchased a costly phaeton and two excellent stallions. He rented several thousand acres from assorted landlords who were content to stay overnight with the Bronsteins if they travelled from afar.

Yanovka marked the edge of Leiba's universe before going to school at the age of six. The Gromokleya colony did not have one of the many officially subsidized schools which taught Russian.[21] Instead there was a traditional Jewish *cheder* where Yiddish was the language of instruction. The sole teacher was Mr Shuler, who came out to see Leiba's mother about arrangements:

> The teacher greeted me with that mildness with which every teacher greets his future pupil in the presence of parents. Mother completed the business arrangements right before me: for so many rubles and so many sacks of flour the teacher undertook to instruct me at his school in the colony, in Russian, arithmetic and the Old Testament in the original Hebrew.[22]

Leiba's qualms about starting school were quietened when he saw before him this inoffensive man trying to ingratiate himself with the Bronsteins. Indeed Shuler was so timid that his wife did not flinch from throwing bags of flour in his face while he was teaching.

Leiba's parents decided that two miles was too far for him to walk daily into the village. Instead he would stay with his aunt Rakhil in the village. The arrangement was concluded without the need for cash to change hands. David supplied his sister Rakhil with sacks of wheat flour, barley flour, buck wheat and millet. The Bronsteins made their payment in a mixture of rubles and flour, which was how things were done in the countryside. Shuler had agreed to introduce Leiba to Russian;[23] but if

Leiba's difficulties with the vocabulary a couple of year later are anything to go by, Shuler himself may not have had the firmest grip on the Russian language.[24] Hebrew was another matter. Shuler would never have gathered pupils without proficiency in that tongue. Leiba himself had to pick up more Yiddish if he was to understand the lessons or get on with the other boys. In the event he stayed at the school for only a few months, subsequently claiming that his lack of linguistic facility prevented him from making close friends.[25] At any rate he felt a permanent gratitude towards Shuler because the short time he spent in his hands gave him mastery of rudimentary skills in reading and writing.

Trotsky had a distinct preference for his father over his mother. He put this with characteristic insouciance: 'My father was undoubtedly superior to my mother in both intellect and character. He was deeper, more reserved, and more tactful. He had an unusually good eye not only for things but also for people.'[26] He was also decidedly frugal. Leiba remembered him declining to get the holes in the sofa repaired:

> The smaller hole was near the chair where Ivan Vasilevich [Greben] sat, the larger where I sat, next to my father. 'This sofa should be re-covered with new cloth,' Ivan Vasilevich used to say. 'It should have had one long ago,' my mother would reply: 'We haven't covered it since the year the tsar was killed [1881].' 'But you know,' my father would justify himself, 'when you get to that damned city, you run all over the place, the horse cabs devour money; you're thinking all the time about how to get back quickly to the farm and forgetting all about what you meant to buy.'[27]

The entire business was run on avoidance of waste:

> My parents generally bought very little, especially in the old days – and father and mother knew how to save their kopeks – but father never made a mistake in what he was buying. He had a feeling for quality in everything whether it was cloth, a hat, shoes, a horses or machinery. 'I don't like money,' he said to me later on, to justify his meanness, 'but I don't like having none of it. It is bad to need money and not have any.'[28]

Leiba hated how David disciplined his labourers. One day he came back from a game of croquet to find a short, barefoot peasant pleading for the return of his cow which had strayed into his fields. David was furious about what had happened; he impounded the animal, shouting: 'Your cow may eat only ten kopeks' worth of grain, but it will do ten rubles' worth of damage.' Leiba was shocked:

The peasant kept on repeating his words, and one could sense the hatred in his pleading. The scene shook me through to the innermost fibres of my body. The croquet-playing mood I had brought from the pitch amid the pear trees, where I had trounced my sisters, immediately gave way to acute despair. I slipped past father, rushed into my bedroom, fell flat on the bed and cried myself into oblivion despite the fact that I was a pupil in the second grade at school. Father walked through the hall into the dining room as the small peasant shuffled behind him up to the doorstep. I could hear their voices. Then the peasant went. Mother came from the mill; I recognized her voice at once and heard the plates being prepared for lunch and my mother calling out for me. But I did not answer, and went on weeping.[29]

She comforted him and tried to find out what was the matter. Leiba refused to speak. The parents whispered between themselves. His mother said: 'Are you upset about the peasant? Look, we gave him back his cow and we did not fine him.'[30] Leiba pretended that the peasant's troubles were not why he was crying, but everyone in the house knew the truth.

His older cousin Moshe Shpentser – Aneta's nephew – sympathized with the boy. On one of his visits from Odessa, Shpentser objected when a foreman whipped a shepherd for leaving the horses out late: 'How disgusting!'[31] Shpentser encouraged Leiba to think critically about his environment. Leiba himself felt sensitive about the poverty of some of his father's labourers. The Bronsteins employed a simpleminded lad, Ignatka, as a shepherd's mate. Ignatka's mother was destitute and was owed a ruble – just one ruble – by the Yanovka farm. She walked three miles in her rags to obtain this paltry sum, but when she arrived there was no one to hand over the money. So she leaned herself against a wall, too timid to sit on the doorstep. She had to wait till it was evening before the ruble was placed in her hands.[32]

Trotsky also described the way justice was dispensed in the Yanovka of his childhood. When a driver stole a bay mare, David Bronstein had no hesitation in sending Alexander, Leiba's elder brother, to catch and deal with him. Two days of searching yielded no result. Alexander returned having failed to find the culprit or exact revenge;[33] and there would have been popular approval if he had gone beyond merely handing over the thief to the authorities: many people enforced the laws of property without recourse to the police or courts. Village ideas of justice were rough and ready. At Gromokleya, in the midst of the agricultural colony, lived a tall fellow with a reputation as a horse thief. (There seems to have been a lot of it about in the area.) His daughter was held in no higher repute and when the cap-maker's wife suspected her of having an affair with her husband, she appealed to local friends for help. Trotsky remembered: 'Returning from school one day I saw a crowd shouting, screaming and spitting as it dragged the young woman . . . down the street.' As it happened, the government inspector was on a visit to the colony at the time. But he refused to intervene. The villagers were left to enforce traditional justice.[34]

As Leiba grew a little older, he was given more freedom at Yanovka and he loved to wander into the farm workshop. This was the domain of the remarkable Ivan Greben, his father's mechanic. He was a jack of all trades and a master of most:

> This was a person of great talent and handsome appearance with a dark red moustache and a French-style beard. His technical knowledge was universal. He could repair steam engines, carry out work on boilers, turn a metal or a wooden ball, cast brass bearings, make spring carriages, mend clocks, tune a piano, upholster furniture or make an entire bicycle except for the tyres. It was on such a contraption that I learned to ride a bicycle when I was between the preparatory and first years. Neighbouring German colonists would bring him their seed-drills and binders to be repaired in the workshop, and they would invite him to go along with them to buy a threshing machine or a steam engine. People consulted my father about farming and Ivan Vasilevich about technology.[35]

Greben was the farm's most valued employee, and when he was called up for military service David Bronstein paid a bribe to secure his exemption.[36] The mill required his regular expertise. Greben had an assistant mechanic, Foma by name. There was also a second miller: this was an ex-cavalryman called Filipp. Then there were the two apprentices, Senya Gertopanov and David Chernukhovski. (Greben eventually fell out with young Gertopanov and got rid of him.)[37]

Unlike most youngsters of the colony, Leiba did not have a life associated mainly with fellow Jews. The Bronsteins increasingly adjusted themselves to the Christian calendar. Their labourers were Christians and Aneta made *kut'ya* – a traditional wheat berry dish – and handed it to them at Christmas, and at Easter she made painted eggs and baked *kulichi* – almond and saffron cakes – for them.[38] And of course Leiba's friendship with the remarkable Ivan Greben, the farm's mechanic, reinforced his fluency in the Russo-Ukrainian dialect. Leiba loved to visit the workshop and be taught some technical skills. Greben and the young workers took him under their wing: 'In many matters I was the apprentice of these apprentices.'[39]

Greben was strict with Leiba.[40] Trotsky remembered him as the embodiment of the virtues of the working man. His demeanour and uprightness were important for him, and Trotsky remembered his physical presence:

> he would smoke and look into the distance, perhaps pondering something or remembering something or simply relaxing without a thought in his head. At such times I used to sidle up to him and affectionately twirl his bushy, auburn moustache around my fingers, or examine his hands – those remarkable, absolutely special hands of a master craftsman. All the skin of his hands was covered with little black spots: these were the tiniest splinters that had irremovably penetrated his body when he was cutting millstones. His fingers were as tenacious as roots but not completely hard; they broadened towards the tips and were very supple, and he could turn his thumb right back so as to form an arch. Each of his fingers was conscious, living and acting by itself; together they formed an unusual working collective. However young I was, I could already see and feel that this hand was not like other hands when holding a hammer or a pair of pliers. There was a deep scar around his left thumb. Ivan Vasilevich had caught his hand with an axe the day I was born and the thumb was hanging almost by the skin alone. My father had happened to see the young mechanic laying his hand on a board and getting ready to chop off his thumb altogether. 'Stop!' he had shouted. 'Your finger will grow back again!' 'It will grow back, you think?' asked the mechanic, and put the axe aside. The thumb really did grow back and worked well except only that it did not turn back as far as the one on his right hand.[41]

This was not only excellent writing: it also showed how respect for workers was among the earliest social attitudes developed by Trotsky.

The memory of Greben's creativity stayed with Trotsky, and perhaps it explains his lifelong appreciation of technical experts:

> Ivan Vasilevich once made a shotgun out of an old Berdan rifle and tried his skill at marksmanship: everyone took turns at trying to put out a candle by striking the primer at a distance of several paces. Not everyone succeeded. My father chanced to come in. When he raised the gun to take aim, his hands trembled and he somehow lacked

confidence in the way he held the gun. But he put the candle out at the first attempt. He had a good eye for everything, and Ivan Vasilevich understood this. There were never any altercations between them, although my father would talk bossily with the other workmen, often rebuking them and finding fault.[42]

Trotsky also recalled how Greben had built a sophisticated pigeon loft under the roof of the machine house and scores of birds were brought from the Dembovski estate to complete the enterprise. Leiba was very excited about the pigeon loft and climbed up a ladder ten times a day to feed the inhabitants with seed and water. Sadly, very soon all but three pairs of pigeons flew.[43] It was one of the few occasions in Leiba's childhood when anything went irretrievably wrong for him. His early years were peaceful, protected and fulfilling.

# 3. SCHOOLING

David Bronstein was determined that his children were going to grow up without his educational disadvantage. He had never been a devout Jew and did not mind sending his offspring to a Christian school if this would help them find a professional career as adults. So when the time came for Leiba to start at secondary school David chose St Paul's Real-schule in Uspenski Street in Odessa. He would have preferred the grammar school (*gimnazia*), which was the city's finest educational institution, but Leiba was a casualty of the quota system applied to Jews since 1887. The authorities were nervous about producing a large number of highly educated Jewish young men. Ministers were not acting only out of religious prejudice. They also worried that Russians and others in general might resent losing places at favoured schools. St Paul's was the next best choice, and a sound one at that. Arrangements were made for Leiba to live with his cousin Moshe Shpentser and his wife Fanni as a paying lodger.[1]

The day of departure was momentous for Yanovka. For Leiba, the trip of over two hundred miles to Odessa at the age of nine was like a journey across an unknown ocean. David Bronstein ordered the horses and carriage to be got ready. There were hugs and tears when he bade goodbye to his mother and sisters. The suitcases were loaded and then, finally, Leiba set off with his father. The colony's tailor had kitted him out smartly for the Realschule. Large pats of butter and bottles of jam were piled into a trunk for handing over to the Shpentsers. Leiba was still crying as he moved off with his father. They travelled for miles over the rough ground of the steppe until they reached the road which was to take them to the nearest rail station at Novy Bug. From there they went by train to Nikolaev on the River Bug where they boarded the SS *Potëmkin*.[2] Leiba absorbed the strange new sounds and sights: the vessel's piercing whistle, the sailors bustling about on deck and lastly the vast flatness of the Black Sea as the vessel turned westward and began its approach to Odessa. On disembarking, they took a horse cab to Pokrovski Lane where the Shpentsers had their apartment. Moshe and Fanni would be his informal guardians in the city for the next five years while he was at the Realschule.

The school was a foundation of the city's German community and it was attached to a Lutheran church. By the time Leiba joined, German boys from Odessa and the surrounding region constituted only a third to a half of the pupils – such was the growing reputation of the teaching staff that boys of diverse national and religious backgrounds applied for admission.[3] Leiba was pleased but apprehensive about joining them. Big city, big school and big parental ambitions. Everything about the situation was unfamiliar for him. He needed to adjust himself to strange ways, to firm discipline and to masters and pupils who would not always treat him kindly. He had to improve his Russian. He also had to learn a new language fast; although Trotsky was not fluent in Yiddish, its linguistic similarity to German must have made this easier for him. He gradually learned to speak Russian almost without a local accent. Recordings of him were made until after the October Revolution, when traces of Odessan pronunciation were detectable; and presumably the heritage of New Russia was more prominent in still earlier years. It would be odd if there was not also a specifically Jewish tinge to his diction since he lodged with Moshe and Fanni Shpentser and came from a family of Jews. But his grammar was always the standard Imperial Russian of contemporary textbooks.[4]

He found help early on. As a newcomer he was assigned to the preparatory class where a German boy – remembered only as Karlson – who had been kept down a year took Trotsky under his protection and taught him the rules of survival.[5] (Leiba had not been allowed into the first year since he scored only three out of five for Russian language and four for arithmetic in the preliminary test. His village schooling left him with a lot of catching up to do.) Carlson was no academic star but was a cheerful fellow whereas Leiba was feeling less than happy. As he walked for the first time with other boys along Uspenski Street on his way to St Paul's dressed in his splendid school uniform, a youthful ne'er-do-well leaned over and spat on his jacket. The shocked Leiba hurriedly removed the stain, but fellow pupils started to yell at him inside the school gates. Already he had broken one of the rules. The Shpentsers did not know that the full uniform was not to be worn by those in the preparatory class. The school inspector told him to see to the removal of the badge, braid and belt-buckle; and the buttons, which had an eagle stamped on them, had to be replaced with ordinary ones made of bone.[6] It was not the easiest of introductions to his academic career. Leiba felt humiliated. Only Carlson's attentiveness made a bad situation bearable.

There were no classes that morning and Leiba joined everyone at a service of induction in the church. He heard organ music for the first time and was thrilled by its sound even though he could not understand a word of what was being said. The preacher was Pastor Binneman who unlike priests of the Russian Orthodox Church had no beard. Carlson told him that Binneman was 'a remarkably intelligent man, the most intelligent man in Odessa'. Leiba took this on trust. Carlson himself, though, was lazy and ineffective at his studies whereas Leiba won praise in next day's mathematics lesson for copying the lesson from the blackboard and was given two fives (the highest attainable mark). He repeated this feat in his German lesson and was again awarded a five.[7] Once taught something, he seldom forgot it. His leanings were mainly towards the scientific side and he loved mathematics. In fact no subject in the curriculum foxed him. It was a rare day in Pokrovski Lane when he returned without having obtained top marks in any test.

Leiba's Odessa home life was a happy one. Moshe was a lively man, interested in ideas and good with children. Early in life he fell foul of the authorities. The result was that he was barred from entering university education. His supposed offence remains a mystery, but Jews of independent mind were hardly to the liking of the governing elite. Moshe took a while to recover from the setback and spent his days translating Greek tragedies. He also studied the past, his favourite author being the German scholar Friedrich Christoph Schlosser.[8] No doubt it was Schlosser's history of the world, translated into Russian, which Moshe used in order to compile statistics and visual charts of his own on the development of humankind from its origins to the present.[9] He had recently married Fanni who was the principal of the state school for Jewish girls in Odessa and it was her salary that kept the couple afloat in the early years of their marriage.[10] Moshe's penchant for drawing up tables and schedules made him useful to her efforts to introduce a rational system of record-keeping. But he needed to build his own career and managed to make a little money by dabbling in journalism. When this failed to bring in enough income, he tried his hand at producing stationery.[11] At last he had achieved success and his business activity was beginning to grow at the time of Leiba's arrival.

Shpentser was to become one of the leading publishers in the south of the Russian Empire. But all this lay in the future. During Leiba's years in Pokrovski Lane Cousin Moshe was still finding his way. He kept his printing press in the apartment and was therefore at home a lot of the time. Leiba was seldom alone when he came back from school.

The apartment was a modest one. Moshe's mother, an elderly lady, was living with them and a curtain was draped across the dining room to give her some privacy.[12] She had her bed there. The normal thing would have been for Leiba to call her Granny. But Leiba had a sense of genealogical propriety. Since Moshe was his first cousin he insisted on referring to the old lady as Aunty.[13] This was also his way of identifying himself as a full member of the Shpentser household. The ties binding him to his own parents were imperceptibly loosening. A second space was screened off for him in the same dining room where he was given a bed and a pair of bookshelves. Moshe helped him with his schoolwork; and, as Trotsky would recall, 'he loved . . . to act the schoolmaster.'[14] This was exactly what Leiba needed to attain his potential.

Moshe and Fanni set about rubbing the rural habits off him. He had to put on his nightclothes at nine o'clock and could no longer go to bed just when he wanted. (The rule was relaxed when he got older and was allowed to stay up until eleven o'clock.) The Shpentsers also worked on his manners:

> It was pointed out to me at every turn not to fail to say good-morning, to keep my hands and fingernails neat and tidy, not to eat with a knife, never to be late for anything, always to thank the servant for her work and not to speak ill of people behind their backs.[15]

To the Bronstein insistence on hard work and reliability were added the Shpentser requirements of urbanity and politeness. This combination never left him, and in 1923 he was to write a whole booklet – *Problems of Everyday Life* – which spelled out evangelically the urgent need to change Russian popular culture.[16]

Fanni and Moshe, obviously, were more like aunt and uncle to him than cousins. They had a baby daughter, Vera, who was three weeks old when Leiba first arrived in Odessa. (She grew up to be the famous Soviet poet Vera Inber.) Leiba was put to assisting with her. The Shpentsers thought this would do him good by stopping him from studying too hard. He loved little Vera even though he occasionally rocked her too hard.[17] He was a model nephew and Fanni recalled:

> I never saw him rude and I never saw him angry in my life. The worst trouble I had with him was that he was so terribly neat. I remember once he had a new suit, and we went out walking, and all the way he kept picking imaginary lint off that suit. I said to him, 'If you do that everybody will know that you have on a new suit.' But it made no difference. He had to have everything perfect.[18]

Just one incident marred the picture when Leiba stole several valuable books from Moshe's collection and sold them to buy sweets. He did not enjoy the experience even before he was caught out – and he could never explain why he had been delinquent. The Shpentsers forgave him and the deed was put behind all of them.[19]

Moshe and his printing equipment initiated Leiba's lifelong fascination with the publishing world: 'I became very familiar with type, makeup, layout, printing, paging and binding. Proofreading became my favourite pastime. My love for the freshly printed page has its origin in those distant schoolboy years.'[20] Leiba was bookish. Often he would plough through works unknown to his teachers – and Fanni and Moshe appreciated his inquisitiveness. Like all the best pedagogues, they could see that they were helping to educate someone of greater potential than themselves.

Leiba became the confidant of the Shpentsers' servant Dasha. They talked in the evenings after supper and Dasha told him about her love life. Soon her place was taken by Sonya from Zhitomir. Leiba used his free time to teach her to read and write. A wet-nurse was hired for little Vera. She too came from Zhitomir and arrived on Sonya's recommendation. Both Sonya and the wet-nurse were divorced. Leiba penned letters to the ex-husbands on their behalf begging financial assistance. The wet-nurse had been in such penury that she had had to give her own child away. Leiba, who was already composing prose with more than a little artistry, wrote about the baby she had lost: 'Our little boy is the only bright star in the dark firmament of my life.' He proudly read it out aloud. The women appreciated his efforts but felt he had not quite understood their emotional predicament:

> And I had occasion to contemplate the complexity of human relations. At dinner Fanni Solomonovna said to me with an odd smile: 'Don't you want some more soup, author?'
> 'What?' I asked in alarm.
> 'Oh nothing. But you composed a letter for the wet-nurse, so that means you're an author. How did you put it: a star in the dark firmament? That's right, an author!' And no longer able to restrain her tone, she burst out laughing.

Uncle Moshe soothed his feelings and advised him in future to let the women write for themselves.[21]

This was a lesson about the power of words which Leiba never forgot. He had written something he knew to be exaggerated but it had impressed others and drawn favourable attention to him. Although he was attracted more to mathematics and science than to literature, it would not take much to alter his preference – and the fact that he spent his schooldays in the home of a publisher reinforced the tendency. Moshe took him out for walks after school. They discussed the plot of Gounod's opera *Faust*. This caused Moshe some embarrassment since he had to explain that Gretchen had a baby outside wedlock. He also told Leiba about other composers. Leiba was entranced, asking whether melodies had simply to be found or needed to be invented. Fanni and Moshe bought and read the latest Russian literature. Leiba heard them talking about it. When the performance of Tolstoy's play *The Power of Darkness* was banned they bought a copy of the text. They thought the scene where a child is strangled was unsuitable for Leiba, but he took it off and went through it while they were out. With their approval he also gained an enthusiasm for Charles Dickens. The Shpentsers gave him a window on to high culture. And he was always to be grateful for the sensitive way they handled him. He remembered Fanni with greater warmth than his own parents.[22] 'It was', he recalled, 'a good intellectual family. I owe it a lot.'[23]

Pastor Binneman wielded the dominant influence at St Paul's, and when he died the boys were led past his open coffin to pay their respects. The experience startled Leiba. Presumably it was the first time he had had such an experience since Jews, unlike Christians in the Russian Empire, did not expose corpses to public view before funerals. Leiba was learning the ways of the Gentiles. He got used to the idea that different peoples had their own customs and practices. Russian was becoming his instinctive medium of expression. At the same time he was being taught universal principles of analysis in geometry and physics. The restricted perspective of Yanovka was receding into the past; and when he went back during the vacations he was starting to look on the farm with alien eyes.

Binneman's brother-in-law Shvannebakh was sacked as the school's director shortly after the funeral and replaced by Nikolai Kaminski, who was the inspector who had told off Leiba on his first day at the school. Kaminski's appointment occurred at the time when the government was introducing a policy of Russification to its schools. Shvannebakh, a German by descent, gave way to a Slav. Kaminski was a physicist with a sharp, falsetto voice which terrified pupils. His calm exterior seemed to Leiba to disguise a condition of constant irritation. According to his later account, he treated everyone he met with an attitude of 'armed neutrality'. Yet Kaminski was not without his enthusiasms. Being a bit of an inventor he delighted in demonstrating Boyle's law with an apparatus he had developed. The display always provoked a certain amount of hilarity and quiet insubordination among the pupils.[24]

Then there were Yurchenko and Zlotchanski who taught mathematics. Yurchenko was a gruff Odessan who was easy to bribe to get him to award higher marks. Zlotchanski was no more refined, being given to hawking and spitting – and out of school hours he was a heavy drinker. Leiba got on well with both of them. History lessons came from a certain Lyubimov. These were less than impressive and Leiba turned for preference to the bookshelves of Uncle Moshe for enlightenment about the Imperial past. Lyubimov, it turned out, was mentally unhinged and he hanged himself from a window. If Lyubimov appeared volatile and eccentric, geography master Zhukovski instilled mortal fear in his pupils of all ages. Leiba would later liken him to an 'automatic meat-mincing machine'. The German language, still a fundamental aspect of the curriculum, was entrusted to Mr Struve. Kindly and well meaning, Struve was distraught whenever anyone scored poorly in academic tests – no other master called forth such affection from Trotsky when he wrote his memoirs.[25]

The new inspector after Kaminski was Anton Krzhizhanovski, who taught Russian literature; he quickly recognized Leiba's writing talent and read out the boy's compositions to the class. Leiba started up a school magazine entitled the *Realist*.[26] (Is it too fanciful to suggest that he was chafing against the received opinions of irrational authority?) Magazines of this kind were usually prohibited in Imperial schools but Krzhizhanovski was benevolent towards the project. Leiba enjoyed the editorial tasks. He also wrote some verses for the first issue. His theme was a drop of water falling into the sea; this served as an allegory for the magazine being a tiny part of the 'ocean of enlightenment'. Krzhizhanovski liked the poem but criticized its metrical inaccuracy, and Trotsky in his autobiography accepted that he never achieved much as a poet. As long as he was doing the criticizing he did not mind appearing less than brilliant.[27] At any rate it is clear that the pedagogical atmosphere at St Paul's was not wholly authoritarian and discouraging to the imagination.

Trotsky could not bring himself to admit this. He recollected nothing negative about the pupils – and by the end of his time he was a leader and not just a mere member of the pack. He portrayed his entire class as the collective victim of the malice and stupidity of those who taught them. If the boys were the proletariat, the masters were the bourgeoisie. Yet it is doubtful that his companions gave him no problems. Odessa was a multinational city of several faiths with greater mutual tolerance than existed in most other important centres of the Russian Empire. But Jews could expect a good deal of personal unpleasantness. The educational establishments were not clear of anti-Semitic jibes. Trotsky made light of what he encountered at St Paul's because of his Jewishness; but his silence cannot be taken as evidence that all had been well.

He liked to give the impression that he was integrated into every common aspect of school activities. This was not so. St Paul's, like all Imperial schools, had to teach religion. Leiba Bronstein entered it as a Jew and did not convert to Christianity. He had to continue his spiritual devotions under the guidance of a rabbi who taught the Jewish pupils, and David Bronstein paid for his services. The rabbi in question failed to make it clear whether the Torah was superb literature or holy writ – and Leiba was later to conclude that he was really an agnostic of some kind.[28] The Jewish boys at St Paul's were sharply distinguished from the Christians. Jews who passed through Odessa's general school system at that time recorded how the masters would often pick on them in lessons. Usually this took the form of teasing. For example, Yuli Martov – then called Tsederbaum and later to be Trotsky's Marxist comrade on the *Iskra* newspaper – was asked in a geography lesson to name the capital of Russia before St Petersburg. He answered Moscow. The master then enquired where the capital had been before Moscow, and Martov correctly replied Kiev. A deluge of sarcasm followed as the master pretended he had expected Martov to say Berdichev. No one in the room needed reminding that Berdichev was a town with a Jewish majority in the Pale of Settlement. Only Jews attending Jewish religious schools completely escaped such treatment.

This does not necessarily mean that Trotsky retained a sense of grievance about how he had been handled. Even at the Realschule he had that self-confidence which stayed with him to the end of his life. He associated himself with rationalism and progress. The chances are that he despised any bullies and teasers as people steeped in ignorance. What is more, he was never one to bear a grudge. As a politician he was to prove extremely slow to display rancour.[29] Contempt was another matter. Trotsky would develop a magisterial capacity to indicate, either casually or with sophisticated contrivance, how he despised certain individuals.

In the second grade, however, his progress at St Paul's was brought to a sudden halt by an incident with one of the masters. It happened like this. The teacher of French was a Swiss called Gustave Burnand. The boys were convinced that he hated all of them. He was believed to have fought duels earlier in his life. This supposedly explained the deep scar on his forehead. Burnand had problems with his digestive system and constantly swallowed dyspepsia tablets to settle his stomach. He had it in for the German students, especially for one called Vakker to whom he gave a very low mark which the class felt was particularly unfair. They decided to 'give him a concert' and made a howling sound as he left the room. Burnand returned to the class with the director, accompanied by the class prefect, and rounded up those deemed to be the main culprits. This group did not include Trotsky, who was allowed home on the day of the offence. The next day Trotsky found that his classmates had unjustly shopped him to the authorities claiming that he was the instigator of the rebellion. In fact his prominent involvement in the troubles had begun late in the process.

A school council was called. Kaminski wished to be seen to be decisive. He called Leiba into his office and demanded to see his parents. Leiba explained that they lived far away. Kaminski requested that his two guardians should come in their place. The decision was announced to them: Leiba Bronstein would be suspended from St Paul's for a short period.

Leiba feared that the worst would befall him when he returned to Yanovka. His father kept his laudatory school reports on display. He appreciated that Leiba was something of a prodigy. His older boy Alexander had done well enough at school to go on to train as a doctor. But Alexander had never been outstanding at school. Leiba was different. Not only was he a gifted adolescent but also he had the ambition to make the most of his talent. The Shpentsers consoled him as best they could. It was obvious to them that an injustice had been done. Moshe said with some solemnity: 'Well, fellow, what do you make of life now?' Leiba understood that this was his normal jocular banter, and started to calm down.[30] Fanni had the practical idea of writing to Leiba's sister so that David could be prepared for the news.[31] In fact David Bronstein bore the news stoically. Perhaps he even admired his son's refusal to become a teacher's pet. He himself had not become a wealthy farmer by failing to stick up for himself. Leiba guessed that he was proud of him for having been some kind of 'cavalry leader' (konovod).[32] In any case Leiba returned to the third grade after his suspension and continued through to the end of the sixth. St Paul's normally released its boys at that point; and the Bronsteins, no doubt relieved that Leiba had avoided further trouble, entered him for the Realschule in Nikolaev for the completion of his secondary education.

# 4. THE YOUNG REVOLUTIONARY

Leiba Bronstein's assertiveness had no political dimension until after he moved to Nikolaev in autumn 1895, a few weeks before his sixteenth birthday. Built at the confluence of the Rivers Bug and Ingul, the city was like Odessa in being a recent foundation. Prince Potëmkin, Catherine the Great's favourite, had established its first administration and drawn up the plans for the original buildings. It was not one of the empire's great and famous cities. But its strategic position for defence against the Turks meant that the authorities never forgot about it and its large army garrison. Fifty miles to the south lay the Black Sea. In the late nineteenth century the cereal trade was booming. Farmers and peasants brought their produce from far and wide to profit from rising prices. Merchants sent shiploads of wheat across the Black Sea for European consumption. Most Nikolaev inhabitants were Russians or Ukrainians but the city also contained other ethnic communities as the existence of a synagogue and a Lutheran church testified. There were two large shipyards as well as a railway station and repair works. Nikolaev had enough wealthy residents to have a cantonment of dachas (or summer houses) on its western outskirts. It had an observatory, a library and a wide central boulevard. Yet it could never pretend to the glamour and excitement of Odessa, and the authorities thought it sufficiently quiet and out of the way for them to deposit political trouble-makers there after a period of Siberian exile. This last feature was about to have a decisive impact on the personal development of young Leiba.

Rooms were found for Leiba before he joined the seventh class at the Nikolaev Realschule. He behaved unobtrusively, resolving to finish his secondary education and fulfil his academic promise. But he relied mainly on knowledge already obtained:

> More and more frequently I played truant. Once the inspector paid me a visit at the apartment to ascertain the reason for my non-attendance. I felt extremely humiliated. But the inspector was courteous and became convinced that proper order prevailed inside the

family I lived with as well as inside my room; he left peaceably. Under my mattress lay several illegal political pamphlets.[1]

Nevertheless he was top of his class.

He picked up the pamphlets in his activities outside school. No longer under the affectionate but firm tutelage of the Shpentsers, he went his own way. Soon he got to know an intellectual Czech in his late twenties called Franz Shvigovski. Leiba had come across Franz's younger brother Vyacheslav in the Nikolaev Realschule. Franz and Vyacheslav held to revolutionary ideas; they had a tolerant attitude to Marxism even while criticizing it as being too narrow a doctrine. They met for discussions in the garden of Franz's small house and horticultural business. Among the friends were former exiles such as Osipovich and Shargorodski. The great topics of contemporary political debate exercised them. Members of the circle shared their books and journals.[2] Leiba, aged eighteen when he joined them, was the youngest. His schoolwork had always been an easy routine for him and now he reserved time for learning about public affairs. He devoured the circle's literature with his usual intensity. The wide cultural focus of the Shpentsers was being narrowed to a concentration on concerns about the political and economic future of Russia and its empire.

The intellectual explorations made a pleasant contrast with the cramping atmosphere he experienced inside the Bronstein family. His father wanted him to train as an engineer and pressed this idea on him on visits to the city. David was not known for his diplomacy nor Leiba for his humility. Like father, like son. Leiba himself, before leaving Odessa, had thought of enrolling in the maths faculty at the New Russia University there. David saw no future in the subject and wanted his boy to opt for a more practical line of training. Their disputes were noisy and bitter, and the elder daughter Elisheba was upset whenever they took place in her hearing.[3]

Worse was the possibility that young Leiba might choose neither option and devote his life to the revolutionary cause. David could sense this from what he witnessed on his trips to Nikolaev. Temptation was ever present so long as he belonged to the group at Shvigovski's. The appeal of radical ideas was strong among young Russians in the three decades before the First World War. They gave little credit to the emperor and his government for the economic and social changes in the country. They saw the Imperial political order as a brake on desirable progress. Thousands of them were joining groups like the one in Shvigovski's garden and experimenting in radical politics. Leiba as a Jew had an additional reason to detest the public status quo. He was anyway a person who made up his mind for himself and treated his parents as a financial resource for achieving his purposes. Thoughts of continuing his formal education started to pall. David visited Leiba frequently, seeking to steer him away from what he thought to be a dangerous path. Now Leiba was taking a risky experiment with his own future. He knew his own mind. His father was middle class and propertied. Shvigovski and his young friends lacked much money but were educated and restless, and Leiba felt an affinity with them. Leiba had no compunction about living at his father's expense while despising his hopes and values. The son, furthermore, was as stubborn as his father. He would no longer be told what to do, and rather than submit to the paternal will he fled his comfortable apartment and took up residence in Shvigovski's house.

David Bronstein for the first time in Leiba's experience cut a sorry figure. Leiba's younger sister Golda followed him into the orbit of revolutionary sympathizers after he introduced her as someone 'showing promise'.[4] The elder boy Alexander might have been a disappointment in his studies, but at least he went on to train as a doctor. The elder daughter Elisheba married a doctor. The younger pair were turning out to be constant trouble. David had got them educated so that they would be relieved of the back-breaking labour he had endured. He was finding that contemporary urban schooling could expose people to unsettling ideas such as he had never known existed, and he did not like these ideas when they were described to him.

The new way of life induced in Leiba a choice of personal identity. By sending him to a Realschule, his parents had made sure he learned proper Russian. This was not the same as wanting him to cease regarding himself as a Jew; it is unlikely that such a thought ever occurred to them. David Bronstein had remained Jewish without being at all devout. But Leiba had been in contact with a culture which eroded the impulse to pay even lip-service to the faith and customs of his forebears. His educational texts had been in Russian. His literary and political influences were Russian. It is true that several of his Nikolaev friends – Ilya Sokolovski, Alexandra Sokolovskaya and Grigori Ziv – were Jews; but they did not talk, read or write in Yiddish. Moreover, they had Russian first names and liked to be called by very Russian diminutives: Ilya as Ilyusha, Alexandra as Sasha, Shura or Shurochka and Grigori as Grisha. Leiba, wanting to be like them, decided that he wanted to be known as Lëva.[5] Pronounced 'Lyova', this was the Russian diminutive of Lev. Semantically it had nothing to do with the Yiddish name Leiba; but it was a common first-name and helpfully it sounded a little the same. His mental horizon was bounded by the entire Russian Empire.

The commune lived a hand-to-mouth existence. Franz Shvigovski, though he employed a worker and an apprentice, had to go on doing manual work in his garden. The Sokolovskis, Ilya and Alexandra, came from a family of middling status and moderate income. Grigori Ziv was a medical student in Kiev and moved away in the university term. Communal conditions were never luxurious but that was the way they all wanted to live.

Lëva had a zeal for studying the books he had missed in his time at school. Among them was *System of Logic* by John Stuart Mill. He also read textbooks such as Tefling's *Psychology*, Lippert's *History of Culture* and Kareev's *History of Philosophy*. These were standard items on the shelves of Russian intellectuals;[6] and members of Shvigovski's small circle were typical in acquainting themselves with ideas within a broad range of general subjects. They aimed to bring together politics, economics, philosophy and sociology. Only once they had digested the textbooks did they feel competent to pronounce on the specificities of Russian Imperial conditions. They did not restrict themselves to works of theory. Like all their contemporaries, they drew intellectual sustenance from creative literature. Lëva was drawn towards writers with a distinctly public agenda; his favourites were Nikolai Nekrasov and Mikhail Saltykov-Shchedrin.[7] Nekrasov wrote poetry excoriating the injustices in contemporary Russia and celebrating those who stood up to their oppressors; Saltykov-Shchedrin, though a loyal subject of the Romanovs, exposed the corruption and ignorance in Russian provincial cities. Neither had much time for the powerful and wealthy in society, and Lëva's choice of reading matter indicated how far he was moving away from the aspirations for him held by his parents.

Only one person in the group of friends, Alexandra Sokolovskaya, had read Marx's *Capital*. She arrived back from her nursing course in Odessa in summer 1896. This was nearly a year after Lëva had joined the Realschule. The group had only a handwritten and scarcely legible copy of *The Communist Manifesto* by Marx and Engels.[8] Grigori Ziv began to consider himself a Marxist.[9] But Lëva resisted Marxism as a world view. His inclination, like many contemporary radicals, was to pick the bits of Marx and Engels he disliked and to discard the others. He was still a free spirit. He would later contend that his anti-Marxism had 'psychological rather than logical roots' and that he had felt 'an inclination to protect my personality to a certain degree'.[10] He did not bother himself with studying Marxist texts but took his knowledge of it from articles in monthly journals. Apparently he felt antipathy to the grinding economic determinism of Russian Marxism at the time. Instead he preferred Nikolai Mikhailovski, who wrote anti-Marxist pieces for *Russkoe bogatstvo* ('Russian Wealth').[11]

Marxism became the dominant trend in the 1890s among the revolutionary intelligentsia in the Russian Empire, and cities such as Nikolaev were behind the times. Books by Karl Marx and Friedrich Engels had long been in circulation in Russia. Volume one of Marx's *Das Kapital* was first translated into Russian in 1872; it was allowed by the censors who thought it an economic tract on industrial development unlikely to do harm in a pre-industrial country. Many Russian socialists liked it because it warned of inevitable social degradation if measures were not taken to prevent the spread of capitalism. They were known as the *narodniki*, taking their name from the word for the people (*narod*). Theirs was a diverse movement united solely by the idea that a future socialist society should be based on the egalitarian, self-governing traditions of the Russian peasantry. They saw the village land commune as a model of how to organize society across the country. Peasant traditions seemed to embody a spirit of fairness, welfare and co-operation. For the narodniks, the widespread practice of redistributing landholdings in accordance with the material needs of households was socialism in embryo.

Capitalist development, they argued, was not unavoidable. Russia could 'leap over' feudalism into socialism. The horrors of human exploitation in the sweatshops of London, Paris, Berlin and Milan did not need to be repeated in Russia. Narodniks differed over how to instigate their revolution. Some wanted to go out to the countryside and learn from the peasantry while urging insurrection against the political and social order. Others formed clandestine parties – and among them there were several who sought to bring down the monarchy by acts of terrorism. The political police – the Okhrana – hunted down the militants regardless of their strategic priorities. But as soon as one organization was crushed, another took its place. Terrorism increasingly took hold. In 1881 a group succeeded in killing Alexander II. Instead of detonating a popular uprising, the assassination caused outrage; and Alexander III, the next emperor, acted severely against all revolutionary activity. The narodniks themselves spent time rethinking strategy. Terrorist activity was not entirely abandoned; a big trial of members of an abortive conspiracy, involving Lenin's elder brother Alexander, took place in 1887. Other advocates of narodnik ideas devoted themselves to investigating and writing about Russian economic conditions and their social consequences. Most militants increasingly wondered whether it might be more practical to conduct propaganda among the working class than among the peasantry.[12]

The early Marxists in the Russian Empire were former narodniks. Chief among them was Georgi Plekhanov. Since the early 1880s he and his Emancipation of Labour Group had lived as political refugees in Switzerland. Their thinking was based on a simple argument. Capitalism had penetrated the Imperial economy to a decisive extent in the past few years. Russia was taking the path of transformation pioneered by Britain, France and Germany. Railways were constructed to link the empire together. An efficient telegraph network was built. Enormous factories with advanced technology were established in St Petersburg and Moscow. Output from Ukrainian mines was hugely expanded. The wheat of southern Russia and Ukraine was being shipped to world markets. The dairy industry in western Siberia produced butter and yoghurt for export to central Europe. These changes, according to Plekhanov, were an incipient economic transformation. Plekhanov and the Emancipation of Labour Group contended that all narodnik strategies were a waste of time. Capitalism could no longer be leapfrogged; it was turning itself into the dominant modality of the economy in the Russian Empire. Indeed one of Plekhanov's supporters, Vladimir Ulyanov (who later came to public notice as Lenin), went further. In a series of articles, culminating in his *The Development of Capitalism in Russia* in 1899, he contended that Russian economic conditions were already hardly different from those in Britain and Germany.

The Shvigovski circle in Nikolaev debated such topics. Chronic dispute arose between Lëva and Alexandra, whom he regarded as an 'obdurate' Marxist. On one occasion when she was wearing a dark-blue dress and kept smoothing her waist as she spoke in one of their frequent altercations – Lëva never forgot this detail – he had stated: 'Marxism is a narrow teaching which splits the personality.' This was a conventional assertion among narodniks. Nikolai Mikhailovski, one of the most influential among the narodnik writers, had contended that Marx, by emphasizing the economic aspect of behaviour throughout society, had developed a theory which segregated the various aspects from each other. Narodniks stressed that revolutionaries ought to be rounded characters who opposed the crushing of individuals under the wheels of a runaway historical tractor. Alexandra faced him down: 'No, that's not the point!'[13] The disagreement got out of control and tempers were lost. The others thought that he was out to annoy her in any way he could. If this was his intention, he succeeded. She told Grisha Ziv: 'I will never, never stretch out my hand to that little boy!' Yet the sexual chemistry was explosive. They were attracted to each other and this was expressed in rivalry. Such was his unruly manner that someone said: 'He'll either turn out a great hero or a great scoundrel; it will be one or the other but he'll definitely rise to greatness.'[14]

Another of his traits was the will to dominate. Like other young men of his generation, he did not like to concede to women. Outspoken female revolutionaries were not unknown; Lëva would cherish some of these later in life – Vera Zasulich, Rosa Luxemburg, Angelica Balabanova and Larisa Reissner. Alexandra was not ready to succumb to the convention of listening to men's wisdom. When Lëva attacked she retaliated.

Lëva prepared himself as if for a military campaign. He scrutinized Schopenhauer's *The Art of Controversy* with the purpose of improving his debating skills.[15] Schopenhauer was frank about wanting to win by fair means or foul. He cited Machiavelli as an authority. For Schopenhauer, all discussion was 'political fencing'. He recommended pushing an opponent's case up to and beyond its desired limits and then pulling it apart. Personal ridicule was highly effective. If people could be needled into anger, they might lose the thread of their arguments. Obfuscation of terminology was another effective ploy. If there was an audience, the aim should be to draw them to one's side by making them laugh. Emphatic diversions and a false display of modesty could also help. Feelings would inevitably be hurt, but the good debater knew how to keep a cool head. Victory, crushing victory, was the only worthwhile objective. There was nothing embarrassing about having a 'despotic' temperament; and Schopenhauer advised that 'a man of high gifts, in his intercourse with others, must always reflect that the best part of him is out of sight in the clouds.' Schopenhauer went on to declare that the ideas of 'ordinary people' counted for nothing. He called for individual genius to be recognized; he saw nothing wrong in being a misanthrope.[16]

Schopenhauer did not belong to the regular armature of Russian revolutionary thought, and Lëva Bronstein did not openly acknowledge his influence on his techniques of argument. Yet he probably found much that he needed for his politics and personality in *The Art of Controversy*. Ziv noticed how he relished wounding his opponents:

As soon as he opened his mouth, not only A. Sokolovskaya but everyone present turned to stone . . . The entire situation and character of the speech made clear that the single aim of his outburst was to spit on and, as painfully as possible, needle A. Sokolovskaya, whose only fault was that she was a Marxist.[17]

Lëva was an intellectual bully; he was a clever young man conscious of his cleverness. This awareness was never to leave him even though he learned to avoid showing off.

Another of his peculiarities was already detectable: his aversion to sentimentality. He took this to an extreme. This impressed itself on the other members of the group when Alexandra Sokolovskaya received news that one of her best friends had been arrested in St Petersburg. Alexandra subsided into depression and did not recover for a long time. Lëva could not understand such sensitivity, telling Grisha Ziv that he himself would never 'experience a feeling of distress' if Ziv were to suffer arrest – and yet the two of them were friends at the time.[18] Ziv concluded:

> Undoubtedly he loved his friends and he loved them sincerely; but his love was of the kind that a peasant has for his horse, which assists the confirmation of his peasant individuality. He will genuinely caress and look after it and happily undergo privations and danger for it; his mind can lovingly even penetrate the horse's very individuality. But as soon as the horse becomes unfit for work, he will unhesitatingly and without a shred of conscience send it to the knacker's yard.[19]

Lëva looked on his revolutionary comrades as the peasant regarded his horse, and none of them was more eager than he for the group to have a practical impact.

From their conversations came a decision to reach out to potential followers. Members decided to form a society and to call it Rassadnik.[20] Liberally translated, it means the Seed-Plot and was a reminder that they had first come together either in the grounds of the Realschule or in the garden of Franz Shvigovski's little house. They made financial contributions to get things going – Lëva himself was not short of funds. They also set about gathering money from sympathizers: this was normal procedure at that time since not a few wealthy citizens either disliked the Imperial political order or wanted to defend themselves against being associated with it in any future revolutionary situation.[21] Lëva wrote an article for a narodnik journal in Odessa and went there to see the editor. Its content did not commend itself for publication.[22] But Lëva went on trying to write and publish. He also took part in the campaign against the Nikolaev Public Library's decision to raise its fees from five rubles per

annum to six. This resulted in victory for the 'democrats', who got themselves elected to the library board in place of the old moneyed and
powerful figures.[23] What they did not know was that they were under
surveillance. The Okhrana kept one of Shvigovski's labourers, a certain
Tkhorzhevski, as its informer. They were living on borrowed time almost
as soon as they started making a name for themselves in the city.[24]

They were thrilled by the stirrings of discontent and protest among
the city's shipyard workers, who objected to their wages and conditions
of employment. But although Lëva could win arguments with a flourish
he started to question his own ideas. Alexandra's standpoint gradually
gained favour with him and the others. He began to accept that the lively
workers' movement was irrepressible. The Marxists were claiming that
liberalism would never win out in Russia. Lëva agreed. He was to sum
up his ideas retrospectively in 1898: 'We'll get by even without liberal
revolutions; we don't need them; we'll go our own way . . .'[25]

Lëva already had contact with groups operating in Odessa and
Yekaterinoslav. He adopted the pseudonym Lvov and encouraged his
comrades to insert themselves into the labour movement under the name
of the South-Russian Workers' Union.[26] The shipyard workforce had a
large skilled component and many labourers were well paid and literate.
Their conditions of labour were not the worst in Europe – they had
already achieved an eight-hour day. But there was discontent with the
general conditions of oppression and injustice among workers, and Lëva
noticed that this was an extension of their religious beliefs. Many of them
were Baptists or evangelical Christians of other sorts; the traditions of the
Orthodox Church did not appeal to them. The Shvigovski circle aimed to
turn this orientation into a revolutionary commitment. They set up a
study circle of twenty workers, calling it a university, and Lëva lectured
briefly on sociology.[27] They lacked much idea about how to avoid detection. They were so proud of their activity that the friends from the
Shvigovski circle had a group photograph taken of themselves – the police
were to make use of the image when they took them into custody. But for
a while Lëva and the others were pleased with the progress they were
making in their proselytizing activity.[28]

Such was Lëva's dedication that he rebuked Grisha Ziv for returning
briefly to university to complete his medical degree.[29] The group's
ambitions widened all the time. On May Day Lëva took the opportunity
to deliver his very first speech. He made it in the woods on the city's
outskirts. He claimed to have felt embarrassed at the time; Grisha Ziv
remembered Lëva's attitude differently, stating that his comrade boasted

that the workers mistook him for the great German socialist orator
Ferdinand Lassalle.[30] It is impossible now to know who was the nearer to
the truth. What is clear is that the group's emphasis was placed on
publishing work:

> Soon we ourselves began producing our own literature. This really
> was the beginning of my literary work. It almost coincided with the
> start of my revolutionary activity. I composed proclamations or
> articles and then wrote out each separate letter by hand for the
> hectograph [a small, rudimentary gelatin duplicator). At that time
> we had no idea about typewriters. I printed the letters with the very
> greatest care, considering it a point of honour to make it possible
> for even a less literate worker to make out any proclamations from
> our hectograph without any trouble. Each page required about two
> hours' work.[31]

Throughout the empire there were similar extensions of Marxist activism.
The Nikolaev circle was learning as it went along how to spread the
political word.

It did so with external assistance. The link was strengthened with
fellow Marxists in Odessa. Experiences were compared; literature was
exchanged. Odessa was a main point of entry for smuggled revolutionary
literature. The Nikolaevites were eager to partake of it. Plekhanov and his
group in Geneva were valued as founders of Marxism in Russia, and their
latest ideas were avidly sought. Lëva sometimes went off to Odessa to
pick up suitcases filled with pamphlets and newspapers printed abroad.
The Nikolaev circle seemed to be making unstoppable progress in its
clandestine activity.

The end, when it came in January 1898, was sudden. Arriving at
Shvigovski's new house in the countryside, Lëva assumed he had found
asylum. He unpacked his bundle of papers and began work on readying
them for distribution. Maria Sokolovskaya, Alexandra's younger sister,
turned up in the middle of this. One of her brothers had been arrested in
Nikolaev. The Okhrana had evidently gathered information on the entire
organization, and Maria felt sure that an agent had tailed her to Shvigovski's. Neither Lëva nor even Shvigovski took her seriously. Maria
insisted. Eventually the three of them took the papers outside and buried
them in a deep pit among some cabbages. After a while Shvigovski decided
that the agent was a figment of Maria Sokolovskaya's imagination. He
retrieved the papers from the pit, leaving them on a water butt at the
entrance to the house.[32] Next day the folly of the three friends was revealed.

The agent had been there all along and was only waiting for back-up to reach him before advancing on the house. Shvigovski, as he was being arrested, whispered to his housekeeper that she should destroy the papers (which had not been noticed by the police) after everyone had departed. The entire revolutionary group was rounded up and carted off to Nikolaev Prison.

# 5. LOVE AND PRISON

Led through the iron doors to his cell in Nikolaev, Bronstein was pleased to find how spacious it was: he had expected worse of the Imperial authorities. His earlier pessimism was then confirmed as he noticed that the room lacked furniture, even a bed. Moreover, he was not alone. Somebody in an overcoat and hat was sitting in the corner. Bronstein assumed that the man was not a revolutionary as he was so poorly dressed – he still believed that people who became Marxist would take care of their appearance. Yet Misha Yavich was a 'political' as well as a worker. They lived together for three weeks. The stove was never properly stoked and the surveillance-hole in the door let in a freezing draught from the outside air. The cold was too great for them to take off their clothes to wash. They were allowed mattresses only at night, and placed them near to the fire when trying to sleep. Following Misha's example, Bronstein made contact with the non-political inmates, whom he paid for a kettle and extra food. What he could not acquire was a pencil since murderers and thieves neither wanted nor needed writing materials. Life without communication was hardly life at all for Bronstein.[1]

He was relieved at being transferred by mail coach, accompanied by two gendarmes, to Kherson, which was sixty miles away. He travelled in hope but the experience was a drastic disappointment because he was put into solitary confinement on arrival, and he spent two and a half months in this condition. Although the new prison was warmer the air was foul. No soap or change of underclothes was provided. Lice crawled everywhere. He had not a single book with him and continued to lack writing materials. For the sake of his sanity he composed revolutionary poems in his head even though, as he later admitted, they were pretty lame.[2] The isolation sharply lowered his morale.[3]

In May 1898 the order came to transport the Nikolaev revolutionaries from Kherson to Odessa. By then all of them, including Alexandra, were in custody. Bronstein and a certain Gurevich were taken together; Ilyusha left next day.[4] The entire group was assembled in Odessa before a decision was made about them. It was a new kind of prison and Trotsky was to remember it almost admiringly as having been designed to the highest current standards of American technology. The building had four storeys. The gangways and stairs were of metal. There were four main blocks, each with a hundred separate cells, and he would recall:

> Brick and metal, metal and brick. Footsteps, blows and movements are acutely sensed throughout the building. The bunks have been constructed into the wall and are put away during the daytime and let down at night. You can hear exactly when your neighbour's bunk is being raised or lowered. The prison warders signal to each other by clanking a metal key on the metal rail of the gangway. You hear that sound practically the entire day. You hear footsteps on the metal stairs just as accurately as footsteps next to you, beneath or above you. All around you there are the noises and sounds of brick, cement and metal.[5]

'And at the same time', Trotsky would add, 'you are completely isolated.' Odessa prison was no holiday camp. Each of the Nikolaev revolutionaries was held in a separate cell in the block reserved for political prisoners. They were guarded by gendarmes rather than by ordinary warders.[6]

Literate inmates communicated by laboriously tapping on the wall in the prisoners' alphabet.[7] The windows were opened to let in fresh air on days of clement weather. When this happened it was possible for the comrades to stand on their stools and converse through the bars. This in fact was strictly forbidden. But the administration was irregular in enforcing its own rules. Every prisoner took on a pseudonym for security. Bronstein called himself Mai, because May was the month when he had arrived at the prison. He was lucky to be assigned cell 179 since it was one and a half times bigger than the average. Soon he largely gave up tapping because he found it brought him little solace and strained his nerves.[8] He also had a problem with the gendarmes, who were not deliberately harsh but talked through the night as if they were sitting in a club. Bronstein wrote to Alexandra in November 1898 about his insomnia. Then he pulled himself up short:[9] 'It's stupid for me to complain to you about all this as if your circumstances are any better; but I'm in such a foul mood that I want to go on complaining to you so that you might feel sorry.'

He was showing off to an attractive young revolutionary. Lev Bronstein was a handsome fellow with the ambitious brilliance that appeals to many women. The feeling was reciprocated. Having teased and provoked her, he had fallen in love. Alexandra fitted the stereotype of the Russian revolutionary: dedicated, determined, altruistic. He knew that she appreciated his talent. He wrote to her without coyness. He called her Shura or Sasha and revealed all his confused emotions to her. He sent her a long message composed in a stream of consciousness. 'Shura,' he wrote, 'I feel bad . . . Not for a very long time have I been in so unpleasant a condition as today.'[10] He also confessed his sadness to a revolutionary called Grinshtein; but he went further with Alexandra: 'You know, Sasha, I'm extraordinarily tied to life. I've had minutes – even an hour or days, months – when suicide would be the most decent outcome; but somehow I have never had the courage for this. Whether it's cowardice, I don't know, but there was something missing.'[11] Perhaps he recognized that he had descended into clichés. Trying for an exalted tone, he commented: 'Doubtless love of life and fear of death are nothing less than the result of . . . natural selection.'[12]

There was showiness and immaturity in these sentiments. He was a self-centred young man. Unconsciously he was trying to induce Alexandra to do more than love him: he wanted her to understand and look after him and perhaps this could be achieved by admissions of weakness. He was never genuinely suicidal; his comment was designed to make her want to protect him. He saw that he had been haughty and unfeeling towards her. What better, then, than to own up to possessing a stony exterior and to say he was 'shedding tears' about this?[13]

He was not trying to mislead her. He simply did not know any other way of expressing himself. He was too self-centred to ask her how she was feeling. She was a sounding board for his thoughts. It would, of course, have been easier if they could have talked directly. He wrote:

> You know, a particular thought enters my head which I'm not going to pass on to you at the moment. Mikhailovski in an article about Lassalle says that one can be more frank with the woman one loves than with oneself; this is to a certain degree true but such frankness is possible only in a personal conversation but not always, only in special and exceptional moments.[14]

Mikhailovski was a Russian revolutionary narodnik, Lassalle a German revolutionary and a Marxist. Bronstein was taking account of them in relation to personal self-development. He was relegating politics to the sidelines of his discussion. Revolution was in his mind but he needed – as he was telling his confidante and lover – to find a way to become a revolutionary and stay true to himself.

Suicidal thoughts were not new to him but, as in summer 1897, he had no sooner stated his purpose than he dismissed it from his mind.[15] He had read great Russian poets of the early nineteenth century such as Pushkin and Lermontov and no doubt he loved their romantic moodiness – just as they in turn had loved Byron and Goethe.[16] But neither Pushkin nor Lermontov was given to physical self-harm. Lëva was young and psychologically edgy despite his outward self-confidence. Until his imprisonment he had lived constantly in a supportive milieu. In Odessa he had been cared for by the Shpentsers; in Nikolaev, as he turned to revolutionary militancy, he had belonged to a commune of friendly, helpful comrades. Prison was different. Its daily routine robbed him of the psychological props he needed. He was surprised by the effects. He was not dreaming up a fictitious state of distress but exaggerating it. Then and later he favoured extreme images and striking turns of phrase. This was no artificial invention. It flowed from the personality of someone who did not feel alive unless he could communicate with others. Solitary confinement was one of the worst conceivable punishments for him.

Writing to Alexandra was one of the ways he found to cope. He was coming to rely on her.[17] His was the push-and-pull of someone who had not learned to disguise or properly examine his feelings. He was a young man who thought his interior life – his thoughts, his fears, his aspirations – to be unique and special; and since he believed himself to be an extraordinary person he did not mind opening his mental world to the woman he trusted.

Despite the difficulties, he was beginning to write his first solid work – and this by itself raised his morale. It was to be a study of the freemasons. He told Alexandra: 'You'll be my first reader and my first critic.' He was planning nothing to match Plekhanov's *Monist View of History* in philosophical scope or Lenin's *Development of Capitalism in Russia* in its exposition of the country's economic present and future. They too were avid controversialists. But their writings had an almost academic ponderousness. Bronstein had no pretensions to doing 'scientific' research.[18] He wrote for immediate political effect and he had a passion for doing this with elegance. The striving after literary accomplishment marked him out, even at this early stage, among Russian Marxists. He was a stylist. He could not bear to write an ugly sentence. This was his talent and his asset; it was also to prove a damaging weakness when his aptitude for exaggerated ridicule caused him to make enemies unnecessarily.

He remained fond of this study in later years. Apparently it compared the masons of history with the contemporary *narodniki*.[19] Bronstein may have wished to expose the mystical and ceremonial facets of freemasons, whom he depicted as a circle of intellectuals trying to subvert the political status quo, and to suggest that the narodniks were no less deluded in their ultimate intentions. He finished the piece to his own satisfaction but never placed it with a publisher. He was to lose it in Switzerland, it seems, when his landlady used it to start the fire in her stove.[20]

The stay in Odessa prison confirmed young Lev in his adherence to Marxism, as he would remember in an early autobiographical sketch: '[The] decisive influence on me was two studies by Antonio Labriola on the materialist conception of history. Only after this book did I proceed to Beltov, to *Capital*.'[21] Labriola was an early Italian Marxist who sought to develop a philosophical framework for an understanding of societies in the process of industrialization. Beltov was the authorial pseudonym of Georgi Plekhanov who was the founding father of Marxism in Russia and wrote on philosophy and economics. Labriola and Plekhanov followed Marx by insisting on the need to ground any analysis of a country's politics in its economic conditions. *Capital*, needless to emphasize, was at the core of Marx's doctrines about the development of a capitalist economy. All the Nikolaev detainees used their time in prison to turn themselves into more informed Marxists. Intellectual preparation was essential if they wished to be regarded as serious followers of Marx and Engels in the Russian Empire.

It was in November 1898 that Lev's mother visited him from Yanovka. Her horror at his imprisonment is readily understandable. This was her adored son and brilliant student. She knew her mind: he ought to give up revolutionary commitments before it was too late. What was he going to live on? His answer was scarcely a consoling one: good people would help him out. She retorted: 'And does this mean that you expect to live on alms?' A blazing dispute broke out between them. In fact they had two such disputes because his mother took a break between attempts to save her boy from his madness.[22] This in itself was unusual. Previously it had been his father who had laid down the law to him. Perhaps David Bronstein recognized that his wife might be better at the arts of persuasion. At any rate a 'pretty nasty scene', as Lev described it at the time, ensued; it ended with him telling his mother that he no longer wanted any help from either of his parents.[23]

David and Aneta Bronstein at last understood that Lev – their Leiba – had made up his mind and that if they stood up to him they would lose him for ever. There was one matter on which they refused to compromise. Their son had told them of his wish to marry Alexandra, and he was too young to do this without parental consent. Among the reasons why his father and mother refused permission was the discrepancy in wealth between the two families. The Bronsteins did not want to see their own property fall into the hands of someone less prosperous than themselves. Probably they suspected Alexandra of scheming in this direction. They took no chances. Their son was behaving in all sorts of undesirable ways. They would at least thwart a premature marriage.

Lev contrasted this reaction with the letter of best wishes he received from Alexandra's father. The words touched him. He told Alexandra that her father was a 'very nice person' who had assured him that he was in no way offended by the intransigence of the Bronsteins. Mr Sokolovski even saw a positive aspect in the rupture between Lev and his parents: no longer would the self-declared fiancés be troubled by the delicate question of 'material inequality'.[24] A total contempt for the social attitudes nurtured at Yanovka welled up inside Lev and remained with him for the rest of his life. In the diary he kept in France in 1935 he asserted: 'There is no creature more disgusting than a petit bourgeois engaged in primary accumulation.'[25] Nobody more closely fitted the description of such an accumulator than David Bronstein, who had built a fine farm through the sweat of his brow and the guile of his dealings. Lev was giving up the comforts which were available through his parents' hard-won wealth, and he felt the better for it. He nevertheless could not have the wedding he wanted. To that extent David and Aneta Bronstein were able to feel a small satisfaction.

Meanwhile Lev and Alexandra languished in the same prison. If he was unable to marry the next best thing for Lev, even if it was far from ideal, was to be placed in a cell next to hers. His request was refused. The only possible rationale for such proximity was to enable communication, and the authorities wanted the exact opposite – and anyway men and women were kept strictly apart in the prison. Consequently Lev's only hope was that she would somehow pass near his cell: 'Were you to come down the stairs for your walk and say something, I would definitely hear.'[26] Otherwise he and she had to put up with things as they were. They had yet to learn the nature of their punishment but knew that, almost certainly, it would involve banishment to Siberia. But for how long? He and Alexandra, he claimed, had earned their 'hour of happiness'. Eventually they were going to live like 'Olympian gods'. He convinced himself that they had suffered a lot in their lives. He tried to cheer himself up: 'Doesn't the thought occur to you that by the time we return from exile we'll have the possibility of legal activity?'[27]

It was in fact another year before they learned of their fate. In November

1898 the Nikolaev group heard that they were to serve a term of administrative exile; Trotsky was sentenced to four years.[28] All of them were quickly moved by train from Odessa to the Moscow Transit Prison and held in the Pugachëv Tower. The historical associations were not lost on the Nikolaevites. Pugachëv had led a huge popular revolt against Catherine the Great in 1773–4, moving rapidly with his ill-trained but powerful forces from the south of the empire. Defeated outside Moscow, he was locked in the tower that subsequently bore his name before being executed on Red Square. The fate awaiting the Nikolaevites was never going to be so severe. The prison governor was a certain Metsger, a Russian of German descent. Metsger expected implicit respect from all inmates and ordered them to remove their hats in his presence. When Trotsky refused to comply, Metsger lost his temper and shouted at him. Trotsky stood his ground: 'I'm not your soldier. Kindly stop shouting at me.' His fellow prisoners showed solidarity. A whistle was blown and they were marched off to windowless punishment cells where the beds had no mattresses. A day later, though, they were restored to the Pugachëv Tower.[29]

As with several such episodes of daring in his life, Trotsky did not include this information in his published memoirs. It had to be dragged out of him by admiring writers. Although he liked to cut a dash in public, he disliked boasting: he preferred others to do the job for him. He was noisy and full of himself. People did not have to wait long before discovering how vain and self-centred he really was.

Peaceful co-operation with Metsger was resumed in the months while the Nikolaev group waited to be sent out to Siberia. They spent their time reading and writing, and they held conversations in their daily periods of physical exercise. Bronstein resumed his attempt to marry Alexandra. They were in love. They had the blessing of Alexandra's father, and David Bronstein was too far away to make any objection. The incentive to hasten things was that the Imperial authorities did not divide married couples in Siberian exile.[30] Permission was granted for the wedding to take place in the Moscow Transit Prison. Since Lev and Alexandra were from Jewish families and in this period there was no civil marriage, a rabbi was contacted to carry out the ceremony.[31] There would have been no difficulty in finding ten Jewish revolutionaries as witnesses in order for the proceedings to have religious and legal validity.[32] The traditional *chupa* was placed over the heads of the betrothed. The obligatory prayers were spoken. The rings were exchanged. Formal submission to the faith of their ancestors was a small price to pay for Lev and Alexandra to become man and wife. It was the last such compromise that either of them would make.

They were revolutionaries who had yet to work out what to do next. They had little idea about the conditions awaiting them and their Nikolaev group had had no contact with Marxist organizations elsewhere in the Russian Empire. Although they had read material smuggled in from 'the emigration' they had yet to announce their existence to the Marxist leaders abroad. Already in Moscow they were rubbing shoulders with militants who knew more about Marxist doctrines and activity in cities larger than Nikolaev. They talked and talked with every fellow revolutionary they came across. They were ceasing to be provincial and fitting themselves out to play their part in the affairs of the Russian Social-Democratic Workers' Party.

# 6. SIBERIAN EXILE

The Nikolaev convict group had yet to be told exactly where they were to sit out their period of exile but first, in summer 1900, the Jews among them were taken to eastern Siberia. Russians at that time were being dispatched to northern Russia so as to be kept separate from prisoners of nationalities which were thought to exert a 'harmful influence'.[1] Leaving Moscow, the Bronsteins journeyed nearly 1,400 miles by train before picking up the Trans-Siberian railway at Chelyabinsk. Another two thousand miles and five and a half days of travelling lay ahead to Irkutsk. At Telma station, thirty-seven miles short of the great Siberian city, the prisoners were removed from their carriage and taken five miles north over the great River Angara to the village of Alexandrovskoe.[2]

The biggest of the region's prisons was to be found there; the Ministry of Internal Affairs had chosen the rural spot precisely because it was distant enough from Irkutsk to make it difficult for a convict to run off and board a train bound for central Russia.[3] (Telma itself was small and was heavily patrolled by gendarmes.) The Alexandrovskoe Central Labour Prison held about 1,300 inmates and the dormitories were overcrowded. But the governor was doing what he could to improve conditions – and a British visitor commented that he looked more like a German orchestral conductor than a gaoler. The diet included meat and soup; sanitary arrangements were reportedly adequate. Men who were serving their entire sentence at the prison received compulsory training in carpentry, tailoring or watch repairs. The aim was to remove the temptation to return to crime after release. Prisoners received a small wage for their work which they could either spend in the internal shop or remit to their families. Yet still it was a place with its own indignities and harshness. Clothing was of a single size, which meant that the shorter inmates trailed their trousers on the ground. Murderers, wearing chains, were usually sent on to heavy labour on Sakhalin island – and they had to trudge hundreds of miles under escort to the Pacific coast.[4]

Bronstein and his comrades, being political offenders, were kept apart from common criminals. They had arrived in plenty of time before the winter and its snow storms. While waiting, they had the same access to books and newspapers as in the Moscow Transit Prison.[5] Lev and Alexandra as spouses had the right to stay together, and she became pregnant with their first child. Then the news arrived that the whole Nikolaev group would be dispatched further north. Several isolated villages had been designated, and the Bronsteins heard that they were to proceed to Ust-Kut. The name meant nothing to them. All north-east Siberia was still a mystery and the little they found out about the climate and the exile regime came from conversations with fellow prisoners.

Ust-Kut was a tiny hamlet in the Kirensk district of Irkutsk province, standing at latitude 57°N. Others in the Alexandrovskoe Prison were even less fortunate and were dispatched to places inside the Arctic Circle. The entire region was grimly cold in winter and unbearably hot in summer. The two of them knew this before their little party and its guards set out for their destination four hundred miles upstream to the north of Irkutsk. Here is how Trotsky remembered the trip:

> We were going down the River Lena. The current bore several barges of convicts slowly along with their convoy of soldiers. It was cold at night, and the heavy coats we covered ourselves with were thick with frost by the morning. On the way, at predetermined villages, one or two convicts were put ashore. It took about three weeks, if my memory serves me, before we came to the Ust-Kut settlement. There I was put ashore with one of the woman exiles, a close associate of mine from Nikolaev.[6]

The last sentence referred to his pregnant wife Alexandra. Just possibly he was trying to spare her feelings at the time of writing. Even so, what misleading primness!

A small revolutionary 'colony' greeted the newly-weds in Ust-Kut. Among them was a Polish cobbler called Miksha with whom the Bronsteins found accommodation. Miksha was an able cook and a heavy drinker. Lev and Alexandra got on well with him despite his fondness for the bottle. (They, of course, had each other whereas he had nobody.) True to his egalitarian precepts, Lev did his share of the housework. His tasks included chopping wood for the fire, sweeping the floor and washing the dishes. Only then would he pull out his books: he had brought a pile of Marx and other socialist tracts with him as well as some foreign literary classics.

The rules of exile allowed visits to neighbouring places on condition that permission was obtained in advance. Thus Bronstein could travel to Ilimsk, ninety-five miles away, where goods and facilities were more plentiful. He went there frequently. In Ilimsk he became acquainted with Vasili Ulrikh, who spent his time translating documents from German and celebrated Marx as a brilliant recorder of the travails of capitalism rather than as an advocate of revolutionary socialism. Nevertheless Bronstein, who was still finding himself in his life and ideas, enjoyed their meetings. He was thirsty for open, intelligent conversation. Ulrikh was anyway not the only interesting local character. Bronstein also made contact with Alexander Vinokurov in Lower Ilimsk. Vinokurov was a medical auxiliary and a person with a wealth of experience of popular conditions in the empire. Another frequent interlocutor was Dmitri Kalinnikov, a doctor who tried to reach out to exiled revolutionaries old and new.[7] Bronstein was still refining what he called his world view, and his knowledge of Marx and Engels remained in need of much hard work.[8] It was useful to try out his thoughts on well-informed local residents, and he never forgot Ulrikh and the other comrades he encountered in Siberia (even though he wrote nothing about them in his published autobiography).

Conditions for exiled revolutionaries were nowhere near as harsh as they were to become under the Soviet order in the 1930s. Grisha Ziv, fellow detainee, recorded:

> [Bronstein] had a very large amount of free time and energy which sought an outlet but had absolutely nothing to expend it on. And he took an active part in all the games and recreations which the exile used as a way of shortening the passage of time. He had a remarkable passion for croquet, perhaps partly because the character of the game – more than any other – gave special latitude to the expression of his natural cunning, imaginativeness and resourcefulness. And it was here, as in every other place and in every matter where the opportunity arose to show his individuality, that Bronstein was organically incapable of tolerating rivals alongside him; and the winning of victory over him at croquet was the surest way of making him into your worst enemy.[9]

Alas, no extant sources tell us who flattened the ground and laid out the lawn in Siberia for Bronstein to indulge his disconcerting competitiveness.

At any rate the detainees were clearly not deposited in conditions of destitution. Often they were the only educated people in the vicinity and had skills in short supply. The state gave them a monthly stipend of thirty-five rubles, which was enough for subsistence; they were also allowed to seek gainful employment. Some did a bit of tutoring. Others worked in libraries, infirmaries and even offices of local government; and Siberian entrepreneurs were frequently eager to hire them. An increasing proportion of exiles did not come from middle-class families, and worker-militants such as Miksha the Pole were able to resume their trades in Siberia or at least adapt their expertise to local economic requirements. Money could also be made by sub-letting rooms in houses where they lived. Nor was Ust-Kut completely cut off from visitors. All convicts being sent down or up the Lena stopped there if only for a break in their long journey.[10] Lev and Alexandra took their opportunities to talk with passers-by. News and advice were exchanged, morale strengthened. Politics were a constant topic of conversation, and revolutionaries carried their disputes with them to their places of detention.

Even so, a communal spirit prevailed in matters of everyday living. Convicts counted on each other for assistance in episodes of ill health, worry or material hardship. The greatest offence of all was to render any help to the police. It was not unknown for informers to be brought before a tribunal of comrades and killed with whatever weapon was available. Lev Bronstein fitted well into this milieu. Even his brashness seems to have mellowed, if only temporarily; one of his later political adversaries, Eva Broido, said in her memoirs that he struck her as 'still a modest man'.[11]

Like other exiles, he looked for opportunities for paid work. Making the most of his schooling in mathematics, he gained employment from a merchant who needed an accountant. Bronstein earned thirty rubles a month for his services, doubling his regular income.[12] But it ended in tears when the employer sacked him. Bronstein made no defence of his conduct:

> It was relatively easy to get permission for a transfer from one place to another from the Irkutsk governor. Alexandra Lvovna and I moved [165 miles] to the east on the River Ilim where we had friends. I worked there for a short while as a clerk to a millionaire merchant. His fur depots, stores and taverns were spread over a territory as big as Belgium and Holland put together. He was a powerful commercial lord. He referred to the many thousands of Tunguses under his rule as 'my little Tunguses'. He couldn't even write his name and had to mark it with a cross. He lived in a mean and miserly fashion the whole year round and then squandered tens of thousands of rubles at the Nizhni Novgorod fair. For a month and a half I worked in his

service. Then one day I entered a pound of red-lead as 'one pud'
[forty pounds], and sent this huge bill to a distant store. This shred-
ded my reputation and I was discharged.[13]

Bronstein had kept accounts for his own father and his lapse of concentration was strangely out of character.

Perhaps he was not performing his duties with due application. The
merchant belonged to the bourgeois class. He was an enemy of socialism.
Why should Bronstein bother to keep in order the books of a millionaire?
Possibly the clerical routine also took up time he wanted to devote to
writing. He recorded that the work 'depressed' him and that his articles
for the *Vostochnoe obozrenie* ('Eastern Review') in Irkutsk offered a preferable source of income. (He erased this comment before publication.)[14]
Bronstein's contact with people in the city had grown since his arrival
in Siberia, and his first literary efforts were quickly recognized as impressive. Soon he was writing regularly under the pseudonym Antid Oto.
His routine involved finishing off his pieces in the evenings after carrying
out his domestic tasks, which became indispensable after the arrival
of the Bronsteins' first child – their daughter Zinaida (or Zina) – on
14 March 1901.

*Vostochnoe obozrenie* was a journal edited by the Irkutsk political
liberal M. Popov, who looked out for promising newcomers. Popov knew
how far he could push the censors and avoided being closed down. The
authorities anyway kept a tighter watch on the press in St Petersburg and
Moscow than in the outlying regions of the empire. The censorship in
Georgia was notoriously accommodating to revolutionary writings; and
although eastern Siberia was a territory inhabited by thousands of con-
victed enemies of the Imperial order, Irkutsk too had a reputation for
being a place where critical thought could be aired with a degree of
impunity. The Ministry of Internal Affairs, moreover, had no objection to
the exiles writing for the legal press. Few had the talent to make a living
at general journalism – their preference was to publish in clandestine
political outlets and to use the abstruse lexicon of their comrades. Trotsky
was different. He loved to appeal to readers outside the revolutionary
milieu. He relished turning out well-polished prose. Young as he was, he
was a master of ridicule and sarcasm. He produced images that made
people see their day-to-day world afresh. Popov snapped him up and
'Antid Oto' had instant success through the pages of *Vostochnoe obozrenie*.

The engineer Moshe Novomeiski was no admirer of Trotsky as man
or politician but attested to the excellence of his journalism: 'These articles

at once attracted attention. Indeed, they transformed the appearance of the paper. I recall how eagerly we all used to await a new number of *Obozrenie* and turn the page to see if there was anything by "Antid Oto", the pseudonym of Bronstein . . .'[15] Acclaim grew for his sketches about the villages, often headed 'Everyday Rural Life' ('Obyknovennoe derevenskoe'). He criticized the heavy drinking and administrative inefficiency in the region and called for a cultural and material improvement in the conditions of the peasantry. He advocated an expanded network of popular schooling. He demanded a proper legal framework. He castigated the chaos of the Imperial postal system (which was a matter of importance for a revolutionary several thousand miles from family and comrades). One of his remedies was a pay rise for postmen.[16] As he got into his stride as a columnist he even wrote about the Siberian prison system. Needless to say, he favoured its reform.[17]

Popov sent him all manner of books for review and Bronstein developed a light, ironic touch as his confidence rose. While disapproving of John Ruskin for 'his reactionary–romantic confusions', he conceded that machines in industrial society had their dark side. Marxists did not readily admit this sort of thing, but Bronstein added that he preferred the pleasure of riding on a 'real horse'.[18] Being the son of a wealthy landowner, he at this stage in his career was not disguising his feelings and memories.

Independence of thought was a matter of pride for him. Hostility to 'individualism' was another. When Popov sent him a collection of the dramas of Henrik Ibsen, he surprised the editor by turning in a dyspeptic piece. In Bronstein's opinion, Ibsen's preoccupation with the fate of individuals was a definite flaw.[19] He was hinting – only hinting – at his Marxist commitment to collective solutions to society's ills. He did, though, recognize the Norwegian dramatist as a cultural giant. He did not accord the same status to several of Russia's contemporary writers. He disliked the ex-Marxist philosopher Nikolai Berdyaev for postulating absolute criteria of truth. He could not stand Konstantin Balmont and his school of 'decadent' literature.[20] He had more time for Gleb Uspenski. It was Uspenski who exposed the unpleasant aspects of peasant life. (Trotsky was scathing, however, about how the publishers put frivolous material in their illustrated page-a-day calendar alongside the item on Uspenski.)[21] In a piece on Siberian rural life Trotsky itemized the rough habits of the local peasantry. The urgent need was for cultural improvement, and for this to happen there had to be a transformation of material conditions and a proper legal framework needed to be introduced.[22]

Quietly he tucked party-political commentary into his pieces. He scoffed at Pëtr Struve, yet another former Marxist, for contending that increased wages for the working class should be the highest public priority. For those attuned to the debates inside contemporary Marxism the implication was easily detected. While advocating more rubles for postmen, Bronstein had never thought that such an outcome would solve the truly basic problems in society. Political transformation – a socialist revolution – was ultimately essential.[23] Not that he failed to praise leading figures from other parts of the revolutionary movement. He cited Nikolai Mikhailovski, an intellectual colossus for narodniks, with enthusiasm when making the point that the 'class in command' would always have opinions different from those of the 'proletariat'.[24] He also paid tribute to Alexander Herzen, who had initiated the fondness for the peasantry's collectivist traditions which was picked up by Mikhailovski. But he rejected any unthinking reverence. There should be no 'cult of the individual' for Herzen: Bronstein insisted that everybody and everything should be subject to constant re-examination.[25] His readers were left in no doubt that the existing order in society could not last for long. They were living in a 'sharply transitional' epoch.[26]

This article was easily decipherable as a call for revolutionary action against the Imperial order. Much more open opportunities for discussion, needless to stress, existed inside the colonies. Disputes between veteran agrarian socialists and Marxist neophytes were common. Each side had its internal divisions. Some Marxists leaned towards a moderate, non-violent set of ideas being proposed in those years by Eduard Bernstein in Germany and – until he abandoned socialism for liberalism – Pëtr Struve in Russia. Others favoured revolution. Only one of the contemporary exiles was renowned outside Siberia. This was the Polish writer Jan Machajski, who argued that the radical intelligentsia, given half a chance, would seek to dominate the workers in whose name they were making revolution. The terrorist–narodniks remained on friendly terms with him and chose to interpret his ideas as being applicable solely to Marxists and not to themselves. Marxists, by contrast, were deeply offended.[27]

Bronstein was open-minded enough to want to meet Machajski, who had been exiled to Vilyuisk, over a thousand miles to the north-east. Both chanced to be on trips to Irkutsk at the same time. Bronstein attended a meeting where the thinker was berating one of Struve's supporters. Arguments bounced off Machajski like 'peas from a wall'. Trotsky intervened, but only weakly. He never recorded what he had said except to note that the two disputants combined momentarily to attack him.[28] Other individuals of Bronstein's acquaintance became famous only many years later. Among them was yet another Pole, Felix Dzerzhinski, who sat round the fire one evening with comrades and recited a poem he had written. Dzerzhinski was sentenced to hard labour in Nolinsk and Kaigorodsk; in December 1917 he would become the founder of Lenin's security police in the wake of the October Revolution. Another outstanding figure was Nikolai Sukhanov. In Siberian exile Sukhanov advocated putting the peasantry at the core of revolutionary strategy; he subsequently became a Socialist-Revolutionary and then a Menshevik. Whereas Dzerzhinski and Trotsky became Bolsheviks in 1917, Sukhanov pitted his political talent against the Bolshevik party – and in later years he became Trotsky's greatest competitor as annalist of Russia in revolution.[29]

The exile colonies themselves embraced a broad ethnic and social mixture. Poles and Jews supplied a disproportionate number of revolutionaries. As the labour movement intensified, moreover, the working-class people who arrived in eastern Siberia were mostly Polish or Jewish since the authorities preferred to dispatch Russian labourers to northern Russia (which was thought less severe).[30]

Bronstein and his group could get nowhere near to the factories – and anyway Siberia had but few of them. They had no access to printing facilities of their own; their communication with Russia had to be circumspect or conspiratorial – and the postal deliveries took weeks to reach them. Yet Bronstein did not yet feel his time was entirely wasted as he educated himself in the Marxist classics. This was how he was to describe the experience to Lenin in 1902:

> I told him how in the Moscow transfer-prison we had collectively studied his book, *The Development of Capitalism in Russia*, and how in exile we had worked on Marx's *Capital* but had stopped at the second volume. We had intently studied the controversy between Bernstein and Kautsky, using the original sources. There were no followers of Bernstein among us. In the field of philosophy, we were impressed by Bogdanov's book, which combined Marxism with the theory of cognition advanced by Mach and Avenarius. At that time Lenin too thought Bogdanov's theories were correct. 'I am not a philosopher,' he said with trepidation, 'but Plekhanov sharply denounces Bogdanov's philosophy as a disguised variant of idealism.'[31]

There is no reason to doubt his account since he was acknowledging his need to keep on learning. He was also indicating how seriously he took his Marxism, reading German as well as Russian texts. And he was asserting that the group's members covered the gamut of Marxist works: economic, political and philosophical. For Trotsky, Siberia was like a free revolutionary university of the taiga, that unwelcoming coniferous zone covering the furthermost rim of the Russian Empire.

Soon he was producing proclamations and leaflets for 'democratic organizations' that sprang up in cities along the Trans-Siberian railway, as he was to recall: 'After a three-year interval, I was rejoining the ranks for active struggle.'[32] It was a period of frantic change for the Bronsteins in every way. In 1902 Alexandra gave birth to their second child. It was another girl, whom they named Nina. Commissions from the *Vostochnoe obozrenie* were plentiful. Contact with the Marxist groups was growing stronger. It looked as if Lev and Alexandra would see out the term of their shared sentence.

Then something happened which changed the course of Lev's life and career:

> In the summer of 1902, I received, by way of Irkutsk, books in the binding of which were concealed the latest foreign publications printed on very fine paper. We learned that a Marxist newspaper, *Iskra* ['Spark'], had been created abroad which set as its object the creation of a centralized organization of professional revolutionaries who would be bound together by the iron discipline of action. There also arrived Lenin's book, *What Is to Be Done?*, published in Geneva, which was entirely devoted to the same question. My handwritten essays, newspaper articles and proclamations for the Siberian Union immediately appeared small and provincial to me in the face of the new and tremendous task confronting us. I had to look for another field of activity. I had to escape from exile.[33]

Impulsively he saw a chance to join up with the leadership of a Marxist organization. If he wanted action on the largest stage available, he needed to move abroad for a while. He knew he had talents as a writer: everyone told him so. He had never lacked confidence or motivation. What had been missing was a strategic focus. Lenin's booklet filled the void.

The Russian Social-Democratic Workers' Party was putting itself on an effective footing at last. Its First Congress, held in Minsk in March 1898, had yielded few results apart from the arrest of nearly all its participants. The doctrines of Marx and Engels as well as the strategy for Marxism in Russia continued to be debated by adherents. Huge diversity of opinion prevailed. Most militants wanted an immediate revolution and regarded political involvement as the priority. When a small grouping of intellectual 'revisionists' dissented from this they incurred the anger of the revolutionaries. Lenin and *Iskra* were determined to root out revisionism. Bronstein wanted to join them.

He later made the claim that Alexandra had wholeheartedly blessed his departure. This is hard to take at face value. Bronstein was planning to abandon her in the wilds of Siberia. She had no one to look after her, and she had to care for two tiny babies all on her own with winter coming on. No sooner had he fathered a couple of children than he decided to run off. Few revolutionaries left such a mess behind them. Even so, he was acting within the revolutionary code of behaviour. The 'cause' was everything for the revolutionaries. Marital and parental responsibilities had an importance but never to the point of preventing young militants from doing what their political conscience bade them to do. All were theoretically in favour of equality between the sexes. But women had to avoid having children if they wished to maintain their freedom as militants. When their men got into difficulties with the authorities it was usually the wives who were expected to deal with the emotional wreckage. It was anyway plain to Alexandra by now, if it had not been before, that her husband was an individual of exceptional promise. The *Vostochnoe obozrenie* had recognized this by making him its columnist. Everyone who met him shared a high opinion of him.

Even if Alexandra really did give her consent, Lev showed little appreciation of the sacrifice he had asked of her. 'Life', he said as if it was a simple matter of fact, 'separated us.'[34] In reality he had chosen to separate himself from his marital and parental responsibilities. Any woman who lived with him had to accept that he would do as he pleased. He must have broken Alexandra's heart even if she had no reason to suspect that the family would not one day be reunited. When writing to him she continued to end her letters with endearments, writing: 'I warmly, warmly kiss you.'[35] The loving relationship, at least on her side, had not ended; but his own attitude was about to change.

# 7. ISKRA

There was an 'epidemic of escapes' from Siberia by the turn of the century and the revolutionaries had to introduce a queuing system to cope with the number of volunteers.[1] This was how Trotsky remembered the scene. Well-established techniques existed for a successful flight. Money had to be given to peasants for their assistance or at least to keep them quiet. Then the long journey began in stages by boat, cart and – if the snow had not yet melted – sleigh. Boatmen and carters passed the escapers 'from hand to hand' and a fee had to be paid each time. Policemen might need to be bribed; this could be risky but usually they were easily corrupted as their salaries were so low. A false identity was essential and the revolutionary parties developed an expertise in procuring or producing blank internal passports. Bronstein quickly acquired one, inscribing his surname as Trotsky.[2] Speculation has accreted to this. Some have suggested it refers to a Polish town where his ancestors had lived before going south to Ukraine. Another suggestion was that Bronstein had remembered the senior supervisor at Nikolaev prison and appropriated his surname as his own. This was what Grisha Ziv assumed; but when he mentioned this to Ilya Sokolovski, who had been with Bronstein at the time, Ilya scoffed and said that their friend had simply acquired a passport from an Irkutsk inhabitant called Trotsky.[3]

By then he and the family were living, with permission, in Verkholensk which had a bigger revolutionary colony than Ust-Kut. The police put the date of his disappearance at 21 August 1902.[4] Trotsky and a Marxist woman, whom he remembered only as 'E.G.', left Verkholensk in a hay cart driven by a friendly peasant. No doubt they had to pay the current rate. The ground was uneven so that the pace was slow, never surpassing ten miles per hour. Trotsky's companion found the trip very uncomfortable and had to try and stifle her groans for fear of discovery. On reaching Irkutsk, Trotsky split from her. Friends in the city made further arrangements, procuring him a ticket for the Trans-Siberian line. He also acquired a suitcase containing 'starched shirts, a necktie and other attributes of civilization' and boarded his carriage without interference from gendarmes. With him he had a copy of Homer's *Iliad* in the Russian hexameters of Nikolai Gnedich. The long journey back from Siberia passed without incident. At every stop on the way there were women selling roast chicken, pork, milk and bread. It was a far cry from the miserable conditions of Ust-Kut. Trains were bringing economic prosperity to the cities along the newly built railway and to its hinterland where agriculture was expanding rapidly. Trotsky observed this and was impressed. Russia and its empire were in the grip of a remarkable transformation.

If he missed his wife and daughters, he did not mention this in his memoirs. He had embarked on an adventure. He enjoyed his family when he was with them but the revolutionary cause and its excitements meant more to him. The journey from Siberia left him emotionally freer than at any time since Nikolaev.

These days of relaxation ended when he alighted in Samara. The *Iskra* group had chosen the city as one of their organizing and distributing centres in Russia. Trotsky contacted their leader Gleb Krzhizhanovski, who called him Pero ('the Pen'), in tribute to his success as a journalist in Siberia. Krzhizhanovski asked him to visit contacts in Poltava, Kharkov and Kiev before moving abroad to get in touch with the editorial board. He did not think much of the efforts of provincial Iskraites. When the time came for his foreign trip he found they had put a schoolboy in charge of planning border crossings. Age was not his only drawback; another was that his allegiance lay not with the Russian Marxists but with the Socialist-Revolutionaries. Under the leadership of Viktor Chernov the Socialist-Revolutionaries were resuming the narodnik idea that the best chance of transforming Russia lay in working among the peasants. Trotsky's temper was not improved at the Austrian frontier where he was put under the escort of professional smugglers who invented unscheduled 'tariffs and norms' for their services.[5] But although his funds were steadily vanishing his confidence remained high. Arriving in Vienna on a Sunday, he thought nothing of demanding that his socialist contacts take him to see Victor Adler. They explained that Adler, leader of the Social-Democratic Party of Austria, disliked being disturbed on his day of rest. Trotsky made such a fuss that they agreed to bring him to Adler's house, and Adler was impressed enough to have a lengthy conversation with him.

Vienna was only a stopover. Soon Trotsky was boarding a train at the West-Bahnhof for Switzerland. Decanting himself in Geneva, he hailed a horse-drawn cab to the lodgings of *Iskra* editorial board member Pavel Axelrod. His funds had completely run out and it was late at night before he reached the district of the Russian 'colony'. The lights were out in Axelrod's flat, so Trotsky knocked loudly, roused him from sleep and asked: 'Are you Pavel Borisovich Axelrod?' Receiving a positive reply, he announced: 'I've come straight from the station. Please pay off the cab driver; I've got no money. I'll be staying the night with you.' Axelrod mildly asked who he was, and after establishing Trotsky's identity he handed over the cash and let him indoors.[6]

It did not take long for Trotsky to understand that *Iskra*'s dynamism lay not in Geneva with Georgi Plekhanov and Pavel Axelrod but in London with their younger editorial colleagues Vladimir Lenin and Yuli Martov. He anyway sensed that Plekhanov, the founding father of Russian Marxism, did not take to him. Lenin was a confident militant from Simbirsk who had started to make a name for himself through his economic and political writings; Martov, a Jewish militant brought up in Odessa, was his bright and energetic associate. The logical step was to move to Britain, where Trotsky arrived in October 1902. He had Lenin's Bloomsbury address in his pocket when he stepped down from the train early in the morning at Victoria Station. The Lenins were still in bed when he reached their door. (This time Trotsky had the money in his wallet for the cab.) The Iskraists in Switzerland had told him to knock three times on the door: this was the code for avoiding unwanted strangers. Lenin was not amused to have his slumber interrupted. His wife went to see what the noise was about, as Trotsky recalled:

> The door was opened by Nadezhda Konstantinovna, who had prob-
> ably been woken by my knocking. It was still early, and anyone more
> accustomed to civilized ways of behaving would have sat around at
> the station for an hour or two rather than knocked on a strange door
> at such an unearthly hour. But I was still charged up with my escape
> from Verkholensk.[7]

He remained proud of his brashness nearly three decades later.

Lenin knew about Trotsky from Gleb Krzhizhanovski's letter and greeted him with the words: 'Ah, the Pen has arrived!'[8] Trotsky threw himself into an account of his experiences, and he was not complimentary about the Iskraites in Russia.[9] He handed over a list of addresses and contact places while explaining which ones were no longer functional; the *Iskra* communication system, he commented, was in 'an extremely weak condition'.[10] This was the report of a man who knew his value to the party and was unafraid to tell unpalatable truths to his seniors. Lenin appreciated such frankness. *Iskra* was not just acquiring a lively, fluent writer but also a practical organizer. Trotsky settled in a colony of friendly companions among whom the closest were Yuli Martov and Vera Zasulich.[11] Lenin acted as his guide around central London, commenting as they walked past the Houses of Parliament: 'Here's their famous Westminster.' He also gained access for Trotsky to the British Museum so that he could fill out his Marxist studies.[12] This was presumably an illicit manoeuvre: indeed Lenin himself had acquired a reader's card under an alias.

The big event for Trotsky was a speech he gave in Whitechapel, where his opponents were the anarchists Nikolai Chaikovski and Varlaam Cherkezov. He was trying out his skills against attractive senior opponents. The audience were émigrés from the Russian Empire. Most of them were Jews and the language was Russian.[13] It was a triumph for Trotsky and he felt as if he was walking on air on the way back from the venue.

His performance persuaded the London *Iskra* group to assign him the task of delivering a speech against the Socialist-Revolutionaries in Paris. He arrived in the French capital in November 1902 and presented himself at the house of an older member of the *Iskra* group – one Yekaterina Alexandrova. She asked a young militant called Natalya Sedova to find a place for him to live. Natalya reported that a room was available in her own house though it was little better than a prison cell. This did not matter to Alexandrova, who was expecting Trotsky to focus on his forthcoming speech.[14] Alexandrova fussed about whether Trotsky was serious in his preparations. When Sedova mentioned that she had heard him whistling in his room, the veteran ordered her to tell him to work hard and quit making a noise. Alexandrova was worrying in vain – Trotsky did everything with ease and could write any piece with enviable rapidity. What is more, the speech was a brilliant success: Trotsky again showed his ability to thrill an audience.[15] Leaving the platform, he went over to sit with Sedova. When she asked his real name he demurred out of considerations of security.[16] But in every other way they were instantly communicative. They went out together in subsequent days as Natalya showed him the sights of Paris.[17] Together they went to hear French socialist leaders such as Jean Jaurès and Jules Guesde. On matters artistic she appreciated his fine taste. He loved the paintings of Murillo – she had brought a photograph album of them back with her from Munich. Both of them read the novels of Octave Mirbeau. They discussed the Russian writer Leonid Andreev.[18]

Trotsky had met the woman who would be his partner for the rest of his life. It disconcerted her that his first question about people was always: 'And what's their attitude to revolution?' She had not yet accepted such a political intensity as normal. But she was smitten. She admired 'his attentiveness, graciousness and difference from the others'.[19] He assumed that she too was intensely confident like he was, and he put her name forward for a role in a production of Maxim Gorki's *The Lower Depths*. Although the proceeds were to go to *Iskra* she refused point-blank to go along with the idea. Lacking his self-assurance, she also hated to 'act a part'.[20] He soon appreciated this characteristic, becoming entranced by a personality so different from his own and yet so cultured and committed. Physically she was a petite woman, only five feet tall, was pale of face and dressed plainly but, as even an unsympathetic observer conceded, 'tastefully'; and a female friend was impressed by her 'exquisitely pro-portioned' figure.[21] She moved gracefully – Trotsky never forgot how beautifully she walked out on to a pier jutting out from the side of a bridge: despite being in her high heels she went out to talk to two boys perched on the pier's end.[22]

The wife and daughters in Siberia were becoming less and less impor-tant for him; but Natalya too had to accept his political priorities and it was not long before he took off to London to consult with Lenin. The two men agreed that Trotsky should to return to Russia and drum up support for *Iskra* with a view to dominating the next Party Congress. Martov, writing from Paris, confided to Lenin on 29 November 1902:

> I don't know whether to insist on his immediate departure. On the one hand, he'd be very useful to us here; on the other hand, he really needs to stay around here for a minimum of 3–4 months to finish his education, especially in his understanding of theory where he had a lot of gaps; and thirdly I fear that the longer he stays here the more he'll be attracted by literary endeavours and the less he'll fancy going to Russia.[23]

Although everyone recognized Trotsky's talent he was not yet the finished article as a revolutionary and there was always the risk that he might fail to develop into the kind of leader which the established Iskraites wanted. He was his own man. The *Iskra* editors trod warily in deciding about him.

It was decided that he was too valuable to be dispatched to Russia. Instead he was asked to visit the Russian Marxist colonies around Europe to campaign for *Iskra*'s ideas in advance of the Second Party Congress. He visited Brussels, Liège, Heidelberg and several other German and Swiss cities.[24] Receiving pay and expenses from the editorial board, he was also sent occasional money orders from his father, who had come to accept that his son's mind was fixed on a political career.[25]

Everywhere he was a success. He wrote a lot on his travels, sticking to political themes and dropping his penchant for literary reviews or philosophical discussions. He mocked Pëtr Struve, Nikolai Berdyaev and other ex-Marxists in his *Iskra* articles. He criticized Russia's factory inspectorate and legal trade unions; he pinpointed the difficulties with Russian officialdom encountered by students, Finns and various social groups. In speeches and in writing he delivered tirades against the Socialist-Revolutionaries, who had emerged as the principal revolutionary rivals to the Russian Social-Democratic Workers' Party. Although Trotsky had little to say in internal party disputes he supported the *Iskra* tenet that it would not do to trail along behind working-class opinion. The duty of Marxists, he stressed, was to work out what needed to be done and to win the 'proletariat' over to their side.[26]

A political alliance was taking shape. When Lenin was on a visit to Paris he bought a pair of shoes which cramped his feet, so he gave them to Trotsky. The shoes seemed to fit Trotsky. But when he and Natalya Sedova went with Lenin to the Opéra Comique Trotsky found they pinched him. Lenin, who had a sadistic sense of humour, laughed as Trotsky hobbled home in pain;[27] but it did not disrupt their co-operation in politics. Echoing Lenin's *What Is to Be Done?*, Trotsky advocated a centralized, disciplined, clandestine party for Russia. He also called for the use of terror in moments of revolutionary upsurge – Lenin quizzed him about this and found that they had the same basic idea. Lenin was the leader but Trotsky had superior talents in certain areas and Lenin was eager to use them.

Trotsky also wanted others to admire his efforts. On 13 February 1903 he sent a letter to his wife Alexandra in Verkholensk about his busy life:

> Why do neither you nor Ilyusha [Ilya Sokolovski] write? Which issues of *Iskra* have you got? I'd like you to read all the issues. I sent issue no. 32 (the latest) to Ilyusha's address a week ago. Do you have *Zarya* ['Dawn', the sister journal to *Iskra*]? I'll try and send the main articles in a binding. There are none of my articles in no. 32: I was away delivering speeches.[28]

*Iskra* and its cause rather than the welfare of his family filled his thoughts. He wrote the letter in invisible ink but the Okhrana had marked him down as a man to be watched carefully, and the amateur nature of Trotsky's precautions made things easy for them. Trotsky was not unusual among leading political émigrés: most of them underestimated the depth of police penetration and manipulation of their activities. He also warned Alexandra against the Jewish Bund. This was a large Marxist organization based in the Pale of Settlement whence his ancestors had fled. The Bundists wanted to enter the Russian Social-Democratic Workers' Party on special terms guaranteeing their right to recruit Jews without reference to the party's other organizations in the region and speak and write in Yiddish freely. Trotsky saw this as despicable nationalism which would only give pleasure to the Zionists; he urged his wife to conduct 'energetic agitation' among the Bundists in Siberian exile to get them to drop their demands.[29]

This was not the only point he impressed upon her. Alexandra had questioned the importance he attributed to oratory in Russian political conditions. Trotsky replied:

> I don't wholly agree with your thoughts on the art of the orator. You think it's not really much use. Obviously you have parliamentary eloquence in mind. But the Rostov events, where Bragin spoke in front of a crowd 20,000–30,000 strong, and other such events are going to get more and more frequent. It's precisely in this revolutionary period that we now need street orators, 'demagogues'.[30]

Trotsky looked forward to applying his newly discovered skills as an émigré lecturer in direct political action in Russia. He did not intend to give up writing: he simply relished the idea of having the chance of testing himself as a Marxist agitator as soon as possible. He knew that he had a special talent, and he wanted to develop it.

Trotsky's insistence on finding his own way to be a revolutionary leader added to Plekhanov's doubts about him. Lenin took the side of his protégé and a tussle began. Plekhanov said Trotsky's articles were full of noise and lacking in content.[31] Lenin, though, wanted him as the seventh member of the editorial board. He acknowledged his shortcomings, especially his ornate style, but claimed to be working to eliminate it.[32] Plekhanov remained opposed: he really disliked Trotsky, as Trotsky was only too aware. The old prima donna disliked another prima donna who was still in an early stage of development. (The story went around that Zasulich had said, 'That young man's a genius,' and that Plekhanov had replied: 'That is something I can't forgive Trotsky.')[33] What is more, Plekhanov regarded Trotsky as Lenin's puppet. If Trotsky were to be admitted to the *Iskra* editorial board as a voting member it would be like giving two votes to Lenin – and Lenin would secure a permanent, reliable majority in disputes. Despite her friendliness with Trotsky, Zasulich sided with Plekhanov. Axelrod refrained from challenging Plekhanov. Not only Lenin but also Martov could hardly believe that Trotsky was being baulked on grounds that were so trivial.[34]

Lenin himself was driven to distraction by Plekhanov. He had his revenge when Plekhanov produced his draft party programme for the perusal of the editorial board. He poked fun at him for failing to mention the need for a 'dictatorship of the proletariat' once capitalism had been overthrown. He found flaws in logic and style and called for their correction.[35]

The Second Party Congress, which opened in Brussels on 17 July 1903, was basically the founding assembly of the Russian Social-Democratic Workers' Party. All the Marxist groups saw the need for a combined political organization, and the *Iskra* board and its practical agents brought delegations together to establish a proper central apparatus and agree on a party programme. Lenin was the leading spirit behind the scenes and was far from impartial in how he made his preparations. Wherever and whenever possible, he gave mandates to *Iskra*'s supporters. He was packing the Congress with individuals who would provide him and his friends with a majority – and among those friends was Trotsky, who visited the Russian Marxist 'colonies' drumming up support for the Iskraites. He was travelling on a false passport in the name of a Bulgarian called Samokliev and his last stopping place before leaving for the Congress was Geneva. He and his companion Dmitri Ulyanov (Lenin's brother) had an adventure on the way to Brussels. They set off to catch the train from Nion, a small village outside the city, so as to throw off any police agents. As an extra precaution they stood on the wrong side of the tracks, but they failed to reach the carriage door in time and caused the guard to halt the train. The guard opined that 'it was the first time he had seen such stupid fellows' and demanded fifty Swiss francs for stopping the train. The Russians, not possessing fifty francs, pretended not to speak French and were eventually allowed to proceed.

The Russian Ministry of Internal Affairs had alerted the Belgian government to the holding of the Congress. Brussels swarmed with clandestine delegates and secret agents. The Congress proceedings were bitter from the start. Days were taken up with challenges and counter-challenges to the mandates of particular delegates. Then the Belgian police intervened. The decision was taken to move the Congress to London where a venue had been found at the English Club in Charlotte Street in Bloomsbury.

High on the agenda was discussion of the party programme. Plekhanov and Lenin took the lead arguing for acceptance of the *Iskra* draft, and they succeeded. Trotsky appeared among the auxiliary forces and *Iskra* carried all before it. It was when debate turned to organizational questions that trouble erupted. One of the largest delegations at the Congress was the Jewish Bund with five members. The Bundists were eager to secure special terms for entrance to the party. Concentrated in the Pale of Settlement, the Bund had more members than any other Marxist organization in the Russian Empire. It demanded exceptional autonomy in its territory. To Iskraites this seemed like nationalism, and they strenuously objected. When a narrow majority turned the Bund down, all the Bundists walked out. This had the effect of strengthening *Iskra*'s dominance for the rest of the Congress. Plekhanov, Lenin and Martov were extremely pleased. Their draft party programme was passed. Their proposed structure for the party was given approval. The Russian Social-Democratic Workers' Party appeared to be emerging from its Congress unified and reinforced.

Suddenly the Iskraites fell out among themselves when Lenin and Martov disputed the definition of a party member in the draft rules. Both supported principles of centralism, discipline and clandestinity. But Lenin stipulated that nobody should join the party without giving a commitment to working actively for it. Martov sensed danger here. Lenin's formula, he claimed, would create a party of full-time revolutionaries whereas what was required was an organization attracting thousands of working-class members. Martov thought Lenin was recommending an authoritarian approach inappropriate for a Marxist party. Lenin's followers called themselves the 'hards' and referred to the Martovites as the 'softs'.

Plekhanov was minded to support Lenin even though he said privately that there was something of the Robespierre about him.[36] The voting was going to be closely contested. Trotsky felt drawn to Martov. Lenin went to him with Pëtr Krasikov to persuade him otherwise. Krasikov did not hold back in his personal criticism of the other *Iskra* editors. Even Lenin winced at his comments. Trotsky refused to budge. The tensions among the Iskraites were becoming intolerable and a separate gathering was held outside the Congress. Trotsky's friend Lev Deich suggested him as chairman: 'I propose to elect our Benjamin.' He judged that both sides would trust Trotsky. The atmosphere was volatile, provoking Lenin to storm out slamming the door. But he did not give up trying to persuade Trotsky to side with the 'hards'. This time he sent his younger brother Dmitri together with Rozalia Zemlyachka. To no avail. Trotsky had made up his mind that Lenin was in the wrong and had to be opposed.[37] He had chosen the winning side. The votes went twenty-eight to twenty-three in Martov's favour. The problem for him was that the election to the central party bodies – the Central Committee and the *Iskra* editorial board – went the other way, and Plekhanov and Lenin held a dominant position in them.

Worse still, neither Lenin nor Martov thought that the Congress had brought their dispute to a close. Lenin went round calling his group the Majoritarians (or *bol'sheviki*) and Martov's group the Minoritarians (or *men'sheviki*) with reference to the recent election. He behaved as if he had the exclusive right to speak in the Russian Social-Democratic Workers' Party's name. Such comportment could lead to an outright split, and Trotsky was depressed.[38] He wrote to Natalya Sedova about the Congress. She had not been present because, despite her inexperience, she had been given the task of going to St Petersburg on a mission to spread *Iskra*'s ideas among industrial workers. She enjoyed acquiring the techniques of disguise for such a mission;[39] but she understood how badly her friend felt about what had occurred in London. For Trotsky, as for all Marxists in Russia, there was only one working class and there should be a unified workers' party. He held his former patron responsible for trying to shatter the common dream.

# 8. CUTTING LOOSE

The months after the Second Party Congress were unsettling for its protagonists. Plekhanov quickly regretted supporting Lenin and moved over to Martov's side, tipping the balance in the party leadership in favour of the Mensheviks. Trotsky was meanwhile hard at work on his *Report of the Siberian Delegation*.[1] It was not a piece he later wanted to advertise because it contained invective against the Bolsheviks. Lenin and his followers reacted fiercely but Trotsky rejected their accusations of unfairness, pointing out that his commentary was based on quotations from Bolshevik doctrine and policy.[2] Martov considered him for inclusion on the *Iskra* editorial board.[3] This was a period when Trotsky, detached from Lenin, drew close to Axelrod. Plekhanov, though, made difficulties by stipulating that he would remain with the Mensheviks only on condition that they kept Trotsky off the *Iskra* board. Martov acceded to the demand while continuing to welcome Trotsky's articles for publication.[4] The hope was that Trotsky would be satisfied with such a compromise. The Mensheviks wanted to go on benefiting from the brilliance of his attacks on the Bolsheviks – one Menshevik, M. S. Makadzyub, purred that nobody could 'speak more sharply about Lenin'.[5]

Makazyub later noticed the 'pride and happiness on [Trotsky's] face' and felt he deserved to be so pleased.[6] For a while Trotsky seemed to have accepted the situation among the Mensheviks, even though a petition was organized in Paris asking Martov to stand up to Plekhanov and incorporate Trotsky on to the editorial board.[7] He did not try to get the sympathy of others for his treatment at Plekhanov's hands. Pëtr Garvi recalled:

> somehow he always knew how to impart 'the pathos of distance' which leaders of a much higher calibre than Trotsky such as Axelrod, Zasulich or Martov did not establish in their relations with comrades. The cold glint of his eyes from behind his pince-nez; the cold timbre of his voice; the cold correctness and sharpness of his speech as 'he writes as he speaks', not in an ordinary conversational manner but

in formulae and pronouncements; and finally the exaggerated care over his external appearance, dress and gestures: all this had the effect of alienating people and even thrusting them away from him.[8]

Trotsky knew he had become one of the recognized leaders of the party.[9]

War broke out between Russia and Japan in February 1904, and he quickly became an uncomfortable partner for Martov when he stirred up a controversy about it among Marxists. Nicholas II believed that his forces were invincible on land and at sea. The Black Sea fleet was dispatched to the other side of the world to deliver a drubbing to a country of 'Orientals' while the Trans-Siberian railway transported troops out to the Far East. Trotsky declared that the Japanese war caused damage to the general national interest – and he was untroubled by fellow Marxists saying that he should concentrate on the specific damage done to the working class. Outraging many Mensheviks, he called for 'Marxist self-criticism instead of "orthodox" self-satisfaction'.[10] Trotsky had little automatic respect for the pieties of the Russian Social-Democratic Workers' Party. He also lambasted those who issued 'a summons to insurrection' and aimed at 'revolutionary dictatorship' – here he had the Bolsheviks in his sights. He showered the party's two internal factions with scorn even while urging the reunification of the party.[11]

The Japanese war, he judged, had brought forward the prospects of revolution in Russia. His first thought was to return and conduct clandestine agitation. First he left Switzerland and moved to Karlsruhe, where he operated again under the alias of Lvov. Fëdor Dan wrote to Axelrod from Geneva imploring him to write to Trotsky and 'cool down his fantasies'. The Mensheviks wanted Trotsky to fulfil his agreement to write pieces for them.[12] In fact Trotsky himself had changed his mind about speeding off to Russia – he was never someone to let others do the thinking for him. Instead he stayed in central Europe where he continued to cause controversy in the party leadership. Always he wrote whatever was in his head. Plekhanov made no effort to get over his dislike of him and demanded that he should be kept off the *Iskra* editorial board; he threatened to resign if the other editors refused.[13] Martov and Axelrod hoped that Trotsky would see their problem and avoid making a fuss. Scarcely had Trotsky confirmed his importance in the party than his status was put under threat. He was anyway fed up with the Mensheviks, wanting a more active revolutionary strategy than they espoused; and he wrote an open letter to express his concerns.[14] The Menshevik reluctance to dispense with his useful talent effectively stopped the dispute in its tracks.[15]

Trotsky moved to Munich in summer 1904.[16] He hated all the factional squabbling and made friends with a lively Marxist émigré based in the Bavarian capital. This was Alexander Helphand, usually known by his pseudonym Parvus. Twelve years older than Trotsky, he had spent some years of exile in Archangel province before seeking refuge in Germany and taking a doctorate in philosophy. Quickly he joined the German Social-Democratic Party and helped to mount the attack on the attempts by Eduard Bernstein to move Marxism away from doctrines of revolution and towards those of peaceful political change. Parvus became a famous 'anti-revisionist'. Although he had not lost interest in Russia he disdained to join either the Bolsheviks or the Mensheviks. His revolutionary strategy was unique in Russian Marxism. He had no time for the middle classes: his idea was that only the workers could dependably lead the revolutionary struggle against the Romanov monarchy.[17] Indeed Parvus called for a 'workers' government' to be established as soon as Nicolas II was overthrown. Trotsky found all this attractive and Parvus became his intellectual mentor, as the Okhrana noted with some alarm.[18] While Trotsky was immersed in the internal disputes of Menshevism he was helping to divide the party and was inadvertently doing the work of the police. The Okhrana had an interest in encouraging factionalism. By joining up with Parvus, Trotsky was concentrating on questions about how to carry out violent revolution against the Imperial order.

Wanting political independence from *Iskra*, he resolved to found his own publishing operation. He decided to approach his father for help with funding. This was a matter requiring delicate handling, and Trotsky talked about inviting him abroad 'to initiate him into the scheme'. Trust would need to be rebuilt between them. Trotsky thought of asking for four or five thousand dollars from the land he expected to inherit in the future. It was a far cry from six years earlier when he had broken with his father and thought he had shunned parental support for ever. Trotsky sent a probing letter to test the mood in Yanovka – unfortunately there is as yet no evidence to indicate David Bronstein's reaction; but certainly, as we have seen, his son had been receiving money from him from time to time since leaving Siberia.[19]

Trotsky dealt with the topic of party organization in a pamphlet entitled *Our Political Tasks*, which was published in Russian by the party's press in Geneva. Signing himself 'N. Trotsky', he dedicated the work to his 'dear teacher Pavel Borisovich Axelrod'. This was the sole sign of modesty: Axelrod's writings exerted little influence on the content. Trotsky referred to himself and his friends as 'representatives of "the minority"'.

Thus he identified himself as a Menshevik of some sort (which would quickly become an embarrassment).[20] He did not bother to discuss fellow Mensheviks; Martov passed without reference. Hardly any Bolsheviks were considered either. The big exception was Lenin: Trotsky intended to prove that the Bolshevik leader's influence was on the wane and that his position had been rendered 'hopeless'. The preface was dated 24 August 1904.[21] This was important because Trotsky was trying to indicate that the year-long 'nightmare atmosphere' in the party was at last over. Russian social-democracy was resurgent as comrades gave up their bickering. Yet Trotsky belied his own confidence by suggesting that Lenin's ideas and activity remained a dangerous distraction. The Romanov autocracy was seeking a way out from its problem through war with Japan. The Russian political situation was unstable. Instead of debating internal organizational questions, the party ought to be studying 'the science of uprisings'.[22]

Lenin, according to Trotsky, had forgotten the need for Marxists to promote 'the independent activity of the proletariat'. Obsessive concentration on centralism and discipline was a damaging feature. Trotsky, abandoning his early admiration of *What Is to Be Done?*, suggested that Lenin was too concerned with the role of the newspaper. It was fatuous to believe that a perfect hierarchical structure was attainable. Alexander Parvus had rightly argued that socialist objectives would never be realized if Marxists gave all their attention to eliminating subversive elements. Leninism was simply impractical. The true emphasis had to be on broad revolutionary initiatives. Strikes and demonstrations should be encouraged without any preordained pattern of activity.[23]

Trotsky laid out a brisk case: 'A barracks regime cannot be the regime for our party just as the factory cannot be its model.'[24] Lenin had acted as if the entire party was simply 'the technical agency attached to a newspaper'.[25] This simply would not do. He had got into such a mess because of his preoccupation with revolutionary intellectuals. His claim to be some new sort of Jacobin showed a misunderstanding of the history of the French Revolution. Maximilien Robespierre had had all the wrong attitudes for a healthy political vision, as evidenced in his declaration: 'I know only two parties, the party of good and the party of bad citizens.' For Trotsky this was senseless intolerance, and he saw the same trait in 'Maximilien Lenin'. Trotsky suggested that if Karl Marx had been living in France under Robespierre his head would have fallen from his shoulders on the guillotine.[26] The Russian Social-Democratic Workers' Party needed to avoid Jacobin suspiciousness. It certainly should not engage in 'theoretically terrorizing' the intelligentsia.[27] Essentially it should dedicate itself to helping to prepare the workers so that they could establish their own dictatorship. Such indeed was the task of Marxists worldwide.

What Lenin was proposing was 'political substitutionism'. There would be no dictatorship of the proletariat under the Bolsheviks but a 'dictatorship over the proletariat'. The party would substitute itself for the workers, the central leadership for the party and the leader for the central leadership. In place of 'proletarian socialism' the followers of Lenin would install mere Jacobinism. He adduced the pamphlets of Bolshevik groups in Ufa, Perm and the mid-Urals as proof of his case, and he noted Lenin's reaction: 'He stays silent.'[28] Lenin with his 'organizational fetishism' would lead to a lack of confidence in the working class. Marxists would look elsewhere to realize their aspirations. Some would become mere reformists, others would turn to anarchism.[29]

This brilliant exposition was prophetic in many basic respects. The October Revolution was to put the Bolsheviks in power, and soon after forming a government they would give up hearkening to popular opinion after millions of workers had turned against them. The 'proletariat' was never given the chance to dictate even the size of its food rations, far less to choose who was going to rule. But the 'prophecy' in 1904 was unintended by its author. At that time Trotsky was writing not about a distant future but about current developments. He overestimated the party's capacity to eradicate factionalism. When ridiculing the Bolshevik leader as a potential dictator, he put the word in inverted commas in order to signify that this was not a realistic possibility. Over the next dozen years the Bolsheviks repeatedly disrupted efforts to unify the party except when, temporarily, it suited their factional purposes. Gradually Trotsky came to learn that Bolshevik doctrines and practices had a force of their own. Even without Lenin's leadership there were plenty of irreconcilables among Bolsheviks who could cause schism, and indeed there were times when the troubles would have been greater if Lenin had not insisted that there were advantages in co-operation with the Mensheviks for tactical reasons. But Trotsky kept up his optimism: he continued to believe that schisms in the party would be swept aside by the pressure of revolutionary events.

By turning on Lenin, Trotsky anyhow won the admiration of Bolshevism's antagonists. Martov offered him an enlarged role in *Iskra* as writer and editor and promised him a post in charge of party pamphlets; he also proposed to set up a 'popular newspaper' under Trotsky's editorial leadership.[30] Trotsky was cautious in his response, agreeing only to a modest level of collaboration with the Menshevik leadership. He knew he could not take on so heavy a load. He hated to be unpunctual in finishing his tasks; and unlike Martov, he was unforgiving of chaos.

While dragging a hot rake over Bolshevism, furthermore, he did not leave Menshevism unharmed. It was an article of faith for him that the 'proletariat' should direct the revolutionary struggle and that the 'bourgeoisie' could never be trusted as allies. Mensheviks wished to avoid giving offence to the middle class: they hoped that Russia's liberals would actively participate in a joint campaign against the autocracy. Trotsky despised the industrialists, bankers and advanced farmers as supporters of the political status quo. Faced with a choice between a popular revolution and their own financial interests, they would ultimately come out on the side of the Romanov dynasty. The liberals were engaging in rhetoric against the Romanovs and in the following year would form the Constitutional-Democratic Party (or Kadets). Trotsky predicted that they would always cave in to governmental pressure. The 'proletariat' ought to go it alone. It had to lead every social group with a genuine dedication to transforming society. No other class could do this. Workers would be the salvation of Russia and then of the rest of the world. Trotsky made a name for himself by denigrating the Russian liberals. Whereas Mensheviks strove to win them over, Trotsky provoked them. He repudiated any tactical alliance with the Kadets. For Trotsky, they were the dregs of public life. The Russian Social-Democratic Workers' Party would do itself a favour by repudiating compromises with them.

Trotsky emerged as a spokesman for Marxists standing between the two factions as they had existed at the Second Party Congress.[31] But while accepting his right to speak out for his beliefs, people often objected to his personal demeanour. He came across as arrogant and insensitive. Alexander Bogdanov, co-leader of the émigré Bolshevik faction, wrote to Lenin's wife Nadezhda Krupskaya about an encounter with him: 'Trotsky came round to see me. I very much dislike him – he's totally uncongenial.'[32] What gave weight to Bogdanov's judgement was the fact that he was among the least censorious of comrades. Martov needled Trotsky with the comment that he was a dilettante. Trotsky responded that Martov was constantly shifting his ground, often under pressure from his brother-in-law Fëdor Dan who was known as the 'little Lenin' of the Mensheviks. The dispute became bitter when Martov held up publication of Trotsky's articles. It seemed evident that this was the price (or 'tribute', as Trotsky put it) exacted by Plekhanov for his own co-operation with *Iskra*. Trotsky accused Martov of being cowardly and disingenuous as an editor.[33] Trotsky's entire career was in the balance. He had fallen out with

Lenin. Then he had done the same with Martov and Dan. And although he was buoyed up by his friendship with Parvus, his new mentor was not someone who made for a quiet existence.

Natalya Sedova, returning from Russia in October 1904, helped to steady Trotsky. He had arranged to meet her off the train in Berlin. Among his first words were that they 'must not be parted ever again'. They were in love. They spent a month in the German capital where he introduced her to the leading German social-democrats who had become his acquaintances such as Karl Kautsky, Clara Zetkin, Rosa Luxemburg and August Bebel. They moved on to Geneva as partners for life.[34]

The marriage with Alexandra Bronstein was over. In his memoirs he claimed that he could 'scarcely conduct a correspondence with her from abroad'.[35] He was inventing an excuse. The plain fact was that he exchanged letters with Alexandra but had dropped her for someone else. Natalya from then onwards was his wife – his second one – in all but law. Alexandra coped as best she could. She accepted that he had found a permanent partner he wanted to live with. The daughters had been her responsibility since he had left Siberia. On her release from exile, she baulked at looking after both of them by herself. She and Trotsky came to an arrangement whereby the younger one, Nina, would stay with her while Zina would go off to Kherson province and be brought up by Trotsky's sister Yelizaveta. Zina would join an 'intellectual, bourgeois-provincial' milieu – this was Natalya's less than felicitous description. Yelizaveta was married to Naum Meilman, who was a doctor as well as an amateur musician. The couple were not without hostility to the tsarist order but they were no way active in this respect.[36] (Not that this stopped the police from searching their house in Kherson in 1906.)[37]

Natalya too came from Ukraine – she always retained more of her 'southern accent', as people in the Russian capital called it, than Trotsky.[38] Her family had owned a farm at Yasinovka in Poltava province and her father, who was of Cossack stock, was manager of a family-owned factory. Natalya had three brothers and two sisters.[39] She lived on the farm only in her early childhood but Yasinovka's countryside never lost its enchantment for her: its tall, pyramidal poplars, of which she was reminded when she saw the oil derricks in Baku; its riverside willows covered in yellow-green powder and the buzzing of millions of bees; its tender roses and flaming lilacs.[40] Natalya was born into the hereditary gentry. They were friends with the family of the renowned Ukrainian anti-tsarist poet Taras Shevchenko.[41] Eventually the Sedovs sold up their estate, as many were doing after the Emancipation Edict of 1861 which released peasants from personal bondage to landowners, and moved to the nearest town. This was Romny, where Natalya was born on 5 April 1882. The Sedovs lived comfortably. But her father died of a heart attack when she was only seven and her traumatized mother perished a few months later. Natalya was brought up by her grandmother and an aunt.

Her relatives sent her off to Kharkov to be educated as a boarder at a private grammar school. The teachers were progressive by contemporary standards and one of them discussed the revolutionary movement with her.[42] Soon she was taking collections for political prisoners and reading banned literature. One of Natalya's own aunts had been a revolutionary and been sentenced to a period of exile in Siberia. (Natalya learned from her about Lev Deich, the famous escaper and revolutionary, who later became a family friend of Natalya and Trotsky.)[43] She was successful at her studies even though the school authorities considered her frivolous. At the age of sixteen she was happy to throw aside her uniform and enrol in the 'higher women's courses' in Moscow. She thrived on visits to theatres, museums and concert halls.[44] Then she took a trip to Switzerland, where she joined Marxist groups in Geneva and was given material to smuggle back to Poltava. She did not take to Swiss life, which reminded her too much of boarding school. More to her liking was Paris, where she aligned herself with the *Iskra* group. Still supported by money from her grandmother, she attended both the Sorbonne and the Higher Russian School. And it was in Paris that she met Trotsky and found her life being swept into the maelstrom of his career.[45]

As the winter of 1904–5 approached, the news she now brought back from her Russian trip was politically encouraging for both of them. Industrial militancy was on the increase. There was restlessness among the peasantry in several provinces. Liberals were stirring themselves into a campaign against the government. In the Polish lands a challenge was made to St Petersburg. The war with Japan was going badly for the Russians and questions of political and military competence were raised. The Russian garrison at Port Arthur was put under siege. Nicholas II's throne and dynasty began to look under serious threat.

In December 1904 an article by Trotsky appeared in *Sotsial-demokrat* ('Social-Democrat') in Geneva. He wrote about street demonstrations in Warsaw and Radom and about a general strike in Baku. He predicted a campaign of 'bestial revenge' by the Imperial government and suspected that Jews would be singled out as scapegoats. A resumption of 'the Kishinëv medicine' could be expected. (Kishinëv was where one of the worst atrocities against Jews had occurred in April 1903.) The military news from the Far East was unrelievedly grim and Trotsky sensed that the situation could spiral out of the authorities' control. He worried that revolutionaries might be tempted to do a deal with the government. This would 'drape a noose round the neck of a Russian people which had already provided so many victims in the struggle for freedom'.[46] At the same time he warned against abstract phrases 'calling for insurrection'; implicitly he even criticized Lenin's preoccupation with 'revolutionary dictatorship'. His article was a synopsis of newspaper reports. He missed the most dangerous phenomenon for the status quo in Russia. This was the industrial trade union led by an Orthodox Church priest, Father Georgi Gapon, and based in St Petersburg. Its members were peaceful and it had legal status. Yet it was about to organize something without precedent: a procession to the Winter Palace on 9 January 1905 to present a petition to Nicholas II asking him to promulgate universal civil rights. Gapon was about to set off a revolutionary eruption.

Despite having underestimated Gapon's importance, Trotsky was readier than his comrades in the party's leading cadre to take advantage of subsequent developments. His intuitions fitted him for roles which were about to gain in importance. He could write and speak with brilliant fluency; he was supremely daring and confident and planned to become an orator for the revolution. At the same time he was a tiresome colleague. He liked to burst the bindings of party discipline. He relished the company of those who appreciated his intellectual vivacity. He treasured his personal independence; he was quicksilver. Trotsky was already Trotsky.

# 9. THE YEAR 1905

Disturbances convulsed the Russian Empire on 9 January 1905 after troops outside the Winter Palace in St Petersburg fired upon an unarmed procession of workers and their families wearing their Sunday best. The massacre of hundreds of innocents caused popular outrage. Strikes broke out in the capital, soon followed by a withdrawal of labour in factories and mines across the country. Concerns arose about the obedience of the soldiers expected to enforce order. The vulnerability of the Imperial political order was heightened by the reverses in the war against Japan which had been going on since the previous year. Liberals and conservatives had traditionally shown suspicion towards rebellious workers. The events of Bloody Sunday changed all that and demands were made for Nicholas II to grant fundamental reforms.

On 9–10 January Trotsky spent a restless night on a train to Geneva after a speaking trip to other Swiss cities. He arrived so early in the morning that the paper boy only had the previous day's press, and the article on Russia therefore referred to the St Petersburg demonstration in the future tense. Trotsky felt able to assume that it had not taken place. He discovered the truth after reaching the *Iskra* office in the city. By then Geneva's Russian revolutionary colony had learned of Bloody Sunday and the public reaction. They could hardly believe that what they had yearned for and predicted for many years seemed at last to be happening: the monarchy and its supporters were in full political retreat. The émigrés always remembered what they were doing when the news came through to Switzerland. Trotsky's reaction was the most dramatic. An announcement was made in the course of an *Iskra* editorial board meeting and the effect on him was instantaneous: he had one of his blackouts.[1] This inherited condition, he believed, was most likely to give trouble when he was already feeling ill or tired. He had been living on his nerves as he inveighed against tsarism, Bolshevism and world capitalism. Perhaps he had also been driving himself too hard.

A new era was dawning in Russia. Revolutionaries of all casts –

Socialist-Revolutionaries, Mensheviks and Bolsheviks – gathered in Geneva's rue Carouge district. They were wondering whether they might soon need to return home. Few yet did so. Their names were on police lists. The authorities more or less coped with the tumult in St Petersburg but were aware that disorder might soon recur. The embers of Bloody Sunday had not been put out.

Nicholas II recognized the power of popular outrage. The Imperial government was under threat. The war against Japan was going disastrously. Russian armed forces had recently been forced back to Mukden, and Port Arthur had been seized by the Japanese army and navy a week before Bloody Sunday. Military success was crucial to Romanov prestige. All sections of society remained furious about the brutal treatment of the 9 January demonstration. Official efforts were made to consult workers in the capital about their grievances, but the massacre had burned itself deep into everyone's consciousness. Urban areas were in tumult. Strikes proliferated. Trade unions, including illegal ones, became ever bolder. In May 1905 a workers' soviet (or council) was elected in Ivanovo-Voznesensk; it quickly made demands on the local textile-factory owners and asserted its influence throughout the vicinity. As yet the peasantry stayed quiet but landowners were worried lest the troubles might spill into the countryside. Anti-government activity was intensifying in Finland, Georgia and the Polish lands ruled from St Petersburg. Clandestine political groups of all kinds were gathering recruits, issuing newspapers and pamphlets and explaining their plans for political change. Even moderate liberals were calling for action.[2]

Trotsky had long sensed that he had the personal potential for open 'mass' politics (as he had indicated two years earlier to his wife Alexandra). He was reckless of the risks in returning incognito. He was on the police lists for immediate arrest. His prominence in emigrant politics only added to the danger, but he did not care. While nearly all the other leaders of the Russian Social-Democratic Workers' Party tarried, Trotsky made swift arrangements for travel. He did not comment on the contrast: that would never be his way. But he surely wondered why so few prominent figures followed his example. Self-sacrifice was in the Russian revolutionary tradition. The individual's safety was meant to be subordinate to the cause. Imperial Russia was cracking apart. Trotsky felt he absolutely had to join the efforts of striking workers to confront the monarchy, generals, policemen and employers. The fact that he was a party leader made no difference. Revolutionary commitment to his way of thinking unavoidably involved danger. Seclusion in Switzerland, France or

Britain was no longer a tolerable option. Revolutionary duty was calling him to action.

He and Natalya made for Vienna where Victor Adler, the leading Austrian Marxist, was helping emigrants obtain money and passports. Trotsky's striking looks were a problem, so Adler arranged a visit by a hairdresser to change his appearance. Natalya then went ahead to Ukraine to find lodgings for them. This was the easiest way to cross the frontier without too much fear of arrest. Once she had found a place in Kiev, Trotsky followed her, adopting the identity of retired Corporal Arbuzov. It was still only February. Trotsky and his partner intended to play a full part in revolutionary politics.[3]

Around a month later they moved on to St Petersburg where Natalya operated as a propagandist in circles of workers employed at the huge Pipe Factory on Vasilevski Island.[4] She had to be still more careful than when she was on her own. As both of them had agreed, Trotsky's security was paramount: he was a leader in the party, she only an ordinary militant. By then he was operating under his new pseudonym of Pëtr Petrovich. Any mistake by her could lead the police to him, and they would not have found it hard to discover his real identity. She was scrupulous about the techniques of 'conspiracy' and all went well until May. Natalya was attending a gathering of revolutionary supporters in woods outside the city when the authorities arrived after a tip-off from an informer. She and others were arrested; but, luckily for Trotsky, her link with him did not come to light. She was sentenced to six months in the House of Preliminary Detention.[5] By her own account, she was treated well enough and was even allowed a bath every day. She set about cleaning up her cell with help from a common criminal; she was always keen on cleanliness in her surroundings.[6] Natalya was released early from prison on condition that she stayed in Tver, a hundred miles north-east of the capital as the crow flies, under regular police supervision.

Trotsky for reasons of his own safety could not see her. Many of his comrades were being arrested as the Okhrana intensified its activity. Feeling the heat, he went off in midsummer and lived incognito in the Finnish town of Rauha. Finland had a degree of autonomy from St Petersburg and the local police were famously loath to search for absconding revolutionaries.[7]

Trotsky was among the earliest to come up with a clear-cut strategy. *Iskra* on 3 March 1905 carried a 'political letter' from him calling for 'an uprising of the whole people' which would produce a Provisional Government and then a Constituent Assembly.[8] A fortnight later he clarified what he meant. Revolution could not simply be unleashed but required organization and planning. The Mensheviks, he stated, were wrong to reject Parvus's ideas about a 'workers' government'. Parvus denied that universal suffrage was an end in itself since the middle class would always find ways to manipulate the electoral system. Freedom could not be begged for: it had to be won. The bureaucracy and officer corps had to be eliminated.[9] What was needed, in fact, was not just an uprising as demanded by the Bolsheviks but a commitment to a struggle to 'make the revolution permanent'.[10] Trotsky picked up the latest version of Parvus's strategy, stressing that the Central Committee should order each of its local committees to establish a 'military organ'. Stormy events were thrusting the proletariat towards a position of 'hegemony' and the party had to be ready to exploit the situation.

He conceded that the projected 'workers' government' would lack the 'social base for an independent Jacobin democracy'. By this he seems to have meant that the Jacobins in the French Revolution had been able to call up support from broad layers of the lower classes throughout the country. The working class in Russia was as yet too small for that purpose. Very well, concluded Trotsky, Marxists in Russia should fight to establish a dictatorship of a revolutionary elite – and it would be a dictatorship led by the Russian Social-Democratic Workers' Party.[11]

Trotsky said little directly about terror. What would have happened if his 'workers' government' had come into existence? Decades later he recalled his basic attitude: 'We too stood for terror but for mass terror realized by the revolutionary class.'[12] In making his case he did not bother with an exegesis of Marx and Engels. While Lenin noisily appealed to the founders of Marxism as his authorities, Trotsky focused on his own intrinsic arguments. He insisted that Marxists could draw lessons from the past, especially the French Revolution. He bridled at the suggestion that he and Parvus propounded ideas which had nothing in common with European social-democracy. He pointed out that the German Social-Democratic Party aimed at 'the conquest of state power by the proletariat' and a 'class dictatorship'. In Trotsky's eyes there should be no 'fetishism' about using legal methods. Nor should people expect the period of revolutionary transformation to be a brief one. A whole epoch of building socialism stretched before the party. Marxists in Russia should commit themselves to the 'uninterruptedness of revolution'.[13]

The Bolsheviks held their own separate Congress between April and May in London to decide strategy; the Menshevik leadership was forever conferring about policies. In fact the Bolshevik faction at Lenin's instigation was moving towards a strategic choice which was close to the Parvus–Trotsky position. Lenin called for a two-stage revolutionary process. The first stage was meant to introduce electoral democracy and capitalist economic development just as Plekhanov had always projected. But Lenin argued that this could happen only if a 'provisional revolutionary democratic dictatorship of the proletariat and the peasantry' were established. He did not trust the middle classes to have any part in Russia's political leadership. Many noted at the time how close this was to Trotskyism. The differences, indeed, were detectable only with an ideological microscope. Whereas Trotsky called for a single stage of revolutionary transformation, Lenin demanded two – and Lenin to this extent could go on claiming to have stuck to Russian Marxist orthodoxy. Another divisive matter was the role of the peasantry. Trotsky mentioned that land reform would be essential to the effectiveness of his 'workers' government'; Lenin wanted a bigger influence for peasants and proposed that the government should be a coalition including the parties with the electoral support of the peasants.

Through the long summer of 1905 the difficulties mounted for the Romanov monarchy. Industrial conflicts were frequent. Disturbances in the armed forces were not uncommon. Provinces in Poland, Georgia and the north Caucasus were becoming almost ungovernable. A general strike was started in early October. Factory workers and radical intellectuals in St Petersburg elected a body which was to become known as the Council (or Soviet) of Workers' Deputies; its functions quickly spread far beyond wage bargaining to basic aspirations of popular self-rule. On 17 October, advised by Count Witte who as Minister of Finance in the 1890s had instigated rapid industrial growth in the empire, Nicholas II yielded ground and issued his Manifesto granting a range of civic freedoms and promising to hold parliamentary elections to a State Duma.

This concession both excited and horrified the revolutionaries. There were signs that broad sections of public opinion were willing to give the benefit of the doubt to the emperor. Trotsky was among those who believed that the monarchy's overthrow and revolution should remain the goal:

On 18 October, the day after the manifesto's publication, many tens of thousands of people were standing in front of St Petersburg University, aroused by the struggle and intoxicated with the joy of their first victory. I shouted to them from the balcony that a half-victory was unreliable, that the enemy was irreconcilable, that there were traps ahead; I tore up the Imperial manifesto and threw the pieces to the winds.[14]

The worst thing that could happen from Trotsky's viewpoint was for workers to drop their political demands for the removal of the dynasty. For a while he based himself in Finland. Natalya, though, was allowed to return legally to St Petersburg and made contact with him. She travelled north to meet him for couple of days in Vyborg – only seventy-six miles from the Russian capital.[15] Meanwhile the revolutionary mood intensified. Trotsky decided to take the risk and engage in open political activity by returning to St Petersburg. Natalya would have liked to do the same but was in poor health at the time.[16] Trotsky chose to focus his efforts in the Petersburg Soviet where he operated under the alias of Yanovski.

The Soviet's elected Chairman was the lawyer Georgi Nosar-Khrustalëv. He belonged to no party and was pleased with the title; he hardly looked like a dangerous subversive with his coiffeured hair and upturned collar.[17] He stayed in place until being arrested on 26 October. Trotsky's critics watched him closely and thought him too keen to take the post vacated by Khrustalëv.[18] He himself was to exaggerate how large an influence he wielded. The Mensheviks and Bolsheviks co-operated better in the Soviet than he claimed, and it would seem that only a few decisions were attributable to him personally.[19] Nevertheless the critics – most of them belonging to factions of the Russian Social-Democratic Workers' Party – usually conceded that he rose to the demands of the situation. Whereas they had talked endlessly about 'mass politics', Trotsky alone had acted. He had found himself as an orator. Without breaking sweat he could stir an audience. He had no difficulty in inspiring people. He was brave. Rather than hiding away he challenged the authorities to close down the Soviet. No leading figure in his party thrust himself into danger as Trotsky did. He was justifiably annoyed when accused of a mere lust for popularity. How did they think revolutions could be made?

Other revolutionary émigrés were stirred to return to Russia when they read the October Manifesto. Its contents meant that they were at last assured of their personal security. Back they came: Lenin, Martov and Chernov. Some of the old precautions were still necessary. The emigrants travelled on false passports. They were careful about where they stayed overnight and who was allowed to know. St Petersburg was the common destination. Lenin, through gritted teeth, acknowledged that his colleague deserved to be leading the Soviet: 'Well, Trotsky has earned it by his ceaseless and brilliant work.'[20] Practically everyone who attended the big meetings in the capital felt the same about him. It was obvious to everyone that the fate of Imperial politics lay in the capital. Newspapers were being founded there. Presses were used overtly by all the revolutionary groups. Parties set up stalls in public. Bookshops stocked subversive literature. Public meetings were held where violent abuse of the dynasty and its supporters occurred. There was a heightened feeling among the Marxists and other rebels that the moment of definitive struggle with the Romanov monarchy was at hand.

An exception was Petersburg Soviet member Roman Gul:

> In his manner of speaking Trotsky was the polar opposite of Lenin. Lenin moved around the platform. Trotsky stood still. Lenin offered none of the flowers of eloquence. Trotsky showered the public with them. Lenin did not listen to himself. Trotsky not only listened to himself but also surely admired himself.[21]

He also noted the care Trotsky took with his appearance down to the fastidious choice of tie. In Gul's eyes he was the epitome of vanity. But Gul could not deny that Trotsky as a public politician put Lenin in the shade.

Now that both of them were back in St Petersburg, life for Trotsky was steadied by Natalya's companionship. They rented a room in the capital under the names of Mr and Mr Vikentev. Their landlord was a speculator in stocks and shares whose affairs were deteriorating in the turmoil caused to the St Petersburg stock exchange in earlier months. He became frantic on discovering that the revolutionaries, reaching out beyond the factory workers, were trying to appeal to concierges. The end of civilization as he understood it appeared imminent. By chance his eyes had lit upon an article by Trotsky. Not knowing that he was speaking at that very moment to the author himself, he shouted: 'If I came across that convict I would shoot him with this!' – and he pulled a gun from his pocket and shook it in the air.[22] For obvious reasons the 'Vikentevs' kept quiet about their political opinions for they had no time to try and find new lodgings. They had little social life even outside the apartment. So long as the Petersburg Soviet existed politics was the all-consuming activity. There were also always articles to write for the daily newspapers and workers' meetings to address. The rented apartment was only a place for them to eat and sleep in.

Trotsky went off each day to the editorial offices of whatever newspaper he was writing for at the time:

In the Soviet I operated under the name of Yanovski, after the village in which I was born. In the press I wrote as Trotsky. I had to work for three newspapers. Together with Parvus I headed the tiny *Russkaya gazeta* ['Russian Gazette'], turning it into a fighting organ for the masses. Within a few days the circulation rose from thirty thousand to one hundred thousand. A month later it had reached half a million. But our technical resources could not keep up with the growth of the newspaper. We were finally delivered from this contradiction only by a government raid. On 13 November, in a block with the Mensheviks, we established a big political organ, *Nachalo* ['The Beginning']. The paper's circulation grew not day by day but hour by hour. The Bolshevik *Novaya zhizn* ['New Life'] without Lenin was rather drab. *Nachalo*, on the contrary, achieved gigantic success.[23]

It was Trotsky who wrote the editorial for the first issue of *Nachalo*;[24] and even if he may well have exaggerated the print run of *Russian Gazette* he was certainly justified in claiming that his ideas were reaching a widening circle of readers in the capital.

The Bolshevik and Menshevik factions were internally divided. Some Mensheviks were attracted to the strategic ideas of Parvus and Trotsky.[25] This horrified Martov, who insisted that some kind of co-operation with the Constitutional-Democrats and other liberals was the best way forward. The Bolsheviks too were in disarray. Most of them wanted nothing to do with the existing labour movement; they even spurned the Petersburg Soviet. They saw themselves as true Leninists and gave primacy to the party rather than to any organizations formed by the workers to represent their interests. Lenin himself was of a different opinion. He wanted the Bolsheviks to exploit all the available opportunities. To him it was self-evident that this meant getting involved in the soviets and trade unions – and it took some weeks for him to persuade his comrades to change their stance.[26] Even Lenin, though, did little but devise strategy and write articles. He did not impress himself on the Petersburg Soviet's activity. He attended a session or two, observed and then left. This left the ground clear for Trotsky. He was the only leader of the Russian Social-Democratic Workers' Party who helped to form the Soviet's core.

The revolutionary situation relieved him of any lingering strains of the polemics about the 'organizational question'. Active politics in Russia were calling out for him and his comrades to participate. He responded more swiftly than any of them. Suddenly he could put theory into practice and it was a liberating experience. Events were bringing workers and intellectuals in their tens of thousands into soviets and other political associations. This was a truly mass phenomenon. Unlike the rest of the leadership of the Russian Social-Democratic Workers' Party, he was under no obligation to refer his actions to a larger group. He was neither a Menshevik nor a Bolshevik. A free agent, he could do and say what he wanted.

He had no ideological inhibitions about plunging into work in the soviets. The Bolsheviks were impeded by their axiom that the workers, if left to themselves, would develop only 'trade union consciousness'. They stood back from involvement with their local soviet unless and until its militants formally accepted the programme of Bolshevism. The Mensheviks were more adaptive; but although they took part in soviet activity, they fretted that the working class might be exposing itself to undesirable danger. Menshevik policy was to let the bourgeoisie act as the vanguard against the Imperial monarchy. Trotsky was delighted that members of the two factions would co-operate with him in the Petersburg Soviet. Distrust between Bolsheviks and Mensheviks persisted and they regularly held separate enclaves. Having the most expansive strategy among the Marxists, Trotsky was pleased that the 'proletariat' of St Petersburg refused to be fobbed off by promises of constitutional reform. Workers did not require to be indoctrinated before coming out on to the streets against Nicholas II. This confounded the Bolshevik analysis. At the same time they paid no heed to the cries for caution, and Menshevik warnings about isolating the working class appeared to be a delusion. Trotsky believed that 'permanent revolution' was in the air.

He underestimated the coercive resources still available to the government. The settling of accounts could not long be delayed. It came in the last month of the turbulent year, as Trotsky was to recount:

> On the evening of 3 December the St Petersburg Soviet was surrounded by troops. The exits and entrances were barred. From the balcony where the Executive Committee was in session, I shouted down to where hundreds of delegates were crowding the hall: 'Offer no resistance, surrender no arms to the enemy.' The arms were only hand-held ones: revolvers. And so in the meeting-hall, which was surrounded on all sides by guards detachments of infantry, cavalry and artillery, the workers began to put their arms beyond use. With skilful hands they struck Mauser on Browning and Browning on Mauser.[27]

The Soviet leadership was arrested. For Trotsky, the revolution was over – if only temporarily.

# 10. TRIAL AND PUNISHMENT

The revolutionary challenge faded in the capital with the arrest of Trotsky and his comrades. Alexander Parvus initially escaped imprisonment and purportedly led the Petersburg Soviet before being taken into custody in December 1905;[1] but really the body had ceased to exist and the authorities were turning their attention elsewhere. The Moscow Soviet organized an uprising at the end of the year but was quickly crushed. Armed forces were deployed against peasant disturbances. The campaign of pacification continued into the following year. This was a lengthy process. Mutinies broke out in the armed forces returning along the Trans-Siberian railway from the disastrous war against Japan. Peasants united against their land-lords and there was violence in the rural areas. When the State Duma met in St Petersburg in April 1906 its biggest group – the Trudoviki – demanded land reform. The Kadets decamped to Finland, calling on people to resist conscription and deny taxes to the government. Emperor Nicholas II called their bluff. The war with Japan had ended with the treaty of Portsmouth in September 1905. Financial loans from France bailed out the economy. The old order was steadily reimposed.

The Petersburg Soviet leaders and militants were held in the Kresty Prison before being transferred to the Peter-Paul Fortress. This was the place where Peter the Great had confined and tortured his son Alexei – and some of the empire's best-known political prisoners were held there in ensuing years. Finally Trotsky and his group were delivered to the House of Preliminary Detention where he was consigned to cell no. 462.[2] Altogether he spent fifteen months in gaol. The detainees were handed prison clothing and told they were to be put on open trial.[3] No one strip-searched them: this never happened to Trotsky until he was taken into custody in Canada in March 1917.[4] They had daily exercise in the yard where they could also confer with each other. They were allowed a stream of visitors. They could read more or less what they wanted, and they found ways to smuggle what they wrote to clandestine revolutionary newspapers: the briefcases of Trotsky's lawyers were handy for this purpose.[5]

In prison he visited the library and borrowed the plays of Shakespeare. For revolutionary pamphlets he had to look elsewhere. But this was no problem as he sent out a request to S. N. Saltykov asking him to get hold of *The Civil War in France* and other works by Marx on the Paris Commune of 1871. He also requested material on the 'agrarian question' in Russia and the rest of Europe. These included controversial books by Karl Kautsky, Pëtr Maslov and Vladimir Lenin.[6] Russian Marxists saw a need to adjust the doctrines of Marx and Engels to the specific conditions in Russia – and Trotsky was later than other leading thinkers in turning to this task. It was not his usual intellectual zone and he never finished his investigation of land rent;[7] his drafts disappeared some time after the October Revolution and he failed to recover them. He was anyway determined to use his time in confinement productively, and he swotted up on what he could to elaborate his revolutionary programme for the party. The result was one of his most influential booklets: *Results and Prospects*. He regarded it as his most complete statement of the theory of permanent revolution until he came back to the subject after 1917.

Trotsky remained an active journalist and was proud of his piece on 'Pëtr Struve in Politics' in which he fulminated against the willingness of prominent liberals to compromise with the government.[8] He was still a figure of public importance and several of his articles reached the metropolitan press. This was not the only way in which he was prolific. Natalya visited him regularly and the two of them were allowed conjugal privacy despite the fact that they were not man and wife under the law. The result was that she became pregnant. It would be her first child; Trotsky was starting a second family.

The Russian Social-Democratic Workers' Party had spent months deciding how to handle the trial of the Petersburg Soviet. Influenced by Martov, the Central Committee told the defendants to state that the Soviet had been formed with the sole purpose of achieving the goals subsequently promulgated in the October Manifesto. If the state punished them, it would be acting merely in a spirit of vengeance. Martov thought the Soviet leaders had suffered enough and ought to try for as light a sentence as they could get. The reality was that a serious challenge to the Imperial order had been made in 1905. The judicial punishment could be very severe. Martov wished to preserve the lives and health of the defendants so as to ensure that they could re-emerge from confinement as useful militants. He wanted no histrionics to get in the way of this goal. Trotsky, however, had his own ideas about how to behave. Having discovered his powers as an orator, he refused to be shackled by the instructions of the

Party Central Committee. He aimed to follow in the tradition of Russian revolutionaries who treated open trials as opportunities for propaganda. Neither Martov nor the Central Committee was going to deflect him. He would speak out against monarchy, government and the entire Imperial order and damn the consequences.

He repeated his concerns about Menshevism to Martov. The Mensheviks were saying nothing about the police and had no plan for 'the organization of revolutionary self-administrations'. Menshevism was relapsing into the strategy and tactics of the Kadets, and Martov's own publications were characterized by 'mannered chatter'. As for Plekhanov, why did he think it was enough to continue writing critical articles about ineffectual German Marxist writers like Eduard Bernstein? While disliking the crudity of Bolshevik polemical tactics, Trotsky felt that Lenin was correct in upholding the requirement for revolutionary optimism. He admitted to Martov that 'as a social-democratic politician I feel myself closer to the [Bolsheviks].' He implored the Menshevik leader not to get angry with him but to respect his sincerity.[9] Trotsky's words, fumblingly expressed, indicated a determination to go on choosing his personal way to advance the revolutionary cause – and there was nothing Martov could do to stop him.

Trotsky's preparations in the House of Detention suffered an unexpected disturbance from another quarter. The publicity about the forthcoming trial induced his parents, whom he had not seen since their visits in the Nikolaev prison, to travel from Kherson province to attend the proceedings. They were understandably worried about the possible outcome, and Trotsky warned them that the judge might sentence him to hard labour. His mother coped by persuading herself that the court might be benign and perhaps even issue a public commendation for his Soviet activities.[10] His father was more realistic and stoical; but at the same he was oddly happy for his son. All this unsettled Trotsky. He was also disconcerted by Alexander Parvus, who often partnered him in the daily exercise period. Parvus aimed to escape from prison before the start of the trial. Trotsky refused to join the conspiracy: he was sticking to his objective of gaining positive attention for the Russian Social-Democratic Workers' Party – and for himself – by speaking out in court. Parvus's plot was discovered when guards uncovered some tools in the prison library. The affair blew over quietly because the governor wrongly suspected that the Okhrana had planted the evidence in order to secure a harshening of the confinement regime.[11]

Police were mobilized throughout the capital for the opening day of the trial on 19 September 1906. The fifty-four defendants carried themselves with dignity. Trotsky's lawyers were A. S. Zarudny and P. N. Malyantovich. Though not his personal choice, they were able professionals who shared a hostility to the Romanov monarchy. They were destined to join the Provisional Government in 1917.[12]

By prior agreement Trotsky and the others made no formal plea. He spoke less stridently than he had threatened to do. He also had one of his fainting fits.[13] Showing a mastery of forensic rhetoric, he declared that it was the Bloody Sunday massacre that had thrust the workers into action: 'We are setting out to demonstrate that the attacking was done by the government, that we were defending ourselves.' The emperor and his ministers had hoped that the trial would split the workers from the revolutionaries 'as Peter denied Christ'.[14] They had not succeeded. The truth was no longer a secret. Only a socialist revolution could protect the interests of working people:

> On one side there is struggle, courage, truth, freedom . . .
> On the other – deviousness, baseness, slander, slavery . . .
> Citizens, make your choice.[15]

This went down well in revolutionary circles. Trotsky had learned that people like to believe that they are not the aggressors in any conflict. They warm to moral denunciations of the enemy; and Trotsky, the reader of Schopenhauer's *Art of Controversy*, refined his expertise in the rhetorical devices of evasion. In any case, he did not want to provoke the judge into silencing him or meting out the heaviest of sentences – at least to this extent he went along with Martov. Outspokenness was not to become suicidal.

The court allowed Trotsky to lay his counter-charges against the Imperial authorities. He declared that the government had colluded in recent pogroms against Jewish communities in the Pale of Settlement. He even admitted that the Soviet had armed itself against such a 'form of government'. When he cross-examined the prosecution witnesses he let loose his armoury of sarcasm, especially against the general of the gendarmes.[16] The press reported his tirades and Trotsky had his days in the political limelight again.

On 2 November the verdict was announced. In the light of all the evidence the defendants were found not guilty of insurrection. But their guilt was affirmed on lesser counts of subversion and they were sentenced to exile for life and to loss of all civil rights. To their obvious relief, they were not going to be consigned to hard labour. Taken from the courtroom, they were deposited in a single large hall in the Moscow Transit Prison to await a decision about their permanent destination. Trotsky was not pleased. The constant noise made by his comrades made writing impossible, and he could not easily live through a day without such activity.[17] He yearned for a quieter routine. He failed to be distracted by another big change in his life in these weeks. Natalya's pregnancy came to its term on 24 November 1906 when she gave birth to a son. They named the boy Lev; inside the family he soon acquired the diminutive of Lëva on the model of his father.[18] Trotsky, though, maintained his concentration on literary work. Even in his memoirs he did not treat the arrival of the child, his first by Natalya, as meriting more than a few words.

*The History of the Soviet of Workers' Deputies* quickly appeared, written mainly by its members as they awaited sentencing. Like the other contributors, he was cautious about what he wrote for fear of helping the case for the prosecution. He repudiated the charge of having tried to organize an insurrection. No evidence had been adduced that the Soviet leadership had delivered weapons to the workers of the capital. He dismissed the trial as a judicial travesty.[19] This was sophistry. Everyone in the courtroom had known that Trotsky had spent the year 1905 urging his comrades to prepare an uprising against the government.

He rejected suggestions that the Petersburg Soviet had failed as a result of restricting its appeal to the workers. The Soviet's very strength, in his opinion, lay in this strategic orientation. 'Bourgeois liberals' would never be any help in overthrowing the monarchy. The Soviet's failure consisted in its not convoking an All-Russia Workers' Congress before the government carried out its mass arrest. Such a Congress would have established an All-Russia Workers' Soviet: 'Needless to say, the essence of the matter does not lie in names or in the details of organizational relations; the task consists in the democratically centralized leadership of the struggle of the proletariat for the transition of power into the hands of the people.'[20] This was not Trotsky at his most elegant. It was as if he became distracted by excitement about the concept. According to him, revolutionaries had to get ready for yet another clash with the Imperial administration. Trotsky had clear objectives. The old army would be dissolved. The 'police–bureaucratic apparatus' would be annihilated. An eight-hour working day would be promulgated. Soviets would be turned into 'organs of revolutionary urban self-administration'. The model would be spread to the countryside where soviets of peasants' deputies would be formed.[21]

In a few paragraphs he sketched out the strategy which he would pursue in 1917. He admitted that his proposals were schematic:

Such a plan is easier to devise than to carry out. But if victory is the destiny of the revolution, the proletariat cannot avoid taking the path of this programme. It will open up revolutionary work such as the world has never yet seen. The history of the [Soviet's] fifty days will appear a pallid page in the great book of the struggle and victory of the proletariat.[22]

It was axiomatic for him that the workers would lead the campaign. Soldiers, peasants and the urban lower classes would be pulled into the struggle: there could be no success without them. If ever Trotsky was prophetic, it was in the brief introduction he composed for the collectively written history of the Petersburg Soviet.

At the turn of the year, the order was made for the onward dispatch of the convicts. Still they did not know where they were being sent; even the officer in command of the convoy claimed that he had not been told.[23] Fourteen exiles including Trotsky were moved out of the House of Detention on 5 January 1907 and deposited in a third-class railway carriage. Each prisoner had his own bunk and could see out of the barred windows.[24] En route they stayed twenty-four hours in Tyumen prison where they ordered goods from the local shops before being moved onwards to Tobolsk by horse-drawn sleighs. There were fifty-two soldiers guarding them. Progress was slow at ten miles a day since it was, after all, the middle of a Siberian winter.[25] Just before reaching Tobolsk they were told which villages they had been allocated to serve out their sentences. Trotsky's group were informed that they would be sent to Obdorsk district, which straddled the Arctic Circle.[26] They received this announcement with anxiety, especially after it was specified that residence would be provided not in the town of Obdorsk, which was the district centre, but three hundred miles further north at Khe. They would have only 'native' fur-trappers as fellow inhabitants. The entire settlement had a mere half-dozen yurts (local tents). It was going to be a gruelling experience: no huts; little regular communication; extreme temperatures in winter and summer.

The only consolation was that their treatment by the military escort softened as the convoy moved northward.[27] Even so, it was heavy going, and they travelled seven hundred miles after Tobolsk before reaching Berëzov in the evening of 11 February, thirty-three days after leaving St Petersburg. They had covered more than fifty miles a day down the rivers Irtysh and Ob since Tobolsk and the authorities granted a period of respite before the final stage of the journey further along the Ob towards Obdorsk.[28] They recuperated in Berëzov prison, which had been cleaned up especially for their arrival. The authorities had laid out a tablecloth for their meals and supplied candles and candlesticks. Trotsky found all this 'almost touching'.[29]

He decided that this was his last chance to make an escape. He had no intention of going on to Obdorsk if he could possibly help it, and deliberately delayed his departure by feigning illness. On advice from a sympathetic doctor he pretended to have sciatica. The medical profession was full of practitioners who hated the government and were willing to aid its enemies. Trotsky, always an effective actor, put on a good enough performance for the police to agree that he was in no condition to make a run for it. After undergoing a medical examination, he was transferred to the hospital and the doctor prescribed regular walks for his patient. Trotsky took his chance to plot with Dmitri Sverchkov, his friend and admirer in the Petersburg Soviet, how he might flee captivity.[30] The easiest route was southward to Tobolsk. But this was equally obvious to the authorities and Trotsky chose instead to head directly west. This covered much more difficult terrain through woods and snow. He was calculating that the forces of law and order would hardly suspect that anyone would be reckless enough to make such an attempt.[31]

Clothes, provisions, false passport and a trustworthy guide were essential, and Sverchkov turned for help to Faddei Roshkovski. Roshkovski was a veteran army officer who had lived in exile in Berëzov for several years and liked to assist the revolutionary cause. Roshkovski found an informant known as Goat's Foot who led him to a willing guide of Zyryan ethnicity. As a precaution, the guide was not told that Trotsky was a political prisoner. Sverchkov's wife made up a sizeable package of food for the trip. A fur coat, fur gloves and fur leggings were obtained for physical survival and disguise. The trip would be by reindeer sleigh. Trotsky agreed with the Zyryan to hand over the fur coat and the deer at the end of their long journey.[32]

They agreed a plan to start their bid for freedom in the middle of an amateur-dramatics production in the garrison hall on 20 February 1907.[33] Trotsky attended the proceedings at first. Seeing that the police chief was present, he told him he was recovered and would soon be able to make for Obdorsk. He slipped away towards midnight and shaved off his goatee at Sverchkov's lodgings before clambering into the sleigh. Trotsky had sported the beard in 1905 and the police knew him by this feature. The physical change and the practical plan worked almost to perfection. The slight snag was that the Zyryan had been drinking heavily and was barely capable of leading the way. Trotsky did not allow this to hold things up:

drunk or sober, the Zyryan had to discharge the assignment. Luck was on their side; nobody noticed Trotsky's disappearance for a whole two days. The police assumed that he was resting at Sverchkov's and the old woman who cooked for them helpfully swore that he was eating everything she put in front of him.[34] The result was disastrous for those he left behind. Sverchkov and friends were arrested and dispatched immediately to the grimness of Obdorsk; the police chief too was apprehended and charged with complicity.[35] Trotsky's comrades had selflessly recognized him as one of the party's prime assets who had to be assisted in rejoining the leadership in freedom abroad. The cause meant everything, even if it involved incurring an aggravated punishment.

The deer moved at a cracking pace.[36] A lot of drinking was done by Trotsky's various guides on the journey. An abstemious person himself, he was astounded that they could swallow shots of 95° proof spirits without a twinge in their facial muscles. Just occasionally they diluted their vodka with tea.[37] Yurt after yurt. Forest, forest, forest. Snow all the way. Towards the end of the journey, Trotsky began to feel guilty about lying to the Zyryan about his identity. But the pangs of conscience passed and he held his tongue.[38]

As they crossed the Urals and entered Archangel province, he sent a telegram to Natalya saying that he was on his way. She was living at that time in Terijoki, just inside the Finnish frontier and only thirty miles north of the Russian capital. He asked her to meet him at Samino on the Vyatka–Kotlas railway. This was still 700 miles to the east of St Petersburg and required her to travel to Vyatka before going on to Samino; meanwhile Trotsky would take the line down from the Kotlas direction. Hurriedly leaving Lëva with friends, she made the trip. In her excitement she became a bit confused, even forgetting the name of the station. This was Trotsky's version of the episode. Natalya recalled it differently, claiming that he had not specified where they should meet up. By chance she overheard a couple of merchants mention that the two trains always crossed each other at Samino, and she sensibly decided to alight there.[39] When Trotsky's train entered the station he looked for her on the platform but did not see her running alongside as she peered into the carriage windows. At last she spotted his baggage and they met up. They embraced and felt completely happy again and triumphant. Then they travelled down the line to Vyatka and on to St Petersburg, staying overnight with friends before Natalya took Trotsky to her rooms in Terijoki and he became properly acquainted with their little son.

Terijoki had been a favourite spot in which revolutionaries could hide and recuperate in 1906, but it was perilous for a well-known absconder to stay there as the government strengthened its campaign of repression. The Trotskys after a few days moved on to Ogilbyu, a Finnish village near Helsinki. As a form of relaxation he wrote up an account of his recent adventures, *There and Back*. Trotsky's booklet contained some of his most glorious depictions of nature – only *My Life* rivals it in this respect. He enjoyed exposing how easy it had been to fool the authorities. There was also a practical purpose. The advance royalties for this piece of writing would pay for their intended flight abroad.[40] Together again, Lev and Natalya went walking in woods of poplar and fir. They threw snowballs. They breathed in the pure air with its tangy aroma from the trees. They had never had a proper 'Russian' vacation together and their Finnish sojourn was the closest they got to this until after the Civil War. Natalya went to Helsinki on household errands and to fetch newspapers and books. Trotsky at the time was fascinated by the German satirical magazine *Simplicissimus* and she brought back copies for him.[41]

Thus they passed their weeks before taking off again into emigration. Trotsky went first, followed by Natalya some weeks later: they travelled independently to avoid trouble from the police, leaving their son Lëva in the safekeeping of their friend Dr Litkens in Finland.[42]

# 11. AGAIN THE EMIGRANT

Trotsky decided to settle in Vienna. His choice of the Austrian capital was a signal that he was eager to stay where his party's émigré factions had their bases. He was going to be his own man. He could get on with his political activity better if he concentrated on what he was good at. He would write and publish intensively. Distant from the party's bickerings in Switzerland, he could do things his own way. This was a time of bitter organizational conflict. Bolsheviks and Mensheviks strove against each other as if their steps towards reunification in 1906–7 in Stockholm and London had never been taken. Both factions were internally divided. Trotsky was appalled, disgusted and alienated. Pleas were made to him to co-operate with one factional group or another. Trotsky turned them down.

Russian political emigrants from the Russian Empire could live unmolested in the Habsburg domains. Imperial rivalry between St Petersburg and Vienna induced the government to treat any enemy of the Romanovs as its friend. Vienna was a centre of European magnificence even though Austria-Hungary was a long way from achieving economic modernization. Germany and Russia exceeded the empire in military might. The Austrian administration, vividly depicted in the novels of Franz Kafka and the essays of Karl Kraus, was notoriously arbitrary and venal. Emperor Franz Joseph I ignored intimations of weakness. Enthroned in 1848, the aged monarch assumed that any current difficulty was of a passing nature. He and his ministers were eager to annex parts of the Ottoman Empire in Europe and to resist any Russian attempt to expand from the east. Franz Joseph had not mounted the throne of his ancestors to oversee its destruction. To Europe's Marxists, though, Vienna was a bastion of the labour movement. The city's suburbs teemed with factories pumping out smoke and producing industrial products. Seven railway stations linked it to the cities of the empire and beyond. Trotsky felt he was moving to one of the great centres of revolutionary struggle. If severe political conflict enveloped Austria, he would be there.

While Trotsky waited for Natalya he looked for lodgings and spent time finishing the account of his escape.[1] This was compulsive activity for him: he was to do the same a decade later when he chronicled his deportation from France and Spain in 1916.[2] He needed the money but he had ulterior motives as well. The drama of his flight from Siberia gilded his status in the party leadership; it also enabled him to win support for the cause by tucking political messages into his prose.

Natalya's route from Finland took her to Berlin, where Trotsky travelled to meet her off the train. Together they sped off to Dresden, where they stayed with Parvus and his wife. Despite his physical bulk, Parvus was an enthusiastic walker and the Trotskys accepted his suggestion of a trip to the mountains of Bohemia above Hirschberg near the border with the Austro-Hungarian monarchy. Every day they talked at length about politics. Parvus liked to hold forth. Belonging to the German Social-Democratic Party, he discoursed on his impressions of its leaders and criticized them roundly for having lost their revolutionary impetus.[3] Trotsky and Natalya knew them too but did not yet have their companion's low opinion of them. They listened respectfully without assimilating Parvus's scepticism. The clean air and the bracing views anyway did all three of them a lot of good – and Trotsky, getting close to his mentor again, was strengthened in his conviction that a 'workers' government' was still the best choice for Russia. Refreshed by the holiday, Trotsky went on a tour of Russian Marxist groups in southern Germany. On his return, Natalya travelled back to St Petersburg to retrieve Lëva and bring him to Austria.[4]

The move to Vienna put them back in touch with old friends. Among them was Semën Klyachko, a Jew from Vilnius who became a respected member of the Social-Democratic Party of Austria.[5] Another resident was Adolf Ioffe, who arrived in 1908 and studied for a medical degree specializing in psychiatry under the direction of the world-renowned Alfred Adler.[6] Ioffe was a prominent militant of the Russian Social-Democratic Workers' Party – and Alfred Adler and his wife were friends of the Trotsky family. Trotsky also renewed his acquaintance with Austrian Marxist leaders such as Victor Adler and his son Friedrich Adler. He became something of a man about town, regularly taking coffee at the Café Central. Whether he ate its famous chocolate cakes is not recorded. While drinking coffee and reading the morning newspaper, though, he could meet up with all the Viennese luminaries of the day including the writers Peter Altenberg, Hugo von Hoffmannsthal and Leo Perutz. Karl Kraus, the prominent satirist and literary theorist, is said to have edited his journal *Die Fackel* on the premises. Trotsky preferred central Europe to the rest of the continent. Berlin in his eyes was infinitely preferable to

London,[7] and he did not have much time for Paris; but it was Vienna that he truly loved. Only Odessa exercised a similar enchantment upon him.

Trotsky travelled to London for the Fifth Party Congress in late April 1907 and gave speeches in Geneva and Paris. He had a lot to say and write. Having started as an opponent of the party's participation in the elections to the first State Duma, he had reconsidered his position and argued for full participation in the subsequent elections. He did not expect much good to come out of the Dumas but saw no sense in boycotting them.[8] *In Defence of the Party*, which he had finished at the start of the year and brought out with more than one publisher in St Petersburg, spelled out his practical recommendations. Marxists, he maintained, had to take whatever opportunities were on offer in circumstances of political retreat. He also more and more emphasized the peasantry's importance to the future success of revolution in Russia. Peasants had to be contacted by the party and persuaded to see their salvation in an alliance with the working class.[9] As before, he rebuked Bolsheviks for their schematic, intolerant manoeuvres and the Mensheviks for their softness towards the liberals.[10] He denied that the Russian Social-Democratic Workers' Party was filled entirely with intellectuals but stressed that more needed to be done to retrieve its old dynamism.[11]

In London he was allowed only a consultative status. This was because he declared himself as belonging to no faction and consequently could not represent any recognized party organization. He can anyway have made few friends by publishing *In Defence of the Party*. He revelled in his solitary status. From the start of the Congress's proceedings he struggled against attempts by the Mensheviks and Bolsheviks to secure dominance over each other.[12] It was annoying for him that a Menshevik referred to him as having been 'leader of the Menshevik faction' in St Petersburg in the last months of 1905.[13] When given the floor he castigated the strategies of both Menshevism and Bolshevism and ended with a summons to full-hearted party unity.[14] He found himself attacked on both sides. He decided it was fruitless to put forward a compromise resolution on party activity in Russia. For this he was attacked yet again.[15] Unbowed, he stepped forward to announce his agreement with Rosa Luxemburg – a Jew from Poland who held simultaneous membership of the German Social-Democratic Party – that the party should show no indulgence to liberals and other 'bourgeois parties'.[16] This served only to induce the Mensheviks and Bundists to gang up on him. Lenin for a few moments warmed to him, announcing a willingness to overlook Trotsky's heresy about 'permanent revolution'.[17]

Trotsky refused the proffered hand from the Bolshevik leadership. Noting that there were disputes among Bolsheviks on both the Duma and the agrarian question, he teased Lenin for voting against his own faction and then accused him of 'hypocrisy'. Trotsky was called to order for this outburst.[18] Even in the debate about the Petersburg Soviet he failed to attract admiration for his prowess in 1905.[19] He made an impact at the Congress without winning friends. His eloquence was recognized but the feeling was strong that the advocate of organizational unification was happiest when causing disruption and controversy.

It was hardly a surprise when Trotsky failed to be elected to the Central Committee at the Congress. Returning to Vienna, he drew the conclusion that he should set himself up as an independent force in the Russian Social-Democratic Workers' Party. The Trotskys hopped from apartment to apartment for a while. At first they lived in the Hütteldorf district. When the rent was raised they moved to Severing and eventually to 25 Rodlergasse, apartment No. 2 in a working-class quarter near the Döbling district. This last abode was a two-roomed place with kitchen and bathroom.[20] Natalya became pregnant in late June 1907 and was delivered of a second son on 20 March 1908. They named him Sergei. The baby did not quickly enjoy the favour of his elder brother Lëva, who complained at being woken at night by the crying. Trotsky too was somewhat disconcerted. Having hoped to retain Natalya as a political partner, he found that she was devoting the hours of daylight to the boys. But she was very determined and set about serious reading when they had been put to bed. The youngsters grew up believing that their mother never slept. Money was not exactly scarce but Trotsky and Natalya had to be careful with it – or at least more careful than had been their custom.[21]

Trotsky's mother and father were among their first visitors from abroad. In 1907 they brought five-year-old Zina Bronstein, Trotsky's daughter by Alexandra, with them to see her father. His family lived a complicated existence. Zina at that time lived with his sister Elizaveta and her husband in their family home on Gryaznaya Street in Kherson. Alexandra wrote regularly to them.[22] Trotsky had not seen Zina since leaving her as a baby in Siberia. She had inherited his colour of eyes and hair and the structure of his face. He immediately attracted her 'burning devotion'.[23]

Trotsky published a collection of his articles from 1905–6, including *Results and Prospects*.[24] For German readers he wrote an expanded version entitled *Russia in Revolution*, which would appear in Russian only in 1922 and is known in English as *1905*.[25] He drew constant encouragement from the French Revolution; and while not wishing to ape the Jacobins and their 'utopianism', he admired their zeal.[26] But what exactly did he mean by this? What was required was a dictatorship of the proletariat led by the Russian Social-Democratic Workers' Party. There should be a 'workers' government'. This would necessitate a strategy of 'uninterrupted revolution' (or 'permanent revolution' as he later called it).[27] He wrote with a broad literary sweep: this was his forte. He refused to bother himself with research on most questions currently bothering the party's intellectual elite. Controversies were raging about epistemology, about the shifting course of Russian agrarian development and about desirable ways of using the State Duma; these became more intense as the participants increasingly recognized that Russia would not soon revert to revolutionary turbulence since the Imperial authorities had recovered their nerve and had succeeded in stabilizing their rule. Trotsky was impervious to fashion. His interest lay mainly in restating and supplementing the strategic case he had sketched while operating in the Russian Empire in 1905.

He emphasized the negative features of Russian historical development. In contrast with western Europe, 'the Russian people had received no cultural legacy' from the Roman Empire. Nor had it experienced the Renaissance. The Mongol invasion in the thirteenth century had had the effect of inducing a hypertrophic growth in state power, a growth that persisted long after Russia regained its sovereignty. Peter the Great's campaign for industrialization required a frenetic increase in the fiscal load and restricted the rise of a Russian middle class. The independent social behaviour which had been crucial to capitalist development and civic resilience in the West had been prevented from taking root in Russia.[28]

Hailed by his readers in later generations as an original analyst of the Russian past, Trotsky in reality was miming ideas formulated by Russia's liberal historians of the Westernizing tendency since the mid-nineteenth century. He himself made no claim to intellectual originality: he would have been ridiculed if he had tried. What he did display was consistency, clarity and verve. The ruling classes were backward in Russia. The peasantry had been stultified. The non-Russians were held in demeaning ignorance. If there was any hope at all, it lay with the working class which was foreordained to take up the struggle.[29] Trotsky insisted that optimism was justified. He argued that Russian 'backwardness' itself could be turned to advantage. He reminded readers that the Paris Commune easily took power in the 'petit-bourgeois' French capital and initiated reforms of a socialist nature. The Commune was crushed after a few weeks of existence. Marxists in Russia would be able to go further and build an entire socialist society – and the fact that the bourgeoisie had not yet properly consolidated itself in power would make this easier to achieve than it was going to be in Britain or the United States. Trotsky adduced Kautsky in support of his confidence.[30]

He did not follow Lenin, Bogdanov and Plekhanov by claiming that his Marxism coherently co-ordinated politics, economics, sociology, culture and philosophy. Intellectually he flitted from topic to topic and felt no stimulus to systematize his thinking. Trotsky came to be revered by Trotskyists as having been on a level with Lenin as a Marxist theoretician before the Great War. Nobody felt this way about him before 1914. Trotsky was respected as an outstanding publicist. He was unrivalled in the party for his cultural range of reference and his elegant, sardonic prose style. No one, furthermore, tried harder to bind the party back together in the early years of the second decade of the twentieth century. The strategic recommendations of Parvus and Trotsky were certainly unique – and Trotsky was alone in proffering them to fellow Russian Marxists after Parvus fled Siberian exile and attended to his business interests in Istanbul and elsewhere. Nobody knew quite what to make of him. Trotsky as a party leader had been an indefatigable unifier and only in the last years before the Great War started to be choosy about who could belong to the Russian Social-Democratic Workers' Party.

He refused to feel downcast by the frostiness of the rest of the leadership towards him. He also admitted that the tone of his criticisms of comrades had caused offence.[31] But he insisted that he acted in the party's best interests: 'Mensheviks? Bolsheviks? I personally am equally close to both of them, I work closely with each of them and am equally proud of every revolutionary achievement of the party regardless of which faction played the leading role.'[32] Party unity remained his preoccupation and his mood was buoyant and optimistic.

His chosen instrument for bringing the party back together was his newspaper *Pravda* ('Truth'). The original idea for this initiative was not his own. Marian Melenevsky, a leading Ukrainian social-democrat belonging to Spilka ('Union'), had gone round cities in Ukraine collecting finance for a publication. Spilka was a Ukrainian Marxist organization and Melenevsky was a successful raiser of funds. Once he had the money, though, he needed a talented editor. Trotsky was an obvious choice, and Melenevsky met up with him in Vienna. Melenevsky strove after greater rights for Ukrainians and gave signs of being a nationalist rather than a Marxist; he saw Trotsky as someone who would undermine the Russian Empire, and Trotsky did not mind who gave him money so long as he kept his political independence. Trotsky and Melenevsky came to an agreement. Melenevsky's comrades in Geneva disliked what had happened and he had to override their objections.[33] Trotsky was delighted. Without having to exert himself in pleading for finance or in uprooting Natalya and the family, he had been given the decisive voice in a new party publication – and he was unconstrained by any need to compromise with the demands of the party's influential factions.

Trotsky had three main collaborators: Adolf Ioffe, Semën Semkovski and Matvei Skobelev. Melenevsky himself played an active role for a while, and Parvus too helped with the commercial side of things.[34] The highly strung Ioffe, a physician and a native of Simferopol near Odessa, was going to Alfred Adler for psychoanalysis while studying psychiatry under him.[35] Ioffe was selfless and well organized, erring always on the pedantic side.[36] His wife helped with the paper's account books.[37] The work was intensive as they had to supply enough copy for bi-monthly publication. Issues were smuggled across the frontier into the Russian Empire through Galicia in the Ukraine and across the Black Sea. Transport of material and people was Melenevsky's speciality.[38] Trotsky concentrated on writing and editing, and he coped easily with the pressure. He was enjoying himself, even squeezing out time to help a clandestine union of Black Sea seamen to publish their news sheet.[39]

He took risks in his correspondence. The Okhrana kept its eye on him even though its agents often misspelled his name as Troitsky. But Trotsky and his associates were not alone in failing to take several elementary precautions. Natalya Sedova, on a later trip to St Petersburg, sent a letter to her husband directly to their family home in Vienna; her only subterfuge was to address the envelope to 'Simon Bronstein', and it did not take a policeman of genius to guess that this might be the revolutionary leader Bronstein-Trotsky.[40] The situation was less dangerous for Trotsky, perhaps, than for other prominent Marxists. In contrast with Lenin and Martov, he was not supervising a network of clandestine organizations in the Russian Empire. Trotsky did not belong to the Central Committee. His main responsibility was to think, write and submit copy on time. He was aware that the Okhrana knew where he lived; he operated on the premise that he and his family should get on with their lives and affairs without excessive concern about the Imperial authorities. He never quite shook off this attitude later in his career when his enemy was not the Okhrana but the murderous NKVD.

*Pravda's* initial finances were not enough to sustain its permanent existence and Trotsky wrote to Maxim Gorki for a subsidy. Gorki was one of the most famous contemporary Russian writers and was willing to subsidize Marxist publications with his huge royalties. Trotsky expressed pride in his newspaper. He claimed that the party leadership pretended to approve of it while obstructing its work. He told Gorki that readers in the Russian Empire responded 'magnificently' to each issue.[41] He sought out every possible source of money, writing to the New York group of the party and explaining that *Pravda*'s debts made it difficult to put out a print run of 8,000 copies.[42] His editorials appealed repeatedly for financial support.[43] He personally sent out reminders to debtors and borrowed 300 crowns from the Austrian social-democrats.[44]

The *Pravda* connection was not the only one that Trotsky resumed with Ukraine. Starting in 1908, he wrote lengthy pieces for *Odesskie novosti* ('Odessa News').[45] He did the same for *Kievskaya mysl* ('Kiev Thought').[46] His recourse to Ukrainian newspapers was purely practical and not a sign of nostalgia. Trotsky was no sentimentalist even though he always loved Odessa. But he had left southern Ukraine for prison and exile early in his life, and he never expressed the desire to return. He had abandoned family and material comfort without regret; he had also ditched his first wife with whom he had fallen in love in Nikolaev. But the reason he wrote for leading newspapers in Ukraine rather than Russia was the practical one that they had asked him to be a contributor. Furthermore, they were based in two of the biggest and most influential urban centres in the Russian Empire and the readership of their journalism was of growing importance. Odessa and Kiev were linked to Vienna by efficient communications. He could rapidly get copy to the newspapers. He could also receive payment with speed, which was crucial for his finances. Although he had to exercise restraint in his articles, his readers understood the hints he dropped. Writing for *Odesskie novosti*, he declaimed: 'I love my country in time – this is the twentieth century which was born in storms and tempests. It hides limitless possibilities within itself. Its territory is the entire world.'[47] This was a discreet way of signalling that he was a socialist and an internationalist.

*Pravda* as an illegal organ attracted plaudits from party militants in Russia, Ukraine and the émigré 'colonies' in Europe. One of them signed herself as 'your Sasha'; her familiar style makes it probable that this was none other than his first wife Alexandra Bronstein. Whoever it was, she reported that the newspaper was doing well in Odessa. Others reported a great demand in St Petersburg.[48] Trotsky succeeded in getting the copies distributed. He had plenty of volunteers to smuggle them into the Russian Empire. It was just about the perfect life for him even though the endless internal wrangles of the Russian Social-Democratic Workers' Party continued to exasperate him.

His geographical distance from the main 'colonies' of revolutionary emigrants eased the pressure to answer questions about his strategy for a 'workers' government'. Many thought that any such regime would need to use massive violence. Did Trotsky advocate terror? Trotsky declined to reply. It is true that he spoke out against 'individual terror' in 1909 when the Socialist-Revolutionaries murdered the police informer Evno Azev, who had penetrated their Central Committee. But then he changed the subject, dwelling on the success of Socialist-Revolutionaries in recruiting among workers; he called on the Russian Social-Democratic Workers' Party to win them over to its cause.[49] Repeatedly he stressed that any worthwhile revolution required sympathy and co-operation from the working class. This gave no clue about how he would go about consolidating a proletarian dictatorship. As soon as he had power in the October Revolution he would openly advocate the application of mass terror against 'enemies of the people'; but in the pre-war years he felt under no obligation to explain himself in advance. He chose not to reveal that when he brandished a word such as 'dictatorship' he meant it in its most literal and merciless sense.

By persevering with his strategic perspective, at any rate, Trotsky rendered himself irretrievably lost to the Mensheviks, and his penchant for a 'workers' government' kept him apart from the Bolsheviks. Yet he was not lost to the party as a whole. He continued to campaign for organizational unity. To many in the party, though, it appeared that Trotsky had no principles.[50] The Bolsheviks simply could not understand how he could advocate a 'workers' government' and yet fail to savage a faction that espoused alliance with the parties of the bourgeoisie. Only one answer to these questions seemed plausible to Bolsheviks: Trotsky was surely more interested in heading a reunited Russian Social-Democratic Workers' Party than in making a revolution. The Mensheviks agreed, overlooking his refusal to entangle himself in organizational intrigues. Both factions anyway disliked him for his vanity. Even his suave standards of dress were annoying. He acquired the reputation of being an adventurer without ideological commitment. In a faction-ridden Marxist movement his openness to all sides in every dispute made him many enemies. He was not to be trusted. On this, Bolsheviks and Mensheviks were at one.

# 12. UNIFIER

Trotsky's unpopularity with the Bolsheviks and Mensheviks diminished but did not extinguish his status as a leader of the Russian Social-Democratic Workers' Party. The Bolshevik Anatoli Lunacharski, organizing a party school on the island of Capri beyond the Gulf of Naples, wrote asking him to give the benefit of the doubt to the project.[1] Good lecturers were at a premium and Trotsky was among the best. He did not go to Capri because, as he told Maxim Gorki, he considered the pedagogical programme to be half baked.[2] He preferred another operation set up by a party group in Nice where he taught about conditions in Austria-Hungary.[3] Then the Bolshevik Forwardists asked him to deliver a course on German and Austrian social-democracy at the school they were founding in Bologna for young Russian recruits. He spent a month with them. Forwardists were on the extreme left of the party and denounced Lenin's encouragement to Bolsheviks to seek election to the Duma and the trade union leaderships. Trotsky sought to get under the skin of the pupils by arguing that if they wanted truly left-wing politics they should espouse his revolutionary strategy. The school organizers quickly intervened and warned the pupils against his heterodoxy. They forgave him simply because he was so good a teacher.[4]

Such was his reputation among European Marxists that he was asked to speak on the Russian question at the Jena Congress of the German Social-Democratic Party in September 1911. Karl Liebknecht was introducing a resolution denouncing Nicholas II's coercive measures in Finland. Material was collected for that purpose, and Trotsky was meant to describe the situation from the local perspective. Suddenly the news came through that Pëtr Stolypin, Nicholas II's prime minister who had presided over significant agrarian reforms, had been assassinated in Kiev. The telegram shook the party leadership's will to go ahead with a debate on Russia. A Russian revolutionary had killed Stolypin. How would it look if another revolutionary from Russia stood forth at Jena and castigated the Russian Imperial authorities? Perhaps Kaiser Wilhelm II, who had warm relations with Nicholas II, would treat any such speech as evidence that the German social-democratic leadership condoned the assassination. August Bebel and others remembered that their party had been made illegal between 1878 and 1890. They wished to give no pretext for the government to outlaw them again. Bebel approached Trotsky and asked his opinion about who might have carried out the killing. For a while there was some worry that it might have been a social-democrat. Bebel also wondered whether the police in Germany might make things difficult for Trotsky.

Trotsky forwent his place on the Congress agenda.[5] This annoyed Liebknecht, who wanted him to go ahead with a condemnation of tsarism. This was a dilemma for Trotsky. Liebknecht tirelessly helped political emigrants from the Russian Empire whenever they encountered problems in Germany. He was also on the left side of the spectrum of opinion in the German Social-Democratic Party just as Trotsky was in his own. Trotsky, though, felt he had to observe political proprieties abroad. In any case, he retained respect and affection for those German social-democratic leaders who found Liebknecht a nuisance. He corresponded with Karl Kautsky. He declined to associate himself with those who claimed that the German social-democrats had abandoned a genuine commitment to revolutionary politics. Refugees from the Russian Empire were among the fiercest critics of Kautsky. They included Rosa Luxemburg, Karl Radek and Alexander Parvus. It was their contention that the party leadership had only a formal adherence to Marxism and revolution while doing little to shatter the Imperial order. Trotsky heard what his friends were saying. Like most other leaders of the Russian Social-Democratic Workers' Party, he thought their critique exaggerated and unfair.

Luxemburg got along well with Trotsky some of the time and approved of measures to bring the Russian Social-Democratic Workers' Party together. But she thought him less than honest as a promoter of harmony. Writing to Luise Kautsky, she strove to enlighten the German Social-Democratic Party about his polemical excesses in the Russian-language party press:

> The good Trotsky is more and more exposed as a rotten fellow. Even before the Technical Committee [of the Russian Social-Democratic Workers' Party's leadership] had got financial independence from Lenin to enable it to give money to *Pravda*, Trotsky blasted away in *Pravda* against this commission and the whole Paris conference in an unheard-of manner. He directly accuses the Bolsheviks and Poles of being 'party splitters' but says not a word against Martov's

pamphlet against Lenin which excels everything else so far in baseness and is obviously aimed at splitting the party. In one word it is a beauty.[6]

Not that Trotsky entirely avoided interfering in the Social-Democratic Party of Austria. He was outraged by the leadership's decision to establish a bakery in Vienna: 'This was the crudest adventure, dangerous in principle and hopeless in practice.' Victor Adler and his associates met him with a 'condescending smile of superiority'; they rejected his argument that they were traducing 'the position of the party of the proletariat in a capitalist society'.[7] Trotsky also objected to the nationalist undertones of Austrian Marxists when they wrote about Austria's rivalry with Serbia. He heard directly from socialists in the Balkans, especially Serbian, how the conservative and liberal press in Belgrade quoted the Viennese *Arbeiter-Zeitung* as proof that the internationalism of the European labour movement was a mere fiction. This drew his ire and he dispatched a critical article about it to Kautsky for publication in *Neue Zeit* in Berlin. After some hesitation Kautsky complied, and the Austrian party leadership were outraged that their guest had been so vituperative. While admitting the factual accuracy of the article, they contended that no one took foreign-policy editorials in *Arbeiter-Zeitung* seriously. There was no meeting of minds. Trotsky pointed out that what was printed in Vienna had an impact in Belgrade; he called on the leadership to show greater intellectual rigour in matters of public debate.[8]

Generally, though, he kept away from the debates of Austrian Marxism. He held resolutely to his own intellectual concerns and ignored the way Otto Bauer, Karl Renner and Victor Adler were imaginatively exploring party doctrine and policy. Living in a vast multinational state such as Austria-Hungary, they contended that Marxists could not properly plan the socialist future unless they took the 'national question' seriously. Their conclusion was an original one. They proposed that, once the revolution happened, each nation would receive the right to elect representatives to its own assembly. The slogan was 'national-cultural autonomy'. Bauer and his fellow leaders expected the national assemblies to balance the power of a unitary elected parliament. Tensions between the two sides of the constitution were expected to be lessened by popular recognition that the socialist government sincerely aimed to treat all nations fairly and with dignity.

While continuing to enjoy meeting Vienna's political and cultural luminaries at the Café Central, he took his sons to the nearby park to play football and handball; and all the family liked to visit the Skobelevs, the Ioffes and their young children. Lëva at the age of three developed a special fondness for the Ioffes' little daughter Nadya.[9] Trotsky decorated the family fir tree at Christmas, but he and Natalya felt distaste for 'the orgy of present-giving'.[10] Atheism was a staple of conversations at home. It was only when they went to the local Christian school that the boys discovered who the Virgin Mary was.[11] Their domestic upbringing could lead to embarrassment outside the apartment. Sergei once blurted out: 'There's no God and no Santa Claus!'[12] Lëva and Sergei grew up with firm opinions, but their father and mother did not equip them with skills in avoiding giving offence. Otherwise the boys took to Vienna like ducks to water – rather too much for Trotsky's liking. He wanted them to go on speaking Russian. He also hoped to inculcate a standard German in them but, going to a local school, they naturally picked up the Viennese dialect. Trotsky took this badly but his friend Alfred Adler admired their linguistic facility, joking that Lëva and Sergei spoke 'like two old cab-drivers'.[13]

Natalya itched to rejoin Trotsky in his political activity and, once the boys were in bed, she went off with him. This worried little Sergei: 'Why are you going to the coffee house?' Natalya replied firmly: 'But look, Serëzhenka [Sergei's nickname], I've done everything necessary for you and now all you have to do is go nicely to sleep.' The retort was immediate: 'But when you're at home you think about me.' Natalya would then come clean: 'I'm going for a bit of relaxation . . . I'll chat with friends and find out what's happening in the world . . . and then tomorrow I'll tell you about it.' Lëva, the elder of the two, sympathized with his brother but already understood that his parents had duties beyond their domestic ones.[14] The boys were well behaved and friends could not remember Trotsky raising his voice to them.[15]

Trotsky continued to work for the legal press in the Russian Empire, turning as ever to journalism whenever a political dispute was getting him down. He had a sharp intuition for a good story. Having attended a lecture by Roberto Michels on the 'characterlessness' of the German bourgeoisie, he offered his own comparison of Germany and Russia. He approvingly cited Pëtr Struve for stating that the Russian bourgeoisie was 'a nonentity'. (Lenin would never have given positive publicity to anything written by Struve. Trotsky made up for his kindliness by saying in a later article: 'Struve's main talent – or, if you like, the curse of his nature – lies in his always having acted "on command".')[16] Trotsky affirmed that the bourgeoisie in Germany had provided the country with towns, with Martin Luther and Thomas Münzer, with the Reformation and with the

1848 revolution. He could see nothing comparable in centuries of Russia's history. At the time of writing the Russian urban middle class was represented, he claimed, by the Octobrist leader Alexander Guchkov. The Octobrists were a conservative party committed to making the Duma system work as well as possible; they were loyal to the monarchy. Trotsky could never resist an opportunity to attack the political and commercial elites in Russia and quipped that Guchkov's sole distinction was to have grown his 'hereditary-merchant's beard'.[17]

While playing on his favourite theme of the peculiarities of Russian historical development, he distracted himself from the urgent questions facing the party. But he had not forgotten them or ceased to care. From Vienna he badgered his correspondents in Switzerland and France about the need for full organizational reunification. As he never failed to insist, a monolithic proletariat required a single party and not an arena of raucous factions. Events began to play into his hand in 1909 when a group known as the Liquidators gained prominence in St Petersburg. Their chief argument was that the clandestine party organizations were no longer making any progress. Comrades should therefore prioritize legal political and social activity. They should stand for election to the State Duma. They should speak at open mass meetings and write for the St Petersburg press. They did not call for the permanent abandonment of the party but wanted to concentrate energies elsewhere. Inspired by Alexander Potresov, one of the founders of *Iskra*, they went on to set up a newspaper – *Luch* ('The Ray') – in St Petersburg in September 1912. This outraged party leaders who regarded the illegal party apparatus as sacrosanct. Even if Potresov and his friends were not seeking to close it down, their policy would have the same result. Every existing faction stood against the Liquidators with some degree of ferocity.

The Leninist Bolsheviks and the Martovite Mensheviks came together at the Central Committee plenum in January 1910. Trotsky simultaneously won a subsidy for his editorial and publishing activity for *Pravda*. But this came at a price. He had to accept Lev Kamenev on to the editorial board.[18] This involved a family complication. Kamenev by then was the husband of Trotsky's younger sister Olga; and when Kamenev moved to Vienna to operate as Lenin's watchdog she naturally came with him. The Bolshevik Anatoli Lunacharski, hostile to Lenin and Kamenev at that time, recalled the denouement:

But so violent a rift developed between Kamenev and Trotsky that Kamenev very soon returned to Paris. I must say here and now that

> Trotsky was extremely bad at organizing not only the party but even a small group of it. He had practically no wholehearted supporters at all; if he succeeded in imposing himself on the party it was entirely through his personality.[19]

Trotsky saw things differently. He had hated Kamenev interfering with the content of his writings – and Kamenev came to see that he was wasting his own time.[20] Yet Lunacharski's basic judgement was a fair one. Trotsky, now thirty years old, lacked the temperament to gather a large team around himself. The unifier par excellence possessed a talent for repelling would-be supporters – and he never seemed to understand that there was a problem. Lunacharski put it down to his 'colossal arrogance'.

Trotsky was equally unpopular with Mensheviks and Bolsheviks. He persisted through 1910 with his campaign for reunification, calling for a full party conference to resolve co-operative arrangements. He ran into trouble for his pains. The Central Committee, led by Mensheviks, treated his plea as a bid to outflank it. He was suspected of personal ambition. Again there were moves to deprive *Pravda* of its official subsidy.[21]

But Trotsky fought back. He declared it madness for the factions to conspire against each other. One party, one working class, one revolution! The common cause required the party to be reunited so as to be able to provide the necessary leadership of the strike movement that was spreading to the factories and mines of the empire. This had to be done with due consideration. Trotsky warned against the kind of party which dominated the workers in thought and deed. He aimed at releasing proletarian initiative and 'self-activity'. The party was 'conceivable only as the organization of the advanced stratum' of the working class.[22] He continued making this case through to the Great War. The aim should be to induce the 'independence' of worker-militants from external supervision. This alone was the way to make revolution happen.[23] The great reason for cheer, he thought, was that a survey of party members in the Russian Empire revealed that most of them professed no factional allegiance.[24] Sectarianism need not be a permanent phenomenon. Trotsky noted that no faction, not even the Bolsheviks, was internally stable. Factions were almost as disputatious as the party as a whole and he hoped to turn this situation to advantage by engineering conditions for reunification.[25]

The contrast with the Bolshevik-Leninists, if not with the other Bolsheviks, lay in the role assigned to the working class. Party newspapers, according to Trotsky, ought not to lead the labour movement but to serve it. This was the recurrent editorial theme in his *Pravda*. He scoffed at the

Socialist-Revolutionaries because they lacked the proletarian base enjoyed by the Russian Social-Democratic Workers' Party. He was keen to welcome recruits from the Party of Socialist-Revolutionaries. He took it for granted that his own party was the natural and inevitable haven for working-class revolutionaries.[26] He shared the old Marxist assumption that the workers were a single social class with uniform interests. It made no sense for them to have a multiplicity of organizations to represent them. More to the point: he had noted the volatility of politics in 1905–6.

The difficulty was that the party was so weak after the suppression of the 1905–6 revolution. Trotsky admitted this. Committees no longer existed in most places and the intellectuals had walked out of social-democracy. It would be fatuous to say that the prospects of revolution were good anywhere. But Trotsky refused to be despondent. The party's priority should be to recruit among the workers.[27] Eventually the mood in the working class would change, and the monarchy would be brought down. It was this belief that sustained his morale. He was to describe Bolshevism and Menshevism as 'purely intelligentsia-based creations'. Such a situation was anathema to the working class. The Russian Social-Democratic Workers' Party should take account of this and put a stop to its internal polemics. Workers would never take the Marxists seriously until they ceased squabbling. The way forward did not lie only in agreements to compromise. Revolution, when it came, would result from class struggle. Workers did not need leading: they had to be encouraged to advance by their own devices. They would find their way forward without tight guidance from the party. Autonomy of action was crucial for the working class.[28] Repeatedly in this period he distanced himself from Bolshevism by such comments.

Trotsky for a while ceased to reply to polemical articles in Lenin's newspapers. Peace had to be worked at, and Trotsky tried to set an example.[29] He was not universally admired for his efforts. Even sympathetic comrades such as Dmitri Sverchkov noticed that many in the party laughed at him. How was it possible to bring together two irreconcilable factions?[30] But Trotsky would not give up the objective. This baffled many in the party. Why did he devote so much time and energy to a lost cause? Some answered that his real purpose was to put himself above and beyond the central party apparatus and to make himself the supreme leader. The Bolsheviks hated him; the Mensheviks at the very least held him in intense suspicion and made moves to withdraw the official subsidy to *Pravda*. Trotsky made a spirited defence – and indeed the accusations were decidedly excessive. The hostility shown towards him demonstrated the validity

1. Trotsky as a youth,
already wearing the pince-nez.

2. Trotsky and his wife Alexandra.
A very serious-minded couple.

3. Vladimir Lenin in 1895, facing the camera of a police photographer and feeling uncooperative.

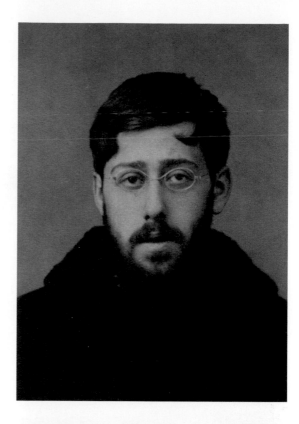

4. Yuli Martov as young man, before he fell out first with Lenin and then with Trotsky.

5. Georgi Plekhanov: never an admirer of Trotsky's talents.

6. Trotsky and his daughter Zina before the Great War. His physical poise and sartorial elegance are remarkable. Zina's fixation with her father is perceptible even in this posed photograph.

7. Lenin in January 1918: his first official portrait as Soviet leader. By then he had grown back the beard he had shaved off to disguise himself before the October Revolution.

8. Trotsky on Red Square in 1919, leaving no doubt about who was in charge of the military group.

9. Trotsky on his train during the Civil War. At work on his papers, he kept a tidy desk.

10. Clare Sheridan striking a melodramatic pose as she regards her bust of Trotsky.

Leiba Trotzky-Braunstein
Kriegs- und Marine-Kommiffar,
der eigentliche Diktator Rußlands.

Ist das ein Menfch? Ein Teufel? Tretet näher!
Ein Bafilisk? Ein tollgeword'ner Faun?
Sagt alles nur in allem: Ein Hebräer —
Ihr werdet feinesgleichen oft noch fchau'n.

11. An anti-Semitic cartoon of Trotsky by Kurfell. In reality, his real nose was neither long nor bent and he never allowed his goatee to become straggly or his hair ill-kempt.

12. Trotsky, probably bored at some political meeting, did a doodle of his own name.

13. Trotsky scribbling about Stalin and generally doodling in 1922, when Stalin was causing difficulties for both Lenin and Trotsky.

of his case that the emigrant 'high-ups' had lost touch with the real party in Russia. All the more reason for him to go on urging that a party conference should be called without delay.[31]

The Russian Social-Democratic Workers' Party was as hard to keep together as mercury on a dish. Alliances and antagonisms were always changing. An odd combination of two contending forces emerged by January 1911, and Russia-based veterans such as Iosif Stalin, then a rising figure in the Bolshevik faction and later to become Trotsky's deadliest enemy, looked with bemusement at the energy being expended by the 'Lenin–Plekhanov block' against the 'Trotsky–Martov–Bogdanov block'. For Stalin, it was a 'storm in a glass of water' as disputes continued to rage about epistemology.[32] The Mensheviks, however, were willing at the time to tolerate Trotsky. So too was Alexander Bogdanov and many other anti-Lenin Bolsheviks. Lenin put his foot down. Resenting Trotsky's success with *Pravda*, he and his own Bolshevik followers started up their own popular newspaper *Rabochaya gazeta* ('Workers' Newspaper').[33]

Trotsky set out his frustrations in the Menshevik newspaper *Nasha zarya* ('Our Dawn') in 1911 since he wanted to reach out beyond his little group of supporters. (He would have done the same in a Bolshevik one if only Lenin had given him an opportunity.) The Russian Social-Democratic Workers' Party suppurated with sectarianism. Faction conflicted with faction. Polemics abounded. Old friendships and associations had collapsed; co-operativeness had faded. This was taking place at the very time when the labour movement in Russia, after a period of torpor, was stirring itself. The industrial downturn had been reversed. Foreign investment was pouring into the country. Vast new metallurgical factories were being built in St Petersburg; textile manufacturing was resurgent in the Moscow region. Wages started to rise again. As fear of unemployment subsided, workers became more militant. The trade unions supported them in their clashes with employers. Trotsky, like fellow leaders of the party, sensed that the period of political retrenchment was coming to an end. Surely his comrades would bury their differences. The revolutionary situation had effected a rapprochement of some sort between the Bolsheviks and Mensheviks. Trotsky, ever the optimist, persuaded himself that the rise in militancy among factory workers and miners throughout the Russian Empire would act as a powerful stimulus to party unity.

Far from taking advantage of the social turbulence, leading Russian Marxists were indulging their inclination towards internal factionalism. The proliferation of groupings continued as disputes intensified among Martov's Mensheviks, Lenin's Bolsheviks, Plekhanovites, Forwardists and

Liquidators. Bizarre émigré misunderstandings and divergences occurred – and the clandestine party organizations in the Russian Empire were exasperated by the wildfire contentiousness. Official Menshevik policy favoured 'neutral' trade unions and the Bolsheviks criticized this for forsaking the party's overriding commitment to politics. In fact, though, Mensheviks who operated in the labour movement rather than framing policy from abroad had turned these unions into 'a surrogate for political organization'; in practice, therefore, they were ignoring their own faction's policy. Meanwhile the Bolsheviks in Russia were supposed to be politicizing the trade unions. Instead they had become so preoccupied with the purity of their political specifications that they drove a wedge between themselves and the party. Furthermore, the so-called Liquidators scarcely practised what they preached. They functioned in close collaboration with party committees; they worked steadily and productively for the party's goals. The Bolsheviks refused to recognize this and subjected the Liquidators to what Trotsky called 'an organizational terror'.[34]

Not that Trotsky was soft on Alexander Potresov and the Liquidators or on those who refused to break with them. He attacked Martov for failing to confront Potresov. The Bolsheviks reproduced Trotsky's argument as proof that they were in the right.[35] At the same time they castigated Trotsky for refusing to allow Kamenev, the Central Committee's appointed representative, to exercise any degree of control over *Pravda* – and they questioned whether Trotsky was fully consistent in his practical handling of Potresov. His behaviour, they said, was 'coquettishness'.[36] Trotsky went his own way. He had no idea how he would get rid of the Liquidators beyond persuading them out of existence. He was sure that the Bolsheviks were excessively belligerent, but he offered no practical alternative.

# 13. SPECIAL CORRESPONDENT

Trotsky lived life on his own terms; the periods of imprisonment and exile were exceptional and even they did not wholly destroy his opportunities for revolutionary activity. Suddenly in January 1912 he was afflicted by personal tribulations. His mouth became so painfully swollen that he took to his bed. It was at this time too that his mother died.[1] Although they had not been close since his early schooldays, the news shook him. His dental trouble worsened so much that he could not speak properly. Weeks passed as the doctors failed to make any improvement. Pavel Axelrod had to help him out with the mounting medical fees.[2] Then the dentist, one of Vienna's finest, broke his drill bit and left it buried in the jaw while extracting a wisdom tooth. Trotsky had no confidence in his assurance that this was nothing to worry about, and consulted another surgeon.[3]

No sooner had his mouth been patched up than his sister Yelizaveta arrived for a fortnight's stay together with her son Alexander. Then Trotsky's father turned up, after a five-year gap, with eleven-year-old Zina Bronstein, and stayed for the entire summer. Trotsky complained to outsiders about the 'waterfall of relatives'.[4] His working routine was disrupted. His stomach gave him pain; he was suffering from stress. David Bronstein assumed the duties of care over the adult revolutionary:

> I went with my father to a professor [of medicine], who opened up my hernia and proposed to perform an operation. Besides that he recommended my going to the mountains (for the sake of my nerves), where there's a health spa. I have put off the operation till the winter and the trip up the mountain until after the Conference. Father at first insisted on making a trip immediately but after staying for his first week with us was convinced I ought not to travel at this point.[5]

Perhaps Trotsky had taken his father along because he needed him to pay for the consultation. His letters hint at a further motive. Trotsky seems to have appreciated being accompanied by someone devoted to his interests.

He was again the centre of attention, and the joint visit to the Viennese professor restored his spirits.

In politics he had much to catch up on. The factions of the Russian Social-Democratic Workers' Party had finally agreed to hold a conference. The exception was constituted by the Bolsheviks, or at least the section of Bolsheviks who followed Lenin. They had stolen a march on everyone else in January 1912 by holding their own gathering in Prague and electing their own Central Committee. This was tantamount to a declaration of independence and was Lenin's way of saying that his was the only legitimate Marxist party in Russia.

Leninists could not care less about the rest of the Russian Social-Democratic Workers' Party. The St Petersburg Bolshevik leadership took Lenin himself unawares by founding a legal newspaper in the capital and calling it *Pravda*. This was a calculated insult to Trotsky, whose own *Pravda* had been published since 1908. Condemning the upstarts, he claimed that 'the Leninist factional–schismatic circle' was deliberately causing confusion in the party. He regretted that he could not take them to court – a curious sentiment in someone who scorned bourgeois law and order. Instead he threatened to complain to the Second International unless the Bolsheviks changed the name of their paper.[6] Founded in 1889 and based in Brussels, the Second (Socialist) International was the co-ordinating body for most of the socialist, social-democratic and labour parties in Europe. Trotsky was hoping to shame the Leninists into ending their disruptive initiative. With the same purpose in mind he wrote to Marxist deputies in the State Duma, arguing that the Bolsheviks were misleading the readers of party newspapers.[7] Lenin enjoyed the fuss. Based in Kraków from summer 1912, he aimed to get the Bolsheviks to operate separately from their Menshevik comrades in the Duma. He regarded an organizational split as the prerequisite for preparing the Bolsheviks for imminent revolutionary opportunities. Trotsky contacted financial supporters imploring them not to treat the 'Leninist conference' as a legitimate expression of the party's opinion.[8] The only alternative was to realize his plans for a larger conference in Vienna.[9]

Bolshevism's effrontery annoyed the rest of the party. There was disbelief that Lenin could sustain his separatism on a permanent basis, and many detested him for the damage he was causing. There was a financial dimension to their hostility. Lenin's Bolshevik sub-faction had made money from bank robberies in contravention of party policy; it had also taken exclusive possession of donations intended for the party as a whole. It had done the same with a double legacy obtained from two naive young women who had been seduced and married by a couple of Bolsheviks. The Russian Social-Democratic Workers' Party had been formally unified at the time. The Mensheviks therefore argued that Lenin had no right to monopolize possession of the proceeds. The dispute had gone on for years and no solution was in sight. An arbitration panel of prominent German social-democrats consisting of Karl Kautsky, Clara Zetkin and Franz Mehring was created. For the Menshevik case to be taken seriously there was advantage in bringing together the anti-Lenin factions for a conference even if the Leninists were unlikely to attend. As patron of the cause of organizational unification, Trotsky had long been pushing for a gathering. He was delighted when Martov agreed to release funds for factions to meet in Vienna in August 1912.

Trotsky's political leverage was strengthening because the Mensheviks could use him for their own purposes. They were more than happy for him to talk to Zetkin and the others about the contested finances.[10] This did not mean that they liked him. They knew that many foreign Marxists regarded him as a force for reason and compromise in the struggle against factionalism.[11] When he wanted, he came across as admirably poised and well mannered. Once he was among the leading figures of the Second International he seemed like one of them – the fact that he sent them no ill-tempered letters was an improvement on many other members of the Russian Social-Democratic Workers' Party leadership.

He volunteered to make the practical arrangements for the Vienna conference, and they took him up on his offer. For over a month he was busy finding places for the delegates.[12] It was a diverse group which gathered in the Austrian capital in August. Apart from Mensheviks there were representatives from the Bund, the Forwardists, the south Caucasus, Latvia, Poland and even the Liquidators. The Leninist Bolsheviks were the only substantial faction absent – and their defiant defence of their own Central Committee was the object of the Conference's contempt. Yet the Conference did not reply in kind by electing its own Central Committee. Instead it modestly formed an Organizational Committee. Conference delegates began to leave before the end of the proceedings. By coming to Vienna, they could feel for themselves how difficult it would be to reconcile the conflicting elements of the Russian Social-Democratic Workers' Party even without Lenin being present. National divergences were damaging to co-ordinated activity. Still more unhelpful were political disagreements stretching between the Forwardists on the left and the Liquidators on the right.

If Trotsky was expecting to be a dominant force in the proceedings, he had forgotten his reception at the Fifth Party Congress. No Menshevik was going to be told by him what to think or do. No Bundist had reason to be fond of him. Marian Melenevsky, who had delivered the Vienna *Pravda* into his hands, took umbrage at his opposition to calls for Ukrainian national assertiveness.[13] Trotsky was defiant. Knowing that no German Marxists were present, he claimed that his ideas were a vital antidote to 'European opportunism'.[14] This was not what he would have wished Karl Kautsky to hear. With nothing to lose, moreover, he rebuked all factions in the party: 'Our old party was a dictatorship of the demo-cratic intelligentsia, standing on the viewpoint of Marxism, over the labour movement.'[15] Trotsky had never minded how much he irritated potential allies. He spoke his mind, thinking that this was what party debates should be all about. The Conference passed resolutions on several broad policies. There was agreement to adopt the Austrian Marxist idea of 'national-cultural autonomy' as the solution to the problems of gov-erning a large multinational state. Each nation was to be allowed to form its own central institutions for the enhancement of its interests. This was anathema to the Bolsheviks who wanted to retain a unitary multinational state after the overthrow of the monarchy but to accord wide powers of regional autonomy in areas where a majority of residents belonged to a nation other than the Russians.

When the Conference drew to a close there was brave talk about the togetherness it had produced. Promises were made to stay true to the spirit of the 'August Block', and Trotsky expressed the hope that the reunification of the Russian Social-Democratic Workers' Party would be the result. Few people, though, felt that much had been achieved. Factional tensions inside the so-called Block persisted. Trotsky had anyway contrib-uted little to the Conference debates. His semi-detached behaviour con-tinued after the delegates departed Vienna. For years he had ignored the Austrian Marxists in their engagement with the national question, and saw no reason to alter his attitude after the Conference. Indeed he resisted being drawn into most of the general discussions that enveloped the Russian Social-Democratic Workers' Party. Bolsheviks and Mensheviks argued noisily about the agrarian question and the national question; they also disputed the nature of contemporary imperialism, militarism and capitalist development. Trotsky by and large kept out of the controversies. Even on organizational problems in the party, his articles only repeated what he had been writing for a long time.

People assumed that Trotsky would get back to his normal editorial obligations at *Pravda* as soon as the Conference was over. This was what he himself thought at the time. Vienna was his zone of comfortable quarantine. He had said what he wanted at the Conference. He had got nowhere. This was coming to be a typical experience for him, and he would surely find solace in his journalism in Marxist newspapers. It came as a surprise to everybody when he announced in September that he would be travelling to the Balkans as *Kievskaya mysl*'s special correspondent. War had broken out that month between the Ottoman central authorities and the Balkan League of Greece, Serbia, Montenegro and Bulgaria. The Turks were at a huge strategic disadvantage. By May 1913 they had been comprehensively defeated and compelled to cede much territory in Europe through the treaty of London; they also had to recognize Albania's independence. Turkish withdrawal quickly proved to be a prelude to military hostilities inside the League. Thus began the Second Balkan War when Bulgaria attacked Greek and Serbian positions in June. Romania too became involved. No state emerged unscathed but the Bulgarians suffered most. An end to the fighting came in July 1913.

Going off to war, Trotsky was not one of those outsiders who developed an enthusiasm for Serbs, Croats or Montenegrins. He went with deep forebodings, as he wrote:

> But when I stood on the bridge in Belgrade I saw the long lines of reservists and civilians with Red Cross armbands when I heard from the lips of parliamentary deputies, journalists, peasants and workers that there could be no retreat and that war would happen within days. This was when I recognized that several people well known to me – politicians, editors and lecturers – were already under arms at the frontier, at the front line, and that they would have to kill and die. At that time war, an abstraction which I so easily speculated about in my thoughts and articles, seemed improbable and impossible.[16]

Later he was to refer to this period of his life as having offered an opportunity to study the arts of war. He persuaded his followers that the experience fitted him out for his appointment as people's commissar for military affairs in March 1918. This was poetic exaggeration. As a correspondent he showed little interest in the tactics or strategy employed by the belligerent forces.

*Kievskaya mysl* was not asking him to put himself in the line of fire, and he sensibly went nowhere near any fighting. (The contrast with his risk-taking in the Russian Civil War was a striking one.) He read no books on the region; he learned no local languages. He felt it was enough for him to go to the Balkans with an open pair of eyes and a ready-made ideology. The fronts were unstable and the battles happened unpredictably; the combatants proved capable of gruesome atrocities against all and sundry. Trotsky reported on the atmosphere and explained the motives of the rebellions against the Ottomans. His articles were as good as anybody's at the time. He travelled to several of the main Balkan cities, sending several dispatches from Sofia and Belgrade. He spoke to as many public leaders as would meet with him – usually he interviewed them about what they hoped to get out of the war politically or territorially. He picked up tips from local journalists; he also took the trouble of talking to soldiers. Although he was always to the rear of the fighting he witnessed plenty of the consequences. Unlike most other reporters, he went into hospitals and talked with the wounded. His descriptions stand the test of time; no one who read his articles in 1912–13 would have been surprised by the ferocity of inter-ethnic violence in the region in later decades.

In one of his dispatches he wrote:

> After they separated the wounded from the dead there was a sorting out between the heavily and lightly wounded. The heavily wounded were left not far from the places of battle in Kirkilios, Yambol and Filippopol while the lightly wounded are being transported to us here in Sofia. Here we have almost exclusively those with 'light' wounds of leg, arm and shoulder.
>
> But these [soldiers] don't feel that they've been lightly wounded. Still covered in the thunder and smoke of a battle which crippled them, they appear like people who have arrived from another mysterious and terrible world. They have lost the thoughts and feelings which would have moved beyond the bounds of the battle they have just experienced. They talk about it and they dream about it in their sleep.[17]

This was understatement used to powerful effect.

In January 1913 he returned to Vienna a chastened man after three months on furlough from *Pravda*. If there was one theme that imprinted itself on nearly all his articles, it was the danger of nationalism in southeastern Europe. The whole region seemed a madhouse to him, and he stressed that nationalist aspirations jeopardized the peace everywhere in the continent. Until he went to the Balkans he had written next to nothing on the national question. His observations had convinced him that war between Austria and Serbia was only a matter of time. His first priority was to secure a European platform for his thinking, and he sought an invitation to speak at the forthcoming congress of the German Social-Democratic Party.[18] He knew more about the dangers in south-eastern Europe than any socialist on the continent apart from those who were natives of the region. He was committed to the Socialist International's opposition in principle to militarism and imperialism. He was at one with the policy that no socialist party should support its government in any future war. But he instinctively understood the need to nail down agreement among the many parties. The German social-democrats were the leading force in the Socialist International. It was Trotsky's urgent task to put aside the internal wrangles of Russian social-democracy and alert comrades in Germany to the need for urgent preventive action.

During his Balkans trip he had left *Pravda* in the care of Semën Semkovski. Now he threw himself back into party journalism. Organizational unity was his principal concern. The episode of military journalism had refreshed him. As frequently happened in his later career, a period away from the internal party hurly-burly built up his energy for the next political campaign. This was both his glory and his weakness throughout his career, for he could never concentrate on being a full-time politician.

He denounced the Leninists for their splitting activity, but he remained an optimist even while railing against the damage they were doing. He made this clear in a letter to Nikolai Chkheidze, a Menshevik deputy in the State Duma whom he aimed to win over to his ideas and whose oratory he admired:

> Lenin's 'successes' do not induce further concerns in my mind. Now is not 1903 or 1908 . . . In a word, *the entire edifice of Leninism at the present time is built on lies and falsification and carries within itself the poisonous inception of its own dissolution.* There can be no doubt that if the other side behaves intelligently, *a cruel dissolution will commence among the Leninists in the very near future*, precisely along the line of the question about unity or schism.[19]

Trotsky was restating what he had said in 1904, when he dismissed the lasting prospects of Lenin and the Bolsheviks.[20] Then in 1905 he had seen how readily the industrial workforce of St Petersburg had come together under the Soviet's leadership. He continued to expect events to force Marxists to combine themselves still more effectively in the next political crisis of the Romanov autocracy.

He planned to help things on their way by getting the August Block to become more resolute in co-ordinating its activities while, he expected, the Leninists fell apart. The workers would respond eagerly to such an outcome.[21] He overrated both the Block's vivacity and the working class's interest in politics.[22] The Bolsheviks, moreover, did not disintegrate. Far from it: Lenin characteristically was exploiting the existence of Liquidators as a reason to write off all Menshevism. Martov played into his hands by refusing to break with the Liquidators; he wanted to uphold the spirit of the August Conference and combine all willing factions. Trotsky was critical. He wrote to *Luch*, the Liquidators' newspaper in St Petersburg, spelling out his terms for stopping his campaign against the group. They had to agree to 'not vilifying the underground, not abolishing the [party] programme, staying true to the old banner'; and he asserted that the August Conference had 'declared uncompromising struggle' against anyone who rejected such a standpoint.[23] Mensheviks felt he merely wanted to mount to 'the peak of power and fame'.[24] Martov thought he lacked a sense of proportion in his attacks on *Luch*; even Axelrod lost patience with him.[25] Marxists wrote to Trotsky from Russia asking why he called for unity in the party and yet was stridently polemical. This was often pointed out to him in complaints from Russia.[26]

The editors of the *Nasha zarya*, the St Petersburg newspaper produced in the name of Menshevik deputies to the Fourth State Duma, told him: 'Not all your latest articles work; they are unsuccessful. "Snout and Snout-beater" doesn't work. The reply to [the Kadet writer] Izgoev also doesn't work. In the polemic with the liberals it is always necessary to remember who reads *Luch* and for whom is it being written.' *Nasha zarya*'s staff were not administered a total brush-off. They recognized that he wrote vividly and soundly about the Duma; but they wanted him to avoid his habitual sharpness.[27]

Unusually, Natalya took Trotsky to task about his manoeuvres in the cause of party unity and told him he was wasting his energy on a lost cause. He ought, she told him, to take a more practical approach. Writing to him from St Petersburg on a trip there in December 1913, she had seen things which he could not; she reported that all his plans were bursting 'like a soap bubble'.[28] A clear split between Mensheviks and Bolsheviks prevailed in the State Duma, in the St Petersburg Marxist press and in the clandestine party networks. Natalya did not describe this in detail and anyway made no progress with him. Once he made his mind up there was no deflecting him. She knew this better than most. Trotsky went on writing about the need for unity and for the rejection of both the Bolsheviks and the Liquidators. He continued to criticize the Mensheviks.

While he had readers in Russia, he neither led a factional grouping of his own nor wanted one. He had never been less influential in the party – and his own Natalya saw why better than he could.

Three things saved Trotsky from becoming demoralized. Two were to the fore: his own cockiness and Martov's need for him to reinforce the case against the Leninists in petitions to the Second International for the Bolsheviks to be constrained to hand over party funds or risk being condemned as undesirable splitters.[29] The third source of encouragement for Trotsky was the situation in the Russian Empire. Industrial workers had caused trouble for government and employers since April 1912 when troops fired upon strikers in the Lena goldfields in Siberia. The years of economic downturn were over and Russia's workforce, now less worried about being made unemployed, was increasingly willing to risk confronting factory owners. Strikes rose from 2,404 to 3,534 between 1913 and the first half of the following year.[30] When demonstrations packed the streets of St Petersburg there were plenty of slogans calling for the overthrow of the monarchy. Radicalism was popular again. Trotsky, from a distance, founded his own legal journal *Borba* ('Struggle') in the Russian capital seeking to enhance support for his ideas. Although it suffered from interventions by the police and from the distrust of established factions (and even of some of his own supporters such as Semkovski), it attracted impressive pieces from several leading Marxists – and Trotsky too contributed his own lengthy articles on the Duma, on the state's budgetary dependence on vodka sales and on the peculiarities of Russian historical development.[31]

Trotsky as well as Lenin was confident that the situation was changing to the advantage of their strategies for revolution. History seemed to be moving in their favour as it had done in 1905. His first editorial for *Borba* indicated a wish to appeal to workers as well as to intellectuals. He insisted that progress for the party would occur only when the working class formed its own opinions and began to struggle for 'general human happiness'.[32] Yet again he called for an end to factionalism. He claimed that organizational unity was a realistic aim since no faction was without its deep internal fissures.[33] He therefore found it tedious to have to bother himself with the Second International's investigation of the Bolshevik–Menshevik dispute. Claims and counterclaims flew through the air. The arbitration panel of Kautsky, Zetkin and Mehring wanted to bring the affair to a conclusion. It was decided that both sides in the Russian imbroglio would meet in Brussels under the surveillance of the Germans in July 1914. The verdict was expected to go heavily against Lenin. Trotsky, if he was going to supply his heavy ammunition for the Mensheviks, would need to disrupt his summer plans and take a trip from Vienna. The meeting did not happen and the trip did not take place. Instead there was war not just in the Balkans but across most of Europe.

# PART TWO

# 1914–1919

# 14. WAR ON THE WAR

The Trotskys lived quietly in Vienna in summer 1914 while a political storm erupted over Europe which ended suddenly in the outbreak of the Great War. Archduke Ferdinand, heir to the Habsburg throne, was assassinated in Sarajevo on 28 June. The Austrian government held Serbia responsible and delivered an ultimatum containing demands which were bound to be rejected. As yet there seemed no cause for alarm. This seemed like yet another dispute in the Balkan peninsula and all such disputes in previous years had ended in compromise.

This time it was different as the European powers spent July in conditions of rising tension. Russia warned the Austrians against military action. The atmosphere worsened when Germany encouraged the Austrians to act on their threats to Serbia. Emperor Franz Joseph needed little encouragement because he judged the state's interests and his personal honour to be under challenge. The Russians sensed that a continental war might be imminent, and Nicholas II ordered the preliminary mobilization of his forces. This only agitated the Austrians and Germans further. The Russians were told to stand down their army or else face war. When Nicholas II ignored the demand, the Germans declared war on Russia. The Austrians, already fighting Serbia, joined them. Neither London nor Paris was willing to see Russia defeated and Germany enabled to dominate central and eastern Europe. Two great coalitions were put together. The Central Powers were led by Germany and Austria-Hungary, the Allies by France, Russia and the United Kingdom. Europe heard the noise of marching feet and trundling trains. But few ministers and diplomats expected that this war would produce a political and social cataclysm across Europe. Most thought it would be of short duration and intensive mobility.

Trotsky let nothing disturb him until the German declaration of war on Russia rendered him vulnerable as a Russian subject living in a state allied to Imperial Germany. Next day, on 3 August, he went to the offices of *Arbeiter-Zeitung*, the social-democratic daily, at Wienzeile and sought out his friend Friedrich Adler. Friedrich's father Victor joined them and suggested that Trotsky should obtain proper guidance about how the Viennese authorities intended to proceed with Russian emigrants like him. Victor, a psychiatrist as well as the country's leading socialist, foresaw mass 'insanity' as the war released nationalist inclinations in society. The fact that Trotsky was a critic of Nicholas II might not save him from incarceration. It could not be discounted that he and his family would suffer at the hands of a vengeful mob. The entire situation was unpredictable. Victor Adler was in no doubt that Trotsky's personal security was under threat. Having contacts at the highest levels of the state administration, in the middle of the afternoon he ordered a taxi and took Trotsky to meet the chief of the political police, Geier. Geier validated Friedrich Adler's pessimism, indicating that there was about to be a mass temporary arrest of residents of Russian citizenship.

Trotsky took the news calmly: 'So you would recommend leaving the country?'

'Absolutely. And the quicker the better.'

'Very well. I shall go to Switzerland with my family tomorrow.'

'Hm! . . . I should prefer it if you would leave today.'[1]

The gentlemanly Geier had no desire to fill Vienna's prisons with foreigners. Trotsky, known as an enemy of Nicholas II, had never figured on the Austrian official list of undesirable aliens. It would be convenient for everybody if he slipped away before measures were taken against him. He hurried home to tell the family. Suitcases were pulled out of storage and rapidly packed with clothes and political files. There was no panic: Trotsky and Natalya were practical, orderly people who led their lives on the assumption that they had to be ready for any sudden emergency. By 6.40 p.m. they were seated on a train leaving Austria for neutral Switzerland.[2]

Their first destination was Zurich, where there was a large community of Russian Marxists and Trotsky could meet up with other veteran comrades. He had lost the fixed centre of his practical revolutionary activity. His *Pravda* was no more, his team of helpers had fallen apart and his financial circumstances were anything but dependable. Worst of all for him was the reaction of most member parties of the Second International to the war. They had vowed to prevent an outbreak of hostilities and to withhold support from their national governments if they went to war. To Trotsky's chagrin this commitment was abandoned. In Germany, France and Britain the ascendant leadership of the main socialist party voted in favour of the military effort. Russian and Bulgaria were among the exceptions; but even in those countries there were plenty of socialists who took up the patriotic cause. The best known of these was Georgi

Plekhanov. Even Bolsheviks such as Grigori Alexinski declared that Germany was the enemy of the Russian people and had to be defeated. Many socialist émigrés from the Russian Empire, who hated Nicholas II, queued to volunteer for service in the French armed forces. The Second International was dead. The German Social-Democratic Party saw itself as postponing revolutionary action until such time as the country was secure against being overrun by the French, British and Russians; the French Socialist Party claimed it was rallying to the side of a government which strove to prevent conquest by Germans.

Anti-war socialists like Trotsky were angry with those parties which had dishonoured the commitments agreed in the Second International. Trotsky himself found just a crumb of comfort in the outbreak of war in Europe. He had nothing to say about military strategy; he had little or no interest in particular rulers, cabinets or high commands. But he was confident that the fighting would enhance the prospects of revolution. He was sure that the 'imperialist war' was the last gasp of global capitalism. The vast military struggle in Europe was about to disrupt the political status quo in every belligerent state. Socialism would arise from the ashes of war as the saviour of humankind.

It was in this mood that Trotsky ran into Hermann Molkenbuhr on a Zurich street. Molkenbuhr was visiting on behalf of the German Social-Democratic Party and canvassing for its policy on the war. Trotsky asked him how he thought things would turn out. Back came the reply: 'We'll finish off France in the next two months and then we'll turn eastward and finish off the armies of the tsar; and within three months – four at the outside – we'll deliver a firm peace to Europe.' Molkenbuhr regarded Trotsky's apocalyptic prognosis as the ranting of a 'utopian'.[3] Trotsky would not be browbeaten. He remembered how in 1905 he had been holed up one day in a Rauha pension-house only to find himself a day later at the Technological Institute in St Petersburg heading the work of the Soviet. That sudden change in circumstances, he thought, would surely happen again. Switzerland, of course, remained a neutral country. Its armed forces were maintained solely to protect its frontiers and cannon practice was regularly undertaken; but the government hoped to keep the country out of the military conflict. The main public discussion was about the surplus of potatoes and the growing cheese shortage.[4]

Like others on the political far left, Trotsky did not discount the prospects of socialist revolution in Switzerland. But after making a careful assessment of the anti-war movement he decided that France would be the better country for him – and anyway *Kievskaya mysl* was asking him to be its war correspondent there. He travelled to Paris on 19 November 1914. A vigorous Russian Marxist group operated there which included Anatoli Lunacharski and Yuli Martov.[5] Trotsky aimed to collaborate on their newspaper *Golos* ('Voice') and was listed among the contributors along with other anti-war Marxists including Yuli Martov, Alexandra Kollontai and Angelica Balabanova. His old friend Axelrod, who sent articles from Switzerland, also appeared on the masthead.[6] He left Natalya to sort out the family's arrangements. When she wrote saying they had run out of money Trotsky contacted Axelrod and asked him to help her to obtain a short-term loan. He also telegraphed *Kievskaya mysl* to get a cheque sent to her.[7] It was not that the Trotskys lacked money in their bank account but that he was encountering difficulty in transferring it to her from Paris.[8]

*Golos* soon changed its name to *Nashe slovo* ('Our Word') and Trotsky made known his desire to join its editorial board. His indication was not without controversy. The editors knew his domineering personality and there was a worry that he might disturb the working atmosphere. But it was recognized that he had unmatched literary flair and was committed to working with every anti-war Marxist from Martov to Lenin. He could hardly be rejected.[9] Not that Martov was pleased with the result. As soon as Trotsky joined the board he insisted on debating Martov's reluctance to break definitively with Plekhanov and all the others who supported the Russian war effort. Board meetings at *Nashe slovo* became occasions for fiery outbursts.[10] Martov had a temperamental distaste for divisiveness and was anyway taking the path of broad organizational tolerance which Trotsky had recommended before 1914. Trotsky no longer accepted the case for a grand inclusiveness. The Great War was the new and fundamental question for the entire party. While Martov was sticking to the old Marxist politics, Trotsky called for a fresh approach. In his eyes, anyone who advocated the patriotic defence of the Russian Empire was to be treated as an outright enemy of the proletarian cause.

For the first time in his career he entered into polemics with Plekhanov, whom he now regarded with utter contempt.[11] As the party's great putative unifier Trotsky had eschewed vituperation with the party's founder whenever possible. He hated factional struggle and his recurrent dispute with Lenin from 1903 was exceptional. Likewise his pre-war denunciation of the Liquidators had not been his usual way of handling internal party disagreements. He turned on Plekhanov in late 1914 over policy towards the war. Plekhanov, without supporting the Imperial monarchy, wanted Russia to defeat Germany. He predicted a Europe under the

German jackboot if the Central Powers were to emerge victorious. He therefore approved of military credits being voted for the Russian government. Trotsky denounced him as a renegade. In his eyes, Plekhanov had descended to a nadir of chauvinism and no longer deserved to be regarded as a comrade. Trotsky had for a long time detested Alexander Potresov and the Liquidators. It came as no surprise to him that nearly all of them became 'social-patriots', and he regularly denounced them. He also fell out comprehensively with Marian Melenevsky, who had helped him become the editor of the Vienna *Pravda*. In 1915 Melenevsky headed the Union for the Liberation of Ukraine and had turned from a Marxist into a nationalist. Trotsky denounced him; Melenevsky replied in kind.[12]

Wartime politics shattered Trotsky's assumption that it was worth holding the Russian Social-Democratic Workers' Party together. He fulminated against any party leader who condoned the voting of financial credits to Nicholas II's government. This was his primary criterion of strategic judgement. Bolsheviks who turned into patriots typically abandoned their factional allegiance, but other party groups were divided by policy disagreements. Much more serious than Plekhanov's writing, from Trotsky's viewpoint, was the editorial line taken by *Nasha zarya*. This was a Menshevik newspaper which, dropping all neutrality, adopted the line that victory by the democratic Allies over the autocratic Central Powers was desirable. Trotsky was enraged. How could the editors not understand that the war was not 'a conflict of political forms'? It had nothing to do with democracy. The two belligerent coalitions were really fighting over markets, territory and global domination. According to Trotsky, this made it nonsense for *Nasha zarya* to blame everything on the German Junkers.[13] At the same time he could not abide Lenin's proposal for a political campaign for Russia's military defeat. Even many Bolsheviks who opposed the war thought this fanatical and senseless. Like Trotsky, they called for criticism of all belligerent powers at one and the same time. Trotsky prided himself on being an internationalist. To him, Lenin's manoeuvres smacked of inverted nationalism. He wrote an open letter on the subject but *Nashe slovo* failed to publish it – or perhaps he himself had second thoughts for some undisclosed reason.[14]

At any rate Natalya and the boys reached Paris in May 1915. War or no war, they were going to have their normal holiday and the family jumped at the offer by the Italian painter René Paress and his Russian wife Ela Klyachko to let them borrow their villa in Sèvres on the southwestern side of Paris. Paress and Klyachko had gone off to Switzerland to get away from the war;[15] Trotsky, though, wished to be as near to the war as possible since he expected revolution at any moment – and he took it as axiomatic that military difficulties for the Allies would bring forward the moment of political explosion. The boys attended the school near the villa until the start of the academic vacation. Having been brought up speaking Russian and the German of Vienna, they now had to learn French from scratch.[16] Political sympathizers in France made efforts to help the Trotskys feel at home. A French worker of their acquaintance brought them an Alsatian named Kiki. Eight-year-old Sergei was enraptured by the dog, which he treated as if she were a human being. He asked his mother to get an extra toothbrush and handkerchief so that Kiki could keep herself clean; he could not understand why she did not speak.[17] The Trotskys had not kept pets in Austria or Switzerland, which may account for Sergei's naivety. But perhaps the boy had received so little attention from his highly political parents that he invented a 'person' to keep him company.

When the summer drew to a close the Trotskys moved to Paris, settling in an apartment in rue de l'Amirale-Mouchez near the Parc Monsouris.[18] It was a matter of honour for the Trotskys that Lëva and Sergei should keep up their Russian and they went to a Russian school in the Boulevard Blanqui. Natalya as usual managed the household while Trotsky drove himself hard at work. He wrote ceaselessly. He did a lot of editing; he gave speeches and rallied supporters. He continued his activity as a reviewer. Being always on the go, he succumbed to a fever which baffled the doctors, and it was Natalya who had to nurse him along.[19] Whether he was fit or unwell, he followed a strict routine. Not for him the hours spent by Martov chatting away in the Café Rotonde. At eleven o'clock every morning he left for the newspaper offices where he would talk about the next issue.[20] He loved the smell of ink in the print room. He adored fingering the newspaper's first copies, still hot and damp from the press.[21] His two boys were at last coming to an age when they could run errands for him, and they liked to deliver his articles to the *Nashe slovo* offices. Sergei made a donation to the newspaper after finding twenty francs in the street.[22] The osmosis of family life was politicizing the lads. (This had a lasting effect on Lëva but not on Sergei.)[23]

One of the workers at the press, a certain Imber, tried to make friends with Sergei but was taken aback by how brusque the boy could be whenever he thought someone was saying something silly. Natalya had a word with her son on the need for greater tact in future.[24] Sergei, of course, had witnessed another member of his family displaying impatience with stupidity.

Both Trotsky and his wife were to claim that they lived frugally in

Paris. There is no evidence for this. In 1914 he dispatched six substantial articles to *Kievskaya mysl*. Such was their success that the newspaper continued to employ him throughout 1915–16; and since the French and the Russians were allies in the war he could rely on money being transferred quickly to his bank account in Paris. The Trotskys were not hard up in wartime France. Although *Kievskaya mysl*, a liberal outlet, brought valuable income he preferred to write for the socialist press. Indeed he always hoped to place articles with newspapers taking the standpoint of anti-war socialism. But he was also willing to deliver articles to newspapers on the political left which had no fixed position on the war. Among these was New York's *Novy mir* ('New World'), which was widely read among the Russian emigrants. Trotsky continued to send material to it across the Atlantic in wartime and did not stint in his warnings about Russian, French and British imperialism.[25] Ziv, Trotsky's old comrade from Nikolaev, who had emigrated and set up a medical practice in New York, supported the campaign against the war and American participation in it; he sent back his best wishes to Trotsky.[26]

Allied governments and commanders censored such news as became available about the fighting; and there was no question of Trotsky going anywhere near any front during the Great War. Yet he keenly reported on the invalids and widows he saw on Paris streets. He needed only a glimpse of tragedy and he could weave it into a tapestry of denunciation of the 'imperialists' and 'capitalists' who had started the military conflict in quest of financial profit. Trotsky felt a strong need to visualize the reality he was trying to describe and analyse: he understood that his readers would be more sympathetic to his political recommendations if he brought the awfulness of the Great War to life for them. He needed to be careful how he phrased his reports for both Paris and Kiev newspapers. There was no point in his writing things that he knew would never be permitted by the French or Russian wartime censorship. His articles for the legal press pushed at the limits of the printable.

Plekhanov accused him of publishing contradictory messages in *Nashe slovo* and *Kievskaya mysl*. Trotsky justifiably retorted that he never allowed his basic thought to be emasculated.[27] Sometimes he went too far for the censors and blank patches had to appear in *Nashe slovo*. Usually, though, he knew how to moderate his language or make it more indirect so as to get his articles published.[28] A game of cat and mouse was going on. Unsurprisingly the Russian ambassador in Paris complained that Trotsky and other anti-war revolutionaries from Russia were undermining patriotism in the Allied countries.

Anti-war socialist internationalists from both France and the Russian Empire met for their discussions at the Quai de Jemmapes in the French capital. Trotsky was a regular. Vladimir Antonov-Ovseenko, one of those who helped him at *Nashe slovo*, attended less frequently since he was usually tied down by editorial duties. Natalya stayed behind to look after the boys.[29] Until Trotsky's arrival it had been Martov who was the soul of the debates. Everyone agreed that he was deeply intelligent and committed – and he sparkled in conversation. Trotsky put him in the shade. Forceful and witty, he was never disabled by the intellectual doubts and comradely inhibitions experienced by Martov. Trotsky liked Martov but had long ago concluded that he lacked the briskness necessary for the making of a revolutionary party and the discharging of the tasks of revolution. Yet there was much they agreed about. The war, they asserted, was the outcome of capitalist and imperialist rivalries which could be terminated only by the installation of socialist governments in Europe. The biggest part of the Second International had irreversibly discredited itself. The job for people such as the Russian and French militants at the Quai de Jemmapes was to construct an international alliance of socialist groups hostile to the war. Groupings and organizations needed to be brought together regardless of national origin. The Great War had to be ended. Europe badly needed the era of socialism to commence.

# 15. DESIGNS FOR REVOLUTION

No group of Trotskyists sprang up in the Great War and Trotsky did not cultivate one. The contrast with other leading lights of the Russian Social-Democratic Workers' Party should not be overdrawn. The number of Leninists had fallen, especially after Lenin called for Russia's military defeat. Nobody any longer talked of the Martovites; and although Plekhanovites continued to exist they were few and weakly organized. Yet no leading party figure was quite as much a soloist as Trotsky.

At the same time he was committed to bringing Europe's anti-war socialists together. The fighting made it difficult for most countries in Europe to host a preparatory meeting. The main possibilities were Switzerland, Scandinavia and Holland, which had preserved their neutrality. Robert Grimm, leader of the Social-Democratic Party of Switzerland and a pacifist, saw it as his political and moral duty to organize a conference. Trotsky picked up rumours about this in December 1914 and wrote to Axelrod enquiring whether they were true.[1] Receiving an affirmative answer, he jumped at the chance to attend. Grimm's proviso was that everyone should avoid causing embarrassment to the Berne authorities in their relations with the Central Powers or the Allies. He sent out invitations simultaneously to Britain, France, Russia, Austria and Germany. Difficulties arose when belligerent governments got wind of the plan and prevented their citizens from attending – and those who arrived could not be sure of being allowed back across their own borders. Some could not come because they had been put in prison. This was true of Rosa Luxemburg and Karl Liebknecht in Germany; and the ten Germans who turned up in Switzerland included only one person – Julian Borchardt – who had voted against the financial credits requested by Wilhelm II's government. Without such credits it would have been impossible to fight the war.

Grimm suffered another shock when the invitees gathered in the little mountain village of Zimmerwald above Berne. He had been hoping for a comradely atmosphere but instead experienced the fractiousness of

Europe's socialist radicals. The Russians gave him most trouble. Lenin got up to his usual tricks by challenging the mandates of his factional adversaries. Grimm soon did not know whether he was coming or going.[2] If anyone could apply a brake to the Leninist mischief it was Trotsky. As a co-editor of *Nashe slovo*, he enjoyed prestige. Lenin thought the same and marked him down as an enemy capable of assembling opposition to Bolshevik scheming. He told Grigori Zinoviev, his closest Bolshevik associate at that time, to minimize any concessions to him in their negotiations.[3] Lenin and Zinoviev intended to make the conference as exclusive as possible; their preference was to have dealings only with those anti-war campaigners who were aiming unequivocally at a revolutionary seizure of power. Trotsky shared the goal of violent revolution with the Bolsheviks but did not want to see the Conference wrecked before it even started. Somehow a coalition of Europe's anti-war socialists had to be agreed, and Lenin's divisiveness needed to be curtailed.

Trotsky was to offer a memorable portrait of the opening day of the Conference on 5 September 1915:

The delegates packed themselves into four stage-coaches and set off up the mountains. Passers-by looked at the unusual procession with curiosity. The delegates themselves joked that half a century after the founding of the First International it was still possible to seat all the internationalists in four charabancs. But there lay no scepticism in these jokes. The historical thread often breaks. In that eventuality a new knot needs to be tied. This is also what we were doing in Zimmerwald.[4]

Thus he claimed that a small gathering in Switzerland was restoring the faith and practices founded by Marx and Engels.

Although he later despised Robert Grimm for his hostility to the October Revolution, at the time he was grateful and respectful towards him. Without Grimm, there would have been no conference – and certainly not one which was attended by socialists from countries fighting on both sides in the Great War. The Russian Social-Democratic Workers' Party could not have arranged it for the simple reason that its anti-war leaders could hardly bear to be in the same room together, far less to draw the leaderships of Europe's radical socialist groups into negotiations. The Zimmerwald Conference participants were a diverse bunch. Most of them were true to the traditions of the Second International and its condemnation of militarism. Some were out-and-out pacifists while others would simply have withheld support for any imaginable war without being anti-war in principle. This could never be said of Trotsky and his Marxist compatriots. They refused to rule out the spreading of socialism by force of arms. They did not declare this in 1915 mainly because their immediate aim was to shatter the capacity of the Central Powers and the Allies to go on fighting.

As the Conference got under way Lenin formed a cabal with Karl Radek. The two of them, along with their adherents, constituted the core of what became known as the Zimmerwald Left. They tried to bully the Conference to toughen its stance on class struggle, violent seizure of power and socialist revolution. A letter came through from the imprisoned Karl Liebknecht urging the need for civil war in the belligerent countries. This raised the spirits of Lenin and Radek. Even if they were not going to dominate the Conference they could realistically hope to push it in the direction of radicalism. The Left produced its own manifesto to counter Grimm's effort to bring all groups together at the Conference.[5] Trotsky supported the contents in most respects and spoke regularly with Radek, who was among his frequent wartime correspondents.[6] (They were almost friends, insofar as either man had any.) He never pretended to be a pacifist even though many people, impressed by his tirades against the war, assumed that he was one. Trotsky, like Lenin and Radek, preached that socialist revolution was the only route to a durable peace, but it was his arguments for peace that tended to capture attention.

Radek failed to persuade Trotsky to co-sign the Left's manifesto and other documents. He was unwilling to draw nearer to Lenin and spoke to others at the Conference about producing their own left-wing manifesto. Zinoviev at this point undertook a rare act of defiance of Lenin, making personal overtures to Trotsky and expressing delight that he was taking 'a small step' towards the Left.[7] It all came to nothing, so Lenin was relieved of the need to sit cosily alongside his old opponent. Trotsky and Lenin resumed their sparring with each other. Lenin criticized Trotsky's dalliance with the peace movement in Europe. Trotsky for his part insisted that the Left at Zimmerwald was stupid in failing to appeal to people who were campaigning against the war but were not Marxists; he also criticized the Bolsheviks for baiting the absent Kautsky. Trotsky thought Lenin obsessive. The time had come to forget Kautsky's initial failure to denounce his own party for voting war credits to the German government. Things had changed. Kautsky was now a vocal critic of the war and of his party's leadership (and in 1917 he was to establish the Independent Social-Democratic Party of Germany). Trotsky and the Dutch radical socialist Henrietta Roland-Holst ended up drafting their own manifesto.[8]

Grimm and his allies anyway easily won a majority for their manifesto. But Lenin, Radek and Trotsky came together to make them sharpen their wording in order to gain general acceptance. The result was that the official manifesto called bluntly for 'uncompromising proletarian class struggle'.[9]

The Zimmerwald Conference ended on 8 September and Trotsky returned to Paris with an enhanced reputation on the far political left even if few people warmed to him on the personal level. He had not spent his entire time ganging up on the rest of the Conference. He had tried to rally as many sympathizers as possible for basic objectives. He had avoided rancour. Any comparison with Lenin at the time would have been to Trotsky's advantage. If a revolution were to break out in Europe there would surely be a need for anti-war radical socialists to stick together – and Lenin's compulsiveness would do only harm. Trotsky had proved his practical potential for leadership in 1905. He could repeat that performance in Russia and, to some extent, even in France. He would bide his time. Detached from factional allegiance, he was free to look for his opportunities with unusual calmness and confidence. He could not care less that he was not elected to the International Socialist Commission created at Zimmerwald. In fact no leader from the Russian Social-Democratic Workers' Party joined it. There would have been endless bickering if one Russian faction was given priority over others, and it was thought better to leave all of them out of the arrangement. The International Socialist Commission anyway had no authority to give orders.

The Zimmerwald Conference was banned from being reported in France. But the censorship office concentrated on the French-language press. To the Okhrana's dismay Trotsky's reports on the proceedings in *Nashe slovo* slipped through the net, and Russian police agents reported to Petrograd that Trotsky was running a 'Germanophile campaign' – in their eyes anyone who criticized Nicholas II and his armies was doing the Central Powers a favour.[10] (Petrograd was the new name adopted for the Russian capital because St Petersburg was thought to sound too Teutonic during a war with Germany.) Word got around among the émigré revolutionary community about what had gone on in Switzerland. The Zimmerwaldists, as the attenders of the Conference called themselves, departed with renewed hope that cracks were about to appear in the popularity of the war in the warring states.

For most socialists it was inconceivable that the old world would emerge unchanged from the Great War. Havoc and misery were only to be expected. What was unusual was the scale of ambition of the belligerent powers. The Central Powers were reviled by the Allies as applying colonial-style methods to the countries they overran. Atrocities were carried out in Belgium. The Allies themselves came in for criticism in Germany and Austria. Hatred of German and Austrian pretensions was such that London and Paris were willing to enhance the authority of the Russian Empire – that bastion of political reaction – in the eastern half of the continent. War aims were steadily revised as the fighting continued. The entire world was going to be affected by the outcome. If Germany lost, it would pay a heavy price. Wilhelm II and his 'Hunnish' ministers were regularly demonized in the Allied press. The German state would almost certainly lose possessions at home and in its external empire. There was also no love for Austria-Hungary, and planning was under way for the dismantlement of the Habsburg domains into separate nation-states. But what if the Allies were trounced by the Central Powers? It was hard to imagine that the British, French or Dutch colonies would remain un-touched. Anti-war socialists took it for granted that a massive reorganiz-ation would be imposed by the victor powers. Annexations would occur; indemnities would be exacted.

Such outcomes were unlikely to be permanent. Lenin spoke about the inevitability of further world wars, but he was hardly the most popular figure among those radical socialists who yearned for peace; this was scarcely surprising since his slogan was for a 'European civil war' to follow the current 'imperialist war'.[11] To men like Trotsky and Martov, as well as to many Leninists, Lenin appeared to have lost touch with political reality. They saw no hope for Zimmerwaldism unless the working class in each belligerent country was offered a less cataclysmic prospect. They believed that the time was overdue to plan seriously for the kind of peace settlement that would stand a reasonable chance of enduring more than a year or two.

Trotsky elaborated his ideas quickly and, as was characteristic, tam-pered little with them subsequently. He hated to waste time on second thoughts; there had to be a big change in circumstances for him to reconsider. In early 1905 he had come forward with his idea for a workers' government. Once he had formulated and argued for it, he assumed he had done enough. This made for a contrast with the other leading Russian Marxist leaders, who were perpetually refining and adjusting their recom-mendations for policy. In the Great War it was the same thing. Trotsky swiftly announced his objectives. His new slogan was 'the United States of Europe'. He concentrated on the new features of the situation around the world. He had been impressed by the federal constitution of the USA and Switzerland. Socialists, he wrote, needed to learn from capitalist achievements. Hungary was a further source of problems as yet under-estimated. Italy and Bulgaria as well as Serbia and Hungary had ambitions of territorial expansion. The solution was the blending of socialism, peace and federation. Each country belonging to such a state would enjoy 'federative autonomy on democratic principles'.[12]

In particular, Trotsky proposed a federal union throughout the Balkans; he declared that Serbia would continue to disturb the rest of Europe if it retained its independence whereas a federation would enable the entire region to engage in rapid industrialization.[13] No solution, he claimed, was possible without socialist uprisings – and the United States of Europe would need to be a dictatorship of the proletariat. Lenin at first entertained the same idea but then dropped it, probably because he wanted to demarcate himself from Trotsky, Luxemburg and others on the left. For Trotsky, this was yet another sign that Lenin was an opportunist, a sectarian and an egomaniac lacking the perspective essential for a successful revolutionary leader.

Works streamed from Trotsky's pen as he strove to prove that capitalism was rotten to the core and inherently militarist. While nation-states covered the map of Europe there could be never be peace. Wars would recur from one end of the continent to the other.[14] Armies were fighting for their nations to acquire capitalist control of empires. Official talk of honour and freedom was mere rhetoric. Capitalism had reached a stage of development where no large territory in the world was immune to imperialist dominance. The war was about retaining or gaining colonial possessions and expanded markets. Trotsky did not work up a detailed economic argument based on empirical information; he left that kind of thing to Lenin, Radek, Luxemburg and Pëtr Maslov. Having set up his analytical framework, he moved on to writing daily commentaries. He continued to write for *Kievskaya mysl*. He had to be subtle in how he reported the grim effects of war on the Western Allies. One article dealt with the number of French women made widows since 1914. Trotsky suggested that the dark colours of mourning had become a fashion in Paris, replacing its colourful high couture.[15] He also described a gambling casino in Monaco. He had the money to travel around the country, and he did not spare his sarcasm when portraying decadence and profiteering among the French middle and upper classes.[16]

He also smuggled overtly political material into his published reports. Once, for instance, he drew a comparison between the French Socialist Party and the German Social-Democratic Party, noting that both had offered support to their government since the beginning of the war. In one respect their positions differed. No German social-democrat served in the war cabinet whereas the French socialists had supplied leading figures Jules Guesde, Marcel Sembat and Albert Thomas as ministers. Trotsky emphasized that the German Social-Democratic Party was not genuinely independent from Germany's ruling classes but had joined the 'imperialist' establishment. But he refused to be pessimistic. Without exaggerating the influence of the imprisoned Karl Liebknecht, he drew attention to the growing sympathy felt for him.[17] This was his way of bringing the news to his readers that socialists in western and central Europe were capable of challenging the pro-war consensus inside governments and among peoples. He also offered a paean to the memory of leaders of the Second International who had opposed militarism: Wilhelm Liebknecht (Karl's father), August Bebel, Jean Jaurès and Édouard Vaillant. Trotsky's implicit anti-war message was unmistakable.[18]

He felt he could not risk attending the second international conference of Europe's anti-war socialists in late April 1916. It was held, like the first at Zimmerwald, in the mountains above Berne. This time the venue was the village of Kienthal. Public criticism of newspapers like *Nashe slovo* was growing in Paris, and Trotsky might have been prevented from re-entering France after the proceedings.

He felt intensely frustrated at the time, but his decision to stay in France was to prove helpful in his later career. The Kienthal debates were still more rancorous than those at Zimmerwald. Again Lenin was the instigator of division. If Trotsky had attended, a clash between the two of them would have been certain. This would have been hard to brush under the carpet in Trotsky's memoirs. Instead he would be able to write: 'The disagreements of essentially secondary importance still separating me from Lenin at Zimmerwald dwindled into nothing in the next few months.'[19] By then an outright split had occurred in the German Social-Democratic Party. Karl Kautsky and Hugo Haase were campaigning against their party's official policy of support for the national war effort. Lenin, though, continued to denounce Kautsky for his failure to denounce the war at its start. He demanded unequivocal adherence to revolutionary objectives and Kautsky and Haase did not satisfy this requirement. Lenin and the Bolsheviks were out for a fight. Zinoviev started things up by attacking Martov and Axelrod for claiming to represent the Petrograd Mensheviks who were supporters of the Russian war effort. Angry exchanges followed. Lenin denounced 'bourgeois-pacifist' schemes to bring the war to an end, and everyone knew that Martov was included among his targets. The conference at Kienthal was a torment for Robert Grimm from beginning to end; and only the fact that Lenin and his ally Karl Radek remained in a minority saved the proceedings from being scuppered by the aggressive Left.[20]

The absent Trotsky in fact was no more eager than Lenin to condone Martov's behaviour. The Petrograd Mensheviks surely had no right to be represented at Kienthal, and the working relationship between Trotsky and Martov at *Nashe slovo* continued to deteriorate. The worst fears of Martov in 1914 were being confirmed. Trotsky may not have been a schismatic à la Lenin but the effect of his presence was to burden every editorial board meeting with fractious accusations.

Meanwhile Trotsky had no organizational links with the party in Russia – what he knew about Russian conditions was derived entirely from the European press. His articles continued to be carried by *Kievskaya mysl* and bankers' drafts reached him from Ukraine. He followed the military aspects of the Great War with less than complete attentiveness. Always in *Nashe slovo* he concentrated on the revolutionary prognosis. His journalism mentioned the deterioration of living and working conditions in France. It covered the conditions of the wounded. It skewered the pretensions of the Allied governments and did not fail to hold up Nicholas II's ministers to ridicule. Without ever saying so, Trotsky assumed that if the situation grew much worse there was bound to be a revolution. The sufferings of factory workers and army conscripts would surely become intolerable. The proletariat would rise against the bourgeoisie. He kept the faith, always emphasizing his sense that the situation was turning in a direction favourable to the advance of European socialism. Others on the radical left were demoralized or distracted. Even Lenin showed a drop in confidence as the war dragged on.[21] Trotsky was as steady as a rock. He had issued his prophecy of imminent revolutionary changes: it was now up to events to fulfil it – and he expected to play a part in the transformation.

Yet nobody knew quite what to make of him. As a party leader he had been an indefatigable unifier and it was only just before the Great War that he started to be choosy about who could belong to the Russian Social-Democratic Workers' Party. His wartime achievement was hardly gargantuan and was limited to his activities as a journalist. No one was predicting that this solitary revolutionary was about to make a name for himself as one of the most influential figures in twentieth-century world history.

# 16. ATLANTIC CROSSINGS

Trotsky had a surprising confidence in 'bourgeois' tolerance, assuming that he was safe in France so long as he stayed within the law. He would have been more worried if he had known how often the Russian government complained to the French about him and his friends at *Nashe slovo*. Russia's embassy in Paris called for the closure of the newspaper and for Trotsky's extradition. Russia was one of the Allies in the war against the Central Powers. France could not easily ignore the pleas from Petrograd if it wanted to conserve the joint military effort. The prolongation of hostilities chipped away at the French government's willingness to shelter revolutionaries actively undermining Russia's war effort.

On 15 September 1916 the order came out of the blue from Louis Malvy at the French Ministry of the Interior that *Nashe slovo* was to be suppressed. Next day Trotsky learned that he was to be deported.[1] Malvy, a member of the Radical Party, had until then declined to arrest those who campaigned against the war. The change of policy burned itself into Trotsky's memory. He was to follow the fortunes of his tormentors over the next few years, noting with satisfaction that Prime Minister Georges Clemenceau soon rid himself of Malvy. In 1917 it was found that Malvy had been subsidizing a newspaper that received secret funding from the German government. Malvy was put on trial and banished from France in 1918 for five years: the man who had deported Trotsky was himself expelled. Then there was the Commissaire de Police who had supplied Malvy with reports on Russian revolutionaries resident in Paris. This was the wonderfully named Charles Adolphe Faux-Pas Bidet. He was to come into contact with Trotsky in 1918 when the roles were reversed. Trotsky by then was people's commissar for military affairs in the Soviet government and Faux-Pas Bidet was in Russia on a secret mission. Captured by Soviet security forces, Faux-Pas Bidet was brought before Trotsky to give an account of himself. Faux-Pas Bidet replied: 'It's the march of events!'[2]

Representations by influential French socialists delayed enforcement of the deportation order. Trotsky protested to Malvy but got nowhere. The anti-war militant Alphonse Merrheim helped by giving the floor to Trotsky at the Committee for the Resumption of International Relations. Trotsky made a fiery speech. He denounced a recent initiative by Camille Huysmans, Secretary of the International Socialist Bureau of the Second International, to organize a conference of socialists from the neutral countries in the war. Trotsky demanded the co-ordination of all socialist parties and groupings hostile to the fighting. The blandishments of 'bourgeois pacifism' should be spurned. Class struggle was essential. The resolutions of the Zimmerwald and Kienthal Conferences should be followed. A Third International had to be created.[3]

Trotsky never received an explanation for why he was being expelled but several accusations were in the air. He was said to be a Germanophile, and it was true that Russian mutineers in Marseilles had been caught with copies of *Nashe slovo*.[4] He was getting desperate. As a last resort he asked permission to move back to Switzerland, where he would be among Russian Marxists who had chosen to see out the war there. The authorities in Berne were less than happy about the potential complication of their relations with Russia and declined Trotsky's request. Malvy lost patience and took the decision to deport him to Spain. A pair of detectives turned up at his latest apartment on rue Oudry with orders for him to accompany them to the French border. He was to leave by train without wife and children. The two detectives avoided personal unpleasantness and chatted to Trotsky as they travelled. They acted surreptitiously and avoided alerting Spain's police; their assignment was to get him on to Spanish territory before returning to Paris.

Trotsky's temporary companions succeeded in their mission. They crossed the northern border between Irún and San Sebastián and left him to his fate. Trotsky hoped to elude surveillance by moving on to Madrid, but the police noticed his presence and he was ordered to leave the country forthwith. Trotsky was to recall this in florid language: 'The liberal Spanish government of citizen Romanones did not give me the time to study the language of Cervantes.'[5] He wrote back frantically to friends in Paris. He appealed to the Spanish authorities. He sought help from Switzerland. Nothing worked: Spain did not want him any more than France did. The authorities considered putting him on a boat to Cuba. This was not to his liking because residence on a Caribbean island would slow down his communications. If he could not find a place in Europe, his next preference was to go to the United States, and his luck changed for the better when he discovered that no objection existed to his landing in New York. Natalya and the boys, however, were still in Paris. His money too was there, and the Spanish police insisted on moving him down south to Cádiz far away from the capital. Trotsky reported the situation to his comrades in Paris and a plan was made for him to meet up with the rest of his family in Barcelona where they would take a passenger liner to the New World.

The Spanish steamship *Montserrat* left Barcelona on Christmas Day (according to the calendar of the Western Churches) 1916.[6] Trotsky claimed they travelled second class.[7] This was one of his silly fibs since he was on record as having occupied a cabin of the first class. The family had paid 1,700 pesetas for second-class tickets but when they turned up to board they discovered that all such berths were occupied, and they were given a first-class cabin at no extra charge.[8]

Trotsky thought it a superannuated hulk;[9] but at least he and his family had decent berths, and they did not mingle with passengers from the lowest decks. Despite being a revolutionary socialist and advocate of proletarian dictatorship, Trotsky felt no impulse to spend time talking to workers. The people the Trotskys met on their own deck were a motley group. Many simply wanted to leave a Europe torn apart by war and had interesting stories to tell. Several of them, including a 'mediocre chess-player' who claimed to be France's finest billiards player, were interested in Zimmerwald. Trotsky made an educated guess at the reason: he had joined a 'steamship of deserters'. He did not really take to them, scoffing that 'they loved to live by dint of their fatherland but not to die for it.' Another traveller was a Belgian who was writing a book on sugar production and thought the fighting might be brought to an end if only there was agreement to divide Belgium. Trotsky met only one person who appealed to him. This was a housemaid from Luxemburg, but he wrote nothing else about her, perhaps because she did not give rise to a mocking anecdote.[10] While noting that some of his fellow passengers were interested in the European anti-war socialist movement, he did not stoop to persuade them about his politics. Trotsky stayed the Olympian observer.

Cut off from the daily news, he spent time keeping up a diary. As the vessel edged its way down Spain's southern coast towards the Atlantic they pulled into Valencia and Málaga. They passed the mountainous outcrop of Gibraltar before stopping at Cádiz, and Trotsky was permitted to go ashore and revisit the city from which he had recently been removed. Then came the voyage across the ocean. The weather was unseasonably mild for the first week. The sun shone bright. Trotsky wrote further entries in the diary while Sergei and Lëva made friends with the Spanish sailors, who told them that they would soon get rid of the monarchy in Madrid.

Natalya was to recall that the men got over the linguistic barrier by drawing their fingers across their throats, and the boys understood.[11]

He arrived in New York to a hero's welcome among emigrant socialist sympathizers from the Russian Empire. He had kept in contact with Lev Deich throughout the war; his years of writing for *Novy mir* meant that he was a known figure on the political far left.[12] But first the family had to disembark. The passengers underwent their sanitary examination while still on board. Natalya was wearing a veil, and the medical officer told her to raise it and made a move to lift up her eyelids to see whether she had trachoma. Her steady dignity dissuaded him and the family was let off the ship without further ado.[13] Trotsky was besieged by journalists wishing to interview him: 'Never under the strictest interrogation by gendarmes did I sweat as now under the cross-fire of these professional specialists.'[14] The political leftists of New York fêted him everywhere. The one exception was a meeting in Cooper Union where the hall was only half full. The speakers spoke in diverse languages and the organizers did not know in detail about his standpoint on the war. But once Trotsky started his contribution no one was left in doubt that an orator of genius was on the platform. Listeners who did not share his opinion admired the brilliance of his performance.[15]

He had experienced nothing like this growing acclaim since 1905 in St Petersburg. *Forverts* ('Forward'), a Yiddish-language socialist newspaper, interviewed him and reported that 'comrade Trotsky will stay with us here for some time,' at least until the end of the war.[16] This newspaper sold 200,000 copies daily so Trotsky became a bigger figure than he had been in any country except his own, at least among emigrants from the Russian Empire. He wrote four articles for its editor. Defending himself against allegations of being an agent of the German government, he denied being pro-German. Trotsky called on workers in America – although, of course, it was only Jewish workers who read *Forverts* – to stand up for internationalist goals.

All went well until the US State Department announced a plot by the Germans to inveigle Mexico into fighting the Americans. Berlin promised, in return for Mexican collaboration, the restitution of New Mexico and large parts of California in the event of the Allies being defeated. *Forverts* and its editor Abraham Cahan adopted an American patriotic position, expressing abhorrence for the German official connivances. Trotsky objected to Cahan taking sides in an 'imperialist war'. He argued that it was no more acceptable for Russian-Jewish American socialists to side with President Woodrow Wilson's administration than it had been for

German social-democrats to vote war credits in 1914. Socialism was not socialism without the internationalist dimension; love of fatherland was a detestable emotion. The goal of socialists ought to be to struggle for revolutions that would relegate all wars to oblivion. Cahan, who was nearly thirty years Trotsky's senior and had once been a revolutionary in the Russian Empire, accepted no lectures from him. A blazing dispute ensued. Trotsky never wrote for *Forverts* again.[17] On a personal level he had trouble with his old friend from Nikolaev, Grisha Ziv, who was working as a doctor in New York. Meeting up with Ziv, Trotsky challenged him to a game of chess. Ziv won. Trotsky hated losing and refused to play him again; he always had to win regardless of the kind of contest.[18]

It was a different matter at *Novy mir*, where he had cultivated contacts since its creation in 1911.[19] His friend Lev Deich had once been its chief editor;[20] his former Paris associate Grigori Chudnovski was still working there. The Bolshevik Nikolai Bukharin was another frequent contributor. *Novy mir* was less sectarian than several Russian-language anti-war publications in Switzerland or France. It was a daily newspaper based at 77 St Mark's Place and had been established under the auspices of the Russian Socialist Publishing Society. It pages were dominated by the news from Russia. It advertised things Russian in New York from bank deposit schemes to a 'convicts' masquerade ball' organized by anarchist refugees from the Romanov monarchy. Though socialist in orientation, it was more like a normal popular newspaper than any Trotsky had written for except *Kievskaya mysl*: the difference was that he could freely visit the premises of *Novy mir* whereas he would have been arrested on sight in Kiev. Trotsky was once again in his element. It did not bother him that he was little known in the broader circles of American socialism. He anyway had scarcely any fluency in English. *Novy mir* offered him a platform to rail against the Great War among Russian, Jewish and German emigrants without being censored. At last he could be as controversial as he wished.

The title of his first article after arrival signalled his militancy: 'Long live the struggle!'[21] Naturally it was not long before a dispute arose. New Yorker Anna Ingerman had suggested that Red Cross doctors should be exempted from the prohibition on socialists taking part in the war. This fired up Trotsky, who declared that the Red Cross was a 'governmental militarist organization'.[22] He had lost any sense of proportion. The Red Cross saved countless hundreds of thousands of wounded soldiers and POWs from misery. They were the conscripts whom Trotsky was hoping to win over. The Russian garrisons in 1917 would have found him less appealing if they had known of his lack of humanity.

The Trotsky family enjoyed their American stay. Chudnovski found them an apartment in the Bronx.[23] While Trotsky worked at *Novy mir*, Natalya and the boys had time on their hands. They enjoyed themselves after the recent domestic disruptions. The boys were entranced by the Manhattan skyline and took to counting the number of storeys on sky-scrapers. Natalya sometimes had to insist that they desist from further 'verification' and come home with her. Some days the three of them went for a spin in a car. A certain Dr Mikhailovsky, presumably one of Trotsky's admirers or possibly a relative, supplied both vehicle and chauffeur. But Lëva and Sergei, having been brought up to treat people on an equal basis, could not work out why Mikhailovsky's man never joined them in the restaurant.[24] This was not the last occasion when Sergei was puzzled by his parents' enjoyment of a middle-class lifestyle.[25] The apartment, costing eighteen dollars a month, was comfortable. It had the latest American furnishings with its fridge, gas cooker and telephone. This was an improve-ment on Paris and Vienna where the family had been unable to phone their friends.[26]

Trotsky gave many public speeches, which helped to pay for his keep. The anarchist Emma Goldman saw him at a meeting and was impressed: 'After several rather dull speakers Trotsky was introduced. A man of medium height, with haggard cheeks, reddish hair, and straggling red beard stepped briskly forward. His speech, first in Russian and then in German, was powerful and electrifying.'[27] He did not confine himself to New York but travelled to Philadelphia and other cities in the American north-east.

His message to socialists in the US reproduced what he had said and written in Europe. The American political far left thirsted for up-to-date information, and Trotsky freely admitted that 'internationalists' were a minority in the European parties. But he insisted that Karl Liebknecht was not alone and that Europe's anti-war movement was gathering in strength. He welcomed the way Karl Kautsky, Hugo Haase and even the arch-revisionist Eduard Bernstein had turned against majority opinion in their parties. He predicted that the trend would intensify. He told his audience that he had witnessed 'the gang of robbers' who led the armies in the Balkan wars of 1912–13. He had entered the current war with the same opinions and had 'seen no ground for changing' them. But good was going to come out of the carnage: 'The future epoch will be an epoch of social revolution.' It was fatuous, he asserted, to think that there would be serious reforms if one side or another won the Great War. The only genuine solution was revolutionary transformation. Trotsky expressed total confidence that this was exactly what was about to happen.[28]

He said more about the war than about Russia; and like everybody else, he was taken aback by news of strikes and demonstrations in Petrograd in the last week of February 1917. Nicholas II knew that his authority had vanished as garrison soldiers joined the rebellious workers. He abdicated on 2 March. His intention was to hand over power to his haemophiliac son Alexei. When no one else would hear of this Nicholas tried to transfer the monarchy to his brother Mikhail. Trotsky and Natalya were as pleased as they had been in January 1905. Their boys too were joyous.[29] Russia yet again was entering a revolutionary phase, and Trotsky felt his predictions were being vindicated.

By then the socialist parties had recovered their confidence. Responding to popular pressure, they organized elections for a Petrograd Soviet of Workers' and Soldiers' Deputies. Liberals were active at the same time; their leaders in the Duma and other public agencies came together to form a Provisional Government. They chose Prince Georgi Lvov, who headed the Union of Zemstvos, as the new premier, but the dominant influence was exercised by the Kadets under Pavel Milyukov (who became Minister for Foreign Affairs). The cabinet promulgated universal civic freedoms. People were given the unencumbered right to think, speak and organize with complete freedom. Lvov and his ministers declared that patience was required in relation to other basic reforms, especially on the agrarian question, until a Constituent Assembly could be elected. They also committed themselves to a policy of national defence, disowning any expansionist ambition for the country. Reassuring messages were sent to London, Paris and Washington that the Russian war effort would at last be undertaken with the entire people behind it. Lvov's cabinet was operating under constraints. The Provisional Government was able to emerge only by permission of the Petrograd Soviet.

Trotsky daily scrutinized the dispatches from Russia at *Novy mir*'s offices. He grew agitated as it became clear that the Mensheviks and Socialist-Revolutionaries were willing to provide the Provisional Government with 'conditional support'. He wanted none of this. The duty of socialists was to oppose the war and struggle for a socialist revolution. Trotsky simultaneously campaigned against the growing movement in the United States to join the Allies against the Central Powers after the Germans had decided to direct their submarines against American shipping. The German plan was to stop supplies getting through to France and Britain. President Woodrow Wilson at the beginning of April secured sanction for entry into the war. A paroxysm of anger afflicted Trotsky. It was bad enough that the Russian Provisional Government was committing itself to fighting the Central Powers. Now the Americans were joining the Allies. The only bright spot in a dark sky, as Trotsky saw it, was the Provisional Government's announcement of a scheme to facilitate the return of all persons persecuted by the authorities before 1917. No conditions were attached to such applications and Trotsky was eager to take advantage of his opportunity.[30]

In a fiery article on 20 March Trotsky rejected the idea that the Provisional Government might save Russia from catastrophe. He pointed to the record of the new ministers. Alexander Guchkov, the Octobrist leader, had always been in favour of imperial expansion and was not going to change his mind as a minister. The Petrograd Soviet under the guidance of the Mensheviks and Socialist-Revolutionaries was wrong to support the government – and Soviet leaders such as Nikolai Chkheidze, whom once he had courted in the State Duma, represented only 'the opportunistic elements of social democracy'. Wars would be eliminated only when socialist revolutions occurred. If the Provisional Government was supplanted in Russia, the German proletariat would follow the example. The Hohenzollerns, the Imperial German dynasty, were right to fear the contagious effect of revolutionary disturbances in Petrograd. Russian workers would show the way. They would not succeed unless they could win the active sympathy of the 'peasant masses'. Trotsky threw up a new slogan: 'Landlord land, not Constantinople!' This was an attempt to expose the fact that the Russian Imperial government had expansionist war aims and wished to seize territory at the expense of the Ottomans. It was not his most vivid piece of propaganda and he quickly dropped it. But he abided by the fundamental idea that the peasants would come over to the political ultra-left if they were promised an end to the fighting on the eastern front (as the Central Powers and the Western Allies called it) and the expropriation of the landed gentry.[31]

Trotsky needed no time to work out his own policy as he had kept it intact since 1905. What was required in his opinion was a 'Revolutionary Workers' Republic'. His hopes were high: 'The Russian proletariat is now throwing a lighted firebrand into the gunpowder store [of social revolution]. To suppose that this brand won't cause an explosion is to flout the laws of historical logic and psychology.'[32]

He was frantic about getting back to Petrograd and secured the necessary documents from the Russian consulate. Then followed the farewell meetings. Until then he had observed some caution in what he said in public; but the night before departure he reportedly told a meeting at the Harlem River Park Casino: 'I want you people to organise and keep on organising until you are able to overthrow this damned, rotten, capitalistic government of this country.'[33] (This sounds like a paraphrase by an Anglophone journalist rather than Trotsky's original words in translation.) Trotsky and the family had been in America for less than three months. They boarded the SS *Kristianiafjord* of the Norwegian-America line on 27 March looking forward to the journey of their lives. Trotsky allegedly shrugged off a warning from the American columnist Frank Harris that he might fall into the hands of the British military when the vessel picked up additional passengers in Halifax, Nova Scotia.[34] Despite the pouring rain, 300 well-wishers saw them off. Flags and flowers were waved as Trotsky was lifted on to the shoulders of friends and carried aboard.[35] Petrograd was surely going to be the culmination of everything they had lived for. A handful of revolutionaries secured berths for the same trip. These included Trotsky's associate Grigori Chudnovski. Another passenger was Andrei Kalpashnikov, who may well have been sent by Allied agencies to keep an eye on Trotsky.[36]

All went well until the vessel anchored in Halifax to pick up additional passengers. As Trotsky had been warned, the Canadian authorities, unlike those in the United States, had long been alert to the danger posed by anti-war socialists. Telegrams passed between Ottawa and London. Once it was established that the notorious Trotsky was in port, an order was issued for his arrest. Trotsky protested loudly and refused to co-operate beyond proving his identity. But he could hardly deny that he had preached fire and brimstone against the Allied cause. He was not the only person pulled off the *Kristianiafjord*. The authorities did the same to seven other passengers suspected of anti-war zealotry. All strongly objected and had to be bodily removed by 'big strapping seamen'. Trotsky shouted and kicked the sailors in impotent fury.[37] He was then subjected to a strip search for the first time in his career of arrests. He hated being touched in this way and bore a grudge for the rest of his life. He and a small group were taken off to a prisoner-of-war camp nearly ninety miles away at Amherst while Natalya and the boys were housed in the Prince George Hotel.[38] Trotsky caused a nuisance, both for his captors and for imprisoned German officers, by conducting anti-war propaganda among the soldiers of the Central Powers.

After protests by the Provisional Government, which was under pressure from the Petrograd Soviet, Trotsky was released and allowed to board another ship, the *Helig Olaf*, to resume the journey with his family. Andrei Kalpashnikov, who had interpreted for the British, recalled the scene: 'As the boat moved away Trotsky shook his fist at the English officers and cursed England.'[39] While moaning about lost time and the lost steamship, he could not know that the *Kristianiafjord* was not the luckiest vessel on the Atlantic run: in June 1917, on its subsequent trip from New York, it was wrecked off Cape Race, Newfoundland as a result of a navigational error.[40]

The Canadian delay meant that Trotsky was coming back to a political situation which had undergone deep change since the fall of the Romanov monarchy. The Provisional Government's authority was weak. The police had fled. The garrison soldiers refused to obey cabinet decrees unless they had the sanction of soviets in Petrograd and the rest of the country. Mensheviks and Socialist-Revolutionaries had no desire to form a cabinet; their doctrines suggested that Russia remained at too rudimentary a stage of industrial and cultural development for it to be sensible to attempt to introduce socialism. They were also reluctant to take responsibility for the country's wartime difficulties. With some reluctance they allowed the Socialist-Revolutionary lawyer Alexander Kerenski to accept a ministerial portfolio. But their preferred strategy was to exert influence rather than to take power – and they insisted on policies of civil freedoms and national defence as the price for their support for the Provisional Government. Even the Bolsheviks were in disarray. While some of them were agitating for a socialist insurrection, the leading figures in their Central Committee, especially Lev Kamenev and Iosif Stalin, broadly shared the idea that 'conditional support' should be offered to the cabinet.

World politics too had changed since Trotsky had departed from New York. German submarines attacked American shipping in a desperate effort to blockade Britain and reduce it to military impotence. Generals Ludendorff and Hindenburg on the western front wanted to cut off Britain and France from supplies being sent from across the Atlantic. The United States declared war on Germany on 6 April, becoming an 'Associated Power' alongside the Allies. Trotsky had taken no part in the politics of the new Russia but he had an unquenchable self-confidence.

# 17. NEARLY A BOLSHEVIK

The last stage of the interrupted journey from New York took Trotsky along the same railway as the emigrants from central Europe had taken. British officials on joint patrol on the Swedish–Finnish border made no difficulty. Allowed on to the train at Tornio, he travelled south in exultant mood. Nothing could now stop him reaching Russia. Crossing the internal Russo-Finnish frontier at Beloostrov, he received a welcome from fellow Marxists Moisei Uritski and G. F. Fëdorov.[1] Uritski belonged to the Inter-districters, who disliked the factionalism of the Mensheviks and Bolsheviks and wanted to unify the Russian Social-Democratic Workers' Party on the basis of forming a socialist coalition government and ending the war; Fëdorov was a member of the Bolshevik Central Committee. No one came on behalf of the Mensheviks: this was an early sign of the turn being taken by politics in the capital. Trotsky arrived at the Finland Station on 4 May, two months after Nicholas II's abdication and a month later than Lenin. The Menshevik and Socialist-Revolutionary leaders of the Petrograd Soviet put on the usual ceremony of welcome. There was applause as Trotsky was carried shoulder-high from the platform. He was a revolutionary hero. He had led the capital's first Soviet a dozen years before. He had served time in prisons and in Siberia. His political writings had brought him fame. Nobody, regardless of party, could match his brilliance as an orator.

Bolsheviks had changed their strategy in the previous fortnight under pressure from Lenin. His *April Theses*, accepted at a factional conference, called for the replacement of the Provisional Government by a revolutionary socialist administration. Essentially Lenin had dropped the 'old Bolshevism' which expected a stage of capitalist development to follow the overthrow of the Romanov monarchy. Now, like Trotsky, the Bolsheviks stood for immediate socialist revolution. Fëdorov had been sent out to greet Trotsky at Beloostrov to explore whether he was amenable to some kind of political collaboration.

The warmth of the reception at the Finland Station hid continuing worries about Trotsky. Mensheviks and Socialist-Revolutionaries detested his revolutionary perspective, and Bolsheviks had yet to be convinced that he was a dependable ally.[2] Trotsky was usually careless about people's attitudes to him. Now he felt somewhat sensitive. He was on his own in Petrograd. His experience as a soviet leader in 1905 counted for little; he had to build a new reputation in an entirely different situation. The Mensheviks and the Bolsheviks were in a full flow of activity and had none of the diffidence they had shown twelve years previously. Politics had entered a phase of extraordinary complexity and Trotsky had yet to show he understood what was happening. This did not deter him. Despite remaining edgy about the Menshevik and Bolshevik factions, he looked at the situation in a positive mood. His emotional eruptions in Halifax had flowed from intense frustration at being prevented from entering the revolutionary whirlwind in Petrograd. He was thirty-eight years old and brimmed with energy and self-belief. He felt he was coming back to fulfil his destiny.

One of his actions in the early days after reaching Petrograd was to contact his brother-in-law Lev Kamenev and his sister Olga. Among his purposes was to find out what the Bolsheviks were doing. Through Kamenev he arranged to pay a visit to the *Pravda* newspaper offices.[3] In fact Trotsky did not confine himself to the Bolsheviks but spoke to all groups in the Russian Social-Democratic Workers' Party unconditionally opposed to the Great War. What is more, bad blood remained between him and the Bolsheviks, and it was far from obvious that Trotsky would ally himself with them.[4]

The Provisional Government was being reshaped after the tumult caused in late April when Pavel Milyukov, Minister for Foreign Affairs, was revealed as having assured the Allies that Russia stood by the expansionist war aims of Nicholas II. Street demonstrations organized by the Petrograd Soviet forced the resignation of Milyukov and Guchkov. Prince Lvov saw no end to the trouble unless the Mensheviks and Socialist-Revolutionaries agreed to join his cabinet. With many misgivings the Soviet leadership acceded. Trotsky had always been hostile to any deal with the liberals and continued to argue for a 'workers' government'. But how was this achievable after the uprising against the Romanov monarchy had failed to put such an administration in power? What factions and groups were worth working with? And what were the best slogans for a campaign against the Lvov cabinet?[5] These were questions which the Bolsheviks had resolved at the conference they had held that had ended a week earlier with a resounding victory for Lenin's *April Theses*. Bolsheviks, despite being a minority in the soviets, were determined to increase their influence with workers, peasants and soldiers as the Provisional Government's difficulties grew. They declared that capitalism doomed Russia to economic and social catastrophe and to a prolonged military bloodbath. The country needed a workers' government.

Trotsky had been of this opinion long before Lenin performed his ideological contortions to justify calling for a socialist revolution. Lenin pretended that a full bourgeois-democratic revolution had already taken place in March. This was a trick for maintaining that he was still sticking to a two-stage revolutionary strategy.[6] He avoided mentioning that he had previously contended that a bourgeois-democratic revolution was possible only if an all-party socialist dictatorship took power and a fundamental agrarian reform was implemented. The nearest he came to admitting that he had changed his mind came with his call for the 'old Bolshevism' to be abandoned. The alternative was to admit to having been wrong: this was not something Lenin ever liked doing. Trotsky did not crow despite years of having been ridiculed for advocating a 'workers' government' – the Bolsheviks had been among those describing him as a crackpot who failed to understand Marxism. Now, after Bolshevism had been redesigned, Lenin and his comrades were calling for the immediate establishment of a 'dictatorship of the proletariat'. Whereas the Bolshevik leadership had to spend time explaining its change of stance, Trotsky could step down from the train at the Finland Station and repeat ideas he had promulgated a dozen years before.

He was in time for the Petrograd Soviet's debate on the governmental pact between liberals and socialists. The scene was a bizarre one. The Soviet had peremptorily installed itself in the Smolny Institute, which had been a girls' secondary school until the February Revolution. Trotsky witnessed his former protégé Matvei Skobelev making the official case for coalition.[7] The Soviet leadership ignored Trotsky: it was all very well to show him respect at the Finland Station but it was a different matter to provide him with a platform for his disruptive political opinions at the Soviet. When word got around the audience that he was present, the shout went up for him to be given the chance to speak. A roar of approval followed as he took the stand. Predictably he opposed the plan for a partnership with the liberals, but he did not indulge in his usual sharpness of expression. He was still feeling his way along the lines of Petrograd politics. He was also nervous – not a condition that usually afflicted him on a public platform. Waving his hands about, he caused his shirt cuffs to protrude too far from the sleeves of his suit, and being a stickler about his appearance he looked uncomfortable with himself and his appearance.[8]

For several weeks he kept his options open, chatting with everyone who might help him build a base from which to campaign without compromising his ideas. In Petrograd he joined the Interdistricters, who were as eager for a rapid socialist revolution as he was. The Interdistricters welcomed Marxists who feared losing their autonomy of thought and action through a fusion with the Bolsheviks. They were not a tautly co-ordinated faction – and they scarcely bothered to spread their network outside Petrograd. In later years Trotsky was depicted as their leader.[9] In fact he was simply the most prominent among several influential figures, and the leadership was of a collective kind. No one dreamed of providing Trotsky with paramount authority.

Other leading anti-war Marxist former emigrants either joined the Interdistricters or else acted independently of any faction. Among them were several contributors to *Nashe slovo* in Paris: Moisei Uritski, Solomon Lozovski, Vladimir Antonov-Ovseenko, Dmitri Manuilski, Miron Vladimirov, Khristian Rakovski, Angelica Balabanova, Grigori Chudnovski, Anatoli Lunacharski, David Ryazanov and Mikhail Pokrovski. There was also his old friend Adolf Ioffe, released from Siberia after the February Revolution.[10] All these dynamic veterans were soon to be incorporated into Bolshevism's uppermost echelons.[11] By joining the Interdistricters Trotsky was reserving substantial freedom of speech and action for himself. At the same time he sought some co-operation with the Bolsheviks and Lenin hoped for the same with the Interdistricters. Lenin's desire was not unanimously shared by the Bolshevik Central Committee; but he persisted, and an appeal was made 'in the name of comrade Lenin and several Central Committee members'.[12] Trotsky played somewhat hard to get. When he spoke at their conference in May he insisted that Lenin should pay a price for any agreement to organizational fusion: 'Bolsheviks have deBolshevized – and I cannot call myself a Bolshevik . . . Recognition of Bolshevism can't be demanded of us . . . The old factional nomenclature is undesirable.'[13]

Trotsky wanted to form a party of all groups who sought the Provisional Government's overthrow and an immediate end to the war. He did not want to join the Bolsheviks. His idea was that the Bolsheviks, the Interdistricters and various 'national' organizations should come together in forming a new party on an equal basis – and he was still not averse to getting the Menshevik Internationalists to join the proposed Organizational Bureau.[14] Lenin was in no position to accept such terms since the Bolshevik Central Committee was jealous of its primacy in the campaign against the government. Trotsky and Lenin agreed to disagree for the moment while co-operating on a practical footing. Meanwhile Trotsky continued to look for opportunities to gain an influential editorial role. The obvious newspaper for him might have been the daily *Novaya zhizn* which criticized the compromises of the Mensheviks and Socialist-Revolutionaries without embracing Bolshevism. Yet knowledge of Trotsky's idiosyncratic strategy for revolution went before him. So too did the memory of his imperious nature. *Novaya zhizn* decided not to include him on its board.[15]

Trotsky was not the only returnee hoping to get a place on the newspaper. Lunacharski, ex-Bolshevik and now a fellow Interdistricter, arranged a meeting in late May to sort things out. Trotsky tried to charm at least one of the editors in advance.[16] The basic snag was political in nature. Trotsky and Lunacharski wanted a government to be formed exclusively from socialists; the editors rejected their case and had no intention of turning over their newspaper to them. There was a frank exchange of opinions. Trotsky was furious with Martov for refusing to break with the majority of the Mensheviks. Sukhanov remembered Trotsky concluding: 'Now I see that there's no longer anything left for me than to found a newspaper together with Lenin.'[17] Trotsky for a while made do with helping to edit *Vperëd* ('Forward') for the Interdistricters with Ioffe.[18] Financial weakness meant that its print run could never match the Bolsheviks' *Pravda* and even undermined the regularity of issues. Trotsky needed a reliable, large-scale outlet for his articles. The process of peace-making with the Bolsheviks continued. Trotsky by early June was telling Sukhanov: 'One must enter such parties and write in such publications where one can be oneself.'[19]

Against such a background it was essential to get the family settled. The Trotskys were staying with Yuri Larin and his family.[20] Larin had always been on the left of the Russian Social-Democratic Workers' Party and had vigorously taken part in its discussions before the Great War. Like Trotsky, he was edging towards Bolshevism. Lame in one leg and terribly short-sighted, he quickly rose to prominence as a Bolshevik writer. He was a better propagandist than a thinker, and his dreamy impracticality made him the last person likely to be appointed to a responsible practical post. Trotsky would subsequently share this verdict. But in mid-1917, newly arrived from across the Atlantic, he was pleased to be offered a room in the Larins' apartment. The situation was hardly ideal but they learned to cope.

Among the advantages of living in Petrograd was the opportunity to resume contact with Trotsky's two girls by Alexandra Bronstein. Zina was sixteen, Nina a year younger. Natalya knew Zina from Vienna; now she met Nina for the first time. Lëva and Sergei, aged eleven and twelve, were frequently abandoned by their parents, who were throwing themselves into political activity. The boys went round to Alexandra Bronstein's apartment and met up with the girls. Zina looked less tense than earlier and Lëva and Sergei adored her.[21] When summer arrived the Trotsky boys stayed in Terijoki on the Gulf of Finland, an old haunt of Trotsky and Natalya, to enjoy some seaside air.[22] There they mixed with Russian middle-class holidaymakers who relaxed as if they were in the Italian coastal towns or on the French Riviera and revolutionary Petrograd was thousands of miles away. The Trotskys took such a lifestyle as a natural feature of their existence. Terijoki had the additional advantage of being in Finland, which was practically ruling itself without regard for the Provisional Government. The parents were confident that their sons would come to no harm there, and Trotsky could get on with his political activity without distraction.

His impact on the politics of the political far left deepened as he spoke at scores of mass meetings. His reputation went before him. People turned out for the pleasure of hearing him. Sometimes the enthusiasm for him was so great that the only way he could leave the Cirque Moderne, the large theatre where many public meetings were held, was by being bodily passed over the heads of the crowd.[23] He did not prepare his speeches in detail: he had no time for that, and anyway he understood that his talent flourished when his words were not confined by a fixed script. Oratory had always fascinated Trotsky, as the letter to his first wife Alexandra in 1903 had indicated.[24] In 1908 he had referred to Jean Jaurès, the greatest speaker on the French political left, as a 'titan'. What impressed him was the ability of Jaurès, physically an unprepossessing man, to produce a captivating display of passion. Trotsky said Jaurès was 'an orator by grace of God'.[25] He was implying that truly great speakers attained their effect without necessarily knowing how they did it. Perhaps this was indeed the case with Jaurès and Trotsky: they left no sign of wondering how they performed what others called their magic. But they also learned by experience. Like the best teachers, they knew what worked and what did not.

Trotsky's habit was to write out a plan of the main points in sequence, marking up the places which he needed to stress.[26] He spoke grammatically. He had exceptional fluency; he was sardonic, persuasive and ebullient. His shock of auburn hair waved in the breeze. He never failed to look dapper in his three-piece suit.[27] With his pince-nez he was an immediately recognizable figure. He was taller than most people in the audience and moved lithely as he picked out the words and themes to stir them. He was fond of gesticulations – this was useful in a period when the loudspeakers delivered a less than perfect sound to a crowd in the open air; and when he wanted to emphasize a point he would fling forward his right arm and direct his forefinger at the audience.[28] He had no compunction about showering his listeners with references to Marx, to current Western politicians, to the in-jokes of Russian revolutionaries. He could convey his general drift with ease. He raced from meeting to meeting as if his life depended on it – and even if he had given the same speech as a few minutes previously he made it feel freshly improvised. His zealous commitment was unmistakable. He was evidently enjoying the new 'mass' politics of Russia.

It was his strategic ideas on politics that Trotsky most eagerly wanted to convey to his listeners and readers. He no longer urged the unification of all factions of the Russian Social-Democratic Workers' Party. For him, as for Lenin, Martov and the other Menshevik leftists were a lost cause. But at the same time he proudly promoted his theory of 'permanent revolution'. This had never been to Lenin's taste, if we disregard a few comments jotted down in 1905 which he kept to himself.[29] Even after the February Revolution he refused to state that Trotsky's scheme had been nearer to what was required than was his own. Trotsky did not argue the toss. Together with his friends he rejoiced that a 'proletarian state' was at last attainable. He felt that his time had come. The revolutionary atmosphere suited a man like Trotsky who would take any risk if he felt that opportunities existed for the advancement of the Marxist cause. Moisei Uritski exclaimed: 'Here's a great revolutionary who's arrived and one gets the feeling that Lenin, however clever he may be, is starting to fade next to the genius of Trotsky.'[30]

Lenin felt no worry about having personal rivals on the political far left. He needed and wanted active, talented associates such as Trotsky. He and Trotsky agreed on a broad agenda for revolution in Russia. The Provisional Government had to be done away with and a 'workers' government' instituted. The era of European socialist revolution had arrived. The Great War would be terminated only when the far leftists came to power and repudiated capitalism, imperialism, nationalism and militarism. There had to be immediate basic reform in Russia. The peasantry should take over the land of the Imperial family, the state and the Orthodox Church. Workers should control the factories. Trotsky would have shared a party with Martov if only Martov had agreed to break with those

Mensheviks who backed the war effort. He parleyed hard along these lines. Martov, though, would not budge and persisted in his opinion that schism inside Menshevism would be a disaster for the socialist movement in Russia.[31] Trotsky was different: he found he liked talking with the Bolsheviks and appearing on platforms with them. The residue of past disagreements was being put aside. Lenin and Zinoviev showed their earnestness by attending the Conference of Interdistricters in late May. Trotsky did not need to make overtures. He could see that the Bolsheviks were no longer behaving like intolerant sectarians and could be a decisive instrument for bringing about the long-predicted 'transition to socialism'. He hoped to join their party and enter its leading cadre.

The whole situation on the anti-war political left was changing rapidly. Bolsheviks and Mensheviks were at last splitting fully into separate parties. Outside the capital a movement for the unification of the Russian Social-Democratic Workers' Party continued, but most local committees had undergone schism by late summer. The Bolshevik party in 1917 was anyway an amalgam of Bolshevisms. Some Bolsheviks flatly rejected Lenin's overtures – Alexander Bogdanov was an outstanding example. He and the writer Maxim Gorki regarded Lenin as a demagogue and misanthrope. But other veterans put aside their past disagreements. Among them was Lunacharski. Bolshevism after the February Revolution drew its analyses and projections into a tighter knot than previously. Party militants sought the overthrow of the Provisional Government and the end of the Great War. All spoke approvingly of the power of the masses. There was agreement that workers and peasants should be encouraged to remake life as they wanted. Factories, offices and farms ought to be reorganized. Differences remained among Bolsheviks – and they were about to be brought to the surface the moment the party seized power. But between February and October the disputes were containable.

Not that Lenin and Trotsky lacked points of difference. Lenin was open to the idea that the Bolsheviks might seize power alone whereas Trotsky strongly desired the next revolution to happen through a combination of groupings on the political far left.[32] There was another difference. Lenin did not wish power to pass to the soviets so long as the Mensheviks and Socialist-Revolutionaries remained in control; Trotsky urged that power should be grabbed from the Provisional Government regardless of who might be controlling the soviets.[33]

Lenin used various slogans. In broad terms he demanded a 'proletarian dictatorship', which was congruent with Trotsky's terminology. Sometimes, though, he wrote about a dictatorship of the proletariat and the poor peasantry – and Trotsky never used such a formula. The two of them were not eager to argue it out: the discrepancies were of no moment to them in the light of their common determination to eject the Provisional Government and install a revolutionary administration. Trotsky's followers later claimed that Lenin alone had to rethink his strategic perspective in 1917.[34] This was misleading. Trotsky had prophesied a revolution led by the industrial workers. What he found in Russia was causing him to modify his analysis. The fate of any government in Petrograd in 1917 depended on how well it was supported by soldiers – and no movement for a seizure of power would be realistic without strong support in the capital's garrisons. By far the largest proportion of men under arms was constituted by peasants. Trotsky saw this and adjusted his strategy so as to include the peasantry as a more decisive factor in his planning. This was a process which brought him closer to Lenin. Like Lenin, he declined to explain his fresh thinking at the time.[35]

The need for a strategic shift, he contended some months later in *From October to Brest-Litovsk*, resulted from the situation provoked by war whereas his previous ideas had been premised upon peacetime conditions.[36] Possibly he would have written more on the topic if he had not been so busy; but at the time he had achieved his main purpose which was to emphasize the broad social support that had enabled the seizure of power.[37] He had never been busier. His life – and Natalya's – was given over to a ceaseless round of public speeches, committee meetings and political negotiations. What dominated his mind was the idea that the Provisional Government had to be overthrown in favour of a revolutionary administration. Fundamental social and economic reform would then be implemented. The European war would be brought to an end. Revolution in Russia would be followed by the overturning of the ruling classes throughout Europe. Failure to act would be a disaster. The counter-revolutionary elements in the former Russian Empire were waiting for their opportunity to strike.

# 18. THREATS AND PROMISES

The Provisional Government's difficulties did not end in May 1917 when Mensheviks and Socialist-Revolutionaries joined it as ministers. Both these parties had their own leftist factions which thought that excessive concessions were still being made to the Kadets, and they campaigned in the soviets for greater radicalism to be shown in external and internal policy. The new socialist ministers resented such criticism. Irakli Tsereteli, a Menshevik, worked hard at arranging in neutral Sweden a conference of socialists from all combatant countries as a means of pressurizing governments to put an end to the war. His party comrade Matvei Skobelev issued regulations enhancing the welfare of the industrial workforce and expanding state regulation of industry.[1] Viktor Chernov, the Socialist-Revolutionary leader and Minister of Agriculture, empowered locally elected committees to transfer uncultivated land to the peasantry.[2] The Kadets found all this exasperating. To them it seemed that Mensheviks and Socialist-Revolutionaries had thrown aside the spirit of compromise needed for a true coalition. The disintegration of the cabinet quickened.

Trotsky clarified his grounds for optimism to Tsereteli: 'When a counter-revolutionary general tries to put a noose round the neck of the Revolution the Kadets will soap the rope for him whereas the Kronstadt sailors will turn up to fight and die . . .'[3] Kronstadt was the island off the coast near Petrograd holding a large naval garrison. Its sailors were well known for distrusting the Provisional Government. Trotsky expressed admiration for them whereas he continually accused the Menshevik and Socialist-Revolutionary leaders of malfeasance. His speeches claimed honesty for the political far left alone, and his personal image down all the decades has suggested that he was indeed a straightforward politician. This is an exaggeration. Trotsky knew how to cut up rough and play the demagogue. He would say almost anything to win workers and soldiers in Petrograd over to the party's side. He feigned outrage when a proposal came forward to bail out the city budget by asking soldiers, who had enjoyed exemptions on public transport, to pay five kopeks for a tram ride. Even his comrade Adolf Ioffe consented to the proposed charge. Workers at that time were having to pay twenty kopeks. It made no great sense to provide the garrison troops, who did no fighting and wanted to avoid being sent to the eastern front, with a privilege denied to the capital's other inhabitants.[4]

Trotsky had never been averse to using demagogic tactics.[5] Now he and his friends on the political far left had the goal of revolution in sight and believed that any methods were justifiable in pursuing it. The Provisional Government in his eyes was guilty of deceiving 'the masses' in the interests of its capitalist masters. His own subterfuges were small by comparison – and they were designed to create a world of justice and honesty for the working class once the Lvov cabinet had been removed from power and 'proletarian autonomy' had been established.

In his speeches and articles he paid little attention to such developments. This was not because he ceased to be a frequent orator or prolific journalist: he had never been busier at both activities.[6] Nor was it only because he believed that the socialist ministers were sponsoring palliatives instead of attempting the necessary general cure for the country's ills. The reason for Trotsky's neglect was his preoccupation with another aspect of the Provisional Government's activity. In June 1917 Alexander Kerenski, a leading Socialist-Revolutionary as well as the Minister for Military Affairs, ordered a resumption of the offensive on the eastern front. For his enemies like Trotsky and Lenin this was proof that the official desire to annex territory had not faded with the resignation of Milyukov and Guchkov. Trotsky prepared a declaration denouncing Kerenski's preparations and this was read out by the Bolshevik caucus at the First Congress of Soviets.[7] The rapprochement of Trotsky and Lenin was solidifying by the day.

Anti-governmental feelings were on the increase among workers, soldiers and sailors. A political demonstration was called by the Bolsheviks in Petrograd for mid-June to protest against the 'capitalist ministers'. The Mensheviks and Socialist-Revolutionaries in the All-Russia Central Executive Committee of the Congress of Soviets outflanked them by banning the demonstration and organizing one of their own. The Bolshevik Central Committee backed down. But Lenin did not despair of destabilizing the Provisional Government. Discussions were started among Bolsheviks to hold yet another demonstration through the capital's streets. Trotsky and the Interdistricters held a simultaneous debate. Close liaison between the two organizations was maintained and the decision was taken to go ahead with an armed demonstration. Although the purpose was not specified, it would not have been an unpleasant surprise for Trotsky and Lenin if the demonstrators went further than simply marching along the Nevski Prospekt. The precedent of the February Revolution was in everybody's mind. If enough workers and soldiers sympathized with the demonstration, the Provisional Government might fall. The sailors of Kronstadt were willing to cross to the mainland to take part. If disturbances occurred, then the Bolshevik party and its allies would improvise a suitable challenge to ministers. The slogan would be 'All Power to the Soviets!'[8]

Trotsky went around instilling enthusiasm for direct action. His printed articles did not spell out what he had in mind because he did not want to provide the Provisional Government with an excuse to take him into custody. When he got up on a platform it was a different matter. Addressing the Kronstadt naval garrison on Anchor Square, he urged the need for the removal of the Lvov cabinet and its Menshevik and Socialist-Revolutionary supporters. The regime he sought to establish would be dictatorial and violent: 'I tell you heads must roll, blood must flow . . . The strength of the French Revolution was in the machine that made the enemies of the people shorter by a head. This is a fine device. We must have it in every city.'[9] Trotsky stood forth as a Jacobin of his time. The Provisional Government saw how things might turn out and issued a prohibition of any such demonstration. At this the Bolshevik Central Committee panicked, worried that the party might be proscribed for subversive behaviour. Lenin, exhausted by his recent efforts, went off to the countryside with his wife Nadezhda and his sister Maria to recuperate. What he had not bargained for was the impatience of the demonstrators gathering in Petrograd. Militants among the workers and sailors continued with the plan for a march. They arrived at the Smolny Institute demanding some kind of sanction from the Bolshevik Central Committee for an armed demonstration.

Trotsky held his nerve while others were becoming flustered. Troops kept pouring on to the streets asking the Bolsheviks to lead them against the Provisional Government. The 1st Machine Gun Regiment was to the fore among the Petrograd garrisons. Sailors from the Kronstadt naval base joined them in the city. The leadership of the Bolshevik party's military organizations was gung-ho for an attempt at fomenting disorder and exploiting it to seize power. Political explosion seemed imminent. News of the forced retreat of the Russian regiments in Galicia widened the disgust felt for the Lvov cabinet. Calls for a new coalition government to be formed from all the socialist parties, including the Bolsheviks and

Interdistricters, were frequently made. The Provisional Government itself had internal problems. Its socialist ministers proposed to grant broad regional autonomy to Ukraine. Liberals regarded this as just the first step towards the break-up of the former Russian Empire. On 2 July they resigned collectively from the Provisional Government and Prince Lvov stood down as premier. Rule over Russia was collapsing into an abyss.[10] Outside the Tauride Palace, where the ministers had their offices, the crowds of protesting workers and soldiers increased in size. It was also there that the Central Executive Committee of the Congress of Soviets was based. Nobody in the ascendant Soviet leadership proved capable of restraining the mood of the gathering political demonstration.

Popular grievances were growing. Food supplies to the cities were dipping. Workers also worried that industrial enterprises were likely to close down, leaving them jobless and destitute. Inflation continued to rise and the incentive for peasants to bring their grain to market diminished. The war was going badly for the government. Garrison troops feared that they would soon be deployed to the carnage on the eastern front. The inclinations of millions of workers, soldiers and peasants turned towards favouring those socialist groups, especially the Bolsheviks, who urged the need for 'radical measures'. The Bolshevik party aimed at the transfer of factories to 'workers' control'. It planned to allow the peasantry to dispose of the lands of the monarchy, the Church and the landed gentry. It claimed to have ways of bringing the Great War to a swift end, demobilizing Russian armed forces and initiating 'European socialist revolution'. It promised that if it came to power it would offer the right of secession to all the peoples of the Russian Empire. It argued that German workers and soldiers would soon be accomplishing their own revolution. Bolsheviks displayed a highly charged confidence. They were sure that a wholly new era in the history of humankind was in the offing.

The Interdistricters met in conference on 2 July while the situation boiled up on the streets of the capital. Trotsky put forward a project similar to the ideas being worked up by Lenin. He concentrated on how to establish a dictatorship of the proletariat and obtain support widely in society. He bothered himself even less than Lenin with economic projects.[11] So much for Trotsky's contention that he was a 'scientific' revolutionary. In fact he was a chancer. This is not the same as saying he did not take ideas seriously. Revolutionary notions filled his mind. What was remarkable about him was that he fervently believed they ought to be tried out. And he judged the moment for experimentation had arrived.

Trotsky was working at fever pitch, treading a fine line between agitating the crowd into revolutionary action and demanding self-restraint when he judged the moment inappropriate for such action. Kronstadt sailors jostled Viktor Chernov, Minister of Agriculture and leader of the Party of Socialist-Revolutionaries, outside the Tauride Palace in Petrograd on 3 July. They hurled abuse at him for refusing to take power in the name of socialism. Their mood was lurching out of control and he was in danger of being lynched. Trotsky was passing by at the time. Immediately he intervened to save Chernov's life. He did not act out of comradely solidarity. His thinking was that Chernov's murder would serve to bring a wave of repression surging over the political forces hostile to the Provisional Government. Trotsky was the hero of the hour. He did not forget to retain the affections of the sailors: 'You have come here, you Red men of Kronstadt, as soon as you heard that danger was threatening the revolution! Yet again Kronstadt has shown itself as a vanguard fighter in the cause of the proletariat! Long live Red Kronstadt, pride and glory of the revolution!'[12] He would need the Kronstadters one day soon. But they had to wait until such a time as he and his comrades appointed.

The Bolsheviks and the Interdistricters had deliberately raised expectations among their supporters, and it was for this reason that the protesters had gathered in Petrograd. At first Trotsky, Lunacharski, Zinoviev and others were pleased about the turmoil. But they became aware that the Provisional Government, despite its difficulties, retained the capacity to quash the projected armed demonstration and had enough loyal regiments to realize its desires. It would have been suicidal for the Bolsheviks and Interdistricters to condone further action on the streets. Appeals were made by both sets of leaders for the crowd to disperse. The objective was fulfilled, but not before many demonstrators made clear their disappointment that the cabinet had not been overthrown. Ministers subsequently accused Lenin and Trotsky of conspiring to take power under the cover of a turbulent march on the Tauride Palace. Both the Bolsheviks and the Interdistricters were vilifying the Provisional Government in the most inflammatory language. They declared that Lvov and his colleagues were betraying the cause of the people and their revolution. What kind of peaceful protest was it when the organizers were asking the thousands of marchers to bring their weapons with them?

Lenin and Trotsky always publicly denied that they had plotted to overthrow the cabinet by violent means;[13] and Lenin was able to stress that he had been absent from Petrograd while the turmoil was brewing in the Russian capital. Trotsky, Lunacharski and Zinoviev could add that they had done more than any Menshevik or Socialist-Revolutionary to prevent the armed march from going ahead. Charge and counter-charge were laid at the time. The cabinet insisted that a *coup d'état* had been intended. The Ministry of Internal Affairs also released evidence from its enquiries into the funding of the Bolshevik party. The allegation was that Lenin and his comrades had received money – 'German gold' – from the Berlin government. Alexander Parvus was mentioned as an intermediary. The evidence was circumstantial but compelling – and this enabled the cabinet to assert that Lenin was not only a subversive but also a traitor. Lenin had broken off his holiday and returned to Petrograd. But on 6 July a warrant was issued for his arrest along with that of Zinoviev. For a few days they remained in hiding in the capital and then fled to Razliv, a village twenty miles to the north. Zinoviev decided to turn himself in to the authorities; Lenin chose to stay on the run and found himself a place of safety in the house of the Helsinki police chief.

There was no evidence, however, that a plan had been elaborated for an uprising – and when Lunacharski after 1917 blurted out that one had existed he was obliged by a furious Trotsky to deny having made such a statement.[14] Nevertheless Trotsky, behind the closed doors of a party gathering in 1920, was to admit that the Bolsheviks and Interdistricters had been using the trouble in Petrograd as a way of 'probing' the possibility of seizing power. Not for several decades, by when he was long dead, were his words allowed into print.[15] The likelihood is that the political far left had indeed been readying itself to exploit any opportunity that might arise. Lenin and Trotsky had no expertise in organizing insurrections, but since the turn of the century they had talked a lot about the need for them. Now they had the confidence in their capacity to improvise an appropriate means to channel the energies of 'the masses' as the Provisional Government's dilemmas were aggravated. A demonstration had brought down the Romanov monarchy. It could just as easily shake down the Lvov cabinet and brush aside the Mensheviks and Socialist-Revolutionaries. The Bolshevik leadership and its allies, including the Interdistricters, resolved to test whether the time had come for an attempt to overthrow the cabinet.

The period of political emergency became known as the July Days. It destroyed any lingering hope in Trotsky's mind that a Soviet government could be formed by the Mensheviks and Socialist-Revolutionaries. He was simultaneously appalled by Martov's refusal to break with the Menshevik party. Trotsky concluded that the political far left had to act as an independent force. He did not yet join the Bolshevik party. But he wrote an open letter on 10 July expressing his solidarity with Lenin. He suggested that if warrants had been issued for Lenin's arrest, then he too should be taken into custody; and he urged the government to do that very thing for the sake of consistency.[16] He was hoping to skew public discussion away from 'German gold' towards the question whether the Petrograd Bolsheviks and their associates had planned a *coup d'état*. He wanted a public trial such as he had undergone in 1906. He knew he could make a great impact again, and he calculated that he could take risks with his personal security: the Provisional Government and its supporters in the Soviet leadership were hardly of a mind to be brutal towards their enemies on the left. He spent a fortnight mocking the authorities. Alexander Kerenski frantically sought to assemble a cabinet. The Menshevik and Socialist-Revolutionary leaders refused point-blank to help him out; the Kadets stuck by their decision to abandon the coalition. The Bolsheviks in Petrograd, if not in the rest of the country, returned to clandestine activity for fear of further reprisals against them. Kerenski, after talking with the army high command, indicated a willingness to deploy force against the soviets. When he became premier on 8 July, he took action.

The 'grey greatcoats' – soldiers loyal to the Provisional Government – arrived at the Larin apartment on 23 July. It was the months of the 'white nights' in northern Russia when the sky darkened for only a short while. Minister of Justice A. S. Zarudny, who had been one of Trotsky's lawyers eleven years earlier, issued the order for his arrest. Natalya heard the men at the door. She touched Trotsky's shoulder and gasped: 'They've come!' Larin went to talk to them. At first they asked for Lunacharski, then for Trotsky. Larin would not let them in. He went to the phone and rang his contacts among the Mensheviks and Socialist-Revolutionaries in the Soviet leadership. No one answered the call. Trotsky's arrest followed and he was taken to the Kresty Prison (where he had last been incarcerated in 1905).[17] The charge against him was that he had abetted the violent challenge to the Provisional Government earlier in the month.[18]

A contrast has often been drawn between Trotsky's courage and Lenin's timidity. The danger to both men persisted as investigators continued their search for evidence of a German financial subsidy. In Trotsky's case, his past association with Parvus was well known and an attempt was being made to prove that money had passed between the two men. The consequences for Trotsky's children were unpleasant: 'What sort of a revolution was this, they asked their mother in reproach, if Papa is put in a concentration camp and then in a prison? Their mother agreed with them that this was not yet a real revolution. But bitter drops of scepticism crept into their souls.'[19] Trotsky was writing as if the Provisional Govern-

ment had initiated his incarceration. He was striving for literary pathos –
and he succeeded with most readers of his autobiography because he
withheld from them the information that he had urged the authorities
to take him into custody. Trotsky's boldness was unquestionable but not
his judgement. It is true that Kerenski would not have let him come
to physical harm, and undoubtedly Trotsky would have led the lawyers
a merry dance at any trial. But once inside prison he was vulnerable to
physical attack by groups of peoples with fewer scruples than the ministers
of the Provisional Government. He was taking a big risk.

On 26 July, three days after Trotsky's arrest, the Sixth Party Congress
opened secretly in Petrograd. Strictly speaking, it was a congress of
'internationalist' Marxists. But nobody at that time seriously expected
that Martov and the left wing of current Menshevism would break away
from the Menshevik faction and join the proceedings. This meant that
the Bolsheviks were the numerically predominant group at the Congress.
Essentially the Interdistricters had agreed to incorporation in the Bolshevik party, for by then there were hardly any joint organizations of
Bolsheviks and Mensheviks. The terms of admittance were generous to
the Interdistricters. The absent Trotsky as well as Moisei Uritski and
Grigori Sokolnikov were elected to the new Central Committee from their
group – and Adolf Ioffe was made a consultative member. Trotsky was
pleased that the political far left was coalescing at last. His prison writings
were automatically carried by *Pravda*. Conditions in gaol were laughably
lax as he and his fellow inmates conducted a vitriolic press campaign
against the Provisional Government. Lëva and Sergei, still perplexed by
events, came with their mother on regular visits. (There is a tone of
self-righteousness throughout Trotsky's memoirs: he refused to allow that
the Kerenski regime had reason to take measures against people who were
plotting its armed overthrow.)

These were worrying times for Natalya, who had already that year
had to console the boys when their father was locked up in a prisoner-of-
war camp in Halifax. She need not have been alarmed. The family, together
with the Ioffes, went off without Trotsky to Terijoki. The two sets of
children strolled out together and came across a couple of Kronstadt
sailors. Finding out who the youngsters belonged to, they tapped the
Trotsky boys on the shoulders and said: 'Don't get upset, lads, we'll soon
come and free your dad, with bayonets and with music.' The children
were tickled by the idea of liberation to the sound of a brass band.[20]

The Provisional Government was in no hurry to put Bolshevik leaders
on trial. Nor did the Ministry of Internal Affairs unduly exert itself to

discover Lenin's hiding place: this would not have been an impossible task since Nadezhda Krupskaya and others went frequently to Helsinki to pick up letters and articles from him and to pass on the news from Petrograd. Kerenski had barely taken over as premier before he was buffeted by a military threat from the political far right. His purpose had been to shore up his administration by getting the armed forces on the German front to send a contingent to suppress trouble from the Petrograd Soviet. His main commander Lavr Kornilov readily agreed and ordered troops to move on the capital by train on 27 August. The compact between Kerenski and Kornilov broke down before the plan could be carried out. Kornilov had been fêted by right-wing enemies of the Provisional Government when he came back from the eastern front; he was widely regarded as the 'strong man' needed to restore order throughout the country. Kerenski, afraid that Kornilov might organize a *coup d'état*, revoked the order for the army contingents to come to Petrograd. At this point Kornilov, deciding that Kerenski was unfit to govern, openly rebelled. Kerenski's situation was so perilous that he turned to socialist agitators, including Bolsheviks, to dissuade the contingents from obeying Kornilov. Their mission was successful. The rebellion collapsed in ignominy and Kornilov was arrested – and the Bolshevik party came back unhindered into public politics.

Abruptly on 2 September Trotsky was given his freedom, and walked out of Kresty Prison. From that day onwards he was the public face of Bolshevism until Lenin emerged from his places of hiding. Whenever the leading Bolsheviks appeared together on the party's behalf it was Trotsky everyone wanted to see and hear.[21] Of the Bolsheviks, neither Kamenev nor Zinoviev came near him in popular appeal. Lenin was secluded in Helsinki and could make no impact except through newspaper articles which were unread by most people. (*Pravda* had a print run of no more than 90,000 copies before the July Days.)[22]

The latest round of elections to the Petrograd Soviet on 1 September had given a majority to the Bolsheviks for the first time. Trotsky was an early beneficiary:

> After my release from the prison of the revolutionary democracy we settled in a small apartment, rented from the widow of a liberal journalist, in a big bourgeois house. Preparations for the October seizure of power were proceeding at full throttle. I became Chairman of the Petrograd Soviet. My name was vilified in every conceivable way. A wall of growing enmity and hatred surrounded us at home. Our kitchen maid, Anna Osipovna, was subject to attack by the

housewives when she appeared at the house committee for our bread. My son was verbally abused at school and called 'the chairman' like his father. When my wife returned from work at the Wood-Workers' Trade Union, the head janitor watched her go by with eyes full of hatred. It was torture to walk up the stairs. Our landlady kept asking us over the telephone whether her furniture was safe.[23]

But he ignored the pressure. He was leading the same organization that had raised him to prominence and influence in 1905. This year was still more propitious: he had already served his time in Kresty Prison before the attempted revolution. He aimed to take the Petrograd Soviet on to a seizure of power and the inception of a socialist order.

# 19. SEIZURE OF POWER

Trotsky's term in Kresty Prison had done him good by giving him a rest from the frenetic political activity that he had been engaged in. But he quickly used up the reserves of energy he had accumulated. Once again he operated at a frantic pace. At this point in his life he still allowed himself a cigarette before making big speeches: he needed the calming effect.[1] His base in September and October was the rooms which the Bolshevik party occupied in the Smolny Institute. The former girls' academy now had an armoured car parked outside its entrance.[2] The symbolism was appropriate. The Bolsheviks were expecting trouble from the Provisional Government and made arrangements for their defence. Soldiers patrolled the entire building.

The Bolshevik party intended the 'mass organizations' – soviets, factory-workshop committees and the other bodies elected by workers, peasants and soldiers – to constitute the core of state power. A revolutionary administration would rule. Lenin, though, looked to other organizations after the July Days when soviets under Menshevik and Socialist-Revolutionary leadership had sanctioned the Provisional Government's suppression of Bolsheviks; he refused to wait for the biggest soviets to acquire a Bolshevik majority. This provoked objections from those Bolsheviks who understood the appeal of 'soviet power' as a slogan. Popular opinion would not move against the soviets. The Bolshevik Central Committee, after a furious campaign by Lenin from Finland,[3] left open the decision about when and how to overturn the Provisional Government. Lenin remained the wild force inside Bolshevism. First he wanted an August Revolution, then he pressed for one in September. It never worried him that Kerenski retained the capacity to strike down any such insurrection in those months.

Trotsky had a better appreciation of the need for flexibility and cunning. At first he refrained from annoying the Mensheviks and Socialist-Revolutionaries unduly. As chairman of the Petrograd Soviet he proclaimed: 'We're all party people, and we've sometimes had to exchange fire. But we'll lead the work of the Petrograd Soviet in the spirit of complete freedom for all party caucuses, and the hand of the Presidium [of the Soviet] will never be the hand which suppresses the minority.'[4] It is hard to imagine Lenin offering similar blandishments to the enemies of Bolshevism. Yet Trotsky was no longer searching for a deal with the Martovites. Nikolai Sukhanov, a supporter of Martov, tried to find out for himself by approaching Trotsky in the Smolny Institute. Trotsky was politely non-committal. Sukhanov drew the obvious conclusion that the Bolshevik leadership refused to court the other parties on the political far left.[5]

Trotsky threw himself into action at the Bolshevik Central Committee, which met in the same building. He joined the *Pravda* editorial board along with fellow Interdistricters Lunacharski and Uritski.[6] Unlike most veteran Bolsheviks, he had not endured years of psychological pressure from Lenin. He had entered the party on his own terms and he performed at the Central Committee as if he had always belonged to it – and he secured the recruitment of Yuri Larin to Bolshevism, obtaining a party post for him as an editor and electoral campaigner.[7] If Trotsky noticed the reservations about him that lingered with leading Bolsheviks, he did not let on. He followed only one ordinance of self-denial by refraining from rubbing the nose of the Central Committee in the fact that Bolshevism had quietly adopted basic elements of the revolutionary strategy he had advocated since 1905. For the moment, at any rate, Bolsheviks were willing to give him the benefit of the doubt because they valued his multifaceted talent. Trotsky was supremely confident and fearless. At last he belonged to a party which stood a chance of realizing the objectives he had set for the Revolution. He had found an instrument for his political ambition and now came into his own as a tactician.

It was his name that tended to appear at the top of the list of people attending the Central Committee.[8] He was put on a working party which included Kamenev and Stalin to draft a declaration to be made on the party's behalf at the Democratic Conference which was being arranged by Kerenski for mid-September.[9] The Provisional Government, never having been elected, lacked political legitimacy. Kerenski's plan was to bring together all parties and organizations from the Bolsheviks on the far left through to the Mensheviks and Social-Revolutionaries on the right with a view to appointing a Provisional Council of the Republic (or Pre-Parliament) with powers to discuss official policies and consult with ministers. Somehow, he hoped, a constructive atmosphere in public life would emerge after the disturbances of the July Days and the Kornilov rebellion.

Trotsky wanted to attend the Democratic Conference only for as long as it took as to denounce Kerenski and proclaim the party's refusal to join the Pre-Parliament; Kamenev's preference was for the Bolsheviks to stay and act as the radical critical opposition at the Conference and in the Pre-Parliament. Kamenev convinced the Bolshevik leaders, who even gave consideration to asking the government to guarantee personal inviolability to Lenin so that he might head the Bolshevik delegation.[10] (Lenin, who had not been consulted, would hardly have agreed.) On 13 September the Central Committee commissioned Trotsky, Kamenev, Stalin, Milyutin and Alexei Rykov to finalize the declaration the party would make to the Democratic Conference. Lenin, still out of sight in Helsinki, warned against any compromise: 'History won't forgive us if we don't seize power now.' The Central Committee met on 15 September to examine Lenin's arguments which, apart from the bizarre claim that the Germans and the British were on the point of signing a separate peace, had not changed a lot since August. Lenin demanded an instant insurrection. The Central Committee disagreed and Kamenev called for the unconditional rejection of Lenin's proposal. This was going too far for the Central Committee majority; instead they simply resolved to prevent sudden disturbances in the garrisons and factories.[11]

Trotsky was helped by the pressure exerted by Lenin. The declaration to the Democratic Conference, read out by Trotsky, included a call for power to be transferred from the Provisional Government to the soviets.[12] But Kamenev's preference for Bolsheviks to sit in the Pre-Parliament prevailed in the Central Committee; and it was confirmed by the Bolshevik faction at the Democratic Conference on 21 September, but only by a vote of seventy-seven against fifty. Evidently a growing body of internal party opinion was moving towards support for an uprising.[13] Trotsky went on co-operating with the Central Committee majority and agreed to represent it in the Pre-Parliament.[14] By 5 October he had nudged the Central Committee towards withdrawing from its proceedings. A horrified Kamenev asked to step down as the party's representative in the Central Executive Committee of the Congress of Soviets.[15] Whereas Kamenev wanted to avoid a rupture with the other socialist parties, Trotsky believed they had betrayed socialism by colluding with the Provisional Government. Trotsky had won the struggle of the brothers-in-law.

He also had duties to fulfil for the Petrograd Soviet. On 9 October he attended to matters affecting soldiers in the capital. Mensheviks and Socialist-Revolutionaries wanted to form a body capable of assisting in the defence of the capital against the Germans. Trotsky replied that only peace on the eastern front could bring this about; he repeated his call for a transfer of power to the soviets. Both sides in the controversy agreed that the Petrograd Soviet needed a new means of co-ordinating activity among the garrison troops.[16]

Lenin remained in hiding but had moved from Helsinki to Petrograd some days earlier, and was determined to present his case to the Central Committee. Trotsky had overturned the policy of collaborating with the Pre-Parliament. Lenin aimed to finish the job. As the trend was for soviets in the provinces to acquire Bolshevik majorities he asked the party leadership: if not now, when? The Central Committee met on 10 October at no. 32 Karpovka and the discussions started in the early evening. Sukhanov, a left-wing Menshevik and the apartment's tenant, had not been told; his wife Galina Flaxerman was a Bolshevik and it was she who made the arrangements.[17] Lenin arrived in a wig – this was not out of vanity but for fear of detection by the security agencies. There were six items on the agenda but all of them were subordinate to one which was not included: the overthrow of the Provisional Government. Lenin harangued those who had been showing an 'indifference to the question of seizing power'. The party, he said, had decided on its answer in principle. Therefore only 'the technical side' of the matter called for proper discussion. The chance would be lost unless urgent action was taken. Lenin declared that the international situation favoured the Bolsheviks. He warned that all could be ruined if the Provisional Government's alleged plan to surrender Petrograd to the Germans was carried out.[18]

The vote, taken in the early hours of 11 October, went ten against two in Lenin's favour.[19] The timing and tactics of a future uprising were left open. The minutes did not record Trotsky's contributions and he was reticent about them in his memoirs. This was not his usual way. It is possible that he had reservations about Lenin, who spoke as if tactical subtleties were a waste of energy. But obviously he approved of the general decision. If this had not been the case his enemies in the 1920s would undoubtedly have reminded him. The two Central Committee members who unequivocally opposed Lenin were Kamenev and Zinoviev, who wrote to leading party bodies emphatically denying that the Bolsheviks had to seize power instantly or else lose all hope of overturning the capitalist order. They pointed out that although most workers and many soldiers in Russia supported the Bolsheviks this was not the same as having the endorsement of a majority of the entire people. They also disagreed that socialist revolution in Europe was truly imminent. They did not exclude the possibility of violent action against the Provisional Government but only in retaliation against an attack by Kerenski. For the moment they proposed adopting a 'defensive position'. Essentially they were accusing Lenin and Trotsky of unnecessary strategic pessimism.[20]

Trotsky, though, was less inflexible than Lenin and sought to build up a regional soviet network of support for a transfer of power at the forthcoming Second Congress of Soviets, initially scheduled to meet on 20 October; he ignored Lenin's demand for an immediate insurrection.[21] On 16 October the Petrograd Soviet established a Military-Revolutionary Committee to co-ordinate the garrisons.[22] Ostensibly no revolutionary initiative was intended and the body did not meet for four days. By then the Bolsheviks had seen how to exploit its existence and secure three representatives in the make-up of its Bureau; the two other members were from the left wing of the Socialist-Revolutionaries, including the Bureau's chairman Pavel Lazimir. Trotsky was pleased with this outcome and liaised closely with the Military-Revolutionary Committee, which took rooms on the Smolny Institute's second floor.[23] The Bolsheviks and their allies visited garrisons under cover of acting in the name of the Petrograd Soviet's plan to save the capital from the Germans. They secured the loyalty of most soldiers. Trotsky raced from regiment to regiment, stressing that only the Bolsheviks and their allies would save troops from being mobilized for the eastern front. He implored his audiences to give their allegiance, as in the early days of the February Revolution, to the Petrograd Soviet. He spoke as its chairman – and he insisted that if the soviets throughout the country held power all the suppurating sores of public life could be cured.

A further meeting of the Central Committee was held on 16 October to resolve contentious matters. Present were party leaders from the Petersburg Committee, the Military Organization, the Petrograd Soviet and various mass organizations.[24] Lenin reported on the previous Central Committee meeting and maintained that compromise with the Mensheviks and Socialist-Revolutionaries was no longer possible; he also proclaimed that revolution was imminent in Germany.[25] Reports by other participants revealed that the prospects for a successful seizure of power in Petrograd were far from good. Central Committee members Milyutin, Zinoviev and Kamenev spoke against Lenin.[26] If Trotsky offered proposals they again remained without mention in the minutes, and the fact that he made no reference to the meeting in his memoirs probably means that he was busy elsewhere, for there was plenty of business requiring his attention in the Petrograd Soviet and the Military-Revolutionary Committee. Lenin was the expert at handling the Bolshevik Central Committee. His force of persuasion was crucial in crushing the opposition led by

Zinoviev and Kamenev while Trotsky worked away at winning over the soldiers of the capital. This time the vote went overwhelmingly in Lenin's favour by nineteen to two with four abstentions.[27]

Lenin's enforced seclusion in the apartment of Bolshevik militant Maria Fofanova on Petrograd's outskirts meant that others took charge of the planning. Yakov Sverdlov, a recently promoted Bolshevik from the provinces, ran the Party Secretariat. Meanwhile Stalin edited *Pravda*. In this situation Trotsky assumed he had an open brief to do whatever he thought useful in the Petrograd Soviet. Co-ordination in the Central Committee was of a loose nature and its leading members made personal judgements on how to proceed. Kamenev felt so much out of joint with party policy that he announced his withdrawal from the Central Committee.[28] He and Zinoviev revealed in the *Novaya zhizn* newspaper that the Bolsheviks were intent on an armed insurrection. Lenin wrote to the Central Committee condemning them as 'strike-breakers'.[29]

Trotsky rebutted Kamenev and Zinoviev in a disingenuous speech to the Petrograd Soviet on 18 October:

> The Petrograd Soviet's decisions are published. The Soviet is an elected institution, every deputy is responsible to the workers and soldiers who have elected him. This revolutionary parliament . . . can have no decisions which are unknown to the workers. We are concealing nothing. I declare on behalf of the Soviet: we have not decided on any armed action.[30]

Thus he succeeded in evading answering questions about what had happened in the Bolshevik Central Committee. Kamenev, frightened by the idea of leaving the Bolsheviks, rose to confirm Trotsky's statement as true, and Zinoviev wrote an open letter in the same vein.[31] This triple solidarity disconcerted Lenin when he heard about it. Did it mean that the seizure of power would not take place? Trotsky arranged a clandestine visit to him and assured him that the insurrectionary objective remained intact. He himself was planning for the action to start hours before the forthcoming Second Congress of Soviets in Petrograd. This would lessen the appearance of an uprising conducted by and for a single party. Lenin's feelings were mollified. Even so, he demanded the expulsion of Zinoviev and Kamenev from the party.

Nerves were jangled at the Central Committee on 20 October. Zinoviev did not attend but Trotsky was present to witness the acceptance of Kamenev's resignation. Stalin thought Kamenev and Zinoviev were being treated harshly; and when his attitude to them in the party press came under criticism he too tried to resign. It had not helped that the interloper Trotsky was his chief opponent. Stalin's request was anyway rejected. Trotsky himself was on ebullient form and he and Ioffe successfully proposed that anyone wishing to join in the activity of the Military-Revolutionary Committee should feel free to do so.[32]

Trotsky was later to describe his tactical preferences as follows: 'The attacking side is almost always interested in seeming on the defensive. A revolutionary party is interested in legal coverings.'[33] This was exactly how he behaved in October 1917 when he led the rising against the Provisional Government. Like a general visiting his troops before a battle, he gave speeches here, there and everywhere in the capital:

> Individually Trotsky, breaking off from work in the revolutionary headquarters [in the Smolny Institute], flew from the Obukhov factory to the Pipe Factory, from the Putilov works to the Baltic works, from the Manège to the garrisons; and it seemed as if he talked simultaneously at all these places. Every Petersburg worker and soldier personally knew and heard him. His influence in those days, both among the masses and at headquarters, was predominant.[34]

He wrote, he orated, he discussed, he organized; he was the greatest all-round activist in revolutionary Russia. Unlike most other revolutionary leaders, he looked more like a runner than a weightlifter. There was a perpetual liveliness about him. When talking to people, he came across as having an artistic sensibility. People noticed how lean his hands were but there was nothing limp about his grip.[35] Trotsky dominated the preparations for armed insurrection.

The Provisional Government's patience was tested beyond endurance by the signs of Bolshevik intentions. On 23 October it ordered the closure of the party's newspapers and sent troops to enforce it. Trotsky issued counter-measures, pretending that he was only trying to defend the Petrograd Soviet. In fact his instructions were entirely offensive. Arrangements were pushed forward on 24 October. Military-Revolutionary Committee members went to garrisons seeking co-operation while Trotsky co-ordinated them from the Smolny Institute. There was a telephone booth in the adjacent room; calls were coming from every part of the city after an intermission earlier in the day when the authorities cut the line. Kamenev surprised him by surmounting his political objections to the insurrection and joining him.[36] Trotsky had been working at full pelt for a whole week. It was clear that the moment of decisive struggle was fast approaching. The capital rumbled with armed activity. Kerenski moved his troops to places of strategic importance. Trotsky and the Military-Revolutionary Committee reacted by dispatching troops to seize the post and telegraph offices, the central banks and telephone exchanges as well as the railway stations. The Tauride Palace fell into the hands of the insurgents.

In the night of 24–25 October Lenin threw caution to the wind and left Fofanova's apartment for the Smolny Institute where he thought he would find evidence of insufficient urgency. He need not have worried. The insurrection had gone too far forward to be halted, and the Provisional Government's efforts were entirely inadequate. It was also clear that the Bolsheviks would be the largest party at the opening of the Congress of Soviets. Lenin and Trotsky spent the day on 25 October making the last dispositions around the capital. The Winter Palace, which had become the seat of the Provisional Government, was stormed; Kerenski fled.

Trotsky declared to the Bolshevik delegation nominated for the Congress: 'If you refuse to waver, there will be no civil war, our enemies will capitulate at once and you will take the place that by right belongs to you!'[37] According to Ioffe's daughter, he 'could hardly remain on his feet through exhaustion'.[38] His nerves were frayed. He lay down on a sofa and, looking over at Kamenev, said: 'Give me a cigarette.' After a couple of puffs he mumbled something to himself and suddenly lost consciousness. It was another of his blackouts. When he came round, Kamenev was fussing over him: 'Perhaps we ought to get you some medicine?' Trotsky demurred: 'It would be a lot better to find some food.' He remembered that he had not eaten for more than twenty-four hours.[39] After snatching a quick meal he was back at work.

The Bolsheviks took the majority of seats on the Congress presidium. Trotsky taunted the Mensheviks and Socialist-Revolutionaries:

An uprising of the popular masses has no need of justification. What has taken place is an uprising and not a conspiracy. We tempered the steel of energy among the Petersburg workers and soldiers. We hammered the will of the masses in the direction of uprising and not conspiracy ... The popular masses moved under our banner and our uprising has won victory. And now the suggestion is being made to us: renounce your victory, make concessions, conclude an agreement ... No, an agreement is no good at this point. To those who have gone out of here and to those who put up proposals [for compromise] we have to say: you are pathetic individuals, you are bankrupts, your role is played out; go off to where you belong from now on, into the waste basket of history![40]

The tirade got under Martov's skin. Unable to contain his anger any longer, he shouted: 'In that case we are leaving!' Mensheviks and Socialist-Revolutionaries took their cue from him and joined the exodus. Trotsky did not disguise his delight.[41]

A government was formed with Lenin as its chairman. On Trotsky's suggestion it was called the Council of People's Commissars – or, using its Russian acronym, Sovnarkom. The entire system of power was to be based on the existing hierarchy of soviets. Decrees were quickly issued on peace, land and the press. Sovnarkom's writ did not as yet run outside the boundaries of Petrograd. The decrees were meant to gather popular support for the Bolsheviks and to encourage 'the masses' to turn the old social system upside down. Socialist revolution had begun in Russia. Lenin and Trotsky expected that the rest of Europe would follow suit. They had made the political gamble of their lives and were supremely confident that they would be confirmed as winners.

# 20. PEOPLE'S COMMISSAR

Most people in Russia and the rest of the world regarded the Bolshevik leadership as a gang of wild incompetents who could never sustain themselves in power. The Soviet rulers were impervious to this; but they knew they quickly had to prove themselves in government and some of the early appointments were more successful than others. Trotsky's aptitude made an immediate, deep impression. He drew upon the skills he had acquired in editing Marxist newspapers before 1917. He mastered a brief with exceptional ease and found it easy to expound it to others. The other side of the coin was his reluctance to seek or accept advice, and he made no attempt to disguise this. He made up his own mind and expected comrades simply to comply with his ideas. He got away with this so long as he and Lenin agreed. Lenin valued his decisiveness, which was a quality he also appreciated in Stalin, Sverdlov and Zinoviev. Despite his own compulsion to poke his nose into other people's business, Lenin recognized that he could not do everything by himself. He needed leaders around him who could impose themselves on difficult situations. Trotsky clearly had an explosive charge of energy which fitted Lenin's requirements to perfection.

After seizing power Lenin and Trotsky left no doubt about the kind of government that they wanted. They would associate only with socialists who supported the Provisional Government's overthrow. They therefore would have nothing to do with the Mensheviks. Martov, the leading exponent of left-wing Menshevism, had walked out of the Second Congress of Soviets. According to Lenin and Trotsky, he had excluded himself from consideration as a partner in government. The Socialist-Revolutionaries had behaved in much the same fashion except that their internal radical faction, known as the Left Socialist-Revolutionaries, had stayed in the Congress. Lenin and Trotsky were willing to countenance coalition only with those left-wing dissenters, and negotiations were initiated to get them to join Sovnarkom.

Lenin came to the Petersburg Party Committee on 1 November and commended Trotsky's campaign against any rapprochement with the

Mensheviks and Socialist-Revolutionaries: 'Trotsky understood this, and from that time there has been no better Bolshevik.'[1] Trotsky in turn defended Lenin against Lunacharski's charge of setting himself up to be dictator:

> No intermediate policy exists. There is no going back. We're introduc-
> ing the dictatorship of the proletariat. We'll force people to work.
> Why did sabotage exist under the terror of the past? Well, here we
> don't merely have terror but rather the organized violence of the
> workers as applied to the bourgeoisie . . . It is necessary to say clearly
> and sincerely to the workers that we are not in favour of coalition
> with the Mensheviks and others; that's not the nub of the matter.
> What counts is the programme. We have a coalition with the peas-
> ants, the workers and the soldiers who are fighting right now . . .
> [We'll] get nowhere if we just keep a few Bolsheviks [in the govern-
> ment]. We seized power and now we must also carry responsibility.[2]

Nobody, not even Lenin, described the communist project so starkly.

Lenin and Trotsky had become the Siamese twins of Russian politics, being joined at the hip in their determination to use ruthless measures including state terror against enemies. They won the day at the Petersburg Committee where there was no trace whatever of Trotsky's old willingness to coax and bargain with Mensheviks. The problem for Lenin and Trotsky was that they could not amass sufficient support in the Bolshevik Central Committee. The dominant opinion was that Bolsheviks in power should form an all-socialist coalition government. The return of Kamenev and Zinoviev to the Central Committee strengthened this tendency. Negoti-ations took place with the Mensheviks and Socialist-Revolutionaries. Lenin and Trotsky were hoist by their own petard: they had deliberately shrouded their intentions in mystery before overturning the Kerenski government and could hardly object if the majority of the Central Com-mittee followed the line of popular aspirations in seeking to set up a cabinet which brought all kinds of Russian socialism together. Power had been seized without a serious strategic discussion about who would be invited to wield it.

About one thing, though, everyone in the Central Committee agreed. This was that Kerenski should be prevented from resuming power. The former premier returned at the head of a Cossack force to the Pulkovo heights outside Petrograd, aiming to crush the Bolsheviks. Red Guard volunteers marched out to confront him. Garrison troops were mobilized. A brief military engagement followed which ended in Kerenski's defeat.

Meanwhile the railway strike called by Vikzhel – the railwaymen's union under Menshevik leadership – petered out almost before it started: the union leadership had overestimated the antagonism of railwaymen to the Soviet government. The Cossack force was routed. The bargaining hand of the Mensheviks and Socialist-Revolutionaries grew weaker. When they demanded the exclusion of Lenin and Trotsky from any coalition it was not difficult for the Bolshevik Central Committee to turn them down.

What shook Lenin was Trotsky's refusal to fill the post he wanted to assign to him. Trotsky desired to handle policy on the press; perhaps his years as a journalist had given him an inclination towards operating in this sector for Sovnarkom. This was indisputably a function of importance, and Lenin issued a decree introducing censorship on 26 October. But he declined to waste his most valuable comrade on such work.[3] He suggested at the Bolshevik Central Committee that Trotsky should head the entire government. Trotsky would have none of it:

> I sprang to my feet in protest – so unexpected and inappropriate did this proposal seem. 'Why ever not?' Lenin insisted. 'It was you who stood at the head of the Petrograd Soviet that seized the power.' I moved to reject his proposal without debating it. And this was what was done.[4]

He was never to explain his reasoning, and – to judge by his account – apparently he did not divulge it at the time. Perhaps he preferred to play a leading role without being the solitary leader. This was a psychological feature that was evident in later years. He may also have been making a political calculation; for when Lenin went on to ask him to take over the People's Commissariat of Internal Affairs, Trotsky again demurred and explained that it would be inappropriate for a Jew to take charge of the police in a society pervaded by anti-Semitism. If Jews were seen to be repressing Russians, a pogrom atmosphere might be provoked. Trotsky insisted that he was making a political and not a personal point.[5]

Instead he accepted the People's Commissariat for Foreign Affairs in Sovnarkom. Lenin had thought this would squander Trotsky's talent but was opposed by Sverdlov:

> 'Lev Davidovich should be pointed against Europe. Let him take charge of foreign affairs.' 'What foreign affairs are we now going to have?' exclaimed Lenin. But with heavy reluctance he agreed. With heavy reluctance I too agreed. Thus, on Sverdlov's initiative, I came to be the head of Soviet diplomacy for a quarter of a year.

> The Commissariat for Foreign Affairs meant freedom from departmental work for me. To comrades who offered their assistance, I almost invariably suggested that they look for a more congenial field for their energy. One of them later in his memoirs gave a fairly juicy report of a conversation he had with me soon after the Soviet government was formed. 'What diplomatic work is there going to be with us?' I said to him, according to his account. 'Look, I'll just issue a few revolutionary proclamations to [foreign] peoples and shut up shop.'[6]

Trotsky was as good as his word in quickly publishing the Allies' secret treaties of 1915 and calling upon workers around the world to rise up against their governments.

Russian anti-Semites had picked out Jews as a race without patriotic commitment to Russia. By becoming the foreign minister for a government more interested in spreading world revolution than in defending the country's interests Trotsky was conforming to a widespread stereotype of the 'Jewish problem'. The truth was that he would inevitably become a figure of hatred among ultra-nationalist political groups in Russia and abroad if he accepted any prominent job in the revolutionary administration. As things stood he had already become the most famous Jew on earth. America's Red Cross leader in Russia, Colonel Raymond Robins, put this with characteristic pungency. Talking to Robert Bruce Lockhart, head of the British diplomatic mission in Moscow, he described Trotsky as 'a four kind son of a bitch, but the greatest Jew since Christ'.[7] Trotsky, furthermore, was merely the most famous Jew in a Sovnarkom where Jews were present to a disproportionate degree. The same was true in the Bolshevik central party leadership. If Lenin were to have dispensed with the services of talented Jews, he could never have formed a cabinet.

The People's Commissariat for External Affairs was very different in its world view from other such ministries. Trotsky and other Bolsheviks focused their minds more on international relations than on foreign policy. Russia for them was just one country among the rest, and they did not intend to give it priority over the tasks of European socialist revolution. The great new era had chanced to start in Petrograd. The old ways of nationalism, imperialism and militarism were declared to be at an end. As if to confirm his perfunctory attitude to the Commissariat, Trotsky seldom worked in the building. It was important for him that he should have his base in the Smolny Institute where Lenin had his office. Routine work was done in the People's Commissariat for Foreign Affairs by

Trotsky's deputy, Dr Ivan Zalkind. This did not mean that the environment was a sleepy one. A lot of innovation in fact took place. The Commissariat created a Bureau of International Revolutionary Propaganda. The Bolsheviks also established a Department of the Press as well as a Department of Prisoners-of-War. Together the three agencies produced newspapers in German, Hungarian and Romanian with the intention of winning over soldiers in the armed forces to the revolutionary cause.[8]

An armistice was arranged on the eastern front. Fighting between Russia and the Central Powers ceased and Sovnarkom set about demobilizing its armed forces. Contact between Petrograd and the rest of the world weakened, but Trotsky assumed that news of the Bolshevik seizure of power would unavoidably be carried by the European press. His hope was that the Russian precedent – he did not call it a model – would be followed. He was waiting for central Europe to throw out its governments and expected the German proletariat to show its mettle. From such revolutions there surely would emerge a permanent peace as a new age dawned. His frustration was that he could not write for German or Austrian papers. The People's Commissar for Foreign Affairs did not stand idly by. He got his functionaries to prepare propaganda suitable for delivery to the regions around the front. Russian soldiers were encouraged to fraternize with troops of the Central Powers. Equipped with material in the languages of eastern Europe, they would be able to spread the communist message. Mutinies against the Hohenzollerns and the Habsburgs were to be fostered. It was hoped that trouble in the armed forces would leach into civilian society. The German high command tolerated this initiative for some weeks. Sovnarkom had desisted from military conflict, releasing Germany's resources to be concentrated on the western front.

Trotsky became ever more boisterous; but, enjoying his partnership with Lenin, he was deaf and blind to the resentments he was stirring in the party leadership. Kamenev, Stalin, Sverdlov and Zinoviev were esteemed by Lenin. Zinoviev had been accustomed to occupying a place as the unofficial deputy leader of the Bolshevik faction in emigration before 1917.[9] Now Lenin consulted Trotsky on every pressing matter of governance. Decrees and announcements had to be prepared at tremendous speed, and Lenin asked Trotsky to correct pieces he was about to publish. When Lenin moved into a larger suite of rooms in order to accommodate the activities of Sovnarkom, he bequeathed a small office to Trotsky; but this room was at the far end of the building from Lenin, so Trotsky was often seen striding down the corridor for consultations.

The Bolshevik elite did not yet recognize the need to make their working conditions as easy as possible; initially they did not even have the sense to employ professional typists.

Trotsky found greater time for his family despite his elevated position in government. The paradox is explained partly by topography. Members of the Soviet political leadership moved their close relatives into the Smolny Institute, where the upper storeys were turned into family apartments as soon as the Mensheviks and Socialist-Revolutionaries had vacated their offices. Bolshevik leaders were less difficult to guard if they stayed inside the building. All of them anyway had to keep in close, regular contact with each other as they consolidated their seizure of power. After his blackout on 25 October, Trotsky had much reason to avoid putting himself under strain by gallivanting about the city. On a normal day he returned home for lunch and took a nap. His adolescent daughters Zina and Nina, who lived with their mother Alexandra elsewhere in the city, became aware of the routine and burst into the apartment before food was served. They had missed their father's presence for most of their lives. Now at last they could be with him even if it meant restricting his time for a siesta. After lunch he would relax on a sofa, sitting the girls next to him and joking with them. If by chance he was not there, Zina and Nina played with their young stepbrothers.[10]

Trotsky had plenty to do beyond his none-too-heavy duties at the People's Commissariat for Foreign Affairs. At Sovnarkom he introduced measures for the establishment of revolutionary tribunals.[11] He was called upon to edit decrees.[12] He was put in charge of arrangements to bring the Russian calendar into line with the rest of the world.[13] He called for 'an energetic purge' of the entire old Military Ministry and for the Latvian Riflemen (who had proved themselves the most effective of the forces serving the communist cause) to be brought to Petrograd to enhance security; he identified other spurts of resistance in the capital and elsewhere.[14] He reported on counter-revolutionary moves in Orenburg.[15] He demanded sterner action against the 'bourgeois press'.[16] More generally he was prolific in suggesting initiatives for other People's Commissariats to act on.[17] His authority and status were not affected when, between mid-November and early December, the Left Socialist-Revolutionaries finally yielded to Bolshevik invitations to join them in a government coalition. The Bolsheviks had made and consolidated the October Revolution; they were of no mind to grant an equal number of places in Sovnarkom to the newcomers. But they welcomed them as comrades. Trotsky had always tried harder than Lenin to ensure that the seizure of power did not appear as a one-party affair, and the formation of a coalition was to his liking.

Public renown went to his head. He had never been an institutional loyalist. His zeal had always been directed at getting everybody ready for revolutionary action. The overturning of the Provisional Government meant infinitely more to him that any fussing about internal party sensitivities – and within a few years he would pay dearly for his insouciance about what the other leading Bolsheviks thought of him. This had always been his way. His inclination was to work out his policy and then impose it with as little delay as possible.

Along with his airs and graces went his alarming tendency to hobnob with foreigners who were no friends of socialism. He could not avoid the company of diplomats in Petrograd when fulfilling his duties in the People's Commissariat for Foreign Affairs. Despite their long-term aim of fomenting revolution throughout Europe, in the short term for pragmatic reasons the Bolsheviks had to steer clear of giving undue offence to the Allies. The geopolitics of Europe were in the balance. While seeking an end to the Great War, Sovnarkom did not wish to give further cause for Britain and France to carry out a military intervention in Russia; for in the winter of 1917–18 there was no telling who might win the war on the western front. As this danger grew Trotsky abandoned his casualness towards his duties in the People's Commissariat for Foreign Affairs. He also spoke regularly to the foreign press in Petrograd; no Bolshevik leader was readier to give interviews.[18] Most correspondents had been unacquainted with him before the October Revolution. All were impressed by the diligence, articulacy and confidence of the man. Standing forth as Sovnarkom's representative, he telegraphed the embassies of the fallen Provisional Government and told them either to support the Soviet 'peace policy' or leave their premises.[19]

Diplomats and journalists of the great powers queued to interview him in his office in the Smolny Institute. They also frequently received the benefit of his wisdom in the family apartment on the top floor – he had never needed an excuse to expatiate on all manner of topics. Visitors were impressed by the modesty of his lifestyle. One of them was the American reporter Louise Bryant:

> During the first days of the Bolshevik revolution I used to go to Smolny to get the latest news. Trotsky and his pretty little wife, who hardly spoke anything but French, lived in one room on the top floor. The room was partitioned off like a poor artist's attic studio.

In one end were two cots and a cheap little dresser and in the other
a desk and two or three cheap chairs. There were no pictures, no
comfort anywhere. Trotsky occupied this office all the time he was
Minister of Foreign Affairs [*sic*] and many dignitaries found it necessary to call upon him there.[20]

Apparently the large red carpet was the sole trace of the Institute's former
dignity.[21]

While Trotsky held forth in Petrograd it was his friend Adolf Ioffe
who negotiated with Germany and Austria-Hungary at Brest-Litovsk near
the eastern front. If the Central Powers threw over the armistice and
invaded Russia, the Bolsheviks wanted to be able to turn to Britain, France
and America for military assistance. It was a bizarre situation. Trotsky's
men were bargaining with the mortal foes of the Allies for a peace which
would enhance the Central Powers' chances on the western front. At the
same time Trotsky and Robert Bruce Lockhart met regularly and the two
got on splendidly.[22] Trotsky also made overtures to the French and the
Americans in Petrograd. He formed a warm relationship with French
military attaché Jacques Sadoul; he even asked America's Red Cross leader,
Colonel Raymond Robins, to use his good offices to get the US Railway
Mission (which had been sent to help the Provisional Government in
restoring Russia's rail network) to give assistance to Sovnarkom.[23] Trotsky
and Lenin simply could not shut up the Russian diplomatic shop in such
circumstances.

Edward Allsworth Ross, reporter for the New York *Independent*,
recorded Trotsky's thoughts on economic regeneration. The People's Commissar emphasized that the Soviet government had no immediate intention of taking all industry into the hands of the state. Bolsheviks aimed
at control rather than ownership. They would limit the scale of private
profit; they would also ensure that factories geared their production to
the needs of social welfare. Capitalism would function within a strictly
imposed framework. Ross reasonably questioned whether entrepreneurs
would agree to operate on such terms. Trotsky retorted that the government would prevent any flight of capital from the country. He admitted
that problems would arise if capitalism endured elsewhere. But he dismissed this as a real possibility after the precedent set by the October
Revolution.[24] Trotsky did not fully deal with Ross's challenge; this was
typical of all Bolsheviks at this time: they were simply hoping for the
best. But a glimmering of Trotsky's hard-headedness appeared in a casual
aside in the same interview. Bolsheviks, he suggested, would apply the

techniques of 'Taylorism' in organizing industrial production – Trotsky had read about F. W. Taylor's experiments in time-and-motion studies in American factories and wanted to apply them in Russia.[25]

By December, however, the Central Powers were making clear that their patience with Sovnarkom was not inexhaustible. The armistice on the eastern front was not enough for them. They demanded a full separate peace treaty so that they could transfer forces to France and defeat the Western Allies. They threatened that the war against Russia would be resumed unless Sovnarkom gave way.

Trotsky had to involve himself in the Brest-Litovsk negotiations. The Germans constituted the leadership of the Central Powers. Their civilian interlocutors were eloquent but behind them, always exerting pressure, were military figures who constantly magnified the German demands. The Austrian representatives were mainly listeners since their forces had been unable to resist Kerenski's offensive in June without reinforcement by Germany's regiments. But the Germans had their own problems. Economic conditions in Germany had worsened. It was also becoming hard to conscript a sufficient quantity of young men fit for military service. There were rumblings of discontent in the factories. The Allies were bearing up surprisingly well and, with America's entry into the war, could only get stronger. Germany's high command, led by Hindenburg and Ludendorff, were becoming agitated. They believed that the only solution was to eliminate the need to fight in the east. The Russian armies were engaged in demobilization at Sovnarkom's behest. The next desirable stage for the Germans was to get a peace treaty signed. Then Hindenburg and Ludendorff could tackle the French and British on the western front with concentrated vigour.

These concerns of the Central Powers were well disguised. As the Germans and Austrians strode to the table for talks they expected to be treated with deference. They acted as if victory was already theirs. They shared the prejudices of their social class. For them, socialists of any kind were hardly human. Russia's communists, who included so many Jews in their leadership, were little better than vermin.

It was a shock for them, therefore, when Trotsky came out to join the Russian delegation at Brest-Litovsk in December. He needed no interpreter. His command of German was good enough for him to understand the nuances of the Berlin and Vienna dialects. His range of cultural references was remarkable; he peppered his remarks with witticisms. He refused to behave as a supplicant. The Germans and Austrians correctly sensed that he was laughing at them. His scheme for the negotiations was characteristically crafty. He obtained agreement that the respective bargaining positions should be publicized, which meant that German and Austrian newspapers would report Trotsky's words; and he snatched every chance to proclaim the ultimate objectives of the Bolshevik party. Whenever the Central Powers hurled demands at him like heavyweight punches, he skipped aside. He asked them questions of his own. He philosophized about the current condition of the world. There he was, the foreign minister of a desperately vulnerable country, talking as if he had no pressing worries. He was the epitome of revolutionary chutzpah. Well dressed and well groomed, he was nothing like the stereotype of the ill-kempt communist. The high representatives of the Hohenzollern and Habsburg thrones had no preparation for confronting such a human phenomenon.

# 21. TROTSKY AND THE JEWS

Trotsky hated it when people emphasized his Jewish background. He had spent his whole revolutionary career striving to escape the bonds of his origins. But he was not naive. He knew that popular interest in him as a Jew was inescapable, and he resigned himself to coping with the consequences.

What did it mean to be a Jew in Russia in the early twentieth century? Under the Tsars to describe someone as Jewish was to describe their religious affiliation rather than their ethnicity. Police and judicial reports as well as the 1897 Imperial census were conducted on this basis. But many Jews, especially in the last decades of the nineteenth century, abandoned their faith. Some converted to Christianity, many more became agnostics or atheists. If they accepted the Christian gospel they had ceased to be Jewish from the standpoint of Imperial law. By entering the Russian Orthodox Church, indeed, they acquired recognition as having become Russian. Under the Soviets, by contrast, Jewishness became a mark of national origin, and individuals of Jewish parentage were categorized as Jews regardless of whether they accepted Judaism as a faith. There had been 5.2 million Jews in the Russian Empire at the time of the 1897 census. Unlike other such large groups, they had no extensive territory where they were the majority – and some Marxists for this reason were reluctant to classify Jews as a nation. Between the official religious and national polarities lay a large number of people who had forsaken religion but still seemed to others to be culturally Jewish. Some followed kosher dietary traditions; others, while eating Gentile dishes, were thought distinctively Jewish because of their social attitudes, their accent or indeed their humour and wit. There was no consensus about what constituted a Jew. Even Jews disagreed on the answer.

Trotsky gave the minimum of his time to the 'Jewish question'. When he filled in official party forms he put down 'Jew' as his nationality;[1] and his full-scale autobiography, published in 1930, made no secret about having been born and brought up Jewish. In his own eyes, though, he had ceased to be a Jew in any important sense because Marxism had burned out the fortuitous residues of his origins. He saw himself, first and foremost, as a revolutionary Marxist; his ancestry, he insisted, was a matter of no account for him.

He called himself an internationalist. This was his way of saying that he was a supranationalist with no desire to acquire a fresh national identity. Although he became a russophone and spoke European languages with a markedly Russian accent, he was not a Russian nor even a Ukrainian except by accident of geography. By political and cultural orientation he was a cosmopolitan. His learning was steeped in the values of the new Russia that was developing in the late nineteenth century, and these were values of progress, enlightenment and science. Born in southern Ukraine, he felt no impulse to seek out the company of its inhabitants. He detested the Ukrainian society he had known with its landlords, capitalists and Imperial administrators. He wanted a new Ukraine as well as a new Russia, a new Europe and a new world. His entire experience in the Balkans convinced him that preoccupations with nationhood posed a deadly danger to humankind. Marxism supplied the ideological prism which helped him predict what the world under socialism would be like. Old values, habits and allegiances would disappear. Trotsky no more expected to live as the son of a Jew than as the son of a wealthy landowner. He aspired to citizenship of a perfect global community when all trace of prejudice and privilege would be removed by policies of universal benefit.

He got round to explaining his position only in 1934, when he was pressed by comrades from the Communist League in the United States:

> I do not understand why I should be considered as an 'assimilator'. I do not know, generally, what kind of a meaning this word holds. I am, it is understood, opposed to Zionism and all such forms of self-isolation on the part of the Jewish workers. I call upon the Jewish workers of France to better acquaint themselves with the problems of French life and of the French working class. Without that it is difficult to participate in the working class movement of that country in which they are being exploited. As the Jewish proletariat is spread in different countries it is necessary for the Jewish worker, outside of his own language, to strive to know the language of other countries as a weapon in the class struggle. What has that to do with 'assimilation'?[2]

This attitude informed his thinking all through his public life. The task of Marxists, he believed, was to expose the iniquities of nationalism and religion. He put himself forward as a socialist, an internationalist and an atheist.

Trotsky's rejection of Judaism by no means meant that he shunned individual Jews. Unconsciously or not, he was drawn to several of them as his closest comrades. Axelrod was a fatherly friend and confidant; Deich was an admired veteran and indefatigable escaper; Parvus was his mentor for several years; Martov had been an associate for a while and Ioffe was a lasting friend. All repudiated their Jewishness. The same was true of Trotsky's friends in Europe where his association with Kautsky and Luxemburg in the German Social-Democratic Party was based on political considerations: their upbringing as Jews was an irrelevance to them. In the Austrian Social-Democratic Party there were Victor and Friedrich Adler – and, of course, he also had other companions in Vienna such as the psychoanalyst Alfred Adler and the émigré Semën Klyachko. All were of Jewish parentage; none wanted to be known chiefly or at all as a Jew. They thought and behaved as citizens of the entire world. This was a widening trend around the turn of the century in culture and science as well as in politics, and Jewish intellectuals were in the forefront of it.

Trotsky also had companions who were cosmopolitans without being Jews. The Bulgarian Khristian Rakovski was an example. Trotsky would cherish him as his best friend after Ioffe's death in 1927. What is more, Trotsky had plenty of associates in the German Social-Democratic Party who had nothing Jewish in their ancestry. He was friends with Karl Liebknecht; he spoke a lot with August Bebel. His intellectual interests were European. Natalya with her interest in French art had encouraged this, and he immersed himself in Europe's literary classics while he lived as an emigrant in Switzerland, Germany and Austria. What is more, there was no trace of Judaism in Trotsky's adult lifestyle. Many secularized Jews continued to observe religious food prohibitions and celebrate traditional feast days. Not so Trotsky. It is true that a rabbi had joined him and Alexandra Sokolovskaya in wedlock.[3] But there had been no choice in the matter for them if they wished to live together in Siberian exile. Imperial law did not recognize civil marriages and since he had not converted to Christianity he had to marry in conformity with Judaism.

After undergoing this formality he reverted to his anti-religious code. On the few occasions when he adduced the words of the Bible he would more often than not use phrases from the New Testament (as when he wrote: 'Go and sin no more!').[4] In any case his second wife Natalya was not Jewish; and his two daughters by Alexandra as well as his two sons by Natalya were given names without association with Jewishness. Instead of calling his first son after his own father, he and Natalya had chosen the name Sergei.

There were many Jews like Trotsky in the Russian Empire who had benefited from an education in the humanities and sciences broader than was available in the Jewish religious schools. Like many bright youngsters, he revelled in the cultural liberation this afforded. He was brash in his cleverness, outspoken in his opinions. No one could intimidate him. Trotsky had these characteristics to a higher degree than most other Jews emancipated from the traditions of their religious community and the restrictions of the Imperial order. He was manifestly an individual of exceptional talent. But he was far from being the only Jew who visibly enjoyed the opportunities for public self-advancement. In later years they were to constitute a model for Jewish youth to follow in the world communist movement when, like communists of all nationalities, they spoke loudly and wrote sharply regardless of other people's sensitivities. Trotsky can hardly be diagnosed as having suffered from the supposed syndrome of the self-hating Jew. Hatred did not come into the matter. He was too delighted with himself and his life to be troubled by embarrassments about his ancestry.

Trotsky was one of those tens of thousands of educated Jews in the Russian Empire who at last could assert themselves in situations where their parents had needed to bow and scrape before Gentile officialdom. Two routes to prominence were available to the young and ambitious. One was legal, the other illegal. As in the rest of Europe, Jews could establish themselves in the professions and in the arts. Quite a number of the Russian Empire's leading doctors and lawyers came from the Pale of Settlement. Increasingly the arts and sciences were also enhanced by the Jewish contribution. The second route was to join the revolutionary parties where Jews constituted a disproportionate element. Young Jewish men and women, trained in the rigours of the Torah, found a congenial secular orthodoxy in Marxist intricacies. Hair-splitting disputes were common to Marxism and Judaism (as they were to Protestantism). Sectarian rivalries were a feature of shtetl life. Faith in a perfect future, once exclusively a religious phenomenon, entered the radical socialist movement.

The Jewish comrades whom Trotsky spurned were those who emphasized their Jewishness, and the Bundists were prime examples. He spoke out against them at the Second Party Congress in 1903. He also attacked Zionism, which was steadily gaining a following in the Pale of Settlement as anti-Semitic pogroms rose in number. For Trotsky, the Zionist was twin to the Bundist. In 1904 he wrote an article for *Iskra* on 'The Dissolution of Zionism and its Possible Successors'. It was Trotsky's most detailed critique of Jewish political separatism. He ridiculed Zionist leader Theodore Herzl for campaigning for a homeland to be granted in Africa for the Jews of Europe and elsewhere. This was a more serious scheme than Trotsky allowed. The British government had made such a proposal to Herzl and for a while there seemed a genuine possibility that it would be realized. As Trotsky predicted, nothing came of it.[5] He was wrong, though, in assuming that Zionism itself would soon fade away. Like most observers at that time, he simply could not imagine a future when the world's great powers would sanction the foundation of the state of Israel in the Middle East.

The intricacies of the Bund's ideas held no interest for Trotsky. He entirely overlooked the fact that even the Bundists – or at least its leaders – were avowed atheists unlike the vast majority of Jews in the Russian Empire or abroad in those years. What worried him about the Bundists was the wish for its members to remain self-consciously Jewish. Trotsky disliked national self-identification among any socialists; he criticized this tendency in his Austrian and Serbian comrades, and he was to lambast the German social-democrats on the same grounds in 1914 when they voted war credits for their government. On the Jewish question, then, he preferred to be the attacker of others rather than a proponent of positive proposals. He castigated the Imperial government for its supposed complicity in the pogroms. He also turned on Pëtr Struve for denying that the Jews had any claim to be recognized as a national group.[6] But he failed to follow this up by examining what constituted nationhood and how territory, belief and tradition contributed to it. He never gave his answers because nobody asked him at the time. Nor was he attracted by the proposal of the August Block to offer 'national-cultural autonomy' to the Jews. He neither approved nor opposed notions of autonomy but steered clear of the discussion. He did not dislike Jews as Jews but felt that national and ethnic assertiveness could not resolve the fundamental problems of the world.

In any case he prophesied that the disappointed left-wing adherents of Zionism would turn to the Bund. Such Jews would at least be seeking their salvation in revolution rather than flight; and he hoped that they might be brought across to the Russian Social-Democratic Workers' Party. But although the Bund fought against Zionism, its ideas in Trotsky's opinion were deformed by nationalism; and this in his opinion was not a desirable way to bring down the monarchy and found a better society. Trotsky saw the Bund as going down the same road as Jósef Piłsudski's Polish Socialist Party in judging people primarily by their national origin.[7]

For tactical reasons, however, he had to liaise with the Bund if the Russian Social-Democratic Workers' Party was ever to be unified, and he stopped expressing overt hostility. All factions, including Lenin's Bolsheviks, accepted the Bundists as an integral section of the party at the Fourth Congress in 1906 (after their walkout from the Second Congress in 1903). He dealt with the Bund by ignoring it so long as Bundists had official recognition as party comrades. He had not changed his mind about them. For Trotsky, they would always constitute a threat to the promise of universal socialism.

The Bund had wielded political influence between the February and October Revolutions of 1917. Its leader Mark Liber was deeply involved in the coalition of socialists which dominated the soviets until the Bolsheviks seized power. Jews were heavily represented in every revolutionary party – Fëdor Dan and Yuli Martov were Menshevik leaders while Abram Gots was in the first rank of the Socialist-Revolutionaries. For a while it seemed that the Jewish question had ceased to be a problem in Russian politics.

Religious Jewry, however, worried about the number of Jews in the leadership of the revolutionary movement. They saw that it could eventually backfire on Jews in general once older popular traditions of anti-Semitism reasserted themselves. A delegation was sent to Trotsky in Petrograd to seek to persuade him to have nothing to do with the Bolsheviks. He listened carefully and, according to a later account, replied roughly as follows: 'It's not my fault that I was born inside a Jewish skin. The workers are dearer to me than all the Jews. And if for the good of humanity it proves necessary for any part of it to perish, then I'd have nothing against the Jewish people in Russia turning out to be that part.'[8] This does not sound like the sort of thing he would have said. Trotsky was generally in favour of allowing each and every national group to pursue its traditions without persecution so long as they conformed to communist political order – and he agreed with the Soviet government's efforts to enable people both to be taught in schools and to have newspapers in their own languages. He also supported measures to recruit young men and women from each national group, giving them ideological training and promoting them to public office. He never mentioned the Jews in this connection, but they fell within the range of official policy aimed at winning the sympathies of non-Russians.

Rabbi Maze in Moscow quipped: 'It's Lev Davidovich Trotsky who signs the mortgage but it's Leiba Bronstein who has to pay up for it.'[9] The cleric was referring to the millions of observant Jews who kept to their faith and dutifully obeyed the secular authorities. Thus it had been for centuries. Then along came the revolutionaries, and among them were many of Jewish origin who promised to build a new society without volunteering the material resources.

Trotsky understood Maze's concerns even while ignoring the general advice. His refusal to head the People's Commissariat of Internal Affairs was not the last time he brought up the matter of his Jewish origins when responding to proposed postings. In 1918 he was to strive, unsuccessfully, against being appointed people's commissar for military affairs in 1918. He would also reject Lenin's proposal that he should become his deputy in the Soviet government in 1922. On all three occasions he adduced his Jewish background as making it inappropriate for him to accept the appointment. Repeatedly he tried to ensure that Jews enjoyed no privileges in the coming Civil War. They had a higher than average rate of literacy and numeracy than the rest of the society and therefore found it easy to gain employment in the Soviet administration. Trotsky did not see this as salutary for the popularity of the Soviet state and wanted to put more of them into the Red Army so as to dispel the popular complaint that they did the bossing around while Russians were doing the dying. The party's leadership was widely identified as a Jewish gang. Trotsky continued to believe that his own prominence in government, party and army did practical damage to the revolutionary cause. When the Civil War was over he told the communist leadership: 'And, well, comrades, after all the work I did in this area I can say with total confidence that *I was right.*'[10]

Jews indeed were widely alleged to dominate the Bolshevik party. In fact several national minorities were heavily represented among the Bolsheviks. Stalin was a Georgian, Felix Dzerzhinski a Pole, Stepan Shaumyan an Armenian. The Baltic peoples too – Latvians and Lithuanians in particular – supplied prominent figures. Such leaders had grown up adding a national or ethnic dimension to their resentment of the Imperial order before 1917. But it was the Jews who attracted the most vituperative commentary, and it is understandable that Trotsky focused his worries on this.

Counter-revolutionary posters were routinely Judaeophobic about Trotsky. A well-known portrait depicted him crouching like a beast waiting to pounce on its victim. In the background stood ordinary Russians suffering from the effects of his policies. The sky had a garish hue. The streets streamed red with blood. Another picture had Trotsky directing a body of Chinese-looking commissars. Such imagery was intended to show that the October Revolution damaged the interests of Russia and its people. The anti-Soviet commander Alexei Kaledin incited his troops by declaring that the Bolshevik leaders were not Russians but Jews – and Lenin and Trotsky headed his list for destruction.[11] The two of them were synonymous with the communist order.[12] An anonymous letter to the Soviet authorities asked:

> Have you gone blind and can't see who's now ruling Russia? ... Trotsky, Sverdlov, Zinoviev and others: they are all full-blooded Jews who have given themselves Russian surnames to trick the Russian people. Trotsky is called Bronstein, Zinoviev is really Liberman and so on. And it's you who prefer the Yid Bronstein – Trotsky – to the Orthodox Tsar.

The writer proclaimed that the time of the Antichrist had arrived.[13]

Trotsky never gave anti-communists the pleasure of witnessing his annoyance, but he acted firmly against all forms of discrimination against Jews. His position appeared in an article he wrote for *Izvestiya* ('News') in October 1919: 'Anti-Semitism is not only a hatred of Jewry but also a cowardice about Jewry.' What he meant by this was that vengeful anti-Semites were scared to compete with Jews in public life. Trotsky denied that the Jews were an especially talented people. He gave a more mundane explanation of their prominence in politics. Jews were predominantly urban residents. The towns were where the sharpest antagonism against the Romanov monarchy had been nurtured. It was therefore logical for Jewry to produce more than its demographic share of revolutionaries in the Russian Empire.[14]

For several years this was all he wanted to say on the Jewish question. The situation would begin to change when factional strife broke out between Trotsky and Stalin in 1923. The public dispute was ferocious, the machinations behind the scenes were even worse. Increasingly the ascendant group in the party leadership was supported by militants who drew attention to Trotsky's Jewish origin. In March 1926 Trotsky wrote to Bukharin, whom he regarded as having a more decent character than anyone else close to Stalin. (Even so, Trotsky felt uneasy touching upon Jewish topics and refrained from dictating to a stenographer.) It had come to his attention that anti-Semitic remarks were regularly being made at meetings of party cells. Someone had allegedly said: 'The Yids are kicking up a row in the Politburo [an inner sub-committee of the Central Committee].' Such an atmosphere was making it difficult for decent Bolsheviks to speak out against anti-Semitism. He appealed to Bukharin, his factional enemy, to intervene and insist on clean methods in political dispute.[15] It would seem that he did not see the point of writing to Stalin on the same subject. Perhaps he thought that it would be a waste of time. In fact Stalin himself had a Jewish associate in the person of Lazar Kaganovich, but he did not find working-class Jews like Kaganovich threatening to his plans for the USSR (the Union of Soviet Socialist Republics, a supposedly 'federal' system). Unaccommodating Jewish intellectuals were a different matter, especially one such as Trotsky who fought against him for power. Stalin turned a blind eye to the outbursts of anti-Semitism which helped him to defeat his antagonist.

Trotsky anyway continued to insist that socialism and not nationhood was the cardinal question of the day. He did not eulogize the Russians; he barely referred to Russia as such. This was not untypical of leading Bolsheviks, including those who had been brought up as Jews. The sole figure in the Central Committee who had leanings in the direction of singling out the Russian people for favour was Stalin.[16] He did this only very cautiously in the 1920s; it was mainly in the following decade that he placed Russians on a pedestal as the primary nation in the USSR. Stalin, a Georgian, to some extent was trying to compensate politically for not being Russian. Trotsky remained a vigorous internationalist. He wrote endlessly about the need for revolution in Europe and Asia. This too was hardly an unusual standpoint to take in the first years after the October Revolution, but Trotsky held to it with remarkable firmness. Lenin frequently commented on the high level of German culture; at times he gave the impression that the Bolshevik revolution in Russia would flounder unless supported by a fraternal revolutionary administration in Germany.[17] There was hardly any trace of this in Trotsky. He remained averse to either extolling or deprecating the qualities of particular peoples and believed that this was the proper approach of a Marxist.

It is true that he identified Russian cultural backwardness, especially among the peasantry, as being a brake on the socialist transformation. He constantly drew attention to Russia's need to modernize its entire society.[18] At the same time he loved the Russian literary classics. But he also adored French novels, was an admirer of Ibsen and was impressed by Nietzsche. He treated all of them as examples of contemporary world culture.

He refined his attitudes over the years without changing his basic standpoint. He wanted the best for all nations in the USSR, including the Jews, and thought this was achievable only by guiding them towards socialism, internationalism and atheism. Not once did he single out Jews as a people with particular needs. Only after Hitler had come to power in the 1930s did he conclude that a specific set of measures had to be designed to avert the extinction of world Jewry.

# 22. BREST-LITOVSK

Trotsky from December 1917 was moving like a weaver's shuttle between Brest-Litovsk and the Russian capital. In Brest-Litovsk he continued to perform the role of confident, untroubled statesman; in the Bolshevik Central Committee in Petrograd he laid bare the imminent danger from the Central Powers. He introduced order and discipline at the diplomatic talks. Everyone understood who held authority among the Russians:

> As chairman of the Soviet delegation, I decided to put an abrupt halt to the familiarity in relations that had imperceptibly developed during the initial period. Through our military people I made it understood that I had no intention of being presented to the Prince of Bavaria. This was taken into account. I demanded separate lunches and dinners on the grounds that we had to consult with each other during the intervals. This too was silently accepted.[1]

Trotsky quickly gauged the distribution of power among the representatives of the Central Powers. The Austrian Foreign Minister Count Ottokar Czernin took his orders from Germany's State Secretary for Foreign Affairs Richard von Kühlmann. Yet Kühlmann himself was weak alongside General Hoffmann – and Hoffmann in turn was merely speaking on behalf of his masters in the German high command on the western front, Paul von Hindenburg and Erich Ludendorff. Trotsky chuckled about this long after 1918; he delighted in exposing the formal pretences – he knew that behind the screen of etiquette it was the naked power of the armed forces that determined what the ministers, diplomats and even emperors ordered.[2]

At the turn of the year the Central Powers presented an ultimatum. The time for Trotsky's eloquence was drawing to a close and the Bolsheviks faced a choice: either they signed a separate peace, pulling Russia out of the Great War, or Germany's forces would be sent over the armistice line. Trotsky was left in no doubt that the Germans would not halt until they took Moscow and Petrograd. The October Revolution would be overthrown.

The Soviet administration's authority in Russia had never been weaker. In November 1917 the elections to the Constituent Assembly gave no party a majority; but the Party of Socialist-Revolutionaries obtained the largest number of seats. This was a rebuff to Sovnarkom because the Bolsheviks secured only a quarter of the vote. The Left Socialist-Revolutionaries had broken with Chernov and the Socialist-Revolutionaries in order to join Sovnarkom; but this split into two conflicting parties came too late for separate candidates to be fielded in the elections. The electorate had no opportunity to distinguish between the left and right wings of the old Party of Socialist-Revolutionaries. At any rate the coalition of Bolsheviks and Left Socialist-Revolutionaries was determined to hold on to power, and it forcibly suppressed the Constituent Assembly on 6 January 1918. The Soviet authorities were being blamed for failing to achieve economic recovery. Peasants withdrew from urban markets. Food supplies disappeared. Factory workers and miners resented the collapse in industrial production and feared mass unemployment. Local soviets resorted to grain requisitioning. Clashes with the peasantry increased. Workers listened increasingly to the Mensheviks. Bolsheviks had made the October Revolution confident that their support in the working class and the peasantry would continue to rise. Their disappointment was intense in the winter of 1917–18.

Trotsky reported on the Brest-Litovsk talks expecting Lenin to concur that the Bolshevik and Left Socialist-Revolutionary coalition should refuse to yield. But Lenin had been reconsidering his policy. He recognized that Russia's army had ceased to exist as a fighting force. The peasants-in-uniform had left the trenches and hurried home to get a share of the land that was undergoing redistribution – the Bolsheviks had encouraged this by setting up a demobilization commission. There was no sign of a popular wish for the war to be resumed: Russians were fed up with the fighting. They wanted peace, and they thought that Lenin's Decree on Peace had promised it to them. Lenin understood all this. His enquiries convinced him that armed conflict with Germany was a practical impossibility. He told nobody for a while as the idea formed in his mind that Sovnarkom should accede to the terms of the Central Powers. His problem was that the two parties in the coalition were committed to waging a 'revolutionary war' if peace failed to come about through the establishment of socialist governments in Europe. Only a few Bolsheviks – Kamenev, Zinoviev and Stalin – had ever been sceptical about the imminence of 'European socialist revolution'.

Most Bolshevik leaders, including Trotsky, thought a separate peace with the Central Powers was an insufferable concession to capitalist imperialism. Trotsky in his public statements made it a matter of principle that the government should sign no separate peace with the Central Powers. He disguised his acceptance that Soviet security was currently unattainable without external assistance. Before joining the negotiations at Brest-Litovsk he had regularly liaised with representatives of the Western Allies with a view to preserving opportunities for military help from Britain and France in the event of a German invasion; and he stuck to this approach through to summer 1918.[3] For years he had been saying that 'Anglo-French' imperialism was just as bad as the German or Austrian varieties. Yet he refused to rule out some kind of deal with London and Paris even if it would not involve a peace treaty. Lenin was right in detecting a whiff of the posturing radical about Trotsky over these months.

The Bolshevik Central Committee became a wrestling match over war and peace. The Left Socialist-Revolutionaries needed no such contest since their party was absolute in its refusal to accede to the terms of the Central Powers. Only Bolsheviks felt that there was any point in a debate, and this was largely the result of Lenin's insistence. After the Constituent Assembly's dispersal it was accepted that the Central Committee should be reorganized. Its members were continually being distracted by their public functions. There was also a geographical factor. The German military threat made it sensible to move the capital from Petrograd to Moscow, leaving a core of party leaders behind under Zinoviev's direction. An inner Bureau was elected consisting of Lenin, Stalin, Sverdlov, Sokolnikov and Trotsky. This would operate in Moscow. The only one of its members who would not be constantly in place was Trotsky, who would have to travel out regularly to Brest-Litovsk.[4] It was a sign of his importance to the party that he was nevertheless included in the Bureau. It was also a reflection of the current agenda of Bolshevism. The question of war and peace dominated everything. As things turned out, the Bureau did not function. Every Bolshevik Central Committee member wanted the opportunity to participate in the debate on war and peace.

Taking his case to the Central Committee on 11 January 1918, Lenin argued that an attempt at 'revolutionary war' would sound the death knell of the October Revolution. The only possible consequence would be a German military occupation. Never one to shrink from bold decisions, Lenin told his comrades to think the unthinkable and accept Germany's terms before they got worse. He was willing to reconsider if the political situation in central Europe were suddenly to change, for he still believed in the imminence of proletarian uprisings in Berlin and Vienna. So if

Germany were to experience a revolutionary upsurge it would behove the Bolsheviks to render whatever military support they could.[5] Trotsky could hardly believe his ears. His partner in the seizure of power in Russia was unilaterally trying to tear up the contingency planning of party and government. Lenin, the opponent of compromise before October 1917, was proposing surrender to one of Europe's great imperialist powers. He and Trotsky had been enemies for years after 1903. They had come together politically in mid-1917. They had co-operated cheek by jowl for three months in Sovnarkom. Now they suddenly fell out, and this had nothing to do with methods or personality. Lenin and Trotsky were embroiled in dispute about the substance of governmental policy.

Trotsky had seen the empty trenches at the eastern front and knew that Soviet Russia could fight nobody. But signing a peace with the Central Powers was a step much too far for him. He advocated the tactic of declaring that the Soviet government would neither make war nor sign a peace. He wanted to use this in his manoeuvres to delay a German offensive. In the meantime he aimed to spread Bolshevik propaganda in Germany. Ultimately he was hoping to encourage radical socialists to undertake a socialist insurrection in Berlin.[6]

The standpoint he took lay midway between Lenin and the Bolshevik left. Bukharin favoured all-out war against Imperial Germany. He and the so-called Left Communists would rather go down fighting than abandon their internationalist commitment – and they were unhappy that Lenin, the leader who had cajoled them into seizing power in Petrograd, was proposing an intolerable compromise. Trotsky's tactic of playing for time was the next most desirable option for them, and the vote went in his favour. Lenin had few supporters. One was Stalin, who argued that there was no genuine evidence of the imminence of revolution in the West. Zinoviev added that Kühlmann would take no notice of the niceties of Trotsky's tactics; he was willing, however, to put the whole matter to a plebiscite. The contributions from Stalin and Zinoviev gave little comfort to Lenin. He distanced himself from Stalin's scepticism about European socialist revolution; he also had no patience with any proposal to hold a plebiscite. Trotsky asked for a decision on revolutionary war. Only two voted in favour; the other eleven, with one abstention, voted against. Lenin then called for a decision on dragging out the negotiations. The discussion went in favour by twelve votes to one. Thus Trotsky's policy of 'neither war nor peace' was confirmed: it was not the result desired by Lenin but it was at least better for him than a decision to go to war.

Trotsky had difficulty in protecting his policy while he was away at

Brest-Litovsk. Lenin was a persuasive debater and had constant access to the Central Committee and its Secretariat. The German ultimatum caused tremors among Bolshevik and Left Socialist-Revolutionary leaders, who had always understood that the October Revolution would need a lot of luck to survive. They and their families lived with suitcases packed in case they had to flee. Questions of Soviet international security acquired an acute seriousness. Georgi Chicherin was made Trotsky's deputy on 29 January 1918 to enable the smooth running of affairs in the absence of Trotsky and Ioffe from the capital: the People's Commissariat had at last moved to the forefront of governmental activities.[7] Lenin, aided by the Central Committee Secretariat, communicated with the rest of the party to make the case for a separate peace. When Left Communists tried to gather support in provincial party organizations for 'revolutionary war' they found little support among factory workers. Lenin's campaign gathered steadily widening support in the Bolshevik party. Among the Left Socialist-Revolutionaries it was a different matter: not one of their leaders or militants would countenance a deal with the Central Powers. But it was the Bolsheviks who mattered, and it was their Central Committee which would take the ultimate decision on war and peace.

The Bolsheviks had consistently declared that they would start a 'revolutionary war' if the German working class, for some unexpected reason, failed to rise up against their government. This had been broadly Lenin's public preference almost until the end of 1917. He did not now disguise his distaste for signing a deal with the Central Powers: it would be an 'obscene peace' with German imperialism. He remained sure that the European proletariat would sooner or later overturn capitalism, and he expressed a willingness to abandon the diplomatic negotiations if an insurrection were to occur. But he was unwilling to bring the October Revolution to perdition by provoking invasion by the Germans.

Trotsky knew as well as Lenin that Sovnarkom would be destroyed in any war with the Central Powers. Travelling regularly between Petrograd and Brest-Litovsk, he saw with his own eyes how defenceless the country had become. The Bolsheviks could not realistically assemble an army against the Central Powers and expect to win the resulting conflict. Trotsky accepted no other option than to drag out the negotiations at Brest-Litovsk. He was more and more comfortable in the role of international statesman. He had got used to economizing on his working time. For years he had written his letters by hand; now he dictated them to short-hand typists.[8] But the Germans and Austrians at Brest-Litovsk regarded him as an upstart who made no secret of his party's devotion to the cause of international revolution. If the Central Powers wanted to defeat the British and the French it was essential to initiate an offensive on the western front before the Americans arrived in force in Europe. As Trotsky saw for himself, the German negotiators were losing patience with his refusal to state whether Russia was going to fight or make peace. Verbal pyrotechnics would not forever put off Germany's plans to invade.

Even Bukharin did not think a revolutionary war could be waged; at the first big discussion at the Central Committee he therefore supported Trotsky's diplomatic manoeuvre until such time as the Germans undertook an offensive.[9] This embarrassed Trotsky a trifle:

> Surely at the present moment the whole question is wrapped up in the correlation of forces. It makes no difference whether we actively participate in the imperialist war or refrain from activity: we will still be taking part in the war. And so we must consider what is most advantageous for us. It's simply utopian to turn all our forces into military forces. Consequently the question of a revolutionary war is an unreal question. The army must be disbanded but disbanding the army is not the same as signing a peace.[10]

For those with ears to hear this was not as hostile to Lenin's standpoint as was widely assumed (and as continues to be assumed). Trotsky was arguing a hard-headed case. While demanding an 'internationalist' perspective, he refused to accept that it was wrong in principle to fight or not fight. His careful argument was that the Bolsheviks would be unintentionally aiding one side or another in the European war whatever they chose to do. It was not a moral but a practical question which had to be answered: what would best facilitate the revolutionary cause?

He came under attack by Stalin, who thought he exaggerated the potential for a European socialist revolution. 'Trotsky's position', he declared, 'is no position at all.' If the party followed Trotsky's advice, it would only worsen the chances of a tolerable deal with the Central Powers.[11] Zinoviev agreed with Stalin. Lenin did not because it was his opinion that the potential for revolution in Europe remained strong; but he argued that the Bolsheviks had to agree to the terms of the Central Powers without delay if they were to avert an invasion of Russia. He could not imagine why Trotsky, a master of revolutionary manoeuvres in 1917, failed to appreciate this.[12] But he could see that 'neither war nor peace' was as good a result as he could expect, and he successfully put forward a motion along these lines.[13]

Trotsky on 24 January 1918 sent a telegram to Vienna requesting permission to visit the Austrian capital 'for the conduct of negotiations with representatives of the Austrian proletariat'. That he would have loved to speak at mass meetings abroad is not in doubt. Yet the wording of the telegram was provocative, and he cannot have been unaware of this. Czernin replied in kind, explaining that Trotsky had no formal powers to represent anybody in any such negotiations.[14] Trotsky went on teasing him and scoffed at the suggestion that considerations of formality had led to the refusal. What was clear was that the Central Powers feared the diffusion of the Bolshevik 'contagion'. They had seen the effects of revolutionary agitation on Russia in 1917. Mass meetings had allegedly turned the heads of the Russian working class. Cities in Germany and Austria-Hungary were experiencing their own turbulence. Strikes were on the increase. Discontent rose with the inadequacy of food rations. There had been mutinies in the French army, and the same might happen in Berlin or Vienna. The last thing that the Central Powers wanted was a fiery speaker such as Trotsky making trouble on their streets.

They also had no wish to let him set their agenda at Brest-Litovsk. Cunningly they had accepted US President Woodrow Wilson's Fourteen Points for a peace settlement to end the Great War. This embraced the principle of national self-determination. The Central Powers professed themselves content to recognize the independence of all European nations, including those in the east of the continent. Berlin and Vienna saw a great chance to make mischief.

Trotsky blustered at the Central Committee meeting which resolved the matter on 23 February. Lenin's campaign was approaching victory. There were no fresh arguments. The only change was the collapse of the pro-war majority in the light of unmistakable signs that the Germans were not going to allow further delay. The vote went seven to four in favour of Lenin. Trotsky refused to alter his opinion and simply abstained.[15] He obdurately insisted that to sign a separate peace was to betray revolutionary principles. He stood down from the Brest-Litovsk negotiations. On 24 February he renounced further struggle and was helpful in discussions about the composition of a fresh diplomatic team. Party policy had been decided and he would not seek to play the disrupter. Stalin welcomed this accommodation, asking Trotsky to stay in post for a few more days. Trotsky agreed; he resisted the temptation to carry on the struggle.[16] So what held him back? He claimed that a revolutionary war could be fought only with a united party. This option was clearly unavailable. He therefore submitted to the Central Committee's authority.[17] More than just a trace of sanctimony inhered in his final speech. There had never been much chance of internal unity being preserved even if the anti-treaty side had won in earlier weeks. Trotsky was posturing. He wished to appear clean and pure, by his own lights, in the future annals of history. He had fought for what he believed in. He had lost the struggle.

The treaty was ratified by the Seventh Party Congress in March 1918. It was at this gathering that the Bolsheviks renamed themselves the Russian Communist Party (Bolsheviks) in order to distinguish themselves from socialist parties in Russia and abroad which dissented from Lenin's doctrines of proletarian revolution. The Congress also gave the opportunity for communist leaders to proclaim their undying commitment to the eventual spreading of revolution westwards. German military power currently made this impossible. The danger for the Soviet state had not been entirely removed. The treaty had stopped the Central Powers from overrunning Russia; but nobody in March 1918 could be entirely confident that the Germans would abide by the treaty, and indeed their forces were to overrun Crimea in April.[18] This was a breach of the agreements at Brest-Litovsk. Even Stalin, arch-proponent of the separate peace, would reconsider his hostility to revolutionary war.[19] It might yet happen that the Bolsheviks would be compelled to defend Petrograd and Moscow against attack. In such an event there would be no doubt about where Trotsky's sympathies would lie. He would love to take on the Central Powers. Lenin called this a breathing space.

Trotsky had suffered a drubbing. Despite emerging as one of the most practically minded Bolsheviks in October and November 1917, he had assumed a wholly unrealistic posture in the Brest-Litovsk dispute. All the time he had known that if it came to a moment of unavoidable decision, the policy of 'neither war nor peace' would not suffice. In Lenin's eyes, therefore, he had wasted everyone's time. Worse than that, he had encouraged others to believe that a 'revolutionary war' was possible despite knowing that Russia no longer possessed serious armed forces. He was just as irresponsible as those out-and-out Left Communists who admitted that war with Imperial Germany would bring catastrophe upon the October Revolution. Trotsky was a bad listener. Indeed his ears were deaf to the case made by others. In any private discussion he wanted to do all the talking. He seldom mixed with other party members outside political meetings. His changes of mind tended to be abrupt – and he did not care to alert his comrades in advance. What is more, he defended his standpoint with ferocity. He was willing, time and time again, to turn the party upside down rather than concede to his opponents. This was his strength when he had ideas that turned out useful for shoring up the revolutionary order. As often as not, though, his brio did more harm than good for his cause.

Robert Bruce Lockhart, head of the British mission in Moscow until his departure from Russia in September 1918, observed how Lenin had acquired a psychological edge over Trotsky in the Brest-Litovsk dispute.[20] The two dominant rulers did not share equal authority. Trotsky could gather up steam for a controversy; he could lead a struggle against Lenin, and was to do this with panache in 1920–21.[21] But he lacked the firmness of purpose that came from deep self-confidence. He blustered. He polemicized with zeal. He acted as if his political life as well as the Soviet administration depended on the success of his proposals. But he had come to sense that he could not supplant Lenin. This was not just a recognition that his comrade of less than a year's duration enjoyed the abundant loyalty of nearly all Bolsheviks. Trotsky had seen Lenin at close quarters more intensely than at any time since 1902–3. He appreciated the intellectual and practical talent of the man. He sensed the will power. He was drawn to the absence of personal vanity. It was as if Trotsky had arm-wrestled with Lenin and lost the trial of strength. Lenin was used to winning and resisted the temptation to appear too triumphant.

Yet Trotsky would not agree to remain as People's Commissar for Foreign Affairs. If he had stayed in post it would have been he who had to go out to Brest-Litovsk and sign the treaty. Trotsky had a strong sense of the theatrical. Much as he liked to strut on the political stage, he was averse to being filmed or photographed putting his name to what even Lenin described as 'an obscene peace'. He was no longer willing to take responsibility for his Commissariat. It was difficult to find a volunteer. In the end the job was assigned to Grigori Sokolnikov; even Lenin, the architect of the Soviet decision to sign the treaty, sidestepped the duty to turn up in Brest-Litovsk.

war in Paris in 1915–16. He had co-ordinated the Petrograd garrisons through the Military-Revolutionary Committee before the October seizure of power. He could fire a gun on hunting expeditions.

Trotsky did not let this bother him. He found the Red Army in a mess and did not mind who heard his opinion of the situation. The founding of the Soviet forces had been announced on 23 February 1918. Its first leaders were good Bolsheviks but hopeless military organizers. Liaison with those commanders willing to serve under Soviet authority was patchy. Plans were endlessly drawn up on paper. The reality was that the old Russian army had disappeared through mass desertions and the process of demobilization promoted by Sovnarkom. Trotsky imparted fresh urgency to the preparations. This was his hallmark. He always acted as if his institution had the crucial role to play in the survival and prosperity of the Soviet state. Making a rapid assessment of the Red Army, he changed policy in favour of attracting experienced officers. He simultaneously extended Kerenski's policy of attaching political commissars to the armed forces at every level of command. Officer and commissar were to work in tandem: the first would supply military expertise while the other supervised his loyalty and spread propaganda to the troops. Trotsky learned on the job how to recruit, train, supply and deploy his armed forces.

He continued to talk to representatives of the Western Allies and on 5 March, only a couple of days after the signing of the separate peace, he asked the Americans whether they would give assistance in the event that Sovnarkom chose to go to war against Germany.[3] The Bolsheviks knew they could not fight unaided. Trotsky was eager to keep up such contact since he still believed the Brest-Litovsk treaty a mistake. He was willing to resume operations against the Germans. Allied diplomats and officers in Moscow understood this and very readily talked to him. The supplementary calculation for Trotsky and the rest of Sovnarkom was that the Bolsheviks needed to discourage an invasion by the Western Allies. Such a crusade became distinctly possible after March 1918. The British sent a force to Archangel with the stated purpose of protecting their military supplies in Russia. A French flotilla landed troops in Odessa. Sovnarkom was thrown into panic by these events, and both Trotsky at the People's Commissariat for Military Affairs and Chicherin at the People's Commissariat for Foreign Affairs did what they could to assure the Allies that Russia's accommodation with Germany was not of a permanent nature. They omitted to add that if ever Sovnarkom were to realign itself with them it would not mean that the Bolsheviks had given up their commitment to international socialist revolution.

# 23. KAZAN AND AFTER

Lenin acted quickly to haul Trotsky back to their shared moorings. He did this by asking him to take over the People's Commissariat for Military Affairs. Adolf Ioffe, Trotsky's old comrade, had come up with the idea and got it approved by the Central Committee members remaining in Petrograd. He wrote to Lenin pressing the case that Trotsky had proved his aptitude for work with the armed forces in course of the October Revolution.[1] Lenin agreed. Trotsky, though, felt tugged in two directions. Although he was minded to stay inside Sovnarkom, he thought it impolitic for a Jew to direct the Red Army. This was the same argument as he had made against becoming People's Commissar for Internal Affairs, and he put up a spirited resistance to the new proposal. Lenin wore him down and Trotsky, after a few days' unemployment, re-entered the Sovnarkom and was confirmed in post on 14 March 1918.[2]

Trotsky was as relieved as Lenin. He had played a leading role in the drama of the October Revolution. A revolutionary state had been established. If he abandoned the Soviet government there was nowhere for him to go if he was to continue to make an impact: he had to find a way of staying with the Bolsheviks. This was easier for him than it was later to seem. Although the treaty had been signed with the Central Powers, nobody could be sure that the Germans would not rip it up and storm into Soviet-held territory. Then Lenin would have a 'revolutionary war' on his hands whether he liked it or not. Alternatively German military power might collapse in northern France and the Russians would be free to rise up against the treaty. Not even Lenin and Stalin regarded the peace as anything but a temporary convenience. Trotsky had reason to think he had not yet lost the contest over foreign and military policy. The immediate future was unpredictable. By taking over the People's Commissariat for Military Affairs, Trotsky would be in a position to raise an armed force to exploit any opportunity to foster 'European socialist revolution'.

His qualifications for the new job were less than impressive. He had reported war from the Balkans before 1914 and observed the effects of

Trotsky used his acquaintance with Robert Bruce Lockhart from Britain, Jacques Sadoul from France and Raymond Robins from America to seek Allied assistance in reorganizing Russia's armed forces. (He obviously enjoyed annoying the German diplomatic and intelligence services.) He took Lockhart out and about in Moscow in his official limousine and explained his readiness to deploy the Red Army against the Germans.[4] He also employed the expertise of Captain G. A. Hill, member of Britain's Special Intelligence Service (soon to be known as the Secret Intelligence Service), in assembling an air force for the Reds.[5] Trotsky said nothing about any of this in his memoirs; by the time he wrote them he needed to keep quiet about his liaisons with the Allies in 1918 for fear of being accused of having betrayed Soviet Russia.

There was no doubting his physical courage. Lockhart recalled an incident when a crowd of Kronstadt sailors gathered in the square outside the Commissariat. The mood turned ugly as the men shouted out their grievances about pay and conditions. Officials in the Commissariat began to panic. These were the same sailors who had done much to destabilize the Provisional Government. Trotsky showed firm resolve in confronting the crowd: 'His eyes were blazing with rage. Out he rushed entirely alone, lashed the sailors with his tongue for a quarter of an hour and sent them away like whipped curs.'[6] This was a true leader of men unafraid to harangue angry servicemen who could have done him lethal damage. He would tolerate no insubordination. From childhood he had seen his father order the farm hands around. Trotsky was created in the same mould. What is more, he was now a revolutionary who expected maximum co-operation from the people in whose name he had helped to seize power. Whenever they disappointed him, he let them know it. He acted on the premise that the 'masses' required strict tutelage.

Gathering and training a Red Army was arduous work. It had not been completed before the summer when a succession of emergencies buffeted Sovnarkom. Trotsky was prominently involved in the first of them. By agreement with the Allies he had allowed a contingent of Czech prisoners-of-war to leave the country and join the armies facing the Germans in France. The first long stage of their journey was to take them along the Trans-Siberian railway to the Pacific. On the way the order came from Trotsky that they should give up their arms. The Czechs wrongly suspected treachery: in fact Trotsky was only taking precautions against being traduced by the Czechs. Thus began the Czech revolt in Chelyabinsk at the end of May 1918. The Czechs, well armed and battle-experienced, turned their trains back into Russia. Arriving in Samara on the River

Volga in south-east Russia, they placed themselves at the disposal of the Committee of Members of the Constituent Assembly (or Komuch). This was the anti-Bolshevik government established in June 1918 by the Socialist-Revolutionaries; its claim to authority rested on the party's success in the elections to the Constituent Assembly. Military conflict between the forces of Komuch and Sovnarkom broke out. The Reds were easily beaten and Czech military strength handed the entire Volga region to the Socialist-Revolutionaries. The Civil War, after several sputtering starts, exploded into life.

Disputes about foreign and military policy had lost any weight. Lenin and Trotsky were back in harness together, and as Lenin's policies became more radical the Left Communists gained confidence that the core of party ideology was restored to life. All Bolsheviks were fighting for each other. The emergency by the Volga was cutting off central and northern Russia from the grain supplies available in the region. Sovnarkom responded by initiating a Food Dictatorship. All private trade in foodstuffs was made a criminal offence and armed squads were sent out to the countryside on a requisitioning mission. Conflict with the peasantry increased. The Left Socialist-Revolutionaries had until then continued to serve Sovnarkom even after resigning their leading posts in the People's Commissariats because of the peace treaty with Germany. Wishing to ignite war with the Central Powers, a group of them under Yakov Blyumkin organized the assassination of the German ambassador Count Wilhelm von Mirbach on 9 July. The entire Party of Left Socialist-Revolutionaries rose in rebellion against Sovnarkom while the Fifth Congress of Soviets met in Moscow in the same week. The Bolsheviks reacted with all their forces, included a regiment of Latvian riflemen. The Left Socialist-Revolutionaries were suppressed.

At an open meeting in Sokolniki on Moscow's outskirts on 6 June, Trotsky had fulminated against those calling for a reversion to a free market in grain. Yes, he admitted, the situation with food supplies was bad in Moscow and Petrograd. He conceded that it was worse again in the rest of Russia. But he insisted that circumstances were even graver in Europe. Showering his audience with the latest official statistics, Trotsky declared that the country had plenty of grain. The problem was how to get it to the cities. He stressed that it was not the Bolsheviks who had introduced the state grain monopoly (although he did not explain why such a monopoly remained essential). He opposed raising the prices paid for the harvest. The only beneficiaries of such a measure, he declared, would be the 'speculators' and 'kulaks'. Trotsky did not define his terms.

Like all his fellow communists, he assumed that merchants and speculators were one and the same thing; and a kulak in Bolshevik parlance was any peasant who was richer than the local average among the peasantry. He did not say why ending the state grain monopoly would be an economic drawback if it increased the delivery of supplies to the urban areas. Trotsky argued that the government's stocks of textiles should be distributed only to the village poor. He announced the need for a violent struggle against those richer peasants who were hoarding their grain, and he called for them to be sentenced to ten years' hard labour.[7]

Trotsky reverted to his vision of the ultimate communist objectives: 'And we say that we want to create on this earth a real paradise for people.'[8] Lenin might have thought this to be a sign of undesirable softness. If he had any doubts on this score they were dispelled by Trotsky's behaviour in the military campaign against Komuch. Arriving in the Volga region, Trotsky called together his commanders and commissars. The Red Army was in a dire situation but he declared that victory was possible if discipline and determination were shown. The Reds had to demand of themselves the utmost dedication if they were to prevail. Morale and co-ordination until then had been poor. Trotsky by his presence began to effect an improvement by holding the line at Sviyazhsk and planning to take Kazan.

He received impatient telegrams from Lenin complaining about the Red operations and demanding an immediate artillery bombardment even if it involved the obliteration of Kazan. The enemy should suffer 'merciless destruction'.[9] Trotsky replied that the Komuch forces had artillery only a little weaker than that possessed by the Reds. More to the point, the quality of the artillerymen on the Red side was inferior. Delay was unavoidable. Trotsky assured Lenin nevertheless that 'the suggestion that I am sparing Kazan is unjustified.'[10] The first military action involving Trotsky was at Sviyazhsk on the other side of the Volga. He spoke to troops at mass meetings, indicating that the survival of the October Revolution was threatened. The power of workers and peasants had to be protected. Confusion still abounded among the Reds. The leading Red commander was Mikhail Muravëv – a Left Socialist-Revolutionary – who deserted and took a contingent of his forces with him. Trotsky refused to let spirits droop. Pistol in hand, he toured the front calling for a redoubled effort against the Komuch army. The Reds secured Sviyazhsk on 28 August. Kazan fell to them on 10 September. It was the first Red triumph of the campaign. Trotsky's name was celebrated in Moscow.

But one incident in those days did him lasting political damage. It centred on the fate of a certain Panteleev who was commissar of the 2nd

Numerny Petrograd Regiment. When the battle around Sviyazhsk appeared to be going against the Reds, Panteleev and his men commandeered a steamship trying to escape upriver to Nizhni Novgorod. The vessel was boarded by other Red units and the fugitives were arrested. Trotsky ordered their summary execution.[11] Hardly had the punishment been carried out than agitation against Trotsky started among Bolsheviks serving in the Red Army. Panteleev had been a Bolshevik. To many party members it seemed that Trotsky, who had joined the Bolsheviks only a year earlier, had stepped over a terrible threshold. Bolsheviks, they maintained, ought to stick together. The really pernicious elements in the Red Army were not the Bolshevik commissars but the Imperial Army officers who were serving in it. The suspicion intensified that Trotsky liked the officer corps more than the party. But Lenin had no concerns. He believed that the mere appearance of the People's Commissar for Military Affairs was enough to steady nerves. He told Trotsky to visit the front yet again, to approach the Red troops directly and to give one of his speeches.[12] Based in Moscow, the Sovnarkom Chairman felt no inhibition in dispensing advice about operational matters beyond his knowledge. Trotsky did not mind. The telegrams from the capital expressed a sense of urgency and mercilessness which he shared; they were also proof of the esteem in which he was held.

The partnership of Lenin and Trotsky was nearly shattered on 30 August when an assassin fired at Lenin outside the Mikhelson Works in Moscow. Badly wounded, he was carried back to the Kremlin for medical treatment. Sverdlov took over co-ordination of the Soviet government and the Bolshevik party, and he wrote to Trotsky: 'Come back immediately. Ilich is wounded; it's uncertain how dangerous things are. Complete calm.'[13] A Red Terror was declared. It was to be carried out by the political police established by Lenin in December 1917. This was the Extraordinary Commission, usually known by its Russian acronym, Cheka; its leader was Dzerzhinski, who quickly acquired a reputation for clinical ruthlessness in suppressing anti-Soviet conspiracies. The Cheka took thousands of captives from the middle and upper classes after the attempt on Lenin's life. Some were immediately shot, others were kept as hostages in case the enemies of Bolshevism planned a series of assassinations. Trotsky fully endorsed the Red Terror and went to see Lenin as soon as his duties permitted. Lenin received the People's Commissar for Military Affairs at the Gorki sanatorium to the south-east of Moscow. Lenin purred with delight listening to Trotsky's stories: 'It seemed to me that he was looking at me with somehow different eyes. He had a way of *falling in love* when they showed him a certain side of themselves. There was this touch in his excited attention of being "in love".[14] If this was not an accurate recollection, it says less about Lenin than about Trotsky who was seldom emotionally attentive to fellow revolutionaries.

What is entirely credible is that Lenin concluded: 'The game is won. If we have succeeded in establishing order in the army, it means we shall establish it everywhere else. And the revolution – with order – will be unconquerable.'[15] Lenin and Trotsky had wanted a civil war in order to have the chance to carry out the irreversible suppression of the enemies of the October Revolution. Neither of them said this directly in public. A secret telegram that Trotsky had sent to Lenin on 17 August 1918 summed up their attitude:

> I consider it unacceptable to let steamers sail [the Volga] under a Red Cross flag. The receipt of grain will be interpreted by charlatans and fools as showing the possibility that agreement can be made and that civil war is unnecessary. The military motives are unknown to me. Air pilots and artillerymen have been ordered to bomb and set fire to the bourgeois districts of Kazan and then to Simbirsk and Samara. In these conditions a Red Cross caravan is inappropriate.[16]

Trotsky did not fight reluctantly; he did not bother with humanitarian considerations and eagerly deepened the political revolution by violent means. Lenin was of the same mind. While convalescing, he wrote *Proletarian Revolution and the Renegade Karl Kautsky*, postulating that Marx's doctrines stipulated the need for armed insurrection and class dictatorship.[17]

In order to regularize political control in the Red Army a Revolutionary-Military Council of the Republic, the RVSR, was established on 2 September, and Trotsky was appointed its chairman with Efraim Sklyanski as his deputy. The Council was empowered to liaise between the commanders and the commissars at every level, overseeing the Revolutionary-Military Councils of the various fronts. It would have made no sense to choose anyone other than Trotsky if party leaders wished to avoid institutional clashes between the Council and the People's Commissariat.[18] Not that there was a careful demarcation of functions. But Lenin was not bothered about this: he admired Trotsky's achievements and trusted him to work out the practicalities.

Lenin's attitude was not shared by the entire leadership. Stalin called for 'reins' to be put on Trotsky before he brought the October Revolution to ruin. Trotsky had issued the original order for Stalin to go to Tsaritsyn, nearly six hundred miles down the Volga from Kazan, to take political charge of the southern front.[19] He quickly regretted this. Stalin behaved like a law unto himself. Trotsky claimed too that the southern front's forces were not as staunch as those which he had trained around Kazan.[20] Stalin aggravated problems by assuming authority over purely military decisions. He established a Revolutionary-Military Council which directed all operations from Tsaritsyn on the Volga. It was not long before Stalin's activity clashed with the central plans agreed by Trotsky and the Commander-in-Chief Jukums Vācietis. Trotsky objected to such insubordination. Stalin retorted that, being on the spot, he needed to assume responsibility for sorting out the complex difficulties in the region around the front. By 4 October 1918 Trotsky had had enough and sent a telegram to Lenin: 'I categorically insist on Stalin's removal.'[21]

The truth was hard to establish in the wartime conditions. Stalin and Trotsky plunged into a sea of vituperative exchanges, always copying them to the Central Committee. The hope of Lenin and Sverdlov was that the two protagonists would calm down and work together amicably. But reports got through to Moscow about the effects of organizational chaos. Stalin's refusal to comply with higher commands were harming the war effort; his temperamental prickliness was evident from his language even before Sverdlov met him to seek a compromise. What is more, it was becoming clear that Stalin engaged in risky tactics which were resulting in huge military losses. Lenin was leaning to Trotsky's side in the tussle. Stalin's reaction was to give quiet support to the party critics of official party policy. Even Lenin did not appreciate how many Imperial officers were being employed in the Red Army. Just as Stalin had conducted military operations as if they were his private affair, Trotsky had steadily built up the command staff with experienced personnel from the armed forces of Nicholas II. He was doing nothing contrary to governmental policy. But he did it on a scale which he did not report to the Central Committee.

He explained to Lenin that the Red Army would collapse without the skills of former Imperial officers, and Lenin decided to support the People's Commissar for Military Affairs. But problems were growing for Trotsky in the party. The Panteleev affair became a chronic sore. Trotsky gained a reputation for being excessively keen on executions as a way of running the armed forces. Stalin was equally ruthless in using repressive measures to secure discipline but at this stage avoided intimidating the political commissars. Most of these were Bolshevik party militants. Every time Trotsky reprimanded or threatened them in the Red Army he strengthened worries about his attitude to Bolshevism. Stalin did not have to stir up or co-ordinate the objections to him. Already in June there had been harsh criticism of Trotsky's methods.[22] The Military Opposition, as it came to be known, arose without artificial stimulation and consisted of a diverse body of Bolsheviks. Some wanted party leaders, not commanders, to lead the Red Army. Others called for the commanders to be elected. Others again believed that a non-centralized system of military organization was desirable. All agreed, though, that Trotsky was a deep threat to the survival of the values of Bolshevism and the October Revolution.

Things might have come to a head in the last couple of months of 1918 if the Bolsheviks had not confronted an even sterner military menace than Komuch had presented in the summer. Admiral Kolchak had busily assembled anti-Bolshevik officers in Omsk in western Siberia. At first he offered his services to the Socialist-Revolutionaries who had fled there after their defeat in the Volga region. Kolchak and his fellow officers had contempt for all politicians, and in November 1918 they set up their own Directory. Kolchak proclaimed himself Supreme Ruler of All Russia and, with British material support, began to advance westward towards the Urals. A fresh front in the Civil War had been opened. Kolchak led the first of the White armies, which took up the colour as standing for purity and patriotism against the internationalism of the Reds.

Trotsky had for some months been worrying about the competence of the Bolsheviks who would have to repel any such attack. His criticisms became the cause for complaints to Lenin by Ivar Smilga and Mikhail Lashevich, two high-ranking party leaders. Neither was a friend of Stalin. Trotsky at the time had dismissed their words as 'coquettishness'. This was a word sometimes applied to Trotsky himself before the Great War, when his opponents had suggested that he paraded as some-one who hated compromising his revolutionary doctrines. Now it was Trotsky who accused his critics of lacking practical seriousness. I. N. Smirnov, who had been a Left Communist in the Brest-Litovsk days and had struggled against Lenin, asserted that the hierarchical regulations in the armed forces were inimical to the comradely traditions of the party. More predictable in their hostility to Lenin was the 'Tsaritsyn group', which assailed Trotsky for being an arch-authoritarian. Trotsky was late to decry them as being Stalinists in the making; but in fact one of them, Sergei Minin, had been a Left Communist and even Stalin's party associate Kliment Voroshilov was far from supporting Stalin in everything he did. Trotsky had quickly squandered the good will he had accrued in the battles for the Volga. Instead of assuaging internal party worries, he had embittered everyone who got in his way. He had proved himself a valiant revolutionary and an adaptable military leader. But his record as a politician was woeful: he punched when he should have embraced.

What saved him at the time was the dire emergency faced by Sovnarkom. Dreadful news arrived in December 1918. Perm, one of the great cities of the Urals, had fallen to Kolchak. The Reds had collapsed into a demoralized heap: the army had retreated headlong and the governmental and party machinery was broken. The way was opened for the Whites to begin their campaign for central Russia. Nobody, not even Stalin, could deny that Trotsky was the man who could rally the forces for the defence of the approaches to Moscow.

# 24. ALMOST THE COMMANDER

Trotsky stopped quarrelling with Stalin for some weeks after the Perm disaster. The central party leadership sent Stalin and Dzerzhinski to investigate the situation in the Urals in January 1919. Trotsky was all in favour, saying there had been too much 'softness' on the eastern front. He urged that Stalin should purge the guilty commissars – as long as Stalin was kept out of military decision-making, Trotsky could find a use for him.[1] The report from Stalin and Dzerzhinski was alarming. The Soviet administration had collapsed. The Red Army was chaotic and demoralized and its discipline had disintegrated. The communist party was unable to help. Stalin and Dzerzhinski wrote that a complete reorganization was necessary to avoid further catastrophes. Hierarchy had to be strengthened. The muddle in the state order had to be eliminated. There had to be a clearer demarcation of responsibilities in party, government and army.[2] The entire party leadership accepted the findings. Such was Trotsky's confidence in Stalin that he wanted to keep him there in place of Mikhail Lashevich and empower him to rectify the situation. He put Stalin's name forward for the same sort of mission in Simbirsk in late March 1919, and he strongly supported Stalin's inclusion in the Revolutionary-Military Council of the south-western front in Ukraine in May 1920.[3]

Nonetheless Trotsky continued to reject Stalin's idea that Bolsheviks necessarily made for better commanders than professional officers; and he had firmly opposed letting Stalin appoint the new military command on the eastern front in the Urals in January 1919.[4] The Military Opposition gathered in strength and asserted that Trotsky had become too big for his boots. Trotsky was reluctant to give an inch. He denied that the supreme military command had interfered unduly on each front. He picked holes in the case against him. Thus he noted that his opponents had called upon him to stop travelling around those fronts and to stay put in Moscow. He expressed doubt whether the Central Committee really wanted this – and he knew what the answer would be after his sterling performance at Sviyazhsk. He also asked who was going to direct the Red Army if the

Military Opposition had its way and there were going to be frequent consultative gatherings of political commissars. According to Trotsky, war did not allow for such time-wasting. He made only one concession, when agreeing that a few more party comrades should be considered for insertion in the supreme command. Sverdlov persuaded him to give postings to Ivar Smilga and Mikhail Lashevich (who subsequently failed to cover themselves with glory at the front).[5]

Trotsky only gradually came to understand that fundamental decisions about how to wage the Civil War lay in the hands of the central party leadership. Since becoming People's Commissar for Military Affairs he had either acted on his own initiative or, at a pinch, turned to Lenin and Sverdlov for help in enforcing his orders. While streamlining and formalizing the hierarchy in the Red Army, he disliked submitting his military preferences to institutional control. He was no more ready than Stalin to receive orders that contradicted his ideas. And he lacked Stalin's cunning; he lacked the talent to manage his own talent.

Through the long winter of 1918–19 the structure of Soviet politics was under renovation. Until then a multiplicity of competing institutions had existed. The result was administrative disorder. Among leading Bolsheviks – Trotsky was one of the exceptions – it became accepted that only one agency, the Russian Communist Party, had the capacity to bring about order. A common call went up for the party to be centralized so that it could control the state organizations and direct the war effort. Since the suppression of the Left Socialist-Revolutionaries in July 1918 the Soviet republic was a one-party state in all but name. Now the Bolsheviks sought to turn the party into the supreme agency of government. Even the central party leadership was reformed. Few Central Committee members could stay in Moscow in wartime. A Political Bureau (or Politburo) was established inside it to manage policy between Central Committee plenums – Trotsky's significance was recognized by his inclusion in the Politburo despite his need to be away from Moscow most of the time; an Organizational Bureau (or Orgburo) was added to handle the internal party administration. Sverdlov's death from influenza in March 1919 reinforced the moves towards the regularizing of procedures.[6]

This had been decided before the Eighth Party Congress met in March 1919. Trotsky had intended to be present in order to speak against the Military Opposition. Kolchak's resumption of his advance stopped him from attending. But Trotsky bombarded the Kremlin with intransigent ideas and refused Zinoviev's plea for a compromise: 'I stand by the viewpoint that we need "to tighten the screws".'[7] Lenin vacillated until

Trotsky explained to him how many former Imperial officers had been recruited to the Red Army and how important a contribution they were making. The Military Opposition's anger was intense and a secret session had to be held at the Congress. It was a heated affair, and Lenin surprised many by attacking the Tsaritsyn group – and Stalin by implication – for the casual waste of Red soldiers on the southern front. But Trotsky's case was not incorporated in its entirety. The Congress underlined the need for a more careful treatment of communists in the armed forces. It also stressed the importance of controlling the command corps. It highlighted the supremacy of the party hierarchy in every aspect of the war effort. This was a lightly veiled warning to Trotsky.[8]

Initially he resented the compromise agreed at the Congress. He should have been grateful. The Congress had calmed his critics sufficiently for a set of procedures to be instituted which preserved his autonomy from control by political commissars at the front. Steadily he calmed down. He understood that the complexity of decisions about strategy, supply and personnel grew as the number of military fronts increased. The Sviyazhsk–Kazan operations had been short lived and simple. Now the Moscow political leadership, the high command and the dispersed Red forces required co-ordination in a sophisticated fashion, and Trotsky accepted that all matters of large importance had to be discussed in the central party leadership. He was usually unable to attend meetings in Moscow, so he made regular use of telegrams to the Central Committee. If a crisis broke out and he needed to take rapid action, he would propose a solution and seek approval. 'I request instructions' became a conventional phrase even for him.[9] Unilateral personal initiatives became fewer and a dependable network of liaison and command was implemented in the Red Army, the People's Commissariats and the Cheka.

Trotsky looked and felt comfortable in his military uniform of a smart dull-green tunic, a cap and a greatcoat. He had always been a sharp dresser and the war, during which he reached his fortieth birthday, allowed him to indulge himself in this respect. He had also been known for exceptional punctiliousness at work, and he brought this quality to his activity in the armed forces. Meetings had to start on time. Reports had to be thoroughly prepared. Clothes and weapons had to be presented clean, smart and ready for use. He was angry with anyone who turned up without their boots polished.

Trotsky did not bother with banter. Reportedly Yuri Pyatakov, a Party Central Committee associate member in 1921, trembled when receiving a telephone call from him.[10] One of the sharpest observers of the Bolshevik wartime scene was Anatoli Lunacharski in the People's Commissariat of Enlightenment. He doubted that anyone else, even Lenin, 'could have coped with the titanic mission [he] took upon his shoulders, with those lightning moves from place to place, those astounding speeches, those fanfares of on-the-spot orders, that role of being the unceasing electrifier of a weakening army, now in one place and then in another'.[11] Lunacharski laced the honey with vinegar:

> He had immense imperiousness and an inability or unwillingness to be in any way kind or attentive to people; the absence of that charm which always surrounded Lenin condemned Trotsky to a certain solitariness. One need only recall that even several of his personal friends (I am speaking of course about the political sphere) turned into his sworn enemies.[12]

Lunacharski, writing in 1923, was referring to the years before 1917 but evidently thought that these were lasting defects in Trotsky's personality.

The People's Commissar travelled on what was called the Trotsky train. He badgered his staff to get it in good order and rebuked them when it did not meet his specifications.[13] Most people thought there was only one locomotive and one set of carriages. In fact he had four locomotives and two whole sets of carriages at his disposal.[14] He had his own bed, desk, chair and sofa. His personal assistants and servants had their own separate space and there were decent cooking facilities. The restaurant-car served as a club for the entire travelling staff. Installed in one carriage was a printing press. Trotsky pump-handled his words into a constant stream of articles; and his press section, officially known as the Campaign Press of RVSR Chairman Trotsky, issued the flysheets and newspapers of his team at each station where they stopped.[15] If the train halted in a city – or even a small village – he would usually deliver a speech. As word about the Soviet administration got about the country, nearly everybody heard at least about Lenin and Trotsky. Whereas Lenin spoke exclusively in Moscow and Petrograd, Trotsky gave tongue to Bolshevism in hundreds of places in European Russia and Ukraine. Workers and peasants who listened to him were frequently entranced, and there was always an eagerness to set eyes on the great man.

The Trotsky train had the following personnel by the end of 1918:

5  Personal assistants

14  Technical staff (including photographer, painter, engraver and treasurer)

4 Office staff of the Train Commander

41 Communications service

12 Finance department

5 Command staff

2 Draughtsmen

17 Typesetting assistants

12 Trotsky's personal bodyguard

35 Military band

6 Cavalrymen of the 1st Moscow Food Supplies Detachment

30 2nd Latvian Riflemen's Soviet Regiment

15 9th Latvian Riflemen's Soviet Regiment

39 Artillerymen of the 3rd Special Tasks Regiment

32 38th Simonovski-Rogozhskii Infantry Regiment

11 Armoured cars unit

14 Restaurant car staff

23 Boilermen and stokers

16 Conductors

8 Grease-men

38 Guards[16]

This was no mere transport facility for the People's Commissar but a full military–political organization.

Trotsky grew in military stature. He could master a strategic or tactical brief in seconds. He demanded and received regular reports from the command staff; he supervised all the fronts from a distance and made frequent visits to each. He learned by intuition and observation. Once he had discharged his military and political duties he liked to write about party policies on international relations, economics, security and politics.

He raised the question of the national composition of personnel in the armed forces. Jews and Latvians were heavily represented in the soviets as well as in the Cheka but not in the Red Army since their literacy and numeracy made them invaluable administrators. In the Red Army it was asked why so few of them made themselves available for active military service. Trotsky was concerned that this had led to 'strong chauvinistic agitation', and the Politburo entrusted him and Ivar Smilga with drawing up measures to rectify the situation.[17] Thus a Jew and a Latvian were asked to broaden the ethnic base of the Red armed forces; there is no evidence that they made any difference but at least they were willing to try. Trotsky baulked Lenin in a further aspect of the national question. In Ukraine the Bolsheviks confronted political rivals in the Borotbists, who were close to the Left Socialist-Revolutionaries on most questions except that they pursued the national interests of Ukrainians. Borotbists were operating legally in the soviets. In Trotsky's eyes they had lurched 'to the right' and relied on 'kulak elements'; he called for them to be outlawed.[18] Lenin, however, wished to incorporate the Borotbist party as a whole in the Russian Communist Party (Bolsheviks) as a means of raising the proportion of ethnic Ukrainians in its postings in Ukraine, and it was Lenin who won the discussion in the central party leadership.[19] Trotsky was more alert than Lenin to the danger that national aspirations might get out of hand in Ukraine. His warnings did not mean he wanted to Russify the Ukrainians: Trotsky welcomed the Ukrainian-language schools, universities and newspapers that were springing up.[20]

He adapted Marxism to his wartime experience. Addressing the General Staff Academy students in 1918, he discoursed on the theme that 'only a class army can be strong.' He did not feel the need to spell out what he meant – perhaps he had no definite idea. He indicated that workers and peasants should be promoted to the heights of the Red Army if they showed talent or potential. But he could not stomach automatic promotion. The armed forces had to be efficient. They needed, above all, to be well led and there was no substitute for professional qualifications. 'Partisan methods' were hopelessly inadequate.[21] He generally found 'Red officers' to be of little use; he preferred to promote NCOs who had proven military experience[22] – and by late autumn 1919 he had secured access to nearly two hundred thousand of them. For Trotsky, this was just as important as securing the services of the sixty thousand officers from the Imperial Army. It also pleased him that workers constituted up to a fifth of the strength of the Red Army.[23] He never forgot his commitment to appealing to the 'proletariat' and enabling it to prove itself in action. These were nothing like the thoughts of a military dictator in the making.

What is more, Trotsky treated former Imperial officers severely until such time as they earned his respect. He took hostages from their families. He was alert to signs of treachery after the spectacular instances when leaders such as Mikhail Muravëv took their troops over to join the anti-Bolshevik forces. He wrote to Stalin expressing his suspicions about Alexander Verkhovski – and he continued to warn about possible disloyalty in the command staff through to 1920.[24] Trotsky's reputation as friend of the tsarist officer corps was widely held among Bolsheviks – and Stalin helped to disseminate it. But it was far from the truth. Trotsky was feared and admired in equal proportions by commanders. Summary executions were one of his favoured measures. He once chided subordinates who omitted to hold a field court-martial before ordering a shooting; but the rebuke was a gentle one since he too wished to terrorize his forces into obedience.[25] Trotsky's emphasis always fell on practical results and he remained a zealot for harsh discipline. He implemented a policy of decimating regiments which deserted or showed cowardice under enemy fire, and the victims included the commanders.[26]

He did a poor job of explaining this to the party. In fact he was not even trying. Disdaining to ingratiate himself with veteran Bolsheviks, he wrote as if they had made little contribution to the October Revolution. His book *From October to Brest-Litovsk*, published in 1919, scarcely mentioned Bolshevik party organizations; and when he deigned to refer to the Bolsheviks he sometimes chose to call them the Maximalists. It was as if he desired to deBolshevize the revolutionary past.[27]

Bolsheviks were eager students of the history of earlier revolutions and were especially drawn to learning lessons from what had happened in France in the years after 1789. The overthrow of the absolute monarchy had been followed by a succession of radical administrations. Maximilien Robespierre had put himself forward as the leader of militant atheism and social transformation, and he strengthened a campaign of terror against the domestic enemies of the French Revolution. Yet his authority was undermined by economic chaos as well as by external intervention; he also never succeeded in extirpating all the political forces ranged against him – and in 1794 he himself fell victim to an order for his execution by guillotine. This febrile revolutionary atmosphere permitted a talented young Corsican officer, Napoleon Bonaparte, to emerge. His military success and his popularity inside the armed forces gained him appointment as first consul by 1799. Making himself emperor in 1804, he sought to turn back many of the radical reforms enacted by preceding regimes. Such an outcome was feared by Bolsheviks after the October Revolution and Trotsky was regarded as the likeliest candidate for the role of the Soviet Napoleon.

The Panteleev affair continued to dog him. As Trotsky's enemies pointed out, though, his general orders kept open the possibility of putting to death communists on active service without due consideration being given to the specific circumstances.[28] His violent language did not help him. When treachery was discovered among ex-Imperial officers on the eastern front, he sent a telegram threatening to shoot commissars who let traitors slip through their hands. Two leading Bolsheviks in the vicinity, Pëtr Zalutski and Ivan Bakaev, treated this as a menace to their lives. Word got about that only Ivar Smilga's intervention had saved Zalutski and Bakaev from being executed. Even *Pravda* printed a version of the story. Trotsky complained vehemently about the article and in points of detail had right on his side.[29] But in one case he genuinely came close to procuring the execution of a prominent communist, Mikhail Kedrov, who led the Revolutionary-Military Council of the northern front above Petrograd. Kedrov in September 1918 refused to accept a redeployment. Trotsky ordered the setting up of a military field tribunal to deal with 'all who dare to shirk their duties and play at opposition'. Trotsky wanted to set a clear lesson: 'Soviet saboteurs must be punished as severely as the bourgeois ones.'[30]

By April 1919 Trotsky had decided that only a Politburo enquiry would enable him to clear his name in the Panteleev affair. Nikolai Krestinski, Leonid Serebryakov and Smilga led the investigations.[31] Krestinski and Serebryakov had been on Trotsky's side in the Brest-Litovsk dispute and were to support him in the internal party controversies in the 1920s; their inclusion in an enquiry into the killing of Panteleev was a sign that the party leadership did not want to harass Trotsky at a time of acute military peril to the Soviet state. Trotsky argued that he had been correct in condoning the decision of the Revolutionary-Military Tribunal to execute the political commissar. He had been shot not as a communist but as a cowardly deserter.[32] In May 1919 he made a further personal attempt to deal severely with a Bolshevik. Trotsky had warned against a certain Panyushkin being assigned to the Red Army. Panyushkin confirmed his worst suspicions by refusing to deliver six hundred deserters to summary justice.[33] Trotsky demanded that Panyushkin should be delivered to the Tribunal of the Republic; after the trouble over Panteleev he proposed that Panyushkin should first be stripped of his party membership – and he took the precaution of getting the Politburo to adjudicate. The Politburo turned him down and Panyushkin was redeployed to the Cheka while remaining a Bolshevik party member.[34] Trotsky was furious and went on collecting evidence about Panyushkin's 'criminal activity'.[35]

Trotsky selected his aides by criteria of ability and did not mind if they had no lengthy previous adherence to Bolshevism. He had picked Efraim Sklyanski as deputy chairman of the Revolutionary-Military Council of the Republic. Brilliant and energetic, Sklyanski had been an active Marxist but not a Bolshevik before the Great War. He had caught

Trotsky's eye in 1917 as an army doctor and a political militant – and his success as a commissar in the military high command immediately after the October Revolution confirmed him as a person of undoubted talent.[36] Trotsky also selected personal assistants such as Mikhail Glazman, Georgi Butov and Igor Poznanski. Glazman was short, youthful and dynamic. He started as Trotsky's travelling short-hand typist. Unflinching in physical combat, he turned himself into a brilliant administrator.[37] Butov and Poznanski had similar qualities. Unfortunately for Trotsky, his choice of subordinates strengthened suspicions about him.

He continued to show great courage. His conduct at Sviyazhsk was known to everyone in the Red Army. Danger existed even in the incident when his train accidentally hit an obstacle at Gorki Station south of Moscow. It was the dead of night and a terrible shaking woke him from his sleep:

> Still half asleep, I summoned up the strength to grope my way along the side of the bed. The familiar rumbling had abruptly stopped; the carriage had turned on its edge, and stood dead still. In the silence of the night, a solitary weak, plaintive voice could be heard. The heavy carriage-doors had been so skewed that they could not be opened; it was impossible get out. No one appeared, and this alarmed me. Was it the enemy? With revolver in my hand, I jumped out of a window and ran into someone with a lantern. It was the train commander, who had been unable to make his way through to me. The carriage was perched on a slope with three wheels dug deep into the embankment and the other three raised high above the rails. The carriage's rear and front platforms had been crumpled. The front grating had pinned down a guard to his platform, and it was his plaintive little voice, like the crying of a child, that was audible in the darkness.[38]

Trotsky did not mention such occurrences in his reports to Lenin: he took it for granted that war was full of them.

He had started to think of himself as a military man. Armed conflict in his eyes made a bond among those who had experienced it. 'Militarism' had always been one of the most pejorative terms among Marxists. Trotsky stood out against the convention. Militarist methods, he decided, were not so bad after all. They induced mental exactitude, verbal concision and practical precision. Life in an army involved being prepared for action and taking responsibility. Trotsky concluded that such qualities would not go amiss in peacetime outside the Red Army.[39]

He had not forgotten the ultimate objectives of Marxism and remained devoted to creating a world without war. He wrote a stirring article on the subject for *Izvestiya* in July 1919 noting that people were saying that military conflict was an eternal characteristic of human societies. Once there had been cannibalism but it had ceased in most communities. Wars of feudal knights had gone into oblivion. More recently there had been the custom of individuals settling their difference by means of duels. This too had been stopped. 'National wars' currently dominated the agenda of world politics but there was no reason for despair. History was moving onward. Marxism taught that 'war was and remains a form of armed exploitation and armed struggle against exploitation.'[40] The conclusion was obvious: as soon as socialism had triumphed around the globe and the proletariat had crushed the bourgeoisie, the objective conditions which bred any type of war would disappear. Although Trotsky lacked a plausible plan for how to put an end to armed conflict, he cherished the vision of a harmonious global society. He had not lost his capacity to dream.

# 25. RED VICTORY

The war between the Reds and Whites peaked in intensity in early 1919. Kolchak, fresh from his success in the Urals, made his dispositions for an offensive in the direction of Moscow. The Whites could also call upon the Volunteer Army, now led by General Anton Denikin after the deaths of its founders Generals Mikhail Alexeev and Lavr Kornilov, which was readying itself to smash down Bolshevism. The government of independent Ukraine rooted out Bolshevik party organizations which sought to implant themselves after the German military occupation had been brought to an end. The British and French gave political and material support to Kolchak and Denikin. The Soviet state covered an area little bigger than medieval Muscovy.

Trotsky was heavily engaged in co-ordinating the Soviet armed forces and so was unable to attend the Eighth Party Congress of the Russian Communist Party in March. He missed the chance to defend his military policy against its critics. His absence also meant that he did not witness the growth of opposition to the way the Soviet state was being reconstructed. A small group known as the Democratic Centralists led by Timofei Sapronov approved of organizational centralization but urged that there should be democratic control from below in party and soviets. They bemoaned the decline in the number of officials who were genuinely elected to their posts; they suggested that dictatorial tendencies had appeared and should be eliminated. Other dissenters in the party wanted to go a lot further. Within a year they were to form the Workers' Opposition. Headed by Alexander Shlyapnikov and Alexandra Kollontai, this group argued that workers and peasants should be empowered to take decisions on the economy. Workers' Oppositionists claimed that their ideas had once been at the heart of the party's doctrines. They urged a reversion to the agenda of 1917. The Democratic Centralists and the Workers' Opposition called the entire central leadership to account. They did not pick on Trotsky any more than on anyone else, but he was a prime object of their anger – and he would have been given a hard time at the Congress if he could have been present.

The Civil War called him away. Central Russia lay directly in the path of Kolchak's forces. Lenin called for the defence of the Revolution as a sense of emergency spread to Moscow. Kolchak sustained his offensive through to May 1919 when the Red Army succeeded in throwing the Whites back across the Urals and pursuing them along the Trans-Siberian railway. The Whites had almost as much trouble from peasant insurrections as from the Red Army. Kolchak was criticized by advisers from the Western Allies, who threatened to cut off foreign aid unless he committed himself to holding elections in the event of his triumph over Bolshevism. His capacity to lead and co-ordinate descended into a shambles. His access to industrial goods vanished as he moved into areas devoid of manufacturing activity. The Reds had a growing numerical advantage in troops and equipment; they also had better facilities for transport and communication. The Whites did not lose all hope even then. At various points along the railway Kolchak ordered a halt and regrouped his army to impede the Reds' forward movement.[1]

Vācietis as Supreme Commander-in-Chief advocated a period of recuperation and training for the Red Army; but Sergei Kamenev, who led the Red forces on the eastern front, and was no relation of the Politburo member, disagreed; his telegrams urged Lenin and Trotsky to resume the advance. Kamenev's zeal commended itself to Lenin, and the Politburo together with Smilga and Lashevich in the Revolutionary-Military Council of the Republic decided to replace Vācietis with Kamenev. The decision annoyed Trotsky, who agreed with Kamenev on the need to appreciate the weariness of the troops as well as the rising danger posed by Denikin's forces as they moved up from the south in a twin-pronged advance through the Donets Basin and Ukraine. As Trotsky later admitted, though, there was also a risk that Kolchak might restore his strength if given a respite over several weeks. The arguments on both sides were finely poised. Stalin sent messages to Lenin dropping heavy hints that Trotsky was getting to big for his boots yet again. In fact Trotsky was brooding. Having lost the struggle to keep Vācietis, he felt undervalued. In a fit of pique he submitted his resignation as People's Commissar for Military Affairs, warning fellow party leaders that they neglected the southern front against Denikin at their peril.

The final straw for him was the recrudescence of objections to his whole way of running the Red Army. He was ill and exhausted; he wanted sympathy and support. Others in the Central Committee disapproved of him but knew that he would be a difficult people's commissar to replace. On 5 July the party leadership was prompted to decide:

The Orgburo and Politburo of the Central Committee, after examining comrade Trotsky's statement and discussing it in all its aspects, has come to the unanimous conclusion that it is in absolutely no position to accept Comrade Trotsky's resignation and comply with his request.

The Orgburo and Politburo of the Central Committee will do everything in their power to make the work on the southern front – work which is now the most difficult, dangerous and important and which comrade Trotsky himself has chosen – the most suitable for his requirements and the most productive for the Republic. In his rank as People's Commissar for Military Affairs and as chairman of the Revolutionary-Military Council, comrade Trotsky is fully able to act also as a member of the Revolutionary-Military Council of the southern front in co-operation with the front commander (Yegorov), whom he himself proposed and whom the Central Committee accordingly confirmed.

The Organizational and Political Bureau of the Central Committee present comrade Trotsky with the full opportunity to use all means for securing whatever he thinks will correct the line in the military question and, if he desires, to try and bring forward the Party Congress.[2]

Even Stalin signed the resolution.[3]

Lenin wrote to Sklyanski: 'Trotsky's illness is a true misfortune at this present moment.'[4] He also handed over a carte blanche of endorsement to Trotsky himself:

Comrades!

Knowing the strictness of comrade Trotsky's orders, I'm so confident – to an absolute degree – that this particular order by comrade Trotsky is correct, sensible and vital for the good of the cause that I unreservedly support the order given.

V. Ulyanov (Lenin)[5]

The idea was that Trotsky could flourish it in the faces of leading Bolsheviks who made difficulties for him. Trotsky never had to use the blank. But his pride had already been salvaged and he agreed to resume his duties.

Nobody by that time could be in any doubt that the Denikin offensive had the potential for success. The Whites had moved smartly from the south, taking Tsaritsyn and Kharkov in the second half of June. It was from Tsaritsyn that Denikin issued his Moscow Directive. Fanning out his forces, he ordered them to seize every railway that led to the Russian capital. Kiev fell to the Whites in late August. Trotsky took his train towards the front. While still feeling a little sore about the recent internal party dispute, he was pleased to find his military ideas being welcomed by political commissars in his many meetings with them.[6] The survival of the Soviet order was on a knife edge and Trotsky rallied the Red Army. It transpired that Denikin had spread his strength thinly. As his forces advanced north from Tsaritsyn he lacked the men and supplies to finish off the Red contingents confronting him and was halted by fierce resistance over two hundred miles to the north outside Saratov.[7] The main thrust by the Whites would therefore have to come through central Ukraine. Trotsky stayed in the vicinity of Kiev, feeling confident about the operation in the Volga region.[8] Ukraine was a different matter. Every province teemed with peasant revolts. Bolsheviks had few ethnic Ukrainians as party members. The Soviet administration had annoyed the peasants by trying to force them into collective farms. Trotsky gave priority to the military and political efforts being made to secure the region for the October Revolution.

Both the Reds and the Whites had problems with peasants who had organized themselves into bands of partisans. Known as the Greens, they fought in defence of rural rights. They rejected the demands being made on them for conscription and grain. The Greens operated in most provinces. Sometimes they were led by anarchists or Socialist-Revolutionaries – and in certain areas such as Ukraine they assembled contingents of tens of thousands of men. Denikin had the reputation of being antagonistic towards the peasants. His army incurred heavy losses as he sought to make his way northward.

The campaign's outcome was put beyond doubt in summer 1919 by a series of exhausting military engagements. There were no protracted battles but the Whites were worsted in clash after clash. The communists made the most of their superiority in manpower, military equipment and communications. The resumption of Red control over the Urals and western Siberia, moreover, somewhat eased the shortage of food supplies to the big Russian cities. Denikin had premised his strategy on the achievement of a quick knock-out blow. When this failed to occur, he had to pull back his forces south towards Crimea. Trotsky and the Reds followed in hot pursuit. As he did so he was re-entering the places of his boyhood. His was not going to be a gentle return, as he indicated in a telegram to Moscow: 'The first requirement is a radical purge in the rear, especially in the big centres: Kiev, Odessa, Nikolaev, Kherson.' He asked for the dispatch of up to two thousand fresh militants from the capital. He argued the special need for 'absolutely reliable Cheka units'. Once re-Sovietized, Ukraine was to be secured for Bolshevism on a permanent basis.[9] The Politburo granted him five hundred militants and endorsed his general plan.[10]

Planning continued in Kiev for strategic dispositions in southern Ukraine. One possibility was to withdraw Red forces from the Black Sea coast. Trotsky sent telegrams to Sklyanski in Moscow about his conclusions but misunderstandings somehow ensued between the Revolutionary-Military Council of the Republic and the Politburo. Trotsky issued Sklyanski with a rebuke: 'You have again fallen into confusion as the result of your inattentive reading of telegrams.' He even accused Sklyanski of sloth.[11] But the moment of tension quickly passed. Trotsky got the munitions he had been requesting for an all-out assault on the positions of the Whites to the south. The Politburo, on receiving up-to-date and accurate reports, 'suggested' that he should give priority to the defence of Odessa; its members assured him that 'our assistance is not far distant.'[12] Trotsky noted that the chief threat to the Soviet administration around Odessa was an uprising of 'colonists'.[13] (Probably they were Germans rather than Jews.) Before he could put his childhood knowledge of the region to further use, he learned that the other half of Denikin's forces was resurgent to the east and had begun to threaten Voronezh near the River Don. Denikin seemed poised to cut off Trotsky and the Reds in Ukraine. 'What's the matter?' Trotsky asked Sklyanski. 'How have we been able to overlook this? Tell the Commander-in-Chief that that things can't be done like this.'[14]

Trotsky was as much to blame as anybody since it had been he who had chosen to concentrate Red forces in Ukraine. Rapid redeployments were essential. Steady progress was being made against Kolchak's forces and final victory became ever more likely. Trotsky, the Revolutionary-Military Council of the Republic and the Red Army high command resumed their mood of calm determination. The Reds mopped up all lingering White forces. They also turned on the peasant forces – the so-called Greens – under Nestor Makhno and Nikifor Grigorev which had until then been co-operating in attacking Denikin's contingents. Trotsky ordered the extirpation of every trace of armed hostility to Bolshevism as the Ukrainian Soviet Republic was re-established. A last battle was fought with Denikin near Orël halfway between Moscow and Kharkov. The Reds won a crushing victory. Denikin, apart from a few attempts at stopping and taking on the Reds, focused his efforts on holding his retreating army together. Morale among the Whites was low and still dropping; but his hope was to gather his officers and troops in Crimea with a view to launching a second great invasion of Ukraine and Russia.

It was at this moment that a third White army emerged from independent Estonia. General Nikolai Yudenich led it. Although his preparations had taken longer than those of Kolchak and Denikin he had spent the time wisely. Prisoner-of-war camps in Germany had been scoured for volunteers to fight the Reds. The Western Allies supplied an abundance of equipment including tanks. Yudenich also recruited Estonians who wanted to ensure that no Soviet regime could be re-established in their homeland. Estonia had been a sovereign state since February 1918 and its inhabitants were determined to maintain this situation. Yudenich's Whites moved eastward in early October 1919 and caught the Bolsheviks by surprise. Trotsky and the Red Army high command were at that time directing operations south of Moscow.

Petrograd stood in Yudenich's path and Zinoviev, who was based there, understood the danger to the city. His pessimistic reports to Lenin induced the central party leadership to give serious consideration to abandoning the city. Trotsky was shocked as he followed the discussion from afar:

> The Petrograd leaders and, above all, Zinoviev were telling Lenin how the enemy's equipment was excellent in every respect – the automatic rifles, tanks, aeroplanes, the British monitors on their flank and so forth. Lenin came to the conclusion that we could take up a successful fight against Yudenich's officer army, which was armed with the very latest technology, only at the cost of stripping and enfeebling the other fronts, especially the southern one. But this was unimaginable. In his opinion there was only one thing to do: abandon Petrograd and cut back the front line. After deciding on the need for such an amputation, Lenin set about winning others over to his side.
>
> When I arrived in Moscow from the south, I firmly opposed this plan.[15]

Lenin and Trotsky fell into acrimonious dispute. The Politburo was split. Not until twenty-four hours later did Trotsky, with help from his political friend Krestinski and his enemy Stalin, win the discussions as Lenin conceded: 'Very well, let us try!'[16]

The Politburo adopted Trotsky's draft decree to 'transform Soviet Russia into a military camp'. Unconscripted men were to be registered for military availability. Talk of evacuating Petrograd was to be regarded as treason. Trotsky promised 'to defend Petrograd to the last ounce of blood, to refuse to yield a foot, and to carry the struggle into the streets of the city'.[17] The peril from the White advance had increased. By the time Trotsky set off for the north, on 16 October, Yudenich had swept eastward to Tsarskoe Selo and was eight miles from Petrograd. No White commander got nearer to one of Russia's two capital cities.

When Trotsky arrived in Petrograd he was unimpressed by the preparations being made by the city authorities. He behaved brusquely towards Zinoviev. Stalin too was deployed by the party leadership to Petrograd, and he distinguished himself by marshalling a group of middle-class citizens in a line in front of the Red forces so as to deter Yudenich from firing on the city's defenders. 'Exemplary' mass executions were another of Stalin's measures.[18] Trotsky offered no objection. At times it seemed that Trotsky and Stalin were competing for the status of the most brutal commissar. At the same time, though, Trotsky found ways to raise the spirits of his own troops. He commissioned Demyan Bedny to write stirring verses for the military operation. (Bedny's wife was anxious about his accompanying the army and Trotsky had had to promise to bring him back to her in one piece.)[19] Trotsky's initiative proved successful when the poet came up with a poem about the Yudenich tanks and the daring of Red artilleryman Vanka in holding up their advance – and the Red Army soldiers responded well.[20] Meanwhile Trotsky struck fear into the hearts of party and soviet officials in the Smolny Institute in Petrograd. He accepted nothing short of total and selfless commitment. Purges of the timid or incompetent were ordered. Where gaps were left, he filled them with the military contingent which travelled everywhere with him on the Trotsky train.

His slogan was: 'We will not give up Petrograd!' When a Red Army regiment scattered under an onslaught by the Whites, Trotsky did not flinch from assuming personal command. He jumped on the nearest horse and chased the retreating soldiers. His orderly Kozlov hurried after him and together they rallied the troops, stiffened the resolve of their commander and reassembled the front against Yudenich.[21] This was the sole time in the Civil War when he had to supplant his 'military specialists' in direct action. Trotsky received the Order of the Red Banner for his bravery and his leadership;[22] it was not the first or last time he exposed himself to danger in the Civil War but the episode secured his reputation among professional commanders – and he deserved his growing accolades as a military leader.

Yudenich, though, had yet to be defeated. Reports were reaching Trotsky that the Finns under General Mannerheim were considering the idea of entering the conflict on the White side. Mannerheim desired to prevent future trouble being spread by Russian communists across a border that was only thirty miles north of Petrograd. Trotsky's answer was that if Finnish forces tried to link up with Yudenich, the Reds would drive them back to Helsinki. The Finnish menace came to nothing. Yudenich had to finish the campaign with his own army. When British officers attached to him advised an immediate, all-or-nothing offensive, he wavered. This was a mistake. The meagre Red military defence was being reinforced by the day. By the time the battle started outside Petrograd, Trotsky had a five-to-one advantage in manpower. Yudenich was losing his Estonian units. Having thrown the Russians out of Estonia, they were averse to fighting for 'Russia One and Indivisible'. Supreme Commander-in-Chief Kamenev took the initiative on 21 October. Yudenich's army was steadily pushed westwards. Desertions were widespread on the White side until the Reds reached the Estonian frontier. The third big White army – and the last – had been worsted on the fields of battle, and the Reds had won their war against the Whites in Russia and most of Ukraine.[23]

There was no time to celebrate. Armed conflicts continued to cover Russian and Ukrainian territory as peasants rose in revolt against the Soviet order with its expropriations and conscriptions. Scarcely had the Red Army defeated Yudenich than it was being sent out to crush the rebellions. The Greens roamed across province after province. Mutinies broke out in Red Army garrisons. Industrial strikes broke out in a rising number of factories and mines. Inter-ethnic and inter-religious clashes also continued to occur in outlying regions. The Bashkirs and Tatars were fighting each other in the southern Urals. Muslim communities fought with Russians in the province by the River Volga.

The remnants of the White Armies had not accepted defeat. As Admiral Kolchak moved eastwards through Siberia, some of his officers wondered how best to regroup themselves and challenge the Reds. Their hopes were undermined by the decision of the United Kingdom and France to halt their intervention in the Civil War. In December 1919 the British withdrew from Archangel, the French from Odessa. Neither Trotsky nor his leading comrades made much comment because they were wary of concluding that the threat of an anti-Bolshevik crusade was over – and anyway their information about the thinking of ministers in London and Paris was scanty. War weariness affected all the great powers. Socialist parties, even if they disliked the dictatorial aspects of Bolshevism, argued against armed attempts to overturn Lenin and Trotsky. Political opposition to military intervention in Soviet Russia was strong and getting stronger. British premier David Lloyd George, Liberal Party leader who won the first post-war election in coalition with the Conservatives in late 1918, successfully argued that the clever way to eradicate the bacillus of revolution was to restore commercial links with Russia and prove by example that market economics worked better for people than state industrial ownership. Geopolitics had turned in favour of the Politburo.

A party which had seemed doomed to defeat in mid-1918 triumphed by dint of determination, organization and leadership. Trotsky frequently highlighted these features of the Red military effort. He also saw the outcome of the Civil War as confirmation of the inevitable global triumph of socialism in Europe and North America; and he gave due weight to the courage of the Red commanders and commissars. Other features were barely mentioned. The Reds benefited from holding on to Moscow and Petrograd. This gave them the logistical advantage of the core of the Russian rail network; it also provided them with a region of dense population from which to conscript their soldiers. Luck too played a part. If the Germans or the Western Allies had been in a position to deploy their forces in central Russia there is little reason to believe that they would have failed to overthrow Sovnarkom. The Reds had come close to defeat several times in the Civil War. But Trotsky never afterwards let himself think that the Whites could ever have gained the upper hand over the Reds. At the time he was franker. Trotsky's appeals and proclamations had told workers and soldiers that the fate of the October Revolution lay entirely in their hands. The Civil War was truly a close-run conflict between the Reds and the Whites.

Just one White army remained a fighting force. Denikin had retreated to southern Ukraine after his disastrous summer campaign. Demoralized by setbacks, he resigned his command and his place was taken by General Pëtr Wrangel in April 1920. This last White army was pushed down into southern Ukraine and regrouped in Crimea. Wrangel yielded at last to advice that the strategy of Kolchak, Denikin and Yudenich had been seriously flawed in its failure to avoid annoying the peasantry. Wrangel promised to leave peasants with the land received through the October Revolution; he took account of political advice from leading liberals. He restored discipline in his army and gathered what armaments and munitions he could lay his hands on. Trotsky failed to take Wrangel seriously. In his eyes the Whites were already defeated and the party's task was to consolidate the Soviet regime, bring about economic recovery and – if at all possible – spread the revolution to other countries in Europe.

# 26. WORLD REVOLUTION

Soviet leaders watched out for any chance to break out of their isolation in Europe. Theirs was an ambition of world revolution. Ideology informed their every step in international relations. A practical reason strengthened their zeal: so long as they ruled the sole extreme-left European state they would remain a likely target for attack by a coalition of capitalist powers. As soon as German military power crumbled in the west – and even a little before – the communist party leadership resuscitated its preparations to spread the revolution westwards. The plan was to form a Third International to supplant the Second. The Bolsheviks believed that the Second International, which combined socialist and labour parties in Europe, had been irretrievably discredited by the support given by most of those parties to their national war efforts. The urgent need was for a fresh global organization dedicated to bringing down capitalism and promoting revolution.

Once the Brest-Litovsk dispute had burned itself out, the differences over foreign policy faded inside the party leadership and Lenin, Trotsky, Bukharin and even Zinoviev and Stalin found themselves largely in agreement. This was no mere display of unity. The emphasis inside the central party leadership was on defending the October Revolution and avoiding risky military initiatives abroad. The Civil War had brought everybody up short. Soviet weakness had been brutally exposed, and the Kremlin leaders on the left of the party dropped their habit of calling for immediate armed action to export revolution westwards. Lenin ceased to be denounced as a political weathervane as it came to be recognized that he genuinely wanted to induce revolutionary upheaval in central Europe as soon as a realistic opportunity offered itself. The Whites had yet to be defeated; Kolchak, Denikin and Yudenich were on the rampage. The entire party agreed that all resources had to be directed at grinding the White armies into the dust. Trotsky shared in this consensus. While travelling around the fronts, he often dreamed up proposals for measures to break the chain of imperialism around the world; but not once did he demand a course of action that could worsen the Red chances of emerging victorious from the Civil War.

Trotsky's memoirs were to contain little about his caution in international relations for two years after the Brest-Litovsk treaty, for he liked to give the impression that his preference in foreign policy was constant in the decades after 1917. This had a claim on the truth for the fundamental objectives he espoused, but it was not wholly accurate. It was only from around 1923 that he pressed the case for gambles on revolutionary action in Europe while knowing that they might jeopardize Soviet military security. In the Civil War he had assumed a more responsible posture.

The preparations for a Third International had been made even before Germany's defeat in November, and Trotsky was involved in them. The expectation was that the comrades in Berlin would require Russian communist assistance whenever they might succeed in carrying out their insurrection and announcing the creation of a Soviet-style regime. As People's Commissar for Military Affairs it was among Trotsky's tasks to strengthen recruitment for the Red Army. Soviet military forces became vastly greater in number than were needed for the Civil War. He and the other Bolshevik leaders were determined to acquire the additional capacity to intervene in central Europe at any time.[1] The People's Commissariat for Food Supplies under Alexander Tsyurupa intensified its effort with the same thing in mind. Warehouses were piled high with grain on the assumption that German workers would need help in feeding themselves if the political far left seized power.[2] Sverdlov gathered a small group of veteran Bolsheviks to draw up the detailed project for a Third International. If ever Trotsky had wondered whether Lenin and Sverdlov had abandoned the commitment to exporting the October Revolution, he now knew the answer.[3]

Red Army responsibilities kept him out of the minutiae of international planning in Moscow after the end of hostilities on the western front. The situation was a complex and fluid one. The Western Allies had not yet finalized their decisions on the peace settlement. The defeated Central Powers were in turmoil. Kaiser Wilhelm II abdicated the German throne and fled to Holland. A government led by the social-democrat Friedrich Ebert took over in Berlin but its legitimacy was challenged by the Spartacus League on the political far left. The Spartacists were led by Karl Liebknecht, Leo Jogiches and Rosa Luxemburg. All had been friends of Trotsky before the Great War, and Trotsky had often partnered Luxemburg in objecting to Lenin's divisive obsessions. Released from prison after the Allied military victory, the leadership of the Spartacus

League campaigned for the replacement of Ebert and his government. Trotsky was delighted. Nothing would have pleased him more than to welcome them as leaders of a Soviet Germany – and the Spartacists were invited to send a delegation to an international communist meeting in Russia which, according to the planning of Lenin and Trotsky, would establish the Third International.

They themselves set about overturning Ebert's government – and they did not trouble to alert Lenin and Trotsky in Moscow. A Berlin rising was hastily organized in January 1919. Luxemburg went along with the venture against her better judgement. Disaster followed. The Spartacists, aiming to repeat the success of the October Revolution in Petrograd, had nothing like the mass support enjoyed by the Bolsheviks in 1917. Their capacity to mobilize the German working class was weak; their political and military preparations were amateurish. What is more, Ebert's social-democratic government was resolute in confronting the Spartacists on the streets and could rely on the loyalty of the armed forces. The unofficial Freikorps, right-wing paramilitary organizations which resented the surrender to the Western Allies in November 1918, came out in force. The Spartacists were gunned down. Liebknecht, Jogiches and Luxemburg were murdered. Their butchered corpses were dumped in the street. The Spartacus League was crushed. The Soviet communist leadership in Moscow received the news with shock and disappointment but refused to let its disappointment deflect it from its own political course.

The Congress which gave rise to the Third International began on 2 March 1919. Despite his commitments at the People's Commissariat for Military Affairs, Trotsky did not want to miss history being made and ensured that he could attend the proceedings in the old Courts of Justice in the Kremlin. Delegates were given no warning that the occasion was going to be used for the official inauguration of a new International. Lenin and Trotsky had cooked up a devious plan. They knew that several foreigners, including German Spartacist representative Hugo Eberlein, wanted more time to settle questions about the status of the gathering. Russian communist leaders trampled on the procedural niceties. They had decades of experience in fiddling the composition and nomenclature of small political gatherings. Lenin had been a notorious manipulator in the Second International; Trotsky, who once had criticized him on these grounds, now offered his full endorsement. They were twin progenitors of the Third International. In order to sharpen its distinction from the Second, they called it the Communist International (or Comintern).

Stormy applause greeted the appearance of Lenin and Trotsky at the opening session. Nearly all members of the Bolshevik pantheon sat alongside them. Bolsheviks had prepared the main documents. The preliminary report was by Lenin, who also wrote the Congress 'theses' on bourgeois democracy and the proletarian dictatorship – no such assembly was thought complete without such an analysis, and it was in any case very desirable as a statement of intent for the new International. The 'platform' was composed by Bukharin. Trotsky delivered a rousing report on the Red Army; he was unapologetic about his internal military policy and expressed his satisfaction in the expansion of Soviet-held territory since 1918:

> Why, Kautsky has even accused us of cultivating militarism! But it seems to me that if we wish to preserve the power in the hands of the workers, then we must show them how to use the weapons they themselves forge. If that is called militarism, then so be it. We have created our own socialist militarism, and we shall not renounce it.[4]

He ended with the declaration: 'We are ready to struggle and die for the world revolution!'[5] Nobody was better able to bring a big meeting to its feet. His bravery in the Civil War was famous and his listeners understood that he meant exactly what he said about self-sacrifice.

The British journalist Arthur Ransome, the only non-communist allowed to be present, witnessed the speech: 'Trotsky, in a leather coat, military breeches and gaiters, with a fur hat with the sign of the Red Army in front, was looking well, but a strange figure for those who had known him as one of the greatest anti-militarists in Europe.'[6] Like many others, Ransome had not read his Russian Marxist pamphlets carefully before 1917. Trotsky had never been unconditionally in favour of peace, still less of democracy and the rule of law. But Ransome otherwise had a sharp eye. When, after four days, the Congress was brought to a close, he reported:

> The conference in the Kremlin ended with the usual singing and a photograph. Some time before the end, when Trotsky had just finished speaking and had left the tribune, there was a squeal of protest from the photographer who had just trained his apparatus. Someone remarked 'The Dictatorship of the Photographer', and amid general laughter Trotsky had to return to the tribune and stand silent while the unabashed photographer took two pictures.[7]

Not for a couple of years had anybody handled Trotsky so brusquely, and he took it all in good part.

Trotsky wrote the manifesto for the Third International, and was asked to read it out to the Congress before it closed on 6 March. This was an unusual duty for an orator whose greatness lay in his brilliant improvisations. He complied with the request because he understood that historic events needed pomp and ceremony. If he had not been in charge of the Red Army he would have loved to devote himself to running the Third International. Instead the task was handed to Zinoviev. Trotsky had to watch developments from afar after the Congress, restricting himself to scrutinizing the shifts in policy and intervening with ideas and advice.

Europe remained politically volatile. In March 1919 two events seemed to confirm communist optimism in March 1919 when sympathizers of the Soviet leadership entered government in both Munich, the capital of Bavaria, and Hungary. The Bavarian revolution was quickly overturned but the Hungarian one proved tenacious. Communist leader Béla Kun set up his administration in Budapest at a time when the Allies were talking of a severe territorial reduction of Hungary as punishment for its leading part in the war against them since 1914. Popular revulsion at the post-Habsburg government had enabled Kun to seize power. Across central Europe there were winners and losers in the peace treaties projected by the military victors. For the Moscow communist leadership this was manna from heaven. Injured national pride in Germany and Hungary in particular could be exploited for internationalist purposes. Kun played the patriotic card while setting about radical communist measures. Banks and industry were taken into state ownership; big landed estates were seized and collective farms began to be established. Kun initiated a Red terror. The prisons teemed with enemies of the regime. Kun put himself forward as the Lenin of Hungary. His hope was that the other countries of central Europe would soon acquire communist governments.

The Kremlin leadership considered how best to give active support to Soviet Hungary. There was a discussion in April 1919. One possibility was to send Ukrainian forces over the border to assist Béla Kun.[8] This was exactly what Kun was demanding since Hungary was half surrounded by enemies. The Romanians and Czechs were pressing on its frontiers; military engagements were intense. There was a possibility that the Serbians too might make a move. Kun pleaded for Moscow to send armed forces to rescue his administration.[9] Jukums Vācietis, Supreme Commander of the Red Army, telegraphed to V. P. Antonov-Ovseenko – the chief political commissar in Ukraine – about how to achieve this. The basic idea suggested by Kun was simply to break across Galicia and Bukovina to Budapest. The risk was that such a move would spark off all-out war with Poland. Vācietis therefore insisted that no territory should be occupied en route if this option were to be chosen. (He obviously assumed that the Poles would be unable to prevent the passage of the Red Army through their territory.) The ultimate problem was that the Civil War in the former Russian Empire was not over. Vācietis pointed to the Don Basin as the immediate and unmistakable priority.[10]

Lenin and Trotsky shared this judgement and ruled out any Hungarian campaign: the first and indispensable requirement was to finish off the Russian Whites. The more they found out about Kun's communist administration, the less confidence they had in his abilities, and their fears proved to have been well founded. Kun and his associate Tibor Szamuely were fanatics eager to out-Bolshevik the Bolsheviks. They hated all compromise. Despite needing the support of the Hungarian peasantry, they proceeded to wage a campaign of unrestrained violence in the countryside. Grain and vegetables were seized without compensation. Catholic priests were hanged. Young men were conscripted.

Kun's regime fell on 4 August as the result of a Romanian invasion. He had brought much misfortune on himself, but the destruction of Soviet Hungary was nonetheless a blow for the Bolsheviks. A day later Trotsky dispatched his conclusions to the Party Central Committee. Béla Kun's overthrow, he argued, indicated that 'Anglo-French militarism' still had life in it. In fact the American administration had in vain nagged the British and French governments to eliminate Hungarian communism. Neither London nor Paris was willing to deploy troops for such a purpose.[11] And although Lloyd George and Clemenceau were pleased by the defeat of the communists, they brought a swift end to the Romanian occupation with its barbarous excesses. Trotsky was seeing an international conspiracy where none existed. But his mistake was understandable. Soviet Russia, Soviet Ukraine and Soviet Hungary had stood alone against the world's great powers; they had thrown down a gauntlet to global capitalism and had to expect a crusade against them. Trotsky asked the Central Committee to look the resultant reality in the face. Measured against the strength of the Western Allies, the Red Army was only a 'modest force'. Europe was currently a lost cause; it might take a whole year or even up to five years for suitable circumstances to come again. Trotsky urged fellow leaders to turn their attention to Asia. An opportunity for revolutionary expansion existed in the east. A base for the Red Army should be built in the Urals with the purpose of starting an offensive war in the near future.[12]

In calling for an 'Asiatic orientation', Trotsky urged the preparation of propaganda and the training of linguists so that the Reds might elicit local support when delivering a 'military blow at India'. He declared that 'the road to Paris and London lies through the towns of Afghanistan, Punjab and Bengal.'[13] This gives the lie to ideas that Trotsky had a strategic obsession with Europe. Doubtless, given a choice, he would have preferred revolution in Germany to anywhere else. This was the entire party's common position, and Trotsky was no different from his fellow leaders in wondering whether the communists would be better advised – at least for the moment – to probe in an easterly direction.

Trotsky's thinking in international relations rested on a few basic assumptions. Since he never spelled them out they have to be cobbled together from his writings in the period. He never recoiled from his belief that the October Revolution was the first great glimmering of the dawn of the global socialist era. Marx and Engels had been proved right in their analysis and prognostication. Trotsky retained his faith in the revolutionary potential of the European working classes and argued that they could be brought to active pursuit of their destiny if only the militants of the political far left would associate themselves with the cause of the Third International. This process would be eased by the trauma being suffered by world capitalism. Economies were in a mess. The great powers, whether the victors or the vanquished in the Great War, were incapable of reintroducing stability – and the Paris peace treaties made the situation irreversibly unstable. Anti-imperialist movements were on the rise outside Europe and North America. Communists had ample opportunity to meddle and to take advantage. Insurrection had to be the objective, especially in Germany. Russia had an importance as the pioneer of a trail that would soon be followed by other countries.

The Red Army consequently ought to be readied for deployment in a 'revolutionary war' in support of risings. This was the internationalist duty of Bolsheviks. It also made pragmatic sense. If Soviet Russia remained an isolated state, it would lack the indispensable asset of economic integration with more advanced societies. Territorial and political security too would stay at risk; the most powerful 'bourgeois' interests would foment public opinion in favour of invading Russia and crushing the Soviet order.

Just as Trotsky and his leading comrades strove to organize communism into a combined offensive against capitalism, he took it for granted that the great powers were at work against the October Revolution. This was again a reasonable hypothesis. The British, French, Japanese and Americans dispatched forces to the former Russian Empire in 1918–19, and their eventual physical withdrawal could not be understood as a permanent acceptance of failure. He continually suspected the worst of the White armies that confronted the Reds. In his eyes they were obviously acting on the orders of one or more great powers. Kolchak, for example, was 'directly an *American* agent'.[14] This was a ridiculous assumption. Yet it was an easy mistake for a Marxist to make. Kolchak, Denikin and Yudenich had served in the Imperial Army, which had been in alliance with France, Britain and the United States. Military and financial supplies had been sent to the Whites. Bolsheviks could not imagine that gifts were offered without heavy conditions. It seemed to follow that the White commanders were acting on orders from abroad and that the Western Allies would exact an economic price for their assistance if the Reds were to be defeated.

The Soviet state as yet had no great network of espionage to help them. Comintern as yet was useless as an organ for espionage in the West; its militants were preoccupied with the forming of communist parties and none of them had posts enabling them to report on discussions in foreign governments. The plenipotentiaries sent out by Sovnarkom had no access to the authorities in Paris, London or Washington. The Politburo had to rely upon Western newspapers (which were hardly unbiased conveyors of news) and upon Western communists (who saw the world through the same ideological prism as the Bolsheviks). Marxist theory at any rate took it for granted that, in the 'epoch of imperialism', the victors in the Great War would seek post-war advantage in a country like Russia with all its vast natural resources. The fact that expeditionary forces were sent from France, Britain, Japan and the United States appeared to confirm this analysis. The Soviet state was bound to cause tremors among those countries, for if Russia succeeded in effecting a break with capitalism, all other capitalist countries were vulnerable to the revolutionary contagion.

At the Second Congress of Comintern, which opened on 17 July 1920, the Bolsheviks appeared to breathe somewhat more easily now that they had won the Civil War. When Trotsky rose to speak at the closing rally the delegates gave him an ovation and sang the Internationale.[15] He condemned the US for seeking world hegemony and predicted war between the Americans and the British. He exulted in the dismantlement of the Russian, Austrian and German empires. He scoffed at Poland as being 'a dirty and bloody tool in the hands of French capital'; he derided France for its dependence on the indulgence of London and Washington. He took pride in the victories achieved by the Red Army and argued that European countries were about to discover that their own economic reconstruction was impossible without access to Russian natural resources.[16]

Equally important to Europe's recovery was a resurgence of German technological dynamism, and Trotsky had this to suggest:

> In order to reconstruct Germany, it must be allowed to live, to feed itself, to work. But if Germany, crucified and oppressed, is not allowed to live, to feed itself and to work, then it will rise up against French imperialism. French imperialism knows only *one* commandment – pay up! Germany must pay! Russia must pay! Therefore all these French profiteers are prepared to put to the torch all four corners of the earth just to get their interest payments.[17]

Europe was on the brink of revolutionary situations in country after country.

Trotsky celebrated the achievements of the October Revolution: military victory in the Civil War had been secured and the beginnings of a socialist economy had been tried and tested. A centralized system of state industrial planning was in prospect. (Trotsky was hoping against hope in this instance, and he was to be gravely disappointed throughout the rest of the 1920s.) Soviet Russia had provided a model for all peoples to copy. The man of iron revealed himself: 'Civil war is on the day's agenda throughout the world.' Even the peasantry in foreign countries were turning towards socialism. Trotsky declared:

> Therefore, comrades, when we look back on our year and a half of work in the Soviet economy, familiar with all its shortcomings, all its privations, we have no cause to cover up these shortcomings. Instead we reveal this picture of our work to our Western brothers, the Americans and other representatives from all countries, all parts of the globe. I think that if anyone came here with doubts at all, he will be convinced that we have chosen the right path. The only possible way out of the world's misery is through a planned mobilization and socialization of the economy, whereby all artificial obstacles and barriers are cleared away and the policy necessary for an integrated economy is followed.[18]

In July 1920 he stood on the summit of an optimism he had last occupied in November and December 1917. Within weeks his confident forecasts were to be rudely shattered.

# PART THREE

# 1920–1928

# 27. IMAGES AND THE LIFE

The Soviet media depicted Trotsky as a dedicated communist internationalist whereas the most extreme enemies of Bolshevism stereotyped him as a bloodthirsty fanatic.[1] Everyone agreed on his importance. When the story spread to Latvia in January 1919 that he had been taken captive, a crowd gathered in the streets of Riga to celebrate.[2] The Cheka was alerted in mid-1920 to a report that Wrangel had sent two of his officers to assassinate Trotsky.[3] The world knew Trotsky and Lenin as towering figures of the Soviet regime. Surely if one of them was removed, the October Revolution would implode?

Lenin and Trotsky remained the principal quarry for foreigners wanting to interview politicians in Soviet Russia. Although Trotsky saw less of visiting journalists during the Civil War, he continued to be sought after. His books went on being translated and distributed in Europe and North America and he wrote some of them for foreign readers in the first instance.[4] He spoke with correspondents whenever he had a moment to himself, and they prized such opportunities highly. They tended to feel a certain gratitude and gave him favourable treatment in their newspapers, and most of them in any case had a distinct sympathy to a greater or lesser extent for the Soviet revolutionary experiment – an exception was William Reswick of the Associated Press agency.[5] Reporters arrived in an increasing number after the defeat of the Whites when Trotsky was frequently in Moscow. Among these travellers were Louise Bryant, Max Eastman, Lincoln Eyre and André Morizet.[6] Trotsky added lustre to his own name by writing prefaces to books by them which promoted the cause of Bolshevik Russia.[7]

H. G. Wells and Bertrand Russell as socialist sympathizers hoped to see him. Their fame gained them access to the communist leadership in Moscow on their mission to understand the nature of communist theory and practice. Trotsky, unlike Lenin, was elusive during their stay because of work in the People's Commissariat for Military Affairs. Russell at last caught up with him at a performance of *Prince Igor* at the opera. He noted how Trotsky had 'the vanity of an artist or actor' in the Napoleonic way he acknowledged the cheers of the audience. They had only a 'banal conversation' before Trotsky was on his way again.[8] Wells was even less fortunate. He had not informed himself as well as Russell about the Bolsheviks and continued to believe that Trotsky had once been a pacifist. He confessed to finding Marx 'a Bore of the extremest sort'.[9] The two British writers returned home appalled by the chaos, oppression and fanaticism they had found in Soviet society, and Trotsky's elusiveness meant that their best-selling accounts conveyed more about Lenin than about Trotsky.[10]

Everyone who made their acquaintance sought to compare Lenin and Trotsky. Robert Bruce Lockhart, head of the British mission, had no doubt that Lenin held the superior authority, but he acknowledged Trotsky's sharp intellect and physical courage.[11] American journalist Louise Bryant put it differently, describing Lenin as the embodiment of revolutionary thought and Trotsky as a man of action.[12] Max Hoschiller disagreed. For him Lenin was 'a primitive', Trotsky a 'sophisticate'.[13]

Applause, though, is often the threshold to abuse. While gathering public plaudits in the October Revolution and the Civil War, Trotsky induced much resentment and suspicion inside the party. He paid little attention to this. Feeling he was right on each and every question, he assumed it was his duty to drag the party over to his standpoint. Yet all this time he was shown a respect at Party Congresses surpassed only by the growing cult of Lenin. Even when he was out of joint with official policy, his seat in the Central Committee and its Politburo was guaranteed. He took his eminence for granted. A vibrant speech by Trotsky was always an occasion savoured even by his Bolshevik detractors – and afterwards he seldom failed to amend the short-hand notes so as to enable the newspapers to publish a coruscating piece of prose. Lenin and Trotsky denied having any interest in their celebrity, but were aware that personal imagery was useful in conveying their political message. In the first couple of years they avoided promoting themselves. They preferred to put up statues to their dead heroes. These included Marx, Engels and even the leader of the ancient slave revolt Spartacus. But once Lenin had nearly died at the hands of an assassin in August 1918, a surge of official devotion to him was sanctioned. Fellow leader Zinoviev hurriedly wrote a concise biography which praised him in terms reminiscent of Christian sainthood.[14]

Although this put Lenin on a pedestal above Trotsky for the first time since the October Revolution, Trotsky did not cease to be fêted in the Bolshevik press. On the first anniversary of the October Revolution in

1918 it was none other than his enemy Stalin who wrote an article for *Pravda* emphasizing Trotsky's contribution to the party's achievement.[15] Appeals were made to Trotsky to supply details for the drafting of a biography. One came from Y. M. Lure, whose draft he thought completely hopeless. Another arrived from V. Nevski, who was starting his career as a historian of Bolshevism. With only a perfunctory attempt at demurral, Trotsky supplied answers to questions by Nevski and others.[16] He also gave up his time to foreigners such as Bessie Beatty and Max Eastman who were intrigued by his life and career. Lenin offered no personal assistance to biographers and walked out of the banquet held for his fiftieth birthday. Trotsky occupied a halfway house: he gave them the information and the access they needed and then left them to their own devices. He rejected requests to check their proofs for mistakes.[17] The reason for his refusal to go any further was not just that he was so busy at the People's Commissariat: he also shared the rest of his party's distaste for direct attempts to draw attention to oneself.

Some communists still felt that Lenin and Trotsky should do more to prevent the trend towards celebrating them as individuals. Angelica Balabanova, secretary to the Executive Committee of Comintern, was among them. She objected to special photographs being taken of the Politburo members.[18] Her expectations were unrealistic. Citizens of Russia and the other Soviet republics needed to know who their leaders were. Only a small proportion of people would get a glimpse of Politburo members. In a society where most citizens remained illiterate, moreover, visual images of the leadership and its policies were crucial if the communist order was to consolidate itself. Posters were produced. Newsreels were made even though the country as yet had an inadequate amount of celluloid to show the film in all cities. Busts and statues were sculpted. The painter Yuri Annenkov executed a marvellous drawing of Trotsky – the original was destroyed in a fire in 1931.[19] Vera Inber, daughter of the Shpentsers and his first cousin once removed, published a poem mentioning him in terms of awe:

> By the light of the lamps –
> A green, green light –
> Usually at the day's end,
> In your six-columned office
> You receive me.[20]

Trotsky, unlike Lenin, travelled to nearly all the European regions of the country under communist rule. Even so, neither Trotsky nor Lenin could count on being recognized. When Lenin was assailed by street robbers in 1919, he failed to convince them that he was head of the Soviet government. But they were certainly the best-known rulers of Russia since Nicholas II and Alexander Kerenski.

At the same time Trotsky kept his close relatives away from prying eyes. This was conventional party practice: only Lenin had a wife who gained political prominence.[21] Nevertheless Natalya, like other spouses of the Soviet communist elite, accepted an official post. Being noted for her interest in Russian culture, she was at first given responsibility for the conservation of artefacts of historical importance – this involved her in planning the nationalization of the landed estates surrounding Moscow.[22] Then, using the surname Trotsky, she took over the Committee of Assistance for Wounded and Sick Red Army Soldiers in 1919.[23] She and Trotsky resisted the temptation to exploit their elevated position to excess. Other couples behaved with less restraint. The Radeks were among the worst, grabbing a grand-ducal set of rooms for themselves in the Kremlin; they revelled in the opportunities for luxury. Natalya thought that the apartment would be better turned into a Romanov museum. Relations between the Radeks and the Trotskys were strained for a while.[24] Natalya was determined to preserve some modesty in her family's lifestyle. When she came across a pleasant tablecloth, she cut it up and sewed shirts for the boys. Lenin noticed and endorsed her determination to avoid waste and excess.[25]

She never joined Trotsky on his train, but her official duties often meant that Lëva and Sergei had to look after themselves. The Trotsky boys made friends with others of their age among the communist elite. The family had moved into the Kremlin on leaving Petrograd. After the attempt on Lenin's life in August 1918 those who had apartments elsewhere in the capital moved into the precinct for safety, and the Kremlin became an exclusive social and political fortress. Young Sergei Trotsky endeared himself to at least one visitor from abroad: 'He . . . is a fine little boy with a broad chest and a straight back. He looks like the heir to the throne in the guise of a peasant.' She noted how he loved to play football with his cousin Alexander Kamenev.[26] The fact that their fathers frequently fell out in the Politburo had no impact on sporting enjoyment.

Lëva and Sergei were growing up robust and independent; the same at first appeared true of their stepsisters, who now hardly ever saw their father after staying behind in Petrograd with their mother when the Soviet government had moved to Moscow. Both young women passionately supported Trotsky's politics. The elder Zina soon left for work on the

Urals front while the younger Nina trained at a higher pedagogical institute. They felt emancipated by the stimuli of the revolutionary environment. Social traditions were being dissolved. Suddenly Nina got married to Man Nevelson, Zina a year later to academic philosopher Zakhar Moglin. Trotsky heard about this only after the ceremonies. He had had no time to spare for the two young women in the Civil War and it was hardly surprising that they took their lives into their own hands. Nina, having been brought up by her mother, coped well. Zina, though, pined for her father; but as yet the consequences of her disrupted childhood had not disclosed themselves in full. Lëva was the only one who would enter adulthood without episodes of volatility, and even he was to leave the debris of emotional turmoil behind him. Trotsky and Natalya as well as Alexandra Bronstein noticed some disturbing symptoms but kept them confidential within the family.

Party etiquette and social civility were only two of the reasons why Trotsky guarded the privacy of his relatives and friends. A third was his experience in the Civil War. Whites routinely shot captured communists; Reds executed counter-revolutionary officers. Civilian hostages were taken by both sides. When Denikin's forces occupied Odessa, they scoured the city and the surrounding provinces for Trotsky's relatives. Anyone bearing the surname Bronstein was in mortal danger. In March 1920 Denikin's men captured Gersh Bronstein and his wife Rakhil with the idea of forcing an exchange of hostages.[27] Since Gersh was the brother of Trotsky's father there was little chance for the prisoners unless a deal was arranged. Trotsky intervened personally on behalf of Moshe and Fanni Shpentser without mentioning that they had been like a beloved uncle and aunt to him. Moshe was arrested by the Ukrainian Soviet authorities. In July 1919 Trotsky, writing to his friend Rakovski that Moshe was a 'capitalist employer', added that he was nonetheless a 'cultured and highly decent person' and should be released.[28] In September 1921 he asked the Ukrainian government to offer material assistance to Fanni who faced a 'heavy winter'; he vouched for her honesty and sincerity, affirming that both she and her husband were apolitical and harmless.[29]

Trotsky's aged father had made his way up from the south in 1920. He had been in mortal peril until the White occupation had been lifted; but the arrival of the Reds led to his farm being confiscated and handed over to Ukrainian peasants. Having lost all his savings, he trudged from Kherson province to Odessa. From there he travelled to Moscow and met his son for the first time since before the Great War. By then he was seventy years old. He could not understand the disturbance to the world he had known and flourished in: 'The fathers toil and toil in order to acquire some comfort for their old days, and then the sons make a revolution.'[30] Yet he was plucky enough, even in old age, to remake his existence. Trotsky found him a post as manager of a state grain mill near the capital. Few were better qualified to do the work, and Alexander Tsyurupa, People's Commissar for Food Supplies, appreciated his agricultural knowledge and enjoyed talking to him.

According to what he told Comintern secretary Angelica Balabanova, Trotsky refused to show any favouritism to his father and would not requisition even a pair of shoes for him.[31] If so, he did not feel the same inhibition about ensuring that his wife and children were kept in bourgeois style – and he had not held back from requesting support for Fanni Shpentser. He may have been putting on a show for Balabanova, who was known for her personal rectitude. Old David Bronstein caught typhus in spring 1922 and died on the day when Trotsky was addressing the Fourth Congress of Comintern.[32] Trotsky's memoirs were grudging in their praise of him. To have built up a farm such as the Bronsteins had in Yanovka was an extraordinary achievement. He had scrimped and saved. He had introduced technical innovations; he had assembled and trained a talented workforce. Trotsky never revealed whether he knew that his father was seriously ill before appearing at the Congress.[33] If he did know, his self-absorption was extraordinary. If he did not know, his lack of concern was equally remarkable.

Not that Trotsky and the rest of the uppermost tier of the Kremlin elite lived by politics alone. Trotsky's brother-in-law Lev Kamenev liked his comforts and pleasures. On a diplomatic mission to London in 1920 he frequented the Café Royal and Claridge's and took trips to Hampton Court and the Isle of Wight. He flirted with women of high society. To one of them he said, 'There is no truth in the world, the only truth is in one's heart.'[34] His wife got wind of this and greeted him frostily on his return to Moscow: 'We don't live *chic* like that in Moscow.' She said to the sculptor Clare Sheridan, his travelling companion from London: 'Leo Kamenev has quite forgotten about Russia – the people here will say he is a bourgeois.' Instantly Kamenev spat on the railway platform 'in the most plebeian way' as if to prove his unspoilt credentials.[35] If his comrades had known how he had spent his time, they might have been sterner with him. If his wife had known exactly how often Mrs Sheridan had gone with him to expensive restaurants, the atmosphere in the marital apartment might have been even frostier.

Although Trotsky was not one for Kamenev's extravagances he too was attracted by beautiful women – and several beautiful women were drawn to him after the October Revolution. He granted time to the same Mrs Sheridan who had incurred his sister's jealousy. Kamenev had commissioned her to produce busts of Bolshevik leaders Lenin, Zinoviev, Trotsky and Dzerzhinski. (She remained coy about how much she was paid.)[36] Sheridan was a cousin of Winston Churchill, who at the time was still calling for a crusade against the Soviet state; she did not let him know where she was going until it was too late for him to stop her. In Moscow, an initially reluctant Trotsky allowed her to work with her clay in his office over several days. They had running tiffs about her efforts, for he felt he had as much right as she to decide what kind of work of art should be produced. She was not a communist or even a leftist intellectual but she felt the force of his personal magnetism. As she measured his face with her callipers, he murmured: 'You're caressing me with tools of steel.'[37] He said of the bust she was working on: 'He looks like a French *bon bourgeois* who admires the woman who is doing him, but he has no connection with communism.'[38]

His flirtatiousness had the intended effect:

> He said, as he watched me: 'When your teeth are clenched and you are fighting with your work, you're still a woman (*vous êtes encore femme*).' I asked him to take off his pince-nez, as they hampered me. He hates doing this, he says he feels *désarmé* and absolutely lost without them. It seemed akin to physical pain taking them off – they have become part of him and the loss of them completely changes his individuality. It is a pity, as they rather spoil an otherwise classical head.[39]

Her desire for him was enhanced by her professional acumen:

> He opened his mouth and snapped his teeth to show me that his underjaw is crooked. As he did so, he reminded me of a snarling wolf. When he talks his face lights up and his eyes flash. Trotsky's eyes are much talked about in Russia, and he is called 'the wolf'. His nose is also crooked and looks as though it had been broken. If it were straight he would have a very fine line from the forehead. Full-face he is Mephisto. His eyebrows go up, at an angle, and the lower part of his face tapers into a pointed and defiant beard.[40]

Obviously the artist fancied her sitter; and he surely knew what he was playing at when, late at night in his low-lit office, he agreed to unbutton his tunic and the shirt beneath to lay bare 'a splendid neck and chest'.[41] He would also come across from his desk and stand behind her with his hands on her shoulders. This was not entirely innocent behaviour.

The rumour spread that they were having an affair. Although she did not confirm this in her memoir she gave a lot of tactile details which in inter-war Britain fell only just inside the boundaries of the seemly – and the liaison would be brought up by Natalya against Trotsky when they had a serious marital rift in Mexico. The rest of his entourage in the 1930s shared the suspicion about the relationship with Sheridan. Nothing was ever proved; and if an affair took place it was a brief one. In mid-1920, when he had to rejoin the Red Army on its Polish campaign, Trotsky invited her to go along with him on his train but she refused.[42] Instead she left for England, published her diary and went on a publicity tour of America. It seemed at the time that Trotsky would proceed unimpeded on his dazzling course across the Soviet political firmament. Such a prognosis was about to be disappointed. The faults in his public personality, already evident to his party enemies, were about to be exposed in full glare. Trotsky had been a revolutionary hero in 1917 and in the Civil War. He had talents in abundance. He never succeeded in balancing them with a sound political intuition in factional strife. The comet was starting its long tumble towards earth.

# 28. PEACE AND WAR

Trotsky was an onlooker during the dispute over dictatorship and democracy between Lenin and Kautsky in 1917–19.[1] He did not seriously try to add his contribution to Marxist theory until the end of the Civil War. But he had been thinking about a big new book even before the defeat of Yudenich. In early 1920, travelling around the country, he dictated notes which he worked up in May. The work was quickly published in Petrograd as *Terrorism and Communism*.

Like the rest of the Bolshevik leadership, he thought the party's policies had been validated by experience. He disdained to argue with Kautsky in the obsessive manner of Lenin. Nor was his book a dour exegesis of the recorded opinions of Marx and Engels. Trotsky put his case starkly and in his own terms:

> The man who repudiates terrorism in principle – i.e. repudiates measures of suppression and intimidation against a determined and armed counter-revolution – must reject any idea of the political supremacy of the working class and its revolutionary dictatorship. The man who repudiates the dictatorship of the proletariat is also repudiating socialist revolution and digging the grave of socialism.[2]

This was all very well if Trotsky meant that revolutionaries had to be willing to use violence against armies in the field. But he and fellow Bolsheviks had gone far beyond this in the Civil War. They had shot innocent hostages. They had stripped large social groups of their civil rights. They had glorified terrorist ideas and gloried in their application. The Bolshevik party had treated even workers and peasants savagely whenever they had engaged in active opposition. Trotsky's earlier ideas about 'proletarian' self-liberation were like old coins that had dropped unnoticed out of his pocket.

A trip to the Urals from February 1920 meanwhile convinced Trotsky that urgent changes in practical policy were essential.[3] Peasants were in revolt against grain requisitioning and military conscription. There were food shortages in the cities. Factories and mines were in disrepair. Workers had left for the countryside to survive the long wartime emergency. The communist party was in poor shape. The soviets and trade unions were ineffectual; transport and communications were in chaos. Wartime measures had secured existing industrial stocks for the Soviet government and had impounded harvests, but they had failed to sustain economic output. Trotsky applied his fecund mind to all such problems.

Now that the outcome of the Civil War was clear in Russia and Ukraine it was time to consider drastic measures for agriculture and industry. One of Comintern's most distinguished theoreticians was the Hungarian communist Györgi Lukács. In 1919 Lukács had produced a pamphlet extolling Soviet reality and claiming that Russia had made a 'leap from the realm of necessity to the realm of freedom' and that the laws of historical materialism were no longer applicable to the country in revolution. 'I remember', Trotsky wrote some years later, 'how Lenin and I laughed on this account and laughed with some bitterness since the realm of freedom was ruled by famine and typhus.'[4] Trotsky drew up a set of theses on the economy and inserted them into a report delivered to the party organization in Yekaterinburg, capital of the Urals region, and subsequently finalized on 10 March 1920. He bluntly stated that the People's Commissariat for Food Supplies was incapable of obtaining enough grain for the cities. There was a dual problem. The Land Decree of October 1917 had transferred the land to the peasants without a mechanism to oblige them to co-operate with the government's requirements; then the Food Dictatorship introduced in mid-1918 lowered the incentive for the peasantry to maintain acreages. Change was desperately needed.[5]

Agricultural collectivization, in the eyes of Trotsky and the whole party, was the solution but this could be undertaken only slowly and in the future. Communists had no alternative but to reward those rural households that produced a decent surplus. Successful farmers should be given industrial products in exchange. This was a rupture with War Communism, as the party's economic policies in the Civil War were to be known. Since 1918 the party had tried to appeal to the poorest and middling peasants whereas Trotsky's project would favour the wealthiest; he was implicitly advocating a pro-kulak line.[6] But how would he obtain products from the factories and mines to exchange for grain? Trotsky called for a shake-up in the entire manufacturing and mining sectors of the economy. He demanded the reintroduction of discipline to enterprises.[7] The principle of competition had to be re-established. Districts, factories and individual workers needed to strive to outmatch each other.[8] 'Model' factories should be established.[9] This was not all. Trotsky's fertile brain was never more productive and he called for the formation of 'labour armies'. Military demobilization had to be halted. Red Army soldiers should be kept in their units and assigned duties connected with industrial recovery. The old ideas about trade union rights had to be abandoned. Martial discipline was essential in places of work.[10]

The Soviet economy, according to Trotsky, had been over-centralized. If it was to recover its dynamism there was a need for the state to devolve powers to regional centres. One of them should be established in Yekaterinburg for the provinces of the Urals. He wanted the first labour army to be run from this city. He also urged that districts should be set in competition with other districts, factories with other factories, individual workers with other workers. The winners would be materially rewarded. Trotsky called it 'socialist competition'.[11]

Central Committee members were horrified by his ideas on the agrarian question, and Lenin charged him with advocating 'free trade-ism' and putting forward extravagant and 'utopian' proposals. This was strong language among communists, who anathematized laisser-faire capitalism.[12] Trotsky really should have known better when offering his scheme to the Central Committee. At the very least he should have canvassed for support in advance of the meeting. War Communism had become the favoured basis for the economy among communists. Solutions to all difficulties were sought in state ownership and control, and concessions to private profit were regarded as reactionary. The kulaks were among the social groups most feared and hated by Bolsheviks and yet Trotsky had suggested using them as the engine of agricultural and commercial regeneration. He had not in fact proposed anything like a return to market economics, so his ideas were not truly the forerunners of the New Economic Policy of 1921.[13] But nobody in the leadership took his side and the proposal fell like a lead balloon – and even Trotsky saw that there was no point in persisting with it.

Trotsky's other suggestions, though, met with a positive reception. He surmounted the worries about labour armies voiced by Lenin with the argument that the economic emergency demanded a drastic response. Lenin, despite distancing himself from the long-term use of militarized labour, condoned the formation of a Urals labour army so long as it was done in agreement with the civilian authorities there.[14] Trotsky, supported by Stalin, won sanction for other such armies to be established.[15]

He also succeeded in convincing the Central Committee that the country's transport needed the same kind of political control that was in place in the Red Army – and he accepted an active role in bringing this about. The reform had been initiated in 1919. Lenin again gave way and the railways and waterways were subjected to army-style discipline; but he regarded it as a temporary measure and did not share Trotsky's belief in the new agency, Glavpolitput, as a permanent section of the Soviet institutional edifice.[16] What brought Lenin and Trotsky back together were the assaults they sustained at the Ninth Party Congress in April 1920. Critics accused them of having unduly authoritarian leanings. Trotsky for once saw that he was becoming politically isolated, and he dropped some of his own more centralizing suggestions in order to cement an alliance with Lenin.[17] Together they made the case for one-person leadership in governmental bodies and for the need to draw up a 'general state economic plan'. This led to some teasing. Someone asked what would happen to Trotsky if Lenin took over the leadership of Sovnarkom by himself.[18] Trotsky declined to react to the joke: he did not mind being mildly self-deprecating but disliked being the butt of other people's ridicule – and he made jibes at his own at comrades in the Central Committee who had obstructed the passage of his ideas.[19]

Otherwise the Party Congress went well enough for him and he returned contented to his duties at the People's Commissariat for Military Affairs. The dangers to Soviet security were not yet over and by spring 1920 the possibility of all-out war with Poland was strong. There had been serious military outbursts since the end of the Great War.[20] The treaties of Versailles, Saint-Germain and Trianon dealt with central and east-central Europe but as yet there was no peace settlement further east. Brest-Litovsk had led to the formation of several states in the lands of the former Russian Empire. Poland, Lithuania, Latvia and Estonia were gradually stabilizing themselves as independent states after the withdrawal of German forces from the east. By the end of 1919 there were Soviet republics in Russia, Ukraine and Belorussia. Formally they enjoyed sovereign statehood but the reality was that supreme control was exercised from Moscow. The whole region was troubled by competing territorial claims and outbreaks of conflict. The biggest question was the demarcation of the western frontier of 'Sovdepia', as foreigners often called the lands ruled by Russia's communists. Warsaw existed in constant fear of what Russia might intend to do as soon as the Red Army was free from the burdens of the Civil War.

The Polish authorities had their own pretensions beyond the territory they governed. In April 1919 they drove the Reds out of Vilnius, capital of the Lithuanian-Belorussian Soviet Republic. Jósef Piłsudski, the army commander, then planned a military campaign to overthrow the Soviet government in Kiev and establish a federal union of Poland and Ukraine.[21] Poles in the distant past had ruled Ukrainian provinces, and a substantial Ukrainian minority inhabited the south-eastern region of the contemporary Polish state. Piłsudski calculated that the acquisition of Ukraine, whose agriculture and industry had thrived before 1914, would provide Warsaw with a defensive outpost against invasion by Soviet Russia. Moreover, Russia would again be deprived of territory, people and economic resources in the west as under the treaty of Brest-Litovsk. Neither Ukrainian popular opinion nor the Polish cabinet were going to be consulted. Piłsudski aimed to present them with a fait accompli. Within a few days he had reached central Ukraine. On 7 May his troops took Kiev. Their advance was so rapid that they caught Soviet soldiers standing by the bus-stops.

The Red Army was mobilized for yet another campaign deep in Ukraine. Trotsky had written cautiously to the Moscow and Petrograd Party Committees predicting that any war with Poland would be 'heavy and lengthy' and that nobody should expect a quick victory.[22] He shared his thoughts with the All-Russia Central Executive Committee of the Congress of Soviets on 5 May, asserting that the Bolsheviks had always tried to maintain peace between Russia and Poland.[23] Piłsudski's invasion of Ukraine was the brutal reaction. The Red Army would hit back but there should be no illusions about the difficulties that lay ahead. Trotsky persuaded himself that Polish workers did not approve of Piłsudski's aggression; but he thought it was a different matter with Poland's peasants, who had 'national prejudices' which gave a distinct advantage to Piłsudski. Hatred of Russians was deep. Polish warmongers, Trotsky assumed, could count on practical support from France and the United Kingdom.

He emphasized that Soviet Russia itself was able to rely on additional support. The veteran anti-Bolshevik General Alexei Brusilov had offered his services against Poland. The Reds eagerly accepted the offer of his expertise. Trotsky denied that this meant that the Bolshevik party had adopted a strategy of 'civil peace' in Russia. Tsarist veterans like Brusilov remained suspect and they would have to work entirely in subordination to the 'proletariat'. In any case, Piłsudski's situation was weaker than it seemed. The Polish situation was reminiscent of Russia under Kerenski. Trotsky claimed that the elites in Warsaw were as divided in their objectives as those in Petrograd had been before October 1917.[24] He wound up his speech with an inspiring declaration: 'The struggle will be awful. But if you ask me about the odds in this struggle, I'll tell you that I have never felt such confidence that we shall emerge victorious, completely crushing the enemy, as in this instance.'[25] Trotsky refused to pretend that the campaign was going to be anything other than arduous, but like Churchill in 1940 he left his audience with an uplifting message of optimism. No one else in the Politburo could perform this feat with such brilliance.

On 10 May 1920 he gave a speech proclaiming a class war: 'Soviet Russia will show you a new kind of war, we'll fight so that the forelocks of the Polish landlords tremble across all Poland, all Europe, the whole world [Stormy applause] . . . We declare to Polish workers and peasants: the struggle we are waging is not against you, friends and brothers, but in the cause of our and your freedom, against our and your enemies, against the oppressors, against the magnate-aggressors.'[26] Preparing for the campaign against the Whites, Trotsky demanded the rapid printing of decrees which were intended to appeal to the 'labouring people'. The Soviet land reform was to be publicized to all people living in the territory to the west of Soviet Russia.[27]

As late as the first week of June 1920 there was no sign that Trotsky seriously contemplated carrying war westward of the old Russian Empire. Nor did he favour military action in the east. He saw that a Soviet-style seizure of power in any of the Asian countries would complicate Russia's geopolitical situation – the British would not sit idly by. Even Azerbaijan, recently conquered by the Red Army, was causing problems for Moscow. Further military expeditions were to be avoided except as a feint designed to exert pressure in negotiations with the United Kingdom.[28]

On 10 June the Reds succeeded in reoccupying Kiev and Piłsudski's forces were forced into headlong retreat. The question arose as to what the Bolsheviks should do next, and Trotsky was reputed to have opposed making an offensive war against Poland.[29] Certainly he had trepidations. They seem to have been military rather than political in nature. He knew how tired his Red Army had become; he doubted it had the energy and material resources for an invasion. Stalin, who was afraid that Wrangel in Crimea might exploit the strategic situation, adopted the same position. Other leading Bolsheviks were even more forthright in opposing the invasion of Poland. Radek was notably sceptical that Polish workers would resist the claims of patriotism. But Lenin was insistent on pressing over the Polish border and trying to take Warsaw; and once Lenin had made this decision Trotsky was as determined as Lenin to see it through. The writings and speeches of party leaders at the time told little about their assumptions about the true purpose of the campaign. Bolsheviks did not advertise the project of breaking past Warsaw to Berlin. Not once did their leaders publicly admit to the goal of 'Sovietization' in central Europe; they understood that the word would be less than attractive to millions of Poles.

The British Foreign Office sought to mediate between Russia and Poland. The Foreign Secretary Lord Curzon evidently expected the Polish collapse to continue and wanted to halt the Red Army's advance. Meeting on 17 July, the Bolshevik Central Committee rejected peace overtures. Trotsky was asked to draw up a proclamation about a lengthy campaign.[30] At the Second Congress of Comintern, starting on 19 July in Petrograd, the mood was exultant as Zinoviev and Lenin explained that world affairs were turning on a new axis. A map was pinned to the wall with flags indicating the lines of the Red Army's advance. Trotsky's military responsibilities did not deflect him from making a brief appearance. He called for communist parties to be established everywhere; he announced that the Polish government of Ignacy Paderewski was suing for peace.[31] The Congress introduced rules stipulating that all member parties should conform to the same organizational principles as the Russian Communist Party. By then Trotsky had raced by train to be near the fighting. On 23 July the western front received orders from Mikhail Tukhachevski, its commander, to cross the River Bug and aim at the total defeat of Poland's armed forces. The Bolshevik party leadership set up a Provisional Polish Revolutionary Committee which drafted decrees on land, industry and security with a view to establishing itself in Warsaw. Among its members were Cheka leaders Felix Dzerzhinski and Jósef Unszlicht.

Lenin goaded commanders and commissars into fomenting an uprising of the Polish, Latvian and Estonian workers and peasants. This was what he meant by 'revolutionary war'. He jotted down the following note to Sklyanski in a planning session: 'Take military measures, i.e. try to punish Latvia and Estland [Estonia] *in a military fashion*, for example by . . . crossing over the frontier somewhere by a [half a mile] and hanging between a hundred and a thousand of their bureaucrats and wealthy people.'[32] He urged that the Polish Revolutionary Committee should encourage Poland's land-hungry peasants to seize landed estates, or at least portions of them, as the Reds moved onward.[33] The 'landlords and kulaks' had to be ruthlessly crushed, and he peremptorily asked his commissars why they were not raising the peasantry against them.[34] He constantly harassed the Red Army: 'If the military department or the Supreme Commander *is not refusing* to take Warsaw, *it must* be taken.'

He allowed no talk of a truce, claiming that such ideas were mere 'idiotism'.[35]

Trotsky and Stalin were almost alone in not receiving wild messages from him, for he knew that they always squeezed the maximum effort from the Red Army. The great prizes of Warsaw and Berlin glistened ahead and the mood of optimism in the central party leadership was almost chiliastic. Central Europe seemed about to turn communist. The Second Congress of Comintern was buoyed up with enthusiasm and sent dozens of foreign delegates back to their own countries to stir up political trouble for governments. Italy and Czechoslovakia might be the next countries to experience revolution.

As the Red Army's advance continued, Trotsky made plain that he wanted to prosecute the kind of 'revolutionary war' which he and other Bolsheviks had wished to fight in 1918 before signing the Brest-Litovsk treaty. Conventional measures of territorial conquest were to be only part of their strategy. The Reds also planned to stir up support among workers, soldiers and peasants. They expected to do this first in Poland and then in Germany. Unlike past invaders from Russia, they looked forward to being greeted warmly as they advanced. Trotsky's articles and speeches tapped out a drum roll against Polish priests and landlords. His call was for the 'masses' to rise up against their national oppressors. He excoriated Poland's government and its army command as being no more than the obedient forward contingent of the world's capitalist great powers. He saw the hand of Paris and London behind Piłsudski's every move. He genuinely judged that Europe was a tinder-box of revolution. The Red Army had only to apply a lighted match and the entire continent would be set ablaze. Such remained his way of thinking throughout his life – he even believed that Finnish peasants in 1940 would welcome Stalin's armed forces as their liberator.[36]

European governments and media recognized that if Poland fell to the Red Army the treaties signed at the Paris Peace Conference over the previous twelve months would be in tatters. This would not be simply a campaign of conquest. Lenin wanted the German communists, who remained a weak presence in public affairs, to ally themselves with the extreme political right. The Freikorps units led by Wolfgang Kapp had tried to seize power in Berlin in March. Lenin's idea was now to assemble all the anti-Versailles groups in an irresistible coalition to liberate Germany from its subjugation. Subsequently, he assumed, the forces of the extreme left and the extreme right would have to fight it out between themselves;[37] but the Red Army, having swept through the Polish lands, would make

itself available to the German communist leadership. 'Sovietization' would
be undertaken on a systematic basis. The war between Soviet Russia and
Poland in 1920 was a struggle about what kind of state order and ideology
would prevail in central and western Europe.

The Reds started as they meant to go on. On taking Białystok, the
Polish Revolutionary Committee nationalized eight factories. The Soviet
ruble was introduced as the local currency. The banks were inspected with
a view to eventual expropriation. Priority was given to workers in the
distribution of food supplies.[38] Trotsky was too busy to involve himself
in civil administration and left such tasks to Dzerzhinski and Julian
Marchlewski on the Polish Revolutionary Committee. He continued to
claim that the military campaign was 'a war forced on us'.[39] This was at
best a quarter-truth. Certainly Piłsudski had invaded Ukraine, but once
he started to retreat the Reds had ignored entreaties for an armistice.

The Red Army entered Poland simultaneously in two groups and
Supreme Commander-in-Chief Sergei Kamenev and Trotsky stayed in
close touch. In the north, pointing his forces directly at Warsaw, was
Mikhail Tukhachevski; in the south was Alexander Yegorov, who was
making a thrust towards Lwów. Strategy was kept under review as the
reports of swift advances arrived from Tukhachevski and Yegorov. The
suddenness of the Red military success meant that no general plan existed.
Trotsky had to communicate regularly with Moscow to finalize a set of
dispositions for the defeat of Piłsudski. Yegorov was ordered to break off
his westward movement and advance in a northerly direction so as to link
up with Tukhachevski. Stalin, however, was in charge of the Revolutionary-
Military Council in the southern military sector. He had long been notorious for ignoring orders from the Politburo and the Supreme Command;
and as Yegorov's armies advanced on Lwów, a vista of military glory
opened before him and Stalin. After Lwów, they might well be able to
continue their campaign and invade Czechoslovakia and Hungary. In any
case it was doubtful that Yegorov would be able to reach the north in time
for Tukhachevski's projected offensive.[40]

Trotsky demanded adherence to the strategy of the Supreme Command. Piłsudski had regrouped his forces across the River Vistula from
Warsaw. The Poles were fighting for national independence and religious
faith. For nearly all of them, the Reds were simply the traditional foe
dressed in revolutionary uniforms. Piłsudski deployed his troops with less
than total brilliance. But the Red troops, exhausted by the campaign and
short of basic supplies, could not give of their best. The battle started on
13 August. Days passed as military engagements taxed the resources of

both sides. By 25 August it was clear that the Reds were defeated. A forced-march retreat took place. The Poles were jubilant: they had saved themselves and the rest of central Europe from Lenin, Trotsky and 'Sovietization'.

# 29. BACK FROM THE BRINK

The Ninth Party Conference took place in Moscow less than a month after the disaster in Poland. Lenin and Trotsky concurred that someone else should take the blame. Stalin's disobedience provided the opportunity. Repeatedly Lenin had protected Stalin from Trotsky's wrath in the Civil War. He himself had blundered badly in insisting on the Polish invasion. He chose Stalin as a handy scapegoat.

Lenin confessed that the Politburo had miscalculated in rejecting Lord Curzon's peace proposal and in assuming that the 'Sovietization' of Poland and Germany would be easily accomplished. The surge of Polish patriotism had come as a surprise.[1] Trotsky took a somewhat different line, suggesting that the Politburo had been duty-bound to test whether European socialist revolution could be achieved:

> Why didn't we enter Warsaw? Because, comrades, the enterprise was not so very simple. We proceeded that way for the reason contained in the report by comrade Lenin. The reason was serious enough and now, looking back and evaluating whether it was a mistake, it's possible to answer in the form of a question: were the July Days [of 1917] or the Revolution of 1905 mistakes or were they not? What was involved was a big attempt to probe the enemy. Nobody would be able to indicate in advance where this attempt should be halted, and it can be said that this experience offers ground for a happier experience.[2]

He stood firm on the correctness of the decision to invade. Simmering with chronic irritation, Trotsky made a personal attack: 'What I have to say is that comrade Stalin undermined me and the Central Committee.'[3] Lenin took Trotsky's side and Stalin felt so humiliated that he demanded the right of reply next day, when he pointed out that he had expressed doubts about the campaign even before it had started.[4]

The Politburo showed caution about the Poles while Soviet armed forces were being directed southward to the Wrangel front. Lenin thought the risk should not be exaggerated; he had learned from Adolf Ioffe, who had conducted peace talks with Poland's diplomats in Riga, that Warsaw feared a resumption of hostilities even more than Moscow did. He felt free to tell Trotsky to concentrate on destroying the last White army in Crimea.[5] Negotiations with the Baltic states were started. Estonia, Latvia and Lithuania were assured that the Kremlin intended no threat to their independence. The key to Soviet international security, though, was to reach an accommodation with the United Kingdom. Bolshevik leaders felt sure that the British and French had instigated the Polish invasion of Ukraine; but they saw that Soviet Russia needed help with its economic recovery. Lenin and Trotsky talked up the advantages to Western countries of regaining access to Russia's natural resources. The Politburo expected in turn to buy industrial machinery and update its technology. Kamenev was sent to London to seek a commercial treaty. The battle of the Vistula had been a crushing defeat; the Politburo had to find a way to secure a breathing space for the country.

Hostility was widespread even though criticism of Trotsky had been muted at the Conference. Glavpolitput annoyed Bolshevik veterans by keeping the party and government out of discussions about transport. Trotsky's advocacy of martial discipline in the running of the railways resuscitated the mutterings that he was lining himself up to be military dictator. So long as he had Lenin's support he was willing to overlook what was being said. But when negative comments spilled out at the Central Committee he lost his temper and filed his resignation from his transport duties on 29 September 1920. The Central Committee turned down his request, promising to ensure that there would be no repetition of such deprecation.[6] Stalin, wounded by accusations made at the Party Conference, was absent and his request to leave the Revolutionary-Military Council of the Republic had been sanctioned by the Politburo at the beginning of the month.[7] Now Trotsky was threatening to walk out.[8] At a time when he had one Politburo member sulking, Lenin could not afford to let a second one go off into seclusion. Nobody doubted that Trotsky was overladen with postings and duties. What is more, he had practically lived on a train for two years and knew more about transport than anyone else in Russia. He was much too valuable to be allowed to stand down.[9]

Unfortunately for Lenin, Trotsky did not forget his idea for all trade unions to be turned into state organizations. He reverted to it at the Central Committee on 8 November, declaring that the entire Revolution would remain under threat until unions were stripped of their current rights and functions. His point was a ludicrously overstated one. Workers were confronting the regime with or without trade unions and a strike movement was spreading from city to city. Trotsky's demand to militarize labour and statify unions was needlessly provocative at such a time.[10]

Lenin and Trotsky clashed in the Central Committee as attempts to formulate a compromise failed. When a vote was taken it was Lenin who won. Trotsky behaved like Lenin in the Brest-Litovsk dispute. Instead of accepting a Central Committee decision he openly attacked it. As he pointed out, this was his right as a party member. Unlike Lenin he showed no guile in explaining himself. His case was a schematic one and he brusquely threw aside objectives such as 'proletarian self-activity'. According to Trotsky, the duty of workers was to do what they were told. Whereas Lenin hoped to control the trade unions by stealth, Trotsky wanted to do it to the accompaniment of bells and whistles. The October Revolution had installed a workers' state. Sovnarkom's policies favoured the interests of the proletariat. Trade unions defended only sections of the working class; it was the government rather than the unions which protected the class as a whole. In this situation it made sense to carry out the 'statification' of the labour movement. Otherwise the unions would continue to support the grievances of working people in conditions of economic collapse. Industrial output would be damaged. Conflict at places of work would increase and the regeneration of factories and mines would be endlessly postponed.[11]

Big meetings of Bolshevik party members were held. The result was inevitable: Trotsky split the party into factions. He was certainly enjoying himself; but oratorical temptation and schematic thinking muddied his sense of political tactics. On 9 December 1920 he asked the Central Committee to relieve him of his post at the People's Commissariat of the Means of Communication, a post he had held since March. Ostensibly he made his request because he was overloaded at the Commissariat for Military Affairs. The real reason was that he wished to engage freely in the trade union controversy.[12] The Central Committee called a Party Congress for February 1921. A fortnight later, with the controversy enveloping them, its members postponed the Congress till March. An open discussion on the trade unions was announced.[13]

Trotsky relished a dispute too much to worry about the consequences. When he was not on a train, he was giving fiery speeches. Bukharin formed a buffer group in an attempt to moderate the factional wildness. All this did was to annoy both Lenin and Trotsky. Alexander Shlyapnikov and the Workers' Opposition plunged into the controversy; they objected to Lenin and Bukharin while reserving their strongest criticism for Trotsky.

The Democratic Centralists joined in. The entire party was caught up in a whirlwind of polemics. Only the Trotskyists and the Workers' Oppositionists believed that trade union policy was the supreme question on the party's agenda. But Trotsky had got the debates that he wanted. The Bolsheviks descended into a pit of factionalism at the very time when the Politburo was called upon to deal with mutinies, strike and rural rebellions. Those party members, including Lenin, who rejected the 'discussion' as a distraction were whistling in the wind. Lenin had criticized Stalin after the Polish war. Now it was Trotsky's turn to feel the heat of his invective. The only solace for Lenin was that Stalin returned to being co-operative, and it was Stalin who organized Lenin's faction for the duration of the trade union dispute.

Although Trotsky contributed to debate on other matters he did not do so with any assiduity. Reconsideration of the party's agrarian policy was in process; and in December, at the Eighth Congress of Soviets, Lenin picked up the abortive suggestion which Trotsky had made in February and proposed offering material rewards to those better-off peasants who increased their output – and delegates gave Lenin a roasting at the Congress.[14] Trotsky might have been forgiven for crowing but he was too deeply immersed in the trade union controversy. Meanwhile the food-supplies crisis deepened. Something drastic had to be done to prevent starvation in the cities. Worse still for the Soviet administration were the intensifying rural revolts. Peasants in Ukraine, the Urals and the Volga region rose against the Bolsheviks and by the start of 1921 the Politburo learned that practically an entire province – Tambov by the Volga – was aflame with rebellion.

On 2 February Lenin returned to the agrarian question at the Politburo. Trotsky had been dispatched four days earlier to inspect industrial conditions in the Urals; he and his companion Zinoviev were strictly forbidden to contribute to the trade union dispute while on their trip.[15] The economic situation called for unity and decisive action and Lenin rebuked the People's Commissariat for Food Supplies for damaging relations with the peasantry. He had Bukharin on his side. Their arguments were effective and assistance to peasants became the agreed priority, and Kamenev and Yevgeni Preobrazhenski were asked to prepare a draft of fresh measures. Absent members, including Trotsky, were to be consulted by telephone.[16] The leadership was being pulled hither and thither in the following days. On 8 February, when the Politburo reconvened, Bukharin was detained elsewhere and Trotsky and Zinoviev had not yet returned from the Urals.[17] Listening to a report from the People's

Российская Социалистическая Федеративная Советская Республика

# Х ВСЕРОССИЙСКИЙ СЪЕЗД СОВЕТОВ Раб., Крест., Красн. и Каз. депутатов.

# АНКЕТНЫЙ ЛИСТ.

С решающим голосом.
С совещательным голосом.

1. Имя, отчество и фамилия *Лев Давидович Троцкий*
2. Возраст *45*
3. Национальность *Еврей*
4. Губерния, от которой делегирован *М. ВЦИК.*
5. Социальное положение *трудовой интеллигент.*
6. а) Ведет ли самостоятельное сельское хозяйство ———
   б) Сколько десятин
7. Партийная принадлежность *РКП*
8. С какого года в партии
9. Профессия *Литератор—журналист—публ.*
10. Указать главные занятия:
    а) до войны 1914 года *Эмигр. литерат. публ.*
    б) до февральской революции ———
    в) до октябрьской революции *парт. раб.*
    г) после октябрьской революции *НКИД, НКПС, НКВоен*
    д) какую должн. занимает теперь *Пред. Реввоенсов, НКВоен*
11. Кем делегирован на Съезд *М. ВЦИК*
12. Как происходили выборы:
    а) на Съезде
    б) в Совете *М. ВЦИК*
    в) в Исполкоме
    г) в армии
13. Участвовал ли в прежних Съездах: 1, 2, 3, 4, 5, 6, 7, 8 и 9-м
14. Место постоянной работы *Москва*
15. Полученное образование: высшее, неокончив. студ., студент, среднее, низшее, внешкольное, читает и пишет, только читает, неграмотный.

Подпись

· декабря 1922 г.

Подпись лица, проверяющего анкету

«Мосполиграф» 1-я Образц. тип. Пятницкая, 71.

14. Trotsky's personal questionnaire at the Tenth Congress of Soviets in December 1922. He omitted, doubtless deliberately, to answer how long he had been in the party. He was less coy about his nationality ('Jew') and his pre-1914 profession ('littérateur'). His claim to have had a higher education was an exaggerated one, since he did not take a university degree.

15. Stalin in 1924: the official portrait of the General Secretary by M. S. Nappelbaum. Easily his most suave image.

16. Khristian Rakovski, one of a small number of Trotsky's friends. Trotsky kept his picture on his desk in Büyükada.

17. Trotsky's address book in 1928–29 in Alma Ata, where he carefully recorded the dates of letters sent and received in correspondence with his supporters. The two pages include the entry for Khristian Rakovski.

18. Trotsky in his cardigan, reading the international communist press in Turkey.

19. Trotsky in his working clothes in Turkey, by the Istanbul photographer Jean Weinberg.

20. Natalya photographed in Paris in the 1930s, as elegant, pretty and demure as ever.

21. Stalin in 1932: already the master of the Soviet Union.

22. The Izzet Pasha house on Büyükada, where Trotsky and his family lived after moving out of the Soviet consulate in Istanbul in 1929.

23. The house at Kadiköy, where the Trotskys lived after the fire in Izzet Pasha in 1931.

24. Trotsky and his son, Lev, in their Turkish days.

25. Zina Bronstein, Trotsky's elder daughter.

26. Sergei Sedov, Trotsky's younger son.

Commissariat of Agriculture, Lenin sketched 'a preliminary rough draft of theses concerning the peasants'.[18] The system of forcible grain requisitioning was to be replaced by a tax in kind. Peasants were to be left with a surplus which, if they wished, they could sell privately. This became the basis of the New Economic Policy (or NEP) and the Politburo set up a working group under Kamenev to elaborate the details.[19] On the need for such a reform there was unanimity among members present and absent.

Trotsky and Zinoviev were back in time for the Politburo's consideration of Kamenev's project on 18 February.[20] A manifesto was to be produced on the deep changes about to be made in state policy. Trotsky was not exactly marginalized from the process, but he was not asked to apply his writing or speaking talents: this was an unusual event in itself. The Politburo as a whole was breaking with economic measures in place since the start of the Civil War or even earlier. Sanction had to be obtained from the forthcoming Tenth Party Congress. Then a legislative programme had to be finalized and the press had to inform the country.

A week later Trotsky noted how strange it was that Lenin, the architect of the NEP, had castigated him as a free trader and a utopian in 1920.[21] He was on weaker ground when he told people privately that the Politburo was only doing what he had urged twelve months earlier. The NEP went far beyond Trotsky's earlier proposal, putting an end to War Communism rather than trying to mend and improve it. Perhaps Trotsky was trying to cheer himself up. By the end of February 1921 it was obvious that his ideas about the trade unions were not going to win a majority at the Party Congress. He had travelled the length and breadth of European Russia and parts of Ukraine. His supporters Preobrazhenski, Serebryakov and Krestinski staffed the Secretariat. He had put his arguments with flair and vigour. Lenin had stayed in Moscow, relying on Zinoviev to take to the railways and state the case on his behalf. *Pravda* reproduced the diverse factional arguments with sufficient even-handedness for the party to make up its mind. Despite the weeks of intensive effort Trotsky had lost. He had spent all that time stressing that the economic situation was dire. His effect was to delay the party's concentration on a practical solution, and meanwhile the Soviet party faced an increasing political and social threat to its existence.

Trotsky's defeat did not guarantee a quiet time for anyone at the Tenth Party Congress, which began on 8 March. It was far from clear how Bolsheviks would react to the NEP. International trade was another difficult topic since Lenin wanted the Congress to agree to industrial concessions being granted to foreign private companies. There would also be debate about international revolution. The fundamental task of Comintern was to seek opportunities to communize Europe and North America; and after the Polish–Soviet War this was going to be difficult because Lenin and Trotsky wished to sign commercial treaties with the United Kingdom and other large trading economies. What is more, the party needed to define its approach to the national question in the post-war situation. A discussion was necessary about how to deal with both the Russians and the other peoples of the Soviet republics. Despite this bundle of controversial topics, the Party Congress turned out rather tranquil. The reason was that its delegates had been facing a threat to the Soviet order for an entire week. On 2 March, after several preliminary tremors, the Kronstadt naval garrison erupted into outright mutiny and arrested its Bolshevik political commissars. Sailors were exasperated by the party leadership's refusal to hearken to their grievances. They hated grain requisitioning and the armed units which stopped people from carrying produce into the towns for purposes of illicit trade. They objected to being bossed by appointed commissars. They were disgruntled about the poverty and disease throughout Russia and Ukraine. They detested being ruled by a single party and called for an elective political system. If the party central leadership conceded such demands it would effectively be overthrowing its own dictatorship. But when officials were sent over the ice of the Gulf of Finland to calm them down, the sailors arrested them and set up a Revolutionary Committee.

Trotsky was deeply involved in the deliberations in Moscow. As people's commissar for military affairs he also stayed in regular contact with the Baltic Fleet command. He was sure, on the basis of past experience, that the centre of any plot would be found abroad.[22] He was no different from other Bolshevik leaders in making this kind of assumption.

On 5 March Trotsky, emancipated from the trade union dispute, told the communist party leadership that the neglect of Kronstadt could cost it dear. There was as yet no plan for dealing with the mutiny and no serious infiltration of agents. Action was urgently necessary.[23] Trotsky instructed Sergei Kamenev, the Red Army's Supreme Commander, to place Tukhachevski in charge of putting down the revolt.[24] Five days later Trotsky remained worried; he informed the Central Committee that he feared it had overlooked the danger from Kronstadt. He ignored his own role in deflecting the party's attention from the rebellions that were incubating. When the spring thaw took place, he warned, the sea ice would melt and the mutineers would be able to communicate with foreign supporters. 'Exceptional measures' were called for.[25] This was the kind of language he had used in the Civil War. Later he contrived to hide what he had said and done about Kronstadt. He was not unusual: the entire leadership drew a curtain across the deliberations and decisions. But Trotsky covered up more than the others did. He was the architect of the mutiny's elimination and when he subsequently started to talk of the need for democracy this became an embarrassment.[26]

Talking to the foreign press at the time, he told lies about the mutineers. He said that they were not the same naval personnel who had helped the Bolsheviks to power in 1917. He alleged that the mutinous sailors of 1921 were casual elements, conscripted at short notice and permanently embittered against socialism – and he accused them of being led by White army officers. He was determined to discredit them in extreme language. His American admirer Louise Bryant was only too willing to reproduce his claims as the absolute truth.[27]

The Tenth Congress had begun with Lenin intoning the litany of mistakes made in the Polish war and in wartime economic policy. At the same time he condemned the Kronstadt mutiny as a 'petit-bourgeois counter-revolution' more perilous than the offensives by the White armies. He assured the Congress that rural revolts would be suppressed with severity. He insisted that the Workers' Opposition's appeal to consult workers and peasants was 'a syndicalist or semi-anarchist deviation' from Bolshevism. He argued strongly for the NEP. He also maintained that economic recovery required acceptance of foreign concessionaires in Soviet industry even if this meant handing over the entire oil industry. Everything he said on these matters could just as easily have been said by Trotsky. The trade union controversy was touched upon only lightly and Lenin's report was approved by an overwhelming majority. Midway through the proceedings the call was made for volunteers to leave Moscow and head north to reinforce the contingent readying itself in Petrograd to take on the Kronstadters. Trotsky, perhaps with a sense of relief, was absent from most of the Congress proceedings. Over the ice went Tukhachevski and the Seventh Army. The leading mutineers were seized and sent to labour camps while ordinary sailors were deployed to other naval units. Resistance was ruthlessly suppressed. Trotsky was pleased with Tukhachevski's performance.

When the trade union question came before the Congress on 14 March there was only perfunctory dispute. The Workers' Opposition and Democratic Centralists were fiery. But their cause was a lost one and they knew it. Lenin's policy was assured of success even before Trotsky had returned to the Congress. Trotsky repeated his point that he had tried to introduce economic reform a year earlier and been harshly rejected despite his prescience. He also criticized the Central Committee motion on the unions for its lack of fluency and angrily objected to Lenin accusing him of breaking party discipline. But the spat fizzled out quickly. Having spent four months urging that his proposals alone could save the situation, he was hardly offering a spirited defence of them; he consoled himself by asserting that the Congress resolution on unions would not survive a year in practice.

When the voting was held for the new Central Committee he came only tenth.[28] Zinoviev, his chef antagonist on his travels, did even worse. But generally Lenin and his group had triumphed and they reduced the number of Trotsky's supporters in the central party leadership. Trotsky himself was untouchable; his friends were not. Yevgeni Preobrazhenski, Leonid Serebryakov and Nikolai Krestinski lost their places in the Central Committee, Orgburo and Secretariat. Krestinski was also dropped from the Politburo. The retaliation against Trotsky could have been even more severe but Lenin advised restraint. So Khristian Rakovski and Karl Radek were retained in the Central Committee. Having helped to put Stalin to shame in the previous year, Trotsky had now let him back into favour. But if he was even slightly disconcerted, he disguised it well. Once the Central Committee had been elected, the Congress passed on swiftly to ratify the Politburo's agreed policy on international trade. In the closing minutes it fell to Lenin to condemn the Workers' Opposition. Trotsky's ally Karl Radek expressed his worry that such intolerance might one day soon be turned against others in the party.

It was a perceptive remark, but Trotsky showed no sign of understanding it. His thoughts were elsewhere. Having become accustomed to power and to plaudits, he had made a fool of himself over the trade unions. Only Kronstadt had rescued him. It was up to him to prove again his worth for the party and for the October Revolution.

# 30. DISPUTING ABOUT REFORM

The Tenth Party Congress was like a quarantine hospital where only a small number of diseases were treatable. Lenin had introduced procedures to ease the economy's ills and to prevent the contagion of the Workers' Opposition; and he had cauterized the wounds of the 'trade union discussion'. The Kronstadt mutiny had drawn the Congress together. But it soon became evident that Lenin's doctoring had produced a less than complete cure.

The entire NEP was put in question as soon as the Kronstadt rebels had been crushed. Bolshevik leaders in Moscow and the provinces took stock of what had been ratified, and many felt discontented. The NEP was only one source of trouble. There were also objections to the scheme to attract foreign concessionaires. Aired at the Congress, the criticism was growing. Less controversial was the series of moves to sign commercial treaties with foreign countries. Kamenev had alluded to them in the last hours of the Congress but had deftly laid his emphasis on revolutionary commitment in a world of capitalist powers – he even contrived to fail to mention that the Anglo-Soviet Trade Treaty was scheduled to be signed on the very day the Congress ended – an indication that even in this case the Politburo was jittery about the party's possible reaction. Then there was the continuing resentment on the part of the Workers' Opposition and the Democratic Centralists of the restrictions on their ability to canvass for their ideas. The worry for Lenin was that he had succeeded only in putting a sticking plaster on the wound of the party's strategic disagreements.

One of his few comforts at the time was that he and Trotsky were of one mind about such questions. Another was that Trotsky had abandoned his obsession with trade unions. He did not change his mind about policy; for him the unions had never been the nub of the matter but now his thinking was focused on how to get the country back on its feet economically. He continued to believe that the unions were 'a dead institution' that would only hamper recovery; eventually he acknowledged that Lenin had been right to tell him: 'The masses won't put up with it!' Trotsky nevertheless also insisted that his own proposal for blending the unions into the structures of government had become a reality within months of the end of the discussion.[1] But he judged it a waste of time to state this except when provoked in private correspondence. His public silence was not a new phenomenon. Once worsted in the Brest-Litovsk controversy back in March 1918, he had immediately stopped canvassing for his 'neither war nor peace' policy – and in that case he subsequently never claimed that Lenin had been in the wrong. Obviously the storm of his logic and invective could blow itself out.

A further matter brought Lenin and Trotsky together at the end of the month. The Comintern leadership had for some weeks been plotting a communist seizure of power in Berlin. This was a daring but unrealistic scheme which was anyhow marred by shoddy planning and implementation. Zinoviev and Radek were the prime movers. No preliminary consultation took place with the Politburo in Moscow. Not even Lenin or Trotsky was initiated. Zinoviev and Radek plunged ahead, sending off Béla Kun in Comintern's name to liaise with the German Communist Party. Kun with his forceful personality and mandate from Moscow overrode the sensible objections of Paul Levi, and he reached out to leading comrades who were eager to attempt a putsch regardless of the chances. The German government brought out the army against the strikers. The communist insurgents were outnumbered. On 31 March the German central leadership had to admit defeat and call off the uprising.

The so-called March Action was a disaster. Trotsky and Lenin were furious about the incompetence of the Soviet instigators and their German accomplices. Harsh words were exchanged behind closed doors. Trotsky said that the Action had involved a dangerous adventurism – and he was annoyed with Kun for going around accusing him of being at odds with Lenin over the Berlin insurrection.[2] Zinoviev and Radek made things worse by seeking a compromise on measures to deal with the consequences for Comintern. According to Trotsky, this only encouraged Kun in his mischief-making.[3] The reality was that Zinoviev, Radek and Kun had presided over a débâcle. Trotsky argued that Germany's ruling 'block' had not been in disarray at the time and could easily deal with any trouble. The German economy had not been faltering. Quite the contrary: it was achieving 'a certain relative equilibrium'. German communists had acted ineptly, putting forward unclear demands which fell short of justifying a seizure of power while alerting 'the counter-revolution' to what was in the offing. The planning was woeful. Paul Levi and other prominent figures on the right wing of the German Communist Party had supplied a similar critique; their only mistake was in making it public. Like Lenin, Trotsky was a centralist and disciplinarian and approved of Levi being punished for insubordination.

Trotsky showed his notes on the Action to Radek, seeking comments in advance of making a speech.[4] This was not his usual procedure but Radek had been his ally in most party controversies since 1917, and he offered his verdict in words which, he hoped, Radek would not object to. Trotsky wanted to avoid any display of division in the Soviet leadership. He also knew that Soviet Russia's security could be damaged if the Russian communist role in March 1921 had become common knowledge. Blame was to be assigned exclusively to the German Communist Party. Lenin and Trotsky worked together in compelling Zinoviev and Radek to toe the Politburo's line.

Lenin could also count on his People's Commissar for Military Affairs to supervise the crushing of resistance to communism in Russia, Ukraine and Siberia. The leading militants of the Kronstadt mutiny were shot, the rest being dispatched to a 'disciplinary colony' at Ukhta in the Russian far north. This was ordered by the Politburo, with both Lenin and Trotsky being present, on 27 April 1921.[5] Trotsky then gave personal attention to Tambov province and its rebellious peasantry. His military protégé Mikhail Tukhachevski was redeployed there in summer 1921 – and Tukhachevski was remorseless in the methods of military terror he used against the insurgents.[6] The communist central leadership said little in public about the fighting, and Trotsky did not take his famous train down to the Volga to inspect Tukhachevski's operations. This was deliberate. The leaders did not wish to be seen trampling on the peasantry's wishes. The Politburo certainly wanted to get popular acquiescence to the NEP. But the priority was to traumatize rural households into submission. Cavalry units were sent to enforce an increase in the peasantry's sown acreage. Their voluntary co-operation could come later.

Trotsky concurred with Lenin over the need to attract capital from abroad, which was one of Lenin's preoccupations. Lenin wanted to open the entire Donets Basin to exploitation by foreign concessionaires; his idea was for entrepreneurs from the advanced economic powers to restore the mines and the farms to full working order. Trotsky had no hesitation in agreeing. He found the criticism of such measures 'ridiculous' and attributed it to local 'patriotism'.[7] He was eager to get German assistance in re-equipping and retraining the Red Army for any future war. The treaty of Versailles placed restrictions on the size and nature of Germany's armed forces. The German government was looking for ways round the obstacle, and Russia was an obvious potential partner. Confidential discussions entered a serious phase in April 1921. Viktor Kopp, the Soviet plenipotentiary in Berlin, wrote to Trotsky confirming that big firms such as Krupp, Albatrosswerk and Blom and Voss wanted to become involved in restoring the Russian armaments industry.[8] Trotsky was far from thinking that the sole route to economic recovery and development was through 'European socialist revolution'.

Many party members, especially those outside Moscow, objected. The Donets Basin had always been highly productive in coal, iron and grain; the granting of concessions to German companies like Krupp would turn them into virtual co-rulers over the region's workers and a large number of the peasants (who would not take kindly to losing the land gained through Lenin's Land Decree). Furthermore, oil extraction and refining was the only advanced industry in Azerbaijan. If the Nobel Brothers' Petroleum Company were to return to Baku, it would be resuming a monopoly it had held before 1917. The question was put as to whether this was what the Bolsheviks had fought the Civil War for.[9]

Lenin and Trotsky held their ground. In trying to make the NEP effective they shared the belief that external assistance was a prerequisite for economic regeneration. They also agreed on the need to give incentives to peasants to trade their agricultural surpluses. Industrial products had to be put on to the market, and on 21 March 1921 Trotsky wrote to Alexander Tsyurupa, People's Commissar for Food Supplies, that the peasantry had to be enabled to buy farming equipment. Soviet factories could not provide this. Imports of foreign technology were therefore crucial.[10] Tsyurupa had been slow to accept the case for scrapping forcible grain requisitioning. Technically competent, he would be an asset for the government so long as he could be weaned away from War Communism. Many other leaders, in Moscow and in the provinces, felt like him. The fact that Trotsky was arguing for help to be given to markets and to peasants was not widely known for the simple reason that his articles for *Pravda* were on other topics. He was usually not one to blench at potential controversy. But he left it to Lenin and Kamenev to make the public arguments for the new agrarian policy; he had plenty of things on his own plate in the People's Commissariat for Military Affairs.

The other reason for passivity was his poor state of health. Whenever active military duty had called, he roused himself to write, speak and travel – and it took some months after the Polish war for him to adjust his style of existence to peacetime. The toll on his health was high and getting higher. By spring 1921 he was exhausted. Professor Guetier, physician to several Kremlin families, put him under orders to take a complete rest.

Trotsky was not the only one taking sick leave. Zinoviev suffered two heart attacks between March and May. Kamenev too had a cardiac problem, and a bout of appendicitis laid Stalin low. Bukharin had returned from convalescence only recently.[11] These men were at the core of the central party leadership. While Lenin shouldered the onus of general strategic oversight, his task was made difficult by outbreaks of disunity. Central Committee member Mikhail Tomski had responsibility for co-ordinating the party's linkage with the trade unions. He had been among Lenin's prominent associates in the dispute of the past winter. The problem for Tomski was that Alexander Shlyapnikov and the Workers' Opposition retained a following in the Metal Workers' Union. Tomski made minor compromises with the union in the interests of collaboration. He had acted without consulting the Politburo and Lenin fell into an incandescent rage to the point of demanding Tomski's expulsion from the Central Committee as a delinquent. Dzerzhinski strongly supported Lenin.[12] The atmosphere cleared only when Lenin calmed down; but he had reason to feel that the party leadership had become dysfunctional. Discipline and co-ordination needed to be restored and the party's general policies had to be confirmed.

The opportunity to fight for the NEP and take stock of the March Action arose at the Tenth Party Conference in May 1921, but Trotsky was still too ill to attend. Agreement on the March Action was easily attained; it was harder to obtain for the agrarian reform. Unease about the concessions made to the peasantry was widely felt in the party. Many Bolsheviks, free to speak their minds behind closed doors, vented their frustrations. They expressed hatred about the return of open markets, land rents, co-ops and kulaks.[13] Other speakers offered a more measured critique. Among them was Preobrazhenski, Trotsky's supporter in the recent 'trade union discussion', who broadly accepted the NEP but wanted to increase the element of central economic planning.[14] Another of Trotsky's political friends, Yuri Larin, complained about an inattention to the needs of Soviet large-scale industry.[15] The situation got on Lenin's nerves. He revealed how difficult it had become to run the party from Moscow when he was left on his own and could not depend on the allegiance of Central Committee members to official policies.[16] Lenin had never previously asked for pity but had become desperate. His emotional plea was his last throw at bringing the Conference to its senses. Nobody else, not even

Trotsky, could have pulled this off. The Conference showed its respect for Lenin and his instincts by ratifying everything he requested.

It was just as well for Lenin that Trotsky was not present, for Trotsky's sympathies were on the side of Preobrazhenski and Larin. Lenin and Trotsky were eager in principle to run the economy according to a fixed state plan. But Lenin thought the conditions had not yet arrived for this whereas Trotsky saw no reason to hold back from introducing central planning controls. Lenin fended him off. But if Trotsky had been in good health he would have made his point at the Conference, and all hope of containing the tensions inside the central party leadership would have been put in jeopardy.

After returning from sick leave Trotsky put forward a paper to the Politburo on 8 August. He went along with Lenin in calling for the extension of the economy's private sector beyond agriculture and trade into industry;[17] he too pushed the case for extending the reach of the NEP. Small-scale entrepreneurs could respond more quickly than large factories to peasant demands. Most of the bigger enterprises had ceased production; output from factories and mines in 1921 was only a seventh of what it had been in 1913. Lively individual producers were vital for getting the wheels of economic exchange between town and countryside moving again. But then Trotsky diverged from Lenin. In his opinion, Lenin had too readily abandoned a commitment to the making of a state 'economic plan'. Trotsky proposed to strengthen the powers of the Supreme Council of the People's Economy. He also suggested that the experts in the State Planning Commission, instead of dreaming up schemes for a distant future, should supply the Supreme Council with a detailed framework for the regulation of the entire economy.[18] He saw this as the best way to accelerate post-war recovery and further development.

He was not putting immediate social needs at the top of his consider-ations. Far from it: in September, while staying in Odessa, he snarled about the food and medicine offered to Soviet children in the Volga region by Herbert Hoover and the American Relief Administration. This was an agency which had shipped indispensable supplies to central Europe from 1919 and was now offering help to Soviet Russia at a time of growing famine in the Volga region. While going along with the Politburo in accepting the offer, Trotsky denounced Hoover as 'our most accursed enemy' and stressed:

Here we need to remember that we are not Hungary. We are not a young Soviet republic. We have been tempered in the struggle against counter-revolution. We have our own special organs; we have the Cheka. The Cheka isn't loved, but then again we don't love the counter-revolution.[19]

If any members of Hoover's mission got up to anything other than food distribution, the prisons of Russia were ready to accommodate them. Assuming that Westerners were out of earshot, Trotsky offered the following explanation of Soviet international economic policy:

But just in the same way [as we are handling the Hoover mission], while concluding agreements with bourgeois governments for concessions lasting ninety-nine years, we offer no guarantee that history won't overthrow the bourgeoisie before that date. We don't answer for history: we answer only for ourselves. In that contingency, of course, we'll have to rip up the agreement about concessions since that will be *force majeure*.[20]

He came to recognize the need to placate public opinion in the United States since Sovnarkom was hoping to get foreign businesses, including American ones, to bid for concessions in Russia and Ukraine. Trotsky was among those who saw no hope of industrial regeneration without capital and expertise being secured from abroad. His Odessa speech revealed his desired strategy even though he pragmatically buttoned his lip. Although Lenin was unbothered by Trotsky's fulminations about Hoover he was disturbed by what he kept saying about state economic planning. The two leaders had never discussed the NEP thoroughly before introducing it. Weaknesses of argument lay on both sides. Lenin, while talking about the NEP as the vehicle for a 'transition to socialism', gave no systematic explanation of the institutional mechanism that would enable this to occur. Trotsky too lacked a comprehensive rationale since he omitted to clarify how the owners of small workshops, whom he wanted to encourage, would benefit from the existence of a State Planning Commission. Lenin sensed that Trotsky might suddenly initiate yet another controversy and split the party. He had yet to be persuaded that he could rely on him again.

Quietly he ensured a diminution of Trotsky's supporters at the next Party Congress, scheduled to start on 27 March 1922. He called in Stalin to send Leninists to regional party organizations before their delegations were appointed. Stalin queried whether this was not banned as factional activity. Lenin took this as a joke, coming from 'an inveterate factionalist'. The Leninists put their candidates into the main positions of authority in the leadership. Trotsky retained his old posts but only two of his supporters in the 'trade union discussion' joined the Central Committee: Andrei Andreev and Khristian Rakovski; he was being put on probation. He behaved discreetly for a change. It was Preobrazhenski on the left who stirred up a fuss by offering a set of critical theses on the agrarian question. Preobrazhenski believed that policy had been skewed in favour of the kulaks. Lenin requested the Politburo to remove this from the Congress agenda; Trotsky did not demur. Debates at the Congress confirmed the line followed since the previous year. Trotsky even supported Tomski's report on the trade unions permitting strikes by workers in state-owned enterprises. But he then caused a flurry by stipulating that experienced specialists and not workers should decide industrial policy. The dispute blew itself out, and Trotsky met with no difficulty when he offered his own report on the Red Army.

Lenin maintained his dominance by arranging a reorganization of the communist leadership. He was suffering from ill health as symptoms of his arteriosclerosis surfaced. Feeling his own growing incapacity, he decided on a reorganization of the central political leadership. He did not yet think his days were numbered. What he wanted was a team who would pull together if and whenever he was temporarily indisposed. To this end he supported the promotion of Stalin to party general secretary. In the previous year the Secretariat had been in the hands of Vyacheslav Molotov. There was agreement that Molotov and his staff had not performed well in their posts, and indeed Stalin had already been helping them out – and the partnership of Stalin and Molotov was set to last for decades.[21] The party required a firm hand at the helm. Stalin was chosen as general secretary at Kamenev's suggestion at the first Central Committee after the Congress.

Sovnarkom also called for attention since Lenin was its chairman. As he felt he was likely to be absent a great deal, he approached Alexei Rykov and Alexander Tsyurupa to be his regular deputies. The two of them could divide responsibilities between them and ensure continuity of governance as the NEP was consolidated. He avoided the obvious big names such as Trotsky, Kamenev and Zinoviev. Trotsky would have made a poor choice for many reasons. As he was to concede, he had his own way of doing things and was unlikely to want to change; he was glad not to have been invited.[22] In any case he had his own vision of the NEP. The weakness of authority for the State Planning Administration, known as Gosplan, continued to rankle with him; and he did not mind telling Lenin that the Politburo should recognize the need for the regulation of investment, production and distribution through a powerful centre.

Trotsky also criticized the Workers' and Peasants' Inspectorate (or Rabkrin) which had been created with Lenin's approval in 1920 to supervise what was going on in the People's Commissariats. Its leader was Stalin. Trotsky believed Rabkrin to be a waste of resources, or worse: the entire institution was useless.[23] For Lenin it was a disturbing reaction. Trotsky had not truly mended his ways; his recent quiescence was deceptive. Internal party trouble remained a distinct possibility.

# 31. THE POLITICS OF ILLNESS

It would have been difficult to slip a cigarette paper between Lenin and Trotsky in foreign policy in early 1922. The British and French were trying to stabilize the post-war political settlement and restore the countries of Europe to economic prosperity, and they planned to achieve this by calling all the European powers to a conference in Genoa. The Soviet leadership determined to send representatives. At first there was talk of either Lenin or Trotsky travelling to Italy, but their physical security was a concern for the Cheka since an assassination attempt was a realistic possibility. Lenin wrote to the Politburo proposing that none of the obvious leaders – Lenin, Trotsky or Zinoviev – should be allowed to go abroad.[1] Georgi Chicherin, Trotsky's successor in the People's Commissariat for Foreign Affairs since 1918, was dispatched instead. The Genoa Conference started on 10 April. The Politburo ordered Chicherin to discover the terms required for Soviet Russia's general diplomatic recognition and reintegration into the global commercial network. The French government disappointed any such aspiration. Short of repealing Sovnarkom's unilateral annulment of Russian state debts, the communists could do nothing to mollify the feelings of France's investors. Lenin did not expect much good to come from Genoa. He insisted that Chicherin should avoid unapproved compromises, and he goaded the Politburo from the Gorki sanatorium into maintaining strategic firmness.[2]

Russia was not the only pariah power in Europe. Germany's democratically elected government too felt badly treated, and the diplomats of both countries met secretly down the Ligurian coast at Santa Margherita. The result was the treaty of Rapallo, signed on 16 April 1922 and designed to facilitate trade. Germany needed Russian natural resources, Russia sought to benefit from German technology. Negotiations also led to collusion to permit German armed forces to conduct their training on Soviet territory – and the Red Army expected to gain important expertise from this arrangement. The Rapallo treaty achieved much progress in the direction of the economic regeneration that Lenin and Trotsky had been seeking for over a year.

They also agreed on how to handle potential resistance from the Russian Orthodox Church. Lenin's instinct was to hammer Christianity while it was too weak to defend itself. Aiming to traumatize the clergy and their believers for generations to come, he called for seizures of ecclesiastical treasures and for show-trials of bishops and priests.[3] Trotsky went along with this but urged that the party should also adopt a more refined strategy for the longer term. A faction had arisen in the Church known as the Renovationists. Its leaders were bent on reforming the structure of internal authority and the liturgy; they were willing to accept the Soviet administration's legitimate right to rule in return for freedom of worship. Trotsky saw a chance to divide and weaken the Orthodox Church by offering favour to the Renovationists. He adhered to the principle that the greater the dissension among the clergy, the stronger the Soviet state. It would take years, perhaps decades, for Marxist propaganda to erode mass belief in the Christian gospels.[4] Lenin saw the point and Trotsky's proposals became official policy.

Then there was the matter of policy towards the other political parties. Here it was Lenin who took the lead, demanding show-trials and executions of prominent Mensheviks and Socialist-Revolutionaries. Trotsky supported him but Bukharin and Radek were unpersuaded. On a trip to Amsterdam for discussions with foreign socialist parties, they gave their word that any such trials would hold back from applying the death penalty. Lenin and Trotsky were furious since they would rather have no dealings with the parties of the old Second International than restrict the freedom of Bolsheviks to carry through a ruthless suppression of the Mensheviks and Socialist-Revolutionaries. The case against these parties was that they had conducted an active struggle against Soviet Russia. It is true that a war took place between Komuch under the Socialist-Revolutionaries and Sovnarkom in mid-1918. Even some Mensheviks had fought against the Red Army. By and large, though, both the parties had helped the Reds against the Whites. What Lenin and Trotsky really wanted in 1922 was to remove the slightest possibility of trouble in the years ahead. There were to be no political competitors for the sympathy of the working class and peasantry.

The show-trial of the Socialist-Revolutionaries began in June 1922. Trotsky with characteristic cynicism urged that it should have 'the character of a finished political production'.[5] He was not bothered about legal procedures: he wanted the Socialist-Revolutionaries punished as an example to all parties hostile to Bolshevism. He delivered a bloodthirsty speech to this effect from the balcony of Trade Unions House.[6] In fact the sentences ordered by the Politburo did not include shootings. Nor did the Politburo grant Lenin's request for judicial proceedings against the Mensheviks. But the campaign of preventive persecution was maintained. In the same month the Cheka rounded up dozens of philosophers, writers and scholars and deported them from Russia on the steamships *Oberbürgmeister Haken* and *Preussen*.[7] The entire party leadership, including Trotsky, endorsed the introduction of comprehensive preventive censorship known as Glavlit in the same summer. The message was conveyed that the communists aimed to put the country into political, ideological and cultural quarantine.

Lenin seemed to have recovered from a winter of ill health but suffered a stroke on 25 May and was sent out to the Gorki sanatorium again. This increased his reliance on Stalin's services. It was Stalin who acted as his main conduit of his ideas to the Politburo, and Lenin was grateful for his willingness to come out and visit him frequently. They conferred about political business and Stalin acquainted Lenin with the latest political news. Lenin ordered a bottle of wine to be placed on the table in readiness.[8] Trotsky never went out to see him. They were comrades rather than friends, and Trotsky felt no tug of sentiment to visit the patient. Anyway he did not expect Politburo members to visit him when he himself was ill; indeed he might well have treated any such visit as an infringement on his writing time. His behaviour towards Lenin was based on the same assumption. Trotsky lacked the rudimentary understanding that he needed to attract the trusting warmth of fellow leaders. Stalin was psychologically cleverer. He was no more a friend of Lenin's than Trotsky was. Lenin privately disliked many aspects of his personality and thought him crude, ill mannered and unintelligent. But he felt he could use Stalin as a political assistant, and Stalin knew that his own best interests lay in liaising with him.[9]

Trotsky's luck changed in late summer 1922 when Stalin ceased to act as the obedient executor of Lenin's wishes. Reports reached the sanatorium that Stalin was behaving imperiously towards Georgian communist leaders who disliked his scheme for the new Constitution. Lenin himself did not wholly approve of Stalin's drafts. Stalin wanted to put all the existing Soviet republics into the Russian Socialist Federative Soviet Republic (RSFSR) and Lenin thought this smacked of 'great-Russian chauvinism'.

Lenin tussled with Stalin over several weeks. In 1918–20 he had assumed that his sporadic difficulties with Stalin were attributable to personal prickliness: he had seldom taken Stalin's proposals on policy with much seriousness. It came as a shock to find that Stalin knew his own mind. Lenin also felt agitated about bureaucratic trends in the party and was starting to query the effectiveness of Rabkrin in cutting red tape in governmental institutions. Stalin was the embodiment of such worries inasmuch as he headed both the Party Secretariat and Rabkrin. What added to Lenin's concern was the fact that Stalin supported the new proposals being made in relation to Soviet foreign trade. Since the October Revolution there had been a state monopoly on imports and exports. Bukharin and Kamenev suggested that the NEP would be enhanced if private traders were permitted to operate again. Their argument was that commercial activity would expand and tax revenues would rise, and the current problem with smuggling would disappear. Lenin was horrified. Having been the principal advocate for deepening the reforming measures in the NEP, he now wanted to set definite limits.

In exasperation he called for the entire Central Committee to be sacked except for Vyacheslav Molotov, Alexei Rykov and Valeryan Kuiby-shev. At a pinch he was willing to allow associate membership for Kamenev, Zinoviev and even Tomski (whom he had tried to remove in 1921). Lenin had lost his sense of proportion. He totally failed to explain why his proposed troika would function better than the existing larger membership. Nor were Trotsky, Stalin, Bukharin and others going to take kindly to their own elimination; and Trotsky would have had every right to ask what he had done recently to deserve losing his Central Committee place. The scheme was anyway impossible under the party rules and Lenin was not the party's dictator. Fellow leaders had grounds for querying his mental stability. But they appreciated that when he calmed down he would remain determined to get his way on the Constitution and on foreign trade. On Kamenev's advice, Stalin agreed that the RSFSR should enter the Union of Soviet Socialist Republics on an equal footing with Soviet Ukraine. This brought back a measure of tranquillity to the leadership even though the Georgian communist leaders remained suspicious of Stalin and predicted that he would continue to bully them.

Lenin, however, continued to oppose the project to abolish the state's foreign-trade monopoly. The longer Lenin brooded on this, the more appealing he found the idea of a rapprochement with Trotsky, who shared his position on imports and exports. Trotsky had failed to win over the Central Committee on 8 August. Lenin complained angrily to the Polit-buro. Kamenev, Bukharin, Zinoviev and Stalin conceded ground by post-poning the final decision for a couple of months. Although Lenin experienced enough of a physical recovery to return to fitful work in Moscow the doctors insisted on a further period of convalescence out at

Gorki. On 12 December, still marooned in Gorki, Lenin sent a message to Trotsky requesting assistance. Trotsky responded positively the same day but made clear that he wanted not merely to preserve the status quo but to place all foreign trade under the authority of the State Planning Commission. Increased excise revenues, he argued, would enable additional investment in industry. Next day a deal was done: Trotsky backed down from his specific demand while Lenin promised an undefined degree of extra authority for the State Planning Commission. Lenin was pleased, writing on 15 December: 'I think we've reached complete agreement. I ask you to announce our solidarity at the plenum.' Faced by the united front of Lenin and Trotsky, the rest of the Central Committee was already backing down before it met. On 21 December Lenin wrote to Trotsky from the sanatorium: 'It is as if we've succeeded by a simple movement of manoeuvre without having to fire a single shot.'[10]

By then he was so frail that he was contemplating the likelihood of his own early death. He despaired of running Sovnarkom simply with Rykov and Kamenev as his deputies, even though he had added Kamenev to this arrangement since April 1922: 'You know them. Kamenev is of course a clever politician but what's he like as an administrator? Tsyurupa's ill. Yes, Rykov's an administrator but he ought to be directed toward the Supreme Council of the People's Economy. You must become a deputy [chairman]. The situation is such that we need a radical personal regrouping.'[11] Trotsky declined the invitation even though, in later years, he was to claim that it was tantamount to a request to agree to be his successor in Sovnarkom.[12] Whether this was really what Lenin had in mind is far from clear: he was a master of the political zigzag. In any case he composed what he could by dictating frantically to his secretaries, about policy and institutions. Over the ensuing weeks he criticized bureaucratic trends in the party and proposed to bring workers into the central leadership as an antidote. He excoriated Rabkrin as a waste of resources. He collected material on the Georgian political situation.

As usual, Lenin hedged his bets. Among his dictated pieces was something that would become known as his political testament. He picked six fellow leaders as his possible successors. These were Trotsky, Stalin, Kamenev, Zinoviev, Bukharin and Pyatakov. None came out well from his assessments. Recognizing Trotsky as 'the ablest person' in the Central Committee, he thought him unduly attracted to 'the purely administrative side of affairs'. A lot of what Lenin said was applicable to himself. He and Trotsky were architects of a kind of state order that had reduced most of the political process to mere administration. No rival political party was allowed to operate. The Cheka and the Red Army eliminated every attempt to resist or obstruct communist rule. The press was in thrall to the Bolsheviks. The judiciary had no independence. Bolshevik veterans monopolized all the great public institutions. What Lenin was pointing to, however, was Trotsky's tendency to dream up policies without taking cognizance of predictable political problems. The trade union controversy was just one example of this. Lenin had made mistakes of the same kind. For instance, he had set up committees of the poor peasants in mid-1918 despite all the evidence that the peasantry as a whole would resent this; and he had refused to abandon War Communism in 1920. But whereas Lenin often moved off the path of error, Trotsky usually had to be dragged off kicking and screaming.

Lenin also cast doubt on Bukharin's credentials as a Marxist. He judged Pyatakov unreliable 'in a serious political question'. While continuing to disapprove of the behaviour of Kamenev and Zinoviev in the October Revolution, he did not want it held against them any more than Trotsky should suffer for not having been a Bolshevik before 1917. Stalin attracted his gravest charge. Lenin complained that he had 'concentrated boundless power in his hands since becoming General Secretary and I am not convinced that he will always succeed in using this power with enough care.' Many communists, had they been privy to Lenin's thinking, would have been surprised that he even considered Stalin as a potential successor. But Lenin had learned much from his quarrels with him in 1922. He felt justified in offering the startling prognosis that Trotsky and Stalin, as 'the two outstanding leaders of the current Central Committee', might clash forcefully and induce a split in the entire party. Such an outcome had to be avoided at all costs. The purpose of Lenin's testament was unmistakable. If and when Lenin died, he believed that the best option for the party would be to secure a collective leadership.

On 24 January 1923, in his sickbed at the sanatorium, he dictated a codicil which upset the balance of his characterizations. Stalin's friend Sergo Ordzhonikidze had used physical violence on one of the Georgian communist comrades in Tiflis. Dzerzhinski and Stalin had condoned it. Lenin needed no second thoughts: 'Stalin is too crude and this inadequacy, which is wholly acceptable in our milieu and in exchanges among us communists, becomes intolerable in the position of General Secretary.' He proposed nothing less than removing Stalin from the Secretariat.

This turn in Lenin's thinking strengthened the bond with Trotsky. On 27 December he had suggested expanding the competence of the State Planning Commission. Stopping short of giving it legislative authority, he agreed to its making regular submissions to Sovnarkom – and he praised its existing leadership. Two days later he recommended letting the State Planning Commission rather than Rabkrin scrutinize the reliability of 'bourgeois' economic experts. He also asked his wife Krupskaya to tell Trotsky that his feelings towards him had not changed since they had first met in London in autumn 1902. Stalin felt the way the wind was blowing and implored Lenin's sister Maria to relay a message to Lenin: 'I love him with all my soul.' Lenin ridiculed these words and would agree only to give a polite response. Stalin tried another tactic on 6 January 1923. If he could not propitiate Lenin, perhaps he could effect a reconciliation with Trotsky. With this in mind he recommended Trotsky's promotion to be Lenin's deputy in Sovnarkom with special responsibility for the Supreme Council of the People's Economy; he also proposed Pyatakov, Trotsky's ally on economic policy, to be elevated to the chairmanship of the State Planning Commission. Trotsky declined the proposal. On 17 January Stalin had another try and said Trotsky should be both deputy chairman of Sovnarkom and chairman of the State Planning Commission.

Trotsky again refused. He too was suffering another bout of ill health and, in the care of Professor Guetier, he wrote to Zinoviev from 'a horizontal position' explaining why he could not be more active.[13] Yet his mental faculties were full of zest. He simply could not see how Stalin's proposal would increase the effectiveness of government; and he asked everyone else to understand his logic. He had said the same to Lenin and nothing had changed in the meantime to convince him to become Sovnarkom's deputy chairman. Trotsky's arguments were cogent but reflected a tactical rigidity. He was turning down a chance to dominate the Soviet government while Lenin was away. Although he was justified in claiming that the proposal fell short of demarcating institutional powers with precision, he was surely wrong to suggest that the problems were insuperable. He looked as if he could not be bothered to help out in what were difficult circumstances for the party. He appeared downright haughty. His enemies were predictably unforgiving in their comments on Trotsky's reaction, and he tried in vain to dispel the impression he had created.[14]

At the time, however, Stalin was in deeper trouble than Trotsky. Having finished an article on Rabkrin, Lenin sought Trotsky's help in getting it published. The Politburo considered printing a fake issue of *Pravda* exclusively for Lenin. The contents would be written so as to stop him worrying about the current political debates and intervening in them. Apparently Trotsky quashed this scheme to deceive Lenin. Then the report

on the Georgian business came up for consideration. Although the Politburo confirmed Dzerzhinski's whitewashing report on Ordzhonikidze's
use of violence, Lenin established a little secretarial group to scrutinize
the materials. He was not going to let Stalin and Dzerzhinski off the hook.
The group got back to him on 3 March. Two days later Lenin wrote a
letter to Stalin demanding an apology for subjecting Krupskaya to verbal
abuse and telling him that otherwise he would break off personal relations
with him. He assured the Georgian communists that he was working for
their cause; he also asked Trotsky to take up the Georgian affair on his
behalf and to involve Kamenev in the campaign against Stalin. Trotsky
agreed without showing any great eagerness: he was always keener to
debate policy than personalities. He also probably thought it was beneath
him to give a lot of attention to the General Secretary: Stalin in Trotsky's
eyes would always be a political mediocrity and intellectual nonentity.

The Lenin–Trotsky alliance was disrupted by the sudden deterioration
in Lenin's physical condition in the night of 6–7 March. Lenin was never
politically active again. On 10 March he suffered another stroke. His entire
right side was paralysed and he lost nearly all capacity for speech. This
hugely complicated the situation. No longer was there the prospect of
Lenin delivering the ideas in his testament to the forthcoming Twelfth
Party Congress. The recommendation for Stalin's sacking would not be
heard.

Georgia, though, retained the potential to cause harm to the General
Secretary. Trotsky received a copy of Lenin's article on the affair on 5 March
but could do nothing until Lidia Fotieva, one of Lenin's secretaries,
revealed that Lenin had wanted it to appear in *Pravda* – and she mentioned
that Lenin had expressed the wish that Trotsky should defend its contents
at the Congress.[15] This impelled Trotsky into action. Stalin had prepared
draft theses on the national question for the Twelfth Party Congress.
Trotsky amended them with gusto in accordance with Lenin's wishes.[16]
Stalin was astute enough to accept the changes – otherwise he might have
strengthened Trotsky's position. What is more, Stalin accused Trotsky of
having deceived the party by failing to talk of the article in a timely
fashion. Trotsky retorted that Lenin had not told him about wanting to
publish it; he suggested that, if necessary, the Congress should decide
whether he had acted properly.[17] Kamenev agreed that the article by Lenin
should be published. The contents contained direct criticism of Stalin and
would help those who thought the General Secretary unfit for office.
Knowing this, Stalin continued to snipe at Trotsky for not disclosing the
article's existence and made it seem almost a breach of party discipline.

To everybody's relief, the dispute appeared settled after a conversation between the two men when Stalin said he would confirm in writing that Trotsky had not misbehaved.

This satisfied Trotsky at the time, but Stalin broke his word and failed to send the retraction.[18] Trotsky was furious about this. He also spoke at the Politburo in favour of clearing the Georgian communist leadership's name against Stalin's charge that it constituted a 'deviation' from Bolshevism. Trotsky castigated the 'excessive centralism' of the Transcaucasian Federation, which governed Georgia, Armenia and Azerbaijan. He demanded Ordzhonikidze's removal from his posting in the region.[19] Kamenev until then had shared Lenin's unhappiness about the way the Georgian Bolshevik leadership had been handled. But at the last moment he declined to support Trotsky. He never explained this. Perhaps he feared the kind of split in the leadership which Lenin had warned against in his testament. He may also have been afraid that Trotsky was bidding to become Lenin's successor. At any rate Trotsky was voted down on every count. In later years he was to be criticized for failing to support the campaign on the national question. This was unfair. He fought early; he fought hard. But he went down to defeat by the Politburo majority.

Stalin could breathe again, and he deviously suggested that Trotsky should deliver the main political report to the Congress. Trotsky declined the honour and Zinoviev took his place. It was as if Trotsky was bedazzled by the cross-cutting lights of too many decisions of a personal nature. He had been handed a chance at least to maintain a measure of pressure on Stalin and he threw it away. Stalin's speech on the national question passed without much controversy. He denounced 'great Russian' chauvinism while castigating nationalism among the non-Russians with equal force.[20] Thus he gave the impression of being even-handed. He also adopted as his own Lenin's proposals for reform in the party; he accepted the scheme to reorganize Rabkrin. He and the rest of the Politburo bought off Trotsky with concessions such as confirming the need for a greater emphasis on central state planning in industry. Lenin would have dealt more aggressively with Stalin; his incapacitation was a catastrophe for Trotsky. Stalin lived to fight another day.

# 32. THE LEFT OPPOSITION

Practically nobody in mid-1923, not even his friends, appreciated that Trotsky lacked a firm desire to be the leader. With Lenin he was routinely mentioned as the co-leader of the October Revolution, and he enjoyed the description. This was different from aspiring to the position of single paramount leader. His self-restraint did not mean that he did not want to lead. If he had the choice, he would handle the process as Lenin had done. There was no need for a special title: Lenin, after all, had never had one. Trotsky liked to think up schemes and take them to the party. His goal, which was doubtless an unconscious one, was to drag the Revolution along with whatever new policy he espoused at any given moment. Whenever he felt like withdrawing from the daily political routine and doing some writing, he did so. He hated days when every hour was filled with meetings. His idea of running the People's Commissariat for Military Affairs was to read reports, give orders and get on with his other interests. He was not lacking in earnestness or self-application but he would operate only on his own terms. Such had always been his way and he never considered changing it.

Not that this stopped the rest of the leadership from regarding him with suspicion. In fact his health had deteriorated again in July and he would scarcely have been able to campaign for supreme power even if he had aspired to it. Natalya was in a still worse condition; she had contracted malaria and had a temperature above 40°. The doctors were worried about both of them, and Trotsky – like Lenin in the previous year – was banned from engaging in 'internal party conversations'. He welcomed his old friend Dmitri Sverchkov for a brief stroll around town and a friendly chat strictly on condition that they did not infringe the medical regime: the leadership had decreed that he should take an 'absolute rest'.[1]

Political pressure continued to be applied to Trotsky. The word was put about that he and Lenin had disagreed about Gosplan. Trotsky replied that he could produce the December 1922 letter from Lenin offering a compromise on state economic planning.[2] Meanwhile the rivalries inside the leadership were in flux. Stalin's dictatorial propensities, rather than the threat from Trotsky, had started to alarm Zinoviev. After several untoward incidents, Zinoviev wrote to Kamenev calling for counter-measures. He was not simply parroting Lenin's testament. Zinoviev objected to Stalin taking decisions without consulting his main comrades.[3] When the leaders dispersed for their holidays, Zinoviev met up in Kislovodsk with Bukharin, Voroshilov, Lashevich and Grigori Yevdokimov and put the case for reining Stalin back.[4] Lashevich and Yevdokimov were Zinoviev's supporters; Bukharin was aligned with nobody, and Voroshilov was consulted despite being close to Stalin. Evidently Zinoviev was trying to fire a shot across the General Secretary's bows. Zinoviev complained that both he and Trotsky, who was no political friend of his, had been unfairly left out of decision-making in the central leadership.[5] The obvious corrective measure was to insert Stalin's critics into the leading party agencies. A plan was put together whose chief feature was to draft Trotsky and Zinoviev into the Orgburo. Stalin took the hint and accepted the proposal, being too wily to react with a refusal. He survived yet again.

Dispute in the leadership was suddenly blown aside by the first economic emergency of the NEP in summer 1923. Food supplies grew scarce as peasants brought less produce to the markets. The payment they received for their harvest had fallen in real terms in relation to the prices of factory goods. Rural households reacted in their traditional fashion by ceasing to trade their grain; they ate more of it themselves, fed it to their livestock or used it to make vodka. The state plainly had to lower the prices charged by its factories for ploughs, buckles, corrugated iron and spades. The peasants had to be tempted back into trading in the towns. The Central Committee met to consider the situation in July to try and resolve the difficulties. Discontent persisted among party leaders. Although they agreed on the need to retain the NEP they disliked appearing indulgent to the peasantry. Least of all did they feel kindly towards the better-off peasant households, which were the ones that bought factory products. Hatred and fear of these kulaks were axiomatic for the party leadership. Nevertheless the shortages in urban grain warehouses compelled the Politburo to cheapen agricultural implements and to import more of them from abroad.[6] The emergency was quickly over. It was given its name by Trotsky: the 'scissors crisis'.[7] His idea was that Soviet state had allowed the 'blades' of industrial and agricultural prices to open too wide.

Trotsky, still convalescing, made no contribution in its resolution but surveyed the débâcle from a distance. But he was quick to offer criticism that a greater amount of central state economic planning would have obviated all the problems. Whether this in itself would have prevented the fall-off in food supplies in midsummer 1923 is a moot point. The Soviet state had caused the crisis. If it had acquired increased powers it might have done still harsher damage to the economic recovery.

Yevgeni Preobrazhenski and Trotsky agreed that the price adjustments had been necessary to sort out the 'scissors crisis'. But they wanted a more durable strategy for economic development. The basic defect of the Politburo's measures, they maintained, was the tying of policy to the retention of the peasantry's consent. Emergencies would recur until the central party leadership moved towards a planned economy. Capital industrial investment had to be raised. Progressive taxation had to be intensified with the pressure being targeted on kulaks and urban merchants. Gosplan had to be ordered to draw up a general economic plan for investment, output and prices. Incentives had to be introduced to make collective farms more attractive to peasants. The Bolshevik left believed that 'bureaucratization' was setting in. A change in economic direction was not sufficient in itself. There also had to be political reform. Party officials currently in post had been seduced by the comforts of power and privilege; they needed to recall the objectives of the October Revolution. Trotsky and his supporters criticized Kamenev, Zinoviev and Stalin indiscriminately. There had indeed been a rapprochement among the ascendant leaders. The Kislovodsk summer deliberations had compelled Stalin to repair his relations with Kamenev and Zinoviev, and Trotsky's disparagement of the so-called troika ruined any chance of isolating Stalin from the other two.

Arguments over foreign policy worsened the atmosphere in the central party leadership. A secret proposal cropped up in late summer 1923 for another attempt at a communist seizure of power in Germany. Trotsky eagerly supported this. Dusting off all his cherished internationalist ideas from the Great War, he stated that the slogan of 'the United States of Europe' had not lost its applicability.[8] Nobody in the Politburo had much confidence in the German Communist Party after the March Action of 1921. But leaders agreed that 'European socialist revolution' was desirable and that every opportunity to facilitate this outcome had to be taken.

Stalin was the solitary doubter. In August 1923, in a letter to Bukharin and Zinoviev, he drew a contrast between contemporary Germany and Russia in 1917. The German comrades were no position to exploit slogans like 'peace' and 'land'. Above all, they did not have most of the working class on their side. It was true that a socialist state – the Soviet republic in Russia – already existed whereas none had existed anywhere before the

October seizure of power. But Stalin asked what military assistance could the Bolsheviks genuinely offer to communists in Germany in the immediate future? He insisted that the likeliest consequence of an uprising would be an overwhelming counter-attack by right-wing social-democrats in alliance with the bourgeoisie.[9] The post-Imperial Weimar Republic was too strong for the German comrades. Stalin, though, was in a difficult position after the Kislovodsk discussions, and he backed down and supported the initiative. Unanimity emerged in the Politburo that an attempt should be made by the German Communist Party to overturn the government in the autumn. Revolutionary optimism prevailed in the Kremlin as the secret policy was elaborated.

Trotsky joined in the debate. He was as lightheaded as everyone else, quietly ditching the sceptical analysis of German communist prospects he had produced two years earlier. Politburo discussions were confined to practical details as representatives of the German leadership in Moscow were consulted. The way forward, it was thought, was to form a Comintern commission and to avoid a repetition of the amateurishness of March 1921. Its members were Zinoviev, Bukharin and Radek as well as Trotsky. Zinoviev wanted the uprising to be based closely on the Russian historical model with German soviets being used as the main instrument for seizing power. Trotsky pointed out that soviets had yet to be created, and he called for factory committees to make the necessary moves – and Zinoviev came over to his standpoint.[10]

The 'plan' rested on the assumption that a successful communist insurrection in Germany would put a blazing torch to the post-war international settlement in Europe. The treaties of Versailles, Trianon and Sèvres would be burned to a cinder. The European great powers would not stand idly by. There would be war and the Red Army would inevitably become involved because the German Communist Party could not prevail without external armed assistance.[11] Trotsky and the rest of the Politburo, when calling for a more active promotion of revolutions in the West, were expressing a readiness to take the gamble. They did not flinch at the prospect of a further European war. Revolutionary gains required sacrifices. Trotsky never explained why he thought Germany in 1923 was a ripe apple for the taking whereas he dismissed the March Action, undertaken only two years earlier, as immature fruit that should never have been touched. Soviet policy was being premised on the urgent need for Russia to break out of its isolation by fostering the creation of communist administrations in the West. Trotsky drove out caution from his thinking – and he was not alone in the leadership in doing this.

Yet it was not a pleasant time in his career. The rest of the Politburo remained nervous about his intentions now that Lenin was out of action. Overlooking their earlier objections to Stalin's domineering tendencies, Kamenev and Zinoviev agreed that Trotsky constituted a threat through his posts in the People's Commissariat for Military Affairs and the Revolutionary-Military Council of the Republic. The Central Committee in plenary session discussed the Council on 25 September. Trotsky's potential to become the Soviet Napoleon was in the minds of many who were present. When criticisms were made of his activity he stormed out of the room. This was inept since it provided his enemies with the opportunity to insert Stalin into the Council, doubtless with the idea of keeping closer control over the People's Commissar for Military Affairs.[12]

Feeling offended and edged out from regular central policy-making, Trotsky wrote an open letter of complaint to the Politburo on 8 October 1923. He had good reason to object to the way Zinoviev, Kamenev and Stalin met outside the formal sessions to fix the agenda. He called for a democratization of procedures throughout the party. He detested the power of committee secretaries. Trotsky contended that organizational change was vital if the party was to discharge its revolutionary duties with competence.[13] A week later his initiative was picked up by forty-six of his leading supporters in Moscow when they co-signed a 'declaration' for circulation among party members. Among the signatories were Yevgeni Preobrazhenski and Leonid Serebryakov and they criticized a range of current trends. They wanted an end to the party's bureaucratization. They ridiculed the leadership's handling of the 'scissors crisis' and urged a stronger commitment to industrial investment and planning. They demanded freedom of expression for dissenting comrades. Several signatories were not unduly bothered about the case for democratization; all of them, though, wanted more radical economic measures.[14] The result was political pandemonium – and Zinoviev, Kamenev and Stalin were alarmed by the threat to their position as so many leading comrades aligned themselves with Trotsky.

His letter had not in fact been carefully co-ordinated with his supporters. But Zinoviev, Kamenev and Stalin believed that he was the guiding spirit of a conspiracy; they also saw Trotsky as completely irresponsible and self-seeking. They had done their best to correct economic mistakes in summer 1923 without his help. Then he had come back and criticized the resident leadership. If he was so clever, why had he not foreseen the 'scissors crisis'? Moreover, he was rocking the boat at the very time when the Politburo was ordering the German communists to organize a Soviet-style revolution. Did he not see the need for unity at a crucial moment? Trotsky had anyway been indifferent to 'internal party democracy' since the October Revolution. He had regularly advocated authoritarian methods and centralistic structures. How could anyone take him seriously now that he was urging democratization? At the same time he occupied a post of sensitivity in the armed forces. Lenin was mortally ill and Politburo comrades knew that his chances of recovery were slim. They asked themselves whether Trotsky was seriously manoeuvring to supplant them with his personal dictatorship.

Trotsky was asked to account for himself on 26 October at an extraordinary joint session of the Central Committee and Central Control Commission attended by representatives of the party's ten largest city organizations. The Central Control Commission had been created in September 1920 to foster fairness in internal party procedures; but, like the Central Committee, its membership was selected in practice for its loyalty to the current official political line. The Politburo majority not only organized its own supporters efficiently but also permitted the Democratic Centralists and Workers' Oppositionists to state their case on the party's internal condition. The leading protagonists, though, were Stalin and Trotsky. Stalin had been chosen to head the attack on a man who stood accused of disruptiveness and disloyalty.[15]

Trotsky and his supporters were beginning to call themselves the Left Opposition. For them, the word 'left' implied sincerity, radicalism and a commitment to the ideals of the October Revolution. There were always going to be too few of them at the session for Trotsky to stand a chance. He used his concluding speech to make a personal statement. He understood that anything he said in public would draw attention to the Politburo's internal disagreements. Yet he felt unable to stay quiet when questions of principle divided the leaders. Only when he had got nowhere in the Politburo did he risk sending his letter on 8 October.[16] He was in the mood for a fight. Zinoviev had made overtures to him through Trotsky's associate Serebryakov in the interests of internal party peace. It had been Zinoviev's idea to reorganize the leadership by adding Trotsky and Bukharin to the ruling troika of Zinoviev, Kamenev and Stalin. Trotsky had also repudiated Bukharin's idea of working in the Supreme Council of the People's Economy on the grounds that he could not combine such a posting with his obligations in the armed forces. Neither Zinoviev nor Bukharin could divert him. Trotsky calculated that he would always lose any vote in the Politburo, Central Committee or Central Control Commission, and he was passionate about the case he was making. As he saw the situation, there was no point in confining himself to discussions in the central party leadership and he had no alternative to writing his open letter and risking a disruptive conflict throughout the party.[17]

He denied heading a group of 'Trotskyists' or being the next Bonaparte; he was willing to step down from the Red Army to prove the point, and anyway the Politburo and Orgburo had always had control over his People's Commissariat.[18] He denied being a military dictator in waiting or even a Trotskyist.[19] Trotsky described the several occasions since October 1917 when 'my Jewish origins' had dissuaded him from accepting important postings from Lenin. It would be imprudent for the Soviet state, he stressed, to have a Jew as its paramount leader.[20] In fact there was not much rhyme or reason in his decisions to take one job or refuse another; and his Jewishness may not always have been the decisive factor in his mind. But his tormented speech to the plenum at least showed a glimmering of self-knowledge. When his enemies said that he was not the man who could ever replace Lenin they were repeating what he himself had already concluded.

The Central Committee and Central Control Committee reprimanded Trotsky and the Declaration's forty-six signatories. Trotsky tactfully abstained in the voting,[21] but he had not given up the fight. The plenum, he noted, had acknowledged the need for greater internal party democracy. He exploited this as constituting official recognition that a 'new course' was essential.[22] He feverishly produced a string of articles for *Pravda*. He declared that 'the role of the apparatus' should not be over-inflated. Discussion and initiative ought to be encouraged at every level of the party. The danger of revolutionary 'degeneration' was a real one. The 'old guard' was especially likely to be vulnerable to it – he noted that there were plenty of precedents in world history. He admitted that democracy could never be perfect. But changes had to be made. Otherwise the current trend in 'apparatus bureaucratism' would induce an increase in factionalism. All but expressly he was putting the blame for recent disputes upon the Politburo majority.[23] His personal authority was such that the leadership did not dare to ban publication. Trotsky himself denied wishing to sack the entire older generation of Bolsheviks as ignorant and incompetent. But things could not go on as in the recent past: 'It is truly naive to think that a secretary, because of his secretarial title, incarnates the whole sum of knowledge.'

The results of the Comintern initiative in Germany were known by early November. It had been hardly less catastrophic than the March

Action. The German Communist Party, aided and guided by Comintern, had organized strikes and demonstrations from 24 October. Trotsky had embraced and kissed Heinrich Brandler, German communist leader, at the Troitski Gates of the Kremlin. His uncustomary display of emotion indicated how much hope he reposed in the forthcoming insurrection. He was all the more disappointed when reports of the defeat reached Moscow. He could and should have known better. He was co-responsible for a débâcle no less predictable than the March Action which he had caustically criticized. In 1923 too the army and police were ready for the insurgents. The working class in Berlin was divided in its loyalties and the German government with its social-democratic ministers was united in its determination to crush the communist rebellion. Brandler was quickly demoralized. Street fighting petered out. Communists in Germany's other cities were still less effective. On 31 October the central leadership officially called off its ill-planned and ill-executed action. Trotsky blamed the German Communist Party for its incompetence. In private as well as in public he never ceased to assert that there had been a genuine chance of a successful uprising.[24]

He brought together his *Pravda* articles on political reform in a booklet entitled *The New Course*. The fractious atmosphere intensified in the party leadership. Lenin was sorely missed. Newspapers disguised how grim his condition had become and the Politburo members themselves continued to hope for a good medical outcome. Only Stalin had cause to fear the possibility of Lenin's recovery. Trotsky at last stirred himself into showing human sympathy by providing Nadezhda Krupskaya with an American idea for her husband's treatment, but he confessed his doubt that it was a genuine cure.[25] He himself was feeling ill again; he felt no impulse to postpone his departure for the south of the USSR for his own period of convalescence. He opted for Sukhum on the Abkhazian coast of the Black Sea. The OGPU (as the Cheka was known from November 1923) wrote to the Abkhazian party leader Nestor Lakoba on 6 January 1924 that doctors had prescribed a break of two months for him and had banned him from doing any work during that time.[26] He had yet to pay the price for the trouble he had caused since October 1923. Zinoviev, Kamenev and Stalin were determined to exact it in his absence. Trotsky had to be stopped. His adversaries sensed that, if they remained inactive, the commotion in the party would continue.

In October 1917 Trotsky had cunningly outmanoeuvred the Provisional Government by pretending that all his measures were purely defensive. In power, he lacked guile in struggle after struggle within the party. By publishing *The New Course*, he had thrown away the advantages of stealth. And having started an ill-prepared offensive, he omitted to give it his all.

Trotsky did not attend when the Central Committee sat in judgement on 14–15 January 1924. Stalin stressed that the ascendant leadership had gone out of its way to conciliate him. Talks had been held with him after the Central Committee meeting in October about state economic planning and a compromise had appeared in sight. But Trotsky wrecked the sub-commission on the internal party situation by insisting on the right to establish 'groupings' (which in the opinion of his adversaries were just another name for factions – and factions had been banned with Trotsky's approval in 1921). Trotsky had then written independently to party organizations. This made for an intolerable atmosphere in the leadership.[27] Zinoviev continued the offensive. Denying that he had artificially set a date for the German communist insurrection, he blamed Trotsky for calling for a 'calendarized programme' of action.[28] The tone was set for the Party Conference, which opened on 16 January. Party secretaries from the provinces were in the majority and victory for the ascendant party leadership was assured.[29] Ridicule was showered upon Trotsky's democratic credentials and Preobrazhenski got nowhere in trying to remove the slurs on the Opposition's reputation. Stalin refused to apologize for the restrictions on democracy in the party. He argued that the USSR faced grave obstacles. It needed to expand and enhance industrial production and educational attainment. It had to prepare against foreign military intervention. It had to renovate the state apparatus and remove the wartime militaristic attitudes from the party. All this, said Stalin, would take time.[30]

He decried Trotsky as a would-be 'superman' and called for him to be reminded of the Tenth Party Congress's secret permission for the removal of any Central Committee member breaching discipline.[31] It was a stupendous turnabout in the fortunes of the great rivals. Lenin had dictated a testament demanding that Stalin be fired from the general secretaryship. Now Stalin was threatening to expel Trotsky from the Central Committee. Nadezhda Krupskaya read out the reports in *Pravda* to her sick husband.[32] Although they were heavily sanitized Lenin appeared to grasp something of what had been happening. Perhaps he sensed that the party split he had predicted was happening. His worries deepened. On 21 January the doctors could do no more with him. In the evening he suffered a massive spasm and died.

Trotsky was travelling through Georgia on his way to Abkhazia when the news reached him. They were halted at the time at Tiflis railway station. Trotsky's aide Sermuks strode into his carriage office with a message from Stalin. Trotsky could tell from his face that a 'catastrophe' had occurred. He passed the piece of paper to Natalya, who had already divined its contents.[33] The Central Committee initially decided to hold the funeral on Saturday in the same week – and the Cheka was ordered to relay this to Trotsky.[34] Trotsky's trip from Moscow had been slowed by heavy snowfalls and it would have been difficult for him to get back in time. As it happened, the funeral took place on the Sunday. Trotsky sometimes later claimed that he had been misled so as to damage his chances of succeeding Lenin. Stalin was indeed capable of such under-handedness but Trotsky was never really sure of what had happened and less than a year before he died he expressed doubts that he had been tricked.[35] In Tiflis, at any rate, he was scarcely in a mood to return to Moscow and instead carried on to Sukhum. Stalin's ally Ordzhonikidze wrote to Lakoba emphasizing the need to prevent any dirty business happening to Trotsky; and OGPU Chairman Felix Dzerzhinski reinforced the message that Trotsky had to receive exceptional care and attention. His physical security was to be a paramount priority.[36]

A Central Committee plenum was held on 29 January, two days after the funeral, mainly to discuss arrangements for ways of commemorating Lenin.[37] A further plenum on 31 January confirmed the resolutions of the recent Conference. The Conference transcripts of the proceedings were sent out to all provincial party committees so that the full nature of the ascendant leadership's objections to Trotsky and the Left Opposition might become widely known.[38] Rykov was made Sovnarkom chairman.[39] A third plenum took place on 3 February and Trotsky was indirectly attacked by the device of a discussion of the 'serious failings . . . threatening the army with collapse'.[40] Stalin expressed concern about the removal of 'Red' commanders from the General Staff. Such commanders were those who had not been officers in the Imperial Army but had been trained and promoted in the Red Army. Sklyanski, Deputy Chairman in the Revolutionary-Military Council of the Republic, attended on Trotsky's behalf. Stalin refused to relent and even asked what use the Red Army would have been if the German Communist Party had indeed seized power and needed Soviet military assistance. Trotsky, he asserted, had been talking 'rubbish'. Lenin had suffered physical extinction; now Trotsky's long political funeral had begun.

# 33. ON THE CULTURAL FRONT

Among the topics holding Trotsky's attention in the south Caucasus was Soviet culture. This did not mean that he had gone soft in his politics. What still counted for him was world revolution, and no human price was too great to pay in the interests of the cause. He displayed his complete moral insouciance when telling his American admirer Max Eastman in the early 1920s that he and the Bolsheviks were willing 'to burn several thousand Russians to a cinder in order to create a true revolutionary American movement'.[1] Russia's workers and peasants would have been interested to know of the mass sacrifice he was contemplating. If the ends were desired, the means had to be willed. Trotsky constantly underlined that the Soviet order could never have emerged without a violent seizure of power, dictatorship, terror and civil war. The Red Army had been obliged to crush the Whites and to fend off foreign military intervention. The party had subsequently to impose a priority for industrial capital investment in economic reconstruction. Trotsky had no patience with calls to indulge popular demands.

He also insisted that there would be no basic improvement until a transformation in social conditions could take place. His was an entrancing vision of the future:

> Man will become incomparably stronger, more intelligent, more subtle. His body will be more harmonious, his movements more rhythmical, his voice more musical; the forms of daily existence will acquire a dynamic theatricality. The average human type will rise to the level of Aristotle, Goethe, Marx. It is above this ridge that new summits will rise.[2]

When Marx had written about the future life of people under communism, he emphasized that everyone would take part in politics as well as engage in manual labour; but there would also be plenty of opportunity for all to read books and to go fishing. Trotsky was influenced by this. He was never a mere pragmatist, opportunist or factionalist. He was a Marxist

believer. He believed in the achievability of a universal order which would
totally liberate the human spirit. For him, progress would not be satis-
factory until the world's artistic and scientific achievements were made
accessible for all working people.

Trotsky agreed with Lenin that literacy and numeracy were a prerequisite for the fulfilment of such ideas.[3] Neither saw hope for revolutionary
advance until the 'masses' could read, write, count and organize themselves. Trotsky fulminated against sloppiness and inefficiency – he was
almost notorious for his outbursts. He admired the working class for its
potential to rise up against its oppressors; he could not abide its frequent
failure to behave in an orderly fashion.

Eager to reform the routines of Russian life, he brought out a booklet
entitled *Problems of Everyday Life* in summer 1923:

> However important and full of life is the need for our work to
> transform culture, it still stands under the sign of European and
> global revolution. We remain soldiers on campaign. We have a rest
> day. Each has to wash his shirt, to trim and comb his hair and first
> and foremost to clean and oil his rifle.[4]

Man, he declared, should 'not live by "politics" alone' and revolutionaries
needed to inculcate the desire for attentiveness to detail. Trotsky wrote
that it was to everybody's advantage that higher standards of hygiene were
attained throughout the USSR. Nobody should drop cigarette butts with
impunity. Swearing had to cease. Heavy drinking ought to be discouraged
and Trotsky proposed the introduction of a total 'anti-alcohol regime'.
He also urged the reinforcement of atheist propaganda. He believed that
the Russian Orthodox Church had a corrupting influence on the working class – and he called for the cinema to be used to wean the people
off religion. Family life too had to be changed. Women should be treated
as equals and encouraged to join the party.[5]

At the same time he aimed to extend the benefits of 'high' culture to
everyone in society. According to Trotsky, 'the development of art is the
highest test of the liveliness and significance of each epoch.'[6] He himself
belonged to the artistic milieu in Russia and Europe. He had reviewed
books, plays and exhibitions. He was a writer of distinction. He did not
feel a day to be complete unless he found time to express his thoughts
elegantly in the pages of his notebooks.

Lenin and the Bolshevik party bothered little about the arts after the
October Revolution. Trotsky and Zinoviev called attention to this neglect
in 1922 when they proposed that the party should seek to gain a productive

rapport with writers and artists. They saw that it would take at least a generation to gain the commitment of bright young authors. The Bolsheviks needed temporary allies. In the interim they would have to make do with 'fellow travellers'. Trotsky and Zinoviev argued as follows. Many intellectuals, without being party members, shared the goals of social and economic modernization and were positive about socialism. If such individuals desisted from criticizing the October Revolution, the censors should leave them alone.[7] Trotsky was no liberal in affairs of culture. He felt that no one in Russia who challenged the Soviet order, even if only in novels or paintings, deserved official toleration. But he wanted a flexible policy of cultural management within this stern framework. He aimed to win the sympathy of those intellectuals who were not the party's foes and might yet become its friends. He approached Kamenev and Zinoviev for help in getting the party to organize a suitable campaign.[8] This in itself was unusual for him. His usual technique was to write a booklet, stir up a controversy and hope for the best. Perhaps he had learned from his defeat in the trade union dispute of 1920–1. (If so, this was a lesson he quickly forgot.)[9]

Trotsky admitted that he had not kept abreast of creative literature since 1914; he recruited the literary critic A. K. Voronski as his expert informant and asked him to compile a list of writers and their works. First of all he wanted to hear about the poet Osip Mandelshtam and the novelist Boris Pilnyak.[10] He also wrote to Italian communist leader Antonio Gramsci for information about Filippo Tommaso Marinetti and the Italian Futurist movement as well as about Gabriele d'Annunzio.[11]

He himself contacted Vladimir Mayakovski and the Futurists in Russia directly after hearing of their growing contribution to contemporary literature. Mayakovski was a poet of technical brilliance who had sided with the Bolsheviks after 1917. Futurism was a trend that predated the October seizure of power and Trotsky recognized that he had to know more about it. (Lenin felt differently: having browsed through some of Mayakovski's poems, he decided it was a waste of money to publish him.)[12] Mayakovski supplied Trotsky with copies of Futurist writings and Trotsky duly read them and asked for a definition of Futurism. Mayakovski obliged, and the two of them enjoyed corresponding for a while.[13] Trotsky was getting into his stride as a cultural campaigner. With his sharp sense of stylistic inadequacy of any kind he wrote to the satirical magazine *Krokodil* ('Crocodile') complaining that its articles were too gloomy. Readers had to be entertained as well as instructed.[14] Trotsky wrote an introduction to a collection of cartoons by Boris Yefimov.[15] No other

Politburo member was interested in this sort of thing. Trotsky understood the importance of caricatures for agitation and propaganda – or agitprop as the Bolsheviks called the process. Yefimov was an artist of exceptional ability – and Trotsky was pleased to add the lustre of his own fame to the cartoonist's publication.

Trotsky's reputation as a reviewer and a literary stylist encouraged writers to approach him for help. Fëdor Sologub, whom he had known in central Europe before the Great War, asked him to put in a word for him to be permitted to travel abroad. Sologub was destitute and thought he might be able to re-establish himself by travelling to Estonia. Trotsky agreed on condition that the author agreed to avoid involving himself in politics,[16] for he was a communist first and foremost and demanded the subordination of artistic aspirations to the demands of politics.

In 1923, after devouring Voronski's list of recommended items, Trotsky published *Literature and Revolution*. He made no reference in it to the reintroduction of state censorship or to the deportation of anti-Bolshevik intellectuals in the previous year. He might have been feeling coy. But this was unlikely for a leader who was usually blunt about what he thought. The more likely reason is that he felt no impulse to comment. The man who urged an increase in state economic regulation was no advocate of complete artistic freedom. He agreed with providing the authorities with the powers to rule on what could be published, and this was to be his attitude in later life. *Literature and Revolution* gave him the chance to express his disquiet about the kinds of literature being produced in Soviet Russia. Although he could see that Vladimir Mayakovski and the Futurist literary school were trying to serve the Soviet cause, he disliked their outlandish imagery and overwrought techniques. While being attracted to the simpler language and metrics of Sergei Yesenin, he criticized him for idealizing 'Russia' and neglecting revolutionary politics. Mayakovski and Yesenin, Trotsky argued, were typical 'fellow travellers' in refusing to incorporate the objectives of Marxism in their poetry. This was harsh on Mayakovski, who wrote paeans of praise to the Soviet order; and when Lenin died in 1924 he hymned him as humanity's gigantic hero and came close to deifying him: 'Lenin lived, Lenin lives, Lenin will live!' But Trotsky's instinct was not entirely awry. Mayakovski soon experienced disillusion with the direction of state policy. He could no longer cope with life as his political enthusiasm left him and in 1930 he committed suicide. Yesenin, who had never tried to ingratiate himself with the regime, had done the same five years earlier.

The poet Valeri Bryusov was one who could be pleased with what

Trotsky wrote about him. Having gone over to the Soviet side, Bryusov was attacked by those he left behind. He had written to Trotsky in gratitude for his kind words of support.[17] The little-known writer Yevgeni Trifonov was less than happy about Trotsky's attack on him in *Pravda*; he wrote to him complaining about the newspaper's refusal to grant him space to reply. It annoyed Trifonov that the People's Commissar for Military Affairs had not deigned to refer to him as 'comrade' even though he was enrolled on the military training course for communists.[18]

Trotsky also paid attention to Alexander Blok – or Mr A. Blok, as he sometimes called him in the booklet – and his 1918 poem *The Twelve*. Written in short stanzas and incorporating Petrograd street argot, it was a stunning artistic triumph. Its subject was a gang of leering, anarchic Red Guards who marauded around the Russian capital in 1917. Trotsky withheld general approval. He thought Blok saw only the seamy aspects of the October Revolution. Such poetry would not further official revolutionary purposes. Trotsky dismissed it as only 'the swan song of individualistic art' and nothing more.[19] Blok at least welcomed certain aspects of the revolutionary upheaval whereas the novelist Andrei Bely was more typical of the pre-revolutionary intelligentsia in condemning the violence and abuse of power. Bely had not a good word to say about the Bolsheviks. Trotsky commented: 'It is not so long ago that Bely wrote some very accurate thoughts about himself – he is always engaged with himself, walking round himself, giving himself a sniff and licking himself.'[20] He had quite a nerve in making such a remark. If literary self-preoccupation was a sign of decadence, Trotsky himself was a recidivist exponent.

*Literature and Revolution*, for all its stylistic brio, was a patchy survey of contemporary prose and poetry. Anna Akhmatova, Osip Mandelshtam and Boris Pasternak were among the greatest poets of the twentieth century, but Trotsky barely mentioned them. Perhaps he had not had time to read them. He produced the booklet in a rush – and he had to revise it in style and substance in subsequent editions. Such material as he included was selected so as to illustrate the general points he was making. Like fellow communist leaders, Trotsky wanted a high culture subordinate to the party's purposes. It would take many years, he assumed, before a 'proletarian culture' would be widely achieved,[21] but he did not want to leave his readers on a note of pessimism. He suggested that Demyan Bedny best embodied the connection between cultural accomplishment and political progress.[22] It requires a cloth ear to imagine that Bedny, who was a purveyor of doggerel verses, deserved this accolade. Even at his best Bedny was scarcely worth anthologizing, and his worst was very poor indeed. It was not until Bedny took Stalin's side against him that Trotsky castigated him for his 'ideological–poetical' emptiness.[23]

That Trotsky in 1923 chose to promote the merits of a mediocre versifier against Alexander Blok and his majestic poetry shows that what mattered most to Trotsky was advancing the revolutionary cause. The imperatives of Soviet governance were blunting his taste. He admired Bedny for praising the working class and the October Revolution and for performing any duty assigned to him. The crudity of Trotsky's judgements was overlooked by later generations because Stalin's cultural policy in the USSR was still cruder and the grim potential of the booklet was masked by the uplifting qualities of his dream of communism. Trotsky also won plaudits for writing something that lay outside the conventional track of official Bolshevism – and the multitude of printings after 1923 indicates that his arguments struck a popular chord. He was always thoughtful, wrapping up his considerations in a bundle that attracted attention from many readers who otherwise would not have taken any Politburo member seriously as a contributor to the basic debate about the future of culture and society. *Literature and Revolution* was essentially a work of political reductionism. When all is said and done, though, it was Trotsky who laid down the philosophical foundations for cultural Stalinism.[24]

The other leaders had no basic objection to what he wrote about everyday life or literature, even though Stalin's entourage blenched somewhat at his puritanical austerity. It was not only what Trotsky wrote but also how much time he spent in writing it that called forth criticism among them. At the Politburo he was asked to run down his rate of booklet production and raise his involvement in practical discussions inside the leadership. His response was an unaccommodating one.[25]

He may well have failed to understand the criticism because even in the Civil War he had gone on writing while efficiently carrying out his military duties. Natalya understood his requirements and helped as she could. In April 1918 she had gone to the Rumyantsev Museum in central Moscow to ask permission to borrow copies of the *Kievskaya mysl* newspaper from 1915–16. He needed them in order to select his best articles for publication in his *War and Revolution* (which appeared in 1922).[26] His military routine precluded him from turning up in person; but most political leaders would not even have dreamed of planning such a project in those circumstances. The onset of peace gave him the chance to dedicate still more of his waking hours to his vocation as a writer. This enthusiasm had become an obsession. In 1926, for example, he published *It Happened in Spain,*[27] which was a lively narrative of the circumstances of his deportation from France and Spain in 1916. Indubitably it had been an important episode in his life. But at the very time he was editing it he faced a drastic challenge to his survival in the Bolshevik party leadership. He pleaded that A. K. Voronski had importuned him to produce the booklet and that the promise of fine black-and-white sketches by K. Rotov was an irresistible inducement.[28] As if a master of the Kremlin would do the bidding of a couple of artistic entrepreneurs! It would anyway have made greater sense for him to concentrate on defeating Stalin and Bukharin.

Likewise he might have found more useful things to do than conduct an enquiry into Lenin's career. His book *On Lenin*, vivid and interesting though it was, took weeks of effort. Trotsky saw it as a way of weakening the attack on him as having been a perpetual anti-Leninist. He filled the pages with fond remembrance of the time he had spent with Lenin from the first meeting in Bloomsbury in 1902 onwards.[29] His capacious mind retrieved his experiences and then ground them down into material for his writings. The work scarcely justified the amount of creative energy he used up in researching, composing and proofing the typescript. He avoided giving the names of those 'moderate' Bolshevik leaders – Kamenev, Zinoviev and Stalin – who had obstructed Lenin's revolutionary strategy in March and October 1917.[30] But anyone who knew anything about the history of the party knew whom he meant. He seemed unaware that he was shutting the door on the lingering possibility of dividing the ruling troika.

Writing anyway often took precedence with him over speaking and organizing; he even allotted time to devising fresh, lengthy prefaces for second and third editions of his booklets in the mid-1920s.[31] He simply loved to be seated at a desk, fountain pen in hand, scribbling out the latest opus. Nobody dared disturb him when the flow of words was forming in his head. He accustomed his family, servants and personal assistants to these habits. Factional organization was never supremely urgent for him since he was doing the right thing by the criteria of the Marxist doctrines that held his allegiance. His whole career seemed to validate this assumption. He had flourished in situations where he grasped unpredicted opportunities and moulded them to his requirements. He had been a revolutionary hero in 1905 and again in October 1917. At any rate he did not care to live except on these terms. He lived as he thought a revolutionary thinker and leader ought to do. He therefore continued to function in this grand manner and he and his group of oppositionists were constantly being outmanoeuvred by the ascendant party leadership. He would rather go down to glorious defeat than modify his style of life and work.

*On Lenin*, in fairness to Trotsky, had a more justified call on his time than his other literary projects. He wrote the bulk of it during his convalescence in Sukhum – the preface was dated 21 April 1924, exactly three months after Lenin's death. This was a period when his enemies were dredging up every moment in his anti-Bolshevik past from the newspaper archives and the party records and hurling them in his face. From being publicly fêted and privately feared, he moved to being the main target of official vituperation. Bukharin was the most determined archer at the highest political level in the press. *Towards the Question of Trotskyism*, which he wrote in 1925, summarized the case against Trotsky. Having been a leading Bolshevik before 1917, Bukharin knew all about the spats between Lenin and Trotsky. Nor did he fail to call attention to the embarrassing items of Trotskyana which Trotsky had omitted to include in his various collected works. As Bukharin pointed out, these lacunae were not accidental. Trotsky had engaged in a distortion of historical truth out of motives of political advantage – and he was easily found out.[32] The Bolshevik past became a battlefield in contemporary communist politics. The exchanges were tedious, the methods underhand on both sides. The stakes of the ideological games could not have been higher. Whoever won would attain supremacy in the party leadership.

In the multi-volume edition of his *Works*, published in Moscow from 1924, Trotsky not only dropped articles but even rewrote several of them.[33] In 1932 he would denounce 'the Stalinist school of falsification' for hiding or altering whatever documents might put Stalin in a poor light.[34] Trotsky's case for the prosecution has entered the canon of Western historiography and has led to the widely held belief that he himself could not have been guilty of similar deceptions. It is understandable that he had acted as he did in the mid-1920s. No one could win the struggle to succeed Lenin without purporting to have been a career-long admirer of Lenin. But that does not make the behaviour admirable or negligible. Thief-taker Trotsky was also something of a felon in matters historical.

At any rate he did not offer *On Lenin* as a piece of thorough research. The sub-title, *Materials for a Biographer*, hinted at this. It was a work written at speed and without reliance on documents. His memory of Lenin was fresh, his political motivation was still fresher. Anecdotes tumbled on to the page. He gave the impression that Lenin and he for most of their political lives had enjoyed a close, vibrant partnership.[35] He told how warmly Lenin had welcomed him to London in 1902. He described his own work for the *Iskra* editorial board. After that he took up historical gymnastics and leapfrogged to the February Revolution, sketching how

Kamenev and Stalin had been slow to adopt a Leninist policy in March 1917. Dealing with the later months of the same year, he recalled how Lenin had wondered aloud what would happen to the Soviet order if the two of them suddenly died. He indicated the episodes in 1917–19 when Kamenev, Zinoviev and Stalin had cut across Lenin's preferences in policy. He just about stayed within the parameters of party decorum and was careful to avoid mention of Lenin's testament. But he wielded his pen in a combative mood. Trotsky was on political campaign.

He wrote with a deft touch, and rather than claim to have been always in agreement with Lenin, Trotsky admitted to occasional collisions. He wanted to appear as the sole political intimate of Lenin who had the necessary qualities of vision, judgement and leadership. None of his adversaries, not even Bukharin, could match the artistry of his polemical style. But victory in the contest for the title of the party's best revolutionary annalist did not help him in the competition to become leader of the Revolution after Lenin's demise.

# 34. FAILING TO SUCCEED

Not before April 1924 did Trotsky pass himself fit to return to Moscow. He had stayed longer than the projected couple of months and had rested – and written – his way back to health. The Thirteenth Party Congress was in the offing. This would be the first big gathering since Lenin's funeral. Trotsky expressed regret about leaving 'the beautiful sun and the beautiful comrades' of Abkhazia.[1] But he could not resume a leading role from there. The telephone and telegraph system was poor and all the important meetings happened in the Soviet capital. His sojourn in the south Caucasus had to come to an end.

He could not resist stopping for a few days in Georgia where he addressed the Tiflis City Soviet on 11 April. He always found public speaking less of a challenge than sitting in meetings. He achieved his customary success despite the depressing theme he had chosen: the recent defeat of the German revolution. He started by claiming to be out of touch with the latest developments – supposedly he had gleaned more from the journalists to whom he had given interviews than they had learned from him.[2] The German comrades, he asserted, had nobody to blame but themselves. The conditions had been right for them to seize power. Most workers were disaffected from the Weimar Republic and the bourgeoisie was internally fragmented. But the communists in Berlin had lacked a tightly organized party such as the Bolsheviks had supposedly possessed in 1917. They also had no leader of Lenin's stature.[3] Trotsky wanted to prove his readiness to play a loyal part in Soviet politics. He did not reveal his private thoughts, for he remained convinced that *The New Course* had offered just criticisms of the ascendant leadership. But recognizing that he needed to behave more adroitly than before, he was readying himself to give an effective performance at the Party Congress.

Arriving in Moscow a few days before it started on 23 May, he resumed attendance at the Central Committee and the Politburo and reoccupied his office in the People's Commissariat for Military Affairs. He knew that people were watching out for any sign of oppositionist activity – and he understood that any blatant move in that direction would backfire after the rebuke he had received from the Party Conference in January. Party veterans were still worried that anti-Bolshevik groups might take advantage of the current political uncertainty: they wanted stability in Soviet public life and looked askance at individuals who put personal ambition before the interests of the Revolution. Lenin was now revered as a kind of secular deity. The name of Petrograd was changed to Leningrad and Lenin's works were treated as holy writ. Trotsky had to show that he was not intending to split the leadership yet again.

Stalin too had to tread carefully. As Nadezhda Krupskaya confirmed, it was the leadership's duty to comply with Lenin's request to relay his testament to the Party Congress – and this was bound to create trouble for Stalin. The Central Committee took the decision to read it out only to the leaders of the local delegations to Congress. They duly gathered for a special meeting and were acquainted with Lenin's deprecatory remarks about the most prominent Bolsheviks. Although Trotsky's 'excessive' administrative zeal was mentioned in the testament it was Stalin who had greatest cause for concern – and this showed in the depressed look on his face while Lenin's criticism was being communicated. Witnesses had never seen him less truculent. As speakers got up to debate the testament there was agreement on the need for a change in the handling of central party affairs. Some delivered signed comments.[4] Stalin survived his ordeal because not enough delegates were willing to have him sacked and in any case the Central Committee expressed its confidence in him. Nobody could fairly cavil about his behaviour since spring 1923, for whereas Trotsky had raised the flag of factionalism Stalin had worked solidly and loyally for the ascendant leadership.[5]

After the defeat of the Left Opposition Trotsky did not even receive voting rights at the Congress,[6] and it was Zinoviev who delivered the political report for the Central Committee. Trotsky joined in the debate on Stalin's organizational report. He adopted a respectful tone as he rehearsed his ideas about the younger generation, factions and economic planning.[7] He was striving to reformulate his recent criticisms in the language being used in Central Committee resolutions. Then he offered a kind of apology: 'Comrades, none of us wishes or is able to be right against his own party. The party in the final analysis is always right because the party is the sole historical instrument given to the proletariat for the solution of its fundamental tasks.'[8] He obviously sensed that he was on parole for his past sins; and from this moment onwards, indeed through to 1933, he was converted to a feeling of party-mindedness that had been notably absent in him since 1917.[9] During his months of reflection in the south Caucasus he had decided to become some kind of Leninist. He never offered a word of explanation for his sudden willingness to bow low before the party. Self-interest must have been a factor. Perhaps also his low morale required him to find an additional rock to base his strategy on; and possibly he no longer felt the impulse to test himself against Lenin, now that he was dead, and could for the first time accept him as some kind of authority.

His public self-abnegation was as extreme as it was uncharacteristic, and he was to prove idiosyncratic in his Leninism in the years ahead.[10] Several leading supporters anyway thought his apology a tactical misjudgement: they willed him to stand proud against his adversaries in the leadership.[11] Trotsky thought caution was required. The ascendant leaders were pleased about his contrition and allowed him to keep his seats in the Politburo and the Central Committee.

Trotsky continued to bide his time before making a further attack on the ascendant party leadership. It was not a condition he found congenial and he threw himself into literary activity. When he went off to Kislovodsk in the north Caucasus for his summer vacation he was ready to dash off a booklet entitled *Lessons of October* (which started in the form of an introduction to a volume in his collected works).[12] He completed it in mid-September 1924 and intended it as a more combative political sequel to *On Lenin*. At the core of *Lessons of October* was the year 1917. With some reason he argued that the party had omitted to conduct a proper study of the October Revolution. He offered up the conclusions he had drawn in the interests of helping the communist cause in the USSR and in countries such as Germany.[13] Repeatedly, he emphasized, Lenin's guidance had been resisted by individuals and groups referred to by Trotsky as Conciliators. Stalin and Kamenev had wanted to compromise with the Provisional Government in March.[14] Then as the party's policy turned towards a seizure of power Kamenev and Zinoviev had striven to disrupt its implementation. They and other Conciliators had continued to work for a deal with the Mensheviks and Socialist-Revolutionaries in November 1917.[15] Trotsky finished with the provocative comment that the party possessed leaders who had not broken with the instincts and doctrines of parties engaged in political struggle against the Bolsheviks.[16]

This pushed Zinoviev and Kamenev deeper into Stalin's arms. What little good Trotsky had done for himself at the Thirteenth Party Congress was tossed aside. *Pravda* was a megaphone for the Politburo's orders of the day. Pamphlets were printed against Trotskyism and Trotsky's record as an enemy of Bolshevism was recounted. Stalin knew how to tighten the screws: he specialized in getting former sympathizers of Trotsky to dish the dirt on him. He also put Trotsky under strict surveillance. This became obvious when the mail sent to his American friend Max Eastman, staying on the Black Sea, failed to arrive from Moscow.[17] This kind of revelation caused Trotsky to refuse an official offer to fit a new telephone in his Kremlin apartment. He exclaimed at the Politburo: 'Phone-tapping is a fact.'[18] Nobody contradicted him.

By now Trotsky and Stalin were deadly rivals. Whenever only one of them attended the Politburo he took a grip on the proceedings. Usually Kamenev would be in the chair, gently coaxing the discussion along. But neither Kamenev nor Zinoviev was a serious contender for the succession. They lacked zest in dealing with communist strategy across the range of public policy. Trotsky and Stalin were a class apart. They were eager initiators of measures and saw through any tangle of complications; they were impatient when unsatisfactory reports were placed before them. They imperiously interrogated experts attending meetings of the leadership. That Trotsky was a possible replacement for Lenin was the talk of all Moscow. Stalin's capacity for the role was not widely touted since Politburo minutes were on a restricted distribution list and he did not have Trotsky's talent for self-publicity; but his potential was none the less for that.[19] He and Bukharin worked closely to undermine Trotsky. Stalin had started to talk about the possibility of completing the 'building of socialism in a single country'. Trotsky claimed that no completion was conceivable until communist revolutions took place in other countries. Lenin had agreed with him about this, but Stalin distorted Lenin's texts so as to claim Marxist-Leninist authenticity for his own policies – and Bukharin asserted that Trotsky's theory of 'permanent revolution', with its alleged distrust of the peasantry, was anti-Leninist.

Zinoviev was still more belligerent in arguing inside the ascendant party leadership for the expulsion of Trotsky not just from the Politburo and the Central Committee but even from the party itself. Stalin saw this as too extreme a measure; he enjoyed playing the role of political moderate and suggesting that measures against Trotsky's supporters should be limited to polemics and sackings. Trotsky was pushed on to the back foot. In late 1924 he got his assistant Mikhail Glazman to trawl through the Bolshevik pre-revolutionary press for articles expressing approval of him.[20] He was retaliating against a campaign of vilification in *Pravda*. Incidents from the past were dredged up and thrown like mud in his face. Full-time official ideologists became involved. When any leading oppositionist spoke up at an open meeting, he would be booed and hissed by an organized claque of supporters of the ascendant party leadership. Trotsky and his associates were denied automatic permission to canvass in the press. Ordinary party members who sympathized with the Left Opposition were expelled from the party or subjected to other punitive sanctions.

Matters came to a head in January 1925 when the Central Committee debated Trotsky's position in the People's Commissariat for Military Affairs. Rather than give his enemies the pleasure of sacking him, Trotsky resigned:

> This decision had been carefully prepared for by the preceding struggle. Along with the traditions of the October Revolution, the epigones [that is, the ascendant party leaders] were above all else afraid of the traditions of the Civil War and my link with the army. I gave up the military post without a fight, even with a feeling of inner relief, so as to wrest from my adversaries' hands their weapon of insinuations about my military intentions. The epigones had first invented these fantastic intentions in justification of their actions and then themselves began to half believe them.[21]

For nearly four momentous years he and the Red Army had seemed inseparable. His achievements in the Civil War had been continually celebrated. Now he kept his seats in the Central Committee and the Politburo, but he was no longer an army man.

Could Trotsky have used the Red Army to secure his return to ascendancy? He would need to have been a different kind of politician even to make such an attempt. He had already told fellow leaders that he did not aspire to a personal paramountcy;[22] and even if he had not been frank with them or himself, it is doubtful that he had the skills to put together an armed coalition that would have done the job for him. The Red Army high command was riddled with ambitious rivalries and there is no evidence that Trotsky was the darling of any group of commanders. It is true that many political commissars were admirers of his. But several of these, including Efraim Sklyanski and Vladimir Antonov-Ovseenko, had already been removed from the armed forces. What is more, Trotsky could count a lot of commissars among his enemies after his imperious conduct of the People's Commissariat in the Civil War. Whereas Napoleon Bonaparte rose to power by dint of the chaos engendered by the French Revolution, the Politburo by the mid-1920s had a tight grip on the Soviet political system. Any attempted coup would have been ruthlessly confronted by party and police. Trotsky in any case was a revolutionary and a Soviet patriot; he was the last person to risk destabilizing the October Revolution by a military adventure.

The party leadership waited four months and then in May appointed him to three jobs when he was made chairman of the Concessions Committee, director of the Electrotechnical Administration and chairman of the Scientific-Technical Administration of Industry. These were not jobs of cardinal political importance but a means of keeping him out of political mischief, and by his own account he threw himself into the new work, took trips to inspect installations in the south and refreshed a personal interest in science which he had developed as a youth when thinking of studying mathematics and physics at the New Russia University in Odessa.[23]

The ascendant party leadership, though, was full of tensions. Zinoviev had attempted to reduce Stalin's power in mid-1923 but had almost immediately been compelled to turn to him as an ally against Trotsky. The thoroughness of Trotsky's defeat in 1924 turned the thoughts of both Zinoviev and Kamenev back to the question of Stalin. The NEP involved concessions to the peasantry. The retreat in the face of rural demands lengthened over the years, and Zinoviev and Kamenev came to believe that Trotsky's early warnings had justification. They shared a growing suspicion that Stalin and Bukharin were abandoning the party's traditional commitment to 'European socialist revolution'. They resented the authoritarian methods of Stalin and Bukharin. From April 1925 they openly attacked them after assembling a group of supporters that became known as the Leningrad Opposition because Zinoviev had his work base in that city. The ascendant leadership was falling apart. Stalin with Bukharin's consent took organizational measures against Zinoviev in Leningrad and Kamenev in Moscow. By the time of the Fourteenth Party Congress in December the schism was clear-cut. Zinoviev offered his own separate political report before going down to a crushing defeat. Stalin and Bukharin were left in control of the Politburo and the Central Committee. They were masters of the Soviet Union by the end of year.

The factional struggle intensified in 1926. Although there was bad blood between the Leningraders and the Trotskyists there was a growing rapprochement in opinion. Trotsky, Zinoviev and Kamenev came together to form the United Opposition in April 1926. They were helped by events in the following month. Against Trotsky's advice, the Politburo had encouraged the Communist Party of Great Britain to co-operate with other groups on the political left. The British general strike in May 1926 was a total failure. Trotsky, Zinoviev and Kamenev pronounced their diagnosis that Stalin and Bukharin were incompetents and compromisers in their handling of Soviet foreign policy and that Comintern was not safe in their hands.

Stalin and Bukharin were ruthless. The last remaining supporters of Zinoviev, including Mikhail Lashevich, were removed from leading posts. Stalin turned on Zinoviev himself and got him demoted from the Politburo. As yet Trotsky remained untouched, retaining his seats in the Politburo and Central Committee despite his continual objections to official policies – and Zinoviev retained his Central Committee membership. But Stalin and Bukharin were out for victory. Trotsky, Zinoviev and Kamenev were accused of factionalism in infringement of the Tenth Party Congress's prohibition. Their disloyalty during months of intense difficulty in international relations was castigated. All of them had once hymned the cause of internal party unity. Instead they had exposed and aggravated tensions among communist leaders, and only the enemies of the USSR could benefit from this situation. The pressure on Trotsky, Zinoviev and Kamenev intensified. In October 1926 Trotsky was expelled from the Politburo just as Zinoviev had been in the previous year. Although the three leading dissenters kept their seats in the Central Committee they had clearly been worsted. Supporters of the ascendant leadership were moved into posts made vacant by the sacking of oppositionists, and several supporters of the United Opposition recanted their opinions rather than break with the official party line. Stalin and Bukharin had triumphed.

If the United Opposition had been created earlier, Stalin would have been helpless against it. Trotsky, Kamenev and Zinoviev would have dominated the Politburo, the Central Committee and Comintern, and Sovnarkom would have been theirs for the taking. Now they faced an uphill struggle. Zinoviev was on record as a critic of Trotsky: he had castigated his 'adventurism' in foreign policy, his excessive inclination towards centralism in political administration and his many clashes with Lenin before and after 1917. Trotsky had replied in kind, denouncing Zinoviev for desertion of Lenin before the October Revolution as well as for his collusion with Stalin and Bukharin in taking the militancy out of the NEP. All such disagreements had been printed in *Pravda*. Trotsky, Zinoviev and Kamenev were now asking everybody to believe that they agreed on the changes needed in party policy. Trotsky could lay claim to some kind of consistency since the formation of the Left Opposition. By aligning themselves with him, Zinoviev and Kamenev called for the democratization of the party and the introduction of restriction of market economics. It was not difficult for Stalin and Bukharin to attribute their alteration of stance to a mere lust for power.

Comintern was not immune to the purging. Steadily the leaderships of the communist parties abroad were changed wherever there was a lack of firm obedience to the Politburo's policies – and Zinoviev's removal made the task an easy one. Unequivocal support for the ascendant leadership's management of the NEP in the USSR was demanded. Criticism of Soviet foreign policy was prohibited. Meanwhile sanctions were being applied against other leading figures in the United Opposition. It would have excited an international scandal if any one of Trotsky, Zinoviev or Kamenev was removed from Moscow or Leningrad. Other leading dissenters were more vulnerable and the vanguard of the United Opposition was deposited in jobs and places where their capacity to disrupt the Kremlin's wishes would be flimsy. At lower levels of the party there occurred a steady purge of oppositionists by the Central Control Commission. Trotsky, Zinoviev and Kamenev lost what had been their automatic freedom to write for *Pravda* and the rest of the party press. They were regularly reviled by official spokesmen who suffered from no such restrictions. Among them was a growing corps of former members of oppositionist factions such as Andrei Bubnov. Trotsky's position was weaker than ever by 1926–7.

Zinoviev, Kamenev and Trotsky for their part were willing pamphleteers and speakers. When Bukharin assailed the bureaucratic propensities of the Leningrad party organization under Zinoviev, Trotsky would have none of it. If the Bolshevik Leningraders were run by their apparatus, then this was true of the entire party. Zinoviev could therefore not fairly be blamed for all the party's ills. Trotsky scoffed at Bukharin's depiction of the Moscow party organization as a bastion of virtue. The fact was that every party organization was being forced to do what its leaders told it to.[24] For a while the United Opposition had the support of Lenin's widow Nadezhda Krupskaya. She and Trotsky had got along well since 1917 despite the recurrent disputes he had had with Lenin, and in 1926 she confided to Trotsky that Lenin had once said of Stalin that 'he lacked even the most elementary human decency.'[25]

Trotsky's coruscating prose has tended to persuade subsequent generations that his descriptions of the ascendant leadership's policies held water. The reality was different and more complex. Stalin and Bukharin were very far from basing their economic strategy on permanently indulging the kulaks. Bukharin had confused everybody by saying that the best thing for agricultural development under the NEP would be for peasants to 'enrich themselves'. The more prosperous peasants were the ones who produced a marketable surplus from their harvest. The entire economy depended on their being successful at this. Bukharin had a habit of over-egging the pudding in his speeches and articles. When the Politburo got round to working out its guidelines for the tax year of 1925–6 he had no trouble in supporting a plan to discriminate heavily against the better-off stratum of the peasantry. What happened was this. The fiscal regime was changed so that kulak households were laden with high tax demands. The poor households, as defined by official categories, were simultaneously given something close to freedom from taxation. Preobrazhenski had stated that the central party leadership should exact a 'tribute' from the peasantry so as to finance industrialization. His proposal urged the expropriation of the grain which would otherwise have been marketed by the wealthier rural households. The Bukharin–Stalin reform of taxation was a big step in the direction of oppositionist policy.

The United Opposition had brought together leaders who disagreed about several policies, and Trotsky had to make compromises in the interests of factional unity. According to him, the Left Opposition had struggled constantly against the policy of ordering the Chinese Communist Party to enter the Kuomintang which was fighting Japanese, American and European efforts to hold China in subjection. The Kuomintang was a coalition containing socialist elements. But Trotsky pointed out that the Left Opposition had always held it in suspicion and argued against the Kuomintang's admission into Comintern. Only Radek and a few of his friends had taken a different line. The Politburo, while Kamenev and Zinoviev were allies of Stalin, had judged the Kuomintang led by Chiang Kai-shek to be the most effective national force against foreign imperialism. The Chinese Communist Party had been diagnosed as too weak to go it alone and had been ordered to seek a provisional agreement with Chiang Kai-shek. When the Left Opposition was joined by the Leningrad Opposition, Zinoviev insisted on following the line set for China by the Politburo, and Radek's coterie had the casting vote. Preobrazhenski and Pyatakov insisted that this should not become a divisive topic for the United Opposition. Trotsky was obliged to back down. It was a compromise he lived to regret.[26]

What kept the alliance of Trotsky, Zinoviev and Kamenev together was their dislike of the Stalin–Bukharin duumvirate and its management of the NEP. Trotsky brought up the recent financial scandals in the party. Gross fraud had been exposed in faraway places, especially in Chita and Kherson. He did this without sentimentality. Although he was a native of

Kherson province, his current interest lay in the generalizations to be made from the evidence. A report by A. G. Shlikhter mentioned that functionaries had been afraid to inform on their party bosses for fear of being subjected to the kind of treatment meted out to oppositionists.[27] For Trotsky this was yet further proof that the Bolshevik party had degenerated since the Civil War. Capitalistic practices and police-style measures were rife. A counter-campaign needed to be started before the current situation got out of hand.

Trotsky was always ready to complain – and he has usually been believed – that Stalin achieved his advance by unfair means. He pointed to the bureaucratic manipulations available to the General Secretary. Stalin, he declared, was not a revolutionary statesman but a mere adminis-trator. Stalin did not go out and address crowds. Stalin could not debate. Stalin was an intellectual pygmy. All he was good at was sitting around in an office and gathering around him a team of protégés who would do his bidding. Personal loyalty to the boss was rewarded by elevation to the highest echelons of bureaucracy in party and government; and he made appointments to the lower ones according to the same criterion. Veteran Bolsheviks who had made the October Revolution and fought the Civil War were systematically tossed aside. Stalin had a distinct preference for the dour kind of administrators, young and devoid of ideological dedi-cation, who had the ruthlessness to carry out his orders without flinching. He had reduced Soviet politics to an administrative process. Trotsky alleged that the makers of the October Revolution and the victorious fighters in the Civil War were being treated as a suspect category. But in accusing Stalin of refusing promotion to experienced revolutionaries Trotsky was firing wildly wide of the mark. The ascendant party leadership was resolute in promoting veteran Bolsheviks. If anyone showed favour to non-Bolsheviks in his entourage, that individual was not Stalin but Trotsky.[28]

# 35. ENTOURAGE AND FACTION

Outside party meetings or work in his commissariat Trotsky saw few people besides his family and his inner circle of technical assistants. He had drawn his aides together in 1918–19: Georgi Butov, Mikhail Glazman, Igor Poznanski, N. Sermuks and Efraim Sklyanski. The little group was not widely popular. They were newcomers to the party; they had joined after becoming attracted to Trotsky and his ideas. They acquired a reputation as candidates to become the adjutants for the Red Bonaparte.

Formed by a process of Darwinian natural selection in the Civil War, his circle contained no one who failed to discharge duties with punctilio. Trotsky demanded a strict regime in his office and was famous throughout the party for his exacting standards. Most Bolsheviks could cope with an atmosphere of chaos around them. Some even thrived on it, thinking that informality in working arrangements reflected a revolutionary dedication. People came and went. They turned up late to meetings – and their chauffeurs turned up late to pick them up. Meetings were noisy and unfocused. It was not unusual for individuals to smoke at Sovnarkom despite Lenin's standing order against the practice. (Dzerzhinski, feared head of the political police, timidly sauntered off to the nearest chimney when desperate for a cigarette.)[1] Lenin was frequently exasperated by the absence of mundane administrative conscientiousness. But even he was outdone by Trotsky, who was a stickler for peace and quiet as he sat at his desk. He would not let his secretaries enter his office without prior permission. He gave preference to one of the maids – a 'matronly peasant woman with a handkerchief tied round her head' – precisely because she walked around very softly.[2]

Stalin worked at disbanding Trotsky's team of assistants. The central authorities expelled Glazman from the party in August 1924 on transparently spurious grounds. Next day Glazman shot himself.[3] Sklyanski was shifted from the Revolutionary-Military Council of the Republic after the dispute with Stalin and assigned to work in the cotton industry. This kept him out of Trotsky's vicinity. On an official business trip to the USA in 1925 he drowned in a lake after a boating accident.[4]

One person inside the outer edge of Trotsky's entourage caused him more problems than arose from any who were members of the Bolshevik party. This was the American writer-turned-communist Max Eastman. Trotsky welcomed him to Russia in 1922 and agreed to his writing a biography of him. Eastman made friends with Trotsky's relatives; he also acquired a lover, Yelena Krylenko, who taught him Russian. Trotsky answered his endless questions in writing and in conversation.[5] Neither man found time to cover Trotsky's whole life and Eastman had to satisfy himself with a book on the early years, *Leon Trotsky: The Portrait of a Youth*.[6] The two men talked over recent political developments. Trotsky recounted the contents of Lenin's testament to him without handing over a physical copy; he needed to make the information public by hook or by crook, and he endorsed Eastman's plan to publish it abroad.[7] *Since Lenin Died*, appearing in Britain a few months after the biography had come out in the USA, became a publishing sensation worldwide. Although Trotsky played the innocent, everyone in the party leadership knew that Eastman was his acolyte. A rumpus broke out in the Politburo. Trotsky was compelled by a majority to repudiate Eastman's book, denounce him as a fraud and deny that Lenin had written a testament.[8]

Eastman, by then based in the south of France, felt hurt by Trotsky's behaviour. Far from acting impulsively, he had taken the trouble to consult Khristian Rakovski, who was the USSR's ambassador in Paris, about how to proceed. Rakovski had read the manuscript and encouraged him to get it published.[9] Later Trotsky privately told his followers that the American was a 'sincere revolutionary', and the message found its way to Eastman in New York in the winter of 1928–9 and he began to work for Trotsky again.[10] Anyway the rest of the entourage always stuck by Trotsky. This was not a sign of his wonderful sociability. He was more like an impersonal planet tugging satellites into his gravitational orbit. He wrote a touching obituary for Sklyanski. But generally he took his helpers for granted until they were removed from him.

His hauteur did not diminish the esteem that his aides felt for him: they had become admirers for life at an early age. It was a different matter with fellow oppositionist politicians. He had never gone out of his way to make friends with people. Politics were his medium of inter-course; he wanted comrades rather than friends. His intimates in public life could be numbered on the fingers of one hand: Khristian Rakovski, Adolf Ioffe and Dmitri Sverchkov. (Alexander Helphand-Parvus had ceased to be on amicable terms with Trotsky long before he died in 1924: his business interests and links with the German government in earlier years had utterly discredited him in Soviet Russia.) None was a Bolshevik veteran, and all of them had opposed Lenin in one way or another before 1917. They wrote affectionately to each other and rallied round whenever one of them was ill. But Trotsky never fully gave himself up to friendship. Years later Max Eastman was to tell Alfred Rosmer in Paris that there was a basic lack of 'a feeling for others as individuals'. Rosmer agreed: 'That's quite true. He has no humanity. It's entirely absent from him.'[11]

Trotsky had known Rakovski – who was of Bulgarian gentry origin – since 1903 and had dedicated *Literature and Revolution* to him as 'fighter, man and friend'. The two of them had liaised on policy towards Ukraine in the Civil War at the time when Rakovski headed the government in Kiev. They agreed about broad lines of policy in the 1920s. Rakovski paid for his support for the Left Opposition by being 'exiled' to postings abroad, eventually serving as Soviet diplomatic plenipotentiary in France between 1925 and 1927. Like Rakovski, Ioffe was a medical doctor and a person of wide cultural interests. Having conducted the early negotiations at Brest-Litovsk in late 1917, he kept in regular contact with Trotsky during the Civil War on matters relating to international policy – and of course he had been a leading light with Trotsky on the Viennese *Pravda* editorial board until being arrested in Odessa in 1912. Ioffe spent little time in Soviet Russia because of his duties as a diplomat in Berlin, Riga, Genoa, Shanghai, London and Tokyo. From a distance he lent what support he could to Trotsky's oppositional activity. Sverchkov too sympathized with his old friend. He and Trotsky met up when political duties allowed. They commiserated with each other in periods of illness. It was a shock to Trotsky when, at the end of the 1920s, Sverchkov announced his sympathy with official party policy and his rejection of the United Opposition.

Rakovski, Ioffe and Sverchkov were seldom geographically near enough for Trotsky to try out his ideas on them before announcing them. He anyway kept his own counsel even in easier times. He was like a hermit who came to the big city only when, in his solitude, he had something important to say.

Other leaders of the Left Opposition and United Opposition included Karl Radek, Yevgeni Preobrazhenski, Leonid Serebryakov, Yuri Pyatakov, Ivar Smilga and Nikolai Krestinski. Radek and Trotsky often agreed about political questions before and after 1917. Both were wittily sarcastic.

Radek, a famous source of jokes about the Kremlin elite, was the more companionable. Free of regular posts in party or government he wrote frequently for *Pravda*. Max Eastman recollected:

> [He] had the attractiveness of a thing you didn't like at first. You thought he was weak-eyed and coarse-lipped, and that you could never endure that old brown stocking of whiskers under his ears and chin. You found that behind the big spectacles his eyes were not watery, but queerly penetrating. You found the coarse lips had a delicate line between them. What you learned to like about them was an expression of serenity. Radek dressed his hollow frame in a strange square costume with unusual flaps and buttons, slick and aristocratic in material, but in design suggesting a New England deacon rather than a Bolshevik agitator.[12]

Preobrazhenski, Serebryakov and Krestinski aligned themselves with Trotsky from the trade union controversy of 1920–1 onwards. This led to their being sacked as Central Committee secretaries. Preobrazhenski was a prime mover in the formation of the Left Opposition, and it was he more than Trotsky who formulated the oppositionist critique of the Politburo's agrarian policy during the NEP. He was never a friend of Trotsky; indeed Trotsky's peremptory style annoyed him.[13]

Pyatakov and Smilga too had personal reservations about him – in Smilga's case it was remarkable that he was willing to accept Trotsky's pre-eminence in the Opposition after their contretemps in the Red Army in 1918–19.[14]

Radek, Preobrazhenski, Serebryakov, Krestinski, Pyatakov and Smilga treated Trotsky as the best available leader but as one who was far from a perfect choice. Yet Trotsky cultivated no political clientele. He wanted a following but would not exert himself in creating one. *The New Course*, indeed, had expressed contempt for Bolshevik veterans. He had accumulated enemies before 1917; many became even more hostile to him in subsequent years. It would not come as a complete surprise in the course of the first five-year plan, which Stalin introduced in 1928 in order to effect the country's rapid industrialization, that practically all Trotsky's principal political associates disowned him as a leader. Even Rakovski made his peace with Stalin. This did not save them from Stalin's punitive zeal in the late 1930s. Radek, Preobrazhenski, Serebryakov, Krestinski, Pyatakov, Smilga and Rakovski died by the executioner's bullet or in a labour camp. Trotsky was more saddened than enraged. He had kept Rakovski's photograph on his desk in emigration; he understood that he would only have appeared in the show-trial of March 1938 after having being physically or mentally tortured.

He did not put himself out by trying to win back that little group of friends and close allies when he fell out with them politically. He seldom even expressed regret. In Trotsky's eyes the error was always theirs. He had small capacity for introspection. With Lenin dead, moreover, he no longer knew anyone whose opinions commanded automatic respect. This was not a new phenomenon in his life. His admiration for Lenin had endured a lengthy period of abeyance, between 1903 and 1917, when he had thought and acted as if only he had the solution to great matters of the day. Like St Simeon of the Desert, he assumed that his solitary occupation of the highest platform was in the natural order of things. But unlike the Egyptian saint he endured no mental or physical torment in pursuit of virtue. He was intensely self-righteous. And he calmly dispensed with people once they had ceased to be of use to him and his cause. This shocked those who had not known him for long. Grigori Ziv before 1917 had witnessed Trotsky's lack of conventional sentiment.[15] He would not have been surprised to learn that his former friend failed in the 1920s to bind together a faction under his own name. Trotsky could inspire by speech, article and booklet. He could light up a topic with his brilliance. He could refute the logic of his adversaries with a flash of criticism or ridicule. What he had always lacked, even before the Great War, was the intuition to sustain a factional group under his leadership.

He refused to make social compromises. He gave up smoking after 1917; he drank alcohol sparingly and only on special occasions. (Lenin did not smoke and took beer in moderation but was a Bohemian in comparison with Trotsky.) He would not tolerate the telling of smutty stories and detested anyone swearing in the presence of women and children – his writings on 'everyday life' came from deep convictions. Nearly all fellow Bolsheviks smoked, drank, swore and gossiped profusely. Stalin's associate Anastas Mikoyan complained that Trotsky had set himself up as a chivalric knight trying to 'stop people speaking Russian'. Mikoyan was referring to Trotsky's aversion to obscene language.[16] Trotsky was never one of the boys, and he always conveyed the impression that he thought himself their superior. Probably he did not do this deliberately but the effect was the same: he alienated potential allies. He could be exasperating even when simply feeling bored. If the Politburo was slow in getting through a tedious agenda he might pull a French novel from his pocket and start reading. Thus he gave out the message that he had better things to do with his precious time than listen to people less intelligent, sharp-witted and capable than himself. Jan Rudzutak, Sovnarkom's Deputy Chairman from 1926, had this out with him: 'Comrade Trotsky, I know you have a clever head; what a pity it belongs to a scoundrel.'[17]

Only his family and friends saw a different side of Trotsky, as Max Eastman recorded:

> He never boasts; he never speaks of himself or his achievements; he never monopolises the conversation. He gives his attention freely and wholly to anything that comes up . . . [As we work together], if I pay him a compliment, he says some little thing, 'I am glad', and then passes on to another subject.[18]

There was indeed a becoming modesty about Trotsky.

Neither in private nor in public, though, did he suffer fools gladly: indeed he did not suffer them at all. He did nothing to correct the impression of being an arrogant know-all. Yuri Pyatakov tried – far too late, in 1926 – to persuade him to be more convivial with a view to winning over the unconverted. Overcoming years of reluctance, he attended an evening get-together; but he stayed only briefly, spluttering to Natalya: 'I can't stand it: the liqueurs, long dresses and gossip; it's been like a salon.'[19] The Kamenevs hosted that particular event. Trotsky's sister Olga was not known as a sybarite and yet Trotsky was rejecting her hospitality as being too bourgeois for him.[20] He omitted to give succour to those leading members of the Bolshevik left who were on his side. Delighting in spelling out his personal opinions, he seldom refrained from assailing the views of others even if they belonged to his own faction. Lenin had been known for listening attentively and avoiding offence to individuals who might want to support him. Preobrazhenski, one of the brightest of his supporters, was to spell this out to him in 1928 after they had been sent into administrative exile.[21] Trotsky, courteous in face-to-face conversations, was a demon with pen in hand.

He anyway lacked the decisiveness for a concerted advance on power. Adolf Ioffe was the only person to tell him to show greater respect for himself. Ioffe recalled that Lenin had privately admitted that Trotsky, not Lenin, had had the correct strategy in 1905. Trotsky had been the man with the best ideas. He had failed to realize his potential because he lacked Lenin's refusal to compromise. Ioffe for many years kept these thoughts to himself. But when determining to kill himself, on 16 November 1927, he decided to press this argument for the first and last time on Trotsky. By then his physical health had been destroyed by tuberculosis, myocarditis, stomach ulcers and polyneuritis. He had been demoralized by being denied permission to carry out official work. The medical commission appointed by the Central Committee had been dilatory; and doctors eventually explained to him that there was no point in seeking a cure abroad. Ioffe had never been emotionally stable but this last note was written in a steady fashion. He was trying to tell his old friend that a different approach to politics was needed if ever Trotsky was going to ascend to the leadership again.[22]

Ioffe had one last request. He asked Trotsky to do what he could to help the wife and two children he was abandoning. He was sceptical that the current party leadership would render assistance. He urged Trotsky to be optimistic, declaring that he had 'no doubt that the moment is not far off when you will again occupy the place which is fitting for you in the party'.[23] By killing himself, he missed the chance to explain what practical measures he had in mind. Trotsky in the second half of the 1920s was fighting fire with fire. By then he was dropping all compromise. Was Ioffe's last letter really a judgement on times past? Or was it perhaps a warning that Trotsky should not be tempted into half-measures again? Or even a plea for him to concentrate more fully on being a politician? Eastman in later life certainly believed that something was lacking in Trotsky as a contender to succeed Lenin. He noted how often his hero withdrew from the field when factional struggle occurred. Illness afflicted him at the worst moments in both 1923 and 1924. Eastman thought Trotsky ought to have accepted Lenin's invitation to become his deputy in Sovnarkom. He chided him for not opening a debate about the testament immediately after Lenin's death.[24]

The Politburo continued to fear that Trotsky might react by turning to the Red Army for further personal advancement. The worry persisted that he might become the October Revolution's Bonaparte, and this was among the reasons why he was sacked from the People's Commissariat for Military Affairs in January 1925. But he made no attempt to rally a body of support from the commanders he had worked with. After losing the Commissariat he did not alter his ways. He was proud of his achievements in the Civil War. Indeed he had come to regard himself as a military man of some kind – when deported from the USSR in 1929 he was to believe that Mustapha Kemal had given him asylum in Turkey because he was a fellow soldier. In every way, though, Trotsky had sought to consolidate the party's control over the armed forces during the NEP. He had overseen the reduction in their size. While striving to raise their technological level, he undertook no special pleading on their behalf in budgetary discussions. Although he approved the joint manoeuvres with the German army on Soviet territory this was not his personal initiative but the official policy of the entire communist leadership in Moscow.

Trotsky anyway did not like to fight dirty. He would not budge when Max Eastman rebuked him for this:

> 'Why this is not an argument, it is a personal attack,' he said, 'I can't reply to a thing like that.' And he spread out his hands as though this proposition were perfectly obvious.
>
> To me it did not seem obvious, and I continued: 'Now, you could take that speech of Stalin's about [the Left Opposition], for instance . . .'
>
> 'What is that?' he asked, and he smiled at my expression. 'I haven't read any of those things,' he explained.
>
> I murmured my amazement, and he spread his hands again in that gesture which indicates that something is quite obvious.
>
> 'Why should I read what they write?' he said. 'They aren't discussing anything that I said. There is no misunderstanding.'[25]

Two years passed before Trotsky accepted Eastman's point, and by then it was already too late. As leader of the Left Opposition he made points to his own intellectual satisfaction with polemical zeal and in fine literary style. Then he left it to his readers to draw their own conclusions. Unwisely he assumed that this was enough.

He claimed in his memoirs that he had lost all influence in the Politburo or the Central Committee in the 1920s. This was untrue. Whenever he sat in the Politburo, especially when Stalin was absent, he took his opportunity to play the boss. He lectured; he interrogated; he expostulated and gave vent to his sardonic wit. His presence could never be ignored.[26]

He failed to canvass opinion properly in the leadership, in his faction or in the party as a whole. Certainly he wrote lots of booklets but this had its drawbacks for others. And it was not without its annoying side. While he was away composing them he was not wholly available for consultations in the leadership. He failed to understand the needs of contemporary politics. Andrei Andreev, an ex-member of the Workers' Opposition who went over to the side of Stalin and Bukharin, told him in 1926: 'Yes, you say you've written a booklet. But who *now* reads *all the books being published*?'[27] Andreev told him that he should stop pretending to be an angel and start making useful, practical proposals. Trotsky took no notice of the advice. He did not mean to be personally offensive and yet he repeatedly injured feelings in any discussion. He was profoundly self-centred. It is true that he was genuinely devoted to Marxism, the October Revolution and world communism. He himself could shake off verbal attacks like dust from a jacket. He simply did not understand that other Bolsheviks were not made like him and that when he ridiculed or castigated their policies, they assumed that he despised them as people – and it was politically foolish of Trotsky to ignore their feelings.

# 36. LIVING WITH TROTSKY

The Trotsky family had occupied a four-roomed apartment in the Kremlin's Cavalry Corpus since moving from Petrograd in 1918. They lived in comfort but without extravagance. Trotsky, like other Bolshevik leaders, had a modest salary. Natalya continued to supervise activity in the country's museums; her monthly income was somewhat less than half of her husband's. As one of the country's most prolific and best-selling authors, Trotsky could have become rich beyond measure. But the acquisition of money meant nothing to him while he had enough to pursue his political priorities. He did not count his pennies, and Eastman noted that he turned over the royalties to his secretaries for safekeeping.[1]

Few foreign visitors understood that the communist elite's members, the nomenklatura, had no need of large bank accounts in order to lead a comfortable existence. If they had high posts in politics, they had access to the USSR's finest facilities free of charge. Their medical needs were automatically satisfied. Their households had cooks, servants and chauffeurs; their food was supplied by the Kremlin, where Abel Enukidze presided over the running of the material supply of the entire precinct.[2] Families of leading politicians dressed neatly – this had always been important for Trotsky, and the photographs of his boys show them well turned out. Like others in the ruling group, he could occupy a dacha outside Moscow or request a vacation in the loveliest spots in the north Caucasus and Abkhazia. He went out hunting for game, which was one of his favourite forms of relaxation after the Civil War, without having to pay a kopek. If he needed a book, he could order it from any number of libraries. His shelves bulged with personal copies sent by publishers. Newspapers and reports from around the world were regularly delivered to him. This was far from being a Spartan lifestyle. Not being eager for luxury, he wanted for nothing.

Like the other Soviet leaders, he kept open house. Children from other families came and went. When Lëva Trotsky at the age of thirteen in 1919 expressed a wish to join the Komsomol – the party's junior organization – none other than Bukharin, soon to become his father's bitter opponent, signed the necessary letter of recommendation.[3]

Rumours persisted about Trotsky and his amours. Good-looking and charismatic, he certainly attracted feminine attention. No sooner had speculation ended about Clare Sheridan than it started up about Larisa Reissner. She was one of the most alluring Bolshevik women. Married to Trotsky's supporter Fëdor Raskolnikov, she was exceptionally beautiful. Her working association with Trotsky had begun in mid-1918 when she went as an agitator to raise morale among Red troops in the Volga campaign. She then accompanied Raskolnikov when he travelled as Soviet plenipotentiary to Kabul. Raskolnikov's posting was a way of removing a known Trotskyist from the political scene in Moscow. Reissner enjoyed herself in Afghanistan, conducting an affair with a local prince. She was an emancipated woman of the sort approved of by Bolshevik feminists such as Alexandra Kollontai. She relished the role of femme fatale and liked to penetrate the higher echelons of the Soviet nomenklatura. She did not just theorize about 'free love': she practised it.[4] On her return to Moscow, she made a play for Karl Radek: she obviously had a penchant for leftists. Radek became infatuated with her.

But Reissner was angling for a bigger catch. Through Radek she passed a message to Trotsky with an extraordinary proposal, even an indecent one. She wanted to have a child by Trotsky. Her idea was to produce offspring 'harmoniously combining the beauty and talent of the mother (Reissner) and the mental genius of the father (Trotsky)'. The promiscuous Radek was not accustomed to being passed over, but he agreed to go on the errand. Trotsky resisted the enticement: 'Calm down, Karl. Tell your beloved that I refuse to become father to her child.' A week later Reissner attended a conference of journalists and writers hosted by Trotsky in the Revolutionary-Military Council of the Republic. She blushed when Trotsky approached her. Trotsky let her down gently, confining himself to topics about literature and Red Army soldiers.[5]

This was the version of events believed by oppositionists in Moscow, including people close to Radek. Women were never Trotsky's main distraction. It was his bouts of ill health that more frequently diverted him from public duties. Physical incapacity became a recurrent problem after the Civil War. Not everyone believed that the cause lacked a psychological dimension. The coincidence of illness with periods of political crisis was remarkable. This had famously occurred from summer 1923 to spring 1924 when he was failing to get his way in Politburo deliberations. Speculation was rife that his ailments were psychosomatic. Such commentary worked best for the weeks after Lenin's death when an open official campaign was maintained against him and his name was dragged through the mud in *Pravda* and booklets and at the Central Committee and the Thirteenth Party Conference. The strain would have shattered the confidence of anyone of less robust temperament, and Trotsky's plaintive address to the Central Committee in October 1923 showed that he indeed felt hurt by the attacks on his motives and integrity even though he quickly recovered some mental poise.

His ill health was anyway not confined to episodes of political crisis; he ailed throughout the decade and the symptoms were not a fiction of his imagination. This is not to say that he did not play up his sufferings. He never slowed down his writing schedule. To complete even the shortest booklet he needed to gather material, consult files, contact libraries and organize his assistants. He then had to draft and redraft. After that he had to liaise with the publishing house and scrutinize proofs. He always had several literary projects on the go, and it was an exceptional month if he failed to submit articles to *Pravda*. Perhaps he was not constantly as unwell as he liked others to believe. Then again, writing was his therapy: it brought salve to his nerves and lessened his physical pain – twenty-four hours without his putting pen to paper was a torment for him.

Natalya never attributed his malaises to hypochondria or some other kind of psychological self-deception. She believed him to be ill whenever he said he was. Poor health had dogged him for years and he took lengthy breaks for convalescence. It was only in the years of the Civil War and the invasion of Poland that he ignored the medical advice. When the survival of the Soviet order was in doubt he was not going to spend his time in bed. From 1921 his physical condition became a preoccupation. He was not alone in the leadership in experiencing severe illness at that time.[6] What distinguished Trotsky from the rest of the Central Committee, apart from Lenin, was the persistence of his problems in subsequent years. Professor Guetier served him throughout this time. Guetier was the favourite doctor of the Trotskys and the Lenins. Despite his wealth of expertise, the causes of Trotsky's afflictions baffled him. Rest was his usual prescription.

The 'concilium' of German medical specialists attending Lenin in 1922 were asked to tend to Trotsky while they were in Russia. They could find nothing organically wrong but had a strong suspicion that he had epilepsy. One of them pointed out to Trotsky that Julius Caesar had been an epileptic. Quick as a shot, Trotsky replied: 'Yes, but the trouble is that I don't happen to be Julius Caesar.'[7] The German specialist was not the first to speculate in this fashion. Grigori Ziv, while training as a doctor in the 1890s, was among the first to make this diagnosis after witnessing Trotsky's fainting fits. Ziv added that Lev Deich, another of Trotsky's friends in the decade before the First World War, said it was 'a well-known and established fact that these faints were epileptic ones'.[8] Ziv's analysis is worth quoting:

> Many traits in his character also involuntarily thrust one towards such a suggestion: his sharply expressed egotism, his over-developed confidence, his extreme and sickly vanity, his proclivity for extravagance in speech, writing and demeanour, a kind of teasing pedantry . . . exhibited even in his precise, careful handwriting.[9]

(Doctors are notorious for their illegible scrawls and it is interesting that Ziv seems to have thought legibility a failing.) The assumption was anyway a widely held one in the 1920s that epilepsy was associated with a specific type of temperament and Dr Ziv was at one with the German specialists in his general diagnosis.

A social stigma was attached to being called an epileptic and sufferers frequently kept quiet about any such diagnosis. Trotsky neither confirmed nor denied the diagnosis but preferred to discuss his medical problem in vague terms. He spoke of fainting fits rather than epilepsy. He disconcerted Clare Sheridan in 1920 when he swayed while standing with his back towards the clay bust she was making of him. She worried that he might fall backwards upon it. Trotsky assured her there was no need to worry by explaining: 'I always fall forwards!'[10]

In any case the doctors were not categorical in their conclusions. Since his collapses did not involve the classic symptoms of convulsions and frothings at the mouth he had grounds for keeping an open mind on the subject. Speculation about his condition leaked out to foreign countries. The London humorous magazine *Punch* carried an anecdote: 'After addressing a meeting for two hours, says a contemporary, Trotsky fainted. A more humane man would have fainted first.'[11] Such public jocularity about a Bolshevik leader's personal condition was impermissible in Soviet Russia. Trotsky made light of his worries. This was unusual for him in matters medical and may be an indication that he was more concerned than he allowed people to believe. He was exceptionally brave on military service; he maundered on almost neurotically about most of his ailments – and Natalya became his chief nurse and confidante during those episodes when he went off to the sanatorium.

If the probability is that Trotsky had epilepsy it was only one among his chronic medical problems. Colitis continued to affect him. His stomach had given him trouble since boyhood and he had a hernia before the Great War. Gout began to bedevil him in the 1920s. He also started to have days when he felt completely lacking in energy. He blamed his ill health on his periods of exile in 1900–2 and in 1906–7. The contemporary evidence scarcely bears this out. Trotsky was in fine shape in Siberia and northern Russia. Apart from when he was in solitary confinement in Kherson in 1898, moreover, the time he spent in prisons was scarcely arduous. The likeliest explanation of his multiple incapacitation is that he had pushed himself to exhaustion by his frenetic pace of work over many years.

Such circumstances were bound to exacerbate his vulnerability to nervous tension. Outsiders to the family knew nothing of this, but Natalya had to cope with it as a regular occurrence. Observing him at close range for a longer period than anyone else, she believed that his outbreaks of mental volatility were caused by physical predicaments. She wrote about his 'nerves' in her diary in 1958: 'L.T. in general was extraordinarily sensitive to physical breakage in his organism; the slightest bout of illness destroyed his equilibrium. He demanded total order and total well-being in his organism.'[12] She took him as she found him, and saw it as her job to serve his needs and to allow him to define what they were. She was also wise. Knowing his mixture of strength and frailty, she strove to ensure that he turned himself out on parade in good shape. The rest she left to her man. The focus in the Trotsky household always had to be kept on Trotsky. The children, both those by Alexandra and those whom he had by Natalya, learned to respect his domestic regime. Whether they were in the Kremlin or at a weekend dacha, they dared not interrupt his pattern of work – and he wrote as much at home as in the office. He got his way without needing to raise his voice. The family seldom had disputes. As they grew up, the offspring deferred to him in politics. Daughters Zina and Nina were avid supporters of the Left Opposition and Trotsky was their hero. Trotsky encouraged their political militancy.

Even so, there were severe problems. Zina's marriage to Zakhar Moglin was brief and disastrous – he disappointed her by showing no interest in communism. The couple stayed together just long enough for her to produce a child, Alexandra, in 1923.[13] Zina's second wedding, to Platon Volkov, lasted longer and produced a son Vsevolod (or Seva) in 1925. But it was a fractious marriage and Volkov left her intermittently.[14] But at least political questions did not divide them: Volkov sided resolutely with Trotsky in the internal party disputes of the 1920s.[15] Alexandra Bronstein,

Zina's mother, tried to help but it was her father whom she wanted most; Natalya believed that Zina loved her father more than she had ever loved either of her spouses. The fact that Volkov campaigned for the Left Opposition stopped him from becoming a rival to Trotsky in Zina's affections. Her admiration for her father bordered on the obsessive. She also had problems with her lungs and had to take frequent periods of convalescence. Nina was the steadier of the two daughters and gave birth to a son, Lev, in 1921 and a daughter, Volina, in 1926. Unfortunately her marriage to Man Nevelson was not a success;[16] she also developed tuberculosis and her health deteriorated drastically in the mid-1920s.

Only one of Trotsky's offspring, his younger son Sergei, failed to show him filial piety. Sergei understood better than Max Eastman how well the Kremlin elite were looking after themselves materially. Brought up on ideas of socialist equality, he took them seriously. He spurned all privileges. He refused to jump the queue for the doctor; he turned down the opportunity to wear smart clothes. When the Moscow Soviet sent a shiny new jacket for him, he announced that he would continue to wear his old one which was patched at the elbows.[17] He rebuked Trotsky and Natalya for their 'bourgeois' lifestyle and despised their cultural tastes. On one occasion he told them off for listening to a radio broadcast of Tchaikovsky's opera *Eugene Onegin*.[18] Sergei thought the Russian musical classics decadent and unacceptable. At the age of sixteen he upped and left home: he had had enough.[19]

His parents told people that Sergei was rejecting the life of the Soviet nomenklatura and had an aversion to politics.[20] Trotsky, Natalya and their elder son Lëva were revolutionary militants whereas Sergei was searching for something different in life. After a while he returned to the family once a week, and Trotsky and Natalya welcomed his visits. (They tried to give him the money for transport across the city but Sergei stuck out for his independence.) 'We have made no protest,' Trotsky said, 'but it's too early – he is too young.'[21] Then Sergei did something quite extraordinary. After becoming fascinated with gymnastics, he signed up with a circus.[22] He wandered around until he met and fell in love with Olga Greber, a librarian, who insisted that he complete his schooling.[23] Sergei resumed intermittent contact with his parents as he settled down with Olga in Moscow and trained as an engineer. His gentleness made him everyone's friend and favourite and he persuaded his parents that his chosen path in life was the right one for him.

Trotsky may have seen something of himself in Sergei. He too had renounced the worldly ambition marked out for him by a domineering father. Like David Bronstein, Trotsky had the sense to let his son find his own career. Natalya cherished her relationship with Sergei: she later confessed to having had a slight preference for him over Lëva.[24] Yet she never came properly to terms with his dislike of revolutionary commitment. Characteristically she opted for a social and political explanation. In her opinion Sergei had been negatively affected by the public atmosphere during the NEP when revolutionary zeal was dissipating.[25] Trotsky and Natalya were children of their times – and, she thought, things changed for the worse in the 1920s. What neither she nor her husband yet believed was that the Bolshevik party elite had undergone an irreversible degeneration. They assumed that that the code of comradely commitment remained in force. Trotsky had not yet got the measure of his enemies. He thought them wrong-headed, stupid or simply inferior to himself. But he gave them the benefit of the doubt for their revolutionary honour. He refrained from castigating even Stalin as a moral degenerate until after he was sent into exile in 1928.

Just occasionally there were undetected intimations of the horrors ahead. A dangerous accident had occurred back in late summer 1924 when the Trotskys were holidaying in Kislovodsk. They had gone out for a day's hunting with the gigantic Nikolai Muralov and Trotsky's personal bodyguard. They had travelled by rail on a open-air trailer. On the way home the trailer had come off the track as it approached the station and the passengers were flung out on to the ground. They escaped with only bruises. When they demanded an explanation they received weak excuses.[26] Subsequently, on 7 November 1927, a shot was fired at Trotsky's limousine as he attended a United Opposition demonstration. There was no proof of Stalin's complicity but Natalya came to believe it was an officially sanctioned attempt at assassination.[27] Kamenev warned Trotsky in 1926 about the danger surrounding him. Assassination was a definite possibility. After helping to set up the United Opposition, he and Zinoviev drew up secret documents blaming Stalin in the event of their 'accidental' death. Zinoviev asked Trotsky directly: 'Do you think that Stalin hasn't discussed the question of your physical removal?'[28] Stalin, according to Kamenev, had once said: 'The finest pleasure is to mark down one's enemy, make one's preparations, take revenge appropriately and go off to bed.'[29]

Even while causing so much trouble for the ascendant leadership, though, Trotsky was treated as belonging to the party elite. In spring 1926, with official permission, he made a trip to Berlin for medical treatment. He and Natalya attended a communist party demonstration at the

Alexanderplatz on May Day; they were present incognito, and the sight of the banners, the enthusiasm and the sheer number of German communists impressed them.[30] They would have been more delighted if Comintern had not, in their opinion, steered the German communists off the path of true Marxism.

# 37. WHAT TROTSKY WANTED

The convention for politicians everywhere is to lay claim to consistency of intent. Trotsky was no different even though he called himself a revolutionary rather than a politician. In his autobiography in 1930 he would represent himself as a constant critic of the basic official measures introduced in the 1920s. He liked to give the impression that he had always fought against market economics.

His was at best a misleading account. Trotsky never called for the NEP to be abandoned even while calling for certain features to be modified or removed. He accepted that the Soviet economy would require a private sector for the foreseeable future.[1] He was proposing his own variant of the NEP and most adherents of the Opposition accepted his basic ideas. The factional disputes of the 1920s were about demarcating the frame of the existing policy and not about destroying it. At least, this was what they contended at the time. Trotsky warned that while supporting the 'prosperous' section of the peasantry the Politburo was increasing the danger from the kulaks. He also claimed that official statistics understated the rise of the kulak.[2] But he stopped a long way short of demanding the immediate comprehensive collectivization of production. He urged the state encouragement of the establishment of agricultural co-operatives. According to Trotsky, this would enable the peasantry to escape the grip of the local kulaks. At the same time he made the case for increasing the taxes on kulak households – and he did not approve of admitting them to the co-operatives unless they could be prevented from exploiting their less well-off neighbours.[3] He also maintained that the isolation of kulaks in each village would help in pushing the middling peasants towards joining co-operatives.[4] He had no illusion about the need for such prodding to be undertaken. The co-operatives, moreover, would succeed only when the factory production in the USSR enabled the 'gradual industrialization of agriculture'.[5]

Such comments were at their clearest in debates at the Politburo or Central Committee. Usually, outside the rough and tumble of face-to-face discussion, he took refuge in vague generalities. He made a single attempt to provide a broad economic prospectus for public consumption. Published in 1925 and reprinted in the following year, *Towards Socialism or Capitalism?* made the case for accelerated capital investment in industry, for a central state economic plan and for collective farms in the countryside. It avoided discussion of possible snags. It offered no desired schedule. Its emphasis fell on the need for the party to choose between the socialist and the capitalist roads to the future.[6]

The introduction of a system of collective farming, Trotsky always contended, should be conducted on a voluntary basis. He avoided Preobrazhenski's provocative talk about making the peasantry as a whole pay for industrial growth.[7] Indeed he avoided the entire topic despite its being at the core of party debate about the NEP. Even so, he scarcely bothered to disguise his contempt for agriculture in discussions inside the leadership – and he sniped at Kalinin in the Politburo for speaking up for farming interests.[8] He wanted the fiscal regime to make it uncomfortable for peasants to stick to household-based farming. This came out in yet another exchange within the leadership:

> *Rykov:* Each peasant raises the question whether, if he doesn't join the collective farm, he will have to pay a tax and bear all kinds of burdens if he doesn't want to do that; it will be a coercive system in my opinion.
> *Kalinin:* Economically coercive.
> *Trotsky:* Not coercive but stimulative.[9]

Trotsky's rejoinder was a slippery one, revealing his impatience as well as his unwillingness to be specific about his ideas on future contingencies. He plainly wanted collectivization to occur sooner than the Politburo majority envisaged. He did not specify his preferred schedule but contented himself with announcing general economic and social objectives.

Trotsky displayed similar restraint when demanding the quickening of Soviet industrialization. He was careful with his words and stuck to vague formulations. He urged increased investment in industrial planning and reasoned that this would benefit the entire economy: 'For a socialist state which is poor in capital the surest methods of raising up agriculture lies in the maximum investment in industry.'[10] He offered no great criticism of the 'nepmen' or the small-workshop owners. He reserved his passion for arguments in favour of a general economic plan; he put the case that Gosplan should direct investment, output and distribution in the manufacturing and mining sector owned by the government. Not once did he call for deprivatization. In his estimation there would be little difficulty in promoting industrial growth. Popular enthusiasm would be abundant. He assumed that the working class would welcome the benefits of higher wages and guaranteed employment. If he thought this to be at variance with the NEP, he told no one about it.

His critique indicated a difference with the Politburo on practicalities but not on questions of strategic principle (and he would work hard to disguise this when he composed his account of the political struggles after the death of Lenin). Looking at the official economic statistics in 1926, he noted that certain sectors of the economy had done better than had been projected in the previous year. Metallurgy and transport had attained a level originally predicted for 1931. Yet the USSR faced a 'famine' of industrial products available to be traded with the peasantry. Trotsky called this 'a basic disproportion' between supply and demand. The Politburo, he argued, was guilty of mismanagement. He urged a faster build-up of investment and output in state-owned factories. Peasants would benefit by being able to buy more urban goods. The period of post-war recovery was coming to an end and a five-year plan for economic development should be enacted. In any case he stated that any plan would need correcting annually in the light of changing conditions. He was offering his ideas not as a finished scheme but as a general basis for the party's perspective on policy.[11]

It remained axiomatic for Trotsky that Soviet Russia had to interact with the world economy in order to achieve industrial competitiveness. When seizing power in October 1917, the Bolsheviks had expected to attain recovery by trading with a Germany which had undergone its own communist revolution. After this failed to happen Lenin coaxed Sovnarkom into seeking strong commercial ties with the Germany of Wilhelm II. Trotsky concurred with him. He and Lenin clashed over policy on trade unions and on state economic planning in 1921–2, but this should not be allowed to obscure their active agreement that the Soviet post-war economy had to attract investment and technology from foreign entrepreneurs. The two of them were at one on the imperative need for concessions.[12]

Another point of agreement lay in their hostility to the growth in what they called 'bureaucratism'. Administrative inefficiency and the sloth and uncooperativeness of administrators were their *bêtes noires*, and Lenin and Trotsky criticized the activity of the Workers' and Peasants' Inspectorate (or Rabkrin). They had a point. Rabkrin was an institutional shambles aggravating the problems it had been created to solve. Indeed the internal life of the party was increasingly bureaucratic by most definitions, and Trotsky had some right to tie his own call for 'democratization' to the last writings of Lenin. The party, moreover, had become highly authoritarian in the way it organized itself. Lenin and Trotsky were diagnosing ailments of the communist order without having a serious cure. This was a state which could not depend on the political loyalty or professional conscientiousness of its own officials. It lacked mechanisms of control such as inter-party competition, an autonomous judiciary, a critical press and an electorate which could throw out the scoundrels. The USSR could not function without supervisory agencies: 'bureaucratism' was written into its genetic structure.

Trotsky passed over other flaws in the Soviet state order without comment. He ignored phenomena such as clientelism in party and government. He did not refer to localism. He had nothing to say about corruption and fraud. He avoided the atmosphere of distrust and apathy engendered by dictatorship, terror and legal nihilism. Trotsky never tried to fix a serious boundary between desirable centralism and undesirable centralist authority. He rejected morality as a subject for proper debate. He accepted and propounded Marxism in its Bolshevik variant as an unchallengeable truth. He thought that his policies were correct. He gave no thought to the possibility that he might be wrong and that other ways of organizing society should be canvassed. Trotsky was straightforwardly a Bolshevik.

It is true that he proposed freer modes of discussion in the party. He also demanded the restoration of the elective principle for party posts and urged that the workers – the 'proletariat' – should be invited to express their opinion on current debates on policy. But his ideas do not point to anything like a stable 'communism with a human face'. He remained proud of the Soviet dictatorship, eagerly defending its ideological intolerance and extra-judicial repression. While breaking party rules by fomenting factionalism, he never suggested that politics should cease to be the privileged activity of a single party. He insisted in the Politburo in June 1926: 'Comrade Dzerzhinski, as you know, I'm not afraid of terror, but we can conduct terror only as a party.'[13] A heated exchange followed:

> *Dzerzhinski:* Trotsky said that one party member is afraid of speaking the truth to another. Tell us, then: who's not speaking to whom? The *apparatchiki* are afraid of Trotsky, and apart from the *apparatchiki* I'll tell you who else is afraid of speaking. Sometimes I'm afraid of speaking. And do you know why? Because I'm afraid of you.

*Trotsky:* Well, I'm not at all afraid of you, comrade Dzerzhinski.

*Dzerzhinski:* I understand. In that respect you're a person without fear or blemish. You're a daring and courageous person whereas I'm afraid of you on behalf of the party.[14]

His enemies had some reason to accuse Trotsky of exploiting each and every failure of the party for his personal purposes.[15]

He asserted the need for democratization and for 'proletarian self-activity'. If the Civil War was the sump that drained away his utopian ideas about the working class, political adversity in the mid-1920s induced him to re-inject them to lubricate his strategic optimism. But at the same time he declared that one could not be right against the party. His thought was a confused and confusing ragbag.

Pragmatic considerations exerted constant pressure on him. Nobody could mount to supreme authority in the USSR without declaring allegiance to the existing state order. There is nothing, though, in Trotsky's private papers to indicate that he acted merely out of calculation. He truly believed, through to the end of his life, that what had been wrought by the Bolsheviks in the half-decade after the October Revolution was a model of communist achievement. He wanted it conserved, imitated and developed. His critique of the ascendant party leadership was not meant to undermine the foundations of the Soviet order – and he never gave any other impression. Trotsky acquired a burning nostalgia for the early revolutionary period. The disputes among the party leaders during the NEP were a struggle of comrades-in-arms. Trotsky recognized no other variant of socialism except Bolshevism. He despised and detested the Socialist-Revolutionaries and Mensheviks as enemies of human progress. He did not object to the show-trial of the Socialist-Revolutionaries in 1922. He did not call for Mensheviks to be released from the Solovki prison island. He was untroubled by the brutal suppression of the Georgian national uprising in 1924.

Trotsky was not oblivious to the concerns of the non-Russian peoples. He consistently advocated that schools, press and cultural development should use the local language; he remained eager for the party to recruit young men and women from the various peoples to serve the revolutionary cause. In 1922–3 his sympathies were with Lenin and against Stalin in the dispute over Georgia. Basically he supported the policy of 'nationalization'. This was not the official name of the party's measures but it was its essence: it involved agreeing that peoples had to be organized on the national principle. In 1927 he called for a fifteen-year plan on the national question. In Ukraine, Trotsky stated, there had to be 'Ukrainiz-ation'. Ukrainians ought to be promoted to office. The Ukrainian language should be spread by schooling and in newspapers and books. His sole reservation – and it was a common party reservation in the 1920s – was that Bolsheviks should keep up a 'merciless struggle against the kulaks'.[16]

Well-off individual farmers were concentrated more heavily in Ukraine than anywhere else in the Soviet Union. Somehow, he assumed, any dilemma would be resoluble. He was always stronger on objectives than on coherent policies. The same syndrome was obvious in his pro-posals for measures on religion. Lenin had initiated a drastic repression against the Russian Orthodox Church in 1922 involving show-trials and execution of bishops as well as the sequestration of ecclesiastical buildings and treasures. He planned to traumatize the Church in Russia for genera-tions to come. Trotsky, while not objecting to this campaign, wanted to reposition the emphasis of policy in the longer term. He urged the fostering of an ecclesiastical reform movement. One already existed in the form of the Renovationists, and Trotsky wanted to use them as a means of causing disruption in the country's largest Christian denomination. He thought that police infiltration should remain a weapon in the Soviet state's arsenal but that religion could not be extirpated by repression alone. Like others in the leadership in the 1920s, he reckoned this was likely to be a lengthy process.

Even in foreign policy he was less out of line with his Politburo colleagues than he pretended in the mid-1920s or in later years. He argued that they had given up the traditional commitment to world revolution. He coupled this with the charge that they were bunglers. He chose two episodes to illustrate his case. The Politburo, he said, had fumbled its orders to the Communist Party of Great Britain in the general strike of 1926 and had overestimated the Chinese Communist Party's strength in Shanghai in 1927 when calling for an insurrection.

Bungling was not the exclusive characteristic of Stalin and Bukharin. In 1923 Trotsky had supported the policy of attempted insurrection in Germany up to the hilt – and only Stalin had raised sensible objections.[17] The ensuing fiasco was as much his fault as anyone else's, which was why increasingly he declined to discuss the episode. In any case he stuck by his original judgement that there had been a realistic chance of a success-ful rising.[18] Likewise he continued to assume that Soviet armed forces would probably have to be deployed if revolution broke out in Europe and that a continental war would ensue.[19] Given though he frequently was to straight-talking about current politics, he gave no indication of these geopolitical calculations. He expected a bloodbath and thought it a price worth paying for the achievement of a communist revolution in Germany. But he understood that it would be impolitic to lay bare his thinking even to the rest of the Bolshevik left; and his near-silence about the German fiasco of 1923 permitted him to concentrate his noise on the United Kingdom and China in 1926–7 since he no longer made a serious direct impact on the course of Soviet foreign policy.

There can hardly be a doubt that Stalin and Bukharin bungled by sending instructions through Comintern for the Chinese Communist Party to organize an insurrection against Chiang Kai-shek and the Kuomintang in April 1927. It was just the excuse that Chiang needed to conduct a bloody suppression of communists in Shanghai and elsewhere. Trotsky was deeply sarcastic at the expense of the Politburo leadership. Yet his own position as critic was not lacking in weakness. Moscow's orders for an insurrection disproved the Opposition's claim that Stalin and Bukharin had abandoned support for world revolution. Furthermore, Stalin and Bukharin were not alone in overestimating the immediate potential of China for communization. Trotsky too misjudged the situation. Far from focusing his revolutionary strategy on Europe and North America, he was generally in favour of promoting revolutions in Asia. When in 1928 he privately debated China with Yevgeni Preobrazhenski, his ally in the Opposition, he stressed his belief that the Chinese Communist Party could have achieved a seizure of power.[20] He had earlier avoided a full public elaboration of his thinking in the mid-1920s – and his subsequent comments arose out of his desire to lambast Stalin and Bukharin. He was consequently selective in his account of the controversy.

The Chinese question, for all its divisiveness on details, involved a broad consensus among leading Bolsheviks regardless of factional allegiance. Despite what Trotsky later wrote, the Politburo's foreign policy was not anti-revolutionary. Dissension in the leadership turned on questions not of principle or basic strategy but of practical contemporary judgement. Moreover, Trotsky covered up his willingness to run risks in pursuit of the grail of 'European socialist revolution'. Having failed to cover himself with glory in 1923, he threw mud at the reputation of fellow party leaders.

The same was true of policy inside the USSR. Although Trotsky was not the father of the NEP he was one of its uncles. Rather than cherish the child he behaved like a stepfather who wanted to disown it. He never lavished praise on it. He behaved as if he believed that if a thing is not perfectly right, it must be wholly wrong. He also appeared to think that he was more truthful and persuasive because he was more quarrelsome.

Being always in a minority in the Politburo and Central Committee, he could not be held to account for official policy. He could supply proposal after proposal without testing them in practice. He could exaggerate his points. He could show disdain for the muddled thinking of his main rivals. He could draw a sharp distinction between what the ascendant leadership was doing and what he would do in its place. In fact the gap between the Politburo and the Opposition was never as wide as he pretended. Trotsky did a brilliant job in convincing people otherwise, and to this day his version of the internal party situation in the 1920s is automatically believed: few observers have troubled to challenge Trotsky as a memoirist or historian.

This is not to deny that Trotsky genuinely believed in the policies he publicly advocated. Not even his worst enemies thought him a complete hypocrite. But although he may have gulled a multitude of people this was only after he had gulled himself. He felt an inner need to sustain his morale. This depended on being able to persuade himself that a chasm existed between his ideas and the politics of the Politburo. His problem was an old one for him. He had become obsessed with a few key ideas. He gave Bukharin the benefit of the doubt about his sincerity but simply dismissed him as misguided, and he contended that Bukharin's policies would lead the country back towards capitalism. He was less kind about Stalin, who he thought had only a lust for power.

Trotsky was far from showing that his ideas would solve the essential problems of the Soviet state order. He spent a lot of his time in disputing, less of it in thinking. Style prevailed over content. He loved an argument; he thrived on that access of adrenalin which occurred whenever he entered the ring against his critics. This involved an ultimate lack of seriousness as an intellectual. Like a lawyer pushing his case to the logical limits, he thought only about what was said in the courtroom. He refused to observe a sense of proportion. He disrespected his opponents, whom he mocked and humiliated. His central argument was that the October Revolution would not have gone to the bad if only his leadership and policies had not been defeated by his internal party enemies. His pamphlets commended themselves to his followers. But most of them were militants who wanted to believe what he had to say. More surprising is the number of people who had no sympathy for communism and yet accepted the idea that the USSR would not have been a totalitarian despotism under Trotskyist rule. There are many reasons for his enduring appeal. He was thrown from the pinnacle of power before his later ideas could be tested in practice. He was a brilliant advocate as writer and orator. He gained sympathy for his personal plight after being deported in 1929. And he died a martyr's death.

He himself always asked to be regarded as a revolutionary idealist. Yet he never faced up to the weakness of his case. The Politburo expanded the frame of the NEP to the maximum size. This was to result in the emergency of 1927–8. Trotsky's policies, if implemented, would have strained the NEP's woodwork to destruction still earlier. His silences and verbal fudgings in the mid-1920s were not accidental. He was more practised at the arts of political manoeuvre, at least in this respect, than his followers understood or wanted to understand.

Trotsky's specific alternatives to the policies adopted by Stalin from 1928, indeed, were to share many of Stalin's assumptions. He called for state economic planning and offered nothing that was essentially different from Soviet practices except the assurance that he would do things less violently and more democratically. These sentiments were not laden with practical specificity. Trotsky said nothing about what he would do if things did not turn out as quickly as he predicted. His thinking was premised on the achievability of success at the first attempt without the need to prepare for other outcomes. In any case, he gave no indication of what he intended to do about the kulaks, priests, ex-Mensheviks and millions of 'former people' (as those who had been deprived of their civil rights under the 1918 Constitution were officially and shockingly termed). It is true that he suggested that he would have moved more slowly and peaceably than Stalin eventually did towards the collectivization of agriculture. But Trotsky never said what he would do if the peasants en masse refused to comply. He also promised to democratize the party. He did not explain how he would react if others engaged in the same kind of factional disruption as he had caused in the 1920s. He committed himself to engineering a global revolution. He offered no analysis of how far he was willing to risk the existence of the Soviet state. Would he gamble with the October Revolution's survival? He offered a prospectus for revolutionary exploration without any guarantee that he would not steer the ship of the USSR off the end of the world.

# 38. LAST STAND IN MOSCOW

The year 1927 marked the tenth anniversary of the October Revolution. It was also the decisive period of struggle between the Politburo and the United Opposition. Trotsky's mood was buoyant. The Politburo had proved its incompetence, in his eyes, beyond peradventure now that Comintern policy in the United Kingdom and in China was in pieces – and Stalin and Bukharin were left fumbling for excuses. The Kremlin's economic supervision was scarcely more impressive. There was a worrying decline in food supplies and a shortage of industrial products. The Politburo's failure was there for all to see. The United Opposition was transmitting its message to the party despite the restrictions on open activity; it offered itself as an alternative leadership more genuine in its commitment to the ideals of the October Revolution and more adequate to the tasks of political management. The combination of Trotsky, Zinoviev and Kamenev would surely overturn the brief supremacy of Stalin and Bukharin.

The Politburo launched a counter-offensive at the plenum of the Central Committee and Central Control Commission in July–August 1927. Trotsky was Stalin's main target. 'And how many years', he asked, 'did comrade Trotsky go a-wandering among the Mensheviks?'[1] Molotov reminded everyone that Trotsky had criticized Lenin's policies in the Great War.[2] Trotsky was also accused of having killed party members in the Civil War,[3] and the general charge was that he was an incorrigible anti-Leninist with an entourage of 'fellow travellers' who subverted party policy.[4] Trotsky and Zinoviev retaliated with an assault on Stalin's record. His softness towards the Provisional Government in March 1917 was rehearsed. His encouragement of the Military Opposition in 1918–19 attracted comment as did his unimpressive recent moves in foreign policy.[5] The exchanges were vituperative as Stalin and Trotsky interrupted each other. Trotsky denied having had serious disagreements with Lenin in the Great War.[6] He recounted how the Politburo under Lenin's chairmanship had asked him to draft many early resolutions of the Communist

International.[7] As regards the execution of communists, he declared that the men had been killed as cowards rather than as party members.[8] He adduced the unconditional affidavit given to him by Lenin after the Panteleev controversy.[9]

Trotsky became a full-time curator of his past life. He was given ample opportunity in the Central Committee and the Politburo to say what he wanted, and he exaggerated and selected in order to strengthen his case. Sergo Ordzhonikidze chaired the plenum. When Trotsky objected to the provocative tactics used by his opponents, Ordzhonikidze – not a man known for his restrained temperament – pointed out that Trotsky himself had been offensive in referring to them as 'Thermidorians'.[10] Ordzhoni-kidze had a point. Thermidor was the revolutionary name of the month in 1794 when the ruling Convention had turned on its radical members and their supporters in the French Revolution. Marxists believed that this was when the bourgeoisie triumphed over the lower social classes through a campaign of savage repression starting with the guillotining of Maximilien Robespierre. Trotsky was suggesting that a similar counter-revolution was under way in the USSR, and Ordzhonikidze and Bukharin had a slanging match with him.[11] The abrasiveness of the party polemics outdid even the Brest-Litovsk dispute. The two sides burned the last bridge standing between them. Only a miracle could have reunited them.

The relentless preoccupation with the party's annals had a rational basis. Stalin needed to ruin Trotsky's record as Lenin's great partner if he was to settle political accounts with him. This required him to show his own credentials for revolutionary leadership. He had to be seen challeng-ing and defeating Trotsky face to face. Trotsky was a brilliant debater, so Stalin used the roughest methods of argument to put him down and made a virtue of his own crudity. He also had a genius for taking small items from the past and repackaging them in a distorted fashion. His effrontery was without limits. Already the discussions had a foregone conclusion since the United Opposition's supporters were in a small minority. No doubt remained by the end of the plenum about who was running the Politburo. Earlier there had been talk about the Stalin–Bukharin duumvirate; but Bukharin's contributions to the plenum were of little weight and Stalin was by far and away the principal prosecutor. Trotsky already appreciated this and spoke of the 'Stalinist faction'.[12] He declared that 'the Opposition thinks that Stalin's leadership is making victory [for the Revolution] harder' and added: 'I sum up: [are we] for the socialist fatherland? Yes. For the Stalinist course? No. We want the party to have the opportunity openly to correct the Stalinist course by means of correcting those appalling mistakes which have led to great defeats.'[13] A voice from the floor interjected: 'It's you who needs correcting!'[14]

Trotsky coined the term 'Stalinist centrism' in the course of the proceedings.[15] This was not just an attempt at analysis but a calculated insult, for no Bolshevik liked to be thought as a mere occupant of the middle ground. Trotsky was fighting for his political life. He therefore refrained from his usual vigorous interventions when the plenum discussed the 'control figures' to be inserted into the state economic plan.[16] Even though industrial planning was one of his cherished topics, he stuck to the core of the disagreements between the Politburo and the United Opposition. Tempers ran high. Ordzhonikidze as chairman of the Central Control Commission read out a list of infringements of party discipline by Trotsky and Zinoviev and rejected Trotsky's complaints about unfairness.[17] The United Opposition was rebuked for its factional activity. Trotsky, Kamenev and Zinoviev were called upon to obey the official party line or else face disciplinary action.

Despite identifying Stalin as the dominant figure in the leadership, however, Trotsky felt that Bukharin's ideas constituted the greater threat to the Bolsheviks and their Revolution. If Stalin was a 'centrist', then Bukharin was leader of the Bolshevik right wing – and Trotsky stressed that the fundamental danger came from that direction. His contradictions did not end there. Knowing Bukharin at a personal level, he appealed in private to his decent side for help in eliminating the use of dirty methods against the United Opposition. Trotsky remarked on the anti-Semitic undertones in local party politics. He also pointed to the disciplinary sanctions being applied to workers who expressed sympathy with the Opposition. Trotsky liked a clean fight. He could not believe that Bukharin would approve of Stalin's machinations. Refraining from dictating his letters to a short-hand typist, he hoped to get the matter resolved without anyone outside the central leadership knowing about it.[18] Bukharin declined to help. Stalin's bile spilled out at the Politburo on 8 September; he shouted at Trotsky: 'You're a pathetic individual entirely robbed of any elementary sense of truth, a coward and a bankrupt, a rascal and a villain who has indulged in saying things that absolutely fail to correspond to reality. That's my answer to you.'[19]

Stalin was getting his own back. At a Politburo session a year earlier Trotsky had proclaimed that Stalin had 'finally put forward his candidature for the role of the gravedigger of the party and the revolution'. Stalin had stormed out on that occasion. Alexei Rykov and Jan Rudzutak persuaded the Politburo to issue a formal rebuke to Trotsky. Pyatakov was present at the meeting and understood that Trotsky had gone beyond sensible bounds. Trembling and sweating, he blurted out: 'He'll never forgive you for this, not you or your children or even your grandchildren.' Even the normally compliant Natalya thought her husband needed to receive the warning.[20]

Constantly outvoted in the Politburo and Central Committee, Trotsky called for the entire party to be acquainted with Lenin's testament and accused Stalin of hiding it.[21] Four years had passed before he had had the gumption to make this demand. He saw a chance of proving that Lenin had no respect for Stalin as a potential party leader. In fact the style of leadership favoured by Trotsky, Kamenev and Zinoviev did not please everyone in the United Opposition. Ioffe wrote to Trotsky on 27 August 1927:

> Is not the Opposition beginning to contain the same regime which is established by the Central Committee majority for the entire party and against which we (the Opposition) are conducting so stubborn a struggle? The top tier of the apparatus decides and all the rest simply accept the decisions. Is it tolerable that the thirteen oppositionist members of the Central Committee and the Central Control Commission should have made a declaration in the name of the whole Opposition without preliminary discussion inside the Opposition either about the fact of the declaration's delivery or about its contents?[22]

Ioffe took seriously the case for 'internal party democracy' and wanted Trotsky, Kamenev and Zinoviev to practise what they preached.

But Ioffe did not represent the entire United Opposition. Several of its leaders had made clear that they cared little for democratization if only a leftward shift in economic policy could be secured. They were not committed democrats. The Politburo knew this, and it was easy for Stalin and Bukharin to accuse Trotsky, Zinoviev and Kamenev of opportunism.

Events in any case were moving faster than either Trotsky or Ioffe had expected. The dispute within the Soviet central leadership shifted to the Presidium of the Comintern Executive Committee on 27 September 1927. Trotsky by then was no longer totally in control of himself. He challenged the Presidium from the outset, declaring that if it too wanted to deliver him a reprimand, it could go ahead. He derided the situation in Comintern: 'Now all organizations only implement things; they no longer have the capacity to discuss or decide.' He mocked the mess made by Moscow in China in recent months. He ridiculed the absence of a proper strategy in the United Kingdom; he scoffed at the Politburo for having permitted the Kuomintang to set up an émigré base and school its cadres in the USSR.[23] The October Revolution was no longer secure: 'Stalin's personal misfortune, which is steadily becoming the party's misfortune, lies in the immense discrepancy between Stalin's intellectual resources and the power that the party-state apparatus has concentrated in its hands.'[24] It was typical of Trotsky to be snobbish about Stalin on cultural grounds. He took it for granted that only someone with his own learning could lead the party.

The measures against the United Opposition intensified. Zinoviev and Kamenev had lost their Politburo places in 1925, followed by Trotsky a year later. In October 1927 their membership of the Central Committee was also brought to an end. Trotsky, Zinoviev and Kamenev no longer held posts of any great political authority but continued to campaign for their policies as best they could. The OGPU systematically undermined their efforts. At one meeting addressed by Trotsky a zealous official switched off the lights. Trotsky declared: 'Lenin said that socialism was the soviets plus electrification. Stalin has already suppressed the soviets, now it's the turn of the electricity.'[25] His wit was as sharp as a razor; his historical fairness was less than absolute for the simple reason that he had done as much as anyone to eliminate the freedom of the soviets.

The Politburo put the OGPU on alert when further oppositionist meetings were arranged. Stalin and Bukharin were eager to avoid strikes and street demonstrations. Informers kept the police in touch with the Opposition's plans and broke up its assemblies in Moscow and elsewhere. But the oppositionists refused to desist from their activities. They posted up notices denouncing the ascendant party leadership. They ran off pamphlets on clandestine presses and distributed them among supporters. They remained in contact by word of mouth in each city and went on sending letters and telegrams to each other. They went to factory gates trying to stir up workers against the Politburo. There was really no other way to save themselves politically; and they persuaded themselves that the working class would rally to their cause if only they could explain their case without interference by the Politburo and the OGPU. It is unlikely that workers felt any greater warmth for Trotsky than for Stalin. But there was undoubtedly much discontent with official industrial policy. Disturbances might easily occur in the factory districts and Trotsky and his friends would be able to exploit the situation. Stalin and Bukharin increased the pressure on the OGPU to disrupt the Opposition's activities.

Trotsky, Kamenev and Zinoviev made a fight of it. On 7 November,

exactly ten years since the Bolsheviks had seized power, the usual cele-
bration took place in Leningrad with a big parade. Supporters of
Trotsky, Kamenev and Zinoviev crowded into the former capital in the
hope of exploiting the opportunity to make a public protest against the
country's rulers. This had happened in February 1917 to the Romanovs.
The Politburo instructed the security police to turn out in force. Gangs
of thugs were also employed. According to Trotsky, the Opposition had
no definite plan:

> This demonstration by an accidental confluence of circumstances
> acquired a wholly unexpected direction. Zinoviev and I together with
> several other persons were travelling round the city by car to see the
> scale and mood of the demonstration. Towards the end of our trip
> we were going past the Tauride Palace where platforms had been set
> up for the members of the Central Executive Committee. Our car
> got caught in front of a rank of police; it was impossible to move
> further forward. Before we could work out how to extricate ourselves,
> the commander rushed over to our car and quite without low guile
> offered to escort us to a platform.[26]

Trotsky and Zinoviev were greeted with rapture by their supporters. Police
agents infiltrated the crowd, vainly seeking to stir up disapproval for the
United Opposition. Zinoviev's spirits rose. Trotsky made a more measured
judgement: he knew that the ascendant leadership would make them pay
for their temporary local triumph.

Stalin and Bukharin, exasperated by the truculence of their adver-
saries, organized a vote to expel the leaders and followers of the United
Opposition from the party. The crucial decision was made by the Central
Control Commission under Ordzhonikidze's chairmanship on 14 Nov-
ember 1927; it was formally ratified by the Fifteenth Party Congress in the
following month. The expulsion was a landmark in Bolshevik history.
The party had been ceaselessly disputatious since the October Revolution.
There had been the Left Communists during the controversy over the
Brest-Litovsk treaty. Then came the Military Opposition, the Democratic
Centralists and the Workers' Opposition in the Civil War, and the last two
of these three continued to function under the NEP. At first the Politburo
had bent over backwards to keep the dissenters in the party while disciplin-
ing them. Troublemakers were demoted; sometimes they were sent out of
the way to Ukraine or to a diplomatic post abroad. The same treatment
had been handed out to the Left Opposition and the Leningrad Opposition
in the mid-1920s. The rhetoric of dissent and counter-dissent had always

been bitter. Now Trotsky, Kamenev and Zinoviev were losing their party cards.

News of the Congress's decision was relayed to Trotsky by telephone and the caller was none other than Bukharin. Trotsky was hosting some young French sympathizers at the time. One of them, Gérard Rosenthal, recorded that Bukharin was upset by what had happened: 'Lev Davidovich, they've expelled you. They're mad in the Kremlin. They won't be able to get along without you. Things must not stay like that. You must return.'[27] Bukharin's expression of sympathy lacked complete cogency. He had spoken out vigorously against Trotsky and had supported punitive measures against him. Nevertheless perhaps a glimmering of understanding about the dangers of his partnership with Stalin was starting to enter Bukharin's mind.

Kamenev and Zinoviev lost their stomach for a fight, and Kamenev quickly announced: 'Now that there's no chance of grabbing power from the current ruling group there's only one thing left: to return to the general harness.' In his own eyes he needed to be linked again to his old team of work horses. Zinoviev took more time to come to the same conclusion. Either shortly before or at the Fifteenth Party Congress, which opened on 2 December, he and Kamenev had their very last conversation with Trotsky. All three understood that they were determining the course of their lives for many years ahead. Kamenev and Zinoviev had a terrible row with Trotsky. Zinoviev, according to Trotsky, adopted a pathetic tone and expostulated: 'Vladimir Ilich [Lenin] in his Testament warned that the relations between Trotsky and Stalin could split the party. Think what a responsibility you're taking on yourself!' It was not that Zinoviev had changed his mind about the United Opposition's basic ideas. But he had convinced himself that 'the very sharpness of the apparatus's struggle against us testified that it's a matter not of conjunctural disagreements but of social contradictions.'[28] Kamenev, Zinoviev and their followers had anyhow come late to the oppositional cause and it was not wholly a surprise that they were departing early. The rumour had been circulating immediately after their expulsion from the party that they would capitulate.[29]

The Central Control Commission's decision to hurl them from the party had already turned them into communist pariahs and deprived them of most of their privileges as Soviet politicians. The loss of status was immediate. Abel Enukidze, whom Trotsky had recently insulted,[30] wrote to him ordering his eviction from the Kremlin. The apartment had come with the rank of Politburo membership, and the only surprise was the delay in his loss of residential rights. Trotsky wrote back on 15 November saying he had already departed from his apartment and was staying with his political ally Alexander Beloborodov on Granovski Street.[31] The Beloborodov apartment had been packed out since the Zinovievs took a room there.[32] Trotsky left the Kremlin on his own. His son Sergei was ill and Natalya was nursing him, and Trotsky indicated that they would therefore wait a few days before leaving.[33]

Trotsky held his nerve. He seemed to thrive in adversity, coming alive as the Politburo majority threw him out into the political cold. His friend Adolf Ioffe experienced a very different reaction. His mental instability was chronic and his physical health had drastically deteriorated in recent years; and the troubles of the United Opposition were like a leaden weight upon his mood. It was in this situation that he decided to take his own life but to give Trotsky a piece of his mind before he carried out the deed.[34] For a while the OGPU denied that Ioffe had left behind a suicide note. But the lie was exposed when a copy reached Khristian Rakovski, who passed it to Trotsky.[35] Ioffe had withheld his advice until it was much too late even from a political viewpoint. Yet he wanted to strengthen Trotsky's determination in the current struggle. He informed Trotsky that he was confident that he would soon return to power.[36] Trotsky badly needed to believe that he had a chance of fulfilling this objective. Ioffe in death lent strength to his combative spirit. Trotsky would, if necessary, stand alone as Lenin had so often done. As Kamenev and Zinoviev edged away from him he held firm to his decision. He would rather go down fighting than surrender to the Politburo majority.

It was a sign of the times that permission had to be obtained for a public funeral at the Novodevichi cemetery. The time was fixed for midday so that most people would be at work, but a vast crowd turned out. At the head of the funeral cortège walked Trotsky, accompanied by Ioffe's widow and Khristian Rakovski. Mounted police tried to hold back the less prominent mourners but the crowd linked arms and forced their way through. Rakovski gave the eulogy. Then Trotsky, his bare head covered with flakes of snow, struck a defiant note in memory of his dead comrade: 'Like you, we swear to continue without weakening right to the end under the banners of Marx and Lenin.'[37] He was not to know that this was the last speech he would make on Soviet soil. Political night was falling on Trotsky and the Opposition.

# 39. ALMA-ATA

The winter of 1927–8 was a time of political emergency in the USSR. The origins lay less in the ascendant leadership's difficulties with the Opposition than in the deepening economic disruption. Stocks of wheat and rye ran dangerously low in city warehouses. It was like the scissors crisis of 1923, only worse. Peasants could no longer buy industrial products at what they considered a fair price and there was a shortfall in factory output for the rural market. The measures taken against the more prosperous peasant households in tax year 1925–6 deepened intransigence in the countryside.

The Politburo wanted Trotsky out of the way while it resolved its problems. He was offered the chance of being sent to Astrakhan, on the north-west shores of the Caspian, for a job in economic 'planning work'. This would not be the harshest treatment. But Trotsky wrote to the Central Committee stating that he preferred outright exile to what he regarded as political hypocrisy. He also objected to Astrakhan on health grounds. If he had a choice about where to go, he would opt for Gagra on the Abkhazian coast or Kislovodsk in the north Caucasus.[1] His combativeness annoyed the Politburo leaders. Since he had turned down Astrakhan, they would see how he liked being dispatched to Alma-Ata in Kazakhstan. Genrikh Yagoda, who was deputy OGPU leader at the time, issued the formal order. Neither Yagoda nor his deputy Vladimir Menzhinski would accept Trotsky's call when he telephoned to protest.[2] The full reasons for dispatching him to Soviet central Asia were not recorded, but probably Stalin understood that undesirable comparisons would be made with Nicholas II if he deposited Trotsky in Siberia. Kazakhstan had long snowbound winters and roadless distances but as yet lacked the connotations of forced labour. Trotsky put on a brave face: 'This is better ... I'm not agreeable to dying in a Kremlin bed.'[3]

Natalya was suffering from influenza and was running a high temperature as the family gathered their belongings. Professor Guetier advised postponing her journey. His common decency had earned the admiration of the Lenins and Trotskys, and it did not occur to him that the Politburo would have no regard for Natalya's condition.[4] Faina Yablonskaya, Alexander Beloborodov's wife, phoned oppositionists telling them the news about Alma-Ata.[5] Well-wishers turned up in Granovski Street with flowers, sweets, books, warm clothes and endless embraces.[6] Trotsky and Natalya appreciated the kindness but needed to get on with their preparations, and working out how to get his bulky personal archive into their trunks.

The OGPU assured the Trotskys that they would not be travelling in the near future. One of Trotsky's former bodyguards, a certain Barychkin, turned up on official duty. He had the impertinence – as Trotsky saw it – to omit to remove his hat. When rebuked, he retreated with 'the look of a whipped dog'.[7] Without warning, on 16 January 1928 Trotsky was told to get ready to be escorted to Kazan Station from where he would be travelling to Alma-Ata. News of what was happening reached supporters of the Opposition, and a crowd of thousands gathered at Kazan Station. Messages about the scene reached the Beloborodovs from young, enthusiastic oppositionists and then from Khristian Rakovski.[8] As a precaution the OGPU avoided conveying the Trotsky family directly to the station. Any riot might turn into a serious political disturbance. Instead the OGPU ferried the group to the Yaroslavl Station in north-central Moscow. From there they were to be taken by train to the Kazan Station and secretly bundled into their waiting carriage.[9] The crowd had no inkling of the ruse. Trotsky's suitcases were heaped by the side of the last carriage where his hunting dog was waiting patiently; the engine was blowing steam but the Trotskys' carriage, with its windows covered with white curtains, was empty. The engine driver turned up but he too was unaware of what was planned. Meanwhile the nearby streets were filling with angry protesters. Posters of Trotsky were stuck up. It looked as if the situation might get out of hand.[10]

Suddenly the OGPU team arrived at the station with Trotsky. They were carrying him since he had made it clear that he would not come voluntarily. The crowd was unaware of what was happening and Trotsky's sons decided to intervene. Lëva was twenty and Sergei eighteen; both were strapping fellows. When Lëva tried to raise a hue and cry Barychkin reached across and put his hand over Lëva's mouth. Sergei, despite wanting nothing to do with politics and planning to stay behind quietly in Moscow, punched Barychkin in the face.[11] His sense of family ties and personal dignity had made him lose his temper. Acting with disciplined restraint, the OGPU succeeded in loading their human cargo in secret. Trotsky, Natalya, Lëva and Igor Poznanski sat in the curtained carriage without anyone knowing they were there. Suddenly at 11 p.m. the engine shunted forward. The crowd at last sensed what had happened. Realizing that there was going to be no inspiring speech from their leader, many of his adherents jumped on to the side of the carriage. Others ran down the platform. But the Kremlin's trick worked and the train quickly disappeared from sight. Voices were raised in favour of starting up a political demonstration even though it was the middle of the night. The idea was to march on the Kremlin. But veteran oppositionists suspected that the OGPU were engaged in a provocation. If a demonstration took place, there would be public disorder. This would provide the ascendant party leadership with material for propaganda against the Opposition. Discretion prevailed and the protesters dispersed quietly to their homes.[12]

As the train proceeded to Ryazan and then to Samara the Trotskys complained about not having the appropriate clothing with them. The situation was remedied before the journey was resumed. They reached Kazakhstan within a few days, having left Russia far behind. At Kzyl-Orda a check was made on them and their conditions by a certain Belski, who headed OGPU operations in central Asia. He was polite but uncommunicative. The Trotskys took their meals in their carriage, finding their fellow passengers uncongenial – or perhaps they needed privacy to talk things over. Natalya shook off her influenza. The fact that her husband was joking and looking on the bright side cheered her up too. He read Marx in German. Planning ahead, he hoped to subsist in Alma-Ata by translating some of these works.[13] The train steadily proceeded as far as Pishpek. Then the last stage of the trip to Alma-Ata was undertaken with horse-drawn carts across the Ala-Too mountains. By then it was Trotsky who was running a temperature, but no respite was permitted.[14] The Trotskys were getting used to being ordered about. They were no longer rulers or even party members but, in the eyes of officialdom, political offenders.

They reached Alma-Ata on the ninth day of their journey from Moscow. The little group and their escort traversed the last stage in a car driven by a driver whose eagerness for speed alarmed his passengers. (He had previously driven armoured cars and evidently relished the opportunity to speed along in a civilian vehicle.) There was snow on the ground. It was 25 January.[15]

As he settled in Alma-Ata, Trotsky fondly imagined that the fate of the Opposition remained at the top of the Politburo's agenda. By then he was lamentably out of touch with events. The leadership's urgent need was to resolve the problem of food supplies. One possibility would have been to relieve the pressure on the kulaks and induce them to trade their cereal stocks. Time was not on the leadership's side. An emergency which had suddenly arisen had to be dealt with rapidly. Stalin decided to take a personal initiative. He did this with stealth. In January 1928 he set off on an inspection of the Urals and west Siberia. This was a region where cereal surpluses had been normal in the past. The recent harvest had not been affected by bad weather. Stalin was confident he would find plenty of grain there – and he assumed that kulaks were the culprits hoarding it. He had resolved to be ruthless with local party and government officials. A capacity to exert pressure was one of his special attributes. Unobserved by his Politburo comrades, he mobilized urban squads. He also offered rewards to poor rural inhabitants willing to point out where the better-off households might have hidden their stocks. Freight trains were filled with wheat and rye seized from the owners. Stalin felt he had done his duty. The immediate threat of hunger in the cities was removed.

The assault on the 'hoarders' severed the frayed cords of rural trust in the Bolsheviks. The peasantry as a whole was determined to hold on to its grain. When cereal stocks fell to a dangerous level in spring 1928, Stalin's former ally Bukharin persuaded the Politburo to adopt remedial measures. These included cutting the prices of industrial goods and importing cheap foreign products. The hope was that peasants would revert to marketing their produce in a voluntary fashion. When this failed to rectify the problem Stalin resumed the political offensive. Already he and the Politburo had introduced a five-year plan for the rapid expansion of industry. Factories were being seized and taken into governmental ownership. Gosplan, the central state planning agency, was instructed to draw up an agenda to prioritize the output of iron, steel and machine-tools. The USSR was set to undergo comprehensive industrialization. The accompaniment to this process would be a 'cultural revolution'. A mass literacy campaign was initiated. Schools and training institutes prolifer-ated. Rapid promotion was offered to talented workers and peasants. Potential points of resistance were attacked. Religious persecution was intensified and there were arrests of nationalists throughout the Soviet Union.

The NEP had been broken. An entire phase of the October Revolution had suddenly come to an end, and the Politburo reinforced the trans-formation across the range of official policies. Stalin had yet to crush Bukharin. The economic troubles caused by violent grain expropriations compelled him to make concessions in the summer months. At least he was free from having to answer Trotsky in public. Stalin and his supporters at the Central Committee plenum took every opportunity to say how they had disproved all the Opposition's claims and predictions. The ascendant party leadership had shown its commitment to radical measures. Trotsky's sniping commentaries in the mid-1920s were rehearsed in his absence and condemned.[16]

Cut off from his usual channels of confidential information, Trotsky wrote almost nothing about this. This was not the only cause of his silence. His daily routine was in turmoil. The family had grown accustomed to the rhythms of a Kremlin existence, and even while staying with the Beloborodovs they had lived in some ease. Now they had to fend for themselves. Natalya had lost the habit of buying provisions and found that the local tradesmen were overcharging her. She quickly adapted, as she always did, but her business with domestic tasks limited the time available to help her husband politically.[17] Sermuks and Butov had tried to join Poznanski in Alma-Ata as Trotsky's assistants. All three were denied official permission to stay. The authorities expected this would reduce Trotsky to political inactivity, but they had reckoned without the contribution of young Lëva, who came into his own as a one-man administrative apparatus.[18] The priority for him and his father was to pick up the threads of the Opposition. Lëva had married young and already had a wife, Anna Ryabukhina, and a baby son whom they named Lev and knew inside the family as Lyulik. Politics, though, now took precedence in Lëva's thoughts. Trotsky was permitted to use the normal postal service. His monthly stipend of fifty rubles and his bank account financed a regular correspondence, and the daily mail usually included ten to fifteen letters from elsewhere in the USSR.[19] His address book shows that he kept in contact with scores of exiled supporters; he updated it as individuals were shifted from place to place.[20] This is not to say that the post was rapid. Trotsky complained that it took weeks for things to be delivered to him.

He was not being put into complete isolation. He enjoyed a correspondence of politics and banter with Khristian Rakovski, his last remaining friend, and their dozens of letters to each other kept up their morale. Rakovski, unlike Trotsky, had accepted a province-level post in economic planning in Astrakhan. The job made few demands on him and he spent a lot of his time reading Charles Dickens and Isaac Babel as well as researching the ideas of the French nineteenth-century socialist Saint-Simon. Rakovski joked about his distance from civilization. Aristotle, he claimed, had designated the Kara-Bogaz Gulf on the mid-eastern coast of the Caspian as the 'start of the underworld'.[21]

Natalya wrote to their supporters on Trotsky's behalf and the Opposition made an announcement. The family supposedly had inadequate access to daily provisions. What is more, Trotsky's intestinal problems were said to have reacted badly to the insanitary conditions in Alma-Ata where malaria had 'entered his organism' and gout was a constant torment – and there was no competent doctor he could turn to. The Opposition asked its supporters to call upon the 'workers' to demand Trotsky's return to Moscow.[22] This was a caricature. The family, as Natalya's notebooks demonstrate, were far from living in squalor.[23] Trotsky even acquired a local secretary, and although he had to assume she was reporting to the OGPU, she carried out her typing duties satisfactorily. It is true that there was much malaria in the city. When Trotsky and Natalya fell victim to malaria they obtained quinine from their son Sergei in Moscow, and this relieved the symptoms at least in Trotsky's case.[24] They could visit the public library and borrow books and back numbers of national newspapers. Among Trotsky's pleasures was to peruse a volume of reproductions of the Mexican muralist painter Diego Rivera which he found in the library; he admired their combination of 'courage' and 'tenderness'.[25]

Trotsky and Lëva went on hunting trips with guns and dogs and came back laden with pheasant, mountain fowl, quail or pigeon. OGPU men accompanied them on an expedition to the salty steppes which lasted several weeks when they slept under the stars or in the huts of the local Kirgiz. They rode after their quarry on the backs of camels.[26] In the summer the family of three rented a reed-thatched house from a peasant fruit-grower up on the nearby hills with a wonderful view of the snow-capped mountains at the end of the Tyan-Shan range. They picked apples and pears for the table; Natalya made jam.[27]

In June 1928 their tranquillity was broken by news from Moscow: Nina Bronstein had died of tuberculosis. Trotsky was working on his critique of the programme of the Comintern's Fifth Congress at the time. He broke off and went into the garden, calling Natalya to join him. They sat on the grass remembering and grieving for Nina. Trotsky moaned: 'I'm so, so sorry for the girl!' It was his first experience of losing a child and he took it badly.[28] Nina, his younger daughter, had been suffering from tuberculosis for several years. She left behind her husband Man Nevelson and their two children Lev and Volina. Nina and Man were supporters of the Opposition, and Man could expect no favours from the Soviet elite in the light of the deportation of Trotsky and other leading critics of the Politburo. Trotsky had spent little time with Nina in recent years; if he felt a pang of guilt when he heard of her death he kept quiet about it. There was anyway no question of the Trotskys returning for

Nina's funeral. Not for the first or last time, Alexandra Bronstein had to cope on her own as a parent. It was something she was long accustomed to – and Trotsky saw no reason why things should not always be like this.

He had plenty on his plate as he concentrated on trying to organize political resistance to Stalin's growing power. He had to cope against a background of defections. News came through that Yuri Pyatakov had surrendered to Stalin and recanted his oppositionist ideas. Trotsky affected indifference. He had often predicted – to Pyatakov's face – that he would turn up in the office even if Bonaparte himself were in power. Trotsky pronounced him 'politically finished'.[29] Serebryakov went the same way as Pyatakov. None of them had been 'Zinovievites'; they had been associates of Trotsky since the days of the Left Opposition. They now saw that Stalin was introducing a lot of the big economic changes which the Opposition had been advocating throughout the 1920s. They had wanted faster industrial growth and a stronger commitment to collective forms of farming; they had yearned for the strengthening of central state planning for the economy. They made their peace with Stalin even though he offered no concessions to their agenda of internal party democracy. Trotsky was angry with the defectors but he refused to be depressed. As he saw it, individual leaders often betrayed their principles. The 'masses' were the sole factor in history which genuinely counted for him. Far from making his peace with Stalin, Trotsky urged an intensified struggle. He expected to be the one who gave the lead. Not everyone took this for granted. He and Preobrazhenski exchanged lengthy messages on strategy, and this plunged them into a dispute about Soviet foreign policy under the NEP. Trotsky's contribution was less than temperate. Even in exile he had no sensitivity to the requirements of leadership. Preobrazhenski objected to his peremptory commentary, declaring that he was ruining the chances of productive discussion in 'our exile commune'.[30]

Kamenev and Zinoviev were readmitted to the party in June 1928; but, as Trotsky learned, Kamenev was not resigned to defeat and next month discussed secretly with Bukharin what to do about Stalin. In September Kamenev met with supporters of Trotsky in Moscow. Agreeing now with Trotsky's assessment of the political situation, he said Stalin had brought the country to the edge of perdition. He also criticized Trotsky as being stubborn and inflexible. The way to return to power was to penetrate the party and the government even at the price of public recantation. Trotsky by implication should do the same and cease castigating people for their 'capitulation'.[31] Zinoviev had similar thoughts and pondered how to put together a 'grand coalition' of Bukharin, Kamenev,

Trotsky and himself against Stalin inside a renovated Politburo.[32] When Kamenev's comments were relayed to Alma-Ata,[33] Trotsky scoffed at their mixture of compromise and manoeuvre.

But at last he was beginning to take the measure of Stalin. In October 1928 when fellow exiles elsewhere in the USSR wrote that they wanted to intensify their protests, he discouraged them. They needed to understand that hunger strikes thousands of miles from Moscow would have no serious impact.[34] But this was just a tactical objection, for he remained recalcitrant in urging the need for the struggle against the Kremlin to be maintained. His intransigence annoyed and alarmed the Politburo majority as its own dispute with Bukharin continued. By continuing to contact and organize his followers, Trotsky remained a menace even in far-distant Alma-Ata. The OGPU came to him on 16 December 1928 and delivered an oral ultimatum: either he desisted from oppositional activity and accepted his political defeat or else the terms of his exile would be altered and he would be sent to a more isolated place of confinement. Trotsky drafted a letter to his followers that he would never surrender to Stalin. He refused to give up what he had been doing for thirty-two years. His 'whole conscious life' had been dedicated to politics and he had no intention of bowing to threats by the police.[35]

The Politburo took over a month to react and discussed the matter more than once. Stalin wanted to deport Trotsky from the USSR. Bukharin, Rykov and Tomski opposed this. But Stalin persisted and on 7 January 1929 he got his way. The decision was taken by a majority to expel Trotsky for 'anti-Soviet work'.[36] There was almost unanimous support for Stalin's action among opponents of those like Bukharin who were now denounced as Rightists. The exception was Sergei Syrtsov who led the party in Siberia – and it was not long before he was rebuked for his audacity.[37]

On 20 January OGPU officer Volynski appeared with armed support and a pair of pointers to announce and carry out the decision. Trotsky was charged with having formed an illegal anti-Soviet party, with being engaged in counter-revolutionary activity and with organizing violent struggle against the authorities. A decree had been passed to expel him from the USSR. Trotsky was requested to confirm his acquaintance with what was being ordered. He signed the form, adding that he was taking cognizance of a decree which was 'criminal in essence and illegal in form'.[38] The house was full of noise and bustle. Trotsky acknowledged that the OGPU men behaved correctly towards him and the family. He had felt no premonition of this outcome: he had probably assumed that, if his punishment was to be increased, he would be sent deeper into central Asia or Siberia. The family packed feverishly so as to be ready, as instructed, early on 22 January. In the middle of winter it was not going to be an easy journey, and all Trotsky's queries about which country he was being sent to were met with a blank response. The truth was that Volynski did not yet know.

When the day came the Trotskys got into a bus which took them up the Kurdai mountain range. The snowdrifts on the summit proved impassable even after a tractor was brought to help. The family were transferred to sleighs. It took seven hours to move nearly twenty miles. Eventually the party descended by car to Pishpek where they were put on a train which then became stuck on a branch line for several days. Trotsky read a book by Anatole France as well as the Russian liberal Vasili Klyuchevsky's classic history of Russia; he also played chess.[39]

Soon they reached what they took to be Kursk province – they were still being kept in the dark about what was happening.[40] At one of their frequent halts Trotsky discovered that the German government had refused to give him the right of residence. The Soviet authorities approached the Turkish government and received a positive response. When Trotsky was told about the plan he exploded with anger and said he would not comply. OGPU officer Bulanov telegraphed to Moscow for consultations and further instructions. The basic plan for deportation to Turkey was confirmed. The train carrying the Trotskys was directed south to Odessa where, still protesting, Trotsky was bundled aboard the steam-ship *Ilich* together with Natalya and Lëva. Trotsky stood majestically by the handrail as they left port. Dressed in a Red Army greatcoat, he waved his military cap in salute and enabled a photographer on board to catch his gesture on camera. The vessel crossed the Black Sea and arrived in Istanbul on 22 February. Apart from OGPU agents the Trotskys were the only passengers as the *Ilich* pulled alongside the quay at Büyük-Dere. Trotsky handed over a letter for the attention of President Mustapha Kemal, explaining that he had not arrived on Turkish soil by his own volition.[41]

A dozen years in active Russian politics were suddenly brought to an end. The Opposition had gone down to defeat. Trotsky, hero of the October Revolution and Civil War, had been brought low. He disguised his confusion with a display of dignity. He could hardly believe that Stalin had emerged as the USSR's supreme leader. He could not imagine a life in permanent separation from revolutionary Russia. Throughout the journey to Turkey he tried to keep up his spirits and give encouragement to his family and the diminishing band of his active followers. Still aged only forty-nine, he was determined to keep up the fight. In his eyes only the Opposition had the ideas which could save the Soviet order from unremitting degeneration.

# PART FOUR

# 1929–1940

# 40. BÜYÜKADA

Turkey's authorities laid down confidential conditions for granting asylum to Trotsky. Moscow had to give an assurance that no attempt would be made to assassinate him on Turkish soil. They also made demands upon Trotsky himself. He had to refrain from interfering in local politics and publish nothing inside the country. Trotsky had fears of his own. Around four thousand White émigrés were living in Turkey and he was worried that an Imperial army veteran might try to kill him. Mustapha Kemal's government was alert to this danger and deported fifty suspects. Everything was done to provide Mr Leon Sedov, Trotsky's new alias outside the USSR, with physical security.[1]

The Trotskys on arrival stayed at the Soviet consulate in Istanbul. This was a temporary arrangement so as to enable the family to search for a more permanent abode. Their first move was to the Tokatliyan Hotel. Trotsky gave an interview to a Turkish newspaper. He also visited the city's historical sites and defied the advice of the police by returning to the hotel on foot. His one slight concession to prudence was to shave off his beard and moustache.[2] After a brief move to a house in the Şişli district he was persuaded that considerations of security required him to move out of the capital. Acting on advice from the authorities, he agreed to live on Büyükada ('Big Island') where a suitable house had fallen vacant. Büyükada, off the south-eastern shore of Istanbul, was the largest of the Princes' Islands (or Prinkipo) in the Sea of Marmara and was their administrative centre. It was where Byzantine emperors and Ottoman sultans had confined their rivals. Kemal's government simply wanted Trotsky to be safe from physical attack and the ferry trip was the sole means of regular transport between the island and the capital. Istanbul was only half an hour away and the postal service was an efficient one: this was very important for Trotsky. Büyükada was the best available option.

The family rented Izzet Pasha, one of the rambling villas taken by wealthy families of Istanbul looking for verdant scenery, fresh air and sunshine. No motorized vehicles were allowed on the island. There was a full range of shops and services – and if the inhabitants wanted they could fish for their food directly off the coast. Izzet Pasha was not in the finest condition of upkeep. But its grounds looked over the sea from a high cliff which offered a splendid vista and meant that the house did not need guarding on the seaward side. Trotsky anyway benefited from round-the-clock protection by the local police.

His health was not perfect: he was troubled by colitis and gout and, like Natalya, he still had not shaken off the effects of malaria picked up in Alma-Ata.[3] But he was fit enough to go on working – he had no other option because his finances depended upon his income from publishers in Europe and North America. The Soviet authorities had equipped him with funds to the value of US$1,500 to facilitate his settling abroad.[4] Such a grant would soon become unimaginable. But Stalin until the mid-1930s worried about what the world thought about how he treated political enemies – and even then he thought it wise to trump up charges of treason against them. Trotsky's money was anyway going to run out fast. According to Natalya, outgoings from the household amounted to roughly US$1,000 monthly; but a secretary later reckoned that the average expenditure in reality was nearer to US$1,500.[5]

Trotsky had a strict routine. He awoke early, usually at four or five o'clock, and put on a blue sweater and a pair of espadrilles before pacing up and down the corridors deep in thought. Everyone heard him on the upper floor.[6] He preferred to commence the day as if in solitary confinement. After breakfast he resumed interaction with others to the extent of dictating correspondence and articles. After a break for lunch he took a siesta and then restarted work in the late afternoon. Meals were communal, and it would be then – especially at dinner – that the household would discuss public affairs. Trotsky encouraged gentle conversation. Family and entourage lived frugally; their only self-indulgence was the international postal service. Nothing was spent on décor.[7] At least one visitor felt that Trotsky and Natalya could have done more to brighten up their surroundings.[8] This idea said as much about the observer as about the observed. Trotsky enjoyed the arts when he had free time, but he was functioning as a full-time writer, politician and fund-raiser. His preoccupation was with the prospects for revolution in Russia and elsewhere.

Natalya and their son Lëva helped Trotsky to maintain a political office. Trotsky suggested that Stalin had assumed this would be a labour beyond their joint capacity.[9] If this was Stalin's calculation he was disappointed. Trotsky created a *Byulleten oppozitsii* ('Bulletin of the Opposition') whose first issue was published in Paris in July 1929 with a print run of around two thousand copies.[10] As Trotsky stipulated, it was printed in octavo size. A small font was selected so as to economize on paper costs. Half the output, though, was printed on expensive thin paper so as to facilitate clandestine carriage to the USSR. The masthead and layout were chosen to distinguish the *Byulleten oppozitsii* from the émigré Menshevik *Sotsialisticheski vestnik* ('Socialist Herald'). Still hoping to win over Soviet officials, Trotsky gave instructions for issues to be sold at kiosks near Soviet embassies and trade missions.[11] He himself wrote most of the articles while Lëva handled the administrative work and Natalya ran the household. The Trotskys were a family on crusade.

They needed support from public opinion in the West. The *Byulleten oppozitsii* denounced German ministers for refusing to honour 'the democratic right of shelter'. He requested, as a minimum, the opportunity to stay at a spa in Germany while consulting doctors about his health. When this was refused Trotsky described Germany's reply as offering him 'the right of the graveyard'. He appealed to lawyer and left-wing social-democrat Kurt Rosenfeld to represent his interests and was furious when Rosenfeld declined.[12] Trotsky's moral outrage chimed oddly with his espousal of scientific, unsentimental Marxism. He had matchless self-righteousness. He was someone who had supplied a rationale for withholding rights from individuals and groups in Soviet Russia. He had made a career as advocate and practitioner of dictatorship. He had regularly insulted democrats and mocked democracy. He had scorned the rule of law. He had preached the desirability of subverting the surviving liberal democracies in Europe, and he had not changed his mind after being deported from the USSR. Trotsky was unwilling to accept that his fanaticism might have consequences: he expected German democracy to welcome him as its exterminator.

Young Trotskyists travelled to Büyükada and supplemented the Turkish police protection. Trotsky was also in need of assistants with political experience of the non-Stalinist far left in Europe. His earliest helpmate was the Czech communist leftist Jan Frankel, who understood several European languages and helped him with the bulging pile of correspondence. He acted as Trotsky's personal bodyguard. He was a fluent Turkish-speaker and dealt with the island's policemen and with the governmental agencies in Istanbul. Aged twenty-three in 1929, he worked himself to the point of exhaustion.[13] Frankel, like everyone in the entourage, carried a pistol. Even Natalya was at the ready to shoot down assailants.[14] Other young sympathizers arrived such as Pierre Naville, Denise Naville and

Gérard Rosenthal from France. Raymond Molinier and his wife Jeanne (née Martin des Pallières) stayed too. They had made the trip to learn from their hero and took notes as he spoke. Trotsky propounded a demanding credo: 'It's useless thinking of making revolution with men for whom their professional life comes first, then their family life and finally the revolution if there's any time left over.'[15]

One thing he could not do without was a secretary qualified to take down dictation. He hired Maria Pevzner, an excellent short-hand typist but not his political follower. (Was she an agent of the OGPU? We still do not know.) She had to be dismissed when the Trotskys ran out of money. The problem was permanently solved only in 1933 when a committed adherent of the Opposition, Sara Weber, turned up in Büyükada. Lëva had vetted her and vouched for her political sincerity. Trotsky embraced her, and she and Natalya – 'a bit haltingly' – exchanged kisses.[16] It was unusual for him to put his arms around a stranger. Despite liking everyone to observe Russian middle-class politesse, he was making an effort in order to make her and her skills welcome. Nobody could address remarks to Trotsky except as 'Lev Davidovich' – he kept his adherents at a social distance. Trotsky's wife by contrast was Natalya to all residents.[17]

Every few days the household went out fishing or hunting. With them was their dog Tosca, a mongrel with pointers in her ancestry. Tosca, however, had also inherited the instincts of her other forebears and liked to wander into any flock of birds and scatter them before Trotsky could take aim.[18] Marine fishing became the most reliable way of supplementing their diet. A Greek fisherman, Charalambos, assisted as they rowed out from the shore and cast their net. Rosenthal recalled:

> We dropped a line fitted with forty odd hooks into the sea. We always brought it back weighed down with lots of mackerel. Sometimes we hung down a net at several lengths from the shoreline. We returned to the coast to gather up some big stones. We came back to throw them into the sea to chase the fish into the nets. Trotsky showed incredible zeal during these exertions. He ran, he got excited and agitated, he recklessly expended his energies. In his eyes, I was lacking in ardour: 'Ah, comrade Gérard, if you do not bombard the bourgeoisie more vigorously it will still have delightful days ahead!'[19]

Trotsky ignored the pleadings of his household for him to avoid risks. Whatever he was doing, he applied an exceptional intensity of effort.

Lëva bridled at the constrictions of life on the island. In August 1929 he had applied, unsuccessfully, for permission to return to the USSR –

he stressed that he had left the country only temporarily and that his young family lived in Moscow.[20] He had not yet completed his education and it was his ambition to train as an engineer. Moscow turned down the request. Lëva decided that if he could not go back to resume his life in the Soviet capital it made sense to move to Germany and study in the Technische Höchschule in Berlin.

There was a further reason why Lëva arrived at this conclusion. He was a young man with a liking for women and they in turn found him attractive. Jeanne Martin took a fancy to him. Soon they were sleeping together and became a permanent couple. Although Raymond Molinier did not obstruct the relationship both Lëva and Jeanne wanted relief from the claustrophobic regime on the island. Trotsky endorsed the idea for reasons of his own. Now that he had a group of foreign assistants he could cope without his son's presence on Büyükada. What is more, Trotsky aimed to enhance his influence in Germany and turn Berlin into the operational base for the *Byulleten oppozitsii* as well as an International Secretariat. Lëva planned to combine his academic studies with political work. He was his father's right-hand man. He understood Trotsky's purposes better than anyone and was an effective organizer. He would be able to supervise Trotsky's affairs in the heart of Europe and make direct links with German sympathizers. There was also the hope that travellers from Russia would make contact. Lëva left Istanbul with his French partner on 18 February 1931.[21]

The son was patient with a father who carped at everything – even the slight misspelling of 'Turkey' in a postcard address earned a tetchy rebuke.[22] There was never any easing of the pressure. Trotsky demanded total devotion to the production of perfect copy. Publication proceeded smoothly. There was only one thing Trotsky had not allowed for. Lëva still felt a longing for Russia and dreamed again of applying to return. Whether he would have returned to his wife Anna or taken Jeanne with him to Moscow is unclear. His relationship with Jeanne was complicated by Molinier's attempt to resume his marriage with Jeanne;[23] and Lëva himself had not seen his son Lyulik since 1929 – and perhaps he also hoped to see Anna. When he mentioned his complicated considerations to his mother in April 1931 she immediately told Trotsky, who wrote: 'You're writing to Mama that you're having thoughts about a return. I'd regard this, chum [*druzhishche*], as a big mistake in every respect. For me personally – from the viewpoint of work and plans for the future – this would be a big blow.'[24] Trotsky needed Lëva's help with finishing his book of the moment. His advice, or rather his plea, to Lëva was for him to apply for an extension of his *Freudenpass* to stay in Germany.[25] Lëva dutifully backed down. If he had followed his inclination it is hard to see how Trotsky's frail international operation in Europe would have survived at that time.

Trotsky kept contact with his offspring in the USSR. Telegrams frequently came through to him from his daughter Zina and his son Sergei. He replied by the same method. Although the contents of messages reaching him were poorly transliterated by the Turkish postal service they kept him abreast of developments in the family.[26]

Zina had a chronic complaint which was diagnosed as the presence of air or gas in the pleural cavities of both lungs. She claimed to feel a lot better and telegraphed her intention to stay in Sukhum till May 1929.[27] Her health was not in fact improving. Further telegrams were exchanged, and Trotsky and Natalya saw no alternative to receiving her in Turkey. He sent a message in October 1930 telling her to ask the People's Commissariat for Internal Affairs for permission to leave for Istanbul. He sent the same request in her name to the same institution.[28] Zina complied and left the USSR to seek the necessary medical assistance after handing her son Seva to the care of her mother Alexandra. At first she was happy in being reunited with Trotsky. She also got on well with her stepmother who had lengthy conversations with her.[29] The blond-haired, plump-cheeked Seva followed her to Turkey and went to a private school where the pupils spoke French (which he had to learn from scratch). He was not keen on the household cuisine and had to be coaxed into eating his food, thus becoming the centre of attention at meal times. At any rate Zina perked up emotionally, though she found the Turkish heat hard to bear.[30]

She adored her father and longed to live within the perimeter of his respect and affection.[31] She aspired to joining in with his political work, but this was a step too far for Trotsky. If she was to carry out serious tasks, Zina would need to be able to run up and down the stairs. According to Natalya, he did not think her health would stand the pressure.[32] Zina tried to prove herself by writing an article, but Trotsky disliked its tone and tactfully rejected it for publication.[33] Natalya's account was loyal to her husband and his memory. She admitted, however, that he had a preoccupation with punctilious discharge of duties, errands and commands.[34] His emotional intelligence was always circumscribed by his personal and political interests. Otherwise he would have found something for Zina to do that did not make her wheeze or get stressed. Natalya continued to talk patiently with her but it was Trotsky who would have made the difference.

Her difficulties were not exclusively physical in nature. This was not openly discussed until 1 March 1931 when a huge fire took place at Izzet Pasha. The wooden structure produced an instant blaze. The household lost nearly all its valuables, including watches, revolvers, shoes and hats. Trotsky in his dressing gown and slippers had not had time to save his library and it was nearly two hours before the Istanbul fire brigade arrived. By then it was too late. As it was, Natalya injured her leg in rushing from the blaze and Trotsky lost nearly all the books he had brought from the USSR. This was a terrible blow for him since they were full of marginal annotations which he had planned to use in future works. But his personal archive survived and this was crucial because its documents were among his weapons in the struggle against the ascendant party leadership; he never ceased stressing that the roots of current difficulties in the USSR lay in policies and practices nurtured by Stalin over many years. The draft of his *History of the Russian Revolution* also escaped the flames: Frankel had rescued it from the burning building – everyone understood that the household's finances depended on that work being published without delay.[35]

Strong suspicion fell upon Zina for having started the conflagration. Her mental ill health was by then unmistakable and there had already been a couple of unexplained fires in the house since her arrival. The homeless Trotskys took refuge in a rented house on the mainland. The new place was in Kadıköy to the south-west of Istanbul and was selected for its seaside position such as Izzet Pasha had commanded. The house was two storeys high and in an even more dilapidated condition than the previous one. Trotsky and Natalya occupied the upper storey. Frankel had the room below near the dining room and kitchen. A cook, a fisherman and a pair of policemen lived elsewhere in the grounds.[36]

Zina was dispatched to Berlin in October 1931 to be treated for the problem with her lung. In the same month Albert Glotzer, an American Trotskyist, turned up to relieve the pressure on Frankel. Glotzer did not seem the ideal assistant for the Old Man. He smoked, could speak neither Russian nor German and by his own admission was poorly informed about Soviet politics. He also turned up at a time when Trotsky was in the last phase of writing his *History of the Russian Revolution* and was loath to be distracted.[37] Trotsky prohibited smoking in the rooms he used but made an exception for Glotzer on his first day with them, even scrounging a cigarette for him from a Turkish fisherman. Thereafter Glotzer had to follow the rules of the house.[38] Perhaps unsurprisingly Glotzer stayed only a month.[39] But in October 1932 there arrived the most remarkable of all Trotsky's aides. This was Jean van Heijenoort. The

Communist League in Paris had intended to send Yves Craipeau but decided that Heijenoort had superior linguistic skills, and these were essential for anyone planning to act in secretarial and organizational capacities. (Craipeau was anyway reluctant to abandon 'action amid the masses'.)[40]

Meanwhile Zina wrote pitiably to Trotsky from Germany. Initially he showed little sympathy; he was more worried about the strain on Natalya, who had to look after Seva until Zina found a Berlin apartment for him and herself. Zina's letters became more and more distressing and the writing of them, at least in Natalya's opinion, was only exacerbating her condition.[41] At last Trotsky began to appreciate the sinister nature of his daughter's condition. She was reaching the edge of mental disintegration.

When told that his daughter had schizophrenia, he was shaken; but, like most people in the 1930s, he had little idea about the nature of the illness.[42] He told his son Lëva about Zina's letters. She wanted to come back to Turkey as her father's 'ally' but he still regarded such a proposal as unfeasible. When the doctors wanted her to return to Russia she refused to take their advice. Trotsky supported the doctors, saying that a stay in a Russian resort would do her good whereas a German one would be 'lethal'. He sent a message to Alexandra Bronstein explaining the situation. Trotsky claimed that he could not properly help Zina unless and until she followed the medical advice, and he asked Lëva to point out to her that her defiance was damaging the health of her relatives. He added that if she failed to comply with his wishes he would effect 'a complete and final break' with her.[43] A more inappropriate way of handling a schizophrenic can scarcely be imagined. It is not known whether Lëva did as he had been asked. It seems unlikely since he was a sensible, caring person. Zina's condition continued to worsen. On 5 January 1933 she could stand it no longer and gassed herself. News of her suicide arrived in Büyükada next day. Trotsky coped with the tragedy by blaming everything on Stalin and his treatment of her.[44]

This accusation, frequently repeated in accounts of Trotsky, was ill aimed. Zina had spent all the time she had wanted in Sukhum; it had been Trotsky who summoned her abroad and not Stalin who had deported her – and it had been Trotsky with whom she wanted to live. Trotsky's attempt to politicize the death was not his finest moment.

Nevertheless he was very upset. Two days passed before he felt able to write to Alexandra Bronstein and tell her: 'Zinushka is no longer alive.' He added: 'I turned to wood.' There followed a misleading account of Zina's travails abroad. He said that he and Natalya had originally supposed that her main problem was tuberculosis. When she transferred to Berlin, the neuropathologists concluded that her greatest need was for 'husband, family, work, duties'. He omitted to mention how much grief had come to Zina through her troubled relationship with him. He ended tenderly, expressing himself like a Homeric bard: 'I strongly, strongly embrace your grey head and mix my tears with yours.'[45] Alexandra did little to spare his feelings in her reply on 31 August. She wanted to know the entire story. Why had he not alerted her to his worries about Zina's mental condition? She already knew, without Trotsky telling her, that some kind of conflict with him had been oppressing their daughter. Zina had written: 'It's sad that I won't be able to go back to Papa any more: you know how I've "adored" him since the day I was born. But now our relations have been definitively wrecked. That's the reason I've fallen ill.' Alexandra had tried to cheer her up, but Trotsky had reserved his attention only for her physical plight; he had ignored the fact that 'she was an adult developed individual' who needed him to interact with her. He had let Zina down badly.[46]

This was a devastating and accurate indictment. Alexandra lightened it somewhat by confessing to sharing his difficulty in opening herself up to others; and she apologized for her 'savagery' towards him. But she did not withdraw her verdict.[47] Although she did not say as much, it must have occurred to her that he had abandoned her and their tiny girls in Siberia in 1902. Now one of them, Zina, had gone to her death when a little dosing of paternal consideration might have made all the difference. Busy he certainly was. Yet he had known that Zina was in deep distress and had failed to discharge a rudimentary human obligation.

# 41. LOOKING FOR REVOLUTIONS

Emergencies in his family had always taken second place in Trotsky's thinking to the political situation in the USSR. Always he wanted to be ready to exploit any weakness in the Kremlin leadership, and it was of crucial importance for him to clarify his revolutionary strategy. On the journey from Kazakhstan to Turkey he had concentrated on the practical difficulties facing him and his comrades in the Opposition. On reaching Büyükada, he needed quickly to take stock of the momentous changes in Moscow. The NEP had been abandoned. Inside the Politburo, Stalin's insistence on minimizing any concessions to peasant opinion initially caused him problems with the Politburo where the majority saw that his campaign in the Urals and Siberia had aggravated rural intransigence. The central party leadership sent factory products to the countryside as a token of official good faith. This was done at the expense of plans for industrial capital investment – and reserves of foreign currency were run down as imports of the goods desired by the peasantry were increased. Bukharin was influential in getting the Politburo to edge away from 'the Urals–Siberian method'. The results were less than encouraging. Word had got around the villages across the USSR about Stalin's violent expropriations. Peasants had no confidence in any reassurance. The problem of food supplies to the towns was no nearer to solution.

Bukharin held the Politburo majority for only a few weeks. As peasants increased their resistance, the party leadership reverted to forcible requisitioning. Stalin grew dominant in the teeth of Bukharin's vigorous criticisms. The Politburo became a battleground between Stalin and Bukharin, and Stalin won every clash. It remained an article of faith for Trotsky and the Opposition that Stalin was a despicable 'centrist' and 'opportunist' who lacked a true commitment to his new policy. Yet Trotsky lost leading supporters in droves. Preobrazhenski, Pyatakov, Radek and Smilga were among them. Bizarrely Trotsky interpreted their surrender as a sign that Bukharin and the 'rightist tail' was conducting an offensive against Stalin and the centrists and that the so-called capitulators were trying to prevent a triumph of the right.[1] This was a gross misreading of the Soviet political situation: Trotsky could not bring himself to recognize that Stalin had Bukharin at his mercy and that the ultra-rapid campaign for industrialization and collectivization would continue. Those who recanted had been impressed by the economic and social transformation brought about by Stalin and the Politburo. They yearned for reintegration into a political movement which they thought to constitute human progress.

The indications of the USSR's economic and cultural transformation seemed compelling to them. They ignored how gravely the peasantry suffered during the introduction of collective farms, how the standard of living in the cities declined and how the network of forced-labour camps – the Gulag – was being expanded. Stalin seemed to be doing many of the things that they had always wanted done. Growth rates in manufacturing and mining output were stupendous. The gross output of the economy rose steeply during the first five-year plan. The entire industrial sector, taken into state ownership and pumped up with increased investment, doubled its output by the end of 1932, and the plan was completed in four rather than the projected five years. Production of coal, iron and steel rose steeply. Metallurgical factories were renovated as the party leadership urged Gosplan to prioritize capital goods. Advanced technology was bought from abroad, especially from the USA and Germany, so that the Soviet economy would benefit from the most up-to-date equipment. Foreign experts were employed. Economic growth involved the construction of new cities such as Magnitogorsk. Thousands of schools were created. A mass literacy campaign was started and newly trained workers were enabled to secure promotion to managerial posts. Official spokesmen proclaimed that the era of making 'the new Soviet man and women' had arrived.

While censuring the small-mindedness of his renegade supporters, Trotsky was not the open-minded intellectual explorer he appeared to be. He was venturing forth with his compass needle locked on the prospect of revolutionary communism. He worked with certain assumptions in analysing European politics. These remained his tools of analysis even when the evidence should have given rise to scepticism.

In the early 1930s he continued to contend that Stalin was not firmly committed to the leftist policy he was implementing. The General Secretary was to be seen as an opportunist, an unprincipled adventurer, a politician who was out merely to maximize his power as the supreme ruler and to serve the interests of the 'bureaucracy'. At best he was a manipulator who knew how to balance one faction against another. Ideas supposedly meant nothing to Stalin except insofar as they advanced his personal interests. The rapid industrial growth sponsored from 1928, according to Trotsky, should not be expected to last. As soon as Stalin defeated Bukharin and the rightists he would revert to the middle-of-the-road Bolshevism which found sustenance among the *apparatchiki*. The chaotic economic conditions would make this happen sooner or later. But Stalin's position would remain unstable. Oppositionists consequently ought to stick to their principles and bide their time. They alone upheld the values of the October Revolution and Leninism. Trotsky was confident that he and his followers would eventually find a way and an opportunity to restore the party to policies worthy of its traditions.

The Opposition had long ago lost official influence in Comintern. Zinoviev was sacked as chairman of its Executive Committee in October 1926 and Bukharin was removed from the Comintern leadership in April 1929. Initially Trotsky's plan was to rally support from real and potential adherents through persistent propaganda through his writings. Now that he was abroad there was no trouble with the Moscow censors. Politically he remained a Soviet loyalist. Comintern was not to be abandoned but conquered. Trotsky did not mind how this was achieved. If support could be found inside the ranks of the parties of Comintern, that was fine. If it was necessary to establish groupings outside those parties, that too was fine. Both methods would assist in disseminating oppositionist ideas among communists and their sympathizers in Europe and around the world.

Trotsky had some explaining to do in 1928–9 as Stalin shifted Comintern policy leftwards and Moscow gave orders to communist parties to prepare themselves for revolutionary seizures of power in the near future. Stalin's group in the Politburo found foreign veterans willing to carry out the newly radical line. They were told to isolate the parties from the rest of the political left – labour, socialist and social-democratic parties – and to treat them as counter-revolutionaries or, in Stalin's phrase, 'social-fascists'. Stalin claimed that only communism offered a bulwark against the political right, and he suggested that Germany was 'ripe' for revolution and that its social-democrats should be brushed aside in the contest for the active sympathies of the working class. Trotsky replied that he had long been proposing that a 'European socialist revolution' was realizable. He accused Stalin of changing his policy in international relations only so as to have a pretext for purging the Bukharinists from Comintern. He cast doubt on the practical competence of Stalin's protégés in foreign commu-

nist parties. He ridiculed the slogan of 'socialism in one country'. Ultimately, Trotsky asserted, Stalin would undertake no initiative which might
imperil Soviet state security.

With this in mind he intensified efforts to attract his own supporters
in Europe. Some of them called on him to form a new International
to supplant Comintern. He would have none of this. Everything had to
be done through existing communist parties with a view to building up
oppositionist strength and effecting 'international unification'.[2] He could
not travel from Turkey and gauge developments for himself on the spot:
he had to rely on reports from foreign enthusiasts. Such information
as he received was not always reliable even when it was not being
supplied by OGPU infiltrators. But he remained confident that he would
survive and flourish. History, he believed, was on his side.

One kind of difficulty he would encounter became obvious after he
had issued an appeal to members of the Leninbund. These were fellow
oppositionists belonging to the German Communist Party. The problem
was that they were more Trotskyist than Trotsky. Extending his analysis,
they declared that the process of 'Thermidorian reaction' had already
matured in the USSR. So the Soviet order was a fully bourgeois one. This
was too much for Trotsky. He denied that a revolution against the Soviet
government and communist party was required.[3] He castigated his leading
German sympathizers for wavering too much and switching from one
obsession to another. He said they had produced a mishmash of ideas
rather than a coherent programme and imposed them on Leninbund
members without broad debate:

> As the Leninbund looks now, it will never guide the German prolet-
> ariat, not even the vanguard of the vanguard. The Leninbund must
> restock its ideological armoury, and must accordingly recognize its
> rank and file. The first prerequisite of this is an ideological clarity
> of line.[4]

This was Trotsky's way of attracting a following in Europe and North
America. He was to be the sole leader. He laid down the line, and others
were meant to follow it without demur.

Trotsky criticized the Leninbund for demanding 'freedom of organization' in the land of the October Revolution:

> The slogan . . . never was and never could be an isolated slogan. The
> permissibility of organization without freedom of assembly, press,
> etc., and also without parliamentary institutions and party struggles.

What is your position on this? In spite of my best efforts I could not make it out clearly.[5]

Trotsky's expostulation shows just how hostile he was to the ideas and institutions of liberal democracy. He was more the conventional Soviet politician than many foreigners imagined. He was spelling out the terms of association for the Leninbund: they had to accept his doctrines or else he would treat them with contempt. As earlier, he consoled himself with the implausible thought that if only the 'workers' were involved in the political debate they would be on his side and would put pressure on the wrong-headed oppositionist leadership.

There was more to it than that. Fresh out of the USSR, Trotsky needed to appear more Leninist than Stalin. Allegiance to Lenin's doctrines and policies was obligatory. Trotsky's notebooks in the 1930s seemingly bear out the genuineness of his affection and respect for the party's founder but it should not be forgotten that when writing his diary he was usually jotting down comments that he expected to work up for publication at a later date. We cannot automatically assume that what he wrote was a reflection of his sincere thought. But the sentiments expressed about Lenin, in general terms, appear believable. On one large matter he asserted himself against Lenin when he sanctioned the reprinting of his old writings advocating 'permanent revolution'.[6] This involved a bit of a risk. The official party leadership in Moscow could give chapter and verse on Lenin's hostility to such ideas before 1917. Trotsky stopped being cautious. Perhaps he felt goaded by Ioffe's advice in his suicide letter.[7] Trotsky may also have wished to mark out a special patch of ground for his followers to gather on. At any rate he offered 'permanent revolution' as a basis for analysis and not as a sacred text. This, he thought, was the way to make sense of the tasks to be discharged by the 'international proletariat'.[8]

Trotsky privately admitted that progress was slow and intermittent. It was not just the Germans and the Russians but the French too who caused him annoyance. Several groups in France were sympathetic to his cause. They were in perpetual conflict with each other and each group was divided by internal rivalries. Trotsky refused to bother himself with Boris Souvarine's organization. (Souvarine was too critical of him.) Trotsky had higher hopes of Albert Treint and thought he might emerge as leader of a combination of supporters of the Opposition. Perhaps, moreover, things might be looking up in Belgium. (Trotsky was not altogether confident about this and his scepticism proved correct.) There was chaos among the comrades in Czechoslovakia.[9] But a letter he sent to supporters in the

USSR was optimistic. 'Lively' groups existed in Belgium and the USA, but practically all foreign groups displeased him for their policy on China, and transatlantic communication was only starting to be organized.[10]

The Opposition had its biggest following in Germany and France – and, of course, the international communist movement since Lenin's time had regarded Germany as the future epicentre of world revolution. Trotsky's followers in France started by being fairly compliant. But the Old Man's bossiness soon began to grate on them. Pierre Naville, Josef Frey and Kurt Landau complained about his 'organizational methods'; and Landau brought up the criticisms of Trotsky made by Lenin in his testament.[11] This hurt Trotsky but failed to induce him to change his behaviour. He always knew best. There were baleful consequences in his handling of the German Opposition. He showed favour to the Sobolevicius brothers Abraham and Ruvim. They were hard-working individuals with the time and the independent means to spend on political work after emigrating from Lithuania. Finance was tight for international Trotskyism and preference was given to individuals who could work for free.[12] The brothers knew how to ingratiate themselves politically. Ruvim informed Trotsky that the Berlin comrades were in a shocking state;[13] and he and Abraham regularly got Trotsky to take their side in the internal disputes of the German Opposition. Trotsky ignored reports that the brothers were causing strife and chaos, and he welcomed them to Büyükada. Natalya had an aversion to them, thinking them jumpy and philistine, but no one could take steps against them until Trotsky learned that Abraham had declared the Soviet five-year plan satisfactorily completed and that Ruvim had repeatedly defended those Trotskyists who had fallen out with Trotsky.[14]

It soon turned out that the Sobolevicius brothers were OGPU agents whose assigned function was to infiltrate and disrupt German Trotskyism. When the truth became evident Trotsky saw no need to apologize for having protected them. He simply denounced them and expected everyone to go on taking his orders. His son Lëva saw that this was provoking resentment among the European comrades.[15] He complained to his father about his irritability and pedantry and called on him to be more tactful. All he received in return was an instruction to be more conscientious.[16]

Believing that the objective of 'European revolution' could be immediately realized, Trotsky called upon the Opposition in Europe to ignore any distraction from the supreme objective. He summarized his opinions in an open letter to the Soviet Communist Party in March 1930, insisting that the Politburo had taken the wrong strategic path by its predominant reliance on force in Soviet society. The result was administrative chaos throughout the USSR.[17] What made things worse was the retention of the 'old theory of socialism in one country'. Stalin in practice did not give priority to the promotion of revolutionary change abroad. Having made stupid errors and often shown a tendency to vacillate under the NEP, the Politburo was confining itself to the tasks of Soviet industrialization and pushing Comintern towards treating the rest of the socialist movement in Europe, rather than the fascists, as the principal enemy.[18] The Opposition had to bestir itself. Its problems of internal strife, organizational disarray and numerical weakness needed only to be temporary. Trotsky saw the solution in terms of class. His European adherents were failing to reach out beyond the intelligentsia. Their 'aristocratic' approach meant that workers were left alone.[19] Proletarian revolutions could not be made without the active involvement of the proletariat. Propaganda and recruitment among the working class were urgent requirements.

Trotsky spent every waking hour contemplating the possibilities. The catastrophic chaos in the global economy after the Wall Street crash of October 1929 did not worry him: it enlivened his sense that a socialist order was about to be achieved. The political and economic disruption in the Soviet Union was of no greater concern. Stalin, the triumphant mediocrity, would surely prove incapable of securing his regime. Trotsky's diary note continued: 'Thus I cannot speak about the indispensability of my work even in relation to the period 1917–1921. But now my work is "indispensable" in the full sense of the word.'[20] Writing for himself, he dropped the modesty of his public discourse. Did he believe what he was telling himself? It could be that his comment was really a way of convincing himself. This was a man who had some personal responsibility for his fall from the pinnacle of power in the USSR. He would not have been human if the thought had not occurred to him that he had made some terrible mistakes. The past was unalterable; but lessons could be learned from it to make a brilliant future.

The leaderships of the official communist parties in Trotsky's estimation were a lost cause. Ernst Thälmann in Germany and Maurice Thorez in France were the embodiment of ineptitude.[21] Despite adopting its radical international policy, Comintern had not a clue how to seize power anywhere. Trotsky suggested that the cynical Stalin probably favoured the installation of a Nazi regime in Berlin precisely because Hitler would crush the communists and relieve the USSR of the obligation to intervene in support of a fraternal revolution.[22] If Stalin had made this calculation he told nobody about it. As usual, Trotsky was caricaturing

Stalin's presumed intentions. Franz Neumann, a member of the German Communist Party leadership, told a different story about Soviet foreign policy. Neumann was worried about the possibility of the Nazis coming to power and took the opportunity to express his concerns to Stalin. The reply surprised him. Stalin said that even if Hitler became Germany's ruler there would be no grounds for pessimism. A Nazi regime would rip up the treaty of Versailles and Europe would be plunged into chaos. The German communists would be able to exploit such a situation for their revolutionary objectives.[23]

Trotsky may have misinterpreted Stalin's thinking but he was right to point to his terrible underestimation of the dangers posed by the Nazis to the entire political left. Bukharin was of the same opinion but no longer had the freedom to express it. Both Trotsky and Bukharin understood that Nazism in power would wreak havoc on the political left. The outlawing and suppression of the communist party would be among Hitler's first measures. Trotsky's *Byulleten oppozitsii* repeatedly warned of the stupidity of concentrating the efforts of Comintern on the struggle against the 'social-fascists'. The times called for some kind of pact between communists and social-democrats in Germany against the Nazi menace. In 1932 he incorporated his conclusions in his booklet *What Next?* The threat of fascism was the greatest presently confronting Comintern. The official Soviet party in its current condition was unfit for global leadership. Instead there had to be 'international control over the Soviet bureaucracy'. There had to be a campaign to introduce 'party democracy' to all communist parties. The Wall Street crash had led to deep and long-lasting economic depression all over the world. The political far right had become a serious contender for power in central Europe. Hitler had to be fought, Stalin to be removed.

In fact Trotsky and Stalin agreed that Hitler was a puppet worked by the hands of German 'finance capital'. Their dispute was about the likely consequences of Nazi political supremacy. Trotsky was quickly vindicated. The Nazis became the largest party in the Reichstag elections of July 1932; they behaved disruptively in the following winter. The economic depression deepened and President von Hindenburg was prevailed upon to appoint Hitler as chancellor in January 1933. A wave of legal and constitutional manipulation was released. Nazi street violence went unpunished. Hitler stood forth as the bringer of order. Blaming the political left for every disturbance, he suppressed the German Communist Party. Those leaders who failed to flee the country were shot or thrown into concentration camps. Stalin was proved right in his prediction that

Hitler would rip up the Versailles treaty and reassert Germany's power in central Europe. His belief that German communism would emerge as the main beneficiary turned out to be catastrophically wrong.

The editorial premises of the *Byulleten oppozitsii* had to be speedily closed down in Berlin and moved to Paris where the International Secretariat had been based since the exposure of the Sobolevicius brothers. The Opposition in Europe and North America had tried to gather its forces at a 'preliminary international conference' in the French capital in early February. Eleven countries were represented and each told a tale of woe. The English had only twenty-seven members. Even the French and the Belgians had recruited a mere hundred apiece. Political disagreements bedevilled attempts to reach out beyond the Trotskyist groupings. The Germans had been disrupted by the machinations of the Soboleviciuses as well as by continuing splits, but they had kept up a lively operation until Hitler's accession to power and accumulated seven hundred members. The Italians, like the Russians, were mainly refugees: Mussolini's police made progress impossible in Rome. The Greeks were now recognized as having the strongest organization with five hundred members, though a tenth of them were in prison. The Spanish had 1,500 members but their leader Andreu Nin had given trouble to the International Secretariat over Trotsky's choices about which groups to support in France. Nin, a Catalan, was not someone who would ever let Trotsky tell him what to do.[24]

Lëva Sedov (he and his brother had changed their surname to match their father's alias) had already made a contingency plan to transfer his operations to Paris and had told Trotsky all about this. Sedov had less faith than his father in the usefulness of the social-democrats as collaborators against the Nazi advance.[25] They agreed about the lack of fighting spirit in the official communist leadership. After the Reichstag fire in February 1933 and Hitler's punitive retaliation against the political left, Sedov announced that he was leaving for France even if Trotsky withheld his approval; he was fed up with the absence of letters from him. The archive was packed up. Jeanne Martin des Pallières hid important papers in her clothing. They escaped in fear of their lives, crossing the border and reaching the French capital on 5 March.[26] Trotsky vented his anger on Lëva, even suggesting that he had failed to prevent the trouble with the Sobolevicius brothers and had behaved like a dilettante. Lëva's frustrations boiled over on receipt of such letters and he tended to write back not to Trotsky but to Natalya explaining how unfairly he was being treated. He was aware that his father had a tendency to pick on those able, diligent assistants – such as himself – who were least deserving of reproach; and this was his way of indicating that enough was enough.

Trotsky never apologized even if, for a while, he desisted from being offensive. Both he and Lëva knew that Lëva was too dedicated to carry out his threats. They felt strongly that the political situation in Europe was on the turn and that it might soon move in their favour. Now that the bankruptcy of Stalin's foreign policy was revealed to everyone, Trotsky intended to stake his claim to leadership of the world communist movement. He acknowledged Lenin's greatness and treasured his memory. But Lenin was dead. It was falling to Trotsky to restore Leninism to Russia and the world. He was hoping against hope. His articles were full of schematic projections, shaky reasoning and ill-considered slogans. Trotsky was an intelligent man: not even his worst enemies denied that. The truth was that the alternative to hope was despair.

# 42. THE WRITER

The one activity in which Trotsky excelled nearly all contemporary politicians was as a literary stylist – only Churchill equalled him. Among the Russians he was without compare. Pavel Milyukov, the leading Kadet, and his liberal colleagues produced impressive historical surveys and memoirs. None had Trotsky's panache. The competition was still weaker on the political left. Socialist-Revolutionary leader Viktor Chernov's autobiography appeared in the West but was not thought worth translating. Most Mensheviks endured the same fate. The only émigré from Russia to achieve an éclat was Nikolai Berdyaev, once a Marxist and later a Christian existentialist philosopher. Berdyaev's account of his life attracted the attention of many reviewers but he came nowhere near Trotsky in size of readership or public acclaim.

Leading writers in Europe and North America made contact with Trotsky. One of the few who made it to Büyükada was Georges Simenon, already world-famous for his Maigret books, who interviewed him for a Parisian daily newspaper in June 1933. Although Simenon was one of Trotsky's favourite authors he feared being misquoted and stipulated that he would answer only three questions and only in writing. He dictated his responses in Russian and had them translated into French.[1] Predictably the result was less than exciting. The German sexologist Wilhelm Reich too expressed a desire to talk with him,[2] but the meeting never happened. While staying in Saint-Palais in the same year, Trotsky received a visit from André Malraux, whose *La Condition humaine* he recommended for translation into English. He and Malraux subsequently fell out over French politics and then about the Spanish Civil War. The two of them were to exchange insults. It is hard to say who was the more blameworthy, but Trotsky had obviously acquired a prickliness that had not been on display in the company of artists and thinkers in pre-war Vienna. His experience of life since 1917 had hardened and constricted his personality.

Asked by a journalist to name his favourite Soviet author, Trotsky chose Isaac Babel. *Red Cavalry*, a brilliant sequence of short stories, had appeared too late for inclusion in Trotsky's *Literature and Revolution*. Babel had fought alongside the cavalrymen in the Polish campaign of 1920 and set his searing tales in their milieu. They are among the finest of the genre in twentieth-century world literature; Trotsky showed his eye for excellence by picking them out as deserving 'the greatest interest'.[3]

French Trotskyists encouraged Trotsky to make contact with André Gide, who published a devastating chronicle of his trip in 1936 to the Soviet Union. Gide wrote of having sent a flattering telegram to Stalin from Tbilisi. It was not flattering enough according to Gide's handlers, who asked him to add the word 'glorious' to 'destiny' in heralding the USSR's future. They declined to dispatch any message unless it was couched in sycophantic language. Trotsky, sitting on the veranda as he read Gide's account of the episode, laughed out loud. Natalya rushed from indoors to find out what the noise was about.[4] Trotsky would not bestir himself to go and make Gide's acquaintance: he expected the mountain to come to Mohammed.[5] Not that he avoided communication with people who spent their days with pens or palettes. He was delighted when the Mexican muralist Diego Rivera wrote to him out of the blue. Trotsky remembered the book of Rivera reproductions he had flicked through in Alma-Ata, and now he invited him to visit him in Turkey.[6] Trotsky also established a rapport with the surrealist painter André Breton. By and large, though, he concentrated on his political campaigning. He wrote absolutely nothing that failed to contribute to that cause.

His book royalties financed his politics, and recollections of his past career were his greatest commercial asset in his quest for commissions. Lenin and Trotsky had led the Bolsheviks in the October Revolution and the Civil War. Trotsky was the sole survivor and his story was highly saleable. Despite having produced accounts of various episodes in his life, he had yet to attempt a consecutive narrative, which strengthened his bargaining hand. His plan was twofold. He would write a full autobiography from birth to the present day, followed by a history of the Russian Revolution from February to October 1917. Initially he published a series of articles sub-titled *Six Articles for the World Bourgeois Press.*[7] Trotsky soon came to his senses and recognized that the condescending title would never attract readers who were not Marxists – and he would be penniless unless he could obtain a wide readership. The autobiography and the history became a daily preoccupation. Much of the research necessitated merely the consulting of his own memory. The trunks of archives he had brought out of the USSR also came into their own. (The Soviet authorities learned from their mistake: no citizen who left the country in the following decade was allowed to carry compromising documents.) His son Lëva sent additional material from Berlin and Paris.[8] Trotsky operated as a writing machine for the good of the Opposition's cause.

Over the years he had made many sketches of his life. He was a resourceful self-plagiarist and pillaged images, turns of phrase and even whole paragraphs for the current projects.[9] He was the literary equivalent of masters of visual collage such as Braque and Picasso. He also had an exact idea about the result he wanted. Commissioning editors urged him to include sensational revelations; they also tried to hold him back from multi-volume editions.[10] Trotsky took little notice, writing what he pleased and at the length he fancied. His mode of composition was laborious. Usually he completed drafts in his own hand, but sometimes he simply dictated to secretaries, expecting them to take down notes or even to copy his words directly on to the typewriter. His methods were nothing if not idiosyncratic. As soon as a full chapter of his *History of the Russian Revolution* was typed up, he took the pages off to his desk and glued them together on a scroll of paper.[11] Why he did this, he never explained. The likeliest motive was that he wanted to have the appropriate balance among the paragraphs. Aesthetic presentation was never far from his mind. Like those poets who have worried about the size of succeeding cantos, he hated to release an unpleasing piece of prose to his readers.

Trotsky struck his desired tone from the earliest drafts. Whenever the secretaries could not keep up he told them to omit a few lines and catch up. He disliked damming himself when in full flood. Sara Weber remembered:

> while dictating L.D. never sat down but dictated *walking* to and fro, at times almost with his back to me . . . L.D. spoke without the use of any notes, at [an] even speed, sentences following smoothly one after the other. A lunch or dinner bell would interrupt the work. At the sound of the bell L.D. would stop dictating, at times in mid-sentence, not to keep the household waiting, and we would descend into the dining room. After lunch and a brief rest, there would often be dictation again. L.D. would ask me at what word we stopped and would go on from there smoothly, uninterruptedly.[12]

He could dictate in Russian, German or French. (He tried to do the same in English, but with unhappy results.) Although he was a stern taskmaster he rarely spoke harshly, preferring to leave the room and calm down.[13]

*My Life*, appearing in 1930, was the first product of his labours; his

*History of the Russian Revolution* was published in three volumes in 1932–3. He suffered a twinge of nerves about writing about himself. Social classes, not individual leaders, were the focus of Marxism, and Trotsky adhered to the tenet that 'great men' do not make history but instead are the tools of historical change. A typical communist anyway thought it poor form to draw attention to oneself in writing. Trotsky communicated his own unease by the tentativeness of the sub-title he chose for the autobiography: *An Attempt at an Autobiography*. He wrote detachedly as though he was depicting a stranger. Behind his rhetorical devices, however, lay a relentless effort to proclaim the rightness of his decisions and actions over the years. Yet the early drafts prove that his nervousness was a genuine feeling. Like Julius Caesar in his *Commentaries on the Gallic War*, Trotsky kept a formal distance between the author and his historical self. He referred to himself in the third person and even adopted the name Grisha for the chapters on his childhood.[14] (Only when he quoted his mother talking to him did he drop this ploy: it would have been silly to have her scolding him as the non-existent Grisha.)[15]

This is a rhetorical technique known as alienation or estrangement. From Caesar to Trotsky it was a self-dramatizing conceit, supplying an aura of modesty to the political image. Although Trotsky restored his real name (or rather his real names and real pseudonyms) to the final text he continued to avoid 'I' to a large extent. This worked wonderfully in the account of Yanovka. Trotsky picked up Leo Tolstoy's devices in *Childhood* and described scenes as if seeing them through the eyes of the boy he had been:

> It was explained to me that telegrams came along a wire but with my own eyes I saw a telegram brought from Bobrinets by a horseman who had to be paid two rubles and fifty kopeks by my father. The telegram was a piece of paper like a letter and there were words written on it in pencil. How did it come along a wire? Did the wind blow it? I was told that it came by electricity. That was even worse. Uncle Abram on one occasion insistently explained to me: 'The current comes over the wire and makes marks on a ribbon. Repeat what I have said.' I repeated: 'A current passes through the wire and makes marks on a ribbon.' 'Repeat!' I repeated: a current passes along the wire and makes marks on a ribbon. 'Do you understand?' Yes, I had understood.[16]

Abram's crotchetiness quelled the boy's curiosity. But not for long. Trotsky dredged up what happened next from his memory:

'But how does a letter result from that?' I asked, thinking of the telegraph blank arriving from Bobrinets. 'The letter comes separately,' my uncle answered. I was puzzled why a current was needed if the 'letter' travels on horseback. But my uncle grew angry at this point: 'Oh, leave the letter in peace,' he cried. 'While I'm trying to explain to you about telegrams, all you can do is go on about letters!' So the question remained unanswered.[17]

The author was a maestro of pithy, elegant prose.

He sustained an appearance of simplicity and straightforwardness as he moved on to his revolutionary career – and the account acquired the pungent qualities of someone paying off old scores. The anecdotes about his conversations with Lenin had bite. The explication of the strategy and intrigue in the Civil War carried the reader along in a splendidly evocative swirl. There have been few better evocations of the emergency which culminated in the decision to introduce the NEP. The pathos of Trotsky's last stand in Moscow in 1928, exile to Alma-Ata and deportation to Turkey was also movingly conveyed. But the special pleading has a wearing effect unless one is already on his political side. The problem lay not in style but in content. This was equally true of *The History of the Russian Revolution*. Both works were written as if only one great outcome was possible in 1917. Reworking ideas from his writings since 1905, Trotsky in *The History* proclaimed 'the law of combined development'. He argued that 'backward' countries might take a different path towards modernity from those followed by their 'advanced' competitors. Russia had been able to learn from the latest political, cultural and technological achievements elsewhere and speed up its own development. It had skipped stages of change experienced in western Europe and north America.[18]

While putting forward his 'law' as an original contribution to Marxist thought Trotsky did not claim that 'combined development' always led to a 'modern' outcome. Backward conditions, he stressed, often enabled the old ruling classes to retain their power, and this is what Nicholas II, the landed gentry and the bourgeoisie had attempted to achieve in the Russian Empire before 1917. The possibilities of effective reactionary politics were many and diverse. Revolutionaries could counteract them only by maintaining a genuine radical commitment and engaging in uncompromising activity. He suggested that the Bolsheviks had proved their worth after the fall of the Romanovs. Lively in his survey of the Imperial past, Trotsky routinized his analysis at this point and chanted the stale mantras about Lenin, the party and the masses as unchallengeable truth. He vilified the socialist opponents of Bolshevism. He disallowed every argument that democracy, civil society or ideological tolerance had anything positive to offer to the Russian people. In most essential respects he was reproducing the dicta of official Soviet accounts by Nikolai Popov and Yemelyan Yaroslavski in the 1920s.

He sparkled when recounting his achievements and those of Lenin. He reproduced what he claimed were the exact words of intimate conversations. How much confidence is to be placed in such gobbets, especially when the words were not overheard by others, is hard to say. Generally he has seldom been faulted for inaccuracy. What is usually overlooked is how blatantly he engaged in evasiveness and selectivity. He eschewed writing about incidents which might undermine his credentials as a friend of the poor and oppressed. Thus he dealt with the Tambov uprising and Kronstadt mutiny in early 1921 by omitting them from his account. *My Life* is a summons for support of the communist cause. It is also a masterpiece of political fudging masked by the artifices of a literary alchemist.

Trotsky edited his drafts systematically. From the start he had played down his father's wealth and the family's Jewishness, and his amendments reinforced this orientation.[19] He also excised a delightful story or two about his nanny Masha. Probably he did not want to seem to have been cosseted as a child. Some of the vibrant dialogue between him and his father's chief mechanic Ivan Greben was removed: doubtless Trotsky wished to avoid coming across as a progeny of the boss class. The names of several acquaintances were erased. In later years he would have done this to protect them against Stalin's security police. This was not a consideration in the Turkish years. More likely he aimed to hide the extent of his interaction with fellow Jews in his early life.[20] Equally important was the wish to minimize past disagreements with Lenin. Here he knew what he was doing even in the first drafts. Always he needed to demonstrate his credentials as a Leninist; he could not afford to boast unduly about being a Trotskyist. He drew a veil over his bitter clashes with Lenin before 1917. He even removed references to his criticisms of the technical shortcomings of the *Iskra* organizers in Russia.[21] He purged the claim that his theory of 'permanent revolution' had been wholly confirmed by history; it was as if he was in two minds about having republished his pre-1917 articles about it.[22]

The mixture of tub-thumping and slipperiness was preserved in *The History of the Revolution*. Ridicule was also to the fore. Nicholas II was called 'dim, equable and "well bred"', his only merit being that he was not personally cruel. Kerenski appeared as a reactionary with a 'little red silk handkerchief'. Stalin was routinely deprecated but mainly he suffered by the paucity of references. (He appeared more frequently in *My Life* where Trotsky, refraining from direct characterization, skewered the General Secretary by reproducing contemporary comments on him by Lenin and others.) Whenever the Mensheviks and Socialist-Revolutionaries between February and October 1917 were mentioned their motives were questioned. Trotsky mocked them pitilessly. For him they were insincere, foolish, vacillators as well as dangerous promoters of a counter-revolution. He saw Kamenev, Zinoviev and Stalin as having behaved little better and he dubbed them the Compromisers, wounding them deftly with pinpricks rather than with a sledgehammer.[23] Thus Lenin and Trotsky emerged as the heroes in the account. Such leaders of the Opposition as had stayed true to Trotsky also earned his praise. The others suffered a verbal cuffing. Trotsky encased his commentary in a vivid exposition of his analysis. Russia, he continued to argue, was too backward for socialism without support from a European socialist revolution. But somehow it had been right for the Bolsheviks to seize power. The achievements of the early Soviet administration were wholly laudable; and if only the 'epigones' of Lenin had not defeated the Opposition, the Leninist heritage would not have been dissipated.[24]

Trotsky was letting his zest for Classical references run away with him. 'Epigones' in ancient Greek usage referred to a younger generation coming after a generation of heroes and sometimes, but not always, it could imply that the youngsters were inferior. The sons of the Seven against Thebes, for example, succeeded where their fathers had failed.[25] Trotsky was wrong to use the term as if the younger generation was wholly without talent, strength or desirable purpose. But he liked the sound of the word: style triumphed in his mind over content. He did not mind what he wrote if he thought it would guard the greatness of the October Revolution.

The Bolsheviks had been accused repeatedly of having organized a conspiracy. Unusually Trotsky did not deny this. Every revolution, he said, needs an insurrection which in turn requires secrecy and 'conscious preparation'.[26] (The official Soviet line by contrast stressed that the collaboration of the leaders, the party and the masses operated entirely in the open.) At the same time he gave the impression that the October Revolution reflected 'mass' opinion. As regards the Second Congress of Soviets, he claimed that 390 out of 650 voting delegates 'fell to the lot of the Bolsheviks'.[27] Yet, as Trotsky made clear, not all those at the Congress who voted for the Bolshevik party were themselves Bolsheviks.[28] He could have gone further and admitted that the Bolsheviks had taken power without support from a majority in society. But this would have counteracted the impression he wished to convey. For him, the seizure of power was the product of unstoppable pressures exerted by workers, soldiers and peasants:

> A revolution takes place only when there is no other way out. And the insurrection, which rises above a revolution like a peak in a mountain chain of its events, can no more be invoked at will than the revolution as a whole. The masses advance and retreat several times before they make up their minds to the final assault.[29]

At least in this respect Trotsky and Stalin put forward similar versions of the history of 1917.

Trotsky's book, though, struck its own note, and no one could accuse him of lacking a sense of humour. He wrote of the bicycle battalion that was among the supporters of the Provisional Government in those last days: 'Let a man find himself, in distinction from others, on top of two wheels with a chain – at least in a poor country like Russia – and his vanity begins to swell out like his tyres. In America it takes an automobile to produce this effect.'[30] He was deadly serious about another thing. No longer under pressure from the Politburo, he felt free to repudiate the official story that the Bolshevik party had led the October Revolution.[31] He also insisted that Lenin's judgement was far from perfect. Lenin had called repeatedly for a seizure of power in August and September.[32] Trotsky's verdict was that the Bolsheviks would have been obliterated if the Central Committee had not turned down Lenin's demand. He also reverted to his earlier emphasis on the importance of the soldiers in the Provisional Government's overthrow. This was his judgement: 'The October Revolution was a struggle of the proletariat against the bourgeoisie for power but the outcome was decided in the last analysis by the muzhik [peasant].' He insisted that the Petrograd garrison of peasant-in-uniform had a decisive impact on the seizure of power.[33]

He had complete control over the Russian printed text of *My Life* and *History of the Russian Revolution*. But this was not where most of his royalties would come from, and the translations into European languages produced some pain for him. London publishers Thornton Butterworth unilaterally replaced the sub-title *An Attempt at an Autobiography* with one of their own, *The Rise and Fall of a Dictator*.[34] His Paris editors at Rieder were little better. Maurice Parijanine, an admirer of Trotsky, agreed to the job on condition that he could add his own explanatory footnotes.

Trotsky howled at the result and wrote to Gérard Rosenthal, lawyer and Trotskyist, listing the inaccuracies and misunderstandings: 'My temperature is rising (without exaggeration!) by the mere act of leafing through this book. You will add these samples to the others while sorting them out, won't you? The insults must be eliminated. (It's to comfort my soul.)'[35] When he threatened to send an open letter of complaint to the newspapers, Rieder gave ground and offered to let him append a declaration explaining his lack of responsibility for Parijanine's insertions. Trotsky was unforgiving and asked Rosenthal to go on 'terrorizing' Rieder.[36] Parijanine, reconsidering his esteem for Trotsky, wrote that no decent translator should be 'the slave of the author'.[37] By the time the case came to court it was too late: Rieder had already put the book on sale.

Trotsky did reasonably well for himself financially and Lëva reported his books as selling decently in Berlin in the early 1930s.[38] Trotsky later attributed such success to Soviet security agents who bought up the copies only to destroy them.[39] He gained his royalties in Germany without getting his desired readership. Generally, moreover, he was less than adept in his business affairs. He signed away 50 per cent of the American rights for his *History of the Russian Revolution* to Charles and Albert Boni of New York. Despite his theoretical contempt for capitalism and capitalists, he naively thought he could get the contract rewritten by appealing to the conscience of the publishers.[40] No one would have taken his father for a ride like this.

Max Eastman went to Büyükada in 1932 so that they could work together on *The History of the Russian Revolution*.[41] Trotsky approved of Eastman's translation. (Evidently he was not proficient enough at English to discern how much slang had been introduced.) Even so, he had his tiffs with Eastman.[42] Trotsky used him as an unpaid literary agent in America. Eastman did not mind the drudgery until Trotsky cut him out of the deal with an American publisher for translating articles for the press, which was especially galling since Eastman was often out of pocket as a result of his efforts – and it was only through him that Trotsky received US$45,000 for the serialization rights of the *History* in the *Saturday Evening Post* alone.[43] But Trotsky refused to give way and Eastman only just stopped himself from exploding, as he later recalled:

> It was one of the few times in my life when I thought of the right thing to say. 'Lev Davidovich, I can only answer you in the words of Lenin.' And I quoted, in perfect Russian from the famous testament: 'Comrade Trotsky is apt to be too much carried away by the adminis-

trative side of things.' At this Trotsky relaxed and dropped back into his chair, laughing genially and completely, as though to say, 'Touché!'[44]

The relationship collapsed. Eastman departed from Turkey a few days later, leaving the Old Man to find others to do his errands.

After the publication of those two books Trotsky was hard pressed to find an equally popular subject. His analyses of the USSR and other political topics did not sell badly. *The Revolution Betrayed*, published in 1937, did well in several languages – the forgiving Eastman returned to translate it into English. But booklets of this kind did not have publishers queuing up to offer lavish contracts.

He had not shot his bolt as a commercial author. A couple of further topics which would net him a decent advance royalty suggested themselves. Trotsky had known Lenin and Stalin. Both lacked adequate biographies. Trotsky yet again could offer the lure of forbidden history. Harper and Brothers in New York paid in advance for an English edition of *Stalin*. The problem was that the project required a huge amount of research. Although he could write quickly he would not dream of delivering a typescript which did not meet his high standards. He was fighting to keep the banner of the Opposition waving in the breeze and to propagate his vision of the future of humankind. The only way he could finance this was by delving into the history of Bolshevism; and Trotsky, by then in Mexico, had to process mounds of documents, relying on his followers in New York to send him books and copy out extracts. It was a gruelling task for a person who at the same time was keeping up correspondence, meeting supporters, devising policies and dictating articles. There were compensations. As he fossicked in the material he came across what he wanted: evidence that Stalin had been a dangerous misanthrope from the day he was born.

His material on Lenin accreted so thickly that he decided to divide it into several volumes, and his old collaborators Eastman and Parijanine agreed to get on with translating the first. The French edition came out in 1936, being sold to unwary purchasers as *The Life of Lenin*.[45] Eastman's English manuscript remained unpublished; it was published more honestly in 1972 as *The Young Lenin*.[46] Midway through his research on Lenin, Trotsky abruptly switched his attention to Stalin, hoping to produce a big book at speed. His American translator for that biography was the writer Charles Malamuth. Things went wrong between them almost immediately. Malamuth, Trotsky told his young American follower Joe Hansen, was

ignorant and pretentious as well as knowing neither Russian nor English.[47]
The bad-tempered cycle of emendation and discussion began yet again.
It was exacting work. There was nothing new in the interpretation and
Trotsky at times did not disguise his distaste for having to pay so much
attention to Stalin. Even so, he held back from declaring his hatred of
the Kremlin dictator. He managed to keep his own emotional balance.
Measured criticism and abundant irony were his preferred mode of attack.
When Trotsky died he was not far off completing the biography; but Stalin
struck Trotsky down before Trotsky could finish off *Stalin*.

# 43. RUSSIAN CONNECTIONS

The Soviet press handled Trotsky inconsistently. At one and the same time he was the USSR's most perilous enemy and its first political non-person. News coverage of his activities was eliminated and his name disappeared from historical textbooks except as a conspirator with foreign powers against Soviet Russia. The briefest announcement of his deportation appeared in the newspapers. A touch of xenophobia crept into public discourse as Trotsky's forenames began to be rendered as 'Lev Davydovich' rather than 'Lev Davidovich' – the spelling now implicitly emphasizing that he came from a Jewish family.[1] In 1932, moreover, an unpublished article, 'On Yudushka-Trotsky's Colour of Shame', by Lenin was revealed.[2] Yudushka was one of the ineffectual members of the unattractive Golovlëv family in Mikhail Saltykov-Schedrin's nineteenth-century novel *The Golovlëv Family*; he was a hypocrite who spoke unctuous, hypocritical nonsense whenever a conflict arose among his relatives. Lenin in 1911 had been comparing him to Trotsky, who was vainly trying to bring harmony to the Russian Social-Democratic Workers' Party. Presumably Lenin or his editorial board had second thoughts about publication because Yudushka or little Judas had a possible anti-Semitic connotation. Stalin had no such inhibition and from the mid-1930s it was common for Trotsky to be mentioned baldly as the Judas of the October Revolution.

The problem for Stalin was that Trotsky still had a political following in the USSR. The OGPU proceeded carefully in arresting the Opposition's active members while leaving ordinary industrial workers untouched. Stalin had thought his plans through. His main objective was to cut every link between Trotskyists and the Soviet working class.[3]

Party spokesmen insisted that Trotsky was spreading his conspiratorial network far and wide. On 8 March 1929 he was denounced as being in league with Winston Churchill and in receipt of 'tens of thousands of dollars' for his services.[4] The accusations mutated in accordance with the shifts in international relations. By mid-1931 it was Piłsudski who was worrying the Politburo, and Trotsky was alleged to be linked to Polish efforts to bring down the Soviet order.[5] Despite this, the consulate-general in Istanbul went on renewing his passport in the name of Lev Davidovich Sedov. This situation lasted for three years. Then on 20 February 1932 the Moscow authorities abruptly revoked his citizenship and rendered Trotsky a stateless person dependent on the mercy of Mustapha Kemal.[6]

The deported Soviet leader might as well have fired his polemical bullets into the earth of Büyükada. The Opposition's residual leaders languished in far-flung, inhospitable places of exile; those who had recanted their 'errors' – Zinoviev, Kamenev, Preobrazhenski, Pyatakov and Radek – were spared such punishment and were allowed back to Moscow so long as they appeared reliably contrite. At the very least they were required to denounce the Opposition in public. Trotsky was one of the recusants. What is more, he proved more resilient abroad than had been anticipated. Despite the OGPU's success in minimizing his contact with the USSR, his ideas remained a danger for the Politburo. Memories were long among leading Bolsheviks. They knew that Trotsky had been an early advocate of a radical strategy and that Stalin had incorporated several of its features in his policies. Stalin had applied these policies in a fashion which caused vastly more hardship than anyone had expected. The official cult of his greatness had the unintended effect of identifying him as the source of people's pain. Stalin prudently prohibited any measured discussion of Trotsky and his ideas. When party officials criticized the wildness of official economic policies it was conventional to accuse them of sympathizing with the deported ex-member of the Politburo on Büyükada.[7]

Trotsky worked at exchanging letters with his followers in the USSR and sending them copies of the *Byulleten oppozitsii*. Soviet politics in his eyes were in a volatile condition. In 1929 it was still uncertain that Stalin's victory over Bukharin was irreversible. Nobody knew for sure that the policies of industrialization would be maintained. While hoping he might be invited to rejoin the leadership in the Kremlin, Trotsky had no thought of reconciliation with Stalin. But perhaps a group of Stalin's supporters, he speculated, would make an approach to him. This explains Trotsky's curious strategy. It is one which nearly all Trotskyists in later generations overlooked; they are not entirely to be blamed since he made his intentions explicit only in his correspondence with Lëva. In October 1932 he wrote: 'We've got to show that we *agree* to work with the Stalinists for the preservation of the USSR.'[8] He was recognizing that he would never regain power by replacing the Stalinist elite with the old elite of the Opposition. The Stalinists were entrenched in all institutions. They were powerful. They had to be won over to the Trotskyist cause.

Trotsky found much to commend in current Soviet policies. He endorsed the rapid industrial expansion – it was only the crudity of Stalin's specific measures he disliked. Similarly he disapproved of the campaign of agricultural collectivization less in principle than on the grounds that it was being waged with gross incompetence and violence. His chief objection to the Politburo, though, lay in its foreign policy under Stalin. He argued that the Soviet leadership gravely underestimated the menace posed by Nazism in Germany.

He was not in favour of using violent methods to remove Stalin. What he had in mind was a political sacking such as Lenin had advocated in his testament.[9] At no point did Trotsky call for a penal sanction. He explained himself in yet another letter to Lëva at the end of the same month:

> We've especially got to pay attention to the talk among middle-ranking bureaucrats that if Trotsky arrives he'll take a cruel revenge. At the moment this is a very important weapon of the Stalinists. Our platform counts entirely on the masses. Our next tactical step must take account of the wall which divides us from the masses.[10]

He was trying to persuade himself, without any evidence, that the functionaries who had supplanted his supporters would consider welcoming him back into the leadership. Perhaps he unconsciously understood this, for at the same time he laid emphasis on an appeal to the 'masses'. Again he was being over-optimistic. Impoverished workers and hungry peasants were unlikely to rally to the cause of a politician who essentially was only promising economic Stalinism at a decelerated pace.

The harsh nature of his communism was demonstrated in his response to Soviet repressive operations after his deportation. When he heard of the show-trials of ex-Mensheviks, ex-Socialist-Revolutionaries and ex-Kadets he raised no objections. He wrote little about the persecution of kulaks, priests and nationalists. He judged them all to be enemies of Bolshevism with the genuine will to carry out the outlandish crimes attributed to them by the USSR's courts. He himself had helped to plan the political stage for the show-trial of the Socialist-Revolutionaries in 1922. He had witnessed and encouraged the tricks of police and prosecutors but did not choose to use his experience in assessing the Kremlin's propaganda about anti-Soviet conspiracies.

His son knew better: 'The trial of the Mensheviks is a complete falsification.' Trotsky would not budge. The case for the prosecution was that Menshevik leaders had established a subversive underground network with foreign links. Trotsky swallowed this whole. Mensheviks in his opinion had 'consciously carried out the instructions of the foreign capitalist high command'.[11] Indeed he blamed Stalin for having given protection to Menshevik economic experts during the NEP. He denied that well-known figures like Nikolai Sukhanov and Vasili Groman would falsely incriminate themselves. It was only much later, in mid-1936, that he issued a formal admission that 'the editorial board of the *Byulleten*' had 'underestimated the shamelessness of Stalinist justice'.[12] This was as near as Trotsky got to a personal apology. The point is that such groups were as uncongenial to him as to Stalin. He himself had been content to see the Kronstadt mutineers and the Socialist-Revolutionary leadership tried on spurious charges in 1921–2. He too had been credulous about international conspiracies where none existed, and he regarded Mensheviks and kulaks as beneath contempt.

To his way of thinking, he had bigger questions to answer about the Revolution. He had always rejected appeals to basic human sympathy as mere sentimentality. What he could not avoid considering was the plight of unrepentant Bolshevik oppositionists. Without them, he would never return to power. He filled the *Byulleten* with reports on the deterioration of conditions inflicted on his exiled and imprisoned adherents. The punishment for continued political activity was made heavier. The messages of an unidentified correspondent signing himself 'Tenzov' left no room for doubt about this,[13] and Trotsky wrote about the cases of maltreatment that came to his attention. But as a moralist he would have been more persuasive if he had shown some concern for the plight of those millions of people outside the Opposition who were suffering dreadfully in the same years. Would Trotsky have avoided Stalin's methods if he had won the struggle for supreme power? It is difficult to believe he would not have reacted harshly to resistance to his policies. Violence was objectively built into the demands of his policies.

He hoped to make use of Yakov Blyumkin, who wrote to him in April 1929 about the fate of the Opposition, in order to break the blockade.[14] Blyumkin was the individual who, as a Left Socialist-Revolutionary, had sought to shatter the treaty of Brest-Litovsk in July 1918 by assassinating the German ambassador Count von Mirbach. Subsequently he had repented – and Dzerzhinski and Trotsky helped to change his mind and get postings for him.[15] Blyumkin joined the Bolsheviks and felt attracted to the Opposition led by Trotsky in the 1920s. While working in Turkey on official OGPU business in summer 1929, he followed up his first letter by effecting an encounter with Lëva Sedov in an Istanbul street. This led to a meeting with Trotsky on Büyükada.[16] Blyumkin carried a letter from Trotsky to the remnants of the Opposition in the USSR.[17] Trotsky intimated that he would soon be publishing a denunciation of 'Radek and Co.' as renegades. Critical times were approaching for the Opposition and the capitulators had to be exposed for failing the test of loyalty to the cause. Trotsky kept up his morale. The apostasy of leading oppositionists relieved him of any pressure to be friendly or accommodating to them. (Not that he had found it hard to resist that kind of pressure.)

The priority, as Trotsky saw it, was to establish firmer links with the USSR. Somehow his adherents had to supply him with 'one or two individuals for organizational work in Berlin and Paris'. Best of all, he thought, would be the exfiltration of a few of those sent to Siberian exile,[18] but he did not explain how this might be achieved.

The fate of Blyumkin, who was a heavy drinker and spoke indiscreetly when drunk,[19] showed the extent of Trotsky's naivety. He should have known that Stalin was suspicious of all known sympathizers of the Opposition and let none of them go to foreign parts without checking up on them. Blyumkin came under investigation after reaching Moscow and the Politburo ordered his execution. The lesson was clear: any contact with Trotsky was to be treated as high treason. It cannot be discounted that Blyumkin was acting out a double game on Stalin's behalf and yet still Stalin had him killed. Whatever was at the bottom of the affair, another threshold of repression had been crossed. Blyumkin's was the first peacetime execution of a card-carrying Bolshevik party member. The General Secretary was not a man to be trifled with: he would now carry out judicial murders if ever his paramountcy came under threat. Trotsky was being put on notice to exercise greater caution when he tried to interfere in Soviet politics. He still did not fully take the hint; he was still thinking in the way he and other emigrants had done before 1917. What is more, he was delighted to receive a smuggled letter from his veteran supporter Viktor Yeltsin in Siberia. It was full of political news – and Trotsky believed this was the start of a regular correspondence between himself and the Soviet oppositionists in confinement or in hiding.[20]

One of his contacts was Eleazar Solnstev, who worked in New York for the USSR's trade organization Amtorg and had been smuggling out the Opposition's material since 1928. Max Eastman used these documents to produce *The Real Situation in Russia*. Ostensibly it was written by Trotsky, but without Eastman's editorial work it could never have appeared. Solntsev returned to the USSR where he was arrested and exiled to Siberia.[21] Another Soviet citizen who liaised with Trotsky was Gavril Myasnikov, who came out to see him on Büyükada. This was a surprise for Trotsky since Myasnikov, a veteran Bolshevik and ex-worker, had suffered at the hands of the central party leadership in the period when Trotsky was one of its leading members. Myasnikov had been on the edge of the Workers' Opposition; the only reason he did not join it was that he thought its demands too restrained. He had been briefly imprisoned in 1923 before being persuaded to work again for the party. But he did not give up his mental independence while carrying out his duties as a Soviet foreign trade representative, which is how he arrived in Istanbul. Trotsky counselled him not to return to the USSR.[22] Myasnikov accepted the advice. If he had ignored it, he would surely have met with the same fate as Solntsev.

Even so, Trotsky's instincts about security precautions remained woeful. He and Lëva kept their Russian contacts to themselves,[23] but this was no solution if they failed to shut Stalin's agents out of their entourage and talked about current general plans. Trotsky and Lëva leaked full buckets of confidential information and uncongenial experiences did little to induce them to improve their procedures.

Soon after arriving in Büyükada Trotsky had received a letter from a certain S. Kharin, a Soviet trade official working in Paris, who purported to be a secret sympathizer and was an acquaintance of Lëva Sedov. Kharin dangled the bait that he would probably spend his summer vacation back in the USSR. He would therefore be able to set up a network of communications.[24] Trotsky swallowed the hook. They corresponded about details for several months. Trotsky solicited Kharin's help with publishing initiatives;[25] he revealed his entire basic strategy and practical planning in his letters.[26] Kharin wrote the correct things about politics and that was enough for the Old Man. For several months Trotsky failed to entertain the slightest suspicion, even though practical chaos occurred which was inexplicable unless Kharin was being deliberately disruptive. Eventually even Trotsky concluded that Kharin was an OGPU agent; he sent out alerts to this effect in matter-of-fact language and confessed to no fault on his own part.[27] As usual, once he had dropped someone, he acted as if that individual had never existed.

Anyone in contact with Trotsky might have been forgiven for wondering whether he properly appreciated the risks he was expecting others to run. A few letters continued to come through to him. There was an anonymous missive on the political situation in January 1930.[28] This was comforting proof that Blyumkin's execution had not stopped the flow of information. Further messages followed. One letter was from 'Svoi' in March 1932;[29] others arrived from 'Gromovoi' in the same year.[30] Both bolstered Trotsky's assumption that support for Stalin was on the wane in the USSR and that the party apparatus was turning against him.[31] 'Tenzov', who had written to Lëva from London in 1930, supplied chapter and verse on difficulties with industrial production and food supplies in February 1933; he added that the non-Russians were stirring themselves against the authorities. The *apparatchiki*, he insisted, were depressed about the general situation.[32]

After the Kharin affair, of course, Trotsky knew that the Moscow communist leadership would try to disrupt and infiltrate his organization abroad. He and his entourage frequently discussed this. But he never let their talk move over into serious preventive action. He did not bother himself with such precautions. Besides, he wanted a pleasant environment for work and leisure throughout the household and was keen to sustain a mood of optimism. He needed to attract fresh faces to carry out all the many tasks. He opined that even if the Kremlin pinned a young agent on him he would win him or her over to his side.[33] Such complacency made his operations vulnerable to penetration by spies and saboteurs, and the OGPU took full advantage. His only excuse was that he had no means of knowing in advance who was reliable and who should be shunned. He had arrived abroad in circumstances different from those which had existed before 1917 when he was always mingling with a big group of Marxists. He had no one to turn to for advice and was frequently fooled by individuals who stayed with him. They included the Sobolevicius brothers Ruvin and Abraham.[34] Another was Jacob Franck. This was a man recommended to Trotsky by Raisa Adler, wife of Alfred, for his linguistic skills.[35] The result was that the OGPU were acquainted Trotsky's plans throughout his Turkish stay and beyond.[36]

Lëva's tiny entourage was penetrated even more damagingly. In 1933 he was approached in Paris by someone he knew as Étienne, who volunteered to work for him. This was Soviet agent Mark Zborowski. His story was that he was a committed Trotskyist from Ukraine who had travelled to France in 1933 to offer his services. He retained Lëva's complete confidence despite the reservations expressed by French comrades. Étienne aimed to become indispensable to Lëva, and he succeeded. Cool-headed and assiduous, he relieved Lëva of many tasks in a heavy workload. Not everyone took to him. It was far from clear where he got his money from or even how he managed to subsist. Lëva's secretary Lola Estrina sympathetically invented jobs for him to do and paid him each time he did one of them. A routine was established: Étienne worked alongside Lëva in the mornings and Lola took his place in the afternoons.[37] Equipped

by his handlers with a camera, Étienne photographed items in the organization's files.[38] Lëva himself lived far from sumptuously. His father sent
him money but expected him to economize. Jeanne Martin, Lëva's partner,
had a small salary which supplemented their income.[39] Étienne's growing
prominence in this situation gave rise to suspicions among French
Trotskyists. Pierre Naville mentioned his worries to Trotsky, only to receive
a dusty retort: 'You want to deprive me of my collaborators.'[40] Scarcely a
secret of international Trotskyism remained closed to Étienne.

Letters from the USSR grew less frequent. 'Svoi' wrote on 25 March
1932 that Rakovski and Sosnovski were not dead and that Muralov had
paid a visit to Moscow before being sent back to Siberia. Police searches
were continuing. Allegedly the talk in the capital was all about Stalin being
'the enemy of October'. There were jokes that Trotsky ought to be asked
to send his directives for the Kremlin's guidance.[41] All this gave Trotsky
heart. But he had almost nobody to dispatch to Moscow (whereas the
Mensheviks, who had been printing their well-informed *Sotsialisticheski
vestnik* since the early 1920s, had dozens of potential couriers). Trotsky's
loose organization grew in size chiefly by recruiting European and American followers. He was getting desperate. He looked for ways to surmount
the difficulty of supplying the *Byulleten* with reports and essays on Russia.
Sometimes he did this by reading the *Sotsialisticheski vestnik*, which was
a regular source of accurate information. He also screened articles in
*Pravda* and other official Soviet newspapers. Reading between the lines,
he was able to guess at much that was going on.[42]

He could no longer pretend to himself that his absence had left an
unbearable vacancy on the Soviet political stage. New approaches had to
be invented. In 1932 he felt he could no longer rule out a reconciliation
of some kind with those who had 'capitulated' to Stalin and the Politburo.
He was turning to an idea he had previously repudiated. This was to
sanction the formation of a 'block' of oppositionists made up from all
the party's old factions. He would even consider reconciliation with the
supporters of Bukharin. Kamenev and Zinoviev could be approached.
The block would not involve an abandonment of mutual criticism and
Trotsky refused to contemplate organizational fusion. The first stage would
simply be to exchange information. Trotsky was evidently despondent
about gaining a toehold in any other way. He let it be known that his
*Byulleten oppozitsii* would publish documents from other factions on
condition that he could comment on them.[43] The plan was well nigh
strangled before birth. The leaders of the other former factions were too
fearful of their lives to have anything to do with it, and just a few dribbles

of information came through to Trotsky from his initiative. 'Block' is much too grand an appellation for what really resulted.

Stalin was therefore worrying unduly about Trotskyist operations at that time. Trotsky's own letters to agent Kharin supplied the proof that Trotskyists were in disorder abroad; and the Opposition's activity in the USSR was pitiful even though Trotsky could not bring himself to admit the fact.

An anonymous Leningrad correspondent in May 1933 reported: 'All opposition is wiped off [*sic*].' He mentioned disgruntlement in the factories and food shortages were reported in the south, but he gave no indication that the Stalin group was in danger.[44] Grounds for optimism had vanished. Some time in 1934 Lëva met up with a sympathizer in Paris who told him that talk of organized resistance to Stalin was exaggerated. Such little political grouplets as sprang up had no following and the old Opposition had lost all capacity to function.[45] Trotsky tried to comfort himself with the thought that he continued to agitate Stalin. He wrote in his diary:

> His craving for revenge on me is completely unsatisfied: there have been, so to speak, physical blows but morally nothing has been achieved. There is no refusal to work, no 'repentance', no isolation; on the contrary, a new historical momentum has been acquired which it is already impossible to halt. This is the source of the gravest apprehensions for Stalin: that savage fears ideas since he knows their explosive power and knows his own weakness in the face of them. At the same time he is clever enough to realize that even today I would not change places with him.[46]

That Stalin by then wanted him dead, there is little doubt. That he cared about Trotsky's feelings of superiority is possible and even likely. That Trotsky and his followers had a 'new historical momentum' is implausible.

At the same time it may be queried whether Trotsky was genuinely reconciled to his own absence from the Kremlin. His diary entry was an attempt at raising morale. He could not go on in life or in politics without feeling that he stood some chance of ultimate victory. If the evidence stood against this, it had to be knocked aside. The fight had to go on. He needed to go on heaping blame on the Stalin gang for all the ills of the years since 1917 if he was to justify his continuing émigré activity. Madness lay in every other direction.

# 44. EUROPE SOUTH AND NORTH

On a quiet day in 1935 Trotsky let his thoughts drift off to the life of Archpriest Avvakum, the leading cleric who had rejected the reforms in the Russian Orthodox Church introduced by Patriarch Nikon in the seventeenth century. Avvakum's punishment was Siberian exile. He and his wife were ordered to proceed there on foot. At one point, as they trudged along, she fell into a snowdrift. 'How long', she cried out, 'is this suffering going to be?' Avvakum gasped that it would last until death. His wife did not flinch: 'So be it, Petrovich, let's be getting on our way.' Trotsky spoke of this to Natalya before confiding to his diary: 'I can say one thing: never did Natalya "reproach" me, never – even in the most difficult hours; nor does she reproach me now, in the most burdensome days of our life when everything has conspired against us.'[1] His self-pity was more understandable than his self-righteousness. Avvakum suffered persecution although he had not harmed a fly, whereas Trotsky had persecuted innocuous people and as yet had suffered nothing like the pain he had inflicted on others. Like Avvakum, he stayed true to his convictions. He admitted to himself that the advance to world revolution might not occur while he was on earth; but he roused himself with the thought: 'I shall still pass into non-existence with indestructible confidence in the victory of the cause I have served all my life.'[2]

No end to his seclusion seemed likely on the tiny island in the Sea of Marmara until late in 1932. Out of the blue he received an invitation to speak to a students' meeting in Copenhagen. He eagerly agreed. The Workers Party had come to power in Denmark and its ministers made it possible for him to make the trip. They overlooked his contempt for both their socialism and their country's democracy – the Mensheviks and Socialist-Revolutionaries could have told them a thing or two about his record in Russia but they were not consulted. Danish social-democrats felt admiration for a man they saw as a victimized hero of the October Revolution. They ignored objections by Prince Aage, cousin to the King of Denmark, that Trotsky had belonged to a Soviet regime which murdered the descendants of the Danish princess who was the mother of Nicholas II.[3] Trotsky enthusiastically set about planning the journey and the lecture. There were no direct ferries from Istanbul to Scandinavia and he had to apply for permission to disembark in France. The Ministry of the Interior in Paris surprised him by giving its consent and allowing him to travel by rail from the Mediterranean south to Dunkirk where he could take a boat to Denmark.[4]

He left Istanbul on 14 November with Natalya and his entourage for a tranquil journey to Naples via Athens on the SS *Praga*. The brief stop in the southern Italian port gave passengers the chance to go sightseeing in Pompeii and Sorrento. From Naples they sailed on to Marseilles. The food had been poor despite the fact that the shipping line was Italian-owned. The little party were glad to set foot on French soil. Comrades from France's Communist League made a fuss of them. Trotsky was lionized by people who regarded him as the embodiment of the best purposes of the October Revolution.

The Communist League took responsibility for his security. Leading members guarded their idol on the train to the north. He was on brilliant form and seemed to tower over them even though he was of average height among the French.[5] Clustered round him, apart from Raymond Molinier and Jean van Heijenoort, were several young French Trotskyists. Lëva Sedov was a constant presence but talked mainly with his mother and in Russian. Natalya fretted that he was visibly getting very tired. She intervened whenever she thought he ought to go and lie down, but she rarely succeeded. The Old Man talked endlessly since he loved an audience. The sole disappointment for his listeners – and it was only a small one – was his refusal to adopt terms of comradely familiarity. Whereas they called each other 'tu' Trotsky insisted on being addressed as 'vous'. Only one of them, Jean Lastérade de Chavigny, ignored Trotsky's expectations of linguistic formality. Perhaps it was significant that de Chavigny was of upper-class social origin. Trotsky chose to overlook what he would other-wise have regarded as impertinence.[6]

The Dunkirk ferry took Trotsky and family to Copenhagen where he was scheduled to deliver his lecture on 27 November 1932. It was his first time on a public platform abroad since 1917. Trotsky put on all his charm, excusing himself for speaking in German. He mentioned the Scandinavian goddess of wisdom Snotra. He quoted from the plays of Ibsen (whom he had reviewed less than favourably in Siberian exile). Not wishing to embarrass his hosts, he kept off international politics in Europe.[7] He complained that his words and deeds in 1917 had been traduced. The

October Revolution had not been an accident. The entire social and economic situation had made it possible for the Bolsheviks to seize power. It had not been the *coup d'état* of a tiny group of armed extremists. Trotsky claimed that his theory of 'permanent revolution' had been proved correct; he recalled his insistence in 1905 that only the proletariat in Russia could make the revolution against the Romanov monarchy and that such a revolution would remain insecure except as 'the first stage of the socialist world revolution'. He repeated his contention in the mid-1920s that Stalin's project for 'socialism in one country' was a 'petit-bourgeois utopia'.[8]

Trotsky identified Aristotle, Shakespeare, Darwin, Beethoven, Goethe, Marx, Edison and Lenin as 'giants of thought and action'; he noted that all had belonged to the upper and middle classes. From among contemporary writers he picked out the bourgeois Sigmund Freud and his 'inspired hand':

> And what has been revealed? Our conscious thought is only a small part of the work of the dark psychic forces. Learnèd [*sic*] divers descend to the bottom of the ocean and there take photographs of mysterious fishes. Human thought, descending to the very bottom of its own psychic resources, must shed light on the most mysterious driving forces of the soul and subject them to reason and to will.[9]

If he wanted to show he was no narrow dogmatist, he succeeded. He brushed aside the conventional notion among Marxists of his generation that politics was generated only by the action of great social forces. Trotsky argued for Freud's ideas about the unconscious to be taken seriously. He ended on a political note by declaring that the time had come to liberate 'the sparks of genius in the suppressed depths of the people'. It would be people from the working class who would supply future intellectual greatness.[10]

The Copenhagen trip compelled a round of economizing on the return of the travellers to Turkey.[11] Trotsky was disappointed that he had not acquired a long-term Danish visa. Geographical proximity made Denmark sensitive to diplomatic pressure from the USSR. If Stalin's greatest personal enemies were to have received political asylum the consequences could have been a rupture of relations between the two countries.

Within months he had better news which came not from Copenhagen but from Paris. Persistent petitioning of the French authorities by Maurice Parijanine and others achieved a reconsideration of his request for a residential visa. The political situation had changed at the beginning of

1934 with the formation of a governmental coalition led by Édouard Daladier and the Radicals. Camille Chautemps, the Minister of the Interior, had been a friend of Khristian Rakovski during his time as Soviet plenipotentiary in France. These connections still counted for something.[12] Chautemps was no admirer of Bolshevism but was willing to issue Trotsky with a *visa de séjour*. Certain conditions were attached. Trotsky had to stay outside the main cities; he had to notify the Sûreté of any proposed movements outside wherever he chose to live. He was on no account to become involved in French politics. Having announced his acceptance of the offer, Trotsky embarked on the steamship *Bulgaria* on 17 July 1933. Accompanying him were Natalya, his entourage and his American follower Max Shachtman (who had been staying with them on Büyükada). Their destination was Marseilles via Piraeus.[13]

Just before they arrived the French authorities insisted on his coming ashore at nearby Ciotat. They feared that White Russian emigrants might make an attempt on his life; there was also a worry about public order if the French Communist Party organized a demonstration against him.[14] The ship dropped anchor short of Marseilles on 24 July. French comrades had arranged a place to stay the night, five or six miles from where they landed. Next morning they went by sea along the coast after hiring a rickety motor boat from Monsieur Panchetti in Cassis. French Trotskyists assembled the documents to supplicate for the revocation of the 1916 ministerial order for Trotsky's deportation. It was at this point that Trotsky found that he had not brought the appropriate papers along with him: 'Oh, what an idiot! I've . . . left them at home [in Turkey].' Panchetti helped to sort things out, although he treated his clients with circumspection, apparently suspecting they might be an international gang of murderers.[15]

Ways were found to get around the difficulty and a plan was put into effect for the Trotskys to make their home in the first instance in Saint-Palais, a small town near Royan on the northern rim of the Gironde. After the move Trotsky and Natalya behaved discreetly when receiving visiting supporters and editing the *Byulleten*. Their compliance was rewarded in November 1933 when the Ministry of the Interior relaxed its conditions of residence. Permission was given for them to move to Barbizon, thirty-odd miles to the south-east of Paris and close to the main road from the French capital to the south of the country. Renting a house on the edge of a forest, they contacted Lëva and other militants who could see them more freely than before. His presence in France was widely known and the French Communist Party as well as the political far right denounced the government for indulging him. So long as his whereabouts remained secret this was not too much of a problem. But the press discovered the Trotskys' address in April 1934, and Trotsky and Natalya moved provisionally to Domène outside Grenoble in southern France. They adopted fresh aliases. Communication with Lëva in Paris became more difficult.

Trotsky had arrived in France at a time of economic and political turmoil. He regarded the troubles as the threshold to the great revolution in Europe he had always dreamed about. The effects of the Great Depression were deep and long lasting. Workers went on strike to seek higher wages in a period of galloping financial inflation. Public life was increasingly polarized and fears grew about the rise of the far right. Pressure grew even in the French Communist Party for an end to Comintern's policy of regarding the Socialist Party rather than the fascist organizations as the main enemy. The German precedent was in everyone's mind. If nothing was done quickly, there was a chance that fascism might come to power in Paris. France was stretched over a political griddle. For Trotsky, the 'contradictions' could be resolved only if 'genuine' communists like his French comrades took power in Paris as he and the Bolsheviks had done in the October Revolution.

He and Natalya, though, were not as content as they might have been. They were living like runaways and his health deteriorated in the first half of 1935. He often spent the day in bed. It was a sign of his poor condition, mentally and physically, that he took up writing a diary.[16] He read a lot of French popular novels and seems to have despised all of them. He listened a lot to music on the radio.[17] Natalya coped most of the time until she too fell ill in May and ran a high temperature. The two of them stayed under the blankets day and night. Trotsky was impressed by her fortitude:

> 'If only you would get well,' she said to me today, lying in bed, 'I have no need for anything more.' She rarely says such things. And she said this so simply, evenly and quietly, and at the same time from such a depth that my whole soul was turned upside down.[18]

Natalya's words expressed love and devotion; they also signalled a degree of bafflement about his lack of a steely will to fight back against whatever it was that afflicted him. The relapse was the longest he had experienced since the mid-1920s. He was now fifty-five years old.

Unlike Trotsky, Stalin doubted that the French far left was any more likely than the German Communist Party had been to achieve a revolution. Collective security became his watchword in Europe in 1934 and he gave orders in the following year for the French Communist Party to liaise closely with the socialists and the liberals against the fascists and their allies in a 'popular front'. This was a somersault in Comintern's policy as the communist leadership in Moscow concentrated on forming an anti-fascist political alliance. The USSR was in danger of military attack by the Third Reich sooner or later. When the socialist Léon Blum led the popular front to electoral victory in France in 1936, the French Communist Party supported the governing coalition. To Trotsky this was further proof of Stalin's betrayal of communist principles. Blum, he believed, would never be strong enough to resist fascism. The only result of the Popular Front government would be a deflection of the working class from making a communist revolution. Trotsky did not on principle reject contact with the other socialist parties: he had criticized Stalin precisely for spurning any collaboration between the German communists and the German social-democrats against the Nazis. But popular fronts, in Trotsky's opinion, erred in the opposite direction. Essentially they were Stalin's device to prevent any great disturbance in Europe while Soviet industrialization proceeded.

According to Trotsky, the diplomatic liaison between Blum and Stalin was being introduced at the very time when revolutionary prospects were strong and getting stronger in France. He expected to be able to make a decisive contribution just as he had done in Russia in the struggle against the Provisional Government. He recorded his thoughts in his diary:

> For the sake of clarity I would put it like this. If I had not been in Petersburg in 1917, the Oct[ober] Rev[olution] would have occurred *on condition that Lenin's presence and leadership existed.* If neither Lenin nor I had been in Petersburg, there would have been no Oct[ober] Rev[olution]: the Bolshevik party leadership would have prevented it from being realized – I have not the slightest doubt about this! If Lenin had not been in Petersburg, I would hardly have coped with the resistance of the party leaders; the struggle with 'Trotskyism' (i.e. with proletarian revolution) would have been engaged from May 1917 and a question mark would have been attached to the outcome of the revolution.[19]

This was honest and accurate. It did not mean that Trotsky felt that he was going to play second fiddle to a greater leader in France in 1935.

He sensed, though, that his French followers might lack the judgement to know when and how to make an attempt on power. Their lack of tactical flexibility irritated him. He told Pierre Naville that he should be shot for saying that communists should oppose demands by the Alsatians for independence.[20] For Trotsky, anything that might help in breaking up bourgeois Europe was to be welcomed. He wrote along these lines to the Central Committee of the Parti Ouvrier Internationaliste on 21 June 1936. His considerations went back to the July Days in Russia in 1917 and he asked his French followers to re-read his *History of the Russian Revolution* for guidance.[21] He believed that they were risking the kind of setback suffered by the Bolsheviks in Petrograd when they prematurely organized an armed political demonstration against the Provisional Government. Flexibility in organization and policy was required. The Blum government was striving to suppress the far right, and the Trotskyists might therefore find themselves fighting on the same side as the Popular Front. Trotsky stressed that the tactic of a general strike would not necessarily bring success for them.[22] Being known for his prescient calls for a surgical offensive against Nazism before 1933, Trotsky acquired a widening audience. Trotskyism in France experienced a surge of popularity as a campaign for recruitment among youngsters produced results. Even so, the French Trotskyists were still only countable in the hundreds.[23]

His son Lëva was among those who chafed against Trotsky's arguments for caution. In 1934 he had disobeyed orders and taken part in a street demonstration in Paris. He was grabbed by a gendarme before breaking free. If he had been arrested the question of his right of residence would have arisen. His bravado was ill advised.[24] Trotsky as a young militant had been like Lëva but now he urged careful political planning: 'We must not let ourselves be directed down this path. On the contrary, we must emphasize the grandiose tasks and difficulties of the enterprise. The precondition for the success of a new general strike are factory committees and soviets.'[25] He understood that the Parti Ouvrier Internationaliste was in no condition as yet to issue a decisive challenge to the French government.[26] He felt he needed to pour cold water on the optimism of his comrades. The problem was that for years he had been declaring France ripe for revolution. They had some justification in asking: if not now, when?

The liaison of the French and Soviet governments was a disaster for Trotsky. He was told by the French government that he was no longer *persona grata*. He was afraid of being deported to one of France's African colonies where he would lose all chance of gearing up his international political apparatus. It consequently came as a relief in May 1935 when he learned that the Labour government in Norway was looking with favour on his request for a residence visa. Although he did not know Norwegian and had only a few active supporters in the country, he could stay in contact with the rest of the world by mail just as he had been doing in France. He thought he could cope. He was far from assuming that democracy would hold out in Norway but as a provisional measure it made sense to make the move. Heijenoort came to see him on 9 June with the news that Oslo had granted the visa.[27] Trotsky and Natalya were used to hoping for the best in Scandinavia. Their part-time servant was away at the time, so Natalya did all the housework and most of the packing until Heijenoort helped a few days later. Trotsky, apart from looking after his political papers, concentrated on how he was going to look on arrival in Norway; he sped off to Grenoble to have his hair, beard and moustache trimmed.[28]

Once more they bade goodbye to their friends and, on 10 June 1936, set off across France bound for Paris. They had Jean van Heijenoort and Jan Frankel as companions and stopped over in Paris where Seva, Zina Bronstein's son, was living with Lëva Sedov. They had not seen young Seva for three years and discovered that he had lost his facility in Russian.[29] The family reunion was brief. Plans were made to keep everyone in touch with each other – Trotsky had to be assured that all would be well with the *Byulleten oppozitsii* and his publishing ventures. Tears were shed, and then it was by train to Antwerp and by ferry to Oslo. The vessel docked in Oslo on 18 June. It was midsummer at longitude 59°N, which the Norwegian capital shared with St Petersburg. To that extent Trotsky and Natalya felt almost at home. They had last experienced such light and such climate in Russia in midsummer 1917. In every other way they felt out of place and vulnerable. Norway's government thought it had discharged its obligations by issuing the visas, and the time had long passed since any Soviet consulate would offer a temporary shelter to the Trotskys. To the rescue came the writer and socialist Konrad Knudsen with the offer of a house in the country forty miles from Oslo. He wanted no payment.

They had arrived just as preparations were being made for the first of the three big Moscow show-trials, involving sixteen defendants. Kamenev and Zinoviev were among them as were past followers of Trotsky such as Sergei Mrachkovski. Trotsky had no way of knowing about the tortures applied to those who appeared in the biggest trials. He commented on the absurdity of the charges in the light of the known facts. He mourned the lapse from revolutionary rectitude of some of his former comrades, accepting that even Zinoviev and Kamenev had once had their merits. All the defendants were found guilty as charged after admitting their guilt. Trotsky, moreover, was officially implicated as leader of an international terrorist conspiracy. On 24 August 1936 he was condemned to death *in absentia*. The Norwegian cabinet felt under pressure to distance itself from him. Regardless of Trotsky's protestations of innocence, ministers had to consider the future of diplomatic relations with the USSR. Their nerve failed them and on 2 September the government put Trotsky under house arrest until such time as a definitive decision might be taken. He was interned in Hurum, which lies between Skoger and Oslo.

Natalya said the new place reminded them of their enforced stay in Halifax, Nova Scotia in 1917. Knudsen did his best. He gave them a radio so that they could listen to foreign broadcasts and get world news; he also left some magnificent flowers in the living room. Yet the isolation bore down on the couple. Trotsky no longer had ready access to facilities for research. Publishers' deadlines were oppressing him. Insomnia returned.[30] Natalya thought he was working much too hard. He took no notice until his old maladies began to drag him down.[31] Natalya, depressed, lashed out at Lëva for being too slow in carrying out his many tasks. Characteristically she soon apologized. The last thing she wanted was to torment her elder son.[32] She sensed that that her husband was descending into one of his lengthy periods of ill health. This could entail months of rest just at a time when he needed to defend himself against the Kremlin's libels. Some days he even lacked the strength to go outside and sit on his chaise longue.[33] Reading was his only solace, and Lëva was asked to send him copies of Malraux, Céline, Simenon and Freud.[34] They made for lighter reading than the reports of the show-trials.

Trotsky and Natalya assumed that they were safer in Norway than they had been in France. They behaved accordingly, leaving the yard gate open day and night. A journalist took advantage of this and crept along the wall to take a photograph. Heijenoort chased him back to the village. On another occasion a couple of harmless drunks turned up.[35] A more welcome visitor was a doctor from Czechoslovakia who carried out some medical tests. He found nothing definite before departing. Rest appeared the finest available medicine and Trotsky's condition gradually improved as he maintained his recumbent regime. The surest sign of amelioration was that he gave up writing his diary.[36]

A volley of counter-shots against the accusations made against him in Moscow was the result. Trotsky was returning to fighting form. He filled the *Byulleten* with exposures of the bizarre lies being told about him and Lëva. He worked frantically to defend his reputation. The terms of his confinement allowed him to communicate with Lëva and his French lawyer Gérard Rosenthal, but otherwise his correspondence was restricted – and the censorship was intrusive. It was essential to clear his name if he was to avoid yet another deportation. He decided to appeal to the League of Nations. The USSR had initiated the setting up of an international tribunal for trying terrorists. Trotsky hoped to use this as a device to refute the Kremlin's allegations, and on 22 October he instructed his Norwegian attorney Michael Puntervold to write to the League's Juridical Section. Nothing good resulted.[37] None of his schemes for survival were working and Trotsky had to depend on what others were doing for him. Without his knowledge something positive was happening on the other side of the Atlantic. Diego Rivera, his favourite Mexican painter, was busily petitioning President Lázaro Cárdenas and the Party of Institutional Revolution to give Trotsky asylum.

The Mexican government had a policy of welcoming European leftist refugees; and as the Spanish Civil War drew to a close with the victory of Franco and the fascists in the following year, Cárdenas was to offer visas to the defeated Republicans.[38] The cabinet was undertaking agrarian reform and striving to stay independent of American capitalism – and he gathered political and cultural support in his country by welcoming eminent anti-capitalist foreigners. Gérard Rosenthal conducted negotiations with the counsellor at the Mexican consulate-general in Paris. Progress was slow because the consul-general spoke no French; but an agreement was made.[39] Trotsky had to promise to keep out of Mexico's politics. Not every Trotskyist approved of the Mexican plan. Max Shachtman wrote that Trotsky's life 'would not be worth a penny there'.[40] Trotsky's own preference had been for a move to the USA but Washington would not hear of it. He had to take what was available, and somehow he would manage. The transatlantic telegraph service would enable rapid emergency communication between the Old and New Worlds; and the ocean-borne postal deliveries were not intolerably slow. The plan was to leave Lëva in France to supervise the *Byulleten* and keep an eye on the activities of Europe's Trotskyists. Things could have been worse. And they would become so over the next few years.

# 45. SETTING UP IN MEXICO

The oil tanker *Ruth* with the Trotskys on board took twenty days to chug its way across the Atlantic. It had been chosen for its inconspicuousness because both the Norwegian authorities and Trotsky's entourage judged it risky for him to take any of the usual cruisers. He and Natalya were the sole passengers. They set sail on 20 December 1936, and, as was his practice when he was removed from opportunities for practical activity, he started a diary. The captain and crew were friendly towards the refugee couple. Trotsky read up on Mexico and flicked through a biography of the Istanbul-born Greek arms dealer and financier Sir Basil Zaharoff – just the sort of historical reading to confirm that international capitalism was rotten to the core.[1] He also drafted a book to be published as *The Crimes of Stalin*.[2] He would have to have been at death's door before failing to write something connected with contemporary Marxism.

The ship dropped anchor on 9 January 1937 off Tampico, the big oil town on the Gulf of Mexico 160 miles to the north-east of Mexico City. The Trotskys worried that an assassin might lurk in wait for them on the quayside. The ship captain, on orders from the Norwegian government, had denied them radio contact with their Mexican friends. The couple could not even discover the terms of the visa being offered to them by the Cárdenas government.[3] Trotsky spoke angrily with the captain and induced him to send a telegram to the Norwegian consul on land. Arrangements were made for a Mexican official to take a boat out to the tanker and pick up the two refugees. On board would be various friends and journalists. Diego Rivera was absent through illness but his wife and fellow painter Frida Kahlo was present. With her were the American Trotskyists Max Shachtman and George Novack.[4] The Trotskys were somewhat appeased but disliked the landscape, which reminded them of the ugly, polluted Baku in Azerbaijan. They cheered up on finding that General Francisco Mugica, Minister of Communications and Public Works, had reserved a comfortable train carriage for them. The reception party made its way to Mexico City and then to Coyoacán on its western outskirts where Frida Kahlo gave them the freedom of her home, the Blue House on Avenida Londres.[5]

The Trotskys had not lived in such comfort since the early 1920s. The garden was full of vivid flowers. Parrots squawked in the trees' foliage. The internal décor of the house combined rustic Mexican and ultra-contemporary styles. The rooms were spacious and airy. Servants were on hand to tend to the needs of residents. Food was plentiful – and Trotsky, whose medical problems had made him picky about his diet, found he took well to Mexico's spicy cuisine. Frida and Diego did not mind how many Trotskyists visited, and Trotsky encouraged them to join the permanent entourage if they had the talent and inclination.

To meet their running expenses he had to go on publishing books of popular appeal. This was never quite enough. He therefore gave paid seminars on current affairs to American students on their trips to Mexico. He also charged for newspaper interviews. When the *Baltimore Sun* sent a man down to talk to him, Trotsky asked for a thousand dollars – a fortune at the time. He failed to understand, according to the journalist, that he was no longer a man of power but only a former 'commissar of all the Russias'.[6] Trotsky was anyway fed up with interviews because he thought that editors too often emasculated his words even if the journalist was conscientious.[7] Books, of course, took a long time to write and he was running out of commercial projects after his autobiography and his history of the Russian Revolution. Even his contracts for biographies of Lenin and Stalin were not going to be a complete solution to his financial problems. At the same time he could not undertake fresh commercial projects until he had met his existing contractual obligations. He therefore decided to make quick money – US$1,000 – by selling copies of his political correspondence from the years 1918–22 to the Institute of Social History in Amsterdam.[8]

The Mexican police provided him with protection round the clock and sent regular reports on him to the government. They were not the only people keeping a watch on him. The Mexican Communist Party was obliged to hold him under surveillance and inform Moscow. Even the US authorities, having barred him from living in the United States, maintained a file on him.[9]

Trotsky settled quickly at the Blue House. His hosts openly identified themselves with Trotsky in his struggle against Stalin and the 'official' world communist movement, and they praised and defended Trotsky at every opportunity. His needs were well looked after. The servants were used to Diego and Frida painting all day long so that nobody thought it odd of him to spend his time reading and writing. He had complete peace for his work.[10] His library of books, diminished on leaving Turkey, was growing again. He always had a book or article on the go. He stayed in touch with his followers by post; he received visitors in the afternoon but only if they applied in advance for an interview. Trotsky usually gave a warm reception to Americans, in the hope that they might be wealthy and make a donation to the cause. The Blue House bustled with people entering and leaving, but the Trotskys themselves had to be cautious about venturing out. It was too dangerous to visit the many sites of cultural interest in Mexico City. They could not even go and admire the brilliant murals of his host Rivera. The deal he had struck was that he would stay out of Mexican public life, and Trotsky stuck to it. He worked up a little Spanish. But he read next to nothing in the language: his chores in writing and organizing allowed no time for this.

He and Natalya had to have some outlet for entertainment and found it in trips to the countryside miles away from the capital. The police were consulted in advance. A car or two, including a Dodge truck, would be organized. Clothes were packed, food was piled into baskets. Then the armed entourage set off. Trotsky liked the ride to Cuernavaca, a town that had given delight to the novelist D. H. Lawrence. Another favourite spot was the mountainous silver-mine city of Taxco which attracted hundreds of American tourists annually. The journeys took several hours in each direction, and for a while the Trotskys could feel free of their worries. The Old Man loved to go searching for rare cactuses just as once he had hunted birds, deer and bears. From no body of knowledge or experience, he would argue with Joe Hansen about the best way to cook hot dogs. The atmosphere was carefree except on the occasion when Harold Robins, an American Trotskyist staying with the Trotskys for a while, opined that Mexican mechanics did not have a clue about mending defective brakes. Trotsky rebuked him for national prejudice. He himself was on the look-out for unusual plants to take back to the garden in Coyoacán. Son of a farmer, he worked off his tensions by digging out the plants and staggering back to the vehicle with them; he resisted offers of assistance from the younger men.[11]

The outings blotted out the woes of the family only temporarily. Lëva remained in France looking after the *Byulleten oppozitsii* and caring for young Seva with Jeanne's help. There was no hope of seeing them again in the near future. Trotsky's time in the Blue House coincided with an intensification of political terror in the USSR. His kith and kin bore the consequences. Sergei Sedov was arrested; he was sent from Moscow to

Siberia on 3 August 1935. By then he had fallen out of love with his wife Olga and, despite continuing to live with her, formed a relationship with Genrietta Rubinshtein who ignored the pleadings of her parents and voluntarily followed him to Krasnoyarsk. He shouted to her from his cell in the transit prison that she should go back to Moscow for her own sake. Soon he was released and allowed to work legally in the city where his technical expertise gained him employment in the goldmine industry.[12] Genrietta, who gave birth to their daughter Yulia in the Soviet capital in 1936, was arrested a year later. Yulia was brought up by her Rubinshtein grandparents and never saw her father.[13]

The Trotskys were distraught about Sergei. They perceived that Stalin was seeking barbaric revenge on Trotsky by persecuting his innocent relatives. The thought occurred to Trotsky that the Bolsheviks in July 1918 had not stopped at executing Nicholas II but had slaughtered every Romanov they could get their hands on. Trotsky had not been privy to the decision on the death penalty. Indeed he had wanted to put the former emperor on public trial and use the proceedings to expose the iniquities of the Imperial order. Yet he stood by what had been ordered by Lenin and Sverdlov in his absence, and he recorded this in his diary on 9 April 1935. The entry for the following day included the comment: 'No news of Serëzha, and perhaps there won't be for a long time.'[14] It is hard to believe that Trotsky in some mental recess was not making a connection between the two situations. He understood that a precedent had been set in the Civil War for relatives of 'enemies of the people' to be exterminated. Trotsky's dignified tone faded at that point and he added superciliously that Sergei could have coped better if he had developed an active interest in politics.[15]

Trotsky's first wife Alexandra Bronstein suffered for her past: she was arrested in 1935 and sent out to a village in Omsk province in Siberia. The security agencies searched their card indexes and rounded up nearly everyone related to Trotsky by blood or marriage. This was repression by genealogy as well as political orientation. For a while Alexandra wrote to Trotsky and he wrote back and sent money orders. The correspondence petered out when the Soviet authorities stopped delivering it. Trotsky knew that no news was bad news. In fact Alexandra survived until 1938. Her troubles had started with a short-lived marriage contracted to keep her and Trotsky together in Siberia – and it was in Siberia that she finally expired.

Concerns in the Trotsky household were focused on relatives caught in the USSR. Less attention was paid to Lëva. This was understandable since he was legally registered as a resident in France and had no trouble from the police. Yet the situation in Europe was worsening for Trotskyists. A series of assassinations took place. Erwin Wolf, a Jew from Czechoslovakia who had worked as Trotsky's personal assistant in Norway, was liquidated in mysterious circumstances after being seized in Spain in July 1937. Rudolf Klement, a German follower who had worked directly for Trotsky in Turkey and France, was killed in Paris in July 1938; it was a grisly murder and parts of his dismembered body were fished out of the Seine over several days. Trotsky assumed that Lëva knew how to look after himself. Neither of them had any excuse for complacency after Ignacy Reiss, a Soviet security officer of Polish nationality, warned leading Trotskyists in spring 1937 that the Kremlin had decided to eliminate all of them.[16] This was to be a priority for the People's Commissariat for Internal Affairs (NKVD), which in 1934 had incorporated the functions previously discharged by the OGPU. If the warning was a true one, it had to involve mortal danger for Trotsky and Lëva. Reiss himself was murdered shortly afterwards. Then an anonymous letter came through to Trotsky stating that a Soviet agent using the alias of 'Mark' had gained a high post in his global political apparatus. Lëva's secretary Lola Estrina was visiting Mexico at the time and Trotsky showed her what he had received. On returning to France, she told Étienne – the NKVD agent Mark Zborowski – about it. Neither Trotsky nor Estrina was the world's most accomplished conspirator, and Lëva was no better.[17]

Correspondence between father and son held to its usual track. Lëva reported on French political developments. He wrote about the local Trotskyists; he also gave an account of the fortunes of the *Byulleten*. He stated that little Seva was doing well. He seldom mentioned how exhausted he himself felt, and whenever he was ill, unlike Trotsky, he made light of his problems. Lëva was a living martyr to the cause of the international Opposition. Jeanne had never been the easiest of partners, and since summer 1936 Lëva had found secret solace in the arms of Hélène Savanier on occasional trips to Antibes – he and Jeanne had stayed with the Savaniers when first they came to Paris as refugees from Germany.[18]

Lëva was less and less able to put up with his father's outbreaks of pique, especially when he accused him of mishandling the French comrades.[19] After Natalya took Trotsky's side in April 1936 Lëva could stand it no longer: 'it seems to me that all Papa's failings are getting worse with age: his intolerance, hot temper, teasing, even crudity and his desire to offend, do down and annihilate.'[20] Why the frequent ruptures of relations with comrades? Why the sharp words to Lëva? Trotsky had to start to accept that 'an organization consists of living people'; he needed to see that individuals reacted by not writing to him about sensitive topics: 'Papa never recognizes when he's in the wrong. That's why he can't bear criticism. When something is said or written to him with which he disagrees he either ignores it entirely or gets back with a harsh reply.'[21] Lëva admitted that the International Secretariat operated poorly. He had never pretended otherwise. His point was that cursing its members would not bring about an improvement.[22]

Lëva also resented his father's condescension and objected to being publicly described as a student. Lëva pointed out to his mother that he was older than Trotsky himself had been when he led the Petersburg Soviet in 1905. This reminded the son of Nikolai Gogol's novella *Taras Bulba* where the hero's mother consistently refers to every adult offspring as a 'young child'.[23] He told Lola Estrina: 'If someone calls me "the son" in your presence, please stop him and say, "You mean Lev Lvovich Sedov, he has a name of his own." '[24] Perhaps he was beginning to be reckless in what he said to people. According to Zborowski, he drank too much and liked gambling at the roulette wheel.[25] Supposedly he had decided that Trotsky's refusal to consider trying to get Stalin killed was mistaken.[26] Zborowski claimed that Sedov wanted him to travel to Moscow, presumably on a mission to carry out the assassination.[27] If all this was true it is hardly surprising that Soviet security forces intensified their effort to eliminate him. Even if Zborowski made it up, feeling that he needed to corroborate the official image of Trotskyists as terrorists, it would still have had the same impact on minds in the Kremlin.

In November 1936 eighty kilos of Trotsky's archive was stolen from the International Institute of Social History at 7 rue de Michelet. The director of the Institute was Boris Nikolaevski. Despite being a Menshevik, he had earned Lëva's trust by lending rare books to him and Trotsky. He was a devoted collector of all material that shed light on Russian revolutionary history and Lëva had decided that his father's files would be safest in his care. The burglars left no sign of breakage on entry. The police were foxed. Sedov informed them that only Nikolaevski, Estrina, Zborowski and Heijenoort knew of the existence of the deposit; and he guaranteed the good faith of all of them.[28] Everyone suspected the NKVD but no one knew how the crime had been planned and undertaken.

By the winter of 1937–8 Sedov's frenetic activity was exacting an intolerable toll when he had to seek treatment for stomach pains. Consulting only a few associates, including Étienne, he went to the Clinique Mirabeau on 9 February 1938; he was sufficiently worried beforehand to write his will and testament on the same day, leaving everything to Jeanne Martin.[29] The Mirabeau was a small hospital, east of the Bois de Boulogne, owned by a Dr Girmonski and staffed by Russians. Lola Estrina's sister-in-law, a doctor, had made a tentative diagnosis of appendicitis and recommended Dr Simkov as a surgeon. Pretending to be a French engineer, Lëva reverted to Russian when he entered the premises. Dr Simkov together with Dr Thalheimer, who worked for several Paris hospitals, thought he had an intestinal occlusion. They operated on him at 11 p.m. The first result seemed positive and Lëva received visits by Lola and Étienne. On 13 February, however, the patient's condition worsened. Getting up in the middle of the night, he tottered naked, febrile and delirious along the corridors. Jeanne Martin, rushing to the ward, was horrified to see he had a wide purple bruise. Dr Thalheimer wondered whether Lëva had tried to take his own life. The decision was taken to give him a blood transfusion. Injections were administered on 15 February. Nothing produced any improvement and the doctors were acting more by guesswork than by scientific conviction. Lëva's intestines were in paralysis. He lost consciousness and entered a coma.[30]

Despite a further blood transfusion, Lëva died at eleven o'clock that morning. His associates, while having no proof, suspected medical foul play. They guarded the corpse until an autopsy could take place. Étienne mentioned that Lëva's health had been poor since the Moscow show-trials and that he had been troubled by fever.[31] Rosenthal recalled this remark soon afterwards. Was Étienne trying to deflect attention from himself?

A telegram was sent to Trotsky and Natalya. The news shattered them and they shut themselves away for days in their bedroom and spoke to no one. When they emerged Trotsky blamed Lëva's death on Stalin and the Soviet security agencies. Proof was hard to come by. The authorities in Paris barely exerted themselves, despite a barrage of requests from Coyoacán, to ascertain the truth. Trotsky suspected that the French government was more eager to sustain good relations with the USSR than to do right by a dead Trotskyist. He may well have been right. France and the Soviet Union were concerting efforts at the time to foster 'collective security' in Europe against German expansionism. At any rate Trotsky accused the clinic and the doctors of being instruments in the hands of Stalin's security forces.[32] Generally he had plenty of grounds for suspecting that a murder had taken place. The NKVD had a larger network of informers and agents in Paris than in any other foreign city after the Spanish Civil War. Étienne may not have been the main procurer of death since there were several other agents who could have organized such an assassination. And Stalin had made little secret of his desire to bring the entire group around Trotsky to extinction.

There remain doubts, though, whether it would have made sense for the NKVD to order the liquidation of Lëva Sedov. Alive he was a source of intimate information about his father's plans since Étienne had permission to open the mail at his own apartment.[33] This facility was destroyed by his death; and when, many decades later, NKVD officers had the opportunity to comment on their European operations they did not boast of having liquidated Sedov.[34] What is more, the hospital's regular doctors were not the only ones responsible for Lëva's care. Having diagnosed an intestinal blockage, they brought in experts from outside when mystified by his unresponsiveness to their treatment. Recalling how Lëva had wandered in delirium around the ward, some of the medical staff were to wonder whether he had administered to himself a dose of some unknown substance in a suicide attempt. His condition perplexed everybody. Gérard Rosenthal was worried enough to persuade his father, a medical consultant, to assist at Lëva's bedside. This would have made it difficult for anyone deliberately to carry out a lethal act of surgery. Furthermore, Lëva's friends ensured that a toxicological analysis was carried out before the cremation.[35]

The younger Rosenthal recorded an open verdict, despite his suspicions about Étienne, but did not deny that the death could have been caused by poisoning. Jeanne Martin, who had been by Sedov's bedside and observed nothing suspicious, was satisfied by the results of the autopsy (which she herself had demanded).[36] The death retains its mysteries to this day.[37] What can be said with confidence, though, is that if he had survived his treatment in the Clinique Mirabeau there would have been attempts on his life in the future. His chances of growing old had always been slim.

Trotsky produced a moving booklet about Lëva. There were hints of guilt feelings arising out of the way he had sometimes handled their relationship. He condemned the Stalin regime for carrying out the crime. Trotsky and Natalya wrote to Jeanne Martin seeking custody of their grandson Seva. They wanted to bring the boy across the Atlantic to Mexico. Jeanne resisted. Tormented by the loss of Lëva, instinctively she hung on to Seva. Trotsky wrote a tender letter to Seva explaining that arrangements were being made for his transfer to Coyoacán, but Jeanne refused co-operation and fled Paris with Seva. Lëva's shocking death brought her to mental disintegration. Her mood became unpredictable. She started using physical violence in disputes with comrades.[38] Trotsky wrote to Étienne and Estrina saying he had totally lost confidence in her – and he called her by her married surname Molinier.[39] Gérard Rosenthal acted as Trotsky's intermediary and lawyer in France. He pointed out to Jeanne that Seva's father might one day emerge from Siberia to reclaim his son. This forced her to face up to the fact that she had no right to continue as the boy's legal guardian. Her opposition crumbled. Alfred and Marguerite Rosmer, who had known Trotsky since before 1917 and were among his ardent French followers, took custody of Seva on the Trotskys' behalf and brought him over to Mexico in August 1939. Trotsky and Natalya became formally responsible for him.[40]

# 46. THE FOURTH INTERNATIONAL

Trotsky had lost a devoted, brilliant son; he and Natalya shut themselves away in their rooms to mourn. Yet he was tough-minded. A week after the telegram from Paris he was asking Étienne-Zborowksi and Lola Estrina about the 'fate of the Bulletin'.[1] An anonymous correspondent in December 1938 was to warn him that Étienne was a Soviet intelligence agent.[2] (The writer of the letter was Alexander Orlov; he claimed to have a relative in the Soviet security services but in fact he was himself a former OGPU officer and a defector.) Natalya took longer to recover, if indeed she ever did in Trotsky's lifetime, and for many months she burst into tears without warning. The house in Coyoacán felt like a prison to her; for whereas the young supporters and guards knew that they were there temporarily, the Trotskys were permanent involuntary residents.[3] Natalya believed that the French comrades were doing too little to find out what had happened in Paris. She was clutching at straws. Trotsky reacted by calling it murder and blaming Stalin as the sole instigator. Although he began to work again he was less communicative with his entourage than earlier when he had prided himself on being prompt and punctilious. His aides noticed that he was leaving his correspondence unanswered on his desk, and discreetly apologized on his behalf.[4]

It was months before he resumed his ebullience. One of his objectives was to co-ordinate the Opposition by forming a new International – the Fourth International – with the aim of supplanting Comintern in the leadership of communism around the world. It had never been realistic for Trotsky to think he might win over the many parties of Comintern. Stalin controlled Comintern's central apparatus in Moscow. People suspected of sympathies with Trotsky had been systematically removed, and the dispute between Stalin and Bukharin in 1928–9 had led to the elimination of all known Bukharinists. Trotsky had held to his illusions until the Nazi rise to power in Germany. The German Communist Party's failure to prevent Hitler from becoming chancellor in January 1933 brought him to the painful conclusion that he had to make an entirely fresh start.

Unfortunately for Trotsky the Opposition had only a small number of supporters in most countries – and in Germany, where Trotsky had concentrated much of his hopes and propaganda, the Nazis quickly extirpated communist groupings. Trotsky's call for a Fourth International did not go uncontested. It was in the nature of the project that he needed the consent of anti-Stalin communist groupings around the world. Not all of them immediately agreed that a break was required with the parties of Comintern. His Spanish followers Arlen and Vela wrote to Trotsky to object to the formation of a new communist party in Germany.[5] But they carried little weight against most Trotskyists in Europe and North America. The way soon became clear for Trotsky to set about providing a strategic rationale and organizational base for his scheme.

The Fourth International was a further five years in gestation while the framework of organization and recruitment was assembled around the world. The new parties had to be persuaded to look outwards; Trotsky insisted that internal divisiveness should be avoided. Communications between him and the national leaderships needed to be as smooth and as rapid as the telegraph, postal services and steamships allowed. In late 1936 the surveillance of his mail in Norway was so blatant that he included pleading messages to the censors in his letters to Lëva.[6] Trotsky and Lëva watched for signs of infiltration by the Soviet intelligence agencies. They frequently speculated that their plans were known in Moscow, especially when they suffered from actions which implied inside knowledge.[7]

All Trotskyist groups were similarly anxious about being penetrated. Internal recriminations were common. Often they were based on nothing more than circumstantial coincidence. Raymond Molinier was widely thought to be a Soviet agent. Gérard Rosenthal came to distrust Lëva's partner Jeanne, and Lëva broke personal relations with him over this.[8] The situation was complicated by the fact that the Opposition's International Secretariat was based in France. Trotsky was later to write that the Secretariat was a mere fiction and really conducted nothing but French activity; he rebuked the French comrades for their bickering and their splits.[9] Molinier did not endure long in his favour. Trotsky in early 1934 had proposed that the Communist League should try to increase its influence by getting its members to infiltrate and radicalize the French Socialist Party. When Molinier rejected the idea he and Trotsky fell into dispute.[10] Jeanne Martin raised the temperature of emotions by expressing a preference for Molinier's policy.[11] This meant that Lëva and Jeanne were at loggerheads. Disputes were personal as well as political. Trotsky had his way in the end and the bulk of French Trotskyists came over to his recommended line of action.

The American far left too attracted sustained interest because he believed its Trotskyists were not exerting themselves to move beyond their sectarian confines. In January 1934 he wrote to his follower Max Shachtman of the Communist League of America proposing the idea of fusing with Albert Weisbord and the Communist League of Struggle. Weisbord, who was an unknown quantity to Trotsky, was notorious for his egomania and fractiousness. For once, Trotsky put his suggestion with a degree of tact.[12] Indeed when the Communist League of America unanimously rejected it Trotsky backed down: 'I am aware that only the League can decide this question. And if you are all against it, there is nothing more for me to say.'[13]

The first gathering designed to prepare the ground for the Fourth International opened in Brussels, after problems with the Dutch authorities made it impossible to meet in Holland, on 28 February 1934. It was a conference of far-left youth organizations. There were a mere fourteen delegates and only Germany, Norway, Holland and the USA were represented. Schismatic tendencies were abundant. Avowed Trotskyists were not the sole participants and not everyone liked the idea of forming a Fourth International even though there was unanimity that the Second and Third Internationals were politically bankrupt. Trotskyists fumbled their way towards the lowest common denominator of the conflicting views. It was the best they could do.[14] Their best was not good enough for Trotsky, who hated the vagueness of the decisions. He wrote to his adherents complaining that they had made too big a concession to non-Trotskyists. The circumstances reminded him of the compromises that had occurred inside the Zimmerwald movement in the Great War. The International Secretariat had a more realistic appreciation of the situation and decide to ignore him. The paradox of these exchanges did not escape Albert Glotzer. He noted that Trotsky had pressed exactly such a conciliatory policy on the Communist League of America. Now Trotsky wanted a sharp demarcation from non-Trotskyists at the world level.[15]

Trotsky's refusal to recognize such contradictions bemused his followers. Most of them as yet did not see how authoritarian he was. Distance increased his crotchetiness. What is more, he felt he had learned from history that indulgence towards opponents was counter-productive. At Zimmerwald it had been Lenin, not Trotsky, who had been the tireless splitter – and Trotsky had come to conclude that Lenin had been right.

Lëva Sedov resented his father's categorical judgements about

European comrades. Trotsky took a shine to Raymond Molinier and rejected every piece of cautionary advice from Lëva. Molinier was a force of nature, bull-headed and thick-set.[16] Lëva stood his ground but Trotsky's response in January 1936 was to accuse his son of bureaucratic stubbornness.[17] Perhaps he also suspected Lëva of a lack of impartiality since he had taken Molinier's wife Jeanne from him. Lëva's judgement, though, was widely shared among French Trotskyists. Molinier was imperious and was frank about it: 'We have Trotsky for our doctrine and Stalin for our methods.'[18] Intellectually he was unimpressive and there were concerns that his financial management was not entirely honourable. This was the opinion of Gérard Rosenthal and the veteran Alfred Rosmer.[19] Although Trotsky began to withdraw support from Molinier in mid-1935 it was only in July 1936 that the International Bureau finally expelled him from its organizations. The Bureau was the Paris-based co-ordinating body for Trotskyist groups, and it liaised with Lëva and Trotsky before moving against Molinier. Trotsky started to describe him as an adventurer; he never admitted the flaws in his earlier firm assessment of him.[20]

The co-ordination of the French comrades was a task beyond even Trotsky, as he told Pierre Naville: 'You know, I've never seen factional struggles like the ones you have. We had a lot of them. It wasn't always soft, oh no! But I've never seen the fierce disputes that you have. That's really extraordinary. How's this possible? This needs to be corrected.'[21]

Trotsky admitted in theory that he could not give specific guidance about matters facing particular Trotskyist groups around the world, and sometimes he refused to hand out rulings. This was not his usual way. More often than not he stuffed his letters with instructions on matters great and small. He meddled even when he lacked rudimentary knowledge of local situations. He also had personal favourites, especially among his supporters in Germany and France – and he did not always make a sensible choice. His trump card in any discussion was his experience in the October Revolution and the Civil War. When a Spanish comrade advocated a policy he disliked in the mid-1930s, he enquired: 'How many comrades in your group have fallen in combat?' The answer was: 'Well, fortunately, none until now.'[22] This was Trotsky's way of putting the comrade at a psychological disadvantage. His self-confidence had frequently turned him into a bungler. Even after almost every European Trotskyist had concluded that the Sobolevicius brothers were Stalin's agents he went on regarding them as sympathizers who had simply gone wrong and 'betrayed' him. He could not bring himself to admit that he had been fooled by them from the start of their apparent support for his cause.[23]

27. Lev Sedov, Trotsky's elder son.

28. Jeanne Martin des Pallières, Lev Sedov's partner.

29. A cartoon of Trotsky in a Fourth International publication.

30. The Blue House at Coyoacán: a mixture of traditional and modern.

31. Trotsky and Natalya on the patio of the Blue House, 1937.

32. Frida Kahlo, painter, host and – for a while – Trotsky's lover.

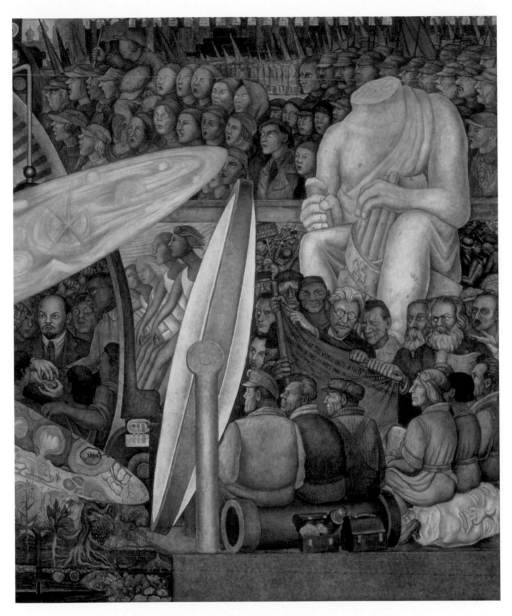

33. A fragment of Diego Rivera's 'Time Machine' mural in Mexico City. Trotsky is depicted holding the Red Flag towards the bottom right-hand side; Lenin is on the left-hand side.

34. Trotsky's office in the villa in Avenida Viena with Clare Sheridan's bust of him standing on the bookcase.

35. Avenida Viena. This is how the Trotsky villa looks today from the outside.

36. Ramón Mercader, Soviet secret agent and Trotsky's killer.

37. A photograph taken of Trotsky shortly after his death.

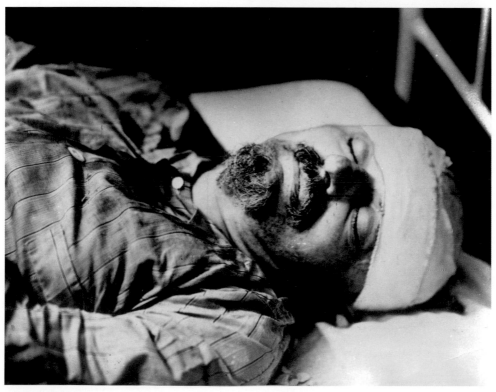

38. The simple monument constructed in Trotsky's memory in the garden of the Avenida Viena villa.

Even when he was not being taken in by agents of the Soviet regime he was not immune to misjudgements about whom to support and whom to ignore among his European followers.

The nascent Fourth International therefore remained a cumbersome entity in logistical terms. Its leader was based in Mexico, its chief editor until his death in 1938 lived in France and its fastest-growing corps of adherents in the USA. Telegrams made this situation only a little easier to handle than it would have been a century previously. Lëva's demise removed a force for mediation between Trotsky and the European groups. The son had even started to write to others in the Coyoacán household such as Bertram Wolfe in search of a more co-operative atmosphere.[24] Measured exchanges became less likely. Trotsky was impatient. He always wanted things to move faster down his preferred track. His impetus came from an intense worry that Trotskyists, especially in Europe, might prove inadequate for what he took to be a 'revolutionary situation'. His little apparatus in Mexico, as he was only too well aware, had severe limitations. More worrying for him were the signs that Trotskyists in France were failing to exploit their opportunities. His comrades conspired against each other. They blustered. They denounced each other and split into grouplets. They were a chaotic presence on the French political far left. They drove Trotsky to distraction.

Stalin had a higher opinion of international Trotskyism; and coming to the Party Central Committee on 3 March 1937 he denounced Trotsky and his associates for assembling a worldwide conspiracy against the USSR. They were not 'a political trend in the working class but an unprincipled gang of wreckers without ideas, diversionists, intelligence agents, spies, murderers, sworn enemies of the working class, acting in the hire of the intelligence service organs of foreign states'. He was quite sure that such activities were co-ordinated. He cited Trotsky and the Fourth International, adding that they were supported by Souvarine's group in France as well as by 'the notorious crook Eastman' in the USA.[25] The fact that Eastman had broken with communism in the mid-1930s did not deter Stalin – and Eastman was denounced by the Communist Party of the USA's *Daily Worker* in 1938 as a British agent. The *Daily Worker* was relying on false testimony forced by torture out of Eastman's old friend Khristian Rakovski.[26]

Global Trotskyism was a lot less substantial than Stalin imagined. This was shown when Spain erupted into civil war after an army revolt in July 1936. The leader of the mutiny was General Francisco Franco, who was determined to rid the country of communists and socialists, restore the authority of the Catholic Church and bring back political order. The Republican government was re-formed under Largo Caballero's leadership and was a left-of-centre coalition. The French 'popular front' cabinet, influenced by the British Conservative administration, pursued a policy of non-intervention. Hitler and Mussolini felt no such inhibition and supplied finance, munitions and air force crews to Franco's forces. Only the USSR and Mexico displayed any support for the Republicans, and the Communist Party of Spain was ordered by Comintern to support the national government. The price Stalin exacted for his assistance to the Republicans was that they should treat the Workers' Party of Marxist Unification (POUM) led by Andreu Nin as a traitorous organization. Nin by then had fallen out comprehensively with Trotsky over Nin's support for the policy of popular fronts in Europe. This did not prevent the Communist Party of Spain from treating Nin and the POUM as Trotskyists. Nin was arrested in May 1937 and killed by Soviet agents shortly afterwards.[27]

The Spanish Civil War put Trotsky into a quandary. While seeing that the POUM was a determined adversary of Comintern, he was not 'hopeful of converting Nin into a revolutionary'. He approved of attempts to 'win him back' but set the condition that he 'must openly unfurl the banner of the Fourth International in Spain'.[28] The POUM, according to Trotsky, was following a policy of 'adaptation, expectation, hesitation, that is to say, the most dangerous of all policies during a civil war, which is uncompromising'.[29] Trotsky continued to carp at Nin while Stalin went about strengthening the influence of the Communist Party of Spain. Neither covered himself with glory. Franco's army took Madrid in November 1936; the Basque territory fell to him in the following year. A drawn-out battle took place by the River Ebro between Republicans and Francoists from July to November 1938. The defeat of the Republicans there determined the outcome of the Spanish Civil War. Franco occupied Barcelona in January 1939. Catalonia was brought to heel by an intensive campaign of repression. The POUM was exterminated.

Trotsky had already privately recognized the numerical weakness of his following around the world. Writing to his adherent James Cannon about American Trotskyists on 10 October 1937, he analysed the difficulties as follows:

The party has only a minority of genuine factory workers. This is an inevitable beginning for every revolutionary workers' party everywhere and especially in the United States. The non-proletarian elements represent a very necessary yeast, and I believe that we can be proud of the good quality of these elements. But the danger is that we can receive in the next period too much 'yeast' for the needs of the party. The disintegration of the Communist Party will probably *begin* not among the workers but among the intellectuals, who are more sensitive to the ideas and less patriotic to the organization.[30]

Trotsky's prediction was that the intellectuals would soon drift away from them. While not wanting to accelerate the process, he was unworried by it since he thought that the working class was the key to ultimate success. He noted that educated Jews constituted a remarkable proportion of his supporters; but it was the 'Jewish masses' on whom he wanted the weight of party activity to be directed. He insisted: 'The unbreakable rule should be: not to command the workers but only to help them, to give them suggestions, to arm them with the facts, ideas, factory papers, and so on.'[31]

This was strange advice from a man who in 1920 had called for the total subjection of the workers' movement to the Soviet state. But Trotsky was being deadly serious, as he explained in his unidiomatic English: 'Many intellectuals and half-intellectuals terrorise the workers by some abstract generalities and paralyse the will toward activity. A functionary of a revolutionary party should have in the first line a good ear and only in the second a good tongue.'[32] The October Revolution's greatest orator insisted that revolutionaries should listen better to their audiences. He was returning to ideas he had purveyed before 1917 when he told the competing factions of the Russian Social-Democratic Workers' Party to cease their bickering and give priority to learning what Russia's workers wanted and to enabling them to achieve this.[33]

Trotskyists disliked publicizing their membership statistics: the numbers were too dispiriting. When the various national 'sections' came together for a conference in Paris in July 1936 they reported confidentially on recruitment. The Dutch claimed 2,500 members, the Americans 1,000 and the Germans as few as 150. (There had been only 750 before Hitler's arrival in power.) The English remained hopelessly divided into three tiny groups. The French, once one of the strongest sections, were in a mess after splits and expulsions – and always more people were leaving than joining. Dutch delegates questioned whether any such conference could sensibly set about founding a new International.[34]

The founding Conference took place in Périgny outside Paris in September 1938. Trotsky in Mexico had to wait for reports. He had supplied the basic documents as guidance for the proceedings and Max Shachtman presided. Twenty-one delegates from eleven countries attended. Among them was Étienne, who had still not been unmasked, as the representative of the 'Russian section'. Pierre Naville changed the venue at the last moment to Alfred Rosmer's house in Périgny in case of an NKVD action. Étienne still enjoyed Trotsky's confidence and was elected to the International Secretariat.[35] Another person, whose loyalty to Trotsky was complete, was a young woman called Sylvia Ageloff: she was inadvertently to have a fatal role in Trotsky's assassination.[36] Not everyone agreed, even at this stage, that it made practical sense to go ahead with proclaiming the creation of a new International. The two Polish delegates, appealing to their direct experience of the labour movement in their country, denied that left-wing workers had abandoned affection for Comintern. They got nowhere. Trotsky ideas were victorious. An Executive Committee of the Fourth International was elected with Trotsky as a secret and honorary member. Étienne insisted on being added from the 'Russian section' – Stalin was going to be kept well informed about the International's plans.[37] If anything, the warnings of the Poles were too weak. Trotsky got his way at the price of political realism and police infiltration.

He himself saw that much needed to be done before the Fourth International could ever rival Comintern in authority, but he chose to think positively. Others felt differently. By 1939 Victor Serge had become so sick of the intrigues among European Trotskyists that he resigned from the Fourth International. Serge was a former anarchist of Russian emigrant parents. He had gone to Russia in 1918, joined the Bolsheviks and served in Comintern before announcing his support for Trotsky's Left Opposition. Arrested in 1933, he was released and allowed to depart from the USSR in 1936. He and Trotsky started to exchange correspondence but Serge was of an independent spirit. Among other things he continued to think that Trotsky had behaved badly over Kronstadt in 1921.[38] As he left the Fourth International he gave Trotsky a piece of his mind. Trotsky had to understand that the conspiratorial atmosphere had 'played a part in the death of Lëv Lvovich [Sedov]'. Serge urged Trotsky to face up to two realities. The first was that he could not run the Fourth International at such a distance; the second that the International as yet had no properly functioning party in its entire membership.[39] Serge was right on both counts, but Trotsky treated him as an unreliable militant in the struggle against Stalinism. Delusion supplanted cool analysis in Coyoacán. Trotsky's basic hope was that events in Europe and North America were on the point of turning in his favour and bringing the working classes to his side. No one had given the Bolsheviks a chance of power in 1916 and yet they made the October Revolution a year later. Trotsky persuaded himself that the same would happen again to the benefit of the Fourth International.

# 47. TROTSKY AND HIS WOMEN

Natalya was Trotsky's anchor in a life of stormy uncertainty and strove to defend him even when she had doubts about his judgement. She told one of his secretaries: 'This is his work; this is his life. My life is to help him do it – to create the conditions for him so that he should not have the slightest difficulties in this, and to live, live by this, and to *delight* in his work, his ideas.'[1] This sentiment does not meet the criteria of later feminist thought. Natalya saw things differently. She regarded herself as a modern woman while counting herself fortunate to have a close, subordinate association with an extraordinary individual. She knew that she lacked his exceptional talent. Assigning herself the role of supporter, she dismissed the calls of the ego.

Her attitude was not an unusual one in the communist party. Bolshevik women who refused to operate in a man's shadow tended to shun a settled partnership. Alexandra Kollontai devoted whole pamphlets to her contention that marriage was a bourgeois trap which true revolutionaries should avoid. Kollontai was listened to and then ignored. Her argument would have gained greater appeal if she had not been extravagantly promiscuous. Lenin regarded her bed-hopping activity with distaste. Age did not weary Kollontai. Entering late middle-age she attracted the company of a man half her years with the suitable surname of Body. Not that Bolshevik veterans were puritanical about extramarital liaisons. Marriage, in fact, was often only a legal convenience for them. Trotsky had gone through a wedding with Alexandra Sokolovskaya purely because they wished to be allowed to stay together in Siberian exile. The same pressure did not exist on him and Natalya, so they never got married. Natalya assumed the functions of other 'wives' of leading Soviet communists. She kept the family together and supervised the household, and any official posts she held were secondary to these functions. The man was the planet, the woman his satellite. For both of them, the revolutionary cause was the sun.

Trotsky's circumstances outside the USSR increased his reliance on

Natalya to secure an orderly domestic environment. Money, meals and housework had to be regularized. The peripatetic existence from Turkey to Mexico was a severe test of her endurance and adaptability. She passed it superbly. Trotsky also had need for a sounding board for his political initiatives. He did not require a proper discussion: he had never been one to consult people before announcing his big decisions. Yet he liked to talk them over with Natalya. She expressed any objections tactfully and then, if they were rejected, she held her peace. It was more important for her that her husband was stable and content than that he was right. She was anyway his admirer. Her whole experience of the years since 1917 had vindicated his career in her eyes.

Although their life had been tumultuous in foreign exile, she had him to herself more than before. Their fellow residents were of a younger generation. Natalya was Trotsky's soulmate. They discussed how they both felt old age creeping towards them. Trotsky worried about his waning physical robustness. Despite his frequent ailments, he was proud of his manly appearance. He anyway exaggerated the extent of his decline. Although he had put on a bit of weight round the waist and his hair had turned grey he remained full of energy on trips to the Mexican country-side. Natalya, trim and petite, continued to move with exceptional grace: this had always been one of her outstanding qualities. They appeared a devoted couple; and if he had indeed had a fling with Claire Sheridan in 1920, no one in Coyoacán knew about it. Trotsky was not noted for taking the feelings of others into account, but he made an exception for his wife, and members of the Coyoacán household noticed how he always attended to her immediate wants and needs at the dinner table and elsewhere.[2]

The diary he kept in 1935 confirms the strength of their bond:

> Human character, its depths and its force, is defined by its *moral* reserves. People completely reveal themselves when they are tossed out of their customary conditions since it is exactly then that they have to resort to their reserves. N[atalya] and I have been bound together for 33 years (a third of a century!), and I am always struck at times of tragedy by the reserves of her nature . . . Whether because our strength is on the decline or for some other reason I would very much like to fix this image of N., albeit partially on paper.[3]

Sometimes when writing his diary, he had an eye on eventual publication in some form. He had done this, for example, in Spain in 1916.[4] There are hints in the jottings he made in France and Norway that he might have wanted to do the same again. Even so, the entry on Natalya is a moving profession of gratitude and love.

Until 1937 she had no serious reason to doubt his fidelity. The ménage had contained attractive young women for several years and he had behaved properly with them. Nor had any of them flirted with him, being in awe of their revolutionary idol. Frida Kahlo was different. She made little secret of her extramarital dalliances, at least when her equally promiscuous husband Diego Rivera was out of sight. For the first time since being sculpted by Clare Sheridan and being propositioned by Larisa Reissner, Trotsky felt exposed to strong temptation. This time he did not resist.[5] Frida was in her early thirties. A street accident had rendered her lame in one leg, but her uninhibited behaviour and vividly coloured clothes appealed to many of the men she sought to seduce. Although her *faux-naïf* paintings were shocking expressions of emotional pain, she otherwise drew no attention to her troubles. She was a hurricane of impulsive, extravagant ideas. She was quite unlike any woman Trotsky had met, and he fell for her. A sexual relationship started some time after mid-April 1937.[6] Trotsky turned into an ageing delinquent who, ignoring all the risks, flung himself into an affair in the Blue House.

Trotsky and Frida planned their assignations with whispers or in notes tucked between the pages of books that he passed to her. Luckily for Trotsky, Diego remained in the dark. Diego was a man of uncontrolled passions and was notorious for threatening people with his pistol. To this extent he was a man of his people. As Frida left the room she would bid him: 'All my love.'[7] She often confined her conversation to English, knowing that Natalya had never learned it. Frida was endlessly coquettish with Trotsky. But then she and her husband Diego were notorious flirts, and for a while no one, not even the eagle-eyed Heijenoort, suspected.[8] Trotsky was behaving with absurd recklessness. Ultimately the important thing in his life was revolutionary politics and it was exactly this which he was putting in jeopardy. He could never have coped without Natalya by his side. Natalya ran the Trotsky household with calm precision and was dedicated to the cause; Frida was an emotional whirligig whose interest in radical politics came a long way after her devotion to painting.

Soon the entire villa knew what was going on. Jan Frankel, bravest of the brave, spoke sternly with Trotsky about the potential political consequences. Moscow would use the occasion to discredit the entire Fourth International. Frankel added that Trotsky was jeopardizing his right to stay in Mexico.[9] Diego Rivera had led the campaign to persuade President Cárdenas to grant him asylum in the first instance. Frankel received a blistering response for his honesty. He returned to his lodgings in the city and never restored personal harmony with Trotsky, who acted as if notions of decorum existed only for others: he seldom moderated the sarcasm at breakfast if ever he discovered that Heijenoort had merely been at the local dance hall the previous evening. He had talked endlessly to them about the need for revolutionaries to dedicate themselves to the cause. He had lectured them as if he was the paragon of virtue. They had wanted to believe in him. He was their inspiration; they had given up the years of their early manhood to Coyoacán, and until this embarrassing episode they had thought their complete faith in him worth while.

It was only a matter of time before Natalya discovered. When this happened she avoided an open dispute but made it plain that the situation was unacceptable. Trotsky was full of contrition. The affair with Frida ended abruptly, and he and Natalya agreed that the best thing for their own relationship would be for him to go and stay on a hacienda near San Miguel Regla, ninety miles north of Mexico City:[10] she wanted him nowhere near her for a while. It seems that it was Frida who brought things to a close. She went round telling people she had grown tired of the Old Man; this was no longer a name of respect or affection and she was underlining the importance of the age gap for her. Trotsky wrote her a long and passionate letter explaining his feelings. Alas, it has not survived. Frida gave the letter to her friend Ella Wolfe, making her promise to burn it rather than let it fall into the hands of others; and Ella, conquering her habit of squirrelling things away, complied with Frida's wishes.[11]

If Trotsky still yearned for Frida, the mood passed: the future, he saw, lay in rebuilding his relationship with Natalya. Out at the hacienda he had time to reflect and to repent. Just before lunch on 19 July 1937 he sat out on the chaise longue while writing to Natalya. Thoughts tumbled on to the page as they occurred to him. This was the first time in his life he had offered a deep apology to any other individual. He was entering untilled territory. Characteristically he chose to explore it in writing; he always felt safest with a pen in his hand. His style was grave and self-deprecating. There was also a trace of jauntiness, as when he complimented himself on having caught the fish he was about to eat. While he rambled on about his experience of the day a touch of self-pity emerged. He told Natalya that his eyes had grown tired in the blazing sun. He needed dark glasses but was out in the back of beyond and could not buy a pair.[12] At the same time he tried to charm his wife by saying that the Lander family – whose acquaintance they had made since coming to

Mexico – had asked them over to breakfast. If Natalya came before Sunday, she was to make sure she packed a dress. Trotsky joked that whereas he could appear in the garb of a 'well-known bandit', a bandit's wife had to dress up.[13]

No sooner had he informed her that he felt well both physically and morally than he saw that he was breaching decent manners in his situation. He admitted to having adopted the tone of a Junker and had written only about himself. This was something Natalya was used to; but for once he saw that he needed to be more solicitous than normal. He added to the letter when lunch was over, mentioning that he was going to take a trip next day to Pachuca and phone her. He asked after health and whether she was suffering from flu; he declared that he wanted 'a fortress, tranquillity, a bit of joy' for her.[14]

He then appended a passage which for years lay in a guarded archive:

> Since I arrived here my poor prick has not once got hard. It's as if it doesn't exist. It too is taking a rest after the tension of the past few days. But I myself – all of me, apart from it – am thinking with tenderness about your sweet old cunt. I want to stuff it, to push my tongue right into its depths. Natalochka, sweetest, I'm going to fuck you hard with my tongue and my prick.[15]

What was he trying to do for himself and for her? How conscious was he of the possible impact of his words? And what was Natalya's reaction? Trotsky in his confused way was trying to do more than express remorse for the wrong he had done to Natalya. He wanted her to know that she was again the sole object of his desire. Trotsky wanted Natalya not merely as a comrade and housewife but as an alluring woman – and he used direct language in conveying this to her. One thing is for certain. Neither of them had lost their zest for lovemaking. Otherwise Trotsky's words would simply have been offensive.

Yet he had not learned his lesson. Scarcely had he managed to compose his peace with Natalya than someone else caught his eye. The young Mexican woman in question lived a few streets away, and he began to visit her. His cover for these planned get-togethers was a clever one. Trotsky and his entourage had come to suspect that a Stalinist group had taken up residence in the building next to the Blue House from where it would be possible to organize an assault. Trotsky devised an escape plan involving a ladder being placed in the far corner of the courtyard. The idea was that if gunmen broke into the Blue House, Trotsky would clamber over the wall. Meanwhile he made four or five pressing propositions to his inamorata which had nothing to do with security; but she ignored his advances. He persisted, telling Heijenoort he wanted to undertake an evening rehearsal of the plan of escape. Heijenoort was not amused, pointing out that the Fourth International could do without a scandal of this kind. Trotsky gave way. It was one of the few occasions when an assistant obliged him to behave in contravention of his wishes.[16]

Heijenoort was losing control of his own emotions. He was a man of exceptional attractiveness to women, bearing a physical likeness to the French film star Jean Marais.[17] The young man had to have some fun. But Heijenoort's idea of a few hours' relaxation was not the same as Trotsky's had been at the same age. The young Trotsky had liked to spend the day visiting an art gallery or an opera house with Natalya. The Old Man was not pleased by Heijenoort's penchant for the dance halls in Mexico City: 'Trotsky did not like me to be out of the house at night. He would be mad; I could feel it. Even if there was nothing that I had to do, he wanted me there. But I went anyway. I needed some kind of release from the tension.'[18] Trotsky would have been still angrier if he had known that he was meeting up with none other than Frida Kahlo. Having got over her passion for the Old Man, she moved on to his handsome acolyte. Heijenoort was footloose and fancy-free after the departure of his wife and son for the USA; he eagerly accepted Frida's invitation to meet up with her and her sister Cristina for an evening in El Salon or Tenampa.[19]

Frida and Heijenoort were soon enjoying a liaison. The young man was fearful of the Old Man discovering what was happening: if Trotsky objected to his going out dancing, what would be his reaction if he found out the identity of Frida's latest paramour? Luckily for Heijenoort, nobody breathed a word of the affair to Trotsky, and it soon petered out. Trotsky's difficulties came not from Frida but from her husband Diego and had nothing to do with sexual matters. Daily contact with Trotsky induced Rivera to want to take part in communist activity and to fight for the Trotskyist cause. This alarmed Mexican Trotskyists, who disliked the painter's bulging ego and assessed his political talent as minuscule. His moods were volatile and his judgement unpredictable. When attacked by fellow Trotskyists, he pulled rank by asking his tenant Trotsky to expel them from the organization. Rivera rejected Trotsky's explanation that he had no authority for such a step: 'But you are the leader!' The painter suspected skulduggery, even accusing Trotsky of setting his followers in Mexico against him. Rivera would not be put off. Convinced that he alone knew how to apply Trotskyism in his country, he set about forming his own grouping. Trotsky loved Rivera's art but was bemused by his public pretensions. Rivera would have been better advised to follow his cultural métier and allow others to tend to politics.

The tensions generated by her husband became obvious to Frida, who wrote to her friend Ella Wolfe insisting that Diego remained loyal to the Fourth International and that he was 'entranced that Trotsky was here'.[20] No one wanted the matter to get out hand, but Diego made it difficult to compose a peace. The growing spat was aggravated by Trotsky's refusal to side with Rivera over the merits of a short article which he wanted to have published. Rivera took umbrage, accusing Trotsky of using Stalinist methods to censor him and calling him arrogant and intolerant. (It must be said that Trotsky would have behaved just like Rivera if his own articles had been rejected.)

Trotsky for a while strove to mollify Rivera's feelings. He wrote to Frida Kahlo seeking her help as an intermediary. Diego believed that Trotsky was denying him an administrative post in the Fourth International. 'And I'm asking you', he wrote to the Old Man, 'why should Diego be [only a] "secretary"?' This exasperated Trotsky, who believed him clearly 'unfit . . . for routine revolutionary work'. He rejected all of Diego's charges. He wrote to Frida that both he and Natalya – evidently Trotsky was stressing that he was not trying for yet another flirtation – had talked things over; they had paid a pleasant visit to Diego. But when Trotsky went alone on a subsequent occasion, a furious dispute broke out and Diego resigned from the Fourth International. Trotsky implored Frida as 'our good and great friend' to intercede.[21] He appealed to various followers to see what they could do to help; he got Heijenoort to ask André Breton to help out.[22] But nothing worked. Trotsky's approach to Frida only stoked Rivera's rage.[23] Exasperated, Trotsky asked Charles Curtiss, a young American visiting Trotskyist grouplets throughout Mexico, to take Rivera aside and calm him down. Rivera explained that he did not really object to Trotsky's methods but simply wanted to retire from politics and devote himself to his painting.[24]

Rivera's brilliance as an artist was beyond question; he had spent years training with the world's greatest contemporary artists in Paris before the Great War. Amadeo Modigliani was his friend and admirer. Rivera had deliberately chosen to use sharp lines and brash colours to convey his message about Mexican history. Trotsky ignored the intellectual content. Rivera's murals traced every ill in the country to the Spanish conquest under Hernán Cortés in 1519–21. Indigenous people constantly appeared as victims – even the Aztec empire was celebrated for its civilization of social harmony. Spaniards were torturers and usurpers, Indians were inheritors of an entirely separate culture of modest splendour. From a Marxist viewpoint this was dangerous nationalism and distorted history. Trotsky as a young man in Nikolaev had abandoned the Russian narodnik fondness for the peasantry; in Mexico he praised Rivera as a pictorial genius and forgot his usual demand that the traditions of the countryside were inimical to progress. If ever it occurred to Trotsky that he was being inconsistent he never said so. The conjunction of political and artistic judgement failed him in Coyoacán. He had needed Rivera for practical reasons and, probably unconsciously, had hooded his sceptical eye.

Trotsky took an initiative in co-writing a 'Manifesto for an Independent Revolutionary Art' with Diego Rivera and the surrealist painter André Breton. Funded by the French government, Bréton travelled to Mexico in February 1938 and met up with Trotsky, who somewhat tactlessly voiced his opinion on the greatness of realist novelists such as Émile Zola. A clash over the merits of realism and surrealism seemed likely. But Bréton was a communist sympathizer and his pictures exhibited sympathy with the plight of working people; he was also an unconditional admirer of Trotsky.[25] The 'Manifesto' bemoaned the 'deep twilight hostile to every sort of spiritual value' in the USSR. It railed against the cultural devastation in the Third Reich. The compilers rejected pleas for 'political indifference' about art but avoided specifying how a revolutionary state should deal with art which espoused politically inconvenient ideas. To that extent it marked no advance on Trotsky's *Literature and Revolution* of 1923. The 'Manifesto' simply called for complete freedom of creation as the prerequisite of great art. It had two mottoes:

The independence of art – for the revolution!
The revolution – for the complete liberation of art!

Only Rivera and Bréton signed the 'Manifesto', presumably so as to make it appear to be the product of artists for artists.[26]

It then turned out that Rivera, far from withdrawing from political activity, was backing General Mugica in the forthcoming elections. A public rupture between Trotsky and Rivera became inevitable. The exasperated Trotsky left it to Heijenoort to win back 'the painter'. Rivera's response was to make bizarre accusations against Trotsky in a letter to André Breton. A copy of it was allowed to fall into Natalya's hands. Trotsky wrote to the grandly named Pan-American Committee of the Fourth International in New York and asked it to issue a statement of support. On reflection he recognized that such a statement would make no practical difference. He chose to interpret Rivera's behaviour as a sign of the times. What was happening, according to Trotsky, was a 'retreat of the intellectuals'. Rivera and others had succumbed to the temptation to 'look for a haven in the bourgeois public opinion of their fatherland'.[27] Trotsky in the early days of their friendship had fostered the idea that the painter was a serious political militant. Diego in his vanity had believed him. Trotsky now had to deal with the consequences of his own social charm. He began to recognize the dangers facing him. Diego was a man who had exerted decisive influence on his being granted asylum in Mexico and getting shelter. Trotsky had also had an affair with his wife. Diego could do much damage by siding with Stalin against the Fourth International and campaigning in Mexico against him.

Frida, who was exhibiting her paintings in New York, was really past caring about political intrigue. Her own relationship with Rivera was in chaos and they divorced in January 1939. Although they married again a year later, Diego never returned to the Trotskyist cause and Frida revised her politics by aligning herself with Mexico's Stalinists. The last work of art she produced before her death in 1954 was an oil painting of Joseph Stalin.[28] Trotsky anyhow could no longer stay in a house provided by Diego, and he gave formal notice of his imminent departure. Tortuous messages passed between them. Diego objected to Trotsky's attempt to use Frida as an intermediary; he refused to calm down.[29] But he also let it be known that Trotsky could stay on despite their continuing disagreement. Trotsky would accept this offer so long as he paid a reasonable rent; he offered 200 pesos a month. Rivera turned down the proposal. At first he did this in his own name. Then he declared that the Blue House was anyway Frida's and not his. Trotsky saw this as a way of putting him under moral pressure to vacate the premises.[30] Standing on his dignity, he secured the tenancy of a nearby villa on Avenida Viena in Coyoacán and moved himself and his household out of the Blue House.

# 48. 'THE RUSSIAN QUESTION'

Trotskyists around the world were not privy to the domestic disturbances in Coyoacán. There was one question that dominated their thinking wherever they lived. This was about the nature of the USSR. Trotsky had no active followers left in the Soviet Union by the mid-1930s. The discussion inside Trotskyism could happen only abroad and predominantly among people who had never been to Moscow. The drama of the October Revolution captivated them from afar. They aimed to imitate the revolutionary achievements of Lenin and Trotsky in their own countries. They had become Trotskyists because as communists they mistrusted the Kremlin's version of communism. They wanted freedom to think for themselves; but in rejecting Stalin they bowed in uncritical admiration for Trotsky and obeyed his intellectual guidance.

Immense changes were taking place in the USSR. The second five-year plan, introduced in 1933, laid emphasis on bringing the newly built factories and mines into regular production. Industrial growth tempos slackened somewhat but remained impressive. The Soviet Union became an ever growing producer of tanks, aeroplanes, lorries and tractors. Stalin put the Politburo under sustained pressure to stick to the general line of economic policy. He regrouped the leadership, inserting newcomers like Nikolai Yezhov and Nikita Khrushchëv whenever he sensed an absence of full commitment among existing comrades. In 1935 the miner Alexei Stakhanov broke records for the amount of coal hewn in a single shift. He was celebrated in *Pravda* and enterprises in all sectors of industry, transport and even agriculture were ordered to find men and women, known as Stakhanovites, to emulate him. Obstacles to the advancing of Stalin's policies in politics, economics and culture were smashed down. The Red Army was modernized in training and equipment. Cinemas and radio stations were built. 'Parks of culture' were laid out for popular recreation. Behind the scenes a bloody mass purge of 'anti-Soviet elements' was undertaken in 1937–8 which became known as the Great Terror. The Gulag was turned into an integral part of the economic transformation as starved convicts felled timber and dug for gold in Siberia. Ostensibly the inmates were benefiting from progressive policies of rehabilitation. Stalin was touted as the architect of an unprecedented revolutionary transformation.

Trotsky's chief work on the contemporary USSR was *The Revolution Betrayed*, published in 1937. His work could no longer spout from his own lived experience and that of his sympathizers. He had to glean what he could from the Soviet official press whose writers were graduates of 'the Stalinist school of falsification'. His argument was as follows. The Soviet Union, despite its defects, remained a 'workers' state'; Stalin and his cronies had failed to carry out a full counter-revolution. The natural resources and the chief economic sectors were state owned. The basic ideology was Marxist. The old capitalist classes had been crushed and preference was being given to raising the cultural level of the 'masses'. The communist party recruited heavily among the working class. The Stalinists, insofar as they had managed to consolidate their power, owed their success to Russia's 'backwardness'. The Soviet proletariat, being a small minority of society in 1917, had lacked the education, training and experience necessary for a comprehensive 'transition to socialism'. At the same time the capitalists had been too weak to reverse the 'gains of October' and the peasants were incapable of sustained resistance. The result was an unstable equilibrium which allowed the 'bureaucratic stratum' to look after its collective interests. Stalin had attained political supremacy by putting himself at the head of the bureaucrats. It was a 'Bonapartist' administration which depended on violent methods for its survival.

What was required to change this situation for the better, so Trotsky had believed in the early 1930s, was for the Opposition to win over the 'healthy' elements in the Soviet communist elite. The *Byulleten oppozitsii* had tried to attract Stalinist functionaries to his way of thinking. He threw this strategy overboard in *The Revolution Betrayed*, deciding that nothing less than a political revolution against the 'bureaucracy' would suffice.

The press in the USSR accused him of conspiring to murder the Kremlin leadership. Nothing could have been further from the truth because Trotsky had ruled out any operation to assassinate Stalin:

> In themselves, terrorist acts are least of all capable of overthrowing a Bonapartist oligarchy. Although the individual bureaucrat dreads the revolver, the bureaucracy as a whole is able to exploit the act of terror for the justification of its own violent activities and incidentally

to implicate its own political enemies in murder . . . Individual terror
is a weapon of impatient or despairing individuals, belonging most
frequently to the younger generation of the bureaucracy.[1]

There was more to this than adherence to conventional Marxist doctrine.
Trotsky could not believe that the killing of such a 'mediocrity' would
make any difference to Soviet politics. At some unconscious level he
seemingly needed the reassurance that great historical forces and not an
individual adversary of comparable talent had brought about his defeat.
The entire Trotskyist movement with the possible exception of Lëva Sedov
accepted this verdict at the time; it was years before Jean van Heijenoort
concluded that it would have been better to try and kill Stalin. In any case
no one worked out how such a goal might be attained.[2]

Trotsky expected that working-class indignation would build up into
rebellion. As yet the peasants had done more than the workers to 'come
out on the road of open struggle'. The urban proletariat, according to
Trotsky, were held back by the belief that a further revolution might rob
them of the achievements of the October Revolution. But revolution
remained inevitable: 'There is no peaceful outcome for this crisis. No devil
ever yet voluntarily cut off its own claws. The Soviet bureaucracy will not
give up its positions without a fight. The development leads obviously to
the road of revolution.'[3] The 'new caste of oppressors and parasites' would
be overthrown by a popular uprising. A fresh communist party belonging
to the Fourth International had to replace the emasculated party of Stalin.

According to Trotsky, the USSR's official propaganda had to be
rejected. He rightly claimed, albeit without any documentary proof, that
the output figures for the Stakhanovite movement were not to be believed;
he saw them as altogether too fantastic.[4] Soviet economic policies were
inept and crude in conception and imposition. Trotsky conceded that a
great industrial base had been laid down and a huge advance had been
made through the mass literacy campaign. But chaos and wastage had
been endemic. The Stalinist elite were by nature conservatives, lacking
the élan needed for a full revolutionary transformation. Agriculture was
in ruins. Literature and other arts had been turned into a travesty of
the cultural changes which were worthy of a socialist society. The alternative was represented by the Opposition, and it was high time for its
ideas to be introduced. Trotsky was offering himself and his followers to
take the place of the Stalinist leadership. Although he was not promising democracy he entertained at least the possibility of restoring 'the
freedom of Soviet parties'. Presumably he had the Mensheviks and the

Socialist-Revolutionaries in mind even if he did not like to name them; and in any event he was not intending to legalize the Kadets. Right to the end of his life Trotsky did not trust the people with unconstrained rights to form or vote for whatever parties they might want.[5]

At the same time he remained a Soviet patriot. If the Third Reich were to attack, comrades should become active in defending the USSR. Trotsky's point was that this would be easier to accomplish if Stalin and his clique had been removed and a new foreign policy established. International military clashes were on the increase. The USSR could not permanently remain uninvolved, and Trotsky warned that Stalin's 'socialism in a single country' doctrine was leading to disaster – among other things it lessened the Soviet Union's attractiveness to workers abroad. The orientation should be changed back to world revolution.[6]

Thus while proclaiming the relentless degeneration of the USSR, Trotsky never ceased to hold a candle for its redemption. What needs to be understood is that he was a man of his time. He believed in 'the decay of the capitalist system, its incurable crisis, its decomposition'. The Great Depression was the latest validation of this Marxist prognosis. He acknowledged 'the constant progress in technique and the remarkable results of certain industrial branches'. But capitalism in his eyes inevitably put a brake on 'the development of the productive forces'. This was his summary:

> The capitalist epoch is characterized, except for the Soviet Union, by a stagnation and decline in the national income, by a chronic agrarian crisis and an organic unemployment. These internal phenomena are inherent in the present phase of capitalism, like gout and sclerosis at a certain age of the individual . . . The [Great War] only worsened the signs of decomposition whose subsequent sharpening is preparing a new war.[7]

All of Trotsky is here. The Soviet Union, he steadfastly asserted, was the sole country capable of avoiding the economic turmoil currently afflicting the world.

He had given up his youth and early manhood to the struggle for revolution in Russia. He and his comrade Lenin had helped to lead the October Revolution and to secure it in the Civil War. He had co-founded Comintern. Together with Lenin he had incarnated the communist cause around the world. For Trotsky to suggest that the Bolshevik seizure of power in 1917 had been a waste of time – or something even worse – would have been like cutting off his own arm. No revolutionary transformation is perfect, and Trotsky saw no need to start a second one from scratch in Russia. The October Revolution had to be rescued and straightened out rather than discarded.

He never said how he thought this could be accomplished. Even in 1917 he had omitted to elucidate his strategy in print: his talent had lain in improvising around a few basic assumptions about the current situation – and this gave him a practical flexibility which even Lenin had lacked. In the late 1930s he had still more reason for reticence. Before the October Revolution his silence had kept the party's enemies guessing. Now political impotence held him back. Although his contact with the USSR had disappeared he continued to place his faith in a popular uprising led by the 'Soviet section of the Fourth International'. This was self-deception on a grand scale. Trotsky himself hinted at this when acknowledging that the so-called section was 'still weak and driven underground'. But even such an admission was nonsense: the 'Soviet section' was a figment of his imagination. The entire Opposition was in the labour camps or had been executed. Trotsky's rhetoric had got the better of him and he insisted that 'the illegal existence of a party is not non-existence.'[8]

Moving on, he declared:

> It is not a question of substituting one ruling clique for another, but of changing the very methods of administering the economy and guiding the culture of the country. Bureaucratic autocracy must give place to Soviet democracy. A restoration of the right of criticism, and a genuine freedom of elections, are necessary conditions for the further development of the country. This assumed a revival of freedom of Soviet parties, beginning with the party of Bolsheviks, and a resurrection of the trade unions. The bringing of democracy into industry means a radical revision of plans in the interests of the toilers.[9]

He did not elaborate what he meant by this. He had not invented objectives like electoral freedom, the struggle with bureaucratism or Soviet democracy; he shared them with every other communist theoretician including even Stalin. Trotsky consistently failed to explain how he would bring these common objectives to fulfilment.

He held to his general analysis of the USSR throughout the late 1930s and saw no need to modify it in the light of what others wrote. There was one major exception to his intellectual fixity. In April 1939 he dropped his commitment to the USSR's territorial integrity. Instead he proposed a new slogan of a 'unified and independent worker-and-peasant Soviet

Ukraine'.[10] He was responding to recent changes in international relations as Hitler's Third Reich conquered and annexed Czechoslovakia. Among the Nazi innovations was the establishment of an autonomous Ruthenian administration in the Czech lands. The Ruthenians are a people closely related to the Ukrainians. Trotsky saw an opportunity for Marxist organizations to stir up trouble for the Germans by resuscitating the political campaign for an expanded Ukraine. What is more, he expressed the hope for a political revolution in Soviet Ukraine by fellow-minded communists. He knew that Ukrainians detested the Stalinist regime in their country. If Soviet Ukraine was to become a bulwark against Nazism in eastern Europe it needed to show its independence from the Kremlin's control.

Any Ukrainian political revolution would inevitably have weakened the USSR's defensive capacity. Ukraine's secession, furthermore, would have caused enormous disruption in Moscow. Trotsky argued that such a disturbance was as nothing compared to the status quo:

> The USSR's enfeeblement, we reply, is being brought about by the ever growing centrifugal tendencies engendered by the Bonapartist dictatorship. In the contingency of war, the hatred of the masses for the ruling clique can lead to the collapse of the social conquests of October . . . The sooner that today's Bonapartist caste is undermined, shattered, swept away and crushed, the sounder will become the defence of the [USSR] and the more secure will become its socialist future.[11]

Trotsky had no confidence in the Red Army in its current condition. A revolution was required to provide the Soviet Union with adequate protection.

His finessing of this standpoint had no impact outside circles of Trotskyists at a time when debates about the USSR were filling the newspapers and journals in the Western liberal democracies. Many prominent writers in France, Britain and the USA showed an enthusiasm for things Soviet. The French writer Henri Barbusse published a biography of Stalin that was so adulatory that it was printed in a massive translation in Moscow. Sidney and Beatrice Webb, leading members of the Fabian Society in the United Kingdom, were fervent admirers who refused to believe anything bad about the Soviet administration. In 1935 they published *Soviet Communism: A New Civilization?* For the second edition they deleted the question mark.[12] Former diplomat Bernard Pares, who had represented the United Kingdom in Russia in the Great War, assured everyone that Stalin nursed a lively concern for justice. In the USA the defenders of the USSR were legion, even including F. D. Roosevelt's future vice-president Henry A. Wallace. The tendency on the political left was to give the benefit of the doubt to Stalin and the USSR at a time when the world economy was suffering from the Great Depression, capitalism was in the doldrums and German, Italian and Japanese territorial expansionism undermined the prospects of global peace.

André Gide's travelogue about his 1936 trip to the Soviet Union had cheered Trotsky up.[13] But Gide was no Trotskyist, and no outstanding literary figure in European or American literature, philosophy or social science was willing to announce adherence to Trotsky's cause. Painters were a different matter: André Breton, Frida Kahlo and Diego Rivera were open, avid admirers in the same decade even if their understanding of the essence of Trotsky's dispute with Stalin was never very profound.

Usually, at any rate, the critics of the contemporary USSR were on the political right and had no time for Trotsky. Stories of the horrors of state terror were regularly traced back to earlier Soviet years, and neither Lenin nor Trotsky was let off lightly. The Right Book Club in the United Kingdom castigated the Politburo past and present. This became an international controversy when the Kronstadt naval garrison mutiny came under resumed discussion. Trotsky's direct involvement was rehearsed. This was a sensitive matter for him. He had been closely involved in the communist leadership's deliberations about how to put down the rebellion but his activity had been secluded from public attention. After being deported from the USSR, when he sought sympathy on the European and American far left, this episode in his career became an embarrassment. The Spanish Civil War aggravated the difficulty. Trotsky denounced Stalin and the NKVD for prioritizing the extermination of rival organizations on the far left in Spain rather than the forming of a broad political and military coalition for the defeat of General Franco and his fascists. The arrest and murder of Andreu Nin figured among the infamies recorded in the *Byulleten oppozitsii*. The fact that Nin had never been a professed Trotskyist allowed Trotsky to claim to be the conscience of the anti-Comintern communist resistance.

Victor Serge, who was released from confinement in the USSR and allowed to emigrate to France in 1936, had a vivid memory of Trotsky's support for the development of the Soviet one-party terror-state. He admired Trotsky for his many achievements and wanted to have amicable political ties to him; but he had not forgotten how he had behaved towards the Kronstadt sailors as well as anarchists and radical socialists in 1921. This annoyed Trotsky. Until Serge's arrival he had got away with the evasive account in his autobiography. Now at last he had to answer the question how it was possible to accept him as advocate of a pluralist socialist system if he had persecuted ordinary sailors who had made exactly this demand in 1921.

The Kronstadt mutineers, Trotsky replied, were not the same sailors who had supported the Bolsheviks in 1917 but cowardly and untrustworthy replacements in league with the enemies of the October Revolution. This was an argument of Jesuitical sophistry. What difference did it make if the sailors were not the same ones? (The truth was that they were the same ones, and Trotsky must have known this full well.)[14] Loyal Trotskyists badgered him to defend himself in greater detail. Trotsky lamely responded that he lacked the necessary materials in Coyoacán; he mentioned that he had asked his son to publish something instead.[15] Lëva had manfully agreed to discharge this unenviable task. He set to work with his father's thoroughness, writing to the French communist Simone Weil with a request for copies of works by anarchist authors. These were among the most powerful critics of Soviet actions against the Kronstadt mutineers.[16] Lëva followed his father's line of interpretation, declaring that the Bolshevik central leaders had had every reason to believe that an international conspiracy was operating against them. Socialist-Revolutionaries abroad had allegedly helped foreign governments to attempt something that might eventually lead to the overthrow of the communists. Lëva insisted that Trotsky had had nothing whatever to do with the suppression of the Kronstadters.

Lëva did not live to complete the piece and steadily the controversy died down. Trotsky declined to return to the topic and maintained an Olympian detachment on the points raised in Serge's articles. His followers raised no objection. As far as they were concerned, Serge had tried and failed to blacken Trotsky's reputation.

There were again signs that some of them did not feel inclined to accept all the tenets of his analysis of the USSR without cavil. American Trotskyism had attracted young thinkers who bridled at any permanent intellectual constraints on them. Even on the 'Russian question' Trotsky's basic standpoint began to come under fire as had happened earlier in the Leninbund.[17] Critics thought that Trotsky underestimated the depth of the Soviet order's transformation and consolidation under Stalin. Whereas he regarded Stalinism as unstable, they suggested that a new class had ensconced itself in power. The terminology varied from writer to writer but the essence of the argument was common. The communist bureaucracy in party, government and police had grabbed inalienable control of the benefits of the country's economy. Repressive violence was ruthlessly used to maintain the new status quo. The bureaucrats – the *apparatchiki* – did not need titled deeds to their property in land, housing and personal accoutrements. They enjoyed privileges without limit and could pass them on to their sons and daughters. The October Revolution, which according to Trotsky could be resuscitated by a political revolution, was already dead. The social and economic foundations had to be dug up and a whole new edifice needed to be built.

Trotsky sometimes edged his way towards revising his own analysis. Even in *The Revolution Betrayed* he admitted the usefulness of an adjective he had been avoiding: totalitarian.[18] This was not a category of Marxist analysis, for it implied a way of looking at modern societies which dropped notions such as social class. Stalin's USSR and Hitler's Third Reich were alike in seeking to remove all obstacles to central state authority. They eliminated democratic provisions for a division of powers. They crushed independent civic associations whenever possible. They instituted police terror. They established concentration camps and arrested or executed adversaries on a mass scale. They introduced a political monopoly over the media. They exalted their ideology and contended that their leaders were comprehensive geniuses. Both Stalin and Hitler had the ambition of remaking citizens after the image of their ideologies and attempted the complete penetration of society by the state.

This theory of a new kind of state was just beginning to be formulated. Trotsky toyed with it but basically used it as a stylistic flourish. He remained true to conventional categories of Marxism. Of course, it was the Marxism of his preference. The long years of deportation and asylum gave him the opportunity to write exactly what he thought, and he never ceased to believe that the world made no sense unless it was recognized that only the proletariat could save it from disaster.

Basically he stuck to what he had been stressing since he had gone into opposition in the early 1920s. The chances of a successful communist revolution in Russia, he asserted, had always been slim without revolutions elsewhere in Europe. He reinforced this determinism in his writings of the 1930s. The thought arose in many minds that this amounted to invalidating the case for the Bolshevik seizure of power in autumn 1917. Millions of people had been killed or afflicted by famine, disease and unfreedom in the USSR. Did not Trotsky see the illogicality of taking pride in the October Revolution while retrospectively pronouncing it to have been futile? He had the ready response that world capitalism had been in a fragile condition since the Great War. Trotsky put all his faith in international revolution. He proposed that communism could be rescued in Russia if revolutionary administrations sprouted up in the nearby countries of advanced capitalism. He fervently hoped for Germany or France to become aligned with the USSR. Then the difficulties of achieving communism in Soviet Russia could be overcome – and it would be demonstrated that the October Revolution had inaugurated a new era for humanity.

# 49. CONFRONTING THE PHILOSOPHERS

The big Moscow trials of 1936–8 were a challenge even to Trotsky's optimism. They were a travesty of judicial process. Defendants were subjected to physical torture or psychological maltreatment before being brought out to testify. Any prisoner who resisted was held back from appearing and was summarily executed. The trials achieved what Stalin wanted at home and abroad. As each indicted group – from Kamenev and Zinoviev in August 1936 to Bukharin in March 1938 – confessed to treason, many influential Western commentators were inclined to believe in the Soviet court system. Among the charges were colluding with foreign intelligence agencies and conspiring to assassinate Stalin and restore capitalism to Russia. The trials incriminated Trotsky as an active plotter. The NKVD was encouraged to make the wildest charges against him. Only when its leader Nikolai Yezhov claimed to have proof that Trotsky had been an Okhrana agent did Stalin overrule him.[1] Trotsky reacted vigorously to the accusations, giving chapter and verse on the preposterous lies underpinning the evidence emitted from the courtrooms in Moscow. He produced countless articles in the *Byulleten*. His son Lëva did the same. It was easy to point to the mistakes about times, places and individuals in the case laid against them by Soviet prosecutors. Trotsky had no reason for fondness towards Zinoviev, Bukharin or even his brother-in-law Kamenev, but he devoted himself to clearing their names as honourable revolutionaries.

He had only limited success in countering the campaign of 'Stalinist falsification'. On the political left in Europe and North America there was much sympathy for the USSR as the world's strongest force against fascism. Stalin was widely admired as a leader who had brought industrial growth and mass education to his people. Most anti-fascists did not wish to query the soundness of the verdicts and accepted that Trotsky must be guilty as charged. It was not just the 'leftists' who disliked Trotsky. Winston Churchill in 1938 told Soviet ambassador Ivan Maiski: 'I hate Trotsky! I've kept an eye on his activities for some time. He's Russia's evil genius, and it is a very good thing that Stalin has got even with him.'[2]

Even so, he stayed an attractive, exotic personality for many readers around the world, including public figures, who had no liking for communism. An impressive number of socialists, liberals and even some conservatives overlooked his advocacy of revolutionary subversion, dictatorship and terror. The American humorist H. L. Mencken wrote offering to donate all his books to Trotsky as well as to purchase and hand over any other literature he might require. Trotsky declined because he did not want to feel obligated to a man he thought a political reactionary. He also turned down the vice-presidency of the Mark Twain Society. This was an easy decision after he discovered that Benito Mussolini and General John J. Pershing were joint vice-presidents.[3] He rejected too the invitation to become rector of Edinburgh University in Scotland.[4] Petitions were meanwhile signed on his behalf. H. G. Wells had induced John Maynard Keynes, Harold Laski and even the Stalin idolator Beatrice Webb to plead for Trotsky to be given asylum in the United Kingdom. (The Archbishop of York refused to indulge Wells but the Bishop of Birmingham signed a petition written by George Bernard Shaw, who took up Trotsky's case despite being yet another worshipper at the shrine of Joseph Stalin.)[5]

The enthusiasm of so many prominent individuals for doing the decent thing by Trotsky says much for civic tolerance in the countries where they lived. It also reflects their naivety. They were blind to Trotsky's contempt for their values. They overlooked the damage he aimed to do to their kind of society if ever he got the chance. Like spectators at a zoo, they felt sorry for a wounded beast. To many he appeared as a kindred spirit who deserved the protection they would expect in the same circumstances. Trotskyists, socialists and liberals came together to form the American Committee for the Defence of Leon Trotsky. Among its members were the American logician and educationist John Dewey, the novelists John Dos Passos and Mary McCarthy, the literary critics Lionel Trilling and Edmund Wilson. The journalist Edward Allsworth Ross, who had interviewed Trotsky in December 1917, joined. So too did young authors who had once been Trotskyists but had come to have doubts about his politics: Max Eastman, Sidney Hook and James Burnham.[6]

Trotsky planned to exploit this breadth of sympathy by offering to undergo examination by a quasi-judicial tribunal to be held in Coyoacán. John Dewey was his favoured choice as chairman. Several of Trotsky's leading supporters in the US thought the entire project was fundamentally flawed. Dewey was in his mid-seventies and had no sympathy for the far left despite having taught both Max Eastman and Sidney Hook.[7] Trotsky insisted that a polite approach should still be made to the great man. Dewey, to the surprise of most people, including his own family, accepted the invitation and arranged to spend several weeks in Coyoacán. His task would be to test the veracity of the allegations broadcast from Moscow. Trotsky would submit his archives to unrestricted perusal; he would appear before the tribunal and allow himself to be interrogated without placing restrictions on what questions were asked. He predicted it would be the judicial sensation of the twentieth century. Among his intimates he compared the project to the cases mounted by Voltaire for Jean Calas in 1762 and by Émile Zola for Alfred Dreyfus in 1898. He badly wanted to clear his name of Stalin's calumnies.[8]

He trusted Dewey as a fair-minded liberal, and they agreed to avoid examining the broadest questions of Trotsky's political and moral record. The proceedings took place in the Blue House. The Commission's composition was agreed in advance. This was done with little fuss even though one of the members, Ferdinand Lundberg, resigned before the first session. Lundberg had come to think, justifiably, that Trotsky was a prime architect of the suppression of civil rights in the USSR which he now, as a victim, complained about.[9] The Commission started its work on 10 April 1937. The defendant and his American inquisitors turned up in three-piece suits. Formality was observed in the interrogation. Verbatim testimony was copied down. This went on for a whole week until Dewey felt he could summarize an agreed verdict. Nobody had been in serious doubt about what it would be. Trotsky was exculpated. The world's news media were contacted. Dewey and the rest of the commission departed and a book of the proceedings was rapidly edited and published, and some of the damage to Trotsky's reputation was repaired.

Dewey's visit reignited Trotsky's intermittent interest in philosophy. It was not the first time that Dewey had had this effect. Max Eastman had been one of his pupils. Like Trotsky, Eastman was a polymath; and he sensed that he had the edge on Trotsky in coming to grips with the epistemology of Marx, Engels and Lenin. Trotsky treated this as impertinence. One day in 1932, while Eastman was staying with him on Büyükada, the two had a dispute: 'Trotsky's throat was throbbing and his face was red; he was in a rage. His wife was worried, evidently, and when we left the tea table and went into his study still fighting, she came in after us and stood there above and beside me like a statue, silent and austere.'[10] Trotsky went down in the younger man's estimation for substituting sarcasm and bluster for rational argument, as Eastman noted in his diary:

I feel 'injured' by his total inward indifference to my opinions, my interests, my existence as an individual. There has been no meeting either of our minds or feelings. He has never asked me a question. He had answered all my questions, as a book would answer them, without interchange, without assuming the possibility of mutual growth.[11]

Eastman had taken many years to understand that his hero had defects of personality.

Trotsky was recognized as one of the world's leading intellectuals. His political and historical writings were renowned. He had published on international relations, the Russian past, terror and Soviet development. Whenever a topic grabbed his attention, as with the arts or with the problems of everyday life in the 1920s, he produced coruscating booklets on the subject. This was more than enough to make him one of the outstanding Marxist writers.

But it did not make him a universal genius, and somehow this nagged at him. If the mathematical logician Bertrand Russell could talk about politics or the novelist H. G. Wells about ideology, it seemed fitting for a revolutionary politician to have his say on philosophy. Another cause of agitation was the trend in official Soviet communism to systematize Marxism-Leninism: everything from social science to epistemology was being incorporated in a unified world view embodied in Stalin's *Short Course* in 1938. Trotsky was trying to catch up on intellectual fashions. Sigmund Freud and his claims about the unconscious had long fascinated him.[12] Trotsky felt that the extreme version of philosophical materialism favoured in Moscow failed to embrace the totality of human affairs; and although he admired the physiologist Ivan Pavlov, he thought there must be more to life than externally conditioned reflexes. At the same time he could not abide the cult of the irrational which was spreading in Europe. He despised Hitler's ideology and its promotion of racial factors as the main determinant of scientific explanation. The Nazis had arbitrarily taken up bits of Darwin while ignoring others. In Trotsky's opinion it was Marx, not any German racialist theoretician, who made best use of Darwinism by applying its insight to the analysis of global economic development.

An indirect stimulus to philosophical study came from inside the ranks of organized Trotskyism. American adherents included some of the brightest young intellectuals of the time. Among them were Sidney Hook, James Burnham and Max Shachtman. While admiring Trotsky's work as a political leader and writer, they hoped to develop a convincing stand-point on philosophy appropriate to the politics of the far left. This meant starting from scratch. The Opposition in the USSR in the 1920s had never concerned itself with such matters. Hook and his contemporaries were free spirits. They would boldly go wherever their speculations took them, and they expected Trotsky to appreciate their endeavour.

They had misjudged him, because he observed the phenomenon with misgivings. Hook's 'Dialectics and Nature', appearing in the *Marxist Quarterly* in April 1937, confirmed his worry about American Trotskyist intellectuals. Unlike Trotsky, Hook had some solid training in philosophy. He also had flair and confidence; he would bow low to no shibboleth, not even to Marx and Engels. His article exposed the incompetence of Engels's writings on dialectical thought and he did not mind if this offended Marxists accustomed to revering the founding fathers. More important to him was the idea of discovering a sound philosophical foundation for Marxism and rendering it invulnerable to ridicule by professional epistemologists, logicians and ontologists. If Marxist thought was genuinely scientific, he argued, it had to be capable of repelling criticism by the professors. Trotsky was appalled. Such revisionism, he believed, was a lightly veiled assault on Marxism regardless of Hook's subjective purposes; and he feared the influence such ideas might have on other Trotskyists.[13] Joe Hansen in a report from New York confirmed that there was indeed a growing tendency for leading Trotskyists to express scepticism about Marxist dialectics and to dismiss Lenin and Trotsky himself as philosophical dunderheads.[14]

Burnham and especially Hook were driving Trotsky quietly mad with anger.[15] His solution was to try and prepare a written response, and to this end he sent requests to New York for books on philosophy to be forwarded to Coyoacán. On one of the lists was Bertrand Russell's *Principia Mathematica*. Trotsky's American followers were mightily impressed that the Old Man's talent stretched to mastering texts of such difficulty. They were misled in this instance. Heijenoort had written a letter in Trotsky's name so as to acquire a copy for himself and not for Trotsky (whose study of philosophy seldom involved reading works by the great philosophers). Still only in his twenties, Heijenoort was quietly probing what was to become his métier as a professional logician; and he exploited his position as Trotsky's secretary to get the material he needed.[16] He felt a growing scepticism about the Old Man's intellectual pretensions. Trotsky told him that Albert Einstein was not a physicist but a mathematician.[17] This was complete nonsense but the Frenchman held his peace. By summer 1939, though, he had had enough of being isolated in Coyoacán, and he told Trotsky that he wanted to do other things with his life elsewhere. He remained a Trotskyist and did not intend to abandon political activity. But he itched to move to New York. Trotsky and he agreed that he would depart as soon as he had obtained a visa.[18]

Meanwhile Trotsky made notes, as was his habit at the start of any large project. He jotted down the following:

> Nevertheless it is precisely because man is inclined to take his own consciousness as the primordial factor – both in relation to his personal subconscious and in relation to the external environment, especially the societal one – that he turns the real relation on its head in diverse areas of science.[19]

This was a bland restatement of the kind of thing said long ago by Marx and Engels. Unlike Lenin in his *Materialism and Empiriocriticism*, Trotsky denied that the human mind, working like a camera on the external environment, automatically receives an accurate image of reality. The process of perception is more complex as well as more crude than that.[20] As Trotsky remarked, a cinema film is simply a moving concatenation of photographic images – and somehow the watching eye omits to notice the celluloid gaps between one image and the next. He deftly summarized the process: 'Our intellect acts exactly like an eye. From a countless number of conditions in the process of development it is capable of capturing and fixing only a limited number of these conditions; this is both its strength and its weakness.'[21] This was the best that Trotsky could come up with. It was not original thinking. But it showed that he could try and break free of the conventional Marxism of his day.

Such moments were few and far between. Usually he focused on politics in his notebooks. Getting hold of Hook's *Towards the Understanding of Karl Marx*, he wrote sharp comments in the margins as he went through it. His suspicion was that Hook and his sympathizers were injecting a subjective strain into Marxism. For Trotsky there could be no dubieties and it was an unchallengeable verity that the proletariat had an objective interest in 'searching for an exit from capitalist chaos'. For Hook, by definition, there were no axioms.[22]

Trotsky had enough sense to see that he lacked the competence to assail the Trotskyist revisionists on matters epistemological and ontological. He was less diffident about disputing questions of political morality. By 1938 he was ready with a booklet entitled *Their Morality and Ours: The Moralists and Sycophants against Marxism*. After a brief exposition of his understanding of dialectics, he turned to more comfortable terrain. As he had done in *Terrorism and Communism* he rejected universal moral concepts. He took the early Protestants as an example: 'Thus the teachings of Christ "purified" by them did not at all hinder the city bourgeois Luther from calling for the execution of revolting peasants as "mad dogs".'[23] According to Trotsky, economic interests and class struggle suffused the way that Christians interpreted the New Testament. They had no difficulty in putting aside their eternal and God-given principles of non-violence whenever their financial wellbeing was threatened; and they did not stop short of resorting to massacres of their enemies. Marxists were much the same in adopting severe measures to protect the interests of revolution. Yes, they engaged in civil wars. Yes, they took and executed hostages in order to beat the counter-revolution. They subordinated moral concerns to the current practical requirements.[24]

He got to one of his main points in an addendum noting that many ex-communists went over to belief in eternal moral truths when they abandoned support for the Stalinist order. These included Eugene Lyons, Walter Krivitsky and Charles Rappoport. Furthermore, several critics of Stalinism who remained communists showed a tendency to do the same. Top of the list were past sympathizers of Trotsky such as Victor Serge ('pedlar of indulgences') and Boris Souvarine (bourgeois 'sycophant'). Basically, according to Trotsky, they had forgotten that 'two classes decide the fate of modern society: the imperialist bourgeoisie and the proletariat'. In a hurrah for Marxist radicalism Trotsky proclaimed:

> Civilisation can only be saved by the socialist revolution. To accomplish the overturn, the proletariat needs all its strength, all its resolution, all its audacity, passion and ruthlessness. Above all it must be completely free from the fictions of religion, 'democracy' and transcendental morality – the spiritual chains forged by the enemy to tame it and enslave it. Only that which prepares the complete and final overthrow of imperialist bestiality is moral, and nothing else. The welfare of the revolution – that is the supreme law![25]

In these five sentences lie all the power, irreconcilability and casualness of Trotsky's intellect.

James Burnham spelled this out in an open letter to him on 1 February 1940. Burnham demonstrated how Trotsky used verbal pyrotechnics to distract from the inadequacies of his philosophical understanding. Every rhetorical flourish – perhaps a brilliant metaphor or a flash of sardonic wit – was employed.[26] Burnham argued that Trotsky's purposes were often polemical rather than fundamentally intellectual. Wanting to crush the Trotskyist opponents of his political purposes, the Old Man attacked them as deviating from the fundamental precepts of Marxism. The dispute about 'dialectics' was a red herring. Burnham repudiated Trotsky's claim that erroneous philosophy was intimately linked to mistaken practical policies. Trotsky, he pointed out, approved of several leading Marxists who did not share his conception of dialectical analysis. Among them was Karl Liebknecht. What is more, there were others who had shared Trotsky's conception and yet had opposed his politics – Burnham adduced Georgi Plekhanov and several Mensheviks.[27]

He then turned to Trotsky's proposition that 'class truth' lay with proletarian revolutionaries operating to philosophical methods and objectives different to everyone else:

> You are on treacherous ground, comrade Trotsky. The doctrine of 'class truth' is the road of Plato's Philosopher Kings, of prophets and Popes and Stalins. For all of them, also, a man must be among the anointed order to know the truth. It leads in a direction diametrically opposite to that of socialism, of a truly *human* society. You issue many warnings to the young comrades of our movement. I add an ominous warning to the list: beware, beware, comrades, of anyone or any doctrine that tells you that any man, or group of men, holds a monopoly on truth, or on the ways of getting truth.[28]

Trotsky, as if to confirm Burnham's assessment, took no serious notice of it: he simply retaliated with a contention of his own: 'Scepticism towards all theories is nothing but preparation for personal desertion.'[29] He had sealed himself in the cave of his fundamental beliefs. He allowed no questioning of them. He bullied followers who dared to object; and he preferred them to leave the Fourth International than to cause him bother.

He had his way in this: Hook, Burnham and Shachtman abandoned Trotsky and the Fourth International. Each did it in his own way. Hook steadily turned into an uncompromising anti-communist just as Trotsky had predicted; he made a renowned career puncturing the pretensions of Marxism past and present and arguing the superiority of liberal and democratic values. Burnham interested himself in applying Marxist categories of analysis to trends in contemporary societies with advanced industrial capacity around the world. He picked up the kind of thinking started by the Polish socialist Jan Machajski (whom Trotsky had met in Siberian exile) and deepened by Italian sociologist Bruno Rizzi in the 1930s. Machajski, Burnham and Rizzi suggested that, as capitalist economic development proceeded, the authority of the managerial stratum increased. They were impressed by the rise in bureaucratic practices. They observed how states were becoming ever more deeply involved in decisions about the economy. Rizzi and Burnham suggested that managers were gradually exercising control even in the Soviet Union at the communist party's expense; both came to reject Marxism as a tool of social science. This was in contrast with Shachtman who tried for the rest of his life to stay within the bounds of Marxist doctrine as he understood it. But Shachtman acknowledged no living Marxist master and never apologized for the affront he had given to Trotsky.

Trotsky wrote *Their Morality and Ours* to attack all his young critics; instead of confronting their intrinsic arguments he deployed his weaponry of sarcasm and ridicule. The Old Man's vanity was bulging. He expected his adherents to publish the work just as soon as he finished editing it. Some of them baulked at this. A world war was raging and they deemed it less than appropriate to give editorial and financial priority to a philosophical diatribe in a magazine they were establishing in New York. Bertram Wolfe led the opposition to Trotsky's request, and was deputed to talk things over with him. Ella Wolfe recounted what happened next:

> So, of course, [Trotsky's] secretary went back and reported what my husband said. We had an appointment Wednesday morning at ten o'clock at his home. And when we arrived at the gate . . . and rang the bell, the servant came out and said Trotsky is too ill to receive you. That was the man's vanity. You know, he didn't think that anyone should say that he couldn't have the first article.[30]

Usually he had only to hint at his displeasure for his acolytes to give way to him. Resistance was an unaccustomed experience. He reacted by sulking.

# 50. THE SECOND WORLD WAR

Trotsky's grip on his followers' allegiance was weakened by disputes in the Fourth International about the geopolitical situation in Europe. For most of the 1930s they had been in awe of his powers of analysis. Trotsky saw the European far right's success as the product of the global crisis in capitalism. He thought fascist leaders were playthings of the interests of big business in their countries just as Stalin was a puppet of the Soviet bureaucracy. Whereas he examined Stalin's every word, though, he felt no urge to study Hitler, Mussolini or Franco. He commented little on the cases of German and Italian aggression. He even wrote about Spanish Civil War almost entirely in terms of Stalin's foreign policy and the machinations of Comintern. His admirers in subsequent generations have unjustifiably treated him as a comprehensive interpreter of all the big events in European politics in the 1930s.

Undoubtedly he had always warned against the dangers of the Third Reich, scorning strategies of containment such as the establishment of popular fronts. All through the decade he said that only communist revolution could save Europe from fascist barbarism. He maintained that nowhere in the world was invulnerable to the onset of authoritarian militarism. He had not only Japan but even the USA in mind. What is more, Trotsky had long given up thinking of the USSR under Stalin as constituting an anti-fascist bulwark. The Politburo, he declared, was preoccupied with Soviet internal interests. Stalin would go to any lengths to stay out of foreign entanglements and his professed commitment to spreading revolution westwards was a deceit. In reality, according to Trotsky, Stalin would countenance a deal even with Hitler if it seemed to guarantee the security of the USSR and his own survival in power. The Kremlin's foreign policy was shifting about in the winds reaching Russia from central and eastern Europe. In the early hours of 24 August 1939, Stalin was present at the signing of a non-aggression treaty with the Third Reich by Molotov and Joachim von Ribbentrop, the German Foreign Minister. The public section of the pact involved an agreement not to attack each other. The two countries also undertook to collaborate in economic relations. Secret protocols divided up Poland into spheres of influence for the Soviet Union and Germany. A diplomatic bomb had exploded in the heart of Europe.

Soviet leaders were hoping that the treaty would deflect Nazi attention for the foreseeable future from aggressive ambitions against the USSR. Hitler invaded Poland on 1 September 1939, rejecting the joint ultimatum of the British and French demanding that he withdraw his forces. The Second World War had begun. The Germans completed their occupation of Polish territory safe in the assurance that the USSR would not intervene against them. While the rest of the world shuddered with shock at the Nazi–Soviet pact, Trotsky pointed out that this outcome proved him right as a prophet.[1]

Stalin held back from invading eastern Poland only because he could not ignore the continuing military threat to him in the Far East. The USSR and Japan had been fighting a border war in Manchuria since July 1938. The Red Army's high command under Georgi Zhukov used tank formations in a war for the first time. It was a perilous geopolitical situation. If Zhukov failed, the Japanese might attempt an attack across Siberia. Stalin contemplated the uncertainties over the ensuing days. His mind was clarified when the Japanese decided in favour of further expansion not westwards to the Urals but southward into China. Tokyo agreed peace terms on 15 September. This freed the Soviet leadership to move forces into Poland's eastern territories. The entire country had now vanished from the map of Europe. As the Red Army completed its occupation, the Sovietization of the territory proceeded. Polish political, military and economic leaders were arrested and either executed or consigned to Siberia. The Moscow newspapers were exultant, praising Stalin the aggressor as continental peacemaker and guarantor of the USSR's security.

There had hardly been time for the world's communist parties to get over their astonishment at the non-aggression treaty. Now they were told to rejoice in Nazi–Soviet collaboration in Poland's dismemberment. The central apparatus of Comintern duly obeyed; but not all communists in Europe and North America toed the official line. Having spent the decade campaigning against the Third Reich, many of them left their parties rather than obey Moscow's instructions. The USSR had become an active ally of the Nazis in all but name.

Trotsky had difficulty in following the course of events from across the Atlantic. Neither Germany nor the Soviet Union was broadcasting exactly what was happening in Poland, and the American press – his main source of information – offered little coverage outside Warsaw. Crisis after crisis developed at lightning speed. There were only three issues of the *Byulleten oppozitsii* in the twelve months after the German invasion of Poland. Even so, Trotsky could have done better than he did. He could no longer summon up the verve and adaptiveness he had displayed in the early weeks of the First World War.[2] As late as 25 September 1939, more than three weeks after the Blitzkrieg on Poland, he saw fit to carry on with a lengthy article on the terms of the non-aggression treaty of August; he felt no compulsion to switch to concentrating on the latest military and political events. The article dourly repeated the rudiments of Trotsky's thinking on 'the character of the USSR'. Admitting that Trotskyists should never stop asking whether their appraisal was the correct one, he declared: 'Just as a tidy housewife never permits cobwebs and rubbish to accumulate, so a revolutionary cannot tolerate lack of clarity, confusion, equivocation. Our house must be kept clean!'[3] The rhetoric was lame. His main point was a lamer one, that the Nazi–Soviet pact and the outbreak of the Second World War should not affect the Trotskyist analysis of the USSR.[4]

He made scant reference to the terrible fate of the Poles as they fell under the combined military yoke. Not a single word on the arrests and shootings. Trotsky, indeed, condoned the likely results of the Soviet operation:

> Our *general* evaluation of the Kremlin and Comintern does not change, however, the particular fact that the stratification of the forms of ownership in the occupied areas is itself a progressive measure. There has to be frank acknowledgement of this. Were Hitler tomorrow to turn his forces in a front towards the East so as to establish 'order' in Eastern Poland, the advanced workers would defend the new forms of property from Hitler introduced by the Bonapartist Soviet bureaucracy.[5]

The mangled terminology came from seeking to say something which, at a certain level, even he found distasteful. This did not stop him saying it. Sticking to his schematic understanding of the war, he made no room for sympathy for the human victims.

The important thing for Trotsky was that the war would shatter political stability in Europe and produce 'proletarian revolution'. What had taken place in Russia in the First World War would happen again elsewhere in the Second. The difference was that the Soviet order now existed. Trotsky called on his followers to support the defence of the USSR in whatever way they could. This was not an invocation to collaborate with the communist parties of the Third International. He stipulated that Trotskyists should fight for the Soviet Union only insofar as this might assist preparations for world revolution.[6] He never explained how such a policy could be realized. He simply recalled that he and Lenin had worked on the assumption that revolutionary administrations could be created across Europe in 1918–20. Germany, Italy, Hungary and Czechoslovakia had had their rumblings at that time. Then capitalist power had reasserted itself. Trotsky could not rule out that the same frustration of communist intentions would recur after the Second World War. What if the working classes disappointed these expectations? Trotsky faced up to this possibility with a frankness he had not previously displayed. He conceded that if the USSR were to survive the world war under Stalin's leadership, then 'it would be necessary in retrospect to establish that in its fundamental traits the present USSR was a precursor of a new exploiting regime on an international scale.'

This conclusion was a deeply disturbing one. The Soviet bureaucracy would have consolidated itself so strongly as to acquire the characteristics of a social class.[7] Trotsky dealt with this topic discursively. He noted that the political theorist Bruno Rizzi had bracketed Nazi Germany and the USSR as examples of the same phenomenon: totalitarianism. Trotsky failed to repudiate the idea out of hand but argued that totalitarianism was 'a condition of acute crisis and not a stable regime'.[8]

He was trying to discover grounds for optimism and still urged the priority of preserving the basic Soviet order. He made just one important qualification:

> The defence of the USSR coincides for us with the preparation of world revolution. Only those methods are acceptable which do not contradict the interests of the revolution. The defence of the USSR is related to the world socialist revolution as a tactical task is related to a strategic one. Tactics are subordinated to the strategic goal and can in no instance become in contradiction to it.[9]

He refused to speculate about future vicissitudes; and, not being in power, he could be as opaque as he liked:

> This kind of 'defence of the USSR' will of course differ, as heaven does from earth, from the official defence which is currently being conducted under the slogan: 'For the Motherland! For Stalin!' *Our* defence of the USSR is being conducted under the slogan: 'For Socialism! For the World Revolution! Against Stalin!'[10]

These were smoke signals rather than practical guidance from the Old Man which could be of use to the Fourth International.

In the same issue of the *Byulleten oppozitsii* he reverted to his customary ridicule of Stalin. He depicted Hitler as the aggressive master, Stalin as the obedient servant. Right to the end of his life he continued to underestimate his enemy in the Kremlin. He dismissed the thought that Stalin behaved autonomously in international relations at this time. Until the fall of France in May 1940, indeed, the Soviet Union derived as much economic and military benefit from the agreements with Hitler as the Third Reich did in the opposite direction.[11]

By then Trotsky had plunged into yet another controversy. Stalin, after gobbling up eastern Poland, turned his attention to Estonia, Latvia and Lithuania. Under the terms of the Nazi–Soviet non-aggression pact, as modified on 28 September 1939, all three states fell inside the USSR's sphere of influence. The Kremlin issued threats to their governments. Baltic ministers were summoned to Moscow, where the intimidation was direct and brutal: they were told they would not leave alive unless they signed a request for incorporation in the USSR. The terrified governments gave way. In June 1940 the Red Army and NKVD moved into their countries to carry out a full 'Sovietization'. Stalin expected the same compliance from Finland but met with stern, unexpected resistance. The Red Army was ordered on to the offensive on 30 November 1939. Finnish forces fought it off. Stalin was furious on learning of the unexpected setback. A Finnish Soviet government had been announced, headed by Comintern official Otto Kuusinen. The 'Winter War' turned into a military stalemate until March 1940, when the Finns agreed to peace talks. The result was a treaty which shifted the USSR's frontier, which till then had been less than an hour's train journey from Leningrad, hundreds of miles further north.

While disparaging the Kremlin's competence, Trotsky had thoroughly approved of the Soviet military campaign in principle. He claimed that 'Sovietization' would have brought inestimable benefit to Finland. The Minority in the Socialist Workers Party in New York – the world's largest surviving Trotskyist organization – objected to this, detesting what they called 'Stalino-imperialism' and rejecting Trotsky's suggestion that the Red Army had triggered a civil war in Finland.[12] What had taken place was Finnish national resistance to invasion. Even the Majority, whose members had stood with Trotsky, queried his information and analysis.[13] Trotsky refused to give way. In a letter to Joe Hansen he noted that even the Mensheviks had admitted that the Soviet–Polish War of 1920 had led to civil war across Poland. He insisted that the same had occurred in Finland. Trotsky continued to hope for a Red Army victory and a Finnish communist insurrection until peace was made between Moscow and Helsinki.[14]

At the same time he inveighed against comrades who took sides in the European war. His intellectual rigidities were on the increase. He was transfixed by memories of the Great War when he, like the rest of the Zimmerwald Left, had called down a plague on all the belligerent powers. Imperial Germany and Imperial Austria had been as bad as Imperial Britain, Imperial France and Imperial Russia. He rehearsed events from earlier communist history – and as usual he gave a biased account. Trotsky recalled the Brest-Litovsk dispute among Bolsheviks in 1918 when Bukharin had stood for revolutionary war despite the military weakness of the Soviet administration. (He omitted to mention that he had taken a standpoint nearer to Bukharin than to Lenin.)[15] Lenin had favoured a separate peace with the Central Powers as a means of saving the October Revolution; he had also stipulated that if socialist revolution were to break out in Germany, the Red Army would be sent to aid German revolutionaries even if it involved sacrificing 'Soviet power' in Russia. Trotsky wanted to apply Lenin's strategy in the Second World War. If the German workers were to rise against Hitler, he wrote to Shachtman, 'we shall say, "We must subordinate the interests of the defense of the Soviet Union to the interests of the world revolution."'[16]

He stressed that he was not calling 'unconditionally for the support of the Kremlin'.[17] This was a justifiable statement at the formal level. But it was a specious argument in 1939–40 when there was not the slightest chance of a German proletarian uprising. Nazi control over society had never been more secure. Trotsky in reality was surreptitiously expressing an absolute commitment to the defence of the USSR. He was willing to allow a frank debate on the matter and urged against applying organizational sanctions against the Minority in the Socialist Workers Party. There was to be no ban on factions and the Minority could even publish an internal party bulletin. Trotsky told Hansen: 'But we are not bureaucrats at all. We don't have immutable rules. We are dialecticians also in the organizational field.'[18] The resultant discussion failed to win over Shachtman, who stood by his criticisms of Trotsky's policy on Ukraine, the Nazi–Soviet treaty and Finland. Trotsky wrote to 'my dear friend' in December 1939, saying he wished he could come to New York for two or three days and persuade him face to face. Alternatively could Shachtman perhaps come to Coyoacán? Trotsky showered Shachtman with praise and entreaties. But in the end he could not help being provocative. He told Shachtman he was standing 'on the wrong side of the barricades' and giving 'courage to all the petty-bourgeois and anti-Marxist elements to fight our doctrine'.[19] Trotsky had shown a proclivity for vituperation and ridicule since his revolutionary youth in Nikolaev. It never left him.

His followers had become Trotskyists because they thought he was the world's greatest anti-fascist. Yet here he was saying that the Third Reich and Republican France were equally bad. The tensions in the Socialist Workers Party intensified. Trotsky grew fearful of losing them from the Fourth International. He told Joe Hansen, his most loyal accomplice in New York, to strive to prevent an organizational split.[20] At least in this respect he was acting more like himself than like Lenin in the First World War. Trotsky added: 'For my part I believe that the prolongation of the discussion, if it is channelized by the good will of both sides, can only serve in the present conditions the education of the party.'[21] Yet Shachtman was beyond caring and walked out of the pro-Trotsky faction of American Trotskyism, never to return. Trotsky had been Russian social-democracy's great unifier before 1914. Now he needlessly made enemies: he had turned into the Lenin of his own wartime International. The difference was that the Second World War did not provide Trotsky with anything like a revolutionary situation to exploit such as he and Lenin had had in 1917.

France fell to the German Blitzkrieg in May 1940. Military occupation followed and the French Trotskyists, who already had to operate secretly because of their anti-war policy, had to fend for their lives. Trotskyism as a world movement was badly damaged. The German comrades had been suppressed in 1933; now the French were being scattered. The British, Dutch and Belgians had never counted for much in the Fourth International. This left the Americans as the only dynamic Trotskyist group working freely – and they were distracted by their multiplying internal divisions. Trotsky's main preoccupation, as always, was with the USSR. He blamed France's capitulation not on the French government or its armed forces but on Stalin. The débâcle, he maintained, was the direct result of the Kremlin's policy of popular fronts. Supposedly the Soviet Union had 'disorientated and demoralized' the 'masses' in Europe by abandoning the strategy of revolution. In 1939 Stalin had turned into an 'agent provocateur in Hitler's service'. Trotsky made the accurate prediction that the next phase in the European war would be a struggle between the USSR and the Third Reich. The Red Army's ineffectualness in the conflict with Finland had encouraged Hitler. The defence of the USSR was unsafe in Stalin's hands. Trotsky repeated his call for 'the Muscovite totalitarian gang' to be removed from power.[22]

On a single big topic he shifted his position. Until the Second World War he had resolutely opposed calls for a Jewish state to be established in Palestine. In a letter to Albert Glotzer in February 1939 he described it as 'a fine trap' for the Jews. But he recognized the growing dangers for Jewish people the world over and told Glotzer, a resident of New York: 'With the decline of American capitalism, anti-semitism will become more and more terrible in the United States – in any case, more important than in Germany.'[23] This defective prophecy needs to be remembered when the case is made for Trotsky's brilliant powers of prediction. Within a year he had changed his mind on Palestine. While reaffirming that proletarian socialist revolution alone would bring the Jewish question to solution, he suggested that a revolutionary administration might agree to grant an independent state to the Jews.[24] German barbarity against European Jewry eroded Trotsky's lifelong hostility to the idea of a homeland for Jews in the Middle East. He did not concede that he had been wrong in the past; and he did not spell out exactly where such a state could be situated. But it was an important change of mind.

His thoughts were becoming distinctly erratic. The Socialist Workers Party had got used to reading his absolute condemnations of the parties of Comintern. Trotsky wrote on 12 October 1939 to J. B. Matthews, Chief Investigator of the US Congress's Committee on Un-American Activities (which investigated foreign subversion of the American Constitution), offering to appear as a witness against the leadership of the Communist Party of the USA. His only condition was that he should be sent the questions in advance.[25] At the same time he expressed pleasure that Comintern's parties on Stalin's instructions remained neutral towards the belligerent sides in the European war. Abruptly in June 1940 Trotsky suggested the need to build bridges towards Comintern. He rebuked Trotskyist leaders in New York for continuing their unconditional attacks on the Communist Party of the USA; he insisted that 'the Stalinists are a legitimate part of the workers' movement' and 'have great courage'. The Fourth International should therefore try to split the 'base' from the official communist leadership.[26] Trotsky insisted that he had not lost his intellectual and political compass, and called on his followers to regard themselves as 'proletarian revolutionary militarists' because one day soon they might have to take up arms against the invaders of the USSR.[27] New York's Trotskyists could be forgiven for thinking he was becoming an unreliable guide in the politics of the far left.

Trotsky wrote to Albert Goldman on 9 July 1940 proposing that the Socialist Workers Party should drop its slogans demanding 'a people's referendum on the war'. This was in line with his wish to hold the labour movement back from supporting the United Kingdom against Germany. He continued to demand that the Fourth International, like the Comintern, should oppose America's entry on the British side. His hope was that a referendum campaign would enable the party to explain 'the futility of their democracy' to American workers.[28]

Meanwhile Trotsky remained convinced that that the USSR would not enter the world war actively on the side of the Third Reich.[29] Even he could not imagine that Stalin would allow himself to stoop so low. Trotsky never explained why: he was simply giving voice to an intuitive feeling. Love of the USSR, despite its faults, lay deep in Trotsky's heart. The last time he wrote on Soviet matters was when he dispatched an open message, printed on the thinnest paper, to 'the workers, kolkhozniks [collective farmers], Red Army soldiers and Red Fleet sailors of the USSR from distant Mexico' in spring 1940. It included fervent declaration of his wish to help with the defence of the USSR. This was the forlorn attempt of a man who must have known that no letter of his would get through to the people he was addressing it to. Or perhaps he was by now cut off entirely from reality. At any rate he foretold that Stalin's press would declare that agents of imperialism had been the carriers of his message.[30] He could hardly have been more wrong. The Soviet media took absolutely no notice and probably the message entirely failed to reach its destination.

# 51. ASSASSINATION

Stalin had not forgotten about Trotsky even though it was years since *Pravda* had reported on his activities. The Great Terror had ended in the final month of 1938 and not a single enemy of Stalin survived in Soviet politics. Trotsky alone remained in operation; and although the Fourth International was weak and divided Stalin was determined to eliminate him. Indeed he had an obsession about him. The Soviet media called Trotsky the most vicious 'enemy of the people' based abroad. While having few illusions about the perils of his situation, Trotsky refused to worry about personal security. Ignoring the advice of his aides, he went on seeing complete strangers alone in his study.[1] He expressed confidence that no one could breach the precautions being taken on his behalf. No one, he claimed, would risk dying in an attempt to assassinate him.[2]

The house in Avenida Viena became a cross between a villa and a fortress. A watchtower was built at the entrance and guard rooms were situated just inside the northern wall. The Trotskys themselves occupied quarters set further inside the courtyard for additional protection. These included Seva's bedroom, Lev and Natalya's bedroom and Trotsky's study. Trotsky's library, the common dining room, the kitchen and bathroom were by the east-facing wall.[3] Rabbits and chickens were kept in the courtyard to supplement the household's diet. Several trees grew in the garden; there was a eucalyptus in the centre as well as a profusion of flowers. The house's brickwork and mortar were of a traditional Mexican kind, strong enough to repel machine-gun fire if not to withstand a bomb blast. An electrical alarm system was installed. Kiosks for the police guards were erected on the outside of the villa. Trotsky knew he could not make the villa impregnable but had ceased to care. The philosopher of revolutionary will was succumbing to fatalism. He no longer minded leaving it to others to build on the political foundations he had laid.

There were moments when he lost his composure. In February 1938, while still residing in the Blue House, he witnessed some large bags of fertilizer arriving for Rivera and inferred that the chemical was intended for use as an explosive. The delivery man claimed to have been sent by the Minister of Communications General Mugica. When this proved to be untrue, Trotsky moved out for several days.[4] He also acted with some care about what he wrote to Trotskyist leaders elsewhere: he had a justified worry that Kremlin agents had gained access to his correspondence, so he used pseudonyms when writing letters. But he was not very inventive about this; he often signed letters as Old Man, a name he had been using off and on since Turkey. Sometimes he called himself Uncle Leon – another transparent nom de plume.[5] He also often signed as Crux, Onken, Vidal and Lund. Trotsky had to contend against the agents of Stalin who were trying to infiltrate his entourage. He also remained under scrutiny by the Mexican police and the American embassy. Stalin was the only one among the watchers who wanted him dead, and Trotsky began to recognize that the NKVD would eventually succeed in carrying out its master's wishes. An inner gloom was descending on him. He had once referred to his living conditions in France as 'a prison situation'; he had hated the way the Sûreté restricted his movements.[6] In Mexico it was his own followers who insisted on confining him, and the dangers were too obvious for him to resist.

He anyway believed that ill health rather than an assassin's bullet might take him off. He wrote out his 'testament' in long hand on 27 February 1940, four months after his sixtieth birthday. This was after Dr Zollinger, his family physician in Mexico, had given him one of his regular medical check-ups. Natalya blamed the doctor for causing her husband to be mentally depressed. Zollinger denied having offered a pessimistic verdict and Trotsky's comments seem to confirm this. Natalya arranged for a further examination with the idea of cheering him up.[7] Although his mood improved he continued writing his will. He included few details, stating only that all his property and future income should revert to Natalya. (He failed to say what was to happen if she were to die before him.) In a note he added: 'My high – and increasingly high – blood pressure is deceiving those near me about my actual condition. I am active and able to work – but the climax is evidently near.' He expected to die of a brain haemorrhage. This was only a guess since he refused to read medical textbooks and suspected that the doctors were not being frank with him. Rather than become a helpless invalid he would prefer to commit suicide; he had an agreement with Natalya about this.

Trotsky admitted to political mistakes while declining to say what they had been. There was, he said, 'not a single blot on my revolutionary honesty', and he added: 'I shall die a proletarian revolutionary, a Marxist, a dialectical materialist and consequently an irreconcilable atheist. My faith in the communist future of humanity is no less ardent and is even firmer today than it was in the days of my youth.' He thought this gave him 'powers of resistance' greater than any afforded by religion. He thanked his friends for their loyalty and paid tribute to Natalya: 'For almost forty years of our life together she remained an inexhaustible source of love, magnanimity and tenderness. She underwent great sufferings, especially in the last period of our lives. But I find some comfort in the fact that she also knew days of happiness.'[8] Trotsky had got over his own distractions of the heart.

His morale rose as he returned to work on the Stalin biography, on the articles for the *Byulleten oppozitsii* and on the disputes with his critics in the Socialist Workers Party. The communal meals enabled him to talk about the great matters of the day. He walked around the garden of his villa to see how the hired labourer was doing his job.[9] Trotsky himself retained responsibility for feeding the rabbits. He also kept up a lively correspondence and his entourage ceased to worry about his mental condition. New recruits came to Mexico and were asked to carry out functions appropriate to their talents. Two of them were to acquire a certain fame in the year 1940. Robert Sheldon Harte was a young American who offered his services as a guard. The twenty-five-year-old Bob, as everyone called him, was a popular fellow. No intellectual, he carried out without complaint any tasks assigned to him. He chatted amiably at meal times. Another newcomer was Sylvia Ageloff. American by citizenship and a qualified secretary, she carried out technical duties for Trotsky. Unlike Harte, she lived outside the villa. Sylvia was a plain-looking woman, aged thirty, who had not had much success with men. She was very thoughtful about politics and, despite belonging to the Trotsky entourage, took the side of the Minority in the dispute among the American Trotskyists.

In the winter of 1939–40 the American Trotskyist Alexander Buchman, a photographer, came down to Mexico to help. He had the expertise to renovate the electrical wiring and rebuild the alarm system so that the household could prevent a break-in and link up with the local police station. In mid-April 1940 he relinquished his duties, being replaced by Harte.[10] It was a fateful change of personnel. Harte was not at all what he seemed. Instead he was a Soviet agent belonging to the Communist Party of the USA. His mission was to liaise with a Mexican assassination squad assembled by the painter David Alfaro Siqueiros, who was a strong supporter of Comintern. Siqueiros, like Rivera, was a muralist. As a veteran of the Spanish Civil War he was also experienced in handling guns and eager to carry out an attack on Stalin's worst enemy.

The firing started before dawn on 24 May, when Siqueiros and around twenty armed men entered the outer gate at Avenida Viena.[11] This should not have been possible but Harte was on duty and let them in. The policemen outside the villa made no fuss, leaving everything to Harte. Siqueiros's gang came in military uniforms. The police later said this stopped them from seeing the need to intervene.[12] Once inside the courtyard they headed for the open area next to where Trotsky worked and slept. For several minutes they shot ferociously in that direction. Trotsky and Natalya dived under their bed. The bullets got near to them and Natalya threw herself over her husband to protect him. The gang's simple plan of attack had been to deliver a concentrated fusillade at the building and leave as fast as possible under the cover of darkness. They fled back to their two large cars without knowing whether they had succeeded. Trotsky and Natalya rushed next door to Seva's bedroom. Hearing the boy crying, they were relieved to find that he had suffered only a graze to his foot. The entourage met in the courtyard trying to work out how their precautions had failed. There was a further mystery. Why had the gang abducted Robert Sheldon Harte?

The Mexican police were determined to undertake a methodical investigation. The identities of the gunmen were unknown although Siqueiros was already the prime suspect. Even Rivera was distrusted because of his ruined friendship with Trotsky. Leading painters seemed especially suspect. Siqueiros and some of his accomplices had sped off to the hills near Tacuba on the north-western outskirts of Mexico City. Theirs had been an attempt of almost comic amateurishness. They had to listen to the radio to discover whether or not they had killed Trotsky.

Colonel Leandro A. Sánchez Salazar, an impressive professional, led the police investigation. The Cárdenas government had been trying hard to prevent any incident such as had now occurred, and it was Salazar who had been in charge of Trotsky's protection. He was called out of his bed within minutes of the shooting and it was not yet dawn when he arrived. The gateway was barred to him: the residents were anxious lest another attack might be imminent and were standing together in the garden with weapons at the ready. Salazar negotiated permission to enter. Young Seva, his foot bandaged, was playing in the open air. Light was beginning to appear in the sky and there was an eerie atmosphere of calm. Trotsky, wearing a dressing gown over his pyjamas, came out with Natalya to greet Salazar. The couple seemed so unperturbed that the colonel wondered whether the shooting had been a put-up job.[13] If he had read his history books he would have known that Trotsky had experienced situations a lot more dangerous even than this one in the Civil War in Soviet Russia.

Salazar and his colleagues formulated two hypotheses in their questioning of the residents. The description of the gang leader fitted Siqueiros closely. Furthermore, Siqueiros had mysteriously disappeared from view. Normally he was a flamboyant figure in the restaurants and bars of Mexico City. A manhunt was started. The entourage was willing to accept the police's guesswork about the painter. The second hypothesis did not please them. This was that Harte had been Siqueiros's accomplice. The police could not see how Siqueiros could have effected the raid without an internal collaborator because there were no signs of a struggle.[14] The residents met the police's suppositions about Harte with condescension. They had got on with Bob, who had shown total loyalty to the cause. They declined to accept that anyone who mouthed Trotsky's slogans could be a Judas. His part in the camaraderie of the villa had surely not been confected. The implications were too ghastly to contemplate. If Bob Harte was a traitor, then who else in the entourage might be lurking with the same intent? The refusal to face up to the possibility of infiltration was about to have lethal consequences.

Not all the Trotskyists were naive. Bob Harte by common consent had omitted to keep the electrical security system working on the night in question and even Natalya, who believed in his innocence, recalled how casual he had been about security.[15] Herbert Solow wrote pointing out his suspicions to Trotsky on 14 June. He also mentioned that a group of Stalinists had been detected at Tacuba only four miles from the centre of Mexico City. This was an odd place for them to live. Solow urged Trotsky to get the police to undertake an immediate investigation. He urged all residents in the Avenida Viena villa meanwhile to stay silent about the abducted Harte.[16]

Harte's fate was revealed when local inhabitants found a corpse at an adobe house outside Tacuba. Siqueiros as well as his limousine had been spotted in the nearby hills, but as yet the police could not lay their hands on him. The investigation quickly turned up interesting details. Siqueiros and friends had taken a three-month lease on the house for forty-five pesos. It was clear that this was where the plotters had been based even if much about the affair remained to be discovered. A black Packard with New York number plates had been reported there in previous weeks. Siqueiros had been seen in town in the same make of car.[17] The authorities approached the house with care in case of booby traps. They came fully armed. But by the time they arrived everyone had fled from the house and Siqueiros was issuing public statements professing his innocence of involvement in any attempt on Trotsky's life. The adobe's contents were turned upside down. The surrounding land was searched. Police reinforcements swarmed over the neighbourhood. The corpse, crudely covered in lime, was identified as belonging to Robert Sheldon Harte.

Colonel Salazar felt he had confirmed the validity of his second hypothesis. Siqueiros had taken Harte off with him as an accomplice and for some reason had decided to murder him. Possibly these were his orders from Moscow. An alternative explanation was that Siqueiros had panicked about having to look after Harte while the police were looking for both of them. When Siqueiros surfaced again in Mexico City he was taken into custody and interrogated. The police lacked the proof that he had murdered Harte. Siqueiros brazened it out and denied having attacked and entered the villa despite all the evidence against him. His fame as an artist made things easier but he did not entirely escape punishment. By the time he was tried in 1941 Trotsky was dead and the Mexican government was embarrassed by the possibility that one of the country's greatest painters might be sentenced to years of incarceration. The decision was to spirit him out of Mexico to Chile, where he stayed for two years before cautiously returning in 1943 and resuming his tempestuous public career.[18]

Trotsky was shaken by the incident at the villa and walked around saying, 'I'm tired, I'm tired.'[19] At the end of July he suffered a recurrence of 'his old and mysterious illness'; there was no fever but he had back pain and a high temperature. He had perked up by 11 August and was spending less time in bed.[20] He was dictating *Stalin* again and conducting a vigorous correspondence with political sympathizers and others. His rage and frustration were sometimes barely containable, and he got them out of his system by firing off a rough letter to his New York translator Charles Malamuth. He was cheered up by visits by admirers, usually from the United States; he rarely passed up the chance to lay out his case for the Fourth International and against Stalinism. No day went by without him putting aside time for reading something about history or current affairs. Alexander Yegorov's account of the southern sector of the front against Poland in the war of 1920 was on his desk – it was exactly twenty years since that fateful summer campaign. Out of the blue he received a gift by post from an admirer: an English-language dictionary of slang. Trotsky tried out the less than couth phrases he learned. On 20 August he wrote to his follower Hank Schultz expressing admiration for the work.[21]

He also prepared a draft article on 'Bonapartism, Fascism, War'.[22] He was on good form and enjoying himself.

The entourage had been hard at work tightening up security arrangements after the Siqueiros attack. Joe Hansen listed them in a letter to fellow Trotskyist Farrell Dobbs. The team bought two second-hand revolvers. They ordered bullet-proof doors for the Trotskys' bedroom. They bricked in and barred some windows; they accelerated the building of an additional watch tower on the north-west corner of the Avenida Viena wall. They constructed extra guard rooms. They rewired the lighting system and installed four external police booths.[23] The defenders aimed to make the villa-fortress impregnable.

Trotsky's letter to Schultz was to be the last he dictated, and the article on Bonapartism, fascism and war had to be edited by others than himself.[24] After a busy morning on 20 August he took his normal siesta. He had only one further item of business that day. He had agreed to have a private meeting in the afternoon with a man he knew as Jacson. This was the boyfriend of Trotsky's occasional secretary Sylvia Ageloff. Jacson frequently accompanied her into the grounds and sometimes left his car behind for the entourage's use when he went on his commercial trips. Once he had turned up to hand over a box of sweets to Sylvia. Sometimes he had arrived while Trotsky was taking his siesta. He varied his timing, no doubt trying to ascertain the sequence of domestic routines.[25] Trying to prove his political seriousness, he had recently accompanied Sylvia to a session with Trotsky where she put the case for the Minority in the dispute of the American Trotskyists. Jacson made a few remarks and laughed. Trotsky brought the discussion to an end after a quarter of an hour saying that he needed to feed his animals. Before leaving with Sylvia, Jacson asked Trotsky to scrutinize a plan for an article he wished to write. Trotsky agreed to do this. The subject was French economic statistics. Trotsky did not think much of the plan, which he found primitive and unconvincing. But he had given his word that he would discuss the contents with Jacson.

By no means everyone close to Trotsky took to Jacson. (Trotsky as usual was hopelessly naive and had no suspicions.) Natalya wondered why Jacson never gave the name of the rich, dishonest businessman he supposedly worked for. Alfred and Marguerite Rosmer were agitated about Jacson. They repeatedly asked why he never revealed what sector of trade he worked in; they noted how elusively he talked about nearly everything.[26]

Arriving at the villa, Jacson was let in as a trusted comrade. Natalya asked him why he was going about in a raincoat on a sunny afternoon.

August in the area around Mexico City can bring heavy thunderstorms, especially from the mid-afternoon onwards, and Jacson replied that a downpour was expected.[27] What no one knew was that he had a mountaineer's ice-axe and a long dagger in his pocket.[28] He had sawn back the handle of the axe to make it less detectable. His aim was to do the deed noiselessly in Trotsky's office and hurry away before detection. If he had used a firearm the noise would have been heard and he would have been apprehended: a guard might even have shot him. Alone with Trotsky, he would take the first opportunity, with either the ice-axe or the dagger, to do the deed. He was fit and strong.[29] He was well trained and cool headed. He was committed to the cause of Comintern.[30] And he had been liaising with officers from the Soviet security agencies under the command of Natan Eitingon on Mexican soil. The time to deliver the decisive blow had arrived.

Jacson met with Trotsky in the office. Trotsky prepared his thoughts as he incautiously glanced again at the pages. This permitted Jacson to leave his chair and walk around the desk. He was carrying his raincoat over his arm so as to have a weapon to hand. The ice-axe was the better of the two to use from behind Trotsky. With a deft movement Jacson drove it into the top of the cranium. The blow was severe but not instantly fatal, probably because the impact was delivered by the wide end. Evidently Jacson had suffered from nervousness at the last moment.

What happened next was described by Jacson under police interrogation:

> I hit him just the once and he gave out a piteous, shattering cry when it happened, at the same time as he threw himself on to me and bit my left hand, as you can see for yourself by these three teeth marks. Then he took some slow steps back from that spot. As soon as they heard the cry, people arrived; because of what had happened I almost lost consciousness and didn't try to escape. Harold [Robins?] got there first and started to beat me with his pistol, and then came [Joe] Hansen and Charles [Curtiss?].[31]

The police arrived from their sentry boxes, grabbed Jacson and took him off injured to their station. An ambulance fetched the wounded Trotsky to the same building.[32] There was next to no chance of a successful outcome despite the presence of five of Mexico City's ablest surgeons led by Gustavo Baz. They carried out a trepanning of the skull. But the wound was too deep. Although Jacson had somewhat botched his act of violence, the ice-axe had penetrated nearly three inches. Blood and cerebral matter had spilled profusely. The right parietal bone was fractured. Trotsky endured all this with exemplary fortitude but the hospital spokesman indicated that the prognosis was 'very grave'.[33] The doctors knew they were handling a man in the ultimate stage of life.

# 52. THE KEEPERS AND THE FLAME

The *New York Times* announced on its front page on Wednesday 21 August 1940: 'Trotsky Wounded by Friend in Home – Is Believed Dying'. By the afternoon American radio stations were confirming that he had breathed his last.[1] It was the most spectacular assassination since the death of Archduke Franz Ferdinand in 1914. The world's press sent its journalists to Mexico. The Coyoacán household, liaising with authorities in the capital, pre-empted them by organizing a funeral the day after the death. It was almost a state occasion. The Ministry of the Interior involved itself in case Stalin's local supporters might attempt a further outrage. Trotsky's corpse was laid out in an open coffin and the hearse was driven slowly through the central streets of Mexico City. Although the deceased had been a militant atheist, 200,000 people – mostly practising Catholics – stood on the pavements to pay their respects or out of curiosity.

The London *Times* editorial on 23 August summarized a less positive mood at the time: 'The murder of Leon Trotsky at Mexico City will relieve the Kremlin of not a few anxieties and will draw few tears from the majority of mankind.'[2] As columnists wrote up their reflections on his extraordinary life, journalists from nearly every country around the globe hurried to Mexico City to report on the murder and its consequences. Opinions inevitably conflicted. Yet few of his detractors, at least those outside the Comintern parties, denied that a star of great magnitude in contemporary affairs had been extinguished. Obituaries narrated his exploits in the October Revolution and the Civil War. His gifts in oratory and leadership were described; his partnership with Lenin was recounted. The decline from supreme power and official approval in the USSR was analysed and the long stay in foreign exile was rehearsed. The attention accorded to Trotsky might have been greater if Europe and the Far East had not been theatres of war. Armies were on the march. Germany and Japan were pursuing their wars of territorial expansion. The political map of the world was being redrawn almost daily. Trotsky's assassination was never going to keep most people's attention for more than a few days.

The Kremlin was jubilant; *Pravda* announced the demise of 'an international spy' and cited American dailies as reporting that the killer, 'one of Trotsky's closest people and followers', was a certain Jacques Mortan Vandendresch. (The Kremlin's fabrications broke down at this point: the nearest name to this used by Jacson in Mexico was Jacques Mornard Vandendresch;[3] but no one anywhere noticed the mistake.) Allegedly the ruling classes in the capitalist countries had lost their truest servant. Not for nothing had Lenin baptized Trotsky 'the little Judas'. Trotsky had been a Menshevik and a counter-revolutionary. He had fought for the interests of tsar, landlords and capitalists. Having infiltrated the Bolshevik party, he had plotted to assassinate Lenin, Stalin and Sverdlov. He had betrayed and sabotaged the Red Army. He had worked as an agent of foreign intelligence agencies since 1921. Britain, France, Germany and Japan had benefited from his services. He had met with a fitting end. Stalin himself edited the text.[4] Official communist parties followed the line established in Moscow, drawing up their sentiments and phrasings from the Soviet central well.

Trotskyists spoke about the deceased as if he had been the greatest man of his time. They declared that there had been nobody like him since Lenin. They tried to amplify publicity for the cause by conveying Trotsky's body to the United States. The US State Department rejected the request: the American authorities were not going to abet mourners in spreading any kind of communism.[5] Whether Natalya would have allowed such transport is anyway unclear. She was hardly in a state of mind to accompany a coffin on a journey of over two thousand miles.

The assassin was continuing to claim to be called Jacson. He had a pencilled letter in his pocket saying he was a Belgian Trotskyist who had come out to Mexico. Allegedly Trotsky had systematically created discord among his followers. This was not all. The killer wrote that Trotsky had inveigled him into consenting to go to the USSR and carry out assassinations. Jacson accused Trotsky of having despised the Mexican government. This much was true since Trotsky hoped for a communist revolution in the country. Also credible was the statement that Trotsky feared being killed by Stalinists. But then Jacson's story entered fantasy. Supposedly Trotsky was scared of being shot by the Minority faction of the Socialist Workers Party. He was a political degenerate in every imaginable way. On learning that Trotsky relied on support from 'a certain foreign parliamentary committee', Jacson decided to take responsibility for eliminating him.[6] The Mexican police disbelieved their captive except insofar as he admitted guilt for the assassination. But who was he really?

Where did he come from and why did he carry out the murder? After several days of questioning the police were getting nowhere as Jacson stuck rigidly to his story.

On 30 August the examining judge took over and invoked his right to begin his proceedings at the Avenida Viena villa. Natalya kept out of the way, too upset to take any part. Trotsky's assistants had left everything in his office untouched. On the table was the draft handed to him by Jacson. There was also an article by Trotsky about the Siqueiros attack. His spectacles lay in pieces; one of the lenses had fallen out. A macabre touch was added to the scene when Jacson was brought from his cell to re-enact the murder for the judge's benefit. He complied uncomplainingly. The authorities ensured that every technical aspect of the crime was investigated. They wanted no repetition of the charges of incompetence levelled against them after the Siqueiros raid.

Trotsky's American lawyer Albert Goldman attended. He had posed friendly questions to Trotsky at the Dewey Commission and now he confronted Trotsky's killer for nearly three hours. The circumstances could not have been more different. Jacson asserted that he had been sent to Mexico by someone belonging to the Fourth International's leadership. Goldman asked sarcastically why, if that had been his mission, he had wasted months before contacting Trotsky. Jacson feigned a defective memory. Goldman persisted. Why could Jacson not remember who had sent him? And why on earth did he not speak to Trotsky or his assistants about the nature of his purported mission? The judge appreciated Goldman's forensic skills and gave him freedom to press his case. Goldman turned on Jacson with a final question: would he not agree that his story would be more credible if the provenance of his instructions had been not the Fourth International but the Soviet security services?[7]

Jacson, despite anticipating a lengthy term of imprisonment, refused to plead for mercy or to divulge any useful information. He stood impassively when the judge sentenced him to twenty years in gaol. He became a model prisoner. But he told no one who he was and on whose orders he had been operating even though it became known that his real name was Ramón Mercader. His conditions of confinement were not severe. He was allowed his own radio, carpet and electrical socket; his cell was left unlocked. A mysterious benefactor supplied him with a monthly allowance of a hundred dollars. Prisoners were allowed to earn money by their labour and Jacson set up his own little radio-repair workshop employing some of his fellows in gaol.[8] Released when his sentence came to an end in 1960, he disappeared from public view. Only years later did it become clear that he had been taken to Moscow where, in secret, he was given a hero's welcome and awarded the rank of KGB general. Mercader found it hard to settle there since the USSR proved a disappointment for him and he successfully petitioned to move to Cuba, where he remained until his death in 1978.

Trotsky's death was an earthquake for the Fourth International and shattered its various component parties and groups around the world. Natalya observed this with helpless disquiet. The Cárdenas government purchased the villa and allowed her to live there rent-free. It was kept almost exactly as it was when Trotsky was alive and was turned into a museum in his memory in May 1946.[9] Joe Hansen, loyal as ever, wrote to Natalya in October 1941 saying that the American section of the Fourth International wished to treat her writings – scant though they were – as programmatic declarations. This was tantamount to saying that Trotskyists were incapable of steering their course without a Trotsky family member at the helm.[10] Perhaps Hansen really meant only that her symbolic imprimatur would make it easier to hold the Fourth International together. Natalya did not respond to his blandishments. She had been widowed and needed to tend to domestic tasks, and there were plenty of difficulties over Trotsky's estate. The result was quickly evident. The *Byulleten oppozitsii* ceased publication after August 1941. Trotsky had been its motor and the rest of the Coyoacán household were incapable of replacing him.[11] In July 1941 the NKVD drew the conclusion that Trotskyists in Mexico no longer constituted a danger. The Moscow file on life in the Avenida Viena was closed down.[12]

Once she had recovered her poise, Natalya was unafraid to express her opinions.[13] The years of living under her husband's shadow were over. She chided Trotskyists who failed to respond promptly to her letters; she contrasted such behaviour with the punctiliousness of her husband and her elder son. She intervened in her own right in political debate. She had always found it hard to swallow Trotsky's belief that the USSR was still a 'workers' state'. For some time after his death this hardly seemed to matter. On 22 June 1941 the Third Reich invaded the Soviet Union; and a few months later, on 7 December, the Japanese air force bombed Pearl Harbor and set off a war with the United States. The USSR, the United Kingdom and America became allies. The Fourth International played a tiny part in the Second World War. Most Trotskyists, including those who had criticized the Soviet attack on Finland in November 1939, were eager to join the fight against militarism and fascism. This wartime activity only delayed the political reckoning, and in 1951 Natalya bluntly told the

Executive Committee of the Fourth International that neither the USSR nor the new 'communist' states of eastern Europe brought any advantage to the working class. She was positively impressed only by Yugoslavia, and she asked the Executive Committee to avoid being hard on Tito.[14] She was less gentle about the Cuban communist experiment under Fidel Castro.

Her influence had by then become negligible, but anyway the Fourth International had declined into impotence worldwide. A dominant faction under Michel Pablo, a militant of Greek origin, polemicized with everyone who opposed it. The factionalists lacked the megaphone of publicity that Trotsky had wielded. But their internal polemics were of paramount importance to them, and they found plenty to dispute.

As Natalya grew into old age she raised her grandson Seva as normally as she was able. After being bundled out of the USSR as a young boy, he had had to endure a series of traumas in Europe and Mexico. He took the Spanish forename Esteban and, feeling no inclination towards political activity, became a painter.[15] Like his uncle Sergei Sedov, he upheld Trotsky's reputation without signing up as a Trotskyist – he described himself as a 'non-practising socialist'.[16] Natalya cherished contact with the people who had known and helped her husband. She suffered constant distress from the absence of news about her relatives in the USSR. Soviet communist leader Nikita Khrushchëv's 'secret speech' in February 1956, when he denounced Stalin as a mass killer, gave her hope that she would learn the truth. It was not to be. The Kremlin stood by the verdict in the first Moscow show-trial that Trotsky was a traitor. Natalya petitioned Moscow in vain. A wall of official secrecy barred her even from discovering that practically the entire family had been exterminated. Just a few survived, and none of these had ever met Natalya while she was a Soviet resident. She died in 1960, deeply mourned by her network of Mexican, French and American friends.

She had witnessed a revival of Trotsky's reputation in the West through the work of his Polish follower Isaac Deutscher, who published a biographical trilogy. He parted company with Trotsky on a number of matters. Chief among them was Deutscher's belief that there could be peaceful evolution towards a more civilized form of communism in the USSR. Generational change in the Soviet political leadership, he thought, would bring about what had proved impossible for the Opposition to achieve. Deutscher's portrait of Trotsky, while not lacking in warts, was basically positive. Albert Glotzer wrote to Natalya urging that it should not be heavily criticized despite its 'stalinoidal' analysis.[17]

The idea again went the rounds on the Western political left that the tragedy of Soviet history lay in Trotsky's failure to win the struggle to succeed Lenin. Works by Trotsky such as *My Life* and *The Revolution Betrayed* were sold widely in many languages. His renewed popularity stemmed from his struggle against Stalin and his grisly death. He convinced those who desired to believe. In 1968, when students in Europe and North America took to the streets against the Vietnam war, Trotsky came into vogue, often among people who were untroubled by the desire to read what he had written and done. Trotskyists drew their information from surviving veteran exponents of Trotskyism – or else they simply dreamed up the Trotsky they wished for. The spurt of popularity did not endure and Trotskyists either gave up on him or relapsed into the sectarian bickering that had characterized them since before the Old Man's murder. Grandiose names were chosen for organizations which were little larger than groupuscules. They rarely included Trotsky in the name of their parties but he was the source of their inspiration. They never came close to taking power anywhere. Trotsky had become a comfort blanket for revolutionaries who did not mind that they were not making a revolution.

Always a fractious lot, Trotskyists spent more time arguing with each other than with the communist parties which submitted to Moscow's leadership. It was not the Fourth International but the Soviet political leader Mikhail Gorbachëv who restored Trotsky's status in Moscow. The death penalty of 1936 was admitted to have been unmerited. Trotsky was exonerated as an honourable Bolshevik who had fallen foul of the monstrous Stalin. A few professional Soviet historians began to publish studies favourable to his career. But the fashion for Trotsky in the USSR faded almost as soon as it had started. The entire Soviet communist order collapsed in 1991. Trotskyism was no more attractive to contemporary Russians than was the blood-soaked religion of the Aztecs. He became an antiquarian curiosity, something to be discussed along with Fabergé eggs, Ivan the Terrible or peasant weaving patterns.

Among the reasons why Trotsky deserves to be rescued from this growing neglect is that he was never quite what he said he was or what others said about him. He was close to Stalin in intentions and practice. He was no more likely than Stalin to create a society of humanitarian socialism even though he claimed and assumed that he would. Trotsky failed to work out how to move from party dictatorship to universal freedom. He revelled in terror. His confident assaults on Stalin in the 1920s and 1930s distracted attention from the implausibility of his own alternative strategy. His followers mistook stated general objectives for personal practices when they wrote their eulogies of him. Trotsky called for unfettered discussion, organization and election; he preached virtues of proletarian self-liberation. His behaviour had been very different in the period of his pomp from 1917 to 1922. He had crushed opposition in party and trade unions. He had trampled on institutional resistance whenever he wanted rapid action and obedience. He had a greater propensity for commands than for discussion; he was arrogant and imperious. Trotskyists invented a man and a leader who bore only an erratic kinship to Lev Davidovich Trotsky.

They naturally regretted his defeats in the factional battles of the 1920s. Most of them accepted Trotsky's apologia with its implication that he had never truly stood a chance. They missed the point. Trotsky's policies lay within the frame of communist authoritarianism and had a genuine chance of victory. Even his Jewish background was a surmountable obstacle. Unfortunately for him, his tactical instincts were weakly developed. He was an inept assembler of supporters. He needlessly alienated far too many people at all levels of the party. He was easily his own worst enemy.

Trotskyists overlooked the inadequacies in their hero's personality and stressed his qualifications for communist leadership. His inner ideological impetus was a constant; his competitiveness and combativeness were extraordinary. His intellect was of a high order. Even his egoism was no barrier to the achievement of political ascendancy. What Trotsky lacked was a willingness to concentrate his efforts. He was a perpetual revolutionary, never a full-time politician. His preoccupation with his writing damaged his capacity to confront a man like Stalin who gave up every waking hour to the advancement of his career and his policies. Neither Trotsky nor Stalin had health of the very best. Trotsky, though, often sank into months of self-appointed repose and rehabilitation. He wanted to be a leader like Lenin whose ideas guided the Soviet state. But Trotsky's notion of leadership was inflexible. He overrated oratory and literary style as attributes of superiority. He disdained the need to fight dirty even though he was far from the cleanest of political figures. The insurmountable hurdle for him in the race for the Lenin succession was the fact that he lacked the overwhelming desire to become the leader. He felt better as a battered contender than as a fighter consumed by ambition to be champion. He did not want paramount authority badly enough.

The USSR after the Second World War had anyway not been as Trotsky had predicted. It had survived and flourished as a state. It had defeated the Third Reich and shown a vitality that took everyone by surprise in the military conflict of 1941–5. The Soviet state's armed forces and heavy industry had made it into a superpower.

Far from sinking into decline, it flourished for decades as a world power – and there had been no political revolution. Stalin died in 1953. His successors, led by Nikita Khrushchëv and Leonid Brezhnev, faced no serious threat to their continued supremacy. Trotskyists turned to Marxist theory and analysis. They produced conflicting analyses of macro-economics around the world. Always they assumed that capitalism was in decline and that a renovated communism, stripped of its Stalinist features, would supplant it. The break-up of the European empires after the Second World War appeared to confirm this analysis. Although the United States currently dominated the global market economy its hegemony would not endure. Nor would the USSR in its current condition. Trotskyists came to no agreement in the defining of the Soviet order. Some held to Trotsky's dictum that it was a degenerated workers' state; they hated to revise the ideas of the Old Man. Others contended that fresh phenomena required fresh thinking. To them it was plain that a new class had emerged in the USSR. A peculiar order had been created which they called state capitalism. If nothing else, Trotsky's leading followers showed a capacity for sophisticated Marxist analysis and a less than refined technique of polemical abuse.

Yet Trotsky's ideas, including those about Russian history, had a lasting impact. His account of the rise of Stalin was always influential. He convinced many outside Marxist circles that the roots of the 'degeneration' of the October Revolution lay in the country's economic and social 'back-wardness'. He also proved persuasive about the 'bureaucratization' of the Soviet order. Not everyone accepted that he had not played a principal role in his own failure to succeed Lenin. Yet his self-serving account of Stalin and Stalinism deeply influenced the discourse of writers on both left and right.

His contradictions were of a sharp nature. If the conditions in Russia were as unpropitious as Trotsky later conceded, then the case for a 'workers' government' in 1917 was demolished. The October Revolution anyway did not start to degenerate only from the mid-1920s. It was flawed from its inception when the Bolsheviks used force against protesting labourers and closed down any soviets without Bolshevik majorities. Trotsky had campaigned before 1917 for the 'proletariat' to liberate itself and make its own revolution. As soon as he had power, he eagerly sup-pressed popular aspirations by violence. He was a ruthless centralizer and a friend of army and police. Nor were his ideas as original as his admirers have claimed. The idea of a proletarian government had been coined by Alexander Helphand-Parvus. The analysis of the peculiarities of Russian historical development before 1917 came from the liberal writer Boris Chicherin. Even Trotsky's interpretation of the USSR in the 1920s owed much to the Mensheviks. His insistence in the last decade of his life that 'Soviet power' had not utterly discredited itself justifiably offended many of his more intelligent followers in his lifetime.

Trotsky was an exceptional human being and a complex one. His strengths were on display in the October Revolution and the Civil War. He inspired a generation of supporters in Russia and abroad. He was a brilliant organizer and orator. His intellectual range was remarkably wide in print and still wider in his private interests. He was an outstanding stylist in print. When he wanted, he could be clear about revolutionary strategy. Once in governmental office, he knew what he wished to do and how to go about doing it. He was unmatched as propagandist for the Bolshevik cause. No one more effectively dragged the Red Army towards acceptance of the need for order. He was like Lenin in having a broad idea about international relations – and he held consistently to putting proletarian revolution in Europe at the head of the Revolution's objectives. The obverse side of the coin was that he was frequently schematic and rigid in his thinking and extremely violent in his practice. He often placed sudden enthusiasms above the sensible requirements for the Revolution's survival. He was brave, impetuous and unpredictable. Trotsky was the holder of an outstanding talent.

He paid the ultimate price for his political struggle against Stalin but not before he himself, while he occupied a position of high power, had carried out campaigns of bloody repression. Most of his immediate family had gone to their deaths because of him. There were exceptions. Daughter Nina was taken away by tuberculosis; daughter Zina committed suicide; and it is not completely discountable that son Lëva was not murdered but died of his medical problems. But most of the husbands, wives and partners of the deceased died in the 1930s as the result of political repression. Trotsky's first wife Alexandra also perished in this fashion. For many Soviet citizens it was enough to carry the surname Bronstein for the NKVD to seize hold of them.

Very few survived and among them were individuals who have figured in this account of the life of Trotsky. Genrietta Rubinshtein was released from a labour camp in 1947. She had suffered punishment for no other reason than that she was the partner of Lëva Sedov. The relief was only temporary. The arrests began again in 1951 and hit Genrietta. Her parents

Moisei and Reiza, who had implored their daughter not to follow Sedov out to Krasnoyarsk, fell victim in the same campaign. Together with their grandchild Yulia they were sentenced to forced resettlement in Siberia.[18] Yulia then travelled further to live with her mother Genrietta 350 miles north of Magadan. The family was allowed back to central Russia only after Stalin's death but was prohibited from residing within forty miles of Moscow.[19] Genrietta finished up in Tallinn. Once she had trained as a chemist, Yulia led a chaotic life. After three marriages she took advantage of the US–Soviet agreements allowing some Jews to emigrate from the USSR and left for New York with her son Vadim in 1979.[20] Vadim – Trotsky's great-grandson – turned to the Jewish faith, joining the devotees of Hasidism. Searching for his personal identity, he emigrated to Israel. There he changed his name to David and, against his mother's wishes, chose a Hebrew forename for his first-born son rather than call him Sergei after his maternal grandfather. He spurned the compensation offered by the Soviet state for the injustice done to the great-grandfather he had never known.[21]

Trotsky had an acute feeling for historical irony. He would surely have noted how the communists came to power determined to extirpate religious faith and yet three generations later one of his own descendants sought comfort in the yarmulke and the menorah. Such an outcome seemed impossible to him in 1917. The Bolsheviks were universal militants. They aimed to turn the world upside down and build a revolutionary society, culture, economy and politics. In their own way they too were fervent believers, and none more so than Trotsky. As he once said, they wished to build paradise on earth.[22] His years of triumph were brief even though his fame lasted longer. Death came early to him because he fought for a cause that was more destructive than he had ever imagined.

# Notes

## Introduction

1. M. Eastman, *Great Companions: Critical Memoirs of Some Famous Friends*, p. 121.

## 1. The Family Bronstein

1. The phrase is taken from L. Trotskii, *Stalinskaya shkola fal'sifikatsii*.
2. L. Trotskii, *Moya zhizn'*, vol. 1, p. 7.
3. *Ibid.*, p. 55.
4. V. N. Nikitin, *Evrei zemledel'tsy: istoricheskoe, zakonodatel'noe, administra-tivnoe i bytovoe polozhenie kolonii so vremën ikh vozniknoveniya do nashikh dnei. 1807–1887*, pp. 686–7.
4. *Ibid.*, p. 1.
5. *Ibid.*, p. 117.
6. *Ibid.*, pp. 686–7.
7. *Ibid.*, p. 654.
8. L. Trotskii, *Moya zhizn'*, vol. 1, p. 56.
9. V. N. Nikitin, *Evrei zemledel'tsy: istoricheskoe, zakonodatel'noe, administra-tivnoe i bytovoe polozhenie kolonii so vremën ikh vozniknoveniya do nashikh dnei. 1807–1887*, pp. 280 and 284.
10. *Ibid.*, p. 162.
11. *Ibid.*, 180.
12. *Ibid.*, p. 116.
13. *Ibid.*, p. 10.
14. *Ibid.*, p. 279.
15. *Ibid.*, pp. 596–7.
16. *Ibid.*, p. 599.
17. *Ibid.*, p. 595.
18. *Ibid.*, pp. 281 and 290.
19. *Ibid.*, p. 454.
20. *Ibid.*, p. 421: the Sabbath lasted until twilight on Saturday so that no serious farm work was resumed until daylight on Sunday.

21. *Ibid.*, p. 289.
22. *Ibid.*, p. 627.
23. *Ibid.*, pp. 539–40.
24. *Ibid.*
25. *Ibid.*, pp. 623–5 and 636.
26. *Ibid.*, p. 282.
27. *Ibid.*, p. 283.
28. *Ibid.*, p. 287.
29. L. Trotskii, *Moya zhizn'*, vol. 1, p. 35.


## 2. Upbringing

1. *Moya zhizn'* draft: Nicolaevsky Collection (HIA), box 312, folder 45, p. 4.
2. Kherson police report to A. M. Yeremin, 16 February 1910: APO (HIA), file XVIIc, folder 2.
3. M. Eastman, *Great Companions: Critical Memoirs of Some Famous Friends*, p. 111. On David Bronstein see N. Sedova's memoir in V. Serge and N. Sedova Trotsky, *The Life and Death of Leon Trotsky*, p. 84.
4. *Moya zhizn'* draft: Nicolaevsky Collection (HIA), box 312, folder 36, p. 125.
5. *Ibid.*
6. *Ibid.*, p. 126.
7. *Ibid.*, p. 115.
8. *Ibid.*
9. *Ibid.*, p. 20.
10. *Ibid.*, folder 38, p. 4.
11. L. Trotskii, *Moya zhizn'*, vol. 1, p. 44.
12. *Ibid.*, p. 50.
13. *Moya zhizn'* draft: Nicolaevsky Collection (HIA), box 312, folder 38, p. 5.
14. *Ibid.*, p. 7.
15. *Ibid.*, p. 6.
16. *Ibid.*, p. 8.
17. *Ibid.*, p. 9.
18. *Ibid.*, p. 12.
19. *Ibid.*
20. L. Trotskii, *Moya zhizn'*, vol. 1, pp. 23–4.
21. V. N. Nikitin, *Evrei zemledel'tsy: istoricheskoe, zakonodatel'noe, administrativnoe i bytovoe polozhenie kolonii so vremën ikh vozniknoveniya do nashikh dnei. 1807–1887*, p. 654.
22. L. Trotskii, *Moya zhizn'*, vol. 1, p. 55.
23. *Ibid.*
24. See below, p. 31.
25. L. Trotskii, *Moya zhizn'*, vol. 1, p. 57.
26. *Ibid.*, p. 35.
27. *Ibid.*, p. 27.

28. *Ibid.*, p. 35.
29. *Ibid.*, p. 104.
30. *Ibid.*
31. *Ibid.*, p. 60.
32. *Ibid.*, p. 104.
33. *Ibid.*, p. 52.
34. *Ibid.*, p. 56.
35. *Ibid.*, pp. 37–8.
36. *Ibid.*, p. 37.
37. *Moya zhizn'* draft: Nicolaevsky Collection (HIA), box 312, folder 37, p. 1.
38. *Ibid.*, p. 54.
39. *Ibid.*, p. 1.
40. *Ibid.*, p. 2.
41. L. Trotskii, *Moya zhizn'*, vol. 1, pp. 38–9.
42. *Ibid.*, p. 39.
43. *Moya zhizn'* draft: Nicolaevsky Collection (HIA), box 312, folder 38, p. 3.

## 3. Schooling

1. M. Eastman, *Leon Trotsky: The Portrait of a Youth* (London edn), p. 23.
2. *Moya zhizn'* draft: Nicolaevsky Collection (HIA), box 312, folder 40 ('Poezdka v Odessu'), p. 1.
3. *Ibid.*
4. Olga Kerziouk and Lena Katz helped me in coming to this conclusion both through their own expertise and by consulting their friends and relatives in Ukraine. The main point is that the residue, whatever it was, remained a small one.
5. *Moya zhizn'* draft: Nicolaevsky Collection (HIA), box 312, folder 40 ('Poezdka v Odessu'), p. 2. Trotsky corrected Kreitser to Karlson in the printed version.
6. L. Trotskii, *Moya zhizn'*, vol. 1, p. 66.
7. *Ibid.*
8. *Ibid.*, p. 62.
9. *Moya zhizn'* draft: Nicolaevsky Collection (HIA), box 312, folder 40, p. 35.
10. *Ibid.*
11. *Ibid.*
12. *Ibid.*, p. 2. I infer from the paragraph that it was Moshe's rather than Fanni's mother.
13. *Ibid.*
14. *Ibid.*
15. L. Trotskii, *Moya zhizn'*, vol. 1, p. 61.
16. See below, p. 314.
17. M. Eastman, *Leon Trotsky: The Portrait of a Youth* (London edn), p. 24. Eastman interviewed the Shpentsers and their daughter Vera for his book.

18. *Ibid.*, p. 25.

19. *Ibid.*, pp. 16–17.

20. L. Trotskii, *Moya zhizn'*, vol. 1, p. 62.

21. *Ibid.*, p. 63.

22. See his comments on her funeral in *Moya zhizn'* draft: Nicolaevsky Collection (HIA), box 312, folder 41, p. 4.

23. *Ibid.*, folder 46, p. 1.

24. L. Trotskii, *Moya zhizn'*, vol. 1, pp. 67–8.

25. *Ibid.*, pp. 68–70.

26. Autobiographical letter to Max Eastman, 25–26 February 1923: RGASPI, f. 325, op. 1, d. 18, p. 2.

27. *Ibid.*

28. M. Eastman, *Leon Trotsky: The Portrait of a Youth*, p. 36.

29. See the observations of M. Eastman, *Great Companions: Critical Memoirs of Some Famous Friends*, p. 114.

30. *Moya zhizn'* draft: Nicolaevsky Collection (HIA), box 312, folder 41, p. 5.

31. L. Trotskii, *Moya zhizn'*, vol. 1, p. 92.

32. *Moya zhizn'* draft: Nicolaevsky Collection (HIA), box 312, folder 41, p. 4.

## 4. The Young Revolutionary

1. L. Trotskii, *Moya zhizn'*, vol. 1, p. 121.

2. Trotsky's autobiographical letter to party historian V. I. Nevski, 5 August 1921: RGASPI, f. 325, op. 1, d. 17, p. 1.

3. L. Trotskii, *Moya zhizn'*, vol. 1, p. 126.

4. G. A. Ziv, *Trotskii: kharakteristika. (Po lichnym vospominaniyam)*, p. 13.

5. L. D. Bronstein to A. L. Sokolovskaya, November 1898: RGASPI, f. 325, op. 1, d.1, pp. 1–18; and G. A. Ziv, *Trotskii: kharakteristika. (Po lichnym vospominaniyam)*, p. 7.

6. Trotsky to V. I. Nevski, 5 August 1921: RGASPI, f. 325, op. 1, d. 17, p. 2. See also G. A. Ziv, *Trotskii: kharakteristika. (Po lichnym vospominaniyam)*, p. 9.

7. G. A. Ziv, *Trotskii: kharakteristika. (Po lichnym vospominaniyam)*, p. 12.

8. Trotsky to V. I. Nevski, 5 August 1921: RGASPI, f. 325, op. 1, d. 17, p. 2.

9. G. A. Ziv, *Trotskii: kharakteristika. (Po lichnym vospominaniyam)*, p. 8.

10. Trotsky's autobiographical letter to Max Eastman, n.d. in 1923: RGASPI, f. 325, op. 1, d. 18, p. 4.

11. *Ibid.*

12. A. Walicki, *A History of Russian Thought from the Enlightenment to Marxism*, pp. 411–13.

13. L. D. Bronstein to A. L. Sokolovskaya, November 1898: RGASPI, f. 325, op. 1, d.1, p. 17.

14. G. A. Ziv, *Trotskii: kharakteristika. (Po lichnym vospominaniyam)*, p. 15.

15. *Ibid.*, pp. 10–11.

16. A. Schopenhauer, *The Art of Controversy*, especially chap. 3.

17. G. A. Ziv, *Trotskii: kharakteristika. (Po lichnym vospominaniyam)*, pp. 14–15.
18. *Ibid.*, pp. 13–14.
19. *Ibid.*, p. 14.
20. Trotsky to V. I. Nevski, 5 August 1921: RGASPI, f. 325, op. 1, d. 17, p. 2.
21. See S. S. Montefiore, *Young Stalin*, pp. 112–27.
22. L. Trotskii, *Moya zhizn'*, vol. 1, p. 124.
23. *Ibid.*
24. *Ibid.*, p. 123.
25. L. D. Bronstein to A. L. Sokolovskaya, November 1898: RGASPI, f. 325, op. 1, d.1, p. 18.
26. G. A. Ziv, *Trotskii: kharakteristika. (Po lichnym vospominaniyam)*, p. 18.
27. L. Trotskii, *Moya zhizn'*, vol. 1, p. 124.
28. G. A. Ziv, *Trotskii: kharakteristika. (Po lichnym vospominaniyam)*, p. 19.
29. *Ibid.*
30. *Ibid.*, p. 20.
31. L. Trotskii, *Moya zhizn'*, vol. 1, p. 133.
32. M. Eastman, *Leon Trotsky: The Portrait of a Youth* (London edn), pp. 110–12.

## 5. Love and Prison

1. 'Otvet na voprosy t. Istmana', February 1923: RGASPI, f. 325, op. 1, d. 18, pp. 16–17.
2. *Ibid.*, p. 17.
3. *Ibid.*
4. Letter to A. L. Sokolovskaya, November 1898, three days after his mother came to visit: RGASPI, f. 325, op. 1, d. 1, p. 15.
5. Letter to M. Eastman (n.d.; this letter is wrongly dated January 1917): RGASPI, f. 325, op. 1, d. 557, p. 101.
6. *Ibid.*
7. Letter to A. L. Sokolovskaya, November 1898: RGASPI, f. 325, op. 1, d. 1, p. 15.
8. Letter to M. Eastman (n.d.): RGASPI, f. 325, op. 1, d. 557, p. 101.
9. Letter to A. L. Sokolovskaya, November 1898: *ibid.*, p. 11.
10. *Ibid.*, p. 12.
11. *Ibid.*, p. 13.
12. *Ibid.*
13. *Ibid.*, p. 14.
14. *Ibid.*
15. *Ibid.*, p. 15.
16. *Ibid.*, p. 14.
17. *Ibid.*
18. *Ibid.*, p. 11
19. *Ibid.*, p. 12.
20. L. Trotskii, *Moya zhizn'*, vol. 1, p. 146.

21. 'Avtobiograficheskie zametki', RGASPI, f. 325, op. 1, d. 14, p. 17. This was a memoir written in Syzran in April 1919.
22. Letter to A. L. Sokolovskaya, November 1898: RGASPI, f. 325, op. 1, d. 1, p. 16.
23. *Ibid.*, p. 11.
24. *Ibid.*
25. L. Trotskii, *Dnevniki i pis'ma*, p. 64. Trotsky disingenuously added that it was in France that he had been able to observe this social type most closely. A more generous interpretation would be that perhaps his childhood was simply remote from his thoughts at the time.
26. Letter to A. L. Sokolovskaya, November 1898: RGASPI, f. 325, op. 1, d. 1, p. 13.
27. *Ibid.*, p. 12.
28. G. A. Ziv, *Trotskii: kharakteristika. (Po lichnym vospominaniyam)*, p. 34.
29. 'Otvet na voprosy t. Istmana', February 1923: RGASPI, f. 325, op. 1, d. 18, p. 18.
30. G. A. Ziv, *Trotskii: kharakteristika. (Po lichnym vospominaniyam)*, p. 35.
31. M. Eastman, *Leon Trotsky: The Portrait of a Youth* (London edn), pp. 130–1.
32. On this see the account of her own prison marriage by Eva Broido in *Memoirs of a Revolutionary*, p. 27.

## 6. Siberian Exile

1. Letter to Ye. M. Yaroslavski, 25 August 1922: RGASPI, f. 325, op. 1, d. 448, p. 4.
2. For details of the last stage of the journey to east Siberia see K. Baedeker, *Baedeker's Russia with Teheran, Port Arthur and Peking: Handbook for Travellers*, pp. 531–2.
3. Letter to Ye. M. Yaroslavski, 25 August 1922: RGASPI, f. 325, op. 1, d. 448, p. 1.
4. J. F. Fraser, *The Real Siberia*, pp. 256–68.
5. *Ibid.*
6. L. Trotskii, *Moya zhizn'*, vol. 1, p. 148.
7. Letter to Ye. M. Yaroslavski, 25 August 1922: RGASPI, f. 325, op. 1, d. 448, p. 1.
8. L. Trotskii, *Moya zhizn'*, vol. 1, pp. 154–5.
9. G. A. Ziv, *Trotskii: kharakteristika. (Po lichnym vospominaniyam)*, p. 41.
10. Letter to Ye. M. Yaroslavski, 25 August 1922: RGASPI, f. 325, op. 1, d. 448, p. 1.
11. E. Broido, *Memoirs of a Revolutionary*, p. 28.
12. *Moya zhizn'* draft chapter: Nicolaevsky Collection (HIA), box 312, folder 50, p. 2.
13. L. Trotskii, *Moya zhizn'*, vol. 1, p. 149.
14. *Moya zhizn'* draft chapter: Nicolaevsky Collection (HIA), box 312, folder 50, p. 2.

15. M. A. Novomeysky, *My Siberian Life*, p. 230. I have corrected Antid Ota to Antid Oto.
16. See, for example, the *Vostochnoe obozrenie* articles in RGASPI, f. 355, op. 1, d. 559, pp. 83–6, 87–93, 151 and 157.
17. 'Penitentsial'nye ideally i gumannoe tyurmovozzrenie', *Vostochnoe obozrenie*, 20 June 1901: *ibid.*, pp. 112–16.
18. 'Poeziya, mashina i poeziya mashiny', *Vostochnoe obozrenie*, 6 September 1901: *ibid.*, p. 173b.
19. 'Ob Ibsene', *Vostochnoe obozrenie*, 22–26 April 1901: *ibid.*, p. 64; 3 June 1901: *ibid.*, p. 96.
20. 'Dve pisatel'skie dushi vo vlasti besa', *Vostochnoe obozrenie*, 25 August 1901: *ibid.*, p. 159; 'Po zhurnalam', *ibid.*, p. 47.
21. 'Otryvnyi kalendar' kak kul'turtreger', *Vostochnoe obozrenie*, 25 January 1901: *ibid.*, pp. 19 and 22.
22. 'Obyknovennoe derevenskoe', *Vostochnoe obozrenie*, 30 May 1901: *ibid.*, pp. 87–93.
23. 'Poslednyaya drama Gauptmana i kommentarii k nei Struve', *Vostochnoe obozrenie*, 5–9 September 1901: *ibid.*, pp. 66–9.
24. 'Pis'ma storonnego cheloveka o pessimizme, optimimizme, XX stoletii i mnogom drugom', *Vostochnoe obozrenie*, 15 February 1901: *ibid.*, pp. 24 and 27.
25. 'Po zhurnalam', *Vostochnoe obozrenie*, 22–26 April 1901: *ibid.*, p. 64.
26. 'Po zhurnalam', *Vostochnoe obozrenie*, 29 March 1901, *ibid.*, p. 49.
27. Letter to Ye. M. Yaroslavski, 25 August 1922: RGASPI, f. 325, op. 1, d. 448, pp. 1–2.
28. *Ibid.*, p. 5.
29. I. Getzler, *Nikolai Sukhanov: Chronicler of the Russian Revolution*, chap. 3.
30. Letter to Ye. M. Yaroslavski, 25 August 1922: RGASPI, f. 325, op. 1, d. 448, pp. 3–4.
31. L. Trotskii, *Moya zhizn'*, vol. 1, p. 167.
32. *Ibid.*, p. 156.
33. *Ibid.*, p. 157.
34. *Ibid.*, p. 159.
35. For example, see 'Sasha' (Alexandra Bronstein) to Trotsky, 11 November 1908: APO (HIA), file XVII, folder 2.

## 7. *Iskra*

1. L. Trotskii, *Moya zhizn'*, vol. 1, p. 158.
2. *Ibid.*
3. G. A. Ziv, *Trotskii: kharakteristika. (Po lichnym vospominaniyam)*, p. 47
4. Police report, 22 August 1902: RGASPI, f. 325, op. 1, d. 2, p. 3.
5. *Moya zhizn'* draft: Nicolaevsky Collection (HIA), box 313, folder 1, pp. 1–2. Trotsky cut most of this information from the published text.

6. D. Sverchkov, *Na zare revolyutsii*, p. 264. Sverchkov claimed that Axelrod loved Trotsky for such 'simplicity' of manner. This may well have been an exaggeration or worse.

7. L. Trotskii, *Moya zhizn'*, vol. 1, p. 166.

8. *Ibid.*

9. Trotsky moderated his first draft for publication. In the rest of this paragraph I follow the excised text of that draft: *Moya zhizn'* draft: Nicolaevsky Collection (HIA), box 313, folder 1, p. 1.

10. *Ibid.*

11. *Ibid.*, p. 5.

12. *Ibid.*

13. *Ibid.*, p. 4. See also E. Goldman, *Living My Life*, vol. 1, pp. 254–5 and 262.

14. N. Sedova, autobiographical typescript begun on 24 December 1941: Trotsky Collection (HIA), box 27, folder 13, p. 8.

15. *Ibid.*, p. 9.

16. *Ibid.*

17. *Ibid.*, p. 10.

18. *Ibid.*

19. *Ibid.*

20. Trotsky's diary in 1935 in L. Trotskii, *Dnevniki i pis'ma*, p. 86.

21. See Yu. V. Got'e, 'Moi zametki', *Voprosy istorii*, no. 11 (1991), p. 151; S. Weber, 'Recollections of Trotsky', *Modern Occasions*, spring 1972, pp. 181–2; A. Glotzer, *Trotsky: Memoir and Critique*, p. 36.

22. L. Trotskii, *Dnevniki i pis'ma*, pp. 86–7.

23. Yu. O. Martov to the London part of the *Iskra* editorial board, 29 November 1902: *Leninskii sbornik*, vol. 4, p. 166.

24. N. Sedova, autobiographical typescript begun on 24 December 1941: Trotsky Collection (HIA), box 27, folder 13, p. 11; *Moya zhizn'* draft: Nicolaevsky Collection (HIA), box 313, folder 1, p. 6.

25. M. Shachtman, 'Natalya Ivanovna Sedoff (Sedova)', p. 3: Albert Glotzer Papers (HIA), box 27. Shachtman took notes from conversations he had with her about her life.

26. See the collection of *Iskra* articles from no. 27 (1 November 1902): RGASPI, f. 325, op. 1, d. 361.

27. *Moya zhizn'* draft: Nicolaevsky Collection (HIA), box 313, folder 1, p. 8.

28. Trotsky to A. L. Bronstein, 10 February 1903 (NS), p. 1: APO (HIA), file XVIIa, folder 1a, p. 1.

29. *Ibid.*, p. 2.

30. *Ibid.*

31. G. V. Plekhanov to V. I. Lenin, beginning of January 1903: *Leninskii sbornik*, vol. 4, p. 211.

32. V. I. Lenin to G. V. Plekhanov, 2 March 1903: *ibid.*, pp. 221–2.

33. A. Lunacharskii, *Revolyutsionnye siluety*, p. 19.

34. *Yu. O. Martov i A. N. Potresov. Pis'ma. 1898–1913*, pp. 36 and 43.

35. *Leninskii sbornik*, vol. 2, pp. 24, 27, 65, 127 and 152.

36. *Moya zhizn'* draft: Nicolaevsky Collection (HIA), box 313, folder 2, p. 7.
37. *Ibid.*, folder 1, p. 5.
38. N. Sedova, autobiographical typescript begun on 24 December 1941: Trotsky Collection (HIA), box 27, folder 13, p. 11.
39. *Ibid.*, p. 12.

## 8. Cutting Loose

1. F. I. Dan to P. B. Axel'rod, 16 October 1903: *Fëdor Il'ich Dan: Pis'ma (1899–1946)*, p. 60.
2. 'Otvet na pis'mo v redaktsiyu' [of *Iskra*]: RGASPI, f. 325, op. 1, d. 561, p. 135.
3. F. I. Dan to P. B. Axel'rod, 2/15 November 1903: *Fëdor Il'ich Dan: Pis'ma (1899–1946)*, p. 63.
4. F. I. Dan to P. B. Axel'rod, 10/23 November 1903: *ibid.*, p. 74.
5. Panin [M. S. Makadzyub] to P. B. Axel'rod, 11 January 1904, p. 1: Nicolaevsky Collection (HIA), box 652, folder 1.
6. Panin [M. S. Makadzyub] to P. B. Axel'rod, 2 February 1904: Nicolaevsky Collection (HIA), box 652, folder 4, p. 11.
7. P. A. Garvi, 'Zapiski sotsial-demokrata' (typescript): Nicolaevsky Papers (HIA), box 55, folder 1, pp. 19–20.
8. *Ibid.*, p. 16.
9. Panin [M. S. Makadzyub] to P. B. Axel'rod, 2 February 1904: Nicolaevsky Collection (HIA), box 652, folder 4, p. 11.
10. 'Nasha "voennaya" kampaniya', *Iskra*, no. 63, 15 April 1904.
11. *Ibid.*
12. F. I. Dan to P. B. Axel'rod, January 1904(?): *Fëdor Il'ich Dan: Pis'ma (1899–1946)*, pp. 77–8.
13. Yu. O. Martov to P. B. Axel'rod, 2 April 1904: *Pis'ma P. B. Aksel'roda i Yu. O. Martova, 1901–1916*, pp. 101–4.
14. F. I. Dan to P. B. Axel'rod, 29 September 1904: *Fëdor Il'ich Dan: Pis'ma (1899–1946)*, p. 110.
15. F. I. Dan to P. B. Axel'rod, 9 October 1904: *ibid.*, p. 122.
16. L. Trotskii, *Moya zhizn'*, vol. 1, p. 191.
17. Z. A. B. Zeman and W. B. Scharlau, *Merchant of Revolution: The Life of Alexander Israel Helphand (Parvus), 1867–1924*, pp. 63–7.
18. Police report, August–September 1904, pp. 1–2: APO (HIA), file XVIIc, folder 2, p. 1.
19. *Ibid.*; and M. Shachtman, 'Natalya Ivanovna Sedoff (Sedova)', p. 3: Albert Glotzer Papers (HIA), box 27.
20. See Ye. M. Yaroslavskii (ed.), *L. D. Trotskii o partii v 1904 g.: broshyura N. Trotskogo 'Nashi politicheskie zadachi'.*
21. N. Trotskii, *Nashi politicheskie zadachi. (Takticheskie i organizatsionnye voprosy)*, p. xi.

22. *Ibid.*, p. x.
23. *Ibid.*, pp. 50 and 55.
24. *Ibid.*, p. 75.
25. *Ibid.*, p. 33.
26. *Ibid.*, p. 95.
27. *Ibid.*, p. 96.
28. *Ibid.*, p. 102.
29. *Ibid.*, p. 107.
30. Panin [M. S. Makadzyub] to P. B. Axel'rod, 16 October 1904: Nicolaevsky Collection (HIA), box 652, folder 4, p. 1.
31. *Ibid.*, p. 2.
32. A. A. Bogdanov to N. K. Krupskaya, 10 July 1904: RGASPI., f. 325, op. 1, d. 212, p. 1.
33. Trotsky to Yu. O. Martov, some time in 1904: Nicolaevsky Collection (HIA), box 51, folder 19, letter one, pp. 1–3 and 5, and letter two, pp. 1 and 3–4.
34. N. Sedova, autobiographical typescript begun on 24 December 1941: Trotsky Collection (HIA), box 27, folder 13, p. 12.
35. L. Trotskii, *Moya zhizn'*, vol. 1, p. 157.
36. N. Sedova, 'Devochki', p. 2: Trotsky Collection (HIA), box 27, folder 13.
37. Kherson police report, 16 February 1910, p. 1: APO (HIA), file XVIIc, folder 2.
38. Yu. V. Got'e, *Moi zametki*, p. 132. On Trotsky see above, p. 31.
39. M. Shachtman, 'Natalya Ivanovna Sedoff (Sedova)', pp. 1 and 3: Albert Glotzer Papers (HIA), box 27.
40. N. Sedova, autobiographical typescript begun on 24 December 1941: Trotsky Collection (HIA), box 27, folder 13, p. 1.
41. *Ibid.*, p. 3.
42. *Ibid.*, pp. 1–2.
43. *Ibid.*, p. 3; M. Shachtman, 'Natalya Ivanovna Sedoff (Sedova)', p. 1: Albert Glotzer Papers (HIA), box 27.
44. N. Sedova, autobiographical typescript begun on 24 December 1941: Trotsky Collection (HIA), box 27, folder 13, p. 4.
45. *Ibid.*, pp. 5–7.
46. *Sotsial-demokrat*, no. 3, December 1904.

## 9. The Year 1905

1. N. Sedova, autobiographical typescript begun on 24 December 1941: Trotsky Collection (HIA), box 27, folder 13, p. 12.
2. A. Ascher, *The Revolution of 1905: Russia in Disarray*, pp. 102–23.
3. L. Trotskii, *Moya zhizn'*, vol. 1, p. 194. His wife's recollection was that they went not to Vienna but to Munich: N. Sedova, autobiographical typescript begun on 24 December 1941: Trotsky Collection (HIA), box 27, folder 13, p. 12. The detail about Adler means that Trotsky was probably right.

4. M. Shachtman, 'Natalya Ivanovna Sedoff (Sedova)', p. 2: Albert Glotzer Papers (HIA), box 27.
5. *Ibid.*
6. Trotsky's 1935 diary in L. Trotskii, *Dnevniki i pis'ma*, p. 130.
7. N. Sedova, autobiographical typescript begun on 24 December 1941: Trotsky Collection (HIA), box 27, folder 13, p. 13.
8. *Iskra*, no. 90, 3 March 1905.
9. Parvus, *Bez tsarya, a pravitel'stvo – rabochee*, pp. 1–4.
10. Parvus, *V chëm. my raskhodimsya? Otvet Leninu na ego stat'i v 'Proletarii'*, pp. 8 and 18.
11. *Iskra*, no. 93, 17 March 1905.
12. Trotsky to J. G. Wright, 2 May 1940, p. 3: Trotsky Collection (HIA), box 13, folder 1.
13. 'Sotsial-demokratiya i revolyutsiya', *Nachalo*, no. 10, 25 October 1905: RGASPI, f. 325, op. 1, d. 563, pp. 15–18.
14. L. Trotskii, *Moya zhizn'*, vol. 1, p. 206.
15. N. Sedova, autobiographical typescript begun on 24 December 1941: Trotsky Collection (HIA), box 27, folder 13, p. 13.
16. *Ibid.*
17. Photograph in L. Trotskii, *1905 God*, opposite p. 200.
18. 'Grisha' to Vilenkina [*sic*] in Geneva, 3 December 1905: APO (HIA), file XVIIc, folder 1.
19. See the convincing review of the evidence by I. D. Thatcher, 'Leon Trotsky and 1905', pp. 248–50.
20. A. Lunacharskii, *Revolyutsionnye siluety*, p. 20.
21. R. B. Gul', *Ya unës Rossiyu: apologiya emigratsii*, vol. 2, p. 252.
22. L. Trotskii, *Moya zhizn'*, vol. 1, p. 203.
23. *Ibid.*, pp. 203–4.
24. 'Nashi zadachi', *Nachalo*, no. 1, 13 November 1905: Nicolaevsky Collection (HIA), box 625, folder 5.
25. I. Getzler, *Martov: A Political Biography of a Russian Social-Democrat*, p. 110.
26. R. Service, *Lenin: A Political Life*, vol. 1, pp. 144–5 and 147.
27. L. Trotskii, *Moya zhizn'*, vol. 1, p. 207.

## 10. Trial and Punishment

1. L. Trotskii, 'Parvus', *Nashe slovo*, no. 23, 24 February 1915: RGASPI, f. 325, op. 1, d. 576, p. 14.
2. N. Trotskii, *Tuda i obratno*, p. 11.
3. See photograph of Trotsky's friend D. F. Sverchkov in L. Trotskii, *1905 God*, opposite p. 216.
4. See below, p. 159.
5. *Moya zhizn'* draft: Nicolaevsky Collection (HIA), box 313, folder 5, pp. 1–2.

6. 'L. Yanovskii' (Trotsky) to S. N. Saltykov, 9 December 1905: RGASPI, f. 325, op. 1, d. 377, pp. 1–2.
7. L. Trotskii, *Moya zhizn'*, vol. 1, p. 215.
8. *Ibid.*
9. Letter to Yu. O. Martov, 12 June 1906: RGASPI, f. 325, op. 1, d. 378.
10. L. Trotskii, *Moya zhizn'*, vol. 1, p. 219.
11. *Ibid.*, pp. 217–18.
12. L. Trotsky, *History of the Russian Revolution*, vol. 3, p. 193.
13. G. A. Ziv, *Trotskii: kharakteristika. (Po lichnym vospominaniyam)*, p. 33.
14. Trotskii, *Itogi suda nad Sovetom Rabochikh Deputatov*, pp. 1–6. Unusually Trotsky's name appeared without forename or initial in this work.
15. *Ibid.*, p. 7.
16. L. Trotskii, *Sochineniya*, vol. 2, book 2, pp. 163–77.
17. D. Sverchkov, *Na zare revolyutsii*, p. 218.
18. L. L. Sedov's 'Freudenpass': Nicolaevsky Collection (HIA), box 356, folder 25.
19. N. Trotskii, 'Sovet i prokuratura', in *Istoriya Soveta Rabochikh Deputatov g. S.-Peterburga*, pp. 319–21 and 323.
20. N. Trotskii, 'Sovet i revolyutsiya. (Pyatdesyat' dnei)' in *ibid.*, p. 21.
21. *Ibid.*
22. *Ibid.*
23. D. Sverchkov, *Na zare revolyutsii*, pp. 220–4.
24. N. Trotskii, *Tuda i obratno*, pp. 13–14.
25. *Ibid.*, pp. 20–1.
26. *Ibid.*, pp. 24–5.
27. *Ibid.*, pp. 25–6.
28. D. Sverchkov, *Na zare revolyutsii*, pp. 225–6.
29. N. Trotskii, *Tuda i obratno*, p. 46.
30. *Ibid.*, p. 51.
31. D. Sverchkov, *Na zare revolyutsii*, pp. 227–8.
32. *Ibid.*, pp. 228–9.
33. Police file on Trotsky: RGASPI, f. 325, op. 1, d. 2, p. 8; N. Trotskii, *Tuda i obratno*, pp. 57–8.
34. L. Trotskii, *Moya zhizn'*, pp. 223–4; D. Sverchkov, *Na zare revolyutsii*, pp. 230–1.
35. D. Sverchkov, *Na zare revolyutsii*, p. 229.
36. N. Trotskii, *Tuda i obratno*, pp. 61–6.
37. *Ibid.*, p. 87
38. *Ibid.*, p. 118.
39. M. Shachtman, 'Natalya Ivanovna Sedoff (Sedova)' (n.d.; typed notes), p. 4: Albert Glotzer Papers (HIA), box 26.
40. N. Sedova, autobiographical typescript begun on 24 December 1941: Trotsky Collection (HIA), box 27, folder 13, p. 17. Trotsky had to be careful about the names he gave in the account in case reprisals were taken against individuals.
41. *Ibid.*
42. *Ibid.*, pp. 17–18.

## 11. Again the Emigrant

1. M. Shachtman, 'Natalia Ivanovna Sedoff (Sedova)' (n.d.; typed notes), p. 4: Albert Glotzer papers (HIA), box 26.
2. L. Trotskii, *Delo bylo v Ispanii*.
3. N. Sedova, autobiographical typescript begun on 24 December 1941: Trotsky Collection (HIA), box 27, folder 13, p. 18.
4. *Ibid.*
5. L. Trotskii, *Politicheskie siluety*, p. 185.
6. N. Ioffe, *Vremya nazad*, p. 13.
7. 'Zatmenie solntsa', *Kievskaya mysl'*, no. 295, 24 October 1908: RGASPI, f. 325, op. 1, d. 568, pp. 21–2.
8. I. D. Thatcher, 'Trotsky and the Duma: A Research Essay', p. 36.
9. N. Trotskii, *V zashchitu partii* (N. Glagolev edn), pp. xiii, 137 and 143.
10. *Ibid.*, pp. xviii–xxi and 2–3.
11. *Ibid.*, pp. 87 and 91.
12. *Pyatyi (londonskii) s"ezd RSDRP. Protokoly*, pp. 15 and 21.
13. *Ibid.*, p. 166.
14. *Ibid.*, pp. 258–66.
15. *Ibid.*, p. 292.
16. *Ibid.*, pp. 397–404.
17. *Ibid.*, p. 443.
18. *Ibid.*, p. 483.
19. *Ibid.*, p. 538.
20. N. Sedova, autobiographical typescript begun on 24 December 1941: Trotsky Collection (HIA), box 27, folder 13, p. 19.
21. *Ibid.*
22. Director of Kherson Province Gendarme Administration to Director of the Special Department A. M. Yeremin, 16 February 1910: APO (HIA), file XVIIc, folder 2.
23. N. Sedova, 'Devochki', p. 2: Trotsky Collection (HIA), box 27, folder 13.
24. N. Trotskii, *Nasha revolyutsiya* (1907 edn), pp. xvi–xvii (preface).
25. L. Trotsky, *Russland in der Revolution*.
26. *Itogi i perspektivy*. Here I use the 1909 edition published by N. Glagolev in *Nasha revolyutsiya*, pp. 236–8.
27. *Ibid.*, pp. 250–9.
28. *Ibid.*, pp. 224–30.
29. *Ibid.*, pp. 231–8.
30. *Ibid.*, p. 278.
31. N. Trotskii, *V zashchitu partii* (N. Glagolev edn), pp. 5 and 8–9.
32. *Ibid.*, p. 82.
33. Letter of M. Bystrytskii-Zhenev to Marfa Osipovna Dunina, 2 January 1909: APO (HIA), file XVIIc, folder 1. Bystrytskii-Zhenev referred to Melenevsky by his pseudonym Basok.

34. N. Ioffe, *Vremya nazad. Moya zhizn', moya sud'ba, moya epokha*, p. 13; recollections of N. I. Sedova in letters to B. I. Nikolaevskii, 2 October and 24 December 1956: Nicolaevsky Collection (HIA), box 628, folder 11.
35. N. Ioffe, *Vremya nazad. Moya zhizn', moya sud'ba, moya epokha*, p. 13.
36. *Ibid.*, p. 20.
37. Trotsky to I. Bisk, 11 June 1908: Nicolaevsky Collection (HIA), box 90, folder 13.
38. Trotsky to A. M. Gor'kii, 20 June 1909, p. 7: Nicolaevsky Collection (HIA), box 652, folder 10.
39. L. Trotskii, *Moya zhizn'*, vol. 1, p. 252.
40. 'Natasha' [N. Sedova] to Trotsky, 12 December 1913: APO (HIA), file XVIIc, folder 1.
41. Trotsky to M. Gor'kii, 9 June 1909: Nicolaevsky Collection (HIA), box 652, folder 10.
42. Trotsky to the New York support group, 11 March 1912: Nicolaevsky Collection (HIA), box 654, folder 1.
43. *Pravda* editorial board's appeal, 26 February 1911: Nicolaevsky Collection (HIA), box 653, folder 2.
44. Trotsky to I. Bisk, 11 June 1908: Nicolaevsky Collection (HIA), box 90, folder 13.
45. The *Odesskie novosti* articles are gathered in RGASPI, f. 325, op. 1, d. 564.
46. The *Kievskaya mysl'* articles are gathered in *ibid.*, d. 568.
47. 'Pis'ma s Zapada', *Odesskie novosti*, 12 April 1908: RGASPI, f. 325, op. 1, d. 564, p. 1.
48. 'Tvoya Sasha' [probably Alexandra Bronstein] to Trotsky, 19 March 1909; I. Boitsov to Trotsky, 14 April 1909: APO (HIA), file XVIIc, folder 1.
49. 'Nekotorye politicheskie itogi. K delu Azefa', *Pravda*, no. 3, 27 March 1909 [9 April 1909]: RGASPI, f. 325, op. 1, d. 566, pp. 37–45.
50. 'K. S.' [I. V. Stalin] to Mr Vel'tman, 31 December 1910: APO (HIA), file XVIIc, folder 1.

## 12. Unifier

1. A. V. Lunacharskii to Trotsky, 26 November 1909: Nicolaevsky Collection (HIA), box 627, folder 5.
2. Trotsky to A. M. Gor'kii, 20 June 1909: Nicolaevsky Collection (HIA), box 652, folder 10.
3. Draft notes for lecture: Nicolaevsky Collection (HIA), box 627, folder 11.
4. A. Lunacharskii, *Revolyutsionnye siluety*, pp. 22–3.
5. *Moya zhizn'* draft: Nicolaevsky Papers (HIA), box 313, folder 6, pp. 14–15. As usual, the draft is fuller than the printed version.
6. R. Luxemburg, 'Letters on Bolshevism and the Russian Revolution', *Revolutionary History*, no. 6 (1996), p. 241. I am grateful to Ian Thatcher for discussing this period of party history with me.

7. L. Trotskii, *Moya zhizn'*, vol. 1, pp. 240–1.

8. *Ibid.*, p. 241.

9. N. Sedova, autobiographical typescript begun on 24 December 1941: Trotsky Collection (HIA), box 27, folder 13, p. 22.

10. *Ibid.*

11. Trotsky to P. B. Axel'rod, 11 June 1912, p. 7: Nicolaevsky Collection (HIA), box 654, folder 4.

12. N. Sedova, autobiographical typescript begun on 24 December 1941: Trotsky Collection (HIA), box 27, folder 13, p. 24.

13. *Ibid.*, p. 27.

14. Trotsky's 1935 diary in L. Trotskii, *Dnevniki i pis'ma*, pp. 19–20.

15. N. Ioffe, *Vremya nazad. Moya zhizn', moya sud'ba, moya epokha*, p. 48.

16. 'Gospodin Pëtr Struve', *Kievskaya mysl'*, 21 April 1909: RGASPI, f. 325, op. 1, d. 568, p. 118.

17. 'Natsional'no-psikhologicheskie tipy burzhuazii', *Kievskaya mysl'*, 25 January 1909: *ibid.*, pp. 86–7.

18. Okhrana report, 24 January 1911, p. 7: APO (HIA), file XVIb(2), folder 1.

19. A. Lunacharskii, *Revolyutsionnye siluety*, p. 21.

20. Trotsky to Duma deputy I. P. Pokrovskii, 5 December 1910: APO (HIA), file XVIIc, folder 2.

21. Letter of *Pravda* editorial board to 'party organizations', 26 November 1911: Nicolaevsky Collection (HIA), box 653, folder 2.

22. 'Pis'mo "Pravdy" k myslyashchim rabochim. Gde zhe nastoyashchii put'?', *Pravda*, no. 14, 24 June/7 July 1910: RGASPI, f. 325, op. 1, d. 567, p. 23.

23. 'Voprosy edinstva', *Bor'ba*, no. 3, 12 April 1914: RGASPI, f. 325, op. 1, d. 574, p. 13.

24. 'Anketa "Pravdy"', *Pravda*, no. 16, 24 September/6 October 1910: RGASPI, f. 325, op. 1, d. 567, p. 50.

25. 'Voprosy edinstva', *Bor'ba*, no. 3, 12 April 1914: RGASPI, f. 325. op. 1, d. 574, p. 15.

26. See 'Pravda svoim chitatelya', *Pravda* [Vienna], no. 1, 3/16 January 1908; 'Nekotorye politicheskie itogi. K delu Azefa', *Pravda* [Vienna], no. 3, 27 March/9 April 1909: RGASPI, f. 325, op. 1, d. 566.

27. 'Anketa "Pravdy"', *Pravda*, no. 16, 24 September/6 October 1910: RGASPI, f. 325, op. 1, d. 567, p. 52; 'Polozhenie v partii i nashi zadachi', *Pravda*, no. 18/19, 29 January/11 February 1911: RGASPI, f. 325. op. 1, d. 566, p. 84.

28. 'Pis'ma ob edinstve', *Luch*, no. 27, 2 February 1913: RGASPI, f. 325, op. 1, d. 573, pp. 10 and 12–14.

29. 'Polozhenie v partii i nashi zadachi', *Pravda*, no. 18/19, 29 January/11 February 1911: RGASPI, f. 325, op. 1, d. 566, p. 95.

30. D. Sverchkov, *Na zare revolyutsii*, pp. 262–3.

31. Open appeal of *Pravda* editorial board to 'party organizations', 26 February 1911: Nicolaevsky Collection (HIA), box 653, folder 2.

32. Iosif [I. V. Stalin] to V. S. Bobrovskii, 24 January 1911: APO (HIA), file XVIIu, folder 1.

33. Okhrana report, 24 January 1911, p. 7: APO (HIA), file XVIb(2), folder 1.
34. 'Neotlozhnye voprosy', *Nasha zarya*, no. 11 (1911).
35. Offprint of *Sotsial-demokrat* (central organ of the Russian Social-Democratic Workers' Party), no. 19, 1911, p. 2.
36. *Ibid.*, p. 3.

## 13. Special Correspondent

1. Trotsky to P. B. Axel'rod, 12 February 1912: Nicolaevsky Collection (HIA), box 653, folder 2, pp. 3 and 7.
2. Trotsky to P. B. Axel'rod, 20(?) February 1912, p. 1: Nicolaevsky Collection (HIA), box 42, folder 8.
3. Trotsky to P. B. Axel'rod, 8 March 1912, p. 1: Nicolaevsky Collection (HIA), box 654, folder 1.
4. Trotsky to P. B. Axel'rod, 20 July 1912, p. 1: Nicolaevsky Collection (HIA), box 654, folder 7; see also Trotsky to P. B. Axel'rod, 8 August 1912: Nicolaevsky Collection (HIA), box 655, folder 1, and N. Sedova, 'Devochki', p. 2: Trotsky Collection (HIA), box 27, folder 13.
5. Trotsky to P. B. Axel'rod, 20 July 1912, p. 1: Nicolaevsky Collection (HIA), box 654, folder 7.
6. Trotsky to the editorial board of 'Zvezda', 29 April 1912: APO (HIA), file XVIIc, folder 1.
7. Trotsky to Duma deputy Voiloshnikov, 29 April 1912 (NS): *ibid*.
8. Trotsky to the New York assistance group, 11 March 1912, pp. 2–3: Nicolaevsky Collection (HIA), box 92, folder 16.
9. Trotsky to the New York assistance group, April 1912: *ibid*.
10. F. I. Dan to P. B. Axel'rod, beginning of September 1911: *Fëdor Il'ich Dan: Pis'ma (1899–1946)*, p. 239.
11. *Ibid.*
12. Trotsky to P. B. Axel'rod, 8 and 16 August 1911: Nicolaevsky Collection (HIA), box 655, folder 1.
13. Basok [M. Melenevsky]'s correspondence with S. Semkovskii, 1912: Nicolaevsky Collection (HIA), box 185, folder 28.
14. G. A. Alexinskii's notes: Nicolaevsky Collection (HIA), box 655, folder 2, p. 6.
15. *Ibid.*, p. 16.
16. 'Balkanskie pis'ma', signed off 28 September 1912: *Kievskaya mysl'*, 3 October 1912: RGASPI, f. 325, op. 1, d. 569, p. 53.
17. 'Ranënye', *Kievskaya mysl'*, 31 October 1912: *ibid.*, p. 99.
18. S. Semkovski to P. B. Axel'rod, 15 January 1913, p. 3: Nicolaevsky Collection (HIA), box 655, folder 3.
19. Trotsky to N. S. Chkheidze, 1 April 1913: Nicolaevsky Collection (HIA), box 656, folder 5, pp. 1–2.
20. See above, p. 82.

21. Trotsky to N. S. Chkheidze, 1 April 1913: Nicolaevsky Collection (HIA), box 656, folder 5, pp. 1–2.
22. For a more positive verdict on the Block's prospects see G. Swain, *Russian Social-Democracy and the Legal Labour Movement*.
23. Trotsky to *Luch* editorial board, 2 April 1913, pp. 1 and 3: APO (HIA), file XVIIc, folder 2.
24. F. I. Dan to P. B. Axel'rod, 11 May 1912: *Fëdor Il'ich Dan: Pis'ma (1899–1946)*, p. 263.
25. Trotsky's quotation in letter to unknown person, probably in 1913: Nicolaevsky Collection (HIA), box 42, folder 24, pp. 1–2.
26. Unknown writer to Trotsky, 22 January 1913, pp. 1–2: APO (HIA), file XVIIc, folder 1.
27. 'A' to Trotsky, 3 March 1913: *ibid.*
28. N. I. Sedova to Trotsky, 12 December 1913: *ibid.*
29. Yu. O. Martov to S. Semkovskii, 31 July 1914: Nicolaevsky Collection (HIA), box 657, folder 5.
30. G. Swain, *Russian Social-Democracy and the Legal Labour Movement*, p. 191.
31. RGASPI, f. 325, op. 1, d. 574. On *Bor'ba* see I. D. Thatcher, 'Bor'ba: A Workers' Journal in St Petersburg on the Eve of World War One', *English Historical Review*, no. 450 (1998), p. 101.
32. 'Ot redaktsii', *Bor'ba*, no. 1, 22 January 1914: RGASPI, f. 325, op. 1, d. 574, p. 2.
33. 'Voprosy edinstva', *Bor'ba*, no. 3, 12 April 1914: *ibid.*, p. 15.

## 14. War on the War

1. L. Trotzky, *Chapters from My Diary*, p. 10.
2. *Ibid.*
3. L. Trotskii, *Moya zhizn'*, vol. 1, p. 271.
4. *Ibid.*, p. 272.
5. Trotsky to P. B. Axel'rod, 10 December 1914: Nicolaevsky Collection (HIA), box 657, folder 6.
6. *Golos*, no. 71, 4 December 1914.
7. Trotsky to P. B. Axel'rod, 11 December 1914: Nicolaevsky Collection (HIA), box 657, folder 6.
8. Trotsky to P. B. Axel'rod, n.d.: Nicolaevsky Collection (HIA), box 43, folder 2, p. 2.
9. A. Lunacharskii, *Revolyutsionnye siluety*, p. 23.
10. *Ibid.*
11. Trotsky to P. B. Axel'rod, 22 December 1914: Nicolaevsky Collection (HIA), box 657, folder 6. Trotsky mentioned Plekhanov en passant in an article on Karl Kautsky: 'Kautskii o Plekhanove', part 3, *Nashe slovo*, no. 117, 19 June 1915: RGASPI, f. 325, op. 1, d. 576, p. 96.
12. M. Melenevsky and others: 'Po povodu insinuatsii N. Trotskogo v gazete

"Golos"', 8 February 1915, pp. 1–3: Nicolaevsky Collection (HIA), box 627, folder 8.

13. RGASPI, f. 325, op. 1, d. 576: 'Nekriticheskaya otsenka kriticheskoi epokhi', part 1, *Nashe slovo*, no. 28, 1 March 1915: *ibid.*, pp. 18–19; part 2, no. 35, 10 March 1915: *ibid.*, pp. 22 and 24.

14. *Ibid.*, p. 71.

15. N. Sedova, autobiographical typescript begun on 24 December 1941: Trotsky Collection (HIA), box 27, folder 13, p. 25.

16. A. Rosmer, 'Durant la Guerre Impérialiste', in M. Nadeau (ed.), *Hommage à Natalia Sedova-Trotsky, 1882–1962*, p. 67.

17. N. Sedova, autobiographical typescript begun on 24 December 1941: Trotsky Collection (HIA), box 27, folder 13, pp. 25–6.

18. A. Rosmer, quoted in P. Naville, *Trotsky vivant*, p. 156.

19. *Ibid.*

20. *Ibid.*

21. *Ibid.*

22. N. Sedova, autobiographical typescript begun on 24 December 1941: Trotsky Collection (HIA), box 27, folder 13, pp. 25–6.

23. See below, p. 118.

24. N. Sedova, autobiographical typescript begun on 24 December 1941: Trotsky Collection (HIA), box 27, folder 13, p. 26.

25. Trotsky to L. G. Deich, 15 July 1915: Nicolaevsky Collection (HIA), box 657, folder 8, pp. 1–2.

26. L. G. Deich to Trotsky, 31 July 1915: Nicolaevsky Collection (HIA), box 658, folder 1.

27. Trotsky to L. G. Deich, 15 July 1915: Nicolaevsky Collection (HIA), box 83, folder 3, p. 1.

28. I. Thatcher, *Leon Trotsky and World War One: August 1914–February 1917*, pp. 25–37. I have drawn copiously on Ian Thatcher's work in dealing with the complexities of Trotsky's wartime writing.

29. A. Rosmer, 'Durant la Guerre Impérialiste', in M. Nadeau (ed.), *Hommage à Natalia Sedova-Trotsky, 1882–1962*, pp. 65–6.

## 15. Designs for Revolution

1. Trotsky to P. B. Axel'rod, 10 December 1914: Nicolaevsky Collection (HIA), box 43, folder 2.

2. *Die Zimmerwalder Bewegung. Protokole und Korrespondenz*, vol. 1, pp. 45–9, 54; V. I. Lenin, *Polnoe sobranie sochinenii*, vol. 49, pp. 115–16 and 128–9.

3. V. I. Lenin, *Polnoe sobranie sochinenii*, vol. 49, p. 78.

4. L. Trotskii, *Moya zhizn'*, vol. 1, p. 285.

5. *Die Zimmerwalder Bewegung. Protokole und Korrespondenz*, vol. 1, pp. 55–6.

6. RGASPI, f. 325, op. 1, d. 394.

7. *Die Zimmerwalder Bewegung. Protokole und Korrespondenz*, vol. 1, p. 141.

8. *Ibid.*, pp. 133 and 137.
9. *Ibid.*, p. 169.
10. Police report to Petrograd, probably 1915, pp. 2b, 3 and 4b: APO (HIA), file XVIIc, folder 2.
11. R. Service, *Lenin: A Political Life*, vol. 2, pp. 79–81.
12. 'Nash politicheskii lozung', *Nashe slovo*, no. 23, 24 February 1915: RGASPI, f. 325, op. 1, d. 576, pp. 9–10; 'Imperializm i natsional'naya ideya', *Nashe slovo*, no. 32, 6 May 1915: *ibid.*, pp. 54–6.
13. 'Natsiya i khozyaistvo', *Nashe slovo*, no. 130, 3 July 1915: *ibid.*, pp. 109–11.
14. 'Nash politicheskii lozung', *Nashe slovo*, no. 23, 24 February 1915: *ibid.*, p. 10.
15. 'Pis'ma s Zapada', *Kievskaya mysl'*, no. 22, 22 January 1916: RGASPI, f. 325, op. 1, d. 571, p. 21.
16. 'Pis'ma s Zapada: u knyazya monakskogo', *Kievskaya mysl'*, no. 191, 10 July 1916: *ibid.*, p. 107.
17. 'Pis'ma s Zapada: brozhenie umov', *Kievskaya mysl'*, no. 133, 18 May 1916: *ibid.*, pp. 92–3.
18. 'Otkhodit epokha', *Kievskaya mysl'*, no. 3, 3 January 1916: *ibid.*, p. 8.
19. L. Trotskii, *Moya zhizn'*, vol. 1, p. 286.
20. *Die Zimmerwalder Bewegung. Protokole und Korrespondenz*, vol. 1, pp. 273–362.
21. R. Service, *Lenin: A Biography*, pp. 127 and 129.

## 16. Atlantic Crossings

1. Okhrana report to Petrograd, 18 September 1916: APO (HIA), file XVIIc, folder 2.
2. L. D. Trotskii, *Chto i kak proizoshlo? Shest' statei dlya mirovoi burzhuaznoi pechati*, pp. 9–10.
3. Comité pour la reprise des relations, 25 September 1916, pp. 1–3: APO (HIA), file XVIIc, folder 2.
4. L. Trotzky, *Lettres aux abonnés de la Vie Ouvrière*, part 3: *L'expulsion de Léon Trotzky*, pp. 13–14 and 20.
5. L. D. Trotskii, *Chto i kak proizoshlo? Shest' statei dlya mirovoi burzhuaznoi pechati*, p. 9.
6. L. Trotskii, *Delo bylo v Ispanii*, p. 120.
7. Trotsky's 1935 diary in L. Trotskii, *Dnevniki i pis'ma*, p. 130.
8. L. Trotzky, *Vingt lettres de Léon Trotzky*, p. 33.
9. L. Trotskii, *Delo bylo v Ispanii*, p. 123.
10. *Ibid.*, pp. 124–6.
11. M. Shachtman, 'Natalya Ivanovna Sedoff (Sedova)' (n.d.; typed notes), p. 6: Albert Glotzer Papers (HIA), box 27.
12. *Novy mir* (New York), 6 December 1916; Nicolaevsky Collection (HIA), box 83, folders 3 and 4.
13. L. Trotskii, *Delo bylo v Ispanii*, p. 147.

14. G. A. Ziv, *Trotskii: kharakteristika. (Po lichnym vospominaniyam)*, p. 67.

15. *Ibid.*, pp. 67–9.

16. J. Nedava, *Trotsky and the Jews*, p. 25.

17. *Ibid.*, pp. 25–6.

18. G. A. Ziv, *Trotskii: kharakteristika. (Po lichnym vospominaniyam)*, p. 76.

19. Trotsky to the New York Group of the Russian Social-Democratic Workers' Party, April 1912: Nicolaevsky Collection (HIA), box 654, folder 2.

20. G. A. Ziv, *Trotskii: kharakteristika. (Po lichnym vospominaniyam)*, p. 57.

21. *Novyi mir* (New York), 16 January 1916, pp. 1 and 4.

22. 'A vsë-taki Klaru Tsetkin naprasno trevozhite!', *Novyi mir* (New York), 16 February 1917.

23. M. Shachtman, 'Natalya Ivanovna Sedoff (Sedova)' (n.d.; typed notes), p. 5: Albert Glotzer Papers (HIA), box 27. According to one report, the Trotskys stayed with relatives who had emigrated from Kherson province: Nathan Sturman, 21 January 2001, recalling the family stories he heard about his great-grandmother Emma Bronstein, who was the niece of Trotsky's father David: RootsWeb.com message board.

24. M. Shachtman, 'Natalia Ivanovna Sedoff (Sedova)' (n.d.; typed notes), p. 7: Albert Glotzer Papers (HIA), box 26.

25. See below, p. 346.

26. L. Trotskii, *Moya zhizn'*, vol. 1, pp. 308–9.

27. E. Goldman, *Living My Life*, vol. 2, p. 596.

28. New York speech (n.d.), RGASPI, f. 325, op. 1, d. 557, pp. 108–21.

29. M. Shachtman, 'Natalya Ivanovna Sedoff (Sedova)' (n.d.: typed notes), p. 6: Albert Glotzer Papers (HIA), box 27.

30. 'Instruktsiya upolnomochënnomu po delam politicheskim emigrantam pri chrezvychainoi rossiiskoi missii v Soedinënnykh Shtatakh': Nicolaevsky Collection (HIA), box 87, folder 13, p. 1.

31. 'Ot kogo i kak zashchishchat' revolyutsiyu', *Novyi mir* (New York), 21 March 1917. His name was given here as Lev N. Trotskii.

32. *Ibid.*

33. J. Nedava, *Trotsky and the Jews*, p. 27.

34. F. Harris, *Contemporary Portraits: Fourth Series*, p. 199.

35. L. Lore, 'When Trotsky Lived in New York', quoted by R. B. Spence in 'Hidden Agendas: Spies, Lies and Intrigue Surrounding Trotsky's American Visit of January–April 1917', *Revolutionary Russia*, no. 1 (2008), p. 47.

36. R. B. Spence, *ibid.*, p. 48.

37. A. Kalpaschnikoff, *A Prisoner of Trotsky's*, p. 223.

38. P. Broué, *Léon Sedov, fils de Trotsky, victime de Staline*, p. 20.

39. A. Kalpaschnikoff, *A Prisoner of Trotsky's*, p. 223.

40. 'Norway Heritage: Hands Across the Sea': http://www.norwayheritage.com/pship.asp?sh=krisf.

## 17. Nearly a Bolshevik

1. L. Trotskii, *Moya zhizn'*, vol. 2, p. 6.
2. L. Trotsky, *The Real Situation in Russia*, pp. 204–5.
3. L. Trotskii, *O Lenine: materialy dlya biografa*, p. 52.
4. N. Sukhanov, *Zapiski o revolyutsii*, vol. 2, book 4, p. 190.
5. *Ibid.*
6. *Sed'maya (aprel'skaya) vserossiiskaya konferentsiya RSDRP (bol'shevikov)*, pp. 67–8.
7. N. Sukhanov, *Zapiski o revolyutsii*, vol. 2, book 4, p. 171.
8. *Ibid.*, p. 172.
9. Trotsky never claimed this.
10. A. Ioffe, 'Avtobiografiya', in N. Ioffe, *Moi otets Adol'f Abramovich Ioffe: vospominaniya, dokumenty i materialy*, p. 53.
11. L. Trotskii, 'Avtobiograficheskie zametki', Syzran, 5 April 1919: RGASPI, f. 325, op. 1, d. 14, p. 18.
12. *Pravda*, 18 May 1917.
13. *Leninskii sbornik*, vol. 4, p. 303.
14. *Ibid.*, p. 302.
15. N. Sukhanov, *Zapiski o revolyutsii*, vol. 2, book 4, p. 190.
16. *Ibid.*, p. 245.
17. *Ibid.*, pp. 245–6. Trotsky disputed whether he had said exactly this; he also claimed that he had already arrived at an understanding with Lenin about jointly founding a newspaper: see *ibid.*, p. 246.
18. A. Ioffe, 'Avtobiografiya', in N. Ioffe, *Moi otets Adol'f Abramovich Ioffe: vospominaniya, dokumenty i materialy*, p. 53.
19. N. Sukhanov, *Zapiski o revolyutsii*, vol. 2, book 4, p. 254.
20. N. Sedova, 'Otets i syn': typescript, 8 June 1940: Trotsky Collection (HIA), box 27, folder 11, p. 6.
21. N. Sedova, 'Devochki': Trotsky Collection (HIA), box 27, folder 13, pp. 1 and 4.
22. *Ibid.*
23. L. Trotskii, *Moya zhizn'*, vol. 2, p. 16.
24. See above, p. 74.
25. 'Kopengagen – Kongress sotsialistov', *Odesskie novosti*, 20 August 1910: RGASPI, f. 325, op. 1, d. 564, pp. 27–8.
26. N. Sukhanov, *Zapiski o revolyutsii*, vol. 3, book 6, p. 188. Sukhanov made it his business to keep a close watch on Trotsky's technique. We know more from Sukhanov than from Trotsky.
27. Herman Axelbank Film Collection (HIA), reel 19: film of Trotsky speaking from the back of a train.
28. *Ibid.*
29. V. I. Lenin, *Polnoe sobranie sochinenii*, vol. 10, pp. 359–62, and vol. 12, pp. 154–7.

30. A. Lunacharskii, *Revolyutsionnye siluety*, p. 24.
31. I. Getzler, *Martov: A Political Biography of a Russian Social-Democrat*, p. 142.
32. N. Sukhanov, *Zapiski o revolyutsii*, vol. 2, book 4, p. 262.
33. *Ibid.*, p. 295.
34. See below, p. 392.
35. Trotsky hinted about his change of stance in *From October to Brest-Litovsk*, chap. 1.
36. *Ibid.*
37. J. D. White, 'Early Soviet Interpretations of the Russian Revolution, 1918–1924', *Soviet Studies*, no. 3 (1985), pp. 348–50.

## 18. Threats and Promises

1. Z. Galili, *The Menshevik Leaders in the Russian Revolution: Social Realities and Political Strategies*, pp. 269–73.
2. G. Gill, *Peasants and Government in the Russian Revolution*, pp. 102–3.
3. L. Trotskii, *K istorii Oktyabr'skoi Revolyutsii*, p. 25.
4. N. Sukhanov, *Zapiski o revolyutsii*, vol. 3, book 7, p. 288.
5. See above, p. 74. The fact that he had put the word 'demagogues' in inverted commas does not, I think, substantially detract from the point.
6. See the articles collected in L. Trotskii, *Sochineniya*, vol. 3, part 1, pp. 45–152.
7. L. Trotskii, *Moya zhizn'*, vol. 2, p. 31.
8. A. Rabinowitch, *Prelude to Revolution: The Petrograd Bolsheviks and the July 1917 Uprising*, pp. 111–34.
9. W. Woytinsky, *Stormy Passage*, p. 286.
10. W. G. Rosenberg, *Liberals in the Russian Revolution: The Constitutional Democratic Party, 1917–1921*, pp. 174–5.
11. N. Sukhanov, *Zapiski o revolyutsii*, vol. 2, book 4, p. 311.
12. *Ibid.*, p. 334.
13. *Ibid.*, vol. 3, book 5, p. 24.
14. RGVA, f. 33987, op. 1, d. 359, pp. 1–2: A. V. Lunacharskii to N. N. Sukhanov, 30 March 1920.
15. *Devyataya konferentsiya RKP(b)*, pp. 25–6.
16. N. Sukhanov, *Zapiski o revolyutsii*, vol. 3, book 5, p. 20.
17. N. I. Sedova, 'Otets i syn' (typescript: 8 June 1940), p. 6: Trotsky Collection (HIA), box 27, folder 11.
18. N. Sukhanov, *Zapiski o revolyutsii*, vol. 3, book 5, p. 43.
19. L. Trotskii, *Moya zhizn'*, vol. 2, p. 11.
20. N. A. Ioffe, 'Ob ottse' (typescript) in N. A. Ioffe Papers (HIA), part 2, p. 3.
21. N. Sukhanov, *Zapiski o revolyutsii*, vol. 3, book 6, p. 182.
22. *Shestoi s''ezd RSDRP (bol'shevikov). Avgust 1917 goda. Protokoly*, p. 41.
23. L. Trotskii, *Moya zhizn'*, vol. 2, p. 11.

## 19. Seizure of Power

1. W. Hard, *Raymond Robins' Own Story*, p. 22.
2. B. Beatty, *The Red Heart of Russia*, p. 190.
3. R. Service, *Lenin: A Political Life*, vol. 2, pp. 201–9.
4. N. Sukhanov, *Zapiski o revolyutsii*, vol. 3, book 6, p. 213.
5. *Ibid.*, pp. 216–17.
6. *Protokoly Tsentral'nogo Komiteta RSDRP(b). Avgust 1917–fevral' 1918*, p. 46.
7. *Ibid.*, pp. 47–8.
8. *Ibid.*, pp. 49, 55, 63, 65 and 66. Admittedly this trend ceased from 24 September: *ibid.*, p, 69.
9. *Ibid.*, p. 49.
10. *Ibid.*, pp. 48.
11. *Ibid.*, p. 55.
12. *Ibid.*, p. 51.
13. *Ibid.*, p. 65.
14. *Ibid.*, p. 67.
15. *Ibid.*, p. 76.
16. A. Rabinowitch, *The Bolsheviks Come to Power*, pp. 231–2.
17. N. Sukhanov, *Zapiski o revolyutsii*, vol. 3, book 7, p. 270.
18. *Protokoly Tsentral'nogo Komiteta RSDRP(b)*, pp. 84–5.
19. *Ibid.*, p. 86.
20. *Ibid.*, pp. 87–92.
21. J. D. White, 'Lenin, Trotskii and the Arts of Insurrection: The Congress of Soviets of the Northern Region, 11–13 October 1917', *Slavonic and East European Studies*, no. 1 (1999), pp. 120–38.
22. A. Rabinowitch, *The Bolsheviks Come to Power*, p. 233.
23. *Ibid.*, pp. 240 and 245; L. D. Trotskii, *Oktyabr'skaya Revolyutsiya*, p. 69.
24. *Protokoly Tsentral'nogo Komiteta RSDRP(b)*, p. 93.
25. *Ibid.*, pp. 93–4.
26. *Ibid.*, pp. 97–9.
27. *Ibid.*, p. 104.
28. *Ibid.*, p. 105.
29. *Ibid.*, pp. 108–11.
30. L. Trotskii, *Sochineniya*, vol. 3, book 2, pp. 31–2.
31. *Protokoly Tsentral'nogo Komiteta RSDRP(b)*, p. 114
32. *Ibid.*, p. 108.
33. L. Trotsky, *History of the Russian Revolution*, vol. 3, p. 259.
34. N. Sukhanov, *Zapiski o revolyutsii*, vol. 3, book 7, p. 287.
35. B. Beatty, *The Red Heart of Russia*, p. 165.
36. L. Trotskii, *Moya zhizn'*, vol. 2, pp. 43–4.
37. *Ibid.*, p. 44.
38. N. A. Ioffe, 'Ob ottse' (typescript) in N. A. Ioffe Papers (HIA), part 2, p. 5.
39. L. Trotskii, *Moya zhizn'*, vol. 2, p. 46.

40. N. Sukhanov, *Zapiski o revolyutsii*, vol. 3, book 7, p. 337. I know that the usual translation is 'dustbin'; but the Russian *korzina* involves something unmetallic and is typically an article of office furniture and has a light and comic implication that has been overlooked.
41. *Ibid.*

## 20. People's Commissar

1. *Peterburgskii komitet RSDRP(b) v 1917 godu*, p. 537.
2. *Ibid.*, pp. 542–3.
3. L. Trotskii, *Moya zhizn'*, vol. 2, p. 62.
4. *Ibid.*, p. 61.
5. *Ibid.*, pp. 62–3. See also below, p. 204–7.
6. *Ibid.*, p. 64.
7. R. H. Bruce Lockhart, *Memoirs of a British Agent*, p. 225.
8. L. Bryant, *Six Months in Red Russia*, p. 200.
9. R. B. Gul', *Ya unës Rossiyu: apologiya emigratsii*, vol. 2, p. 256. The author saw a lot of Zinoviev in 1918–19.
10. N. Sedova, 'Devochki': Trotsky Collection (HIA), box 27, folder 13, p. 4
11. *Protokoly zasedanii Soveta Narodnykh Komissarov RSFSR: noyabr' 1917–mart 1918 gg.*, pp. 43–4.
12. *Ibid.*, p. 20.
13. *Ibid.*, p. 25.
14. *Ibid.*, pp. 32, 37 and 61–2.
15. *Ibid.*, p. 36.
16. *Ibid.*, p. 75.
17. *Ibid.*, p. 28.
18. L. Bryant, *Six Months in Red Russia*, p. 145; L. Bryant, *Mirrors of Moscow*, p. 140.
19. Russia: Posol'stvo (HIA), box 1, folder 7: Russian embassy in Paris to Russian embassy in Washington, 23 November (6 December) 1917; Russian embassy in Rome to Russian embassy in Washington, 24 November (7 December) 1917.
20. L. Bryant, *Six Months in Red Russia*, p. 145.
21. R. H. Bruce Lockhart, *Memoirs of a British Agent*, p. 230.
22. *Ibid.*, pp. 245–6.
23. W. Hard, *Raymond Robins' Own Story*, pp. 97–9.
24. Edward Alsworth Ross, 'A Talk with Trotzky', *The Independent*, December 1917, pp. 407 and 423.
25. *Ibid.*, p. 423.

## 21. Trotsky and the Jews

1. For example, this was Trotsky's entry on the questionnaire at the Thirteenth Party Congress in 1924: RGASPI, f. 52, op. 1, d. 71, p. 366.
2. L. Trotsky, 'On the "Jewish Problem"', *Class Struggle*, no. 2 (1934).
3. M. Eastman, *Leon Trotsky: The Portrait of a Youth* (London edn), p. 119. Eastman interviewed Alexandra Bronstein about her life with Trotsky.
4. N. Trotskii, *V zashchitu partii* (N. Glagolev edn), p. 119.
5. 'Razlozhenie sionizma i ego vozmozhnye preemniki', *Iskra*, no. 56, 1 January 1904: RGASPI, f. 325, op. 1, d. 561, pp. 91 and 94.
6. 'Gospodin Pëtr Struve', *Kievskaya mysl'*, 21 April 1909: RGASPI, f. 325, op. 1, d. 568, p. 117.
7. 'Razlozhenie sionizma i ego vozmozhnye preemniki', *Iskra*, no. 56, 1 January 1904: RGASPI, f. 325, op. 1, d. 561, pp. 93–5.
8. J. Leibovits (Santa Barbara, California), 'Otkrytoe pis'mo L'vu Trotskomu', 23 March 1933: Nicolaevsky Collection (HIA), box 305, folder 59, p. 1.
9. *Ibid.*
10. Concluding speech to joint session of Central Committee and Central Control Commission, 26 October 1923: RGASPI, f. 17, op. 2, d. 104, p. 44.
11. *Pis'ma vo vlast', 1917–1927. Zayavleniya, zhaloby, donosy, pis'ma v gosudarstvennye struktury k bol'shevistskim vozhdyam*, p. 30
12. *Ibid.*, pp. 45 and 57.
13. *Ibid.*, p. 95.
14. 'Krasnaya armiya v osveshchenii belogvardeitsa', *Izvestiya*, 16 October 1919.
15. Trotsky to N. I. Bukharin, 4 March 1926: Trotsky Collection (HIA), box 9, folder 48, p. 2.
16. R. C. Tucker, *Stalin as Revolutionary*, pp. 377–90; M. Agursky, *The Third Rome: National Bolshevism in the USSR*, chaps 3–4.
17. R. Service, 'Bolshevism's Europe', in S. Pons and A. Romano (eds), *Russia in the Age of Wars, 1914–1945*, pp. 73–80.
18. See above, p. 109 and below, p. 402.

## 22. Brest-Litovsk

1. L. Trotskii, *Moya zhizn'*, vol. 2, p. 90.
2. See the report in the *New York Times*, 24 December 1918.
3. See below, p. 196.
4. *Protokoly Tsentral'nogo Komiteta RSDRP(b). Avgust 1917–mart 1918*, p. 166.
5. *Ibid.*, pp. 168–9.
6. *Ibid.*, pp. 170–1.
7. *Protokoly zasedanii Soveta Narodnykh Komissarov RSFSR: noyabr' 1917–mart 1918 gg.*, p. 308.
8. L. Bryant, *Six Months in Red Russia*, pp. 145–6.

9. *Protokoly Tsentral'nogo Komiteta RSDRP(b). Avgust 1917–mart 1918*, p. 170.

10. *Ibid.*

11. *Ibid.*, p. 171.

12. *Ibid.*, p. 172.

13. *Ibid.*, p. 173.

14. Trotsky to O. Czernin, January 1918: Trotsky Collection (HIA), box 4, folder 23.

15. *Protokoly Tsentral'nogo Komiteta RSDRP(b). Avgust 1917–mart 1918*, p. 215.

16. *Ibid.*, pp. 222–4.

17. *Ibid.*, p. 234.

18. B. Pearce, *How Haig Saved Lenin*, p. 32.

19. *ITsKKPSS*, no. 4 (1989), p. 144.

20. R. H. Bruce Lockhart, *Memoirs of a British Agent*, p. 320.

21. See below, p. 279.

## 23. Kazan and After

1. A. A. Ioffe to Lenin, 11 March 1918, reproduced in V. Krasnov and V. Daines (eds), *Neizvestnyi Trotskii. Krasnyi Bonapart. Dokumenty, mneniya, razmyshleniya*, p. 20.

2. Committee and Central Control Commission joint meeting, 26 October 1923: RGASPI, f. 17, op. 2, d. 104, p. 43b.

3. W. Hard, *Raymond Robins' Own Story*, pp. 134–5.

4. R. H. Bruce Lockhart, *Memoirs of a British Agent*, pp. 271–2 and 274–5; W. Hard, *Raymond Robins' Own Story*, pp. 202–3.

5. G. Hill, 'Go Spy the Land', part 5, p. 7: typescript for BBC serial (HIA).

6. R. H. Bruce Lockhart, *Friends, Foes and Foreigners*, p. 120.

7. L. Trotskii, *Na bor'bu s golodom*, pp. 5–29: speech in Sokolniki, 6 June 1918.

8. *Ibid.*, p. 55.

9. RGASPI, f. 325, op. 1, d. 403, p. 65.

10. *Ibid.*, p. 66.

11. Trotsky's speech to joint plenum of Central Committee and Central Control Commission, 5 August 1927: RGASPI, f. 17, op. 2, d. 317 (V-iii), p. 69.

12. Lenin to Trotsky, 22 August 1918: RGVA, f. 33897, op. 2, d. 25.

13. Ya. M. Sverdlov to Trotsky, 31 August 1918: Trotsky Collection (HIA), box 5, folder 92.

14. Trotsky's 1935 diary in L. Trotskii, *Dnevniki i pis'ma*, p. 84.

15. *Ibid.*, p. 120.

16. Trotsky to V. I. Lenin, 17 August 1918: RGVA, f. 33987, op. 1, d. 23.

17. V. I. Lenin, *Polnoe sobranie sochinenii*, vol. 37.

18. R. R. Reese, *The Soviet Military Experience: A History of the Soviet Army, 1917–1991*, p. 10.

19. Trotsky to unknown person: RGASPI, f. 17, op. 109, d. 4, p. 60.

20. Trotsky to V. I. Lenin and Ya. M. Sverdlov, 23 October 1918: *ibid.*, pp. 80–1.
21. Trotsky to V. I. Lenin, 4 October 1918: *ibid.*, p. 64.
22. See the report of the Vyazma party organization, 17 June 1918: TsGASA (Volkogonov Papers), f. 8, op. 1, d. 310, p. 1.

## 24. Almost the Commander

1. Trotsky to V. I. Lenin, 1 January 1919: RGASPI, f. 17, op. 109, d. 42, p. 42.
2. I. V. Stalin, *Sochineniya*, vol. 4, pp. 197–224.
3. RGVA, f. 33897, op. 2, d. 87, p. 172, and d. 100, p. 264.
4. Trotsky to V. I. Lenin, 1 January 1919: RGASPI, f. 17, op. 109, d. 42, p. 2.
5. Trotsky to the Central Committee, March 1919, pp. 1–2: Trotsky Collection (HIA), box 4, folder 80.
6. R. Service, 'From Polyarchy to Hegemony: The Party's Role in the Construction of the Central Institutions of the Soviet State, 1917–1919', *Sbornik*, no. 10 (1984), pp. 70–90.
7. Trotsky to the Central Committee, March 1919: Trotsky Collection (HIA), box 4, folder 80, p. 8.
8. F. Benvenuti, *The Bolsheviks and the Red Army, 1918–1922*.
9. See, for example, his telegram to E. M. Sklyanskii and V. I. Lenin, 6 August 1919: RGVA, f. 33897, op. 2, d. 32, p. 290.
10. S. Liberman, *Building Lenin's Russia*, p. 73.
11. A. Lunacharskii, *Revolyutsionnye siluety*, pp. 27–8.
12. *Ibid.*, pp. 21–2.
13. Trotsky to RVSR Train Commander, 1 September 1918: RGVA, f. 33897, op. 2, d. 39, p. 182.
14. Trotsky's letter to Charles Malamuth, 21 October 1939: Trotsky Collection (HIA), box 11, folder 60, p. 1.
15. RGVA, f. 33987, op. 2, d. 3, p. 124 reverse.
16. RGVA, f. 33987, op. 2, d. 47, pp. 63–74.
17. Politburo meeting, 18 April 1919, item 3: Trotsky Collection (HIA), box 9, folder 12.
18. 'Nashe otnoshenie k borotbistam', unpublished paper, December 1919: Trotsky Collection (HIA), box 9, folder 35.
19. R. Service, *Lenin: A Biography*, p. 403.
20. Trotsky's notes for his report on 'Our Military Construction and Our Fronts', October 1919: RGASPI, f. 325, op. 1, d. 62, p. 100.
21. Stenographic record of Trotsky's report on the position at the fronts: RGASPI, f. 325, op. 1, d. 54, pp. 6, 11 and 14–17.
22. *Ibid.*, pp. 14–17.
23. Data prepared for Trotsky in October 1919. The numbers were evidently rather approximate: RGASPI, f. 325, op. 1, d. 62, pp. 68, 89–93.
24. Trotsky to I. V. Stalin, n.d.: RGVA, f. 33897, op. 1, d. 102, p. 357; Trotsky's secret order, 9 May 1920, RGVA, f. 33897, op. 3, d. 46, p. 192.

25. Trotsky to Revolutionary-Military Council of the Second Army: RGVA, f. 33897, op. 2, d. 32, p. 74.
26. R. R. Reese, *The Soviet Military Experience: A History of the Soviet Army, 1917–1991*, pp. 13–16.
27. L. Trotsky, *From October to Brest-Litovsk*. See also L. Trotskii, *K istorii Oktyabr'skoi Revolyutsii*, which was published in 1918.
28. Voroshilov's submission to the Central Committee of 29 July–9 August 1927: RGASPI, f. 17, op. 2, d. 294, pp. 200–1.
29. Trotsky to Central Committee, December 1918: Trotsky Collection (HIA), box 4, folder 79, pp. 1–2.
30. RGASPI, f. 17, op. 109, d. 14, p. 20.
31. Politburo meeting, 20 April 1919, item 10; Trotsky Collection (HIA), box 9, folder 10.
32. Trotsky's written submission to the Central Committee meeting, 29 July– 9 August 1927: RGASPI, f. 17, op. 2, d. 294, p. 198.
33. Telegram to E. M. Sklyanskii for Lenin, 2 May 1919: RGASPI, f. 17, op. 109, d. 42, p. 30.
34. Politburo meeting, 7 May 1919, item 2: Trotsky Collection (HIA), box 9, folder 11; Trotsky to E. M. Sklyanskii, 7 May 1919: Trotsky Collection (HIA), box 4, folder 54.
35. Trotsky to E. M. Sklyanskii, 16 May 1919: Trotsky Collection (HIA), box 4, folder 56.
36. L. Trotskii, 'Sklyanskii pogib', *Pravda*, 29 August 1925; V. I. Lenin to E. M. Sklyanskii, 28 November 1917: Trotsky Collection (HIA), box 7, folder 1.
37. L. Trotskii, *Politicheskie siluety*, pp. 225–6.
38. L. Trotskii, *Moya zhizn'*, vol. 2, p. 252.
39. Trotsky's private notes for his report on 'Our Military Construction and Our Fronts', October 1919: RGASPI, f. 325, op. 1, d. 62, p. 14 *et seq.*
40. 'Glubokomyslie pustoslovie', *Izvestiya*, 24 July 1919.

## 25. Red Victory

1. E. Mawdsley, *The Russian Civil War*, pp. 148–9.
2. *The Trotsky Papers*, vol. 1, pp. 590 and 592.
3. *Ibid.*, p. 588.
4. *Ibid.*
5. *Ibid.*
6. *Ibid.*, pp. 596 and 598.
7. E. Mawdsley, *The Russian Civil War*, pp. 171–3.
8. Trotsky to V. I. Lenin by telephone, 6 August 1919: *The Trotsky Papers*, vol. 2, p. 628.
9. *Ibid.*, p. 630.
10. Politburo minute, 6 August 1919: *ibid.*, p. 636.

11. Trotsky to E. M. Sklyanskii for the Central Committee, 7 August 1919: *ibid.*, p. 642.
12. V. I. Lenin and L. B. Kamenev (for the Politburo) to Trotsky, 7 August 1919: *ibid.*, p. 640; L. B. Kamenev, E. D. Stasova and V. I. Lenin (for the Politburo), 9 August 1919: *ibid.*, p. 644.
13. Trotsky to E. M. Sklyanskii and V. I. Lenin, 6 August 1919: *ibid.*, p. 638.
14. Trotsky to E. M. Sklyanskii, 10 August 1919: *ibid.*, p. 648.
15. L. Trotskii, *Moya zhizn'*, vol. 2, pp. 154–5.
16. *Ibid.*, p. 155.
17. *Ibid.*
18. I. V. Stalin to V. I. Stalin, 30 May 1919: RGASPI, f. 558, op. 1, d. 627, p. 1.
19. Trotsky to Mrs Bedny and Y. M. Sverdlov, 8 September 1918: f. 17, op. 109, d. 14, p. 19.
20. L. D. Trotskii, working notes (1927): RGASPI, f. 325, op. 1, d. 365, p. 29. See D. Bednyi, 'Tan'ka-Van'ka', in D. Bednyi, *Sobranie sochinenii*, vol. 2, p. 314.
21. L. Trotskii, *Moya zhizn'*, vol. 2, pp. 160–1.
22. Conferment of the Order of Red Banner, 20 November 1919: TsGASA, f. 55, op. 1, d. 9.
23. E. Mawdsley, *The Russian Civil War*, pp. 200–1.

## 26. World Revolution

1. V. I. Lenin, *Polnoe sobranie sochinenii*, vol. 50, p. 186.
2. *Ibid.*
3. RGASPI, f. 17, op. 84, d. 1 (meeting held on 28 September 1918).
4. *Founding the Communist International: Proceedings and Documents of the First Congress, March 1919*, p. 88.
5. *Ibid.*, p. 89.
6. A. Ransome, *Russia in 1919*, p. 217.
7. *Ibid.*, p. 220.
8. S. I. Aralov to V. I. Lenin, 21 April 1919: RGASPI, f. 325, op. 1, d. 404, p. 91.
9. B. Kun to V. I. Lenin, 30(?) April 1919: RGASPI, f. 325, op. 109, d. 46, p. 2.
10. J. Vācietis and S. I. Aralov to V. P. Antonov-Ovseenko, copied to Lenin and Trotsky, 23 April 1918: RGASPI, f. 325, op. 109, d. 46, pp. 4–5; B. Kun to Moscow, 30(?) April 1919: RGASPI, f. 325, op. 109, d. 46, p. 2.
11. R. Service, *Comrades: Communism: A World History*, p. 88.
12. Letter to the Central Committee, 5 August 1919: RGASPI, f. 325, op. 1, d. 59, pp. 1–3.
13. RGASPI, f. 325, op. 1, d. 59, pp. 3–4.
14. Trotsky to the Central Committee, 5 August 1919: Trotsky Collection (HIA), box 4, folder 93, p. 2.
15. *The Communist International in Lenin's Time: Workers of the World and Oppressed Peoples Unite! Proceedings and Documents of the Second Congress, 1920*, p. 784.

16. *Ibid.*, pp. 785–9.
17. *Ibid.*, pp. 789–90.
18. *Ibid.*, pp. 791–2.

## 27. Images and the Life

1. See above, pp. 205–6.
2. A. A. Ioffe to Trotsky, 30 January 1919: RGVA, f. 33897, op. 3, d. 2, p. 1.
3. M. Latsis to the VCheka Special Department, 2 June 1920: RGVA, f. 33897, op. 3, d. 46, p. 319.
4. See L. D. Trotskii's comment in *Oktyabr'skaya Revolyutsiya*, p. 7 that he had written the work chiefly for 'foreign workers'.
5. W. Reswick, *I Dreamt Revolution*, pp. 78–9.
6. L. Bryant, *Mirrors of Moscow*, especially p. 140; M. Eastman, *Leon Trotsky: The Portrait of a Youth*; L. Eyre, *Russia Analysed*; A. Morizet, *Chez Lénine et Trotski. Moscou 1921*.
7. A. Morizet, *Chez Lénine et Trotski. Moscou 1921*, pp. viii–xi.
8. R. W. Clark, *The Life of Bertrand Russell*, p. 469.
9. H. G. Wells, *Russia in the Shadows*, p. 78.
10. *Ibid.*; B. Russell, *The Theory and Practice of Bolshevism*. See also B. Russell, *The Autobiography of Bertrand Russell, 1914–1944*, pp. 141–51.
11. R. H. Bruce Lockhart, *Memoirs of a British Agent*, p. 238.
12. L. Bryant, *Mirrors of Moscow*, p. 131.
13. M. Hoschiller, *Le Mirage du soviétisme*, p. 55.
14. G. Zinoviev, *Vladimir Il'ich Lenin*. See N. Tumarkin, *Lenin Lives!*, p. 84.
15. I. Stalin, 'Oktyabr'skii perevorot', *Pravda*, 6 November 1918.
16. Trotsky to V. I. Nevski, 5 August 1921: RGASPI, f. 325, op. 1, d. 17.
17. See for example Trotsky to M. Eastman, 23 May 1923: RGVA, f. 4, op. 14, d. 13s, p. 21.
18. A. Balabanoff, *Impressions of Lenin*, p. 128.
19. W. O'Rourke to Usick [*sic*], 24 August 1940: Trotsky Collection (HIA), box 24, folder 14.
20. V. Netrebskii, *Trotskii v Odesse*, p. 9.
21. R. MacNeal, *Bride of the Revolution: Krupskaya and Lenin*, chap. 7.
22. N. Sedova, autobiographical typescript begun on 24 December 1941: Trotsky Collection (HIA), box 27, folder 13, p. 12.
23. Draft order, December 1919: RGVA, f. 33897, op. 3, d. 120.
24. A. Ransome, *Russia in 1919*, p. 52.
25. N. I. Sedova, 'Otets i syn' (typescript: 8 June 1940), p. 12: Trotsky Collection, box 27, folder 11.
26. C. Sheridan, *From Mayfair to Moscow*, p. 78.
27. RGVA, f. 33897, op. 2, d. 113, p. 39.
28. RGVA, f. 33897, op. 2, d. 32, p. 247.
29. RGVA, f. 33897, op. 1, d. 450, p. 223.

30. N. Sedova's memoir in V. Serge and N. Sedova Trotsky, *The Life and Death of Leon Trotsky*, pp. 83–4.
31. A. Balabanoff, *Impressions of Lenin*, p. 133.
32. L. Trotskii, *Moya zhizn'*, vol. 2, p. 37.
33. *Ibid.*
34. *Ibid.*, pp. 27, 30, 34–6 and 47.
35. *Ibid.*, p. 75.
36. *New York Times*, 15 October 1921.
37. C. Sheridan, *From Mayfair to Moscow*, p. 129.
38. *Ibid.*, p. 140.
39. *Ibid.*
40. *Ibid.*
41. *Ibid.*, p. 148.
42. *Ibid.*, p. 138.

## 28. Peace and War

1. See above, p. 223.
2. Trotsky, *Terrorism and Communism*, p. 23.
3. See his notes in RGASPI, f. 325, op. 1, d. 67, p. 9.
4. Trotsky to L. L. Sedov, 7 March 1931: Nicolaevsky Collection (HIA), box 308, folder 87, p. 1.
5. Theses for report to the Yekaterinburg party organization, February–March 1920: RGASPI, f. 325, op. 1, d. 67, pp. 4–6.
6. 'Tezisy doklada L. D. Trotskogo', 10 March 1920 (Yekaterinburg): *ibid.*, pp. 4–6.
7. Untitled draft, March 1920, *ibid.*, pp. 9–10.
8. 'Trudovoe sorevnovanie', March 1920(?): *ibid.*, p. 37.
9. Theses for report to the Yekaterinburg party organization, February–March 1920: *ibid.*, pp. 6–7.
10. Notes in RGASPI: *ibid.*, p. 10.
11. 'Pochemu nuzhny oblastnye tsentry?': *ibid.*, pp. 27–8; 'Trudovoe sorevnovanie': *ibid.*, p. 37.
12. Trotsky's letter to unknown person, 25 February 1921: RGVA, f. 33987, op. 1, d. 439, p. 176; L. Trotskii, *Desyatyi s"ezd RKP(b)*, pp. 349–50.
13. J. Channon, 'Trotsky, the Peasants and Economic Policy: A Comment', *Economy and Society*, no. 4 (1985), pp. 513–23; F. Benvenuti, 'Il dibattito sui sindicati', in F. Gori (ed.), *Pensiero e azione di Lev Trockij*, pp. 262–3.
14. V. I. Lenin to Trotsky, 12 January 1920: RGASPI, f. 325, op. 1, d. 405, p. 10.
15. *Leninskii sbornik*, vol. 38, pp. 298 and 300; R. Service, *Lenin: A Political Life*, vol. 3, pp. 106–7.
16. *Leninskii sbornik*, vol. 38, pp. 298 and 300.
17. *Desyatyi s"ezd RKP(b)*, p. 199.
18. *Ibid.*, p. 157.

19. *Ibid.*, pp. 190 and 195.
20. N. Davies, *White Eagle, Red Star*, pp. 74–95.
21. *Ibid.*, pp. 100–1.
22. Letter to the Moscow Committee and the Petrograd Committee of the Russian Communist Party (Bolsheviks), 2 May 1920: Trotsky Collection (HIA), box 4, folder 42.
23. L. Trotskii, *Voina s Pol'shei*, pp. 6–9.
24. *Ibid.*, pp. 12–13.
25. *Ibid.*, p. 14.
26. L. Trotskii, *Rech' t. Trotskogo na massovom mitinge v gor. Gomele, 10 maya 1920 g.*, p. 15.
27. Trotsky to the RVS of the western front, 19 May 1920: RGVA, f. 33987, op. 3, 46, p. 260.
28. Trotsky to G. V. Chicherin (copied to Lenin, Kamenev, Krestinski and Bukharin), 4 June 1920: Trotsky Collection (HIA), box 4, folder 22, p. 1.
29. A. Balabanova to B. I. Nikolaevskii, 30 March 1957: Nicolaevsky Collection (HIA), box 292, folder 2.
30. Central Committee plenum, item 18, 16 July 1920: *ITsKKPSS*, no. 1 (1991), p. 122.
31. *The Communist International in Lenin's Time: Workers of the World and Oppressed Peoples, Unite! Proceedings and Documents of the Second Congress, 1920*, pp. 171–5.
32. V. I. Lenin's note to E. M. Sklyanskii, some day in August 1920 before the 26th: Trotsky Collection (HIA), box 7, folder 31.
33. Lenin to I. T. Smilga, copied to Radek, Dzerzhinski and the Polish Central Committee, 20 August 1920: *ibid.*, folder 58.
34. Lenin to V. P. Zatonskii, 19 August 1920: *ibid.*, folder 84.
35. V. I. Lenin's note to E. M. Sklyanskii, 17 or 18 August 1920: *ibid.*, folder 35.
36. See below, p. 478.
37. V. I. Lenin, *Polnoe sobranie sochinenii*, vol. 41, p. 458; and his political report to the Ninth Party Conference, RGASPI, f. 17, op. 1, d. 5, p. 346.
38. I. I. Kostyushko, *Pol'skoe byuro TsK RKP(b), 1920–1921 gg.*, pp. 21–2.
39. Trotsky's appeal to Red Army soldiers, 13 August 1920: RGVA, f. 33987, op. 3, d. 46, p. 724.
40. N. Davies, *White Eagle, Red Star*, pp. 211–20.

## 29. Back from the Brink

1. *Devyataya konferentsiya RKP(b)*, p. 26.
2. *Ibid.*, pp. 25–6.
3. *Ibid.*, p. 77.
4. *Ibid.*, p. 82.
5. Lenin to Trotsky, 10 October 1920: RGASPI, f. 325, op. 2, d. 473.
6. Central Committee plenum, 29 September 1920: RGASPI, f. 17, op. 2, d. 36, p. 3.

7. Politburo meeting, 1 September 1920: RGASPI, f. 17, op. 3, d. 106.

8. Central Committee plenum, 29 September 1920: RGASPI, f. 17, op. 2, d. 36, p. 3.

9. *Ibid.*

10. V. I. Lenin, *Polnoe sobranie sochinenii*, vol. 42, p. 235.

11. This remained Trotsky's belief in 1926 long after he had dropped other ingredients of his argument: Trotsky to A. V. Lunacharskii, 14 April 1926: Trotsky Collection (HIA), box 11, folder 56.

12. RGASPI, f. 17, op. 2, d. 45, item 5.

13. Central Committee plenum, 24 December 1920: RGASPI f. 17, op. 2, d. 48, items 2 and 5.

14. Central Committee plenum, 27 December 1920: RGASPI, f. 17, op. 2, d. 49, item 1; V. I. Lenin, *Polnoe sobranie sochinenii*, vol. 42, pp. 179 and 180–1.

15. RGASPI, f. 17, op. 3, d. 127, p. 1.

16. RGASPI, f. 17, op. 3, d. 128, item 2.

17. RGASPI, f. 17, op. 3, d. 131, p. 1.

18. V. I. Lenin, *Polnoe sobranie sochinenii*, vol. 42, p. 333.

19. RGASPI, f. 17., op. 3, d. 131, item 1.

20. *Ibid.*, p. 1.

21. Letter to unknown person, 25 February 1921: RGVA, f. 33987, op. 1, d. 439, p. 176.

22. Trotsky to Baltic Fleet command, 1 March 1921: RGASPI, f. 17, op. 109, d. 89, p. 11.

23. Trotsky's order, 5 March 1921, reproduced in V. Krasnov and V. Daines (eds), *Neizvestnyi Trotskii. Krasnyi Bonapart. Dokumenty, materially, razmyshleniya*, p. 339.

24. 5 March 1921: *ibid.*, pp. 340–1.

25. Trotsky to the Politburo, 10 March 1921: *ibid.*, p. 346.

26. See below for the subsequent public discussion, p. 403. In his autobiography he evaded the topic: see L. Trotskii, *Moya zhizn'*, vol. 2, chap. 38.

27. L. Bryant, 'Mutiny of Kronstadt Doomed', *Washington Times*, 16 March 1921.

28. *Desyatyi s"ezd RKP(b). Stenograficheskii otchët*, p. 402.

## 30. Disputing about Reform

1. Trotsky to A. V. Lunacharskii, 14 April 1926: Trotsky Collection (HIA), box 11, folder 56.

2. Materials for a report on the March Action, 9 April 1921: RGASPI, f. 325, op. 1, d. 86, p. 1; Trotsky's letter to V. I. Lenin, 3 July 1921: *ibid.*, p. 72.

3. Trotsky to V. I. Lenin: RGASPI, f. 325, op. 1, d. 406, pp. 73–4.

4. 'Martovskoe revolyutsionnoe dvizhenie v Germanii: zametki dlya sebya', 19 April 1921: RGASPI, f. 325, op. 1, d. 292, pp. 1–7.

5. Politburo meeting, 27 April 1921: RGASPI, f. 17, op. 3, d. 155, item 11.

6. *The Trotsky Papers*, vol. 2, pp. 480–2.

7. Exchange of messages, 28–29 March 1921: RGASPI, f. 325, op. 1, d. 408, p. 198.
8. W. Kopp to Trotsky, 7 April 1921: Trotsky (HIA), box 5, folder 64.
9. RGASPI, f. 17, op. 2, d. 59, p. 1; *Desyatyi s"ezd RKP. Mart 1921 g. Steno-grafcheskii otchët*, pp. 473 and 491.
10. GARF, f. 3316s, op. 2, d. 83, pp. 2–4.
11. RGASPI, f. 46, op. 1, d. 3, p. 16.
12. *Ibid.*, p. 18.
13. See especially the speeches of Vareikis, Chubar, Khramov and Pintsov: RGASPI, f. 46, op. 1, d. 2, pp. 118–19, 146, 158 and 174.
14. Tenth Party Conference: RGASPI, f. 46, op. 1, d. 2, p. 91.
15. RGASPI, f. 46, op. 1, d. 2, p. 124.
16. RGASPI, f. 46, op. 1, d. 3, pp. 16 and 18.
17. Theses on the NEP: RGASPI, f. 325, op. 1, d. 88, p. 4.
18. *Ibid.*, pp. 1–5.
19. Speech of 7 September 1921 to the Odessa City Soviet: *Petlya vmesto khleba*, pp. 9 and 11.
20. *Ibid.*, p. 10.
21. R. Service, *The Bolshevik Party in Revolution: A Study in Organisational Change*, pp. 176–7.
22. L. Trotskii, *Moya zhizn'*, vol. 2, pp. 214–15.
23. Trotsky to V. I. Lenin, 18 April 1922: RGASPI, f. 325, op. 1, d. 407, pp. 44–5.

## 31. The Politics of Illness

1. *ITsKKPSS*, no. 4 (1990), p. 189.
2. R. Service, *Lenin: A Political Life*, vol. 3, pp. 240–1.
3. *ITsKKPSS*, no. 4 (1990), pp. 191–3.
4. *Ibid.*, p. 194.
5. Trotsky to the Politburo: Trotsky Collection (HIA), box 5, folder 32.
6. Ya. Leibovits, 'Otkrytoe pis'mo L'vu Trotskomu', p. 1.
7. L. Chamberlain, *The Philosophy Steamer: Lenin and the Exile of the Intelligent-sia*, pp. 137–9.
8. *Izvestiya Tsentral'nogo Komiteta KPSS*, no. 4 (1991), pp. 187–8.
9. M. I. Ul'yanova, *Izvestiya Tsentral'nogo Komiteta KPSS*, no. 12 (1989).
10. *The Trotsky Papers*, vol. 2, p. 788.
11. L. Trotskii, *Moya zhizn'*, vol. 2, p. 216.
12. *Ibid.*, p. 217.
13. Trotsky to G. E. Zinoviev, 22 February 1923: RGVA, f. 4, op. 14, d. 13s, p. 17.
14. Trotsky to all Central Committee members, 20 January 1923: Trotsky Collection (HIA), box 5, folder 13, pp. 1–4.
15. L. Fotieva to L. B. Kamenev, 16 April 1923: Trotsky Collection (HIA), box 8, folder 47.

16. Trotsky to Central Committee, 16 April 1923: Trotsky Collection (HIA), box 5, folder 17.
17. Trotsky to Central Committee, 17 April 1923: Trotsky Collection (HIA), box 5, folder 18.
18. Trotsky to I. V. Stalin, 18 April 1923: Trotsky Collection (HIA), box 4, folder 74.
19. Trotsky to Central Committee, 28 March 1923: Trotsky Collection (HIA), box 5, folder 16.
20. *Dvenadtsatyi s"ezd RKP(b)*, pp. 479–95.

## 32. The Left Opposition

1. Trotsky to D. F. Sverchkov, 31 July 1923: RGASPI, f. 325, op. 1, d. 457, pp. 1–2.
2. Trotsky to Central Committee, 15 June 1923: Trotsky Collection (HIA), box 5, folder 19.
3. *Izvestiya Tsentral'nogo Komiteta KPSS*, no. 4 (1991), pp. 179–91.
4. R. V. Daniels, *The Conscience of the Revolution. Communist Opposition in Soviet Russia*, pp. 196–9.
5. *Izvestiya Tsentral'nogo Komiteta KPSS*, no. 4 (1991), pp. 179–91.
6. 4 July 1923: RGASPI, f. 17, op. 2, d. 100, pp. 2–3.
7. G. Sokolnikov at Politburo meeting, 26 October and 2 November 1925: *Stenogrammy zasedanii Politbyuro TsK RKP(b)-VKP(b), 1923–1938 gg.*, vol. 1, p. 359.
8. Trotsky, draft article, 29 June 1923: RGVA, f. 4, op. 14, d. 13s, pp. 56–61; Trotsky at Central Committee plenum, 23 September 1923: RGASPI, f. 17, op. 2, d. 101, p. 11.
9. Zinoviev read out the letter at the joint plenum of the Central Committee and the Central Control Commission, 5 August 1927: RGASPI, f. 17, op. 2, d. 317 (V-iii), p. 22.
10. Stalin's speech to the joint plenum of the Central Committee and the Central Control Commission of 29 July–9 August 1927: RGASPI, f. 17, op. 2, d. 304, pp. 99–101.
11. Zinoviev's speech (confidential printed version) to the joint plenum of the Central Committee and the Central Control Commission of 29 July–9 August 1927: RGASPI, f. 17, op. 2, d. 317 (V-iii), p. 22.
12. Central Committee plenum, 25 September 1923: RGASPI, f. 17, op. 2, d. 103, items 2 and 3.
13. *Sotsialisticheskii vestnik* (Berlin), 28 May 1924.
14. R. Service, *The Bolshevik Party in Revolution: A Study in Organisational Change*, pp. 198–9.
15. Central Committee and Central Control Commission joint meeting, 26 October 1923: RGASPI, f. 17, op. 2, d. 104, p. 26.
16. *Ibid.*, pp. 39, 39b and 40.

17. *Ibid.*, pp. 40b, 41 and 43b.
18. *Ibid.*, p. 42.
19. *Ibid.*, p. 43.
20. *Ibid.*, p. 43b.
21. *Ibid.*, p. 75.
22. 'Novyi kurs', *Pravda*, 8 December 1923.
23. *Ibid.*
24. G. Rosenthal, *Avocat de Trotsky*, p. 74.
25. Trotsky to N. K. Krupskaya, 16 November 1923: RGVA, f. 4, op. 14s, d. 17s, p. 290.
26. A. Belenkii to N. Lakoba, 6 January 1924: Nestor Lakoba Papers (HIA), box 2.
27. I. V. Stalin at the Central Committee plenum, 14–15 January 1924: RGASPI, f. 17, op. 2, d. 107, pp. 14–17.
28. I. V. Stalin at the same plenum: *Ibid.*, pp. 94–6.
29. See the list of delegates in *Trinadtsataya konferentsiya RKP(b): byulleten'*.
30. RGASPI, f. 17, op. 2, d. 107, pp. 93–101 and 151–6.
31. *Ibid.*, pp. 100–1.
32. R. Service, *The Bolshevik Party in Revolution: A Study in Organisational Change*, p. 193.
33. L. Trotskii, *Moya zhizn'*, vol. 2, pp. 249–50.
34. Central Committee plenum, 22 January 1924, item 1/7: RGASPI, f. 17, op. 2, d. 110, p. 1; RGVA, f. 33987, op. 3, d. 80, p. 587.
35. Trotsky to C. Malamuth, 21 October 1939: Trotsky Collection (HIA), box 11, folder 60.
36. S. Ordzhonikidze to N. Lakoba, 18 January 1924, Nestor Lakoba Papers (HIA), box 2; F. Dzerzhinski to N. Lakoba, 18 January 1924: *ibid.*; E. A. Kvantaliani, Chairman of the Georgia Cheka, to N. Lakoba, 27 January 1924: *ibid.*
37. RGASPI, f. 17, op. 2, d. 111, p. 1.
38. *Ibid.*
39. *Ibid.*, p. 2.
40. RGASPI, f. 17, op. 2, d. 113, p. 1.

## 33. On the Cultural Front

1. M. Eastman, *Love and Revolution: My Journey through an Epoch*, p. 333.
2. L. Trotskii, *Literatura i revolyutsiya*, p. 190.
3. V. I. Lenin, *Polnoe sobranie sochinenii*, vol. 45, pp. 390–7; L. Trotskii, *Literatura i revolyutsiya*, p. 142.
4. L. Trotskii, *Voprosy byta: epokha, 'kult'turnichestva' i eë zadachi* (3rd edition), p. 3.
5. *Ibid.*, pp. 7, 32–3, 43, 47–8, 51, 54 and 74.
6. L. Trotskii, *Literatura i revolyutsiya*, p. 5.

7. *Vserossiiskaya konferentsiya R.K.P. (bol'shevikov). 4–7 avgusta 1922 g. Byulleten'*, bulletin no. 3, pp. 80 and 82.

8. Letter to L. B. Kamenev, probably 1922: RGASPI, f. 325, op. 1, d. 450, pp. 2a/b.

9. See above, pp. 307–9.

10. Letters to A. K. Voronski, 10 and 11 September 1922: RGASPI, f. 325, op. 1, d. 450, pp. 3 and 4.

11. Trotsky to A. Gramsci, 30 August 1922: RGVA, f. 4, op. 14, d. 13s, p. 154.

12. V. I. Lenin, *Polnoe sobranie sochinenii*, vol. 45, pp. 363–4.

13. RGASPI, f. 325, op. 1, d. 449, pp. 1 and 2–4.

14. Letter to *Krokodil*, 7 June 1923: RGASPI, f. 325, op. 1, d. 456, p. 1.

15. *Ibid.*, d. 338.

16. F. K. Sologub to Trotsky, 28 September 1920; Trotsky to F. K. Sologub, 30 September 1920: GARF, f. 3430s, op. 1s, d. 19, pp. 1 and 2. See also Trotsky to F. K. Sologub, 4 October 1911: RGASPI, f. 325, op. 1, d. 599, p. 1.

17. V. Ya. Bryusov to Trotsky, 6 April 1922: RGVA, f. 33987, op. 3, d. 2, pp. 70–1.

18. Ye. Trifonov to Trotsky, RGVA, f. 4, op. 14, d. 13s, p. 225.

19. L. Trotskii, *Literatura i revolyutsiya*, pp. 86 and 233.

20. *Ibid.*, p. 36.

21. *Ibid.*, pp. 140–3 and 151–2.

22. *Ibid.*, pp. 157–8.

23. Trotsky to the Politburo, Presidium of the CCC and Executive Committee of Comintern, 6 September 1927: Trotsky Collection (HIA), box 12, folder 42, p. 9.

24. Only when Bedny took Stalin's side against the Opposition did Trotsky issue a negative verdict on his literary qualities: working notes of 1927 in RGASPI, f. 325, op. 1, d. 365, p. 29.

25. A. Andreev and Trotsky at Politburo meeting, 3 June 1926: *Stenogrammy zasedanii Politbyuro TsK RKP(b)-VKP(b), 1923–1938 gg.*, vol. 1, p. 778.

26. Yu. V. Got'e, *Moi zametki*, p. 132. The author, the library's director, was the person who received Natalya Sedova.

27. L. Trotskii, *Delo bylo v Ispanii (po zapisnoi knizhke)*.

28. *Ibid.*, p. 5.

29. L. Trotskii, *O Lenine: materialy dlya biografa*, pp. 10–11.

30. *Ibid.*, p. 66.

31. L. Trotskii, *Voprosy byta: epokha 'kult'turnichestva' i eë zadachi* (3rd edition), p. 3. The first preface was dated 4 July 1923, the second 9 September 1923.

32. N. Bukharin, *K voprosu o trotskizme*.

33. Ian Thatcher gives the outstanding discussion of this textual revision in *Leon Trotsky and World War One: August 1914–February 1917*, pp. 73–5.

34. L. Trotskii, *Stalinskaya shkola fal'tsifikatsii*.

35. L. Trotskii, *O Lenine: materialy dlya biografa*: see especially, p. vii.

## 34. Failing to Succeed

1. *Zarya Vostoka*, 12 April 1924.
2. L. Trotskii, *Na putyakh k evropeiskoi revolyutsii. (Rech' v Tiflise, 11 aprelya 1924)*, p. 3.
3. *Zarya Vostoka*, 12 April 1924.
4. RGASPI, f. 52, op. 1, d. 57, pp. 112, 122 and 183–4.
5. *Ibid.*, p. 186.
6. *Trinadtsatyi s"ezd RKP(b). Mai 1924 goda. Stenograficheskii otchët*, p. 754.
7. *Ibid.*, pp. 146–56.
8. *Ibid.*, p. 158.
9. See below, pp. 437–8.
10. See below, p. 392.
11. See below, p. 365.
12. L. Trotskii, *Sochineniya*, vol. 3, part 1: *1917: Ot fevralya do oktyabrya*, pp. ix–lxviii.
13. L. Trotskii, *Uroki Oktyabrya*, chap. 1.
14. *Ibid.*, chaps 4–5.
15. *Ibid.*, chaps 6–7.
16. *Ibid.*, chap. 8.
17. M. Eastman, *Love and Revolution: My Journey through an Epoch*, p. 414.
18. Politburo and Central Control Commission Presidium, 8 September 1927: RGASPI, f. 17, op. 163, d. 705.
19. Even so, the leaders of province-level party committees were given confidential copies in the 1920s: see R. Service, 'The Way They Talked Then: The Discourse of Politics in the Soviet Party Politburo in the Late 1920s', in P. Gregory and N. Naimark (eds), *The Lost Politburo Transcripts*.
20. Trotsky to Mikhail Glazman, 26 December 1924: Trotsky Collection (HIA), box 4, folder 25.
21. L. Trotskii, *Moya zhizn'*, vol. 2, p. 261.
22. See above, p. 309.
23. L. Trotskii, *Moya zhizn'*, vol. 2, p. 261.
24. Trotsky to N. I. Bukharin, 'K voprosu o 'samokritike', 8 January 1926: Trotsky Collection (HIA), box 9, folder 47, pp. 1–4.
25. Trotsky's 1935 diary in L. Trotskii, *Dnevniki i pis'ma*, p. 77.
26. Trotsky to the Chinese Left Opposition, 5 August 1931, p. 1: Trotsky Collection (HIA), box 11, folder 31.
27. Trotsky to N. I. Bukharin, 'K voprosu o 'samokritike', 8 January 1926: Trotsky Collection (HIA), box 9, folder 47, pp. 1–4.
28. See above, pp. 234–5.

## 35. Entourage and Faction

1. R. Service, *Lenin: A Biography*, p. 330.
2. C. Sheridan, *From Mayfair to Moscow*, pp. 136–7.
3. L. Trotskii, *Politicheskie siluety*, p. 224.
4. L. Trotskii, 'Sklyanskii pogib', *Pravda*, 29 August 1925.
5. Trotsky to M. Eastman, February 1923: RGASPI, f. 325, op. 1, d. 18.
6. M. Eastman, *Love and Revolution: My Journey through an Epoch*, p. 402. Eastman disowned the US edition of *Leon Trotsky: The Portrait of a Youth*, published in 1925, because of the poor proof-reading and wanted the British edition to be regarded as authoritative.
7. M. Eastman, *Love and Revolution: My Journey through an Epoch*, p. 443.
8. *Ibid.*, pp. 446–7.
9. *Ibid.*, p. 443.
10. Trotsky to N. I. Muralov, 11 September 1928: Trotsky Collection (HIA), box 11, folder 65; M. Eastman, *Love and Revolution: My Journey through an Epoch*, p. 512.
11. M. Eastman, *Great Companions: Critical Memoirs of Some Famous Friends*, p. 123.
12. M. Eastman, *Love and Revolution: My Journey through an Epoch*, p. 352.
13. See below, p. 372.
14. See above, p. 225.
15. See above, pp. 45–6.
16. *Kak lomali NEP*, vol. 4 (joint plenum of the Central Committee and the Central Control Commission, 16–23 April 1929), p. 246.
17. Politburo meeting, 8 September 1927: *Stenogrammy zasedanii Politbyuro TsK RKP(b)-VKP(b), 1923–1938 gg.*, vol. 2, p. 597.
18. M. Eastman, *Great Companions: Critical Memoirs of Some Famous Friends*, p. 113.
19. V. Serge and N. Sedova, *The Life and Death of Leon Trotsky*, p. 121.
20. On Olga Kameneva see above, p. 264.
21. E. A. Preobrazhenski to Trotsky, n.d.: Trotsky Collection (HIA), box 12, folder 4, p. 3.
22. L. Trotskii, *Portrety revolyutsionerov*, pp. 334–43.
23. *Ibid.*
24. M. Eastman, *Love and Revolution: My Journey through an Epoch*, p. 425.
25. M. Eastman, *Since Lenin Died*, pp. 93–4.
26. See *Stenogrammy zasedanii Politbyuro TsK RKP(b)-VKP(b), 1923–1938 gg.*
27. Politburo meeting, 3 June 1926: *Ibid.*, vol. 1, p. 778.

## 36. Living with Trotsky

1. M. Eastman, *Leon Trotsky: The Portrait of a Youth* (London edn), p. 196.
2. R. Service, *Stalin: A Biography*, p. 233.
3. N. Ioffe, *Moi otets Adol'f Abramovich Ioffe: vospominaniya, dokumenty i materialy*, p. 38.
4. A. I. Boyarchikov, *Vospominaniya*, pp. 149–50.
5. *Ibid.*, pp. 150–1.
6. See above, p. 289.
7. M. Eastman, *Love and Revolution: My Journey through an Epoch*, p. 409.
8. G. A. Ziv, *Trotskii: kharakteristika. (Po lichnym vospominaniyam)*, p. 33.
9. *Ibid.*
10. C. Sheridan, *From Mayfair to Moscow*, p. 144. They spoke in French: 'Je tombe toujours en avant.'
11. *Punch*, 21 January 1920.
12. N. Sedova, 'A Page to the Diary', Coyoacán, July 1958: Trotsky Collection (HIA), box 27, folder 19, p. 2 (in Russian).
13. N. Sedova, 'Devochki', p. 4: Trotsky Collection (HIA), box 27, folder 13.
14. *Ibid.*
15. *Ibid.*, p. 5.
16. *Ibid.*
17. M. Shachtman, 'Natalya Ivanovna Sedoff (Sedova)', p. 7: Albert Glotzer Papers (HIA), box 27.
18. *Ibid.*, p. 8.
19. Trotsky's remark to Max Eastman, *Leon Trotsky: The Portrait of a Youth*, p. 49.
20. Trotsky's 1935 diary in L. Trotskii, *Dnevniki i pis'ma*, p. 91.
21. Trotsky's remark to Max Eastman, *Leon Trotsky: The Portrait of a Youth*, p. 49.
22. Trotsky's 1935 diary in L. Trotskii, *Dnevniki i pis'ma*, p. 91.
23. Testimony of Yulia Axelrod, Sergei's daughter, who learned about this from her mother: Yulia Akselrod, untitled memoir (n.d.), no. 3, p. 21: Yulia Akselrod Papers (HIA). See also her commentary on Sergei's diary in Yulia Akselrod Papers (HIA), p. 40; and P. Broué, *Léon Sedov, fils de Trotsky, victime de Staline*, p. 32.
24. She told this to Max Shachtman: see his 'Natalia Ivanovna Sedoff (Sedova)', p. 4: Albert Glotzer Papers (HIA), box 27.
25. *Ibid.*, p. 7.
26. N. Sedova, draft article 'Vinovnost' Stalina', 18 April 1942: Albert Glotzer Papers (HIA), box 16, p. 2.
27. *Ibid.*
28. Trotsky's 1935 diary in L. Trotskii, *Dnevniki i pis'ma*, pp. 72–3.
29. *Ibid.*, p. 94.
30. *Ibid.*, p. 110.

## 37. What Trotsky Wanted

1. The scholars who first pointed this out were R. B. Day, A. Nove and R. W. Davies.
2. Politburo meeting, 10 December 1925: *Stenogrammy zasedanii Politbyuro TsK RKP(b)-VKP(b), 1923–1938 gg.*, vol. 1, pp. 458, 463 and 464; Politburo meeting, 5 July 1926, *ibid.*, vol. 2, pp. 225–7.
3. Politburo meeting, 28 June 1926: *ibid.*, vol. 2, pp. 162–3.
4. Politburo meeting, 5 July 1926: *ibid.*, p. 244.
5. Politburo meeting, 28 June 1926, *ibid.*, p. 160.
6. L. Trotskii, *K sotsializmu ili kapitalizmu? Planovoe khozyaistvo Gosplan SSSR*, pp. 1–61. Published also in *Pravda* and *Izvestiya*, 1–22 September 1925.
7. *Kak lomali NEP. Stenogrammy plenumov TsK VKP(b), 1928–1929*, vol. 4, p. 607 (Declaration of Bukharin, Rykov, Tomski, 9 February).
8. Politburo meeting, 25 February 1926: *Stenogrammy zasedanii Politbyuro TsK RKP(b)-VKP(b), 1923–1938 gg.*, vol. 1, p. 616.
9. Politburo meeting, 2 August 1926: *ibid.*, vol. 2, pp. 326–7.
10. Politburo meeting, 25 February 1926: *Ibid.*, vol. 1, p. 640. See also pp. 638–9.
11. 'Popravka tov. Trotskogo k proektu rezolyutsii t. Rykova o khozyaistvennom razvitii SSSR', 12 April 1926: Trotsky Collection (HIA), box 15, folder 15, pp. 1–5.
12. See above, p. 285.
13. Politburo meeting, 14 June 1926: *Stenogrammy zasedanii Politbyuro TsK RKP(b)-VKP(b), 1923–1938 gg.*, vol. 2, p. 109.
14. *Ibid.*, pp. 109–10.
15. *Ibid.*, p. 110.
16. 'Zametki na natsional'nom voprose', 5 May 1927: RGASPI, f. 325, op. 1, d. 157, pp. 4–5.
17. See above, p. 306.
18. G. Rosenthal, *Avocat de Trotsky*, p. 74.
19. Zinoviev's speech (confidential printed version) to the joint plenum of the Central Committee and the Central Control Commission of 29 July–9 August 1927: RGASPI, f. 17, op. 2, d. 317 (V-iii), p. 22.
20. Trotsky Collection (HIA), box 12, folder 4, letter 1 (n.d.), p. 1.

## 38. Last Stand in Moscow

1. RGASPI, f. 17, op. 2, d. 292, p. 108.
2. RGASPI, f. 17, op. 2, d. 290, pp. 279–80.
3. RGASPI, f. 17, op. 2, d. 291, p. 50.
4. *Ibid.*, pp. 51–2.
5. RGASPI, f. 17, op. 2, d. 293, p. 175; RGASPI, f. 17, op. 2, d. 304, pp. 99 and 100–1.

6. RGASPI, f. 17, op. 2, d. 306, pp. 79–85.
7. RGASPI, f. 17, op. 2, d. 293, p. 155.
8. RGASP, f. 17, op. 2, d. 294, pp. 198–9.
9. RGASPI, f. 17, op. 2, d. 317 (V-iii), p. 69.
10. *Ibid.*, pp. 6 and 8.
11. *Ibid.*, p. 97.
12. Politburo meeting, 8 and 11 October 1926: *Stenogrammy zasedanii Politbyuro TsK RKP(b)-VKP(b), 1923–1938 gg.*, vol. 2, p. 361 (complaint by A. A. Solts).
13. RGASPI, f. 17, op. 2, d. 293, p. 175.
14. *Ibid.*
15. *Ibid.*, p. 170.
16. RGASPI, f. 17, op. 2, d. 317 (V-ii), p. 47 lists him as present during the session but does not record him as having intervened in the debate.
17. RGASPI, f. 17, op. 2, d. 317 (V-iii), p. 8.
18. Trotsky to N. I. Bukharin, 'K voprosu o 'samokritike', 8 January 1926: Trotsky Collection (HIA), box 9, folder 47, pp. 1–4.
19. Politburo meeting, 8 September 1927: *Stenogrammy zasedanii Politbyuro TsK RKP(b)-VKP(b), 1923–1938 gg.*, vol. 2, p. 594.
20. Trotsky's 1935 diary in L. Trotskii, *Dnevniki i pis'ma*, p. 97; N. S. Sedova to S. Weber, 14 July 1935: Trotsky Collection (HIA), box 26, folder 32, p. 2.
21. Politburo meeting, 8 September 1927: *Stenogrammy zasedanii Politbyuro TsK RKP(b)-VKP(b), 1923–1938 gg.*, vol. 2, p. 596.
22. A. A. Ioffe to Trotsky, 27 August 1927 in N. Ioffe, *Moi otets Adol'f Abramovich Ioffe: vospominaniya, dokumenty i materialy*, p. 100.
23. RGASPI, f. 325, op. 1, d. 170, pp. 1–2, 4 and 7.
24. *Ibid.*, p. 11.
25. G. Rosenthal, *Avocat de Trotsky*, p. 22.
26. L. Trotskii, *Moya zhizn'*, vol. 2, p. 278.
27. G. Rosenthal, *Avocat de Trotsky*, p. 26. Rosenthal did not explain how he came to know Bukharin's exact words. Presumably they were passed on by Trotsky; they were published forty-eight years after the event. Pierre Naville, another witness of the phone call, recorded Bukharin's words only slightly differently: 'It's not possible to have you expelled from the party!': *Trotsky vivant*, p. 18. But according to Naville, it was Trotsky who said that the Kremlin leaders had lost their heads.
28. 'Zhazhda vlasti' (draft: n.d. but certainly after the publication of *The Revolution Betrayed*): Nicolaevsky Collection (HIA), box 354, folder 37, pp. 2–3.
29. P. Naville, *Trotsky vivant*, p. 56.
30. Politburo meeting, 8 September 1927: *Stenogrammy zasedanii Politbyuro TsK RKP(b)-VKP(b), 1923–1938 gg.*, vol. 2, pp. 366–7.
31. Letter to A. Enukidze, 15 November 1927: Trotsky Collection (HIA), box 12, folder 39.
32. P. Naville, *Trotsky vivant*, p. 56.
33. Letter to A. Enukidze, 15 November 1927: Trotsky Collection (HIA), box 12, folder 39.

34. RGASPI, f. 325, op. 1, d. 479, p. 1.
35. L. Trotskii, *Moya zhizn'*, vol. 2, p. 283.
36. RGASPI, f. 325, op. 1, d. 479, pp. 3–4.
37. G. Rosenthal, *Avocat de Trotsky*, p. 30.

## 39. Alma-Ata

1. PA TurFIL, f. 1, op. 3, d. 59, p. 77. I am grateful to Tanya Okunskaya for sharing with me a copy of this document.
2. Diary notes of L. L. Sedov on the journey to Alma-Ata (typescript): Nicolaevsky Collection (HIA), box 303, folder 3, p. 1.
3. N. Sedova, fragmentary draft addendum to 'Tak eto bylo' (apparently November 1940): Trotsky Collection (HIA), box 27, folder 12.
4. N. Sedova's memoir as reproduced in L. Trotsky, *Moya zhizn'*, vol. 2, pp. 285–6.
5. A. I. Boyarchikov, *Vospominaniya*, pp. 135–6.
6. N. Sedova's memoir as reproduced in L. Trotsky, *Moya zhizn'*, vol. 2, p. 286.
7. Trotsky's 1935 diary in L. Trotskii, *Dnevniki i pis'ma*, p. 93.
8. N. Sedova's memoir as reproduced in L. Trotsky, *Moya zhizn'*, vol. 2, p. 286.
9. Diary notes of L. L. Sedov on the journey to Alma-Ata (typescript): Nicolaevsky Collection (HIA), box 303, folder 3, p. 2.
10. A. I. Boyarchikov, *Vospominaniya*, pp. 135–6.
11. Trotsky's 1935 diary in L. Trotskii, *Dnevniki i pis'ma*, p. 93.
12. A. I. Boyarchikov, *Vospominaniya*, pp. 137–8.
13. Diary notes of L. L. Sedov on the journey to Alma-Ata (typescript): Nicolaevsky Collection (HIA), box 303, folder 3, pp. 4–6.
14. *Ibid.*, pp. 6–7.
15. *Ibid.*, p. 7.
16. *Kak lomali NEP. Stenogrammy plenumov TsK VKP(b), 1928–1929*, vol. 2, pp. 268, 358–9, 395, 439, 620 and 629.
17. Diary notes of L. L. Sedov on the journey to Alma-Ata (typescript): Nicolaevsky Collection (HIA), box 303, folder 3, pp. 6–7.
18. N. Sedova to J. Hansen, 11 November 1940: Joseph Hansen Papers (HIA), box 33, folder 14.
19. L. Trotsky, *Moya zhizn'*, vol. 2, pp. 295–7.
20. Nicolaevsky Collection (HIA), box 355, folder 26.
21. K. G. Rakovskii to Trotsky, 17 February 1928: Nicolaevsky Collection, box 356, folder 7, p. 5; 'Rakovskii, Khr. Georg.', *ibid.*
22. See above, note 1.
23. RGASPI, f. 325, op. 1, d. 481, p. 8. See also N. I. Sedova in V. Serge and N. Sedova Trotsky, *The Life and Death of Leon Trotsky*, pp. 159–60.
24. S. L. Sedov and A. Sedova to L. L. Sedov, 17 March 1928: Trotsky Papers (HL), T1222.

25. Trotsky to D. Rivera, 7 June 1933: Nicolaevsky Collection (HIA), box 308, folder 72.

26. L. D. Trotskii, *Chto i kak proizoshlo? Shest' statei dlya mirovoi burzhuaznoi pechati*, p. 12. This episode does not appear in *Moya zhizn'*.

27. L. Trotsky, *Moya zhizn'*, vol. 2, pp. 295–7.

28. N. Sedova, 'Devochki', memoir written in 1941 or 1942: Trotsky Collection (HIA), box 27, folder 13, p. 1.

29. Trotsky to A. G. Beloborodov, 17 March 1928: Albert Glotzer Papers (HIA), box 1.

30. E. A. Preobrazhenski to Trotsky, n.d.: Trotsky Collection (HIA), box 12, folder 4, p. 3.

31. *Kak lomali NEP. Stenogrammy plenumov TsK VKP(b), 1928–1929*, vol. 5, pp. 620–2.

32. *Ibid.*, vol. 4, p. 696 (Zinoviev's notes on Kamenev's record of his conversation with Bukharin in July 1928).

33. *Ibid.*, vol. 5, p. 620.

34. Trotsky to fellow oppositionists in exile, 1 October 1928: RGASPI, f. 325, op. 1, d. 481, p. 96.

35. This letter was drafted in invisible ink and addressed to the central leaderships of the party and Comintern; it was written into a copy of the diary of the poet Alexander Blok: *Dnevnik Al. Bloka*, pp. 121, 125 and 135. Whether it was subsequently distributed is unknown. This copy is held at the Hoover Institution Archive.

36. *Kak lomali NEP. Stenogrammy plenumov TsK VKP(b), 1928–1929*, vol. 4 (joint plenum of the Central Committee and the Central Control Commission, 16–23 April 1929), pp. 316 (Rykov), 405 (Molotov), 717 (endnote 265).

37. Ordzhonikidze at the Central Control Commission, 23 October 1930: *Stenogrammy zasedanii Politbyuro TsK RKP(b)-VKP(b), 1923–1938 gg.*, vol. 3, p. 242.

38. L. D. Trotskii, *Chto i kak proizoshlo? Shest' statei dlya mirovoi burzhuaznoi pechati*, pp. 17 and 19. This booklet offers a slightly fuller account of the expulsion than the one provided in Trotsky's full autobiography.

39. L. Trotskii, *Moya zhizn'*, vol. 2, p. 315.

40. L. D. Trotskii, *Chto i kak proizoshlo? shest' statei dlya mirovoi burzhuaznoi pechati*, p. 21.

41. *Ibid.*, pp. 8–9.

## 40. Büyükada

1. Ö. S. Coşar, *Troçki Istanbul'da*, pp. 14–33. I am grateful to Harun Yılmaz for supplying me with the contents of this book. On the Sedov pseudonym see the Soviet consul-general's statement: Nicolaevsky Collection (HIA), box 303, folder 1.

2. Ö. S. Coşar, *Troçki Istanbul'da*, pp. 62–6.

3. L. L. Sedov to 'Tenzov', May/June 1930: Nicolaevsky Collection (HIA), box 368, folder 29; Trotsky to L. L. Sedov, 7 April 1931: Nicolaevsky Collection (HIA), box 308, folder 87.
4. N. Sedova in V. Serge and N. Sedova Trotsky, *The Life and Death of Leon Trotsky*, p. 163.
5. M. Eastman, *Great Companions: Critical Memoirs of Some Famous Friends*, p. 116.
6. G. Rosenthal, *Avocat de Trotsky*, p. 95.
7. *Ibid.*, p. 72.
8. M. Eastman, *Great Companions: Critical Memoirs of Some Famous Friends*, p. 117.
9. Trotsky's 1935 diary in L. Trotskii, *Dnevniki i pis'ma*, p. 74.
10. Trotsky to S. Kharin (Paris), 29 May 1929: Nicolaevsky Collection (HIA), box 307, folder 56.
11. Trotsky to L. L. Sedov, May 1929: Nicolaevsky Collection (HIA), box 312, folder 4.
12. *Byulleten' oppozitsii*, no. 1/2 (July 1929), pp. 6–8.
13. A. Glotzer, *Trotsky: Memoir and Critique*, p. 35.
14. *Ibid.*, p. 48.
15. G. Rosenthal, *Avocat de Trotsky*, pp. 72–3.
16. S. Weber, 'Recollections of Trotsky', *Modern Occasions*, spring 1972, p. 181.
17. A. Glotzer, *Trotsky: Memoir and Critique*, p. 84.
18. *Ibid.*, p. 52.
19. G. Rosenthal, *Avocat de Trotsky*, p. 96.
20. L. L. Sedov to the OGPU Collegium, 14 August 1929: GARF, f. 3316s, op. 2, d. 83.
21. J. van Heijenoort, *With Trotsky in Exile: From Prinkipo to Coyoacán*, p. 7.
22. Trotsky to L. L. Sedov, 11 June 1931: Nicolaevsky Collection (HIA), box 309, folder 22, p. 2.
23. P. Broué, *Léon Sedov, fils de Trotsky, victime de Staline*, p. 90.
24. Nicolaevsky Collection (HIA), box 309, folder 2.
25. *Ibid.*
26. Nicolaevsky Collection (HIA), box 306, folders 70–5 and 93–4. One of Sergei's telegrams ran as follows: 'vse zederowi rabotain poslal pisma krepka zeluiu sergoz'. This quasi-Russian gibberish means something like the following: 'All are well. I'm working. I've sent letters. Big kiss. Sergei.'
27. *Ibid.*, folder 94.
28. Nicolaevsky Collection (HIA), box 311, folders 41 and 45.
29. N. Sedova, 'Devochki', memoir written in 1941 or 1942: Trotsky Collection (HIA), box 27, folder 13, p. 5.
30. *Ibid.*
31. *Ibid.*
32. *Ibid.*
33. *Ibid.*, p. 7.
34. *Ibid.*, p. 6.

35. Trotsky to Yelena Krylenko and Max Eastman, 3 March 1931: Nicolaevsky Collection (HIA), box 307, folder 61, p. 1.
36. A. Glotzer, *Trotsky: Memoir and Critique*, pp. 34–5.
37. *Ibid.*, pp. 37–9.
38. *Ibid.*, p. 37.
39. *Ibid.*, p. 60.
40. Y. Craipeau, *Mémoires d'un dinosaure trotskyste: secrétaire de Trotsky en 1933*, pp. 97–8.
41. N. Sedova, 'Devochki', memoir written in 1941 or 1942: Trotsky Collection (HIA), box 27, folder 13, p. 6.
42. Trotsky to L. L. Sedov, undated [?1932]: Nicolaevsky Collection (HIA), box 309, folder 87.
43. Trotsky to L. L. Sedov, 22 December 1932: Nicolaevsky Collection (HIA), box 310, folder 54, pp. 1–4.
44. Trotsky to L. L. Sedov, January 1933: Nicolaevsky Collection (HIA), box 310, folder 58.
45. Trotsky to A. L. Bronstein, 8 January 1933, reproduced in V. Krasnov and V. Daynes (eds), *Neizvestnyi Trotskii. Krasnyi Bonapart: Dokumenty, mneniya, razmyshleniya*, pp. 497–8. Alexandra Bronstein repeated the letter from memory when talking with Nadezhda Ioffe in Kolyma in 1936: N. Ioffe, *Vremya nazad. Moya zhizn', moya sud'ba, moya epokha*, pp. 49–50.
46. A. L. Bronstein to Trotsky, 31 August 1933, pp. 1–3: bMS Russ 13.1 T12608, Trotsky Papers (HL). I must record that Isaac Deutscher's quotations from this poignant letter are inaccurate. For a full account of the many factual errors in his trilogy on Trotsky see J. van Heijenoort, *With Trotsky in Exile*, pp. 151–5.
47. *Ibid.*, pp. 4–6.

## 41. Looking for Revolutions

1. 'Zhalkii dokument', Nicolaevsky Collection (HIA), box 312, folder 4.
2. Draft of first circular letter [?1931]: *ibid.*, box 313, folder 17.
3. Trotsky to Executive Committee of the Leninbund, copied to *La Verité*, *Lutte des Classes*, *Le Communist*, the *Militant* and the National Committee of the Communist League (USA), 29 August 1929: Albert Glotzer Papers (HIA), box 1, p. 1.
4. *Ibid.*, p. 2. The English here is lumpy; I have reproduced the translation sent to the Communist League in the USA.
5. *Ibid.*, p. 1.
6. The introduction to the French edition is dated 1931: Nicolaevsky Collection (HIA), box 344, folder 39, pp. 1–2.
7. See above, p. 365.
8. Trotsky to A. Treint, 22 September 1931: Nicolaevsky Collection (HIA), box 311, folder 42, p. 1.

9. Trotsky to S. Kharin, April 1929: Nicolaevsky Collection (HIA), box 307, folder 50, pp. 1–2.
10. This was a letter he entrusted to Yakov Blyumkin, whom he met on Büyükada: *ibid.*, folder 10, pp. 1–2. See below, pp. 402–3.
11. Trotsky to L. L. Sedov, 5 May 1931: Nicolaevsky Collection (HIA), box 309, folder 5.
12. Trotsky to L. L. Sedov, 26 May 1932: Nicolaevsky Collection (HIA), box 310, folder 4.
13. R. Sobolevicius to Trotsky, 25 December 1931: Nicolaevsky (HIA), box 306, folder 81.
14. L. L. Sedov to A. Sobolevicius, 18 December 1932, and R. Sobolevicius, 16 December 1932: Nicolaevsky Collection (HIA), box 311, folders 32 and 40.
15. Trotsky to L. L. Sedov, 11 June 1931: Nicolaevsky Collection (HIA), box 309, folder 22, p. 2.
16. Trotsky to L. L. Sedov, 13 June 1931: Nicolaevsky Collection (HIA), folder 23.
17. 'Otkrytoe pis'mo chlenam VKP(b)', 23 March 1930: Nicolaevsky Collection (HIA), box 313, folder 29, p. 3.
18. *Ibid.*, p. 10.
19. Trotsky to L. L. Sedov, 3 September 1931: Nicolaevsky Collection (HIA), box 309, folder 53.
20. L. Trotskii, *Dnevniki i pis'ma*, p. 123.
21. Trotsky to L. L. Sedov, 23 June 1931: Nicolaevsky Collection (HIA), box 309, folder 27.
22. Trotsky to L. L. Sedov, 13 October 1931: *ibid.*, folder 60.
23. M. Buber-Neumann, *Von Potsdam nach Moskau*, p. 284
24. A. Swabeck, 'Report of Preliminary International Conference [of the] International Left Opposition (Bolshevik-Leninists), Held February 4 to 8, 1933', pp. 1–6: Arne Swabeck Papers (HIA), box 6, folder 20.
25. L. L. Sedov to Trotsky, 2 February 1933: Nicolaevsky Collection (HIA), box 306, folder 24.
26. P. Broué, *Léon Sedov, fils de Trotsky, victim de Staline*, p. 113.

## 42. The Writer

1. *Paris-Soir*, 16–17 June 1933.
2. L. L. Sedov to Trotsky, 13 December 1933: Nicolaevsky Collection (HIA), box 306, folder 54, p. 1.
3. Trotsky to the Sweden-based Russian journalist S. A. Tsion, 16 December 1933: Nicolaevsky Collection (HIA), box 13, folder 8.
4. Trotsky to Lev Sedov, 29 November 1936: Trotsky Papers (HL), T10183.
5. The sexologist Wilhelm Reich wanted to meet him but did not make the journey: L. L. Sedov to Trotsky, 13 December 1933: Nicolaevsky Collection (HIA), box 306, folder 54.

6. Trotsky to Diego Rivera, 7 June 1933: Nicolaevsky Collection (HIA), box 308, folder 72.

7. L. D. Trotskii, *Chto i kak proizoshlo? Shest' statei dlya mirovoi burzhuaznoi pechati.*

8. A. Glotzer, *Trotsky: Memoir and Critique*, p. 38.

9. See for example 'Avtobiograficheskie zametki' (written in Syzran in 1919): RGASPI, f. 325, op. 1, d. 14; Trotsky's letter-memoir to V. I. Nevski, 5 August 1921: *ibid.*, d. 17; his letter-memoir to M. Eastman, February 1923, *ibid.*, d. 18.

10. See Max Eastman's reports and advice to Trotsky: Nicolaevsky Collection (HIA), box 305, folder 35 (17 September 1934) and folder 36 (23 December 1934).

11. Draft chapters: Nicolaevsky Collection (HIA), boxes 332–43. See also N. S. Sedova to S. Weber, 12 November 1959: Trotsky Collection (HIA), box 27, folder 5.

12. S. Weber, 'Recollections of Trotsky', *Modern Occasions*, spring 1972, p. 182.

13. *Ibid.*; L. Trotskii, *Delo bylo v Ispanii*, p. 153: he read Edgar Allan Poe to improve his English.

14. *Moya zhizn'* draft: Nicolaevsky Collection (HIA) – see, for example, box 312, folders 36–9.

15. *Ibid.*, folder 39. Nonetheless he remembered his mother calling him Lëva (Russian) rather than Leiba (Yiddish).

16. L. Trotskii, *Moya zhizn'*, vol. 1, pp. 34–5.

17. *Ibid.*

18. L. Trotsky, *History of the Russian Revolution*, vol. 1, chap. 1. See B. Knei-Paz, *The Social and Political Thought of Leon Trotsky*, pp. 89–90.

19. *Moya zhizn'* draft: Nicolaevsky Collection (HIA) – see, for example, box 312, folder 39.

20. *Ibid.*, folders 36–40.

21. *Ibid.*, box 313, folder 1 (chap. 9), p. 1.

22. *Ibid.*, folder 5, p. 1.

23. Referring to a Central Committee meeting on 24 October 1917, Trotsky said simply: 'Stalin was not present at the session. Generally speaking he did not appear at Smolny, spending his time in the editorial office of the central organ': L. Trotsky, *History of the Russian Revolution*, vol. 3, p. 159.

24. See below, pp. 456–7.

25. I am grateful to Keith Sidwell for sharing his knowledge of ancient Greek culture with me.

26. L. Trotsky, *History of the Russian Revolution*, p. 161. See also pp. 198 and 272–3.

27. *Ibid.*, p. 281.

28. *Ibid.*

29. *Ibid.*, p. 159.

30. *Ibid.*, p. 200.

31. *Ibid.*, p. 264.

32. *Ibid.*, p. 266.

33. *Ibid.*, pp. 269–70.
34. L. Trotsky, *My Life: The Rise and Fall of a Dictator* (Thornton Butterworth: London, 1930). The US edition was loyal to Trotsky's intentions: *My Life: An Attempt at an Autobiography* (Charles Scribner's Sons: New York, 1930).
35. G. Rosenthal, *Avocat de Trotsky*, p. 112.
36. *Ibid.*, p. 113.
37. *Ibid.*, p. 115.
38. 'Agenturnoe delo po nablyudeniyu trotskistskoi literatury za rubezhom', TsAFSB, f. 17548, d. 0292, t. 1, pp. 185–8.
39. Trotsky Collection (HIA), box 11, folder 49: Trotsky's letter to Suzanne La Follette, 4 July 1937.
40. M. Eastman, *Love and Revolution: My Journey through an Epoch*, p. 554.
41. M. Eastman, *Great Companions: Critical Memoirs of Some Famous Friends*, p. 114.
42. See above, p. 339.
43. M. Eastman, *Love and Revolution: My Journey through an Epoch*, p. 554.
44. M. Eastman, *Great Companions: Critical Memoirs of Some Famous Friends*, pp. 119–23.
45. *Vie de Lénine*, trans. M. Parijanine, revised and approved by the author (Rieder: Paris, 1936).
46. *The Young Lenin*, ed. and annotated by M. Friedberg, trans. M. Eastman (Doubleday: New York, 1972).
47. Trotsky to Joe Hansen, 8 March 1939: Joseph Hansen Papers (HIA), box 34, folder 2.

## 43. Russian Connections

1. See the OGPU decision, 18 January 1929 in L. Trotskii, *Dnevniki i pis'ma*, p. 43.
2. V. I. Lenin, *Polnoe sobranie sochinenii*, vol. 20, p. 96.
3. OGPU circular, 21 February 1929: *'Chekisms': A KGB Anthology*, pp. 107–9.
4. *Pravda*, 8 March 1929.
5. *Pravda*, 2 July 1931.
6. Trotsky's passport: Nicolaevsky Collection (HIA), box 303, folder 7; L. Trotskii, *Byulleten' oppozitsii*, no. 27 (March 1932), p. 1.
7. L. M. Kaganovich at Politburo, 4 November 1930: *Stenogrammy zasedanii Politbyuro TsK RKP(b)-VKP(b), 1923–1938 gg.*, vol. 3, p. 152.
8. Trotsky to L. L. Sedov, 9 October 1932: Nicolaevsky Collection (HIA), box 310, folder 40.
9. Trotsky to L. L. Sedov, 17 October 1932: *ibid.*, folder 42.
10. Trotsky to L. L. Sedov, 30 October 1932: *ibid.*, folder 48.
11. L. Trotskii, 'Deistvitel'noe raspolozhenie figure na politicheskoi doske. (K protsessu men'shevikov)', *Byulleten' oppozitsii*, no. 21/22 (May–June 1931), pp. 35–6.

12. 'Ot redaktsii', *Byulleten' oppozitsii*, no. 51 (July–August 1936), p. 15.
13. 'Tenzov' to L. L. Sedov, February 1933: Nicolaevsky Collection (HIA), box 375, folder 1.
14. Ya. Blyumkin to Trotsky, 2 April 1929: Nicolaevsky Collection (HIA), box 374, folder 48.
15. Ya. Blyumkin, 'Avtobiografiya', pp. 1–4, signed 13 June 1928: FSB central archives reproduced in Volkogonov Papers (HIA), box 3, reel 2; G. Rosenthal, *Avocat de Trotsky*, p. 103.
16. G. Rosenthal, *Avocat de Trotsky*, p. 103.
17. A précis of this message, apparently, is given in Nicolaevsky Collection (HIA), box 307, folder 10, pp. 1–2.
18. *Ibid.*
19. Agenturnoe donesenie, 16 September 1929: FSB central archives reproduced in Volkogonov Papers (HIA), box 3, reel 2.
20. V. M. Yeltsin to Trotsky, April 1929: Nicolaevsky Collection (HIA), box 374, folder 47.
21. M. Eastman, *Love and Revolution: My Journey through an Epoch*, pp. 510–12.
22. P. Avrich, 'Bolshevik Opposition to Lenin: G. T. Myasnikov and the Workers' Group', *Russian Review*, vol. 43 (1984), pp. 1–29.
23. See report on Conference of Sections for the Fourth International, 29–31 July 1937, p. 1: Charles Wesley Ervin Papers (HIA).
24. S. Kharin to Trotsky, 31 March 1929: Nicolaevsky Collection (HIA), box 305, folder 54.
25. *Ibid.*, folders 55–7.
26. Trotsky to S. Kharin, Nicolaevsky Collection (HIA), box 307, folder 50.
27. Message entrusted to Blyumkin: see above, note 17.
28. Unnamed correspondent to Trotsky, 21 January 1930: Nicolaevsky Collection (HIA), box 567, folder 62.
29. 'Svoi' to Trotsky, 25 March 1932: Nicolaevsky Collection (HIA), box 306, folder 84.
30. 'Gromovoi' to Trotsky 15 September 1932: Nicolaevsky Collection (HIA), box 305, folder 42.
31. *Ibid.*
32. 'Tenzov' to L. L. Sedov, February 1933: Nicolaevsky Collection (HIA), box 375, folder 1.
33. J. van Heijenoort, *With Trotsky in Exile: From Prinkipo to Coyoacán*, p. 101; A. Glotzer, *Trotsky: Memoir and Critique*, p. 78.
34. See below, p. 440.
35. A. Glotzer, *Trotsky: Memoir and Critique*, p. 78.
36. There is some controversy about whether such individuals came to Trotsky as agents or were 'turned' after joining him. Trotsky as well as Deutscher assumed the latter without any convincing evidence for their choice. More likely, as Glotzer and Heijenoort contended, the individuals were agents from the very start of their contact with Trotsky.
37. L. Yakovlev [L. Estrin], 'Leon Sedov', pp. 1–2.

38. TsAFSB, f. 17548, d. 0292, t. 2, pp. 159–65.
39. L. Yakovlev [L. Estrin], 'Leon Sedov', p. 6.
40. J. van Heijenoort, *With Trotsky in Exile: From Prinkipo to Coyoacán*, pp. 101–2.
41. Nicolaevsky Collection (HIA), box 306, folder 84.
42. Trotsky seldom referred to *Sotsialisticheski vestnik* except in non-public correspondence: see in particular his letter to L. L. Sedov, c. 1932: Harvard File (Nicolaevsky Collection), no. 10107.
43. *Ibid.*
44. Unamed correspondent to L. L. Sedov, May 1933, p. 1: Nicolaevsky Collection (HIA), box 375, folder 3. The letter is in English for some unknown reason.
45. L. L. Sedov's notes on his conversation with 'X', 1934: Nicolaevsky Collection (HIA), box 375, folder 6, p. 1.
46. Trotsky's 1935 diary in L. Trotskii, *Dnevniki i pis'ma*, p. 94.

## 44. Europe South and North

1. Trotsky's 1935 diary in L. Trotskii, *Dnevniki i pis'ma*, p. 124.
2. *Ibid.*, p. 119.
3. *Time*, 5 December 1932.
4. Y. Craipeau, *Mémoires d'un dinosaure trotskyste: secrétaire de Trotsky en 1933*, p. 108.
5. *Ibid.*
6. *Ibid.*, p. 109.
7. L. Trotsky, *In Defence of the October Revolution*, pp. 1–4.
8. *Ibid.*, pp. 16–17.
9. *Ibid.*, p. 33.
10. *Ibid.*
11. Trotsky to Lev Sedov, 26 December 1932: Nicolaevsky Collection (HIA), box 43, folder 36.
12. Y. Craipeau, *Mémoires d'un dinosaure trotskyste: secrétaire de Trotsky en 1933*, p. 109.
13. A. Glotzer, *Trotsky: Memoir and Critique*, p. 180.
14. G. Rosenthal, *Avocat de Trotsky*, p. 149.
15. Diary notes of L. L. Sedov on the journey to Alma-Ata (typescript): Nicolaevsky Collection (HIA), box 303, folder 3, pp. 1–7.
16. Trotsky's 1935 diary in L. Trotskii, *Dnevniki i pis'ma*, pp. 60 ff.
17. *Ibid.*, pp. 90–1.
18. *Ibid.*, p. 136.
19. *Ibid.*, p. 84.
20. P. Naville, *Trotsky vivant*, p. 83.
21. Trotsky to the Central Committee of the Parti Ouvrier Internationaliste, 21 June 1936, p. 1: Trotsky Collection (HIA), box 12, folder 1.

22. *Ibid.*
23. G. Rosenthal, *Avocat de Trotsky*, p. 117.
24. A. Glotzer, *Trotsky: Memoir and Critique*, p. 183.
25. Trotsky to the Central Committee of the Parti Ouvrier Internationaliste, 21 June 1936, p. 1: Trotsky Collection (HIA), box 12, folder 1.
26. *Ibid.*
27. L. Trotskii, *Dnevniki i pis'ma*, pp. 130 and 141.
28. *Ibid.*, pp. 141–2.
29. *Ibid.*, p. 143; J. van Heijenoort, *With Trotsky in Exile: From Prinkipo to Coyoacán*, p. 77.
30. N. I. Sedova to L. L. Sedov, 17 September 1936, pp. 1–2 and 4: Nicolaevsky Collection (HIA), box 362.
31. N. I. Sedova to L. L. Sedov, 30 October 1936, pp. 1–2 and 4: *ibid.*
32. N. I. Sedova to L. L. Sedov, 8 and 24 November 1936: *ibid.*
33. N. I. Sedova to L. L. Sedov, 24 November 1936: *ibid.*
34. N. I. Sedova to L. L. Sedov, 30 October and 8 November 1936: *ibid.*
35. Trotsky's 1935 diary in L. Trotskii, *Dnevniki i pis'ma*, p. 133.
36. *Ibid.*, p. 134.
37. Account given by Trotsky in letter to the Juridical Section, 31 March 1938: Trotsky Collection (HIA), box 11, folder 53, p. 1.
38. G. Rosenthal, *Avocat de Trotsky*, p. 178.
39. *Ibid.*, pp. 178–9.
40. M. Shachtman to L. L. Sedov, 23 November 1936: Nicolaevsky Collection (HIA), box 362, folder 121.

## 45. Setting up in Mexico

1. Trotsky's 1937 diary in L. Trotskii, *Dnevniki i pis'ma*, p. 137.
2. Trotsky to L. L. Sedov, 16 January 1937: Trotsky Papers (HL), T10195.
3. Trotsky's 1937 diary in L. Trotskii, *Dnevniki i pis'ma*, p. 146.
4. L. Trotskii, 'V Meksike': Nicolaevsky Collection (HIA), box 354, folder 37, p. 124.
5. *Ibid.*, pp. 124–5.
6. Wilbur Burton (journalist) to the *Baltimore Sun*, 5 November 1937: Alexander Buchman Papers (HIA), box 1.
7. Trotsky to J. Hansen, 11 November 1938: Joseph Hansen Papers (HIA), box 34, folder 2.
8. Trotsky to J. Frankel, 21 December 1937: Trotsky Collection (HIA), box 10, folder 23.
9. US Government Surveillance file: Joseph Hansen Papers (HIA), box 70, folder 8, pp. 1–15.
10. Interview of Vsevolod Volkov by Norman Melnick, *San Francisco Examiner*, 8 August 1988, p. 2.
11. H. Robins, untitled recollections: Trotsky Collection (HIA), box 31, folder

4, pp. 8–10 and 15; interview of Vsevolod Volkov by Norman Melnick, *San Francisco Examiner*, 8 August 1988, p. 2.

12. S. L. Sedov to G. M. Rubinshtein: Sergei Sedov Papers (HIA), folders 1 (4 August 1935), 2 (12 August 1935) and 21 (23 September 1935); Yulia Akselrod, untitled memoir (n.d.), no. 3, pp. 21–2 and her extracts and comments from S. L. Sedov's diary, p. 44: Yulia Akselrod Papers (HIA).

13. Yulia Akselrod, untitled memoir (n.d.), no. 1, p. 4: Yulia Akselrod Papers (HIA).

14. Trotsky's 1935 diary in L. Trotskii, *Dnevniki i pis'ma*, p. 102.

15. *Ibid.*, p. 114.

16. G. Rosenthal, *Avocat de Trotsky*, p. 207.

17. *Ibid.*, pp. 263–4.

18. P. Broué, *Léon Sedov, fils de Trotsky, victime de Staline*, pp. 116–17.

19. Trotsky to L. L. Sedov, 14 January 1936: Trotsky Papers (HL), T10140.

20. L. L. Sedov to N. I. Sedova, 16 April 1936: Nicolaevsky Collection (HIA), box 367.

21. *Ibid.*

22. *Ibid.*

23. L. L. Sedov to N. I. Sedova, 12 May 1937: Nicolaevsky Collection (HIA), box 567, folder 78.

24. L. Yakovlev [L. Estrina], 'Leon Sedov', typescript apparently composed before 4 May 1975: Trotsky Collection (HIA), box 29, folder 5, p. 6.

25. 'Agenturnye doneseniya Zborovskogo M. G.', TsAFSB, f. 31660, d. 9067, pp. 122–3 – reproduced in the Volkogonov Papers (HIA), box 3, reel 2.

26. *Ibid.*, p. 98.

27. *Ibid.*, p. 72.

28. 'Affaire Sedov, Cabriolage des Archives Trotsky', Préfecture de Police, Seine (Dept) (HIA): police reports of 8, 9 and 17 November 1936.

29. Trotsky Collection (HIA), box 28, folder 8.

30. G. Rosenthal, *Avocat de Trotsky*, pp. 230–3.

31. *Ibid.*, pp. 233–4.

32. *Ibid.*, pp. 254–60.

33. *Ibid.*, p. 262; L. Yakovlev [L. Estrina], 'Leon Sedov', typescript apparently composed before 4 May 1975: Trotsky Collection (HIA), box 29, folder 5, p. 2.

34. P. Sudoplatov, *Special Tasks: The Memoirs of an Unwanted Witness – A Soviet Spymaster*, pp. 82–3.

35. L. Estrina to Trotsky, 21 February 1938: Nicolaevsky Collection (HIA), box 92, folder 3.

36. 'Rappel des faits de J. M. [Jeanne Martin des Pallières]', 18 February 1938, pp. 1–4: Nicolaevsky Collection (HIA), box 92, folder 4.

37. See P. Broué's summary in *Léon Sedov, fils de Trotsky, victime de Staline*, pp. 254–9. Broué got medical and toxicological experts to examine the evidence in the 1980s and was convinced that Sedov had indeed been murdered.

38. S. Weber to L. Estrina, 9 August 1938: Nicolaevsky Collection (HIA), box 92, folder 3.
39. Trotsky to Étienne and L. Estrina, 17 February 1939: *ibid.*
40. G. Rosenthal, *Avocat de Trotsky*, pp. 298–303.

## 46. The Fourth International

1. Trotsky to Étienne and L. Estrina, 23 February 1938: Nicolaevsky Collection (HIA), box 92, folder 3.
2. 'Orlov' to Trotsky, 27 December 1938: Trotsky Collection (HIA), box 13, folder 63.
3. Sara [Weber] to Lola Estrina, 13 August 1938, p. 1: Nicolaevsky Collection (HIA), box 92, folder 3.
4. *Ibid.*
5. Trotsky to J. Frankel, 12 April 1933: Trotsky Collection (HIA), box 10, folder 22.
6. Trotsky to L. L. Sedov, 12 November 1936: Trotsky Papers (HL), T10181.
7. *Ibid.*
8. G. Rosenthal, *Avocat de Trotsky*, pp. 221–3.
9. Trotsky to Mill [*sic*], 2 June 1937: Nicolaevsky Collection (HIA), box 308, folder 17, pp. 1–2.
10. I. Deutscher, *Trotsky: The Prophet Outcast*, pp. 271–2.
11. P. Broué, *Léon Sedov, fils de Trotsky, victime de Staline*, p. 192.
12. A. Glotzer, *Trotsky: Memoir and Critique*, p. 188: Trotsky to Shachtman, 20 January 1934.
13. *Ibid.*, p. 190.
14. *Ibid.*, pp. 195–8.
15. *Trotsky's Writings: Supplement II, 1934–1940*, pp. 448–54.
16. Y. Craipeau, *Mémoires d'un dinosaure trotskyste: secrétaire de Trotsky en 1933*, p. 90.
17. Trotsky to L. L. Sedov, 14 January 1936: Trotsky Papers (HL), T10140.
18. See G. Rosenthal, *Avocat de Trotsky*, pp. 223–5.
19. *Ibid.*
20. *Ibid.*, p. 226.
21. P. Naville, *Trotsky vivant*, pp. 136–7.
22. Rosenthal, *Avocat de Trotsky*, p. 73.
23. 'Declaration Regarding the Case of Senin and Weil', 27 February 1937: Joseph Hansen Papers (HIA), box 69, folder 34, pp. 1–2.
24. L. L. Sedov to 'Braun' (Wolfe), 16 April 1937: Joseph Hansen Papers (HIA), box 28, folder 3, p. 2.
25. M. Eastman, *Love and Revolution: My Journey through an Epoch*, pp. 625–6.
26. *Ibid.*, p. 626.
27. D. Cotterill, 'Serge, Trotsky and the Spanish Revolution', in *The Serge–Trotsky Papers*, pp. 116–19.

28. Trotsky to V. Serge, 5 June 1936: *ibid.*, p. 67.
29. L. Trotsky, 'A Strategy for Victory', in *The Spanish Revolution*, p. 245.
30. Trotsky to James Cannon, 10 October 1937: Joseph Hansen Papers (HIA), box 69, folder 1, p. 1.
31. *Ibid.*, p. 2.
32. *Ibid.*, p. 3.
33. See above, p. 119.
34. Report on the Conference of Sections for the Fourth International, 29–31 July 1937, pp. 1–4 and 6–8: Charles Wesley Ervin Papers (HIA).
35. P. Broué, *Léon Sedov, fils de Trotsky, victime de Staline*, p. 245.
36. See below, p. 489.
37. I. Deutscher, *Trotsky: The Prophet Outcast*, pp. 419–22.
38. The controversy between Trotsky and Serge about Kronstadt occurred after Serge announced his break with the Fourth International: D. Cotterill in *The Serge–Trotsky Papers*, p. 22.
39. Viktor Serge to Trotsky, 18 March 1939: Nicolaevsky Collection (HIA), box 306, folder 76.

## 47. Trotsky and His Women

1. N. I. Sedova to S. Weber, 4 November 1942: Trotsky Collection (HIA), box 26, folder 32.
2. M. Eastman, *Great Companions: Critical Memoirs of Some Famous Friends*, p. 123.
3. 5 April 1935: L. Trotskii, *Dnevniki i pis'ma*, pp. 115–16.
4. See above, pp. 318–9.
5. See above, pp. 265 and 342.
6. J. van Heijenoort, *With Trotsky in Exile: From Prinkipo to Coyoacán*, p. 110.
7. *Ibid.*, p. 112.
8. *Ibid.*, p. 111.
9. A. Burdman Feferman, *Politics, Logic, and Love: The Life of Jean van Heijenoort*, p. 145.
10. J. van Heijenoort, *With Trotsky in Exile: From Prinkipo to Coyoacán*, p. 112.
11. I have searched Ella Wolfe's papers in the (vast) Wolfe Collection in the Hoover Institution Archives without finding a trace of the letter.
12. Trotsky to N. I. Sedova, 19 July 1937: Trotsky Papers (HLA), bMS Russ 13.1 (10622), p. 1.
13. *Ibid.*, pp. 1–2.
14. *Ibid.*, p. 3.
15. *Ibid.*, p. 4.
16. J. van Heijenoort, *With Trotsky in Exile: From Prinkipo to Coyoacán*, p. 118.
17. A. Burdman Feferman, *Politics, Logic, and Love: The Life of Jean van Heijenoort*, pp. 175–6.
18. *Ibid.*, p. 170.

19. *Ibid.*, pp. 170–1.
20. F. Kahlo ('Friduchin') to E. Wolfe, 13 [no month given] 1938, p. 2: Bertram D. Wolfe Collection (HIA), box 158.
21. Trotsky to F. Kahlo, 12 January 1939: Trotsky Collection (HIA), box 11, folder 31, pp. 1–4.
22. See for example Jean van Heijenoort's letter to André Breton, 11 January 1939: Charles Curtiss Papers (HIA).
23. Trotsky to the Pan-American [*sic*] Committee of the Fourth International, 22 March 1939: *ibid.*
24. Charles Curtiss, memorandum of conversation with Diego Rivera, 20 January 1939: *ibid.*
25. J. van Heijenoort, *With Trotsky in Exile: From Prinkipo to Coyoacán*, pp. 121–2.
26. www.marxists.org/subject/art/lit_crit/works/rivera/manifesto.htm.
27. Trotsky to J. Cannon, 27 March 1939: Trotsky Collection (HIA): box 9, folder 56, pp. 1–5.
28. It is nowadays on display in the Blue House, Coyoacán.
29. Trotsky to the Pan-American Committee of the Fourth International, 22 March 1933, Charles Curtiss Papers (HIA), folder 1, p. 2.
30. Trotsky to C. Curtiss, 14 February 1939: Charles Curtiss Papers (HIA), folder 1.

## 48. 'The Russian Question'

1. L. Trotsky, *The Revolution Betrayed*, p. 216.
2. A. Burdman Feferman, *Politics, Logic, and Love: The Life of Jean van Heijenoort*, pp. 140 and 142. See also above, p. 433.
3. L. Trotsky, *The Revolution Betrayed*, pp. 215 and 217.
4. *Ibid.*, pp. 63–5; draft article 'Stakhanovskoe dvizhenie': Trotsky Collection (HIA), box 28, folder 5, p. 1.
5. L. Trotsky, *The Revolution Betrayed*, p. 190.
6. *Ibid.*, pp. 170–6.
7. He wrote this for the preface of the 1936 French edition of *Terrorism and Communism*.
8. L. Trotsky, *The Revolution Betrayed*, p. 217.
9. *Ibid.*, p. 218.
10. 'Ob ukrainskom voprose', *Byulleten' oppozitsii*, no. 77–78 (May–June–July 1939), p. 6.
11. *Ibid.*, p. 7.
12. S. and B. Webb, *Soviet Communism: A New Civilization?*; S. and B. Webb, *Soviet Communism: A New Civilization*.
13. See above, p. 399.
14. I. Getzler, *Kronstadt*, p. 257.
15. Trotsky to Comrade Wasserman, 14 November 1937: Trotsky Collection (HIA), box 12, folder 62.

16. Lev Sedov to Simone Weil, 1 November 1937: Nicolaevsky Collection (HIA), box 368, folder 48.
17. See above, p. 391.
18. L. Trotsky, *The Revolution Betrayed*, p. 210.

## 49. Confronting the Philosophers

1. N. I. Yezhov to K. Ye. Voroshilov, 28 October 1938: RVGA, f. 33987, op. 3, d. 1103s, pp. 146–7. Yezhov fell from power a few days later. Perhaps the letter was a sign of his desperation at the time.
2. Maiski's diary, 23 March 1938. This reference comes to me by courtesy of Gabriel Gorodetsky in his draft translation of the original work.
3. A. Glotzer, *Trotsky: Memoir and Critique*, pp. 40–1.
4. Trotsky's 1935 diary in L. Trotskii, *Dnevniki i pis'ma*, p. 123.
5. A. Glotzer, *Trotsky: Memoir and Critique*, pp. 42–3.
6. Joseph Hansen Paers (HIA), box 69, folder 64.
7. M. Eastman, *Love and Revolution: My Journey through an Epoch*, p. 499.
8. Trotsky to Suzanne La Follette, James Cannon and Max Shachtman, 15 March 1937: Trotsky Collection (HIA), box 11, folder 48.
9. F. Lundberg to S. La Follette, 4 March 1938: Nicolaevsky Collection (HIA), box 134, folder 18.
10. M. Eastman, *Great Companions: Critical Memoirs of Some Famous Friends*, p. 114.
11. *Ibid.*, pp. 114–15.
12. Trotsky's 1935 diary in L. Trotskii, *Dnevniki i pis'ma*, p. 119.
13. See Hook's recollections of the period, including his account of van Heijenoort's subsequent disclosures to him: *Out of Step: An Unquiet Life in the Twentieth Century*, pp. 242–3.
14. Hansen to Trotsky, 23 June 1939: Joseph Hansen Papers (HIA), box 34, folder 2, p. 2.
15. S. Hook, *Out of Step: An Unquiet Life in the Twentieth Century*, p. 242.
16. *Ibid.*, pp. 242–3.
17. J. van Heijenoort, *With Trotsky in Exile: From Prinkipo To Coyoacán*, p. 145.
18. J. van Heijenoort to Joe Hansen, 24 July 1939: Joseph Hansen Papers (HIA), box 34, folder 7.
19. Notes on dialectics, 1939–40: Trotsky Collection (HIA), box 21, folder 6, p. 2.
20. *Ibid.*, p. 6.
21. *Ibid.*, p. 8.
22. Trotsky's copy of the book was taken to New York in 1939 by Jean van Heijenoort, who some years later deposited it in the Hoover Institution Archives: S. Hook, *Towards the Understanding of Karl Marx: A Revolutionary Interpretation* (HIA safe), p. 34.
23. L. Trotsky, *Their Morals and Ours: The Moralists and Sycophants against Marxism*, p. 10.

24. *Ibid.*
25. *Ibid.*, pp. 40–51.
26. Appendix in L. Trotsky, *In Defence of Marxism*, p. 233.
27. *Ibid.*, p. 239.
28. *Ibid.*, p. 246.
29. Trotsky to Albert Goldman, 9 August 1940: Trotsky Collection (HIA), box 9, folder 78, p. 2.
30. Ella Wolfe, Oral History, tape viii, pp. 12–13: Bertram D. Wolfe Collection, box 185.

## 50. The Second World War

1. 'Stalin – intendant Gitlera', *Byulleten' oppozitsii*, no. 79–80 (August–September–October 1939), p. 14.
2. See above, chap. 14.
3. L. Trotskii, 'SSSR v voine', *Byulleten' oppozitsiya*, no. 79–80 (August–September–October 1939), p. 2.
4. 'The USSR in War' (typescript): Nicolaevsky Collection (HIA), box 355, folder 16, pp. 1–3.
5. L. Trotskii, 'SSSR v voine', *Byulleten' oppozitsiya*, no. 79–80 (August–September–October 1939), p. 9.
6. 'The USSR in War' (typescript): Nicolaevsky Collection (HIA), box 355, folder 16, p. 13.
7. *Ibid.*, p. 6.
8. *Ibid.*, p. 9.
9. L. Trotskii, 'SSSR v voine', *Byulleten' oppozitsiya*, no. 79–80 (August–September–October 1939), p. 8.
10. *Ibid.*, p. 9.
11. H. P. von Strandmann, 'Obostryayushchiesya paradoksy: Gitler, Stalin i germano-sovetskie ekonomicheskie svyazi. 1939–1941', in A. O. Chubaryan and G. Gorodetsky (eds), *Voina i politika, 1939–1941*, p. 376.
12. Joseph Hansen to Trotsky, April 1940, p. 1b: Joseph Hansen Papers (HIA), box 34, folder 3.
13. Joseph Hansen to Trotsky, 1 January 1940: *Ibid.*
14. Trotsky to J. Hansen, 5 January 1940 (mistyped as 1939): Trotsky Collection (HIA), box 10, folder 88.
15. See above, p. 211.
16. Trotsky to M. Shachtman, 6 November 1939: Trotsky Collection (HIA), box 12, folder 13, p. 3.
17. Trotsky to M. Shachtman, 6 November 1939: *Ibid.*, p. 4.
18. Trotsky to J. Hansen, 18 January 1940: Albert Glotzer Papers (HIA), box 13.
19. Trotsky to M. Shachtman, 6 November 1939, p. 1, and 20 December 1939: Trotsky Collection (HIA), box 12, folders 13 and 14.
20. Trotsky to J. Hansen, 18 January 1940: Albert Glotzer Papers (HIA), box 13.

21. *Ibid.* The identity of the person who put Trotsky's letter into such contorted English is unknown.
22. 'Declaración a la Prensa: El Papel del Kremlin en la Catastrofa Europea', 17 July 1940: Joseph Hansen Papers, box 69, folder 53, pp. 1–2.
23. Trotsky to A. Glotzer, 14 February 1939: Trotsky Collection (HIA), box 9, folder 59.
24. SWP discussions with 'Lund' (Trotsky): 15 June 1940: Trotsky Collection (HIA), box 22, folder 13, p. 22.
25. Trotsky to J. B. Matthews, 12 October 1939: Trotsky Collection (HIA), box 12, folder 53.
26. SWP discussions with 'Lund' (Trotsky): 15 June 1940: Trotsky Collection (HIA), folder 13, p. 22.
27. SWP discussions with 'Lund' (Trotsky): 12 June 1940: *ibid.*, p. 5.
28. 'Lund' (Trotsky) to Albert Goldman, 9 July 1940: Albert Glotzer Papers (HIA), box 13.
29. SWP discussions with 'Lund' (Trotsky), 12 June 1940: Trotsky Collection (HIA), box 22, folder 13, p. 5.
30. 'Vas obmanyvayut! Pis'mo v SSSR', apparently 23 April 1940: Joseph Hansen Papers (HIA), box 69, folder 45.

## 51. Assassination

1. H. Robins, untitled memoirs, p. 2: Trotsky Collection (HIA), box 31, folder 4.
2. E. Sedov, 'Mi Abuelo, Mexico y Yo', *Contenido*, November 1970, p. 64. Trotsky said: 'There aren't a lot of such individuals' (*No abundan esos individuos*).
3. Joseph Hansen Papers (HIA), box 69, folder 63: 1970 sketch of house and notes on building works.
4. Trotsky to James Cannon, 15 February 1938: Trotsky Collection (HIA), box 9, folder 54. No proof of an assassination attempt at this time has yet emerged from the Soviet archives.
5. See for example his letter to P. Frank and R. Molinier, 1 July 1940: *ibid.*, box 10, folder 15.
6. Trotsky's 1935 diary in L. Trotskii, *Dnevniki i pis'ma*, p. 72.
7. J. Hansen to Usick [*sic*], 21 September 1940: Trotsky Collection (HIA), box 22, folder 4.
8. 'My Testament', 27 February to 3 March 1940: Joseph Hansen Papers (HIA), box 69, folder 44.
9. N. I. Sedova to Sara Weber, 14 April 1940: Trotsky Collection (HIA), box 26, folder 32.
10. Suzi Weissman, 'A Remembrance' (of her friend Alexander Buchman): typescript, 2003: Alexander Buchman Papers (HIA), pp. 1–2.
11. See the varying estimates of Trotsky's guards in Joe Hansen's memorandum, 30 June 1940: Joseph Hansen Papers, box 70, folder 3.

12. L. A. Sánchez Salazar (with Julián Gorkin), *Así asesinaron a Trotski*, pp. 24–5.
13. *Ibid.*, pp. 25–7.
14. Joseph Hansen, memorandum (30 June 1940): Joseph Hansen Papers (HIA), box 70, folder 3.
15. N. Sedova, 'Otets i syn', Trotsky Collection (HIA), box 27, folder 11, p. 9.
16. Herbert Solow to 'Cornell' (Trotsky), 14 June 1940, pp. 1–2: Albert Glotzer Papers (HIA), box 13.
17. J. Hansen to Albert Goldman, 30 June 1940: *ibid.*
18. P. Stein, *Siqueiros: His Life and Works*, pp. 125, 129–30 and 131.
19. N. Sedova, 'Otets i syn': Trotsky Collection (HIA), box 27, folder 11, p. 9.
20. Farrell Dobs to 'Dear Comrade', 16 August 1940: Trotsky Collection (HIA), box 24, folder 13.
21. Trotsky to Hank Schultz, 20 August 1940: Trotsky Collection (HIA), box 12, folder 10.
22. J. Hansen to Usick, 21 September 1940: Trotsky Collection (HIA), box 22, folder 24.
23. J. Hansen to Farrell Dobbs, probably July 1940: Trotsky Collection (HIA), box 24, folder 12, pp. 1–2; Joseph Hansen Papers (HIA), box 69, folder 63: 1970 sketch of house and notes on building works.
24. Trotsky to Hank Schultz, 20 August 1940: Trotsky Collection (HIA), box 12, folder 10.
25. N. Sedova to C. James, 17 October 1940: Joseph Hansen Papers (HIA), box 70, folder 20, p. 1.
26. *Ibid.*
27. V. Serge and N. Sedova Trotsky, *The Life and Death of Leon Trotsky*, p. 267.
28. Ice-axe is a more accurate term than ice-pick, which in the 1930s referred to the small implement used by barmen to shatter a cube of ice to put into drinking glasses.
29. See the photos after p. 84 in J. R. Garmabella, *Operación Trotsky*.
30. L. Mercader, 'Mi hermano Ramón no era un vulgar asesino', *El Mundo*, July 1990, p. 17.
31. L. A. Sánchez Salazar with Julián Gorkin, *Así asesinaron a Trotski*, pp. 149–50.
32. *Ibid.*, p. 119.
33. *Ibid.*

## 52. The Keepers and the Flame

1. J. van Heijenoort, *With Trotsky in Exile: From Prinkipo to Coyoacán*, p. 192.
2. 'Trotsky', *The Times*, 23 August 1940.
3. L. A. Sánchez Salazar with Julián Gorkin, *Así asesinaron a Trotski*, p. 5. This glitch was itself evidence of Soviet involvement in the assassination.
4. *Lubyanka: Stalin i NKVD–NKGB–GUKR 'Smersh', 1939–mart 1946*, pp. 182–4. The article was dated 16 August 1940. Presumably this was a

technical error. Possibly – just possibly – it means that a successful assassination was already anticipated in the Kremlin.

5. US State Department records: Joseph Hansen Papers (HIA), box 70, folder 8.

6. Trotsky Collection (HIA), box 24, folder 5, pp. 1–4.

7. Albert Goldman to Felix Morrow, 31 August 1940: Trotsky Collection (HIA), box 24, folder 14, pp. 1–4.

8. 'Recontres avec Trotsky et son Meutrier' (typescript: Paris, n.d.), p. 4: Augustin Souchy Papers (HIA).

9. N. I. Sedova to S. Weber, 12 November 1959: Trotsky Collection (HIA), box 27, folder 5.

10. J. Hansen to N. I. Sedova, 24 October 1941: Joseph Hansen Papers (HIA), box 33, folder 14.

11. *Byulleten' oppozitsii*, no. 87 (August 1941).

12. Decree of 7th Department, NKGB, 1 July 1941: TsAFSB, f. 17548, op. 0292, t. 2, p. 368 in the Volkogonov Papers.

13. N. I. Sedova to S. Weber, 4 November 1942: Trotsky Collection (HIA), box 26, folder 32.

14. N. I. Sedova to the Executive Committee of the Fourth International, 9 May 1951: *ibid.*, folder 13.

15. N. I. Sedova to Sara Weber, October 1955: Trotsky Collection (HIA), box 27, folder 4.

16. Interview by N. Melnick, *San Francisco Examiner*, 8 August 1988, p. 2.

17. A. Glotzer to N. I. Sedova, 25 May 1954: Albert Glotzer Papers (HIA), box 26.

18. Yulia Akselrod, untitled memoir (n.d. but after 2000), no. 1, p. 1: Yulia Akselrod Papers (HIA).

19. *Ibid.*, no. 3, pp. 2–3, 4–5, 7 and 9.

20. *Ibid.*, no. 1, pp. 2 and 6; Yu. Aksel' [Aksel'rod], 'Istoriya moego odinochestva', *Iskusstvo kino*, no. 4 (1990), p. 103.

21. Yulia Akselrod, untitled memoir (n.d.), no. 1, p. 6, and no. 2, pp. 6, 9 and 18: Yulia Akselrod Papers (HIA).

22. L. Trotskii, *Na bor'be s golodom*, p. 55: speech in Sokolniki, 6 June 1918.

# Select Bibliography

Items relating to Trotsky's career fill rooms in dozens of the world's archives. Works by Trotsky run into their thousands and are catalogued in L. Sinclair, *Trotsky: A Bibliography* (Scolar: Aldershot, 1989). Works on Trotsky run into the tens of thousands. The following list is restricted to those archives, books and articles used in the course of writing this biography.

## Archives

Gosudarstvennyi Arkhiv Rossiiskoi Federatsii (Moscow) [GARF]
Hoover Institution Archives, Stanford University, Stanford [HIA]
    Yulia Akselrod Papers
    Arkhiv Parizhskoi Okhrany [APO]
    Herman Axelbank Film Collection
    Alexander Buchman Papers
    Charles Curtiss Papers
    *Dnevnik Al. Bloka* (with Trotsky's coded message)
    Charles Wesley Ervin Papers
    Albert Glotzer Papers
    Joseph Hansen Papers
    George A. Hill Papers
    N. A. Ioffe Papers
    Nestor Lakoba Papers
    Boris Nicolaevsky Collection
    Préfecture de Police, Seine (Dept)
    Russia: Posol'stvo
    Sergei Sedov Papers
    Augustin Souchy Papers
    Arne Swabeck Papers
    Trotsky Collection
    Volkogonov Papers
    Bertram D. Wolfe Collection

Houghton Library (Harvard University, Cambridge, MA) [HL]

## Trotsky Papers

National Archives (London) [NA]

Partiinyi arkhiv Turkmenskogo filiala Instituta Marksizma-Leninizma (Ashgabat) [PA TurFIL]

Rossiiskii arkhiv sotsial'no-politicheskoi istorii (Moscow) [RGASPI]
Especially:
fond 17 (Central Committee and Politburo)
fond 46 (Tenth Party Conference)
fond 52 (Thirteenth Party Congress)
fond 325 (L. D. Trotsky)

Rossiiskii Gosudarstvennyi Voennyi Arkhiv (Moscow) [RGVA]
Examined in the Volkogonov Papers

Tsentral'nyi Arkhiv Federal'noi Sluzhby Bezopasnosti Rossii (Moscow) [TsAFSB]
Examined in the Volkogonov Papers

## Trotsky's Printed Works

*1905 God*, 4th edn (Gosizdat: Moscow, 1922)

'Avtobiograficheskaya zametka,' *Proletarskaya revolyutsiya*, no. 3 (1921)

*Chapters from My Diary* (The Revolutionary Age: Boston, MA, 1918?)

*Chto i kak proizoshlo? Shest' statei dlya mirovoi burzhuaznoi pechati* (H. Vilain: Paris, 1929)

*Delo bylo v Ispanii (po zapisnoi knizhke)*, with illustrations by K. Rotov (Krug: Moscow, 1926)

*Desyatyi s"ezd RKP(b). Mart 1921 g. Stenograficheskii otchët* (Gosizdat: Moscow, 1963)

*Dnevniki i pis'ma*, ed. Yu. Fel'shtinskii (Ermitazh: Tenafly, NJ, 1986)

*From October to Brest-Litovsk* (n.p.: Aegypan Press, n.d.)

*History of the Russian Revolution*, vols 1–3 (Sphere: London, 1967)

*In Defence of Marxism*, ed. M. Shachtman (New Park Publications: London, 1971)

*In Defence of the October Revolution* (Union Books: London, 2002)

*In Defense of Marxism (Against the Petty-Bourgeois Opposition)* (Pioneer Publishers: New York, 1942)

*I Stake My Life! Trotsky's Address to the New York Hippodrome Meeting*, introduced by M. Shachtman (Pioneer Publishers: New York, 1937)

*Itogi suda nad Sovetom Rabochikh Deputatov* (Tip. V. Ivanova: Kazan, 1907)

*Iz istorii odnogo goda* (Novyi mir: St Petersburg, 1905)

*K istorii Oktyabr'skoi Revolyutsii* (Izd. Russkoi Sotsialisticheskoi Federatsii: New York, 1918)

*K sotsializmu ili kapitalizmu?* (Moscow–Leningrad, 1925)

*K sotsializmu ili kapitalizmu?* (Moscow–Leningrad, 1926)

*Lessons of October*, trans. J. G. Wright (Pioneer: New York, 1937)

*Lettres aux abonnés de la Vie Ouvrière*, part 3: *L'expulsion de Léon Trotzky* (Quai de Jemappes 96: Paris, 1916)

*Literatura i revolyutsiya* (Krasnaya nov': Moscow, 1923)

*Moya zhizn': opyt avtobiografii*, vols 1–2 (Granit: Berlin, 1930)

*My Life: An Attempt at an Autobiography* (Charles Scribner's Sons: New York, 1930)

*My Life: The Rise and Fall of a Dictator* (Thornton Butterworth: London, 1930)

*Na bor'bu s golodom. Rech', proiznesënnaya 9 iyunya 1918 g. na narodnom sobranii v Sokolnikakh* (Kommunist: Moscow–Petrograd, 1918)

*Na putyakh k evropeiskoi revolyutsii. (Rech' v Tiflise 11 aprelya 1924)* (Krasnaya nov': Moscow, 1924)

*Nasha revolyutsiya* (N. Glagolev: St Petersburg, 1907)

*Nasha revolyutsiya* (N. Glagolev: St Petersburg, 1909)

*Nashi politicheskie zadachi. (Takticheskie i organizatsionnye voprosy)* (Partiya: Geneva, 1904)

*Nemetskaya revolyutsiya i stalinskaya byurokratiya. (Zhizhennye voprosy nemetskogo proletariata)* (A. Grylewicz: Berlin, 1932)

*Novyi Kurs* (Krasnaya nov': Moscow, 1924)

*Ocherki gruzinskoi zhirondy* (Gosizdat: Moscow, 1925)

*Oktyabr'skaya Revolyutsiya* (Kommunist: Moscow–Petrograd, 1918)

*O Lenine: materialy dlya biografa* (Gosizdat: Moscow, 1924)

*Permanentnaya revolyutsiya* (Granit: Berlin, 1930)

*Perspektivy russkoi revolyutsii*, 2nd edn (I. P. Ladyzhnikov Co-operative: Berlin, 1917)

*Petlya vmesto khleba* (Penza Gubkbom of the RKP: Penza, 1921)

*Politicheskie siluety*, ed. V. I. Miller (Novosti: Moscow, 1990)

*Portrety revolyutsionerov*, ed. Yu. G. Fel'shtinskii (Moskovskii rabochii: Moscow, 1991)

*Prestupleniya Stalina*, ed. Yu. G. Fel'shtinskii (Izd. gumanitarnoi literatury: Moscow, 1994)

*The Real Situation in Russia* (Harcourt, Brace: New York, 1928)

*Rech' t. Trotskogo na massovom mitinge v gor. Gomele, 10 maya 1920 g.* (Gomel, 1920)

*The Revolution Betrayed: What Is the Soviet Union and Where Is It Going?* (Doubleday, Doran: New York, 1937)

*The Revolution Betrayed* (Dover: New York, 2004)

*Russland in der Revolution* (Kaden: Dresden, 1910)

*Sochineniya*, vols 2–21 (Gosizdat: Moscow, 1924–7)

'Sovet i prokuratura. (Pyat'desyat' dnei)', in *Istoriya Soveta Rabochikh Deputatov g. S.-Petersburga* (N. Glagolev: St Petersburg, 1906?)

'Sovet i revolyutsiya. (Pyat'desyat' dnei)', in *Istoriya Soveta Rabochikh Deputatov g. S.-Petersburga* (N. Glagolev: St Petersburg, 1906?)

*The Spanish Revolution (1931–1939)* (Pathfinder: New York, 1973)

*Stalinskaya shkola fal'sifikatsii* (Granit: Berlin, 1932)

*Terrorizm i kommunizm* (Gosizdat: Petersburg [*sic*], 1920)

*Their Morals and Ours: The Moralists and Sycophants Against Marxism* (New Park: London, 1968)

*Towards Socialism or Capitalism?*, trans. R. S. Townsend and Z. Vengerova, with a preface specially written by the author for the English edition (Methuen: London, 1926)

*The Trotsky Papers, 1917–1922*, vols 1–2, ed. J. M. Meijer (Mouton: The Hague, 1964–71)

*Trotsky's Diary in Exile: 1935*, trans. Elena Zarudnaya (Harvard University Press: Cambridge, MA, 1969)

*Trotsky's Notebooks, 1933–1935: Writings on Lenin, Dialectics, and Evolutionism*, trans., annotated and introduced by P. Pomper, Russian text annotated by Yu. Felshtinsky (Columbia University Press: New York, 1986)

*Trotsky's Writings: Supplement II, 1934–1940*, ed. G. Breitman (Pathfinder Press: New York, 1979)

*Tuda i obratno* (Shipovnik: St Petersburg, 1907)

*Uroki Oktyabrya* (Berlinskoye Knigoizdatelstvo: Leningrad, 1924)

*V zashchitu partii* (Glagolev: St Petersburg, 1907)

*Vie de Lénine*, trans. Maurice Parijanine, revised and approved by the author (Rieder: Paris, 1936)

*Vingt lettres de Léon Trotzky*, introduced by A. Rosmer (La Vie Ouvrière: Paris, 1919)

*Voina i revolyutsiya*, vols 1–2 (Gosizdat: Moscow–Leningrad, 1924)

*Voina s Pol'shei* (Literaturno-izdatel'skii otdel PU RVSR: Moscow, 1920)

*Voprosy byta: epokha 'kul'turnichestva' i eë zadachi*, 3rd edn (Gosizdat: Moscow, 1923)

*V zashchitu partii* (Delo: St Petersburg, 1907)

*V zashchitu partii* (N. Glagolev: St Petersburg, 1907)

*The Young Lenin*, ed. and annotated by M. Friedberg, trans. M. Eastman (Doubleday: New York, 1972)

## Prefaces or Chapters by Trotsky and Books written jointly with others

L. Trotskii and G. Zinov'ev, *Boi za Peterburg. Dve rechi* (Gosizdat: Petersburg [*sic*], 1920)

Ya. Shafir, *Ocherki gruzinskoi zhirondy*, introduced by L. Trotskii (Gosizdat: Moscow, 1925)

L. Trotskii and Kh. Kabakchiev, *Ocherki politicheskoi Bolgarii* (Gosizdat: Moscow–Petrograd, 1923)

K. Marks, *Parizhskaya Kommuna* (Levenshtein: St Petersburg, 1906)
    [with Domov] *Yubilei pozora nashego (1613–1913)* (Pravda: Vienna, 1912)

## Periodicals

*Bor'ba* (Vienna)
*Byulleten' oppozitsii* (Berlin, then Paris)
*Iskra* (Munich and elsewhere)
*Izvestiya* (Petrograd, then Moscow)
*El Mundo* (Madrid)
*Novyi mir* (New York)
*Pravda* (Petrograd, then Moscow)
*Pravda* (St Petersburg)
*Pravda* (Vienna)
*Proletarskaya revolyutsiya* (Moscow)
*Punch* (London)
*San Francisco Examiner* (San Francisco)
*Sotsial–demokrat* (Paris and elsewhere)
*Vorwärts* (New York)
*Vostochnoe obozrenie* (Irkutsk)
*Vperëd* (Paris)

## Other Publications

M. Agursky, *The Third Rome: National Bolshevism in the USSR* (Westview Press: Boulder, CO, 1987)

M. A. Aldanov, *Sovremenniki* (Slovo: Berlin, 1928)

A. Allfrey, *Man of Arms: The Life and Legend of Sir Basil Zaharoff* (Weidenfeld & Nicolson: London 1989)

Yu. Aksel' [Aksel'rod], 'Istoriya moego odinochestva', *Iskusstvo kino*, no. 4 (1990)

A. Ascher, *Pavel Axelrod and the Development of Menshevism* (Harvard University Press: Cambridge, MA, 1972)

A. Ascher, *The Revolution of 1905: Russia in Disarray* (Stanford University Press: Stanford, CA, 1988)

K. Baedeker, *Russia with Teheran, Port Arthur, and Peking: Handbook for Travellers* (T. Fisher Unwin: London, 1914)

A. Balabanoff, *Impressions of Lenin*, trans. Isotta Cesari (University of Michigan Press: Ann Arbor, 1964)

A. Balabanoff, *My Life as a Rebel* (Hamish Hamilton: London, 1938)

B. Beatty, *The Red Heart of Russia* (The Century Co.: New York, 1918)

D. Bednyi, *Sobranie sochinenii*, vols 1–8 (Khudozhestvennaya literatura: Moscow, 1963–5)

F. Benvenuti, *The Bolsheviks and the Red Army, 1918–1922*, trans. Christopher Woodall (Cambridge University Press: Cambridge, 1988)

F. Benvenuti, 'Il dibattito sui sindicati', in F. Gori (ed.), *Pensiero e azione di Lev*

*Trockij. Atti del convegno internazionale per il quarantesimo anniversario della morte di Lev Trockij*, vol. 1 (Olschki: Florence, 1983)

A. di Biagio, *Le origini dell' isolazionismo sovietica: l'Unione Sovietica e l'Europa dal 1918 al 1928* (FrancoAngeli: Milan, 1990)

A. I. Boyarchikov, *Vospominaniya*, introduced by V. V. Solovëv (AST: Moscow, 2003)

E. Broido, *Memoirs of a Revolutionary*, trans. V. Broido (Oxford University Press: London, 1967)

T. Brotherstone and P. Dukes (eds), *The Trotsky Reappraisal* (Edinburgh University Press: Edinburgh, 1992)

P. Broué, *Léon Sedov, fils de Trotsky, victime de Staline* (Éditions Ouvrières: Paris, 1993)

P. Broué, *La Révolution en Allemagne* (Minuit: Paris, 1971)

P. Broué, *La Révolution Espagnole (1931–1939)* (Flammarion: Paris, 1973)

P. Broué, *Trotsky* (Fayard: Paris, 1988)

L. Bryant, *Mirrors of Moscow* (Th. Setzer: New York, 1923)

L. Bryant, *Six Months in Red Russia: An Observer's Account of Russia Before and After the Proletarian Dictatorship* (George H. Doran: New York, 1918)

M. Buber-Neumann, *Von Potsdam nach Moskau. Stationem eines Irrweges* (Stuttgart, 1957)

N. Bukharin, *K voprosu o trotskizme* (Gosizdat: Moscow, 1925)

A. Burdman Feferman, *Politics, Logic, and Love: The Life of Jean van Heijenoort* (A. K. Peters: Wellesley, MA, 1993)

J. Carmichael, *Trotsky: An Appreciation of His Life* (Hodder & Stoughton: London, 1975)

E. H. Carr, *Foundations of a Planned Economy, 1926–1929*, vol. 2 (Macmillan: London, 1971)

*The Case of Leon Trotsky: Report of Hearing on the Charges Made against Him in the Moscow Trials* (Harper: New York, 1937)

L. Chamberlain, *The Philosophy Steamer: Lenin and the Exile of the Intelligentsia* (Atlantic Books: London, 2006)

J. Channon, 'Trotsky, the Peasants and Economic Policy: A Comment', *Economy and Society*, no. 4 (1985)

*'Chekisms': Tales of the Cheka. A KGB Anthology*, ed. V. Mitrokhin (Yurasov: London, 2008)

A. O. Chubaryan and G. Gorodetsky (eds), *Voina i politika, 1939–1941* (Nauka: Moscow, 1999)

F. Chuev (ed.), *Molotov: Poluvlastitel'nyi Vlastitelin* (Olma-Press: Moscow, 1999)

R. W. Clark, *The Life of Bertrand Russell* (Knopf: New York: 1976)

*The Communist International in Lenin's Time: Workers of the World and Oppressed Peoples Unite! Proceedings and Documents of the Second Congress, 1920*, ed. J. Riddell (Pathfinder: London, 1991)

Ö. S. Coşar, *Troçki Istanbul'da* (Kitas: Istanbul, 1969)

Y. Craipeau, *Mémoires d'un dinosaure trotskyste: secrétaire de Trotsky en 1933* (L'Harmattan: Paris, 1999)

R. V. Daniels, *The Conscience of the Revolution: Communist Opposition in Soviet Russia* (Harvard University Press: Cambridge, MA, 1960)

N. Davies, *White Eagle, Red Star: The Polish-Soviet War, 1919–20* (MacDonald: London, 1972)

R. W. Davies, *Soviet Economic Development from Lenin to Khrushchev* (Cambridge University Press: Cambridge, 1998)

R. W. Davies, 'Trockij and the debate on industrialisation in the USSR', in F. Gori (ed.), *Pensiero e azione di Lev Trockij. Atti del convegno internazionale per il quarantesimo anniversario della morte di Lev Trockij*, vol. 1 (Olschki: Florence, 1983)

R. B. Day, *Leon Trotsky and the Politics of Economic Isolation* (Cambridge University Press: Cambridge, 1973)

*Desyatyi s"ezd RKP(b). Mart 1921 g. Stenograficheskii otchët* (Moscow, 1963)

I. Deutscher, *Trotsky: The Prophet Armed, 1879–1921* (Oxford University Press: London, 1954)

I. Deutscher, *Trotsky: The Prophet Outcast, 1929–1940* (Oxford University Press: London, 1963)

I. Deutscher, *Trotsky: The Prophet Unarmed, 1921–1929* (Oxford University Press: London, 1959)

*Devyataya konferentsiya RKP(b) Sentyabr' 1920 goda. Protokoly* (Gosizdat: Moscow, 1972)

*Devyatyi s"ezd RKP(b). Mart–aprel' 1920 goda: protokoly* (Gosizdat: Moscow, 1960)

*Dvenadtsatyi s"ezd RKP(b). 17–25 aprelya 1923g. Stenograficheskii otchët* (Gosizdat: Moscow, 1968)

M. Eastman, *Great Companions: Critical Memoirs of Some Famous Friends* (Museum Press: London, 1959)

M. Eastman, *Leon Trotsky: The Portrait of a Youth* (Greenberg: New York, 1925)

M. Eastman, *Leon Trotsky: The Portrait of a Youth* (Faber & Gwyer: London, 1926)

M. Eastman, *Love and Revolution: My Journey through an Epoch* (Random House: New York, 1964)

M. Eastman, *Marxism, Is It a Science* (W. W. Norton: New York, 1940)

M. Eastman, *Since Lenin Died* (Boni & Liveright: New York, 1925)

A. Etkind, *Tolkovanie puteshestvii* (Novoe literaturnoe obozrenie: Moscow, 2001)

*Evrei Odessy i Yuga Ukrainy: istoriya v dokumentakh*, vol. 1 (Mosty kul'tury: Odessa, 2002)

L. Eyre, *Russia Analysed* (New York World: New York, 1920)

*Fëdor Il'ich Dan: Pis'ma (1899–1946)*, ed. B. Sapir (Stichting International Instituut voor Sociale Geschiedenis: Amsterdam, 1985)

*Founding the Communist International: Proceedings and Documents of the First Congress, March 1919*, ed. J. Riddell (Pathfinder: London, 1987)

P. Frank, *La Quatrième Internationale: contribution à l'histoire du movement trotskyste* (Maspero: Paris, 1969)

J. F. Fraser, *The Real Siberia. With an Account of a Dash through Manchuria* (Cassell: London, 1902)

Z. Galili, *The Menshevik Leaders in the Russian Revolution: Social Realities and Political Strategies* (Princeton University Press: Princeton, NJ, 1989)

J. R. Garmabella, *Operación Trotsky* (Editorial Diana: Mexico City, 1972)

I. Getzler, 'The Communist Leaders' Role in the Kronstadt Tragedy of 1921 in the Light of Recently Published Archival Documents', *Revolutionary Russia*, no. 1 (June 2002)

I. Getzler, *Kronstadt, 1917–192: The Fate of a Soviet Democracy* (Cambridge University Press: Cambridge, 1983)

I. Getzler, *Martov: A Political Biography of a Russian Social-Democrat* (Oxford University Press: Oxford, 1967)

I. Getzler, *Nikolai Sukhanov: Chronicler of the Russian Revolution* (Palgrave: London, 2002)

G. Gill, *Peasants and Government in the Russian Revolution* (Macmillan: London, 1979)

A. Glotzer, *Trotsky: Memoir and Critique* (Prometheus Books: New York, 1989)

E. Goldman, *Living My Life*, vols 1 and 2 (Pluto: London, 1987)

F. Gori (ed.), *Pensiero e azione di Lev Trockij. Atti del convegno internazionale per il quarantesimo anniversario della morte di Lev Trockij*, vols 1–2 (Olschki: Florence, 1983)

J. Gorkin, *El asesinato de Trotski* (Círculo de Lectores: Barcelona, 1970)

Yu. V. Got'e, *Moi zametki*, ed. T. Emmons and S. Utekhin (Terra: Moscow, 1997)

R. B. Gul', *Ya unës Rossiyu: apologiya emigratsii*, vols 1–3 (Most: New York, 1984–9)

W. Hard, *Raymond Robins' Own Story* (Harper & Brothers: New York, 1920)

F. Harris, *Contemporary Portraits: Fourth Series* (Brentano's: New York, n.d. [c. 1923])

J. van Heijenoort, *With Trotsky in Exile: From Prinkipo to Coyoacán* (Harvard University Press: Cambridge, MA, 1978)

S. Hook, *Out of Step: An Unquiet Life in the Twentieth Century* (HarperCollins: New York, 1987)

M. Hoschiller, *Le Mirage du soviétisme* (Payot: Paris, 1921)

I. Howe, *Trotsky* (Fontana Books: London, 1978)

A. A. Ioffe, *1883–1927: diplomat revolyutsii: sbornik rabot* (Iskra Research: Cambridge, MA, 1998)

N. Ioffe, *Moi otets Adol'f Abramovich Ioffe: vospominaniya, dokumenty i materialy* (Vozvrashchenie: Moscow, 1997)

N. Ioffe, *Vremya nazad. Moya zhizn', moya sud'ba, moya epokha* (Biologicheskie nauki: Moscow, 1992)

*Istoriya Soveta Rabochikh Deputatov g. S.-Peterburga* (N. Glagolev: St Petersburg, n.d. [1906?])

*Kak lomali NEP. Stenogrammy plenumov TsK VKP(b), 1928–1929*, vols 1–5, ed. V. P. Danilov, O. V. Khlevnyuk and A. Yu. Vatlin (Mezhdunarodnyi fond 'Demokratiya': Moscow, 2000)

A. Kalpaschikoff, *A Prisoner of Trotsky's*, Foreword by D. R. Francis (Doubleday, Page: New York, 1920)

B. Knei-Paz, *The Social and Political Thought of Leon Trotsky* (Oxford University Press: Oxford, 1978)

L. Kolakowski, *Main Currents of Marxism*, vol. 2: *The Golden Age* (Oxford University Press: Oxford, 1978)

I. I. Kostyushko, *Pol'skoe byuro TsK RKP(b), 1920–1921 gg.* (Institut slavyanovedeniya RAN: Moscow, 2005)

V. Krasnov and V. Daynes (eds), *Neizvestnyi Trotskii. Krasnyi Bonapart: Dokumenty, mneniya, razmyshleniya* (Olma-Press: Moscow, 2000)

*Kronshtadtskaya tragediya 1921 goda: dokumenty v dvukh knigakh*, ed. V. P. Kozlov and I. I. Kudryavtsev, vols 1–2 (ROSSPEN: Moscow, 1999)

V. I. Lenin, *Polnoe sobranie sochinenii*, vols 1–55 (Gosizdat: Moscow, 1958–65)

*Leninskii sbornik*, vols 1–50 (Gosizdat: Moscow, 1922–85)

R. Lévy, *Trotsky* (Librairie du Parti Socialiste et de l'Humanité: Paris, 1920)

S. Liberman, *Building Lenin's Russia* (Hyperion: Westport, CT, 1978)

R. H. Bruce Lockhart, 'Bolshevik Aims and Bolshevik Purposes, 1918–1919' (n.pub.: n.p., n.d.)

R. H. Bruce Lockhart, *Friends, Foes, and Foreigners* (Putnam: London, 1957)

R. H. Bruce Lockhart, *Memoirs of a British Agent* (London, 1932)

D. W. Lovell, *Trotsky's Analysis of Soviet Bureaucratization* (Croom Helm: London, 1985)

*Lubyanka: Stalin i NKVD–NKGB–GUKR 'Smersh', 1939–mart 1946*, ed. V. N. Khaustov, V. P. Naumov and N. S. Plotnikova (Materik: Moscow, 2006)

A. Lunacharskii, *Lunacharskii, Revolyutsionnye siluety* (Tip. '9-e Yanvarya': Moscow, 1923)

R. Luxemburg, 'Letters on Bolshevism and the Russian Revolution', *Revolutionary History*, no. 2/3 (1996)

K. McDermott and J. Agnew, *The Comintern: A History of International Communism, 1919–1943* (Macmillan: London, 1993)

R. H. McNeal, *Bride of the Revolution: Krupskaya and Lenin* (University of Michigan Press: Ann Arbor, 1972)

*Yu. O. Martov i A. N. Potresov. Pis'ma. 1898–1913*, ed. I. Kh. Urilov (Sobranie: Moscow, 2007)

E. Mawdsley, *The Russian Civil War* (Allen & Unwin: London, 1987)

L. Mercader, 'Mi hermano Ramón no era un vulgar asesino, sino una persona que creía en la causa del comunismo', *El Mundo*, July 1990

'*Milaya moya Resnichka!. .' Sergei Sedov. Pis'ma iz ssylki*, ed. Ye. V. Rusakova, S. A. Lar'kov and I. A. Flige (Nauchno-Informatsionnyi tsentr 'Memorial': St Petersburg; Hoover Institution Archives [Stanford University], 2006)

A. Morizet, *Chez Lénine et Trotski. Moscou 1921* (La Renaissance du Livre: Paris, 1922)

M. Nadeau (ed.), *Hommage à Natalia Sedova-Trotsky, 1882–1962* (Les Lettres Nouvelles: Paris, 1962)

N. Naimark and P. Gregory (eds), *The Lost Politburo Transcripts: From Collective Rule to Stalin's Dictatorship* (Yale University Press/Hoover Institution: New Haven, CT, 2008)

P. Naville (ed.), *Pierre Naville, Denise Naville and Jean van Heijenoort, Leon Trotsky: Correspondence 1929–1939* (L'Harmattan: Paris, 1989)

P. Naville, *Trotsky vivant* (Julliard: Paris, 1962)

J. Nedava, *Trotsky and the Jews* (Jewish Publication Society of America: Philadelphia, 1971)

V. Netrebskii, *Trotskii v Odesse* (Inga: Odessa, 2003)

V. N. Nikitin, *Evrei zemledel'tsy: istoricheskoe, zakonodatel'noe, administrativnoe i bytovoe polozhenie kolonii so vremën ikh vozniknoveniya do nashikh dnei. 1807–1887* (Novosti: St Petersburg, 1887)

A. Nove, *Studies in Economics and Russia* (Macmillan: London, 1990)

M. A. Novomeysky, *My Siberian Life*, trans. A. Brown (Max Parrish: London, 1903)

A. Pantsov, *The Bolsheviks and the Chinese Revolution, 1919–1927* (Curzon: Richmond, Surrey, 2000)

Parvus, *Bez tsarya, a pravitel'stvo – rabochee* (Partiya: Geneva, 1905)

Parvus, *V chëm. my raskhodimsya? Otvet Leninu na ego stat'i v 'Proletarii'* (Partiya: Geneva, 1905)

B. Pearce, *How Haig Saved Lenin* (Macmillan: London, 1987)

*Peterburgskii komitet RSDRP(b) v 1917 godu. Protokoly i materialy zasedanii*, eds. T. A. Abrosimova, T. P. Bondarevskaya and A. Rabinowitch (Bel'veder: St Petersburg, 2003)

*Pis'ma P. B. Aksel'roda i Yu. O. Martova, 1901–1916* (Russkii revolyutsionnyi arkhiv: Berlin, 1924)

*Pis'ma vo vlast' 1917–1927. zayavleniya, zhaloby, donosy, pis'ma v gosudarstvennye struktury i sovetskim vozhdyam*, ed. A. Ya. Livshin and I. B. Orlov (ROSSPEN: Moscow, 1998)

E. Pizzi de Porras, *Cinco Días en México* (Alvarez Pita: Havana, Cuba, 1939)

*The Platform of the Left Opposition (1927)* (New Park: London, 1963)

M. Polishchuk, *Evrei Odessy i Novorossii: sotsial'no-politicheskaya istoriya evreev Odessy i drugikh gorodov Novorossii, 1881–1904* (Mosty kul'tury: Moscow, 2002)

*Protokoly Tsentral'nogo Komiteta RSDRP(b): avgust 1917 g.–mart 1918 g.* (Gosizdat: Moscow, 1958)

*Protokoly zasedanii Soveta Narodnykh Komissarov RSFSR: noyabr' 1917–mart 1918 gg.* (ROSSPEN: Moscow, 2006)

*Pyatyi (londonskii) s"ezd RSDRP. Protokoly. Aprel' mai 1907 goda* (Gosizdat: Moscow, 1963)

A. Rabinowitch, *The Bolsheviks Come to Power: The Revolution of 1917 in Petrograd* (W. W. Norton: New York, 1976)

A. Rabinowitch, *The Bolsheviks in Power: The First Year of Soviet Rule in Petrograd* (Indiana University Press: Bloomington, IN, 2007)

A. Rabinowitch, *Prelude to Revolution: The Petrograd Bolsheviks and the July 1917 Uprising* (Indiana University Press: Bloomington, IN, 1968)

K. Radek, *Pampflety i portrety* (Gosizdat: Moscow, 1927)

A. Ransome, *Russia in 1919* (B. W. Huebsch: New York, 1919)

R. R. Reese, *The Soviet Military Experience: A History of the Soviet Army, 1917–1991* (Routledge: London, 2000)

W. Reswick, *I Dreamt Revolution* (Henry Regnery: Chicago, 1952)

W. G. Rosenberg, *Liberals in the Russian Revolution: The Constitutional Democratic Party, 1917–1921* (Princeton University Press: Princeton, NJ, 1974)

G. Rosenthal, *Avocat de Trotsky* (Laffont: Paris, 1975)

A. Rosmer, 'Durant la Guerre Impérialiste', in M. Nadeau (ed.), *Hommage à Natalia Sedova-Trotsky, 1882–1962* (Paris, 1962)

A. Rosmer, *Moscou sous Lénine: les origines du communisme* (P. Horay: Paris, 1953)

B. Russell, *The Autobiography of Bertrand Russell, 1914–1944* (Little, Brown: New York, 1951)

B. Russell, *The Theory and Practice of Bolshevism* (Allen & Unwin: London, 1920)

J. Sadoul, *Notes sur la révolution bolchevique (Octobre 1917–Janvier 1919)* (Éditions de la Sirène: Paris, 1919)

L. A. Sánchez Salazar (with Julián Gorkin), *Así asesinaron a Trotski* (Populibro: Mexico, 1955)

A. Schopenhauer, *The Art of Controversy* (University of the Pacific Press: Honolulu, HI, 2004)

S. Schwarz, *The Russian Revolution of 1905* (University of Chicago Press: Chicago, 1967)

*Sed'maya (aprel'skaya) vserossiiskaya konferentsiya RSDRP (bol'shevikov). Petrogradskaya konferentsiya RSDRP (bol'shevikov) Aprel' 1917 goda. Protokoly* (Gosizdat: Moscow, 1958)

V. Serge and N. Sedova Trotsky, *The Life and Death of Leon Trotsky*, trans. A. J. Pomerans (Basic Books: New York, 1975)

*The Serge–Trotsky Papers*, ed. and introduced by D. Cotterill (Pluto Press: London, 1994)

R. Service, *The Bolshevik Party in Revolution: A Study in Organisational Change* (Macmillan: London, 1979)

R. Service, 'Bolshevism's Europe', in S. Pons and A. Romano (eds), *Russia in the Age of Wars, 1914–1945* (Feltrinelli: Milan, 2000)

R. Service, *Comrades: Communism: A World History* (Macmillan: London, 2007)

R. Service, 'From Polyarchy to Hegemony: The Party's Role in the Construction of the Central Institutions of the Soviet State, 1917–1919', *Sbornik*, no. 10 (1984)

R. Service, *Lenin: A Biography* (Macmillan: London, 2000)

R. Service, *Lenin: A Political Life*, 3 vols (Macmillan: London, 1985, 1991, 1995)

R. Service, *Stalin: A Biography* (Macmillan: London, 2004)

R. Service, 'The Way They Talked Then: The Discourse of Politics in the Soviet Party Politburo in the Late 1920s', in P. R. Gregory and N. Naimark (eds), *The Lost Politburo Transcripts: From Collective Rule to Stalin's Dictatorship* (Yale University Press/Hoover Institution: New Haven, CT, 2008)

Ya. Shafir, *Ocherki gruzinskoi zhirondy* (Gosizdat: Moscow, 1925)

C. Sheridan, *From Mayfair to Moscow* (Boni & Liveright: New York, 1921)

*Shestoi s"ezd RSDRP (bol'shevikov). Avgust 1917 goda. Protokoly* (Gosizdat: Moscow, 1958)

R. M. Slusser, *Stalin in October: The Man Who Missed the Revolution* (Johns Hopkins University Press: London, 1987)

J. D. Smele and A. Heywood, *The Russian Revolution of 1905: Centenary Perspectives* (Routledge: London, 2005)

R. B. Spence, 'Hidden Agendas: Spies, Lies and Intrigue Surrounding Trotsky's American Visit of January–April 1917', *Revolutionary Russia*, no. 1 (2008)

R. B. Spence, 'Interrupted Journey: British Intelligence and the Arrest of Leon Trotsky, April 1917', *Revolutionary Russia*, no. 1 (2000)

I. V. Stalin, *Sochineniya*, vols 1–12 (Gosizdat: Moscow, 1946–51)

P. Stein, *Siqueiros: His Life and Works* (International Publishers: New York, 1994)

I. N. Steinberg, *In the Workshop of the Revolution* (Gollancz: London, 1955)

*Stenogrammy zasedanii Politbyuro TsK RKP(b)-VKP(b), 1923–1938 gg.*, ed. K. M. Anderson, A. Yu. Vatlin, P. Gregory, A. K. Sorokin, R. Sousa and O. V. Khlevniuk, 3 vols (ROSSPEN: Moscow, 2007)

H. P. von Strandmann, 'Obostryayushchiesya paradoksy: Gitler, Stalin i germano-sovetskie ekonomicheskie svyazi. 1939–1941', in A. O. Chubaryan and G. Gorodetsky (eds), *Voina i politika, 1939–1941* (Nauka: Moscow, 1999)

P. Sudoplatov, *Special Tasks: The Memoirs of an Unwanted Witness – A Soviet Spymaster* (Little, Brown: London, 1994)

N. Sukhanov, *Zapiski o revolyutsii*, 3 vols (Politizdat: Moscow, 1991)

D. F. Sverchkov, *Na zare revolyutsii*, 3rd edn (Komissiya po Istorii Oktyabr'skoi revolyutsii i Rossiiskoi Kommunisticheskoi Partii: Leningrad, 1925)

G. Swain, 'The Disillusioning of the Revolution's Praetorian Guard: The Latvian Riflemen, Summer–Autumn 1918', *Europe–Asia Studies*, no. 4 (1999)

G. Swain, *The Origins of the Russian Civil War* (Longman: London, 1996)

G. Swain, *Russian Social-Democracy and the Legal Labour Movement, 1906–14* (Macmillan: London, 1983)

G. Swain, *Trotsky* (Longman: London, 2006)

N. S. Tarkhova, 'Trotsky's Train: An Unknown Page in the History of the Civil War', in T. Brotherstone and P. Dukes (eds), *The Trotsky Reappraisal* (Edinburgh University Press: Edinburgh, 1992)

*Terrorism and Communism: A Reply to Karl Kautsky*, foreword by M. Shachtman (University of Michigan Press: Ann Arbor, MI, 1961)

I. D. Thatcher, 'Bor'ba: A Workers' Journal in St Petersburg on the Eve of World War One', *English Historical Journal*, no. 450 (1998)

I. D. Thatcher, *Late Imperial Russia: Problems and Perspectives* (Manchester University Press: Manchester, 2005)

I. D. Thatcher, 'Leon Trotsky and 1905', in J. D. Smele and A. Heywood, *The Russian Revolution of 1905: Centenary Perspectives* (Routledge: London, 2005)

I. D. Thatcher, *Leon Trotsky and World War One: August 1914 to February 1917* (Macmillan: London, 2000)

I. D. Thatcher, *Reinterpreting Revolutionary Russia: Essays in Honour of James D. White* (Palgrave: London, 2006)

I. D. Thatcher, 'The St Petersburg/Petrograd Mezhraionka, 1913–1917: The Rise and Fall of a Russian Social-Democratic Workers' Party Unity Faction', *Slavonic and East European Review*, no. 2 (2009)

I. D. Thatcher, *Trotsky* (Routledge: London, 2003)

I. D. Thatcher, 'Trotsky and the Duma: A Research Essay', in I. D. Thatcher (ed.), *Regime and Society in Twentieth Century Russia* (Macmillan: London, 1999)

I. D. Thatcher, 'Uneven and Combined Development', *Revolutionary Russia*, no. 2 (1991)

*Trinadtsataya konferentsiya RKP(b): byulleten'* (Gosizdat: Moscow, 1924)

*Trinadtsatyi s''ezd RKP(b). Mai 1924 goda. Stenograficheskii otchët* (Gosizdat: Moscow, 1963)

R. C. Tucker, *Stalin as Revolutionary, 1879–1929* (W. W. Norton: New York, 1973)

N. Tumarkin, *Lenin Lives! The Lenin Cult in Soviet Russia* (Harvard University Press: Cambridge, MA, 1983)

N. Ustryalov, *Hic Rohdus* [sic], *Hic Saltus* (n. pub.: Harbin, 1929)

N. A. Vasetskii, *Trotskii: opyt politicheskoi biografii* (Respublika: Moscow, 1992)

A. Vatlin, 'The Testing-Ground of World Revolution Germany in the 1920s', in T. Rees and A. Thorpe (eds), *International Communism and the Communist International, 1919–1943* (Manchester University Press: Manchester, 1998)

D. Volkogonov, *Trotskii: politicheskii portret*, vols 1–2 (Novosti: Moscow, 1992)

*Vserossiiskaya konferentsiya R. K. P. (bol'shevikov). 4–7 avgusta 1922 g. Byulleten'* (Gosizdat: Moscow, 1922), bulletin no. 3

*Vserossiiskaya Konferentsiya Ros. Sots.-Dem. Rab. Partii 1912 goda*, ed. R. C. Elwodd (Kraus International: London, 1982)

A. Walicki, *A History of Russian Thought from the Enlightenment to Marxism* (Oxford University Press: Oxford, 1980)

S. and B. Webb, *Soviet Communism: A New Civilization?* (Longmans, Green: London, 1935)

S. and B. Webb, *Soviet Communism: A New Civilization* (V. Gollancz: London, 1937)

H. G. Wells, *Russia in the Shadows* (Hodder & Stoughton: London, 1920)

J. D. White, 'Early Soviet Historical Interpretations of the Russian Revolutions, 1918–1924', *Soviet Studies*, no. 3 (1985)

J. D. White, 'Lenin, Trotskii and the Arts of Insurrection: The Congress of Soviets of the Northern Region, 11–13 October 1917', *Slavonic and East European Review*, no. 1 (1999)

B. D. Wolfe, *Strange Communists I Have Known* (Stein & Day: New York, 1965)

E. Wolfenstein, *The Revolutionary Personality: Lenin, Trotsky, Gandhi* (Princeton University Press: Princeton, NJ, 1967)

W. Woytinsky, *Stormy Passage: A Personal History through Two Russian Revolutions to Democracy: 1905–1960* (Vanguard Press: New York, 1961)

Ye. M. Yaroslavskii (ed.), *L. D. Trotskii o partii v 1904 g.: broshyura N. Trotskogo 'Nashi politicheskie zadachi'* (Gosizdat: Moscow, 1928)

Z. A. B. Zeman and W. B. Scharlau, *The Merchant of Revolution: The Life of*

*Alexander Israel Helphand (Parvus) 1867–1924* (Oxford University Press: Oxford, 1965)

*Die Zimmerwalder Bewegung. Protokole und Korrespondenz*, ed. H. Lademacher, 2 vols (Internationaal Instituut voor Sociale Geschiedenis: The Hague, 1967)

G. Zinoviev, *Vladimir Il'ich Lenin* (Petrograd, 1918)

G. A. Ziv, *Trotskii: kharakteristika. (Po lichnym vospominaniyam)* (Narodopravstvo: New York, 1921)

G. I. Zlokazov and G. Z. Ioffe (eds), *Iz istorii bor'by za vlast v 1917 godu: sbornik dokumentov* (Institut Rossiiskoi Istorii RAN: Moscow, 2002)

# Index